The Complete Visual C# Programmer's Guide

From the Authors of C# Corner

Bulent Ozkir

John Schofield

Mahesh Chand

Mike Gold

Srinivasa Sivakumar

Shivani Maheshwari

Saurabh Nandu

Levent Camlibel

Microgold Software Inc.—Publishing Division

Trademarks

About the Authors

S. Bulent Ozkir

Bulent is a software engineer and consultant from Turkey who is an experienced Microsoft developer. He is currently working for Microsoft Arabia as a consultant. In the past he has worked for Deutsche Telecom T-Systems as project manager on MOF, ITIL, TCO, MSF, and service management topics. He has also worked as a consultant lieutenant for the Turkish Army Land Forces Computer Center and as a senior support engineer for Microsoft Turkey for two years. In his spare time after graduating, he worked for three years at various positions at a software development company named Intertech and at a TV manufacturer named Vestel. In his career, which spans a little more than six years, he has worked with several Microsoft technologies, including Visual Basic, Visual C++, Visual Interdev, JavaScript, VBScript, Java, ASP, DHTML, COM+, TCP/IP, SMS, Exchange, Proxy, IIS, Site Server, Windows 3x/9x/ME/NTx/2000/XP, MCIS, ASP+, and SQL Server. His background includes a BA in computer science, and he holds an MCSE+ in Internet technologies and an MCSD in Visual C++. He has also written several articles on MSDN related to support issues. He is thinking of completing an MBA program soon if he finds free time. You can reach him at bulentozkir@hotmail.com.

"I would like to thank the Microsoft staff for their support and Mike, Mahesh, and Levent for performing a great job on the book (a really admirable job!). I dedicate my modest works to my dad, Mahmut, to my mom, Sevim, to my sister, Esra, to my love, Vildan, and to the people who try to amend the world to being a worthwhile spot to live in the universe."

John Schofield

John is an independent consultant with more than 12 years' experience with C/C++ on the OS/2 and Windows NT platforms. In the early 1990s he developed GUI applications using IBM's Open Class libraries and Microsoft's MFC library. John has spent the past six years designing and coding multitiered, distributed applications using COM/DCOM/ATL. Since 1996, he has been contracting in the southern United States and California. He holds an honors degree in film from York University in Toronto. Any time away from the computer is spent daydreaming about living under palm trees in Belize and never seeing snow again.

"I would like to thank my wife, Phyllis, for her love, support, and encouragement. She sacrificed her sabbatical to allow me to dedicate my efforts to writing my chapters for this book. She also provided invaluable assistance with the editing of my work."

"I would also like to thank Mahesh Chand, the founder of C# Corner, for giving me the opportunity to contribute to this book."

Levent Camlibel

Levent Camlibel holds a master's degree in economics and industrial management. He is also a PhD candidate in the Department of Economics at Clemson University in South Carolina. He is the founder and admin of C#Turk.com, a Turkish C# site. He has been programming in Visual Basic, COM/COM+, and database for more than seven years. He has also worked on many dynamic, database-driven Web and Windows applications. He is currently working with C# and ASP.NET. His expertise is VB, C#, ASP, and ASP.NET. You can reach him at leventc@clemson.edu.

He'd like to thank his wife for giving him all the love, support, and understanding when he was working on this book. A special thank-you goes to Professor Steve Davis for giving Levent the opportunity to work with the latest software and development environment on many computer-related projects.

"I dedicate my work in this book to my wife and son."

Mahesh Chand

Mahesh is a founder of C# Corner (http://www.c-sharpcorner.com) and Mindcracker (http://www.mindcracker.com). He has more than six years of programming experience with Microsoft technologies. Mahesh's background includes a master's degree in computer science and applications and a BSc in mathematics and physics. He is a Microsoft Certified Professional in Visual C++ and also an author of *A Programmer's Guide to ADO.NET in C#*.

Mike Gold

Mike Gold is the president of Microgold Software Inc. and creator of the UML tool WithClass. Mike's company is a Microsoft VBA Partner and a Borland Tools Companion Partner. He has been programming Windows applications for about 11 years and has consulted for financial companies such as Merrill Lynch and Chase Manhattan. Currently he works for Identix Corporation and resides in Manhattan. He looks forward to the possibilities in C# and .NET.

"I dedicate the book to my wife, Vered Gold, who continued to inspire me to finish this book. I would also like to dedicate the book to my family; they have always supported me in my various endeavors."

Saurabh Nandu

Saurabh Nandu currently lives in Bombay, India. He is the founder of www.MasterCSharp.com, which concentrates on teaching C# and .NET. He worked on HTML, JavaScript, Flash 5.0, and Java before he started programming in Java and C#. After being influenced by the power and flexibility of .NET, he sticks to working as a freelance writer and reviewer on .NET and related technologies for many books and Web sites and has worked as a technical reviewer of many books. He is currently working as technical evangelist at YesSoftware Inc.

"I would like to thank my friend Nanu Jogi, without whose direction I

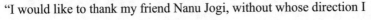

never would have begun working on the .NET platform. I would also like to thank my family, especially my brother Pritesh, for their support, without which I would not have been here."

Shivani Maheshwari

Shivani Maheshwari currently works in Bangalore, India. She has done her engineering from REC Bhopal. She has also worked with C#, .NET, Java, WAP, XML, ColdFusion, VB, and other middleware technologies.

"I would like to thank Mahesh for inspiring me to work with .NET technology and to move forward with it. I would like to dedicate my work to my parents. They are my inspiration at every stage of my life."

Srinivasa Sivakumar

Srinivasa Sivakumar is a software consultant, developer, and writer. He specializes in Web and mobile technologies using Microsoft solutions. He has co-authored *Professional ASP.NET Web Services*, *ASP.NET Mobile Controls—Tutorial Guide*, *.NET Compact Framework*, *Beginning ASP.NET 1.0 with VB.NET*, *Visual Basic .NET Threading Handbook*, *Beginning ASP.NET 1.0 with C#.NET*, *Professional ASP.NET Security*, *Professional ASP.NET Web Services with VB.NET*, and *Professional .NET Network Programming* for Wrox Press and written technical articles for C-SharpCorner.com, ASPToday.com, CSharpToday.com, and .NET Developer. In his free time, he likes to listen Tamil soundtracks, especially ones sung by Mr. S.P. Balasubramaniyam. A list of his published materials is available at www3.brinkster.com/webguru/.

"I'd like to dedicate my section of this book to my wonderful daughters, Sruthi and Anusri (God's wonderful gift to me and my wife). Your smiles inspire me and your day-to-day growth and learning amazes me."

Editors and Technical Reviewers

Craig Breakspear

Craig has been developing software for more than 10 years. Craig has a master's degree in information technology from American Intercontinental University. A father of two wonderful boys, Craig is currently employed with Extreme Logic, a Microsoft consulting firm based in Atlanta.

"I am very excited about the new .NET Framework and look forward to the next few years of .NET development."

Dipal Choksi

Dipal Choksi has a bachelor's degree in computer engineering. She has experience in Visual Basic, Visual C++, Java, Directory Services, and ASP projects. Dipal is a frequent contributor to the C-SharpCorner Web site.

Foreword

C_Sharp (or C#) is one of the newer entries in the object-oriented (OO) language sweepstakes. It is much easier to learn than C or C++, which are its clear ancestors, and has a great deal in common with Java. In fact, much of C#'s syntax is identical to Java syntax.

If you were having trouble getting your arms around OO programming in earlier languages, you will probably embrace C# much more easily. Its syntax is simpler and it is much harder to write crash-causing code because at long last *there are no pointers!*

Learning C# can be a real joy compared to languages like C++. It is elegant and compact and very easy to program using Visual Studio .NET. This book will lay the groundwork for almost everything you will ever need to know about programming C#. The eight authors have covered almost every facet of C# programming in Windows and .NET.

But C# can be more than a Java "me-too" language, because it is closely tied to both Windows and the .NET platform. And of the languages supported under .NET, you will quickly make C# your first choice because it makes OO programming so simple. Using C#, you can write elegant Windows client GUI programs, servers, middleware for transmitting objects and data, and almost any other kind of program you can imagine.

You will see that C# programs consist entirely of classes and their instances, and that the dreaded global variable has vanished into the mists of history. You can discover that C# not only supports but actively encourages both inheritance and interfaces to write powerful programs more easily.

This book brings together all of these important ideas in a single reference. It covers the language, the Visual Studio .NET programming suite, compiling, debugging, Windows applications, databases, ASP.NET, security, Web services, SOAP, and .NET Remoting, all in a single complete (if only somewhat large) reference.

Over time, you will probably add to your bookshelf other books on specific C# programming topics or on modern programming methodologies like Design Patterns, but this book is a fundamental C# reference for your bookshelf, and it ought to be there as one of the first.

James W. Cooper
Wilton, Conn.
July 2002

Contents

Chapter 1:
Introduction

Microsoft defines C# (pronounced *C sharp*) as "a simple, modern, object-oriented, and type-safe programming language derived from C and C++. It combines the high productivity of Visual Basic and the raw power of C++." Over the last two decades, C and C++ programmers alike have enjoyed programming with two very powerful languages, but developing enterprise-ready applications in either of these languages is complex and time consuming. As a rapid application development (RAD) language, Microsoft Visual Basic does serve its purpose in generating Windows applications, but it lacks the flexibility and power that C and C++ offer to developers.

C# takes an intelligent approach by combining both the flexibility of C and C++ and the RAD support found in Visual Basic. In fact, Anders Hejlsberg, the chief architect of the C# language, reviewed a number of existing languages before writing down the C# specification. As you dive deeper into C#, you find many features similar to those of other languages like Object Pascal, Modula, Oberon, Smalltalk, and Java. It's commonly accepted that object-oriented languages aid in productivity and produce scalable and efficient enterprise solutions. Since C# is fully object oriented, it derives the same benefits any other object-oriented language does. Although C# supports object-oriented behavior such as instantiation, interfaces, polymorphism, encapsulation, and inheritance, some of the features of object-oriented languages that lead to poor application architecture such as multiple inheritance have been intentionally left out, promoting better-designed applications.

Support for modern programming concepts such as type safety, automatic memory management (sometimes referred to as garbage collection), overflow checking, attributes, events, delegates, properties, and indexers make C# one of the best languages to develop and deploy applications for the Microsoft .NET platform. The ability to call and use unmanaged native code directly from C# classes is yet another powerful feature that allows you to interoperate and reuse your existing legacy code.

Services provided by the underlying .NET platform, such as automatic memory management, security, and a huge base class library (BCL), make developing applications in C# a less code-intensive job.

Because C# was primarily written for the .NET platform, it supports a large part of the Common Language Specification (CLS); hence C# is now touted as the best language for developing applications for the .NET platform. Microsoft's support and enthusiasm in promoting the new C# language along with the recent ratification of C# as a standard by the European Computer Manufacturers Association (http://www.ecma.ch/) definitely should encourage you to consider C# when choosing a language for .NET platform programming.

Visual C#

As mentioned earlier, C# in the .NET environment supports RAD of Windows applications. The drag-and-drop approach for creating applications in Visual Basic also applies to C#. Actually, Visual C# gains all its Windows functionality from the base class libraries, so graphical user interface APIs like GDI+, ASP.NET Web forms, and Windows forms are fully supported. The programming model exposed by these APIs is so consistent that the approach to developing Visual C# applications is similar to developing applications from the command prompt. The latter part of this book concentrates on developing applications based on Visual C#.

Visual Studio .NET

One of the biggest benefits of developing with Microsoft technologies is the wide array of rich development tools available from Microsoft. Visual Studio .NET (VS.NET), the latest version of the Visual Studio development suite, is no exception.

Microsoft offers VS.NET in various forms to suit the needs of different levels of users. Integration is one of the key features of VS.NET. The single integrated development environment (IDE) supports development in any of the managed languages, also enabling seamless development using multiple languages in the same project. Bundled with the IDE is the bitmap editor, the Hypertext Markup Language (HTML) editor, the Extensible Markup Language (XML) editor, and the XML schema editor. The SQL Enterprise manager, Microsoft Message Queue manager, and other server resource managers have also been built into the IDE so you never need to leave the IDE while developing applications! Another more notable feature is the cross-language VS.NET debugger. The VS.NET debugger can help you easily debug console applications, libraries, windows applications, ASP.NET Web applications and more.

The VS.NET IDE is a tool you need to master to rapidly develop enterprise applications from the .NET platform. Throughout this book you will see examples of developing applications using the VS.NET IDE.

Intended Audience

The content of this book has been carefully crafted to meet the requirements of beginner to intermediate-level developers. The initial chapters help beginners gain a deep understanding of the C# language and the .NET platform. Slowly, the book delves into more complex issues and applications that help you as you develop applications. The authors have taken special care to explain the intricacies of each topic they have taken on, hoping to enrich your reading experience in the process. Beginners are advised to brush up on object-oriented programming concepts before working with this book.

Prerequisites

The authors suggest minimum system requirements or prerequisite knowledge as follows:

- At least one year of work experience with an object-oriented programming language such as C++, Object Pascal, or Java
- Windows 2000 with Service Pack 2 or Windows XP Professional
- Internet Explorer 6.0
- MSDE or MS SQL Server 2000
- Visual Studio .NET (version 1.0.3705)

Basic knowledge of a RAD tool such as Visual Studio, Visual Basic, or Delphi is helpful but not mandatory.

Online Source Code

Source code for all examples discussed in this book is contained on the CD in the back of this book and is also downloadable from the C# Corner Web site (http://www.c-sharpcorner.com/cspub/). The code on this site is updated periodically to account for changes to Visual C#.

Scope of Content

This book's 26 chapters provide a fairly detailed view of the .NET environment. The first eight chapters introduce you to C#, the .NET Framework, and the IDE so you get a basic feel for the power of the language and environment. Then the book explores Windows programming, database access, Web programming, graphic programming, mobile programming, XML, and the many avenues that C# and .NET allow you to control in the programming world. Each topic was written by the C# Corner author with the strongest experience in the subject.

Chapter 1: Introduction

This chapter gives you a quick tour of the features of the book, the C# Corner Web site, and the source code downloads and also summarizes the content of the book by chapter.

Chapter 2: .NET and the .NET Framework

Chapter 2 discusses the .NET Framework and its components. After finishing this chapter, you should have a fair grasp of the .NET architecture and how it works.

Chapter 3: Hello, C#

This short chapter shows you the basics of a simple "Hello, World" application. From this chapter you learn how to write your first C# program and compile and run it from the command line. You also gain an understanding of the components of a simple .NET program.

Chapter 4: Compiling and Debugging

The topics of compiling and debugging warrant discussion before you start writing real programs. In this chapter, you learn about C# compiler options and the ILDASM utility that can be used to view the metadata of an assembly and to disassemble an assembly IL code. This chapter also covers CorDbg, DbgCLR, and Visual Studio .NET debugging options.

Chapter 5: C# Language Programming

This chapter covers C# and the syntax of the language. It covers value and reference types, control statements of the language, and object-oriented features of the language. In this chapter you will gain the knowledge needed to understand the many program examples contained within the book.

Chapter 6: System I/O and Streams

As the chapter title implies, system I/O streams are the focus here; you learn to read, write, and process streams to and from the system I/O. This chapter also includes classes related to file and directory operations and text reader and writer operations.

Chapter 7: Exception Handling

As a modern, object-oriented language, C# provides a professional way to handle errors through exception-handling classes and various exception-handling techniques. This chapter explains the language's exception-handling capabilities—important because the robustness of the software you develop depends on how effectively the program deals with exceptions.

Chapter 8: Visual Studio .NET IDE

VS.NET is the latest version of Microsoft's Visual Studio suite. Integration is the key tenet of this IDE; all the tools you require to develop applications on the .NET platform have been packed into a single IDE, making VS.NET a powerful, indispensable tool. This chapter introduces you to the VS.NET IDE and defines its various windows, menus, and options.

Chapter 9: Windows Programming

In this chapter, you learn to write GUI applications in VS.NET using Windows forms and controls. You begin by writing a simple Windows application with few controls; then you move on to gain an understanding of the basic structure of Windows Form classes in the .NET class library and of various Windows controls.

Chapter 10: Database Programming Using ADO.NET

In this chapter, you learn the basics of ADO.NET, the data providers, and the classes provided in the .NET class library; you also learn how to use various data providers to access different data sources. The chapter demonstrates how to use common data classes such as DataTable, DataView, DataSet, DataViewManager, DataRow, and DataColumn. Finally, you learn to write database applications using VS.NET wizards and tools such as Server Explorer and the DataForm wizard. This chapter covers the OLE DB, Open Database Connectivity (ODBC), and Structured Query Language (SQL) data providers.

Chapter 11: An Introduction to ASP.NET

Here you start your journey with a brief history of Web programming technologies and the origin of ASP.NET. Then you get a glimpse of the advantages and limitations of ASP.NET and learn the difference between Active Server Pages (ASP) and ASP.NET before you take on the topic of server controls and a basic "Hello, World" example with Notepad and VS.NET.

Chapter 12: Advanced ASP.NET

This chapter covers basic ASP.NET server controls. Server controls bring lots of excitement to the Web development community, and the DataGrid control in particular reduces much of the work required for programmers to present data. Chapter 12 also explains advanced ASP.NET topics such as validation, session state options, output and data caching and authentication.

Chapter 13: .NET Web Services

Web services represent a great advance in the distributed computing architecture, providing significant flexibility when you work with multiple platforms and tools. Chapter 13 shows how to build ASP.NET Web services with text editors and VS.NET. You also see the different data types you can pass into Web services and learn to customize the look and feel of Web services with a C# feature called *attributes*.

Chapter 14: XML.NET

XML is the standard way of exchanging data between different platforms. Unlike its predecessors, XML is extensible (as you might have inferred from the name), meaning that XML.NET classes let you exploit the language and its promising, derivative techologies. As XML evolves by demand, so does the XML.NET. XML has different aspects that will help you simplify the development maintenance cycle. Chapter 14 focuses on XML basics, the relationship between XML and .NET, XML-related classes, and how to read and write XML documents. This chapter also shows how to use XML in database applications using ADO.NET.

Chapter 15: GDI+ Programming

The new GDI+ signifies a big improvement over the former graphics device interface (GDI) library, giving you a host of namespaces and classes to make graphics programming quicker and easier. In this chapter, you learn to use the Graphics class and paint to a Graphics surface. We also show you how to use GDI+ on the Web, how to do animation, and how to utilize sound.

Chapter 16: Threading

This chapter discusses multithreading classes provided by the .NET runtime library and how to write multithreaded applications. Threads are an easily implemented mechanism to create simultaneous operation of processes. Multiple threads can go a long way toward maximizing an application's performance.

Chapter 17: Windows Services

Windows services are applications that run in a Windows session in the background. This chapter explains the basics of Windows services and Windows services–related classes provided by the .NET runtime library. Here you also learn to write Windows services in .NET.

Chapter 18: COM Interoperability

Chapter 18 addresses how to use unmanaged code from managed code using Component Object Model (COM) components, ActiveX controls, and a function from the native dynamic-link library. The .NET interoperability services help bridge the gap between managed and unmanaged code. When using .NET interop services, the .NET application pays a performance penalty because the class to the COM component goes through the process of marshaling. You'll touch on all these details in Chapter 18.

Chapter 19: TCP/IP and the Internet

Suite components of TCP/IP, the most widely used protocol among private and public networks, are the bricks and mortar of all networked applications. The .NET Framework provides a robust and versatile set of classes to develop programs for networked applications. Most of the other classes of interest such as those available in Simple Object Access Protocol (SOAP) and ASP.NET use the .NET TCP/IP classes through inheritance, aggregation, or composition. The .NET Framework classes provide the necessary infrastructure for them to hook into the network wiring. In this chapter, you learn how to program with raw sockets, Transmission Control Protocol/User Datagram Protocol over Internet Protocol, and other Internet-related .NET Framework classes. With this chapter, you can gain some experience developing networked applications by examining some real-world exercises, such as a File Transmission Protocol (FTP) client and server, and a simple chat client program such as an Internet Relay Chat client.

Chapter 20: Strings and Arrays

Chapter 20 takes a look at the concepts of strings, arrays, and regular expressions. It also examines the Array, ArrayList, String, and StringBuilder classes and how to use them.

Chapter 21: Miscellaneous Topics

This chapter covers some miscellaneous topics omitted from other chapters—topics such as the advantages of Diagnostic classes such as Debug, Process, ProcessThread, Switch, TraceListener, EventLog, and PerformanceCounter. This chapter also explains using the Environment class, working with the Buffer class for memory manipulation, performing math with the Math class, generating random numbers with the Random classes, manipulating the Windows registry with the

RegistryKey class, working with timers, using directory services, taking advantage of reflection, and using Windows Management Instrumentation.

Chapter 22: Security in .NET

Security is another big issue in .NET. The .NET Framework separates the logical security behavior covered by role-based security and the permissions a segment of code has during execution. In this chapter, you learn the basics of security and how to use the security-related classes.

Chapter 23: SOAP and .NET Remoting

Welcome to the concepts of SOAP, .NET Remoting, ASP.NET Web services, and HailStorm. This chapter begins with the basic theory behind remoting, gives a brief introduction to SOAP and the available classes in the .NET Framework library, and follows with developing real-world applications with the .NET SOAP classes.

Chapter 24: Mobile Programming

Chapter 24 teaches you the basics of mobile programming within the .NET Framework and how to take advantage of using the Mobile Internet Toolkit. We take a brief look at the basic controls provided by the toolkit, including mobile pages, interface controls, validation, and utility controls. In the end, you learn how to employ these controls and tools to write some real-world mobile applications.

Chapter 25: .NET Remoting

This chapter takes you through the remoting framework in .NET, giving developers enough of a foundation from which to address the majority of their problem domains. The designers of the .NET Remoting Framework have delivered an easily implemented, adaptable architecture that can meet most of the demanding challenges you'll face. Not only can sinks and proxies be customized or extended, but channels can also be designed and coded using any protocol desired. The remoting framework is truly an extensible architecture.

Chapter 26: Packaging and Deployment

The final chapter covers what is necessary to deploy your .NET applications. It begins by telling you which files you need to deploy to get your .NET applications to run. It shows you the simplest deployment scenario of copying a file. It then continues to describe the basic unit of a deployed application—the .NET assembly—and how to use it as a private program or as a shared program. You learn about the global assembly cache, its role in shared assemblies, and how to create strong-named assemblies that provide uniqueness and security. You will also learn about different deployment packaging options, such as the cabinet file, the Microsoft Windows Installation file, and the Merge Module, and you'll learn what is the best time to use each. You'll delve into how the VS.NET IDE makes it easy to package and deploy your .NET applications with the setup wizard. Finally, the chapter wraps up with a discussion of how to deploy ASP.NET applications.

Summary

Visual C# is an exciting new language with a powerful framework behind it. As you go through this book, you will find that you have the power at your fingertips to create applications for all aspects of programming in a fraction of the time it took you in previous development environments. Also you will find Visual C# and the .NET Framework extensible, robust, well architected, and extremely flexible.

The next chapter provides you with an introduction and precursory understanding of .NET and the .NET Framework.

Chapter 2:
.NET and the .NET Framework

Introduction to .NET

Is .NET another framework promising to heal the world's software ills? No, but it goes a long way toward curing the complexities of implementing distributed computing. The framework, in fact, is not .NET, but only the foundation of Microsoft's .NET vision. That vision, encapsulated in a single phrase, is software that can be executed any time, in any place, and on any device. A more technical definition is transparent application collaboration in a device-independent, distributed environment. From a developer's perspective, this vision is constructed on a foundation of the following five elements: tools, technologies, servers, services, and smart devices.

Tools

Visual Studio .NET will certainly be the preeminent tool for .NET developers. The integrated development environment (IDE), familiar to so many developers, is now a truly integrated environment to seamlessly create Windows- or Web-based applications or middle-tier infrastructure. Visual Studio .NET (VS.NET) will ultimately be released in three versions: Professional, Enterprise Developer, and Enterprise Architect. Numerous other tools also exist to aid in the generation of such things as Web service proxies (wsdl.exe) and C# wrappers for Component Object Model (COM) objects (tlbimp.exe). Finally, there are two software development kits (SDKs) at present—the framework SDK and the Mobile Internet SDK—and an interesting third offering on the horizon. Currently in pre-beta, the ObjectSpaces SDK uses an Extensible Markup Language (XML) vocabulary to convert objects into sets of database tables. It supposedly will support inherited, nested, and contained objects. As .NET matures, you can expect a wave of tools and SDKs to flood the market.

Technologies

The technologies figuring most prominently in the .NET vision are six key protocols or technologies that the World Wide Web Consortium (W3C), the European Computer Manufacturers Association (ECMA), Microsoft, and IBM have already accepted or are currently considering as standards.

XML, the W3C standard for formatting structured data according to a set of rules, lies at the core of .NET. Configuration files use XML. Five namespaces in the .NET class library are devoted to creating and querying XML streams and documents. (A *namespace* is a string identifier, wrapping classes to reduce the potential of class name conflicts across multiple dynamic-link libraries or DLLs.)

Simple Object Access Protocol (SOAP), a proposed W3C standard built on XML, is designed to define communication between loosely coupled applications across any platform. .NET's Web services implement SOAP over Hypertext Transfer Protocol (HTTP) as the default protocol.

Web Services Description Language (WSDL), another proposed W3C standard, describes what functionality a Web service provides and what arguments and methods are available to the consumer.

Universal Description, Discovery and Integration (UDDI) is a means for providing a directory of Web services. It allows providers to advertise Web services and consumers to locate them. There are plans to submit this specification, which IBM and Microsoft have adopted, to a standards body in the future.

C# is the new and premier programming language of .NET. Heavily influenced by C++ and Java, it is a powerful, object-oriented language that will feel familiar to developers migrating from those languages. Proof of the elegance of C# will be evident through this book.

The **Common Language Infrastructure (CLI),** which is currently before the ECMA for acceptance, is an umbrella that covers the definition of .NET and numerous subspecifications that make up the comprehensive, robust framework. As this is the heart of the chapter, the CLI and its various components will be dealt with in detail in subsequent sections.

Servers

The servers are a suite of enterprise applications to administer and facilitate business functions. The following servers are available for supporting or hosting the .NET Framework:

Windows XP Advanced Server, or Windows 2000 Advanced Server, is the .NET platform to host Microsoft's suite of enterprise servers.

SQL Server 2000 is Microsoft's fully XML-enabled relational database.

Exchange Server 2000 handles messaging and collaboration.

Host Integration Server 2000 is the result of the evolving SNA Server to access mainframe applications and databases.

Commerce Server 2000 builds e-commerce Web applications.

Application Center 2000 deploys and manages Web applications.

BizTalk Server 2000 accelerates the building of business processes and document interchange.

Internet Security and Acceleration Server 2000 provides Web caching and firewall services.

Mobile Information Server 2001, the latest of the .NET servers, provides wireless access to information.

Services

.NET My Services, formerly HailStorm, is Microsoft's strategy to secure revenue on a subscription basis. The vision encompasses a set of Web services that can be invoked over the Internet by any subscribing client's application. It promises to deliver enhanced convenience and utility to business and to the consumer. This new approach to using the Web is largely untried and unproven.

Microsoft currently offers two services in this manner. The first, .NET Passport, is a suite of authentication and encryption services that has single-point access over the Internet. The Passport client, using any device, is granted access to any Passport Web site without requiring a login. Required authentication takes place in the background, between the Passport Web site and the Passport server.

The second service, .NET Alerts, is an opt-in, push notification service. An Alerts client, for example, who requests a notification if a specified stock reaches a stated price, would automatically be notified by his broker when that price is reached. Used in conjunction with the Passport service, the Alerts server is aware of the devices associated with the client and sends notification through the device currently in use—for example, it calls a client who is on the phone or sends e-mail notification to a client who is typing on a laptop.

It is important to understand the distinction between a Web site, a Web service, and .NET My Services. A *Web site* is the presentation of an application that users can interact with over the Internet. A *Web service*, on the other hand, is a new, innovative interaction between two or more applications over the Internet. Web services (covered extensively in Chapter 13) are based upon XML and SOAP messages using HTTP as the transport mechanism. Finally, *.NET My Services* is primarily a Microsoft business strategy that happens to use Web services as a medium.

Smart Devices

Smart devices access and present data in the appropriate form for a particular device anytime and anywhere. In reality, the device is as thick as a brick; the *software* is smart. Microsoft's vision of smart devices has ambitions to be hardware *and* software smart. The following capabilities are among the components that make up that ambition:

- The logged-on user's preferences are understood. Alerts and information are tailored to location and type of device in use.
- The device responds to bandwidth constraints, to take advantage of the type of Internet connection when sending and receiving information.
- Information can be accessed anytime and anywhere in a device-appropriate form.
- When a device detects another device, it can send information in the format that is most appropriate to that device. Devices interrogate each other to determine which services are available.

Benefits of the .NET Framework

C#

C#'s design started on a blank page, taking into account the current state of programming languages. The designers drew on the strengths of existing languages and avoided their flaws. What emerged is a full-featured, object-oriented language of rare beauty and grace. Based on C, C++, and, most would say, Java, C# is a strongly typed language that C++ and Java developers will find very familiar. It is easy to learn and has none of the backward-compatibility issues of C or C++. Created for the .NET environment, C# has a thoroughly modern syntax with accessors (properties), a concept borrowed from COM, and new operators, such as *implicit* and *explicit*. While affording easy access to the framework's class library, it also allows direct memory and pointer access with the *unsafe* keyword. There is also talk of extending language support to templates, or parameterized types.

Among the stated design goals of the C# inventors, Anders Hejlsberg, Scott Wiltamuth, and Peter Golde, was the creation of a modern, simple, general-purpose programming language. They also intended to craft a language flexible enough to handle the contradictory demands of hosted and embedded systems running on distributed networks. As you become familiar with C#, you might agree that the inventors have more than succeeded.

You should be aware of an important limitation of C#: When exceptional or time-critical performance is required, it is probably wise to retreat to C or C++. In the C# specifications submitted to the ECMA, the section outlining C#'s design goals clearly states that C# is not intended to compete directly with C or assembly language on performance or executable file size.

Managed Code

Managed code is simply code written to execute in the .NET environment. Managed code offers a few benefits in terms of integrated security, type-safe code, and automatic memory allocation and deallocation.

In the .NET world, there is no *delete* keyword. No longer are hours, if not days, spent tracking down a stubborn memory leak. Memory allocation and deallocation is done via the common language runtime (CLR). This garbage collection is handled by the System.GC, which periodically walks the heap to clean up obsolete objects. Although you are not required to dereference objects with *null*, it is still good programming practice to do so; and it delivers added benefit in that the Garbage Collector (GC) is given early notice that the object is not needed.

Security is integrated into .NET from the ground up. With .NET comes support for role-based security and code access security. In traditional *role-based security*, authentication (the verification of a person or process) and authorization (a means of determining that a person or process is permitted to perform a requested process) are carried out by any one of many commonly used mechanisms, such as .NET Passport, NTLM, or an application-defined mechanism. *Code access security* takes a different approach. The idea behind this .NET innovation is that code itself can be malicious, as any victim of a virus or worm will attest. Code access security allows code behavior to be restricted by varying degrees, depending on the code's origin and identity.

Currently, most application boundaries are normally confined to the process level. Any communication outside of the process requires specialized handling such as a COM component. Application domains, a concept introduced in .NET, permit multiple applications to run in a single process. Before managed code runs, it goes through a verification procedure to establish that it will not access memory or perform an action that would cause the process to crash. If the code passes this verification, it is said to be *type safe*. Type-safe code allows the CLR to define application domains, which carry the same level of isolation and protection as a process. While not totally free of charge, interapplication communication, across application domains, avoids most of the performance penalties associated with interprocess communication.

Cross-Language Operation

The hurdle of calling methods across different languages is almost as high as the barrier to interaction between different operating systems. TCP/IP aided in communication between operating systems, just as COM components went a long way to facilitate cross-language conversations. But there were constraints. Visual Basic only has signed integer and long data types, while Unicode characters are not native to C++. In many instances, performance would suffer as data was converted or cast back and forth. In .NET, all compliant languages are equal; and, with Microsoft Intermediate Language (MSIL), all operating systems are potentially equal as well. Efforts toward platform independence are taking shape with the Mono Project, a .NET implementation on Linux. A .NET-compliant language is one that adheres to the Common Language Specification (CLS) and the Common Type System (CTS) laid out in the CLI. It is now possible to have C#, managed C++, and VB.NET code in the same module. Other compliant languages include J# (Java Sharp), Cobol, and Perl. MSIL has made programming languages transparent. Systems can be developed in the language or languages of choice.

Of course, becoming a compliant language might force some concessions to be made. Visual Basic appears to have mutated to such an extent that VB.NET could qualify as a new .NET language along with C#. C++ is confined to single inheritance. In all likelihood, other languages that adhere to the CLS will have minor restrictions placed upon them.

This newfound freedom may come at a cost. It brings to mind an old adage in the C world: C gives the developer plenty of freedom—enough to hang himself! In the same way, developing an application in multiple .NET languages sows the seeds for project failure. An application written using C#, VB.NET, J#, Cobol, and Perl requires an army of skill sets, rather than a cohesive team, to maintain the code.

C# will likely be the language of choice for most projects, because of current and future features such as the unsafe keyword and possible support for templates. Other serious contenders are probably VB.NET and J#.

The Class Library

What can be said about the framework's class library? It is extensive and extensible. There is finally a consistent method to access system resources spanning the many .NET-compliant languages. Certainly, at first glance, the number of namespaces, classes, and interfaces can be daunting, and here seasoned C++ and Java developers will hit a learning curve. Developers migrating to the .NET Framework from C++ or Java should have an easier transition because they have already grasped object-oriented concepts. Those coming from a procedural language world, such as Visual Basic and Cobol, face a much sharper bend on the road to mastering the .NET Framework.

The class library is broken down into a hierarchy of namespaces. Each namespace's name describes its general purpose. Contained in each namespace are the classes and interfaces, which define specific behaviors and data that contribute to the namespace's functionality. The class library is not language specific and may used by any of .NET's compliant languages.

In conjunction with the CLR, the class library supports not only dynamic runtime binding but also dynamic compile-time binding. Although the term *compile-time binding* is open to debate, the practice isn't. If an object is not present, it is possible for an application to obtain the source code and compile it on the fly. Calling the compiler, in the System.CodeDom.Compiler namespace, with either a string or a file name returns a reference to the executable code. The results can then be loaded and the object's methods executed, thus giving a whole new meaning to late binding.

The class library is a comprehensive implementation that addresses 80 percent of problem domain needs with an out-of-the-box answer. But, as is always the case, a customized solution is the only alternative in some situations. In designing the class library, the developers paid a great deal of attention to extensibility. The library features a rich set of *virtual* and *abstract* classes and methods, as well as a wide range of interfaces to tackle any customization requirement.

Deployment

Windows application distribution has always been fraught with potential disaster. COM executables and DLLs have to be registered. Likely, every developer has had nightmares involving the Windows registry. Did I register everything? Are all the proxy/stubs accounted for? And that's only for local machine registry—in DCOM the proxy/stub has to be registered on both client and server machines. And if you're using a customized surrogate, you had better start writing an installation application. Microsoft describes this situation as "DLL Hell."

Updating shared DLLs is also a form of DLL Hell and commonly creates havoc. The newer DLL versions overwrite the current ones, or registration conflicts occur. The newer versions are backward-compatible with only some of the existing software. Consequently, some applications run normally while others inexplicably crash. Tracking down which DLL is the culprit and where the bug is can be a long, agonizing task. .NET eliminates the clash of old and new with assemblies.

An *assembly*, the name .NET uses for an executable or DLL, contains a *manifest* and *metadata* in addition to the compiled source code. Together, the manifest and metadata fully describe the contents of the assembly. Each assembly is a self-contained unit with compiled source code, a full description of the code and its dependencies, a version number, and security settings. Assemblies can be private or shared. In most cases, to install private assemblies, it is a simple matter of using XCOPY. To uninstall, use DEL. Shared assemblies require a bit more work and are discussed in detail in Chapter 26. Shared assemblies are installed in the global assembly cache (GAC).

Common Language Infrastructure

In previous sections, terms such as *CLI* and *CTS* have been bandied about without any explanation. Beginning with this section, we'll start to explore what makes .NET run. The CLI can be broken down into three main components:

Common Type System. The CTS lays out the basic data types in order for compiler designers to build a .NET-compliant language.
Common Language Specification. The CLS establishes the minimum set of rules to promote language interoperability. In conjunction with the CTS, it describes the contract all compilers must meet when targeting .NET.
Virtual Execution System. The VES is responsible for loading and running programs and providing services for those programs.

These three elements, and the use of metadata by the VES, constitute the CLI. Without putting too fine a point on it, the CLI can almost be thought of as specifications for a virtual operating system or machine. In the Windows world, the CLI comes to life in the CLR.

Metadata

Aside from the three main components, a fourth component in the CLI is *metadata*, or data about data. From a CLI perspective, metadata is information about every element in an assembly. The importance of metadata cannot be overstated. One feature of .NET that is well known to Java developers but unknown in the C++ world is *reflection*, the ability to interrogate assemblies and objects at runtime. Reflection enables dynamic creation and invocation.

Enough metadata is in an assembly that the CLR can control all aspects of execution, including loading, execution, and inspecting the execution state (i.e., walking the stack); enforcing security; and establishing runtime context boundaries (i.e., where one application domain begins and another ends).

Common Type System

The CTS is one of the cornerstones of .NET. This type system permits .NET to support multiple languages—a reasonable expectation, considering that languages have great difficulty interoperating if they are based on dissimilar types. This multilanguage support must take into account both procedural and object-oriented languages. How is this accomplished? The quick answer is that all types are objects.

Although the CTS is a hierarchy of types, as shown in Figure 2.1, it can be distilled down to two root types: value and reference. The single most distinguishing feature between these basic types is memory allocation. Value types are allocated on the stack, while reference types are allocated on the heap.

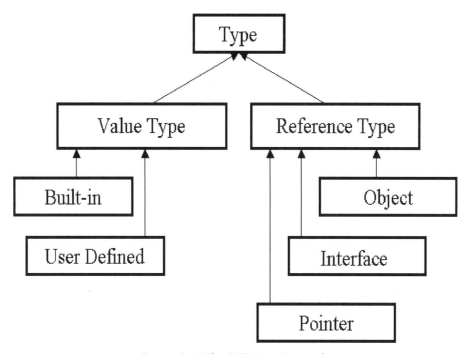

Figure 2.1: The CTS Type Hierarchy

Although accurate, the earlier statement that all types are objects is somewhat misleading. For each value type, the CTS supports a corresponding reference type. Therefore 2.ToString() is a valid statement.

The *built-in* value types consist of primitive types such as integers and longs. *User-defined* value types are types such as structures and enumerations. An *object* reference type can be said to be a class. An *interface* reference type has no implementation but simply defines method and property signatures that must be implemented by an object. A *pointer* reference type is a value that identifies a memory location in the heap.

Common Language Specification

The CLS defines the minimum requirements that must be realized before a language is considered .NET compliant. It is primarily of use to language and framework designers. It specifies a minimum subset of CTS types to be supported and a set of usage rules. From an application developer's perspective, where language interoperability is crucial, Table 2.1 lists the types supported by the CLS. This is likely to be the only instance where the CLS need be consulted.

MSIL Assembler Name	Class Library Name	Type	Description
bool	System.Boolean	Value	values either true or false
char	System.Char	Value	Unicode character (16 bits)
class System.Object	System.Object	Reference	base object of all classes
class System.String	System.String	Reference	Unicode string (16-bit characters)
float32	System.Single	Value	IEEE 32-bit float
float64	System.Double	Value	IEEE 64-bit float
int16	System.Int16	Value	signed 16-bit integer
int32	System.Int32	Value	signed 32-bit integer
int64	System.Int64	Value	signed 64-bit integer
natural int	System.IntPtr	Value	signed integer, natural size
unsigned int8	System.Byte	Value	unsigned 8-bit integer

Table 2.1: The CTS type hierarchy

Supported CLS types are only a small subset of defined CTS types. Keep this in mind if language interoperability is a requirement. C# supports unsigned and signed values, whereas VB.NET supports only signed types. Therefore, to be CLS compliant, a C# component should expose only signed types and use unsigned types only with an accessibility level of *private* or *internal* or as locally scoped variables. (This rule is opposite for int8 or Byte, whose unsigned value is CLS compliant and whose signed value is not).

Common Intermediate Language

The Common Intermediate Language (CIL), more commonly known as Microsoft Intermediate Language (MSIL) or simply Intermediate Language (IL), is a CPU-independent instruction set that allows .NET to support multiple languages. It also has the potential to be operating system–independent as long as the platform can host an implementation of the CLI. The major difference between IL and Java's byte code is that IL is only an intermediate step on the path to execution. The Java Virtual Machine runs an application by interpreting its byte codes. .NET compilers, on the other hand, produce an assembly that is loaded by the CLR at runtime.

Common Language Runtime

The CLR provides the environment in which managed code is executed. In addition to implementing the CLI, the CLR adds Windows-specific functionality, such as security, GUI capabilities for the Win32 environment, and COM interoperability. Again, without stretching the point too far, the CLR may be perceived as a virtual machine but, in fact, it isn't. The CLR reads an assembly and compiles it to the native instruction set of the processor, via a Just-In-Time (JIT) compiler, prior to execution.

Figure 2.2 shows the sequence of steps taken to compile an assembly.

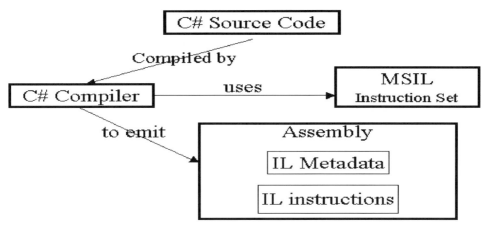

Figure 2.2: The C# Compiling Sequence

Before an application can run in the .NET environment, a runtime host, which is a stub of unmanaged code, must load and initialize the CLR. An example of such a host is aspnet_isapi.dll, an Internet Server API extension DLL that loads the CLR and creates the application domain for an application's subsequent ASP.NET Web requests. Various runtime hosts are currently distributed with the .NET Framework, including one for Microsoft Internet Explorer and one for all shell executable applications. It is likely that future versions of operating systems that support the CLR will have any required runtime hosts built in.

The sequence of loading and executing an application is graphically illustrated in Figure 2.3.

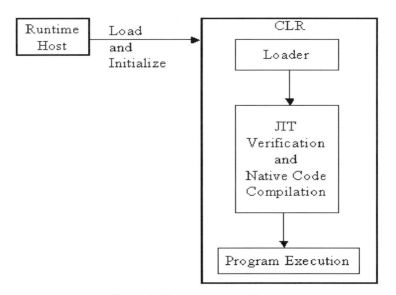

Figure 2.3 Running an Application

Once the CLR has been loaded and initialized and an application domain created, the application is ready to run. At this point, the CLR loads the application in the domain and then verifies that the IL compiled code is type safe. If verification fails, an exception is thrown. Verification can be skipped if a security policy (see Chapter 22 for a detailed explanation) is in place to do so. Once verification succeeds or is skipped, the JIT compiler compiles the IL to native code.

Not all the code in an assembly is verified and compiled at the outset. The JIT converts the IL to native code as an object's methods are called during program execution. The resulting native code is cached and used for subsequent calls of the method. It does this by marking the method, which in turn points subsequent calls to the binary code.

A Customized Runtime Host

Earlier we mentioned that any managed application currently requires a runtime host. In designing a customized runtime host, a number of considerations should be taken into account. One of the benefits of .NET is side-by-side execution, where a number of versions of the CLR can run simultaneously. This is true for a computer, but only a single version of the CLR can be hosted by a process. Therefore, only assemblies compiled for the loaded CLR version will run as expected. Another consideration is determining which CLR build to use: a workstation build or a server build. The workstation build, mscorwks.dll, provides optimal performance for client applications. The server build, mscorsvr.dll, optimizes parallel GC on multiprocessor machines. The mscoree.dll, located in the System32 directory, uses a *startup shim* to load the type of CLR build specified by the runtime host.

As we create the customized runtime host, note that the sample application is fairly complex and requires a substantial knowledge of .NET and VS.NET configuration. Also, some understanding of COM interoperability, running unmanaged and managed code in the same process, is needed to fully benefit from the example. Readers who are new to .NET may wish to return to the example once they have completed the appropriate chapters and have a better appreciation of the relationship between the operating system and the CLR.

The customized runtime host consists of three projects: (1) an unmanaged executable, RuntimeHost.exe; (2) a managed-code DLL (class library), AppDomainCreatorLib.dll; and (3) a managed-code executable, ManageCodeExecutable.exe. Before launching into the code, we'll take a minute to set up the projects.

Project Setup for RuntimeHost Application

Each project's output has been configured to place the compiled code into the RuntimeHost/Debug directory; thus, the code can be run from any of the projects without having to copy various DLLs or executable files to multiple directories. Another option is to register the assemblies in the GAC (see Chapter 26 for a more detailed explanation). Also, the startup program for the managed-code modules points to RuntimeHost.exe. The AppDomainCreatorLib project is initially compiled as a managed-code DLL, which is then employed to generate a typelibrary with the tlbexp.exe utility.

The AppDomainCreatorLib and ManagedCodeExecutable project property pages should resemble the displays shown in Figures 2.4 and 2.5, respectively.

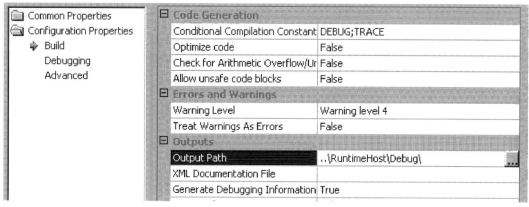

Figure 2.4: DLL and Executable Output Path

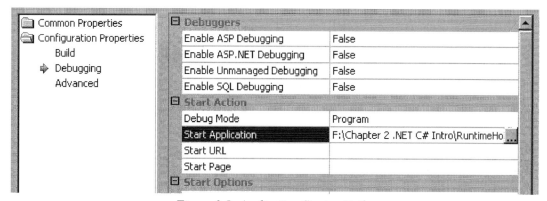

Figure 2.5: Application Startup Path

If the Debug Mode drop-down list (Figure 2.5) in either the AppDomainCreatorLib or ManagedCodeExecutable projects contains anything but "Program," change it. In addition, the Start Application path is hard-coded and therefore must be changed to reflect the actual directory of the RuntimeHost.exe.

A couple of default settings must be changed to debug the application from any of the projects. The managed-code projects, AppDomainCreatorLib and ManagedCodeExecutable, must enable unmanaged debugging, whereas the unmanaged project, RuntimeHost, has to be set to mixed debugging (Figure 2.6).

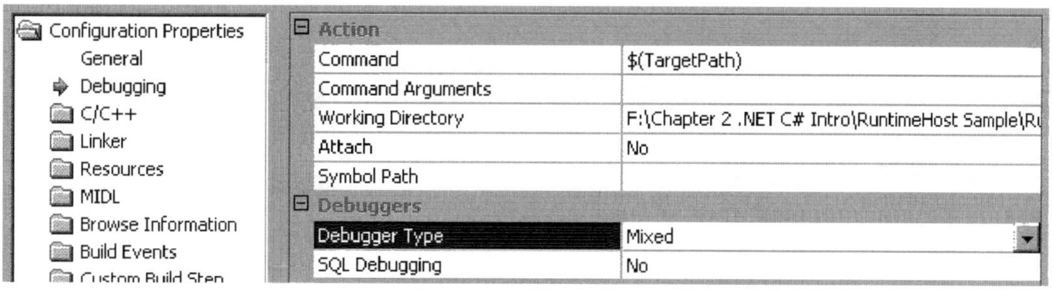

Figure 2.6: Unmanaged Project with Mixed Debugging Enabled

The final property configuration, required to run this application from any of the projects, is in the AppDomainCreatorLib and ManagedCodeExecutable project settings. The command line arguments, highlighted in Figure 2.7, need the .NET version and the server type. Indeed, if the version of the .NET assemblies does not correspond with v1.0.338, then the Command Arguments setting in the RuntimeHost project *must* change to the .NET version on the user's machine.

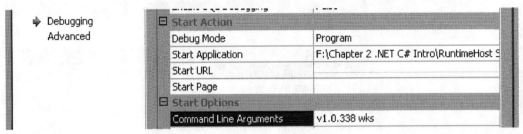

Figure 2.7: Required Command Line

The compilation order is also important so that the AppDomainCreatorLib's essential typelibrary is generated without unnecessary recompiling. First, compile the two managed code projects, AppDomainCreatorLib and ManagedCodeExecutable. Then, open a console window and switch to the RuntimeHost project's debug directory. Create a typelibrary by typing the following command.

```
tlbexp AppDomainCreatorLib.dll /out:AppDomainCreator.tlb
```

Copy the typelibrary into the RuntimeHost project's root directory and then compile the RuntimeHost executable. The application can now be run from any of the three projects.

Project Code

The process created by the runtime host ultimately contains seven application domains: the default domain and six domains created in the AppDomainCreatorLib. Once created, each of these six application domains starts an instance of the managed executable, ManagedCodeExecutable.exe. The output from the three projects (shown in Figure 2.8) is trivial but serves to demonstrate the point of several managed executables running in a single process.

```
file:///f:/Chapter 2 .NET C# Intro/RuntimeHost Sample/RuntimeHost/Debug/ManagedCodeExecutabl...
args label is - RuntimeDomain0.
args label is - RuntimeDomain1.
args label is - RuntimeDomain2.
args label is - RuntimeDomain3.
args label is - RuntimeDomain4.
args label is - RuntimeDomain5.
```

Figure 2.8: RuntimeHost Output

Working in the opposite direction of program execution, we'll first look at the managed executable located in the ManagedCodeExecutable project. Only the main method is shown in Listing 2.1, as any class and namespace would suffice.

Listing 2.1—ManagedExe.cs

```
static int Main( string[] args)
{
    Console.WriteLine( "args label is - {0}.",
            AppDomain.CurrentDomain.FriendlyName);
    return( 0);
}
```

As is evident from the output in Figure 2.8, each managed executable simply writes its application domain's name to the console window and terminates.

The core of the projects is the unmanaged stub, RuntimeHost.cpp, located in the RuntimeHost project. The source code for this unmanaged stub appears in Listing 2.2.

Listing 2.2—RuntimeHost.cpp Source Code

```
#include <mscoree.h>

//Without renaming the "ReportEvent" a C4278 warning is generated
//by the compiler
#import <mscorlib.tlb> rename( "ReportEvent", "RuntimeReportEvent")
using namespace mscorlib;

//Without the pragma a C4192 warning generated by the compiler
#pragma warning( disable: 4192)
#import <mscoree.tlb>

#import "AppDomainCreator.tlb"
using namespace AppDomainCreatorLib;

int _tmain( int argc, _TCHAR* argv[])
{
int             ret = -1;
TCHAR*          pszVersion = NULL; //_T("v1.0.3328")
TCHAR*          pszServer = NULL; //_T("wks")
ICorRuntimeHost *punkHost = NULL;
HRESULT         hr = E_FAIL;

        if( argc != 3)
        {
                return( ret);
        }

        pszVersion = argv[1];
        pszServer = argv[2];
        hr = CoInitializeEx( NULL, COINIT_APARTMENTTHREADED);
        //loads CLR into the process -
        //Ex requires _WIN32_DCOM preprocessor define
        hr = CorBindToRuntimeEx( pszVersion, pszServer,
                            STARTUP_LOADER_OPTIMIZATION_MULTI_DOMAIN |
                                    STARTUP_CONCURRENT_GC,
                            CLSID_CorRuntimeHost,
                            IID_ICorRuntimeHost,
                            (void **)&punkHost);
        if( SUCCEEDED(hr))
        {
                IUnknown    *punk = NULL;

          //GetDefaultDomain returns E_UNEXPECTED if Start() not called
        punkHost->Start();
        hr = punkHost->GetDefaultDomain( &punk);
        if( SUCCEEDED( hr))
        {
          _AppDomain *punkDefDom = NULL;

              //Get the actual AppDomain
            hr = punk->QueryInterface( __uuidof(_AppDomain),
                                            (void**) &punkDefDom);
          if( SUCCEEDED( hr))
          {
          _bstr_t bstrName = "AppDomainCreatorLib.AppDomainCreator";
          _bstr_t bstrAssembly = "AppDomainCreatorLib";
```

```
        _ObjectHandle *punkHandle = NULL;

        punkHandle = punkDefDom->CreateInstance( bstrAssembly,
                bstrName);
          if( punkHandle != NULL)
          {
             _variant_t var;

               VariantInit( &var);
                  //Get the actual IUnknown
                  //for AppDomainCreator
               var = punkHandle->Unwrap();
             if( var.punkVal != NULL)
             {
                _AppDomainCreator *punkCreator = NULL;

                     //With .NET you'll never have to use another
                     //variant after this.
                     hr = var.punkVal->QueryInterface(
                           __uuidof(_AppDomainCreator),
                           (void**)&punkCreator);
                if( SUCCEEDED( hr))
                {
                     //Call to create multiple, managed code AppDomains
                       hr = punkCreator->CreateAppDomain(
                                         _bstr_t("RuntimeDomain"), 6);
                     if( SUCCEEDED( hr))
                     {
                          punkCreator->Release();
                          ret = 0;
                     }
                }
             }
          }

          punkDefDom->Release();
       }

       punk->Release();
    }

    punkHost->Stop();
    punkHost->Release();
      CoUninitialize();
  }

      return( ret);
}
```

Nothing unusual surrounds the host's entry point, a standard C/C++ main method that can be compiled either for single- or multiple-byte characters. In this case, the preprocessor #define is Unicode. As stated earlier, the CLR version and build are assigned from the command line arguments. CoInitializeEx is called; but note that the program runs without a problem if CoInit isn't called. One can only assume that the following call initializes the COM subsystem if it hasn't already initialized. CorBindToRuntimeEx is the method that loads and initializes the CLR. Each parameter is optional and the CLR loader uses a default value if none is provided.

Use of the first parameter is obvious: If the value is NULL, the latest version of the CLR is used.

Options for the second parameter, the build type, are WKS or SVR. In the face of a NULL value, the workstation build is loaded. Additionally, the workstation build is used on a single-processor machine, even if SVR is specified, because mscorwks.dll is the always the best performer on a single-processor box.

The third parameter applies to automatic allocation and deallocation of memory ("garbage collection" or GC) and the assembly loader. GC has two modes: concurrent and nonconcurrent. Concurrent GC operates on background threads instead of user threads, making applications with a user interface more responsive. Nonconcurrent GC should be employed by server applications for better performance. The assembly loader flag determines whether assemblies are treated as *domain neutral* when loaded. This idea is similar to the concept of a dynamic-link library as compared to a statically linked library. In our example, if the loader flag had specified a single domain, a copy of the executable file would have been loaded and run each time an application domain requested an instance. In a domain-neutral environment, the executable code is shared. As is usually the case, there are tradeoffs. Domain-neutral processes tend to consume less memory but have slower performance.

The fourth and fifth parameters specify the class ID (CLSID) and interface ID (IID) of the ICorRuntimeHost interface. The last parameter provides an address for the interface pointer. In all the documentation we've read, the ICorRuntimeHost->Start() call isn't required to start the CLR; but without it, the HRESULT returned by the GetDefaultDomain() is E_UNEXPECTED. The documentation states that the CLR is started upon the creation of the first application domain. It may very well be that the default domain isn't created on GetDefaultDomain() but on the later call to QueryInterface(). This isn't an unreasonable supposition, as will be seen later in the chapter.

Once the default domain's interface is obtained, the time has come to create our own application domains. The AppDomainCreator object can be instantiated in the default domain. This is accomplished by calling the default domain's CreateInstance method with the assembly name and the class name. An ObjectHandle is returned and unwrapped. Unlike System.Runtime.Remoting.ObjectHandle, which returns an object, the unmanaged Unwrap() returns a VARIANT data type. An IUnknown is extracted from the variant and QueryInterface returns an _AppDomainCreator interface. In calling the CreateAppDomain method, we enter the realm of managed code. The parameters specify the domain name and the number of domains to be created. The AppDomainCreatorLib project (Listing 2.3) is responsible for creating multiple application domains.

Listing 2.3—AppDomainCreator.cs

```
using System;
using System.Runtime.InteropServices;
using System.Security.Policy;

[ClassInterface( ClassInterfaceType.AutoDual)]
public class AppDomainCreator
{
        public void CreateAppDomain( string appDomainName, int appDomCnt)
        {
                if( ((appDomainName == null) ||
                        (appDomainName.Length == 0)) ||
                        (appDomCnt <= 0))
                {
                Exception exc = null;

                        exc = new Exception( "Invalid parameters.");
                        throw( exc);
                }

        Evidence    evid = null;
        string      currentDir = null;

                evid = AppDomain.CurrentDomain.Evidence;
                currentDir = Environment.CurrentDirectory;
```

```
for( int x = 0; x < appDomCnt; x++)
{
AppDomain        appDom = null;

        appDom = AppDomain.CreateDomain( appDomainName +
                                 x.ToString());
string assembly = null;

        assembly = currentDir + @"\" +
                    "ManagedCodeExecutable.exe";
        appDom.ExecuteAssembly( assembly , evid, null);
}
    }
}
```

Upon entering the CreateAppDomain method, we are working with managed code, although the method was called from unmanaged code. Any invalid parameters cause an exception to be thrown. The application domains are created using the static method AppDomain.CreateDomain and the returned reference is used for the ExecuteAssembly method. It should be noted that the returned reference isn't the actual object, but rather a proxy similar to a COM proxy in an "out-of-proc" component. The only other point of interest in this method is the Evidence object in the System.Security.Policy namespace. Evidence, along with code groups and membership conditions, goes into setting the rules applied by the CLR's security policy. Looking at the class as a whole, another aspect of note is the ClassInterface attribute.

ClassInterfaceAttribute can be applied to assemblies or classes. Used in conjunction with tlbexp.exe, it facilitates the generation of unmanaged COM class interfaces. Only those class methods that are public and nonstatic and that have had the ClassInterfaceAttribute value set to ClassInterfaceType.AutoDual, will be generated by tlbexp.exe.

Before you leave this section, Listings 2.2 and 2.3 warrant another look. Notice in Listing 2.2 (the unmanaged host) the number of directives. To simply compile the runtime host requires a number of #includes, #pragmas, and #imports, not to mention the libraries needed by the linker. Now consider Listing 2.3, in which simple "using" statements identify a class' namespace. There may also be the need to attach the odd reference to an assembly. The .NET Framework is so clean, so simple.

Summary

Will .NET and the .NET Framework succeed? Many think so. The .NET Framework provides a powerful platform with which to develop distributed systems. .NET won't remain static. As the potential of networking and the Internet becomes more sharply apparent, as hardware capabilities advance and speeds increase, as new demands are placed upon technology by businesses and consumers, .NET will evolve and continue to offer benefits to users, businesses, and developers.

For users, the major benefits remain a bit distant. In the future, .NET will change the way digital devices and users interact. Users will be authenticated from any location. Their preferences and permissions will be transparently attached to an invoked application. Information, whether it takes the form of text, handwriting, speech, audio, or video, will be presented with the appropriate view for the device. A device's firmware will transparently be updated with new software, doing away with the need to manually download upgrades and fixes.

For businesses developing applications, the costs incurred by development and deployment will plummet. Those fully exploiting .NET's capabilities will find that painful and expensive sectors such as customer service become a pillar of customer loyalty, with online problem resolution taking place between smart devices, rather than frustrated, harried individuals.

Finally, and importantly, Visual Studio .NET and the framework's class library benefits developers by allowing them to concentrate on solving the problem domain, not the myriad of technical challenges surrounding the domain. When technical obstacles do arise, the framework has been designed to readily adapt and facilitate a customized solution.

For those who have been exposed to .NET and didn't immediately skip to the next chapter, we hope we have not been too tedious rehashing the fundamentals. If this is your first introduction to .NET, read on. We are sure you'll be intrigued by the possibilities and potential of the .NET vision in general and the .NET Framework in particular. The next chapter introduces C# with the standard "Hello, World" console application to get you started in the future of software development with .NET.

Chapter 3:
Hello, C#

This short chapter based on the classic "Hello, World" sample program familiarizes you with the language syntax and introduces the command line compiler. It illustrates how to write a C# program and compile it from the command line by exploring some of the basics of C# programming and compiler options. After completing this chapter, you will know how to write a simple program in C# using a text editor and compile it from the command line.

C# Compiler

Although we assume you are using Visual Studio .NET, there is another way for you to get the C# compiler and compile your programs from the command line. The command line C# compiler comes along with the .NET Framework Software Development Kit (SDK). The URL for retrieving these files can be found in the Downloads section of the Web site C# Corner (http://www.c-sharpcorner.com).

Hello, C#

As we discussed in the previous chapter, you can use any text editor to type C# programs. After typing the code, save it with the .cs extension and compile it from the command line using the C# compiler called *csc*.

Listing 3.1 shows the Hello, C# program. Type this program in a text editor such as Notepad or in the Visual Studio .NET editor. The output of the program in Listing 3.1 to the system console produce "Hello, C#!" after it is compiled and run.

Listing 3.1—"Hello, C#" Example

```
using System;
class Hello
{
 static void Main() {
  Console.WriteLine("Hello, C#!");
 }
}
```

Save the file as hello.cs and compile it from the command line using the C# compiler, using the following syntax:

```
csc hello.cs or C:\temp> csc hello.cs
```

Make sure the file path is correct.

If you don't find csc.exe in your current directory, provide the full path of csc.exe. For example, if your csc.exe is in C:\Program Files\.NET\Exes\, then compile your code from the command prompt using this command:

C:\Program Files\.NET\Exes\csc.exe C:\hello.cs

After compiling your code, the C# compiler creates an executable file called hello.exe in the bin directory. Figure 3.1 shows the executable file as it is running.

Figure 3.1: "Hello, C#" Output in Command Line

Description of "Hello, C#"

The first line of your program is *using System*.

```
using System;
```

As we discussed in Chapter 1, the .NET Framework class library is defined in namespaces. The class keyword is similar to the C++ class keyword and is used to define a new class that is followed by a class name. For example:

```
class Hello
{
   ...
}
```

The next line of code may consist of the static void Main() function, but this depends on what form of the Main method you are using. The different forms of the Main method are discussed later in this chapter.

In C# every application must include a static Main() or an int Main() method. This method is similar to the main() function of C or C++. This is the entry point of an application. Although an application can have multiple Main methods, you can assign only one of them as the application's entry point. For example:

```
static void Main()
{
   Console.WriteLine("Hello, C#!");
}
```

The next line of code uses the System.Console class to write output to the console. WriteLine(), a method of the Console class, writes a string followed by a line terminator to the console. The Console class defined in the System namespace contains methods to read and write from the console. We discuss this class in more depth in the system I/O chapter.

Compiler Options

When you compile a C# program, the compiler doesn't generate a native (executable) file that is executed directly by the system; rather, it generates a Common Intermediate Language file, which is read by the Common Language Runtime at runtime and then executed. Table 3.1 lists several compiler options you can use in your command line along with the C# compiler and describes what they do.

Option	Meaning
/target:exe	Default output option to build an executable file
/target:library	Builds a DLL with manifest
/target:module	Builds a DLL with no manifest
/target:winexe	Hides console windows for windows applications
/doc	Sends source code comments to an XML file
/out	Specifies the program's name (by default the name of the executable file or the DLL is the same as the class name)

Table 3.1: Compiler Command Line Options

The Multiple Faces of the Main Method

The Main method has a few different declarations from which you can choose. Some of its declarations are discussed here.

The first version of the Main method is the *void* type. This method contains no return and no arguments. The second version of the Main method has no returns but takes arguments, and the third type returns an integer value but no arguments. The different versions of the Main method are shown in Listing 3.2.

Listing 3.2—Different Versions of the Main Method

```
// static Main no return, no arguments
static void Main()
{
        Console.WriteLine("Hello, C#!");
}
// static Main no return, arguments
public static void Main( string[] args)
{
        Console.WriteLine("Hello, C#!");
}
// static Main no return, arguments
public static int Main()
{
        Console.WriteLine("Hello, C#!");
        return 0;
}
```

Command Line Parameters

One form of the Main method plays a vital role when you need to process command line parameters. This Main method takes an argument of a string array. For example:

```
// static Main no return, arguments
public static void Main( string[] args)
{
```

```
        Console.WriteLine("Hello, C#!");
}
```

Let's look at a sample of passing a string array and writing out the arguments. Listing 3.3 shows such an example.

Listing 3.3—Hello.cs Command Line Arguments

```
using System;
class Hello
{
        // static Main no return, arguments
        public static void Main( string[] args)
        {
                for (int i=0; i<args.Length; i++)
                {
                        Console.Write("Args {0}, {1}", i, args[i]);
                        Console.Write("\n");
                }

        }
}
```

When you run the hello.exe generated by the program shown in Listing 3.3, the output looks like that shown in Figure 3.2 (after you press ENTER in the command line).

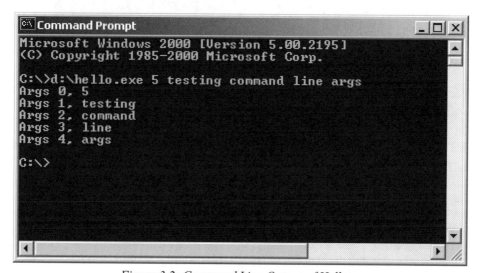

Figure 3.2: Command Line Output of Hello.cs

Another interesting example presented in Listing 3.4 takes three arguments. The first argument is either Add or Subtract, and the second and third arguments are two numbers. If the first argument is Add, the output is the sum of two numbers. If the first argument is Subtract, the output is the difference of two numbers.

Listing 3.4—Add and Remove Arguments from Command Line

```
using System;
class Hello
{
        // static Main no return, arguments
        public static void Main( string[] args)
        {
                int num1 = Convert.ToInt16(args[1]);
```

```
        int num2 = Convert.ToInt16(args[2]);
        int result;

        if (args[0] == "Add")
        {
                result = num1+num2;
                Console.WriteLine(result.ToString());
        }

        if (args[0] == "Subtract" )
        {
                result = num1-num2;
                Console.WriteLine(result.ToString());
        }
    }
}
```

Figure 3.3 shows the results of executing hello.exe from compiled Listing 3.4 and passing in the arguments to Add and Subtract 23 and 3 from the command line.

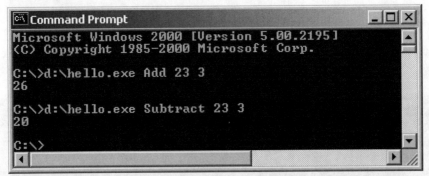

Figure 3.3: Output from Using Add and Remove Arguments in the Command Line

Referencing an Assembly from the Command Line

The core functionality of the System namespace resides in mscorlib.dll, which is available to a program without referencing it. Thus, if you are using only the System namespace, you do not have to pass any assembly information as a command line argument. However, if you are using any other assemblies such as System.Drawing or System.Windows, you need to pass the assembly information as an argument.

For example, if you are using the Windows.Forms namespace in your program, you need to reference the system.winforms.dll assembly as a command line argument.

```
csc /r:system.winforms.dll myforms.cs
```

Summary

The C# compiler comes along with the .NET Framework SDK. You can install the C# compiler in one of two ways: either install the .NET SDK or install VS.NET. Writing a "Hello, World" sample in C# is quite similar to writing one in C++ or Java. The Main method is the entry point of any application. You can pass your command line arguments in the Main method and use them in your application.

In the next chapter, we talk about the C# language in much more depth and teach you how to write applications using that language.

Chapter 4:
Compiling and Debugging

Introduction

We generally write programs in higher-level languages such as C# or Java because they are easier to work with and are more readable than assembly language or machine code. Therefore, using a higher-level language makes a programmer's task easier and less prone to error. However, because the computer understands only binary code, we must somehow convert the source code files of a higher-level language into code the machine can understand. This process is called *code compilation*, and the program that converts the source code into machine code is called a *compiler*.

C# runs on top of the .NET Framework, taking advantage of features such as automatic garbage collection and base class libraries. Hence the .NET Framework adds another level of abstraction between the machine and the C# code. All languages on the .NET platform, including C#, compile into Microsoft Intermediate Language (MSIL) code instead of machine code. MSIL code is just like assembly-language code, but it's highly optimized and diversified to support a variety of programming languages. The MSIL is considered an intermediate language because at runtime the MSIL code is compiled into machine-level code by the Just-In-Time (JIT) compiler. Unlike the one-step approach of the C/C++ compiler, which converts source code directly into machine-level code, C# takes a two-step approach. First, the C# compiler compiles the source code into MSIL code; then, at runtime, MSIL code gets converted into machine-level code by the JIT compilers provided by the .NET Framework.

The .NET Framework provides three JIT compilers: StandardJIT, PreJIT, and EconoJIT. StandardJIT, the default JIT compiler, is generally used to compile all your normal .NET applications. PreJIT, as the name suggests, compiles all the MSIL code into machine-level code at once during installation. This compiler can be very useful when you want to use an application frequently. The EconoJIT compiler is used with handheld systems, personal digital assistants, and other systems that have limited resources. It is optimized to save memory but takes a bit longer to execute code.

Using the C# Command-Line Compiler

The C# language can be compiled into MSIL using either the Visual Studio .NET (VS.NET) integrated development environment (IDE) or the command-line compiler. Even users of the VS.NET IDE may find the various aspects of command-line compiling interesting because it helps them understand the C# compiler and its capabilities.

The C# compiler is contained in the file csc.exe and gets installed when you install the .NET Framework. Even though it is a command-line compiler, you can use it to compile all kinds of C# applications—for example, console applications or Windows forms applications (Visual C#). The C# compiler is generally located within the

<drive>:\<windows>\Microsoft.NET\Framework\<version>\ folder, so on a typical Windows 2000 machine the path to the compiler is found in c:\WinNT\Microsoft.NET\Framework\v1.0.3328\.

To run the C# compiler, you must first open the DOS console containing the Command Prompt/MS-DOS Prompt. Then you navigate to the directory containing the source code files, and finally you compile the source files. Try calling the csc compiler from the command prompt, as follows: c:\>csc. If you get a error such as *'csc' is not recognized as an internal or external command, operable program or batch file,* you must set the environment variables for the compiler in one of two ways. If you have installed VS.NET, search for and run the file vsvars32.bat; if you only have the .NET Framework, then search for and run the file corvars.bat.

C# Command-Line Compiler Options

Chapter 3 explained how to compile a simple console application by passing the compiler a single parameter (the name of the file to compile). When you have to compile complex applications, you need to pass several other parameters to the compiler. Let's address each of the C# compiler options.

The @ Option

As shown in Listing 4.1, the @ option is used to specify a response file (denoted with the extension .rsp) that contains the compiler options to be used while compiling.

The response file is a normal text file that can contain compiler switches and/or file names to be compiled. The pound symbol (#) is used to write comments. Writing options in a response file is similar to typing them at the command prompt. Specifying these options in a response file comes in handy when you want to perform complex compilations during application design. For example, if you have to specify many assemblies to be referenced in your application, a normal compile statement would span many lines! You can write a response file containing the reference to all the assemblies and reuse this file every time you compile the code.

You can specify additional options along with the response file. The compiler processes these options sequentially as they are encountered. Therefore, command-line arguments can override previously listed options in response files. Conversely, options in a response file will override options listed previously on the command line or in other response files.

Listing 4.1—Sample Response File (winform.rsp)

```
#Sample file containing general compiler options for Windows forms
#Usage: csc @winform.rsp yourCode.cs
#Usage 2: csc @winform.rsp /out:MyApplication.exe yourCode.cs

/target:winexe
/r:System.dll;System.Windows.Forms.dll;System.Data.dll;System.Drawing.dll
```

The /? or /help Option

The /? or /help option displays on the console a list of all the compiler options and their usage.

The /addmodule Option

The /addmodule option prompts the compiler to import metadata from the specified modules into the assembly you are compiling. You can specify two or more modules in a single statement by separating them with a comma or a semicolon, as shown.

```
csc /addmodule:module1.netmodule;module2.netmodule myAssembly.cs
```

The /baseaddress Option

The /baseaddress option lets you specify in hexadecimal, decimal, or octal form the preferred memory base address at which the .NET runtime should load your dynamic-link library (DLL).

```
csc /t:library /baseaddress:0x1111000 urClass.cs
```

Generally, the base address is determined by the .NET runtime. This option is ignored if your output file is not a DLL.

The /bugreport Option

As its name suggests, the /bugreport option is used to report source code bugs. It creates a text file containing the source code; versions of the operating system, compiler, and .NET runtime; and the programmer's description of the problem and the expected result. The following example shows how to use the /bugreport option.

```
csc /bugreport:report.txt myCode.cs
```

The /checked Option

Sometimes the results of an integral value fall outside the permissible range of the data type and cause a runtime exception. The /checked option eliminates the potentially drastic effects that can occur when a value falls outside the range allowed. For example, the range of the type Int16 extends to 32767. Generally, during runtime, if a variable of type Int16 is assigned a value greater than 32767 and if that value is not within the scope of the *checked* statement, the variable's value is automatically set to zero and the program executes normally. If it's important for you to that you always have the right value assigned to your variables, then compile with the option /checked+. This results in a runtime exception every time the variable exceeds its maximum value.

The /codepage Option

The /codepage option is useful when you have written source code in code pages in a format other than Unicode or UTF-8. Code pages are character sets, and they vary for different languages. For example, the Hindi language has multibyte characters. The /codepage option takes the ID of the code page to be used to compile the source code.

The /debug Option

You can use the /debug option to produce additional debugging information for your application. This option accepts either + or – to indicate creation or omission of debugging information. To expand the functionality, you can specify /debug:full to create debugging information along with capabilities of attaching it to a debugger. As an alternative, /debug:pdbonly does not allow you to debug the source code if you attach the debugger to a running program. The pdbonly option will only display assembly code from the running program

The /define Option

When you use preprocessor directives in your code, you can define multiple symbols for your program via the /define option. Preprocessor directives are used to perform conditional compilation—that is, they mark sections of the code to be compiled as per the options defined during compilation time. For example, suppose you mark the debugging counters and trace statements with the DEBUG preprocessor directive. Only if you define the DEBUG directive during compile-time (as shown) will these statements get compiled.

```
csc /define:DEBUG;Test myCode.cs
```

The /doc Option

The /doc option allows you to produce an Extensible Markup Language (XML) file containing the documentation you have defined within your source code using the special documentation comments. This option does not work when you are using the /increment+ option. An example of the syntax follows.

```
csc /doc:MyCode.xml myCode.cs
```

The /filealign Option

The /filealign option lets you specify the size of different sections within the compiled file. The sizes you can specify in byte form are 512, 1024, 2048, 4096, 8192, and 16384. If a section cannot fit within the given size, then two or more sections will be created in multiples of the size specified. This option is useful, for example, if your code is to be used on small mobile devices.

The /fullpaths Option

Enabled by default, the /fullpaths option is used to show the full path to the source code file that is causing errors or warnings during compilation.

The /incremental Option

The /incremental option incrementally builds your applications and can be used along with the /debug+ option. The first time you use this option along with the compiled assembly, an .incr file is created to contain all the information about the current build. The next time you compile your code, only those portions of the code that have changed are recompiled and the .incr file will be updated. This option has significant impact only when you compile many small files.

The /lib Option

You use the /lib option to specify additional directories where the compiler can find the libraries to be referenced during compilation. If you store your DLL assemblies in various directories, use this option to supply the C# compiler with the path to those directories, as in the following example:

```
csc /lib:c:\csharp\libraries /r:myLibrary.dll myCode.cs
```

The /linkresource Option

The /linkresource option provides a link to the resource file in the assembly you are compiling. It does not store the resource file within the assembly; it only provides a reference to the resource file. Therefore, you must distribute the resource file along with your application files. The following example shows how you might use this option:

```
csc /linkresource:myrs.resource myCode.cs
```

The /main Option

The /main option is useful only when you compile an executable (.exe) application and your source code has multiple classes that define the Main method. Because an application can have only one entry point, you use this option (as shown in the example) to specify to the compiler which class's Main method should be treated as the entry point into an application.

```
csc /main:myCode myCode.cs yourCode.cs
```

The /nologo Option

You use /nologo to suppress the Microsoft banner that usually appears every time you use the compiler.

The /nostdlib Option

If you have created your own System namespace implementation, you may use the /nostdlib option to prevent the compiler from loading the mscorlib.dll that holds the System namespace.

The /noconfig Option

The /noconfig option prevents the compiler from using the global and local response files defined within the csc.rsp file. If you do not need the default compiler options that are defined in csc.rsp, you can use the /noconfig compiler option.

The /nowarn Option

The /nowarn option forces the C# compiler to suppress the specific warnings you've specified. The C# reference documentation lists all the numbers associated with C# warnings. With /nowarn, you can specify the number of any warning you don't want to display during compilation. The following example shows how to compress the warning CS0029 – *Cannot implicitly convert type 'type' to 'type'*:

```
csc /nowarn:29 myCode.cs
```

The /optimize Option

The /optimize option allows the compiler to optimize compiled code to make it execute faster and more efficiently. Use this option when compiling the release versions of your assemblies.

The /out Option

You use the /out option to specify the output file name of the file compiled by the C# compiler. As shown in the following example, you can also specify the path name along with the file name after the out directive to specify where the compiled file will be stored:

```
csc /out:.\bin\website.dll /t:library myCode.cs
```

The /recurse Option

The /recurse option is used to compile all files bearing the specified file name within the specified directory and its child directories. You can also use wild cards to specify the names of files to be compiled, as shown in this example:

```
csc /recurse:*.cs /out:myCode.dll /t:library
```

The /reference Option

The /reference option is used to reference the external assemblies you have used in your code. The compiler reads the public type information from the external assemblies and provides the necessary metadata within the assembly you are currently compiling. The following example shows the syntax used with /reference:

```
csc /reference:urCode.dll myCode.cs
```

The /resource Option

You can use the /resource option as shown to embed the resource file within the assembly you are compiling.

```
csc /resource:fileres.resource myCode.cs
```

Unlike the /linkresource option that merely links the resource file, /resource actually embeds the resource into the assembly.

The /target Option

You use the /target option to tell the compiler which of four kinds of output files you want to produce:

exe—a console application (.exe).
winexe—a Windows application (.exe).
library—a library DLL (.dll).
module—a .NET module (.netmodule).

The example specifies creation of a Windows application:

```
csc /target:winexe /out:Application.exe myFile.cs
```

The /unsafe Option

When you have included unsafe code (e.g., pointers) within your C# source code, the source code will not compile unless you use the /unsafe option.

The /utf8output Option

The /utf8output option is used for situations in which the output generated by the compiler does not render properly on certain international language packs. You may use this option to redirect the output to a separate file in UTF-8 format.

The /warn Option

With the /warn option, you can set the warning level displayed by the C# compiler. Values range from *0,* which turns off the warnings, to *4,* which reports all warnings and includes additional information.

The /warnaserror Option

The /warnaserror option reports all warnings as errors at compile-time. When you use this option, any warning issued by the compiler causes the code not to compile.

The /win32icon Option

You use the /win32icon option as shown to specify inclusion of an icon file when you compile a Windows executable file.

```
csc /win32icon:myApp.ico /target:winexe /out:Application.exe myCode.cs
```

This option gives the Windows application the desired look in Windows Explorer.

The /win32res Option

You use the /win32res option to include a Win32 resource file in your compiled code. The Win32 resource file can contain icons, cursors and bitmaps. An example of the syntax for this option follows:

```
csc /win32res:oldres.res /target:winexe myCode.cs
```

To include .NET resource files rather than Win32 resource files, use the /addresource option.

Tools and Utilities in the .NET Framework

The .NET Framework Software Development Kit (SDK) installs a host of tools and utilities to help you program more efficiently. The SDK includes wrapper creation tools for interoperating with existing unmanaged code, tools that help you discover and use Web services that are based on Simple Object Access Protocol (SOAP), and tools that enable you to configure security for managed code. This section provides an overview of the Intermediate Language Disassembler (ILDASM) and other debugging tools provided with the .NET Framework.

Using ILDASM to Disassemble and Display .NET Metadata

All the languages on the .NET platform compile into MSIL and are subsequently compiled into native code at runtime by the JIT compiler. The Intermediate Language (IL) includes a very powerful feature for accessing its internal metadata called reflection. The Reflection API provided by the .NET runtime enables a programmer to discover and invoke public types of an assembly at runtime. The ILDASM tool can be used to view the metadata contained within a .NET file and to disassemble a .NET assembly or module into IL code.

Viewing the Contents of a .NET Portable Executable File

To start ILDASM, choose Run from the Start menu and type *ILDASM*. Once you've started the ILDASM tool, choose Open from the File menu. Navigate to the "Hello, C#" program created in Chapter 3 and select it. You should see a window similar to the one shown in Figure 4.1.

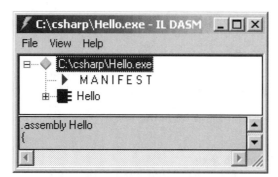

Figure 4.1: ILDASM Tool

The figure shows a couple of symbols along with some names. Table 4.1 lists all the symbols and their meanings. Once you have reviewed at them, you will understand some of the contents shown in Figure 4.1.

Image	Description
▶	Indicates that more information is available
◗	Indicates a namespace
▤	Indicates a class
▤	Indicates a value type (structure)
E▤	Indicates an enumeration
I▤	Indicates an interface
■	Indicates a method
S	Indicates a static method
◆	Indicates a field
◈	Indicates a static field
▼	Indicates an event
▲	Indicates a property
▸	Indicates a manifest or class information

Table 4.1: ILDASM Symbols

To view the manifest of the assembly, double-click on the Manifest item in ILDASM. The resulting display is reproduced in Figure 4.2.

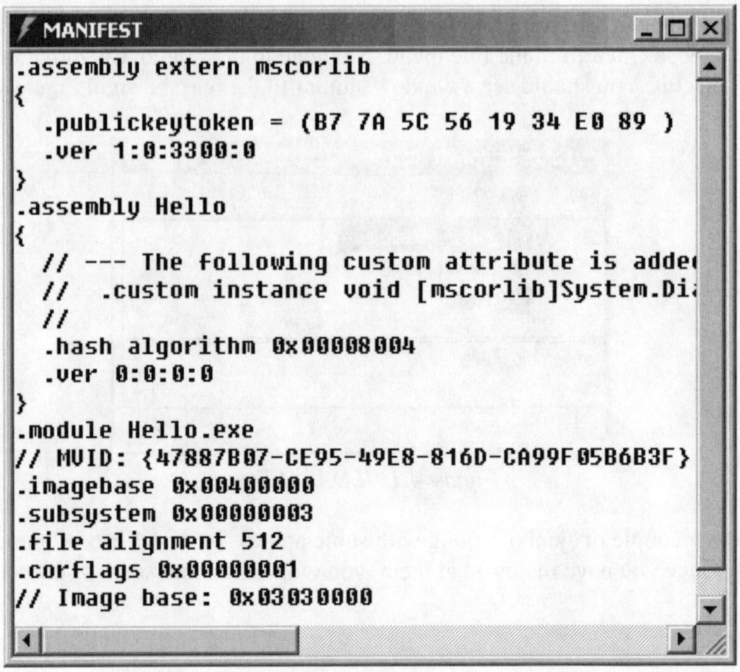

```
MANIFEST                                      _ □ ×
.assembly extern mscorlib
{
  .publickeytoken = (B7 7A 5C 56 19 34 E0 89 )
  .ver 1:0:3300:0
}
.assembly Hello
{
  // --- The following custom attribute is added
  //   .custom instance void [mscorlib]System.Di
  //
  .hash algorithm 0x00008004
  .ver 0:0:0:0
}
.module Hello.exe
// MVID: {47887B07-CE95-49E8-816D-CA99F05B6B3F}
.imagebase 0x00400000
.subsystem 0x00000003
.file alignment 512
.corflags 0x00000001
// Image base: 0x03030000
```

Figure 4.2: Hello, C# Class's Manifest

The manifest of a portable executable (PE) file provides some important information about the files dependencies, version, and culture. This metadata within the manifest makes every .NET PE file self-describing.

The first section of the manifest begins with .assembly extern mscorlib, indicating that the Hello class uses classes (e.g., System.Console) that are stored in the mscorlib assembly. The publickeytoken (a public key only available in cases of strong-named assemblies—you'll learn more about this in Chapter 26) and version of the mscorlib assembly are also embedded in this section of the manifest. Having this version information stored in the manifest solves some of the versioning problems otherwise encountered when different version of the same assembly are present. The .NET runtime can easily check the assembly manifest for version information and then load the correct version of the assembly.

The next section, which contains .assembly Hello, is the *assembly manifest* of the assembly Hello. This section is only present in assemblies—that is, modules do not have this section. The assembly manifest contains the culture, version, hash algorithm for encryption, publickeytoken, and other important metadata about the assembly. Since in this case we have not specified any special version or culture settings on the assembly, the default version of 0:0:0:0 is applied.

The section containing .module Hello.exe states that the assembly is stored within the PE file called Hello.exe. The remaining sections contain other relevant metadata used by the .NET runtime.

To explore the various contents of the assembly, click on Hello to expand and view its internal members. Figure 4.3 shows the contents of the Hello assembly.

Figure 4.3: Contents of the Assembly

From the figure we can make out that the assembly contains a single class called Hello. Double-click the line that starts with *.class private auto* to find the definition of the Hello class, as presented in Figure 4.4.

```
Hello::.class private auto ansi beforefieldinit      _ □ X
.class private auto ansi beforefieldinit Hello
        extends [mscorlib]System.Object
{
} // end of class Hello
```

Figure 4.4: Hello Class Definition

The figure shows that Hello is a private class that extends the System.Object class from the mscorlib assembly. You might remember that all classes in the .NET Framework extend the System.Object class directly or indirectly. Hence, even though the class is not explicitly extended in the source code, the C# compiler automatically extends the class from System.Object.

The next line in Figure 4.3 contains .ctor: void(), the default constructor for the class. The C# compiler automatically adds this line too, if you do not define a constructor for the class. The default constructor is always public and takes no parameters. Figure 4.5 shows the definition of the default constructor for the Hello class.

```
Hello::.ctor : void()                                          _ □ X
.method public hidebysig specialname rtspecialname
        instance void  .ctor() cil managed
{
  // Code size         7 (0x7)
  .maxstack  1
  IL_0000:  ldarg.0
  IL_0001:  call          instance void [mscorlib]System.Object::.ctor()
  IL_0006:  ret
} // end of method Hello::.ctor
```

Figure 4.5: Default Constructor

The first section regarding code size indicates that the constructor occupies 7 bytes of MSIL. The .maxstack 1 section indicates that only one operand at a time can be pushed onto the virtual stack for computation. Next, the directive ldarg.0 loads the class's *this* pointer on the virtual stack. On line IL_0001, the System.Object class constructor (or base class constructor) is called. Finally, on line IL_0006, the method returns from the constructor.

Lastly, to examine the Main method of the class Hello, double-click the Main:: void() line from the screen shown in Figure 4.3. Perhaps you have already noticed the symbol to the left of this line that signifies the method is static.

Figure 4.6 shows the contents of the Main method.

```
Hello::Main : void()                                              _ □ ×
.method private hidebysig static void   Main() cil managed
{
  .entrypoint
  // Code size          11 (0xb)
  .maxstack   1
  IL_0000:  ldstr       "Hello, C#!"
  IL_0005:  call        void [mscorlib]System.Console::WriteLine(string)
  IL_000a:  ret
} // end of method Hello::Main
```

Figure 4.6: Definition of the Main Method

You can see from the top line of the figure that Main is a private, static method that returns a void. The .entrypoint section tells the .NET runtime that this method is the entry point for the assembly and that the .NET runtime should begin executing code starting with this method. The // Code size section indicates that this method occupies 11 MSIL bytes, and the .maxstack section indicates that at a given time, a maximum of 1 byte can be loaded on the virtual stack. The line IL_0000 loads the string "Hello, C#!" on the virtual stack. (Because static methods don't have a *this* pointer, the variables get loaded on the stack first; otherwise, the this pointer is loaded first.) On line IL_0005, the WriteLine(string) method of the class System.Console from the mscorlib assembly is called and the string is displayed on the console. Finally, on line IL_000a, the method returns. Thus ends your brief tour of the Hello class.

Emitting IL from a .NET PE File

The ILDASM tool can also be used to emit the IL code from a .NET PE file. To decompile a file, load the file into ILDASM as indicated above and select Dump from the File menu. You are presented with a dialog box similar to that in Figure 4.7. From this dialog box, select the options you require (the default options are sufficient in most cases) and click OK.

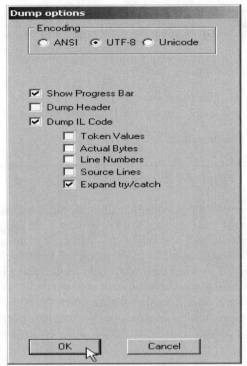

Figure 4.7: Dump File Dialog Box

Next, you are presented with the File Save dialog box. Type an appropriate file name and click OK to save the IL code for your PE file. Two files get created when you click OK: the IL file (Hello.il) and a resource file containing resources for your assembly (Hello.res).

Now open the Hello.il file in notepad to view its contents. Within the Main method definition in this file, find the following line:

```
IL_0000:  ldstr      "Hello, C#!"
```

Change it to read as follows and save the file:

```
IL_0000:  ldstr      "Hello World"
```

Now bring up the command prompt window and navigate to the directory where you saved the Hello.il file. Run the ILASM tool (IL Assembler) to compile the IL file into a .NET PE file that contains the change you have made. Before you run the ILASM tool, be sure you have closed the ILDASM tool running on the Hello.exe file; otherwise, Hello.exe remains locked and the new file won't be generated. Issue the command ilasm hello.il to compile the IL code into a PE file. Finally, run the file Hello.exe to view the reflected changes you made in the IL (shown in Figure 4.8.).

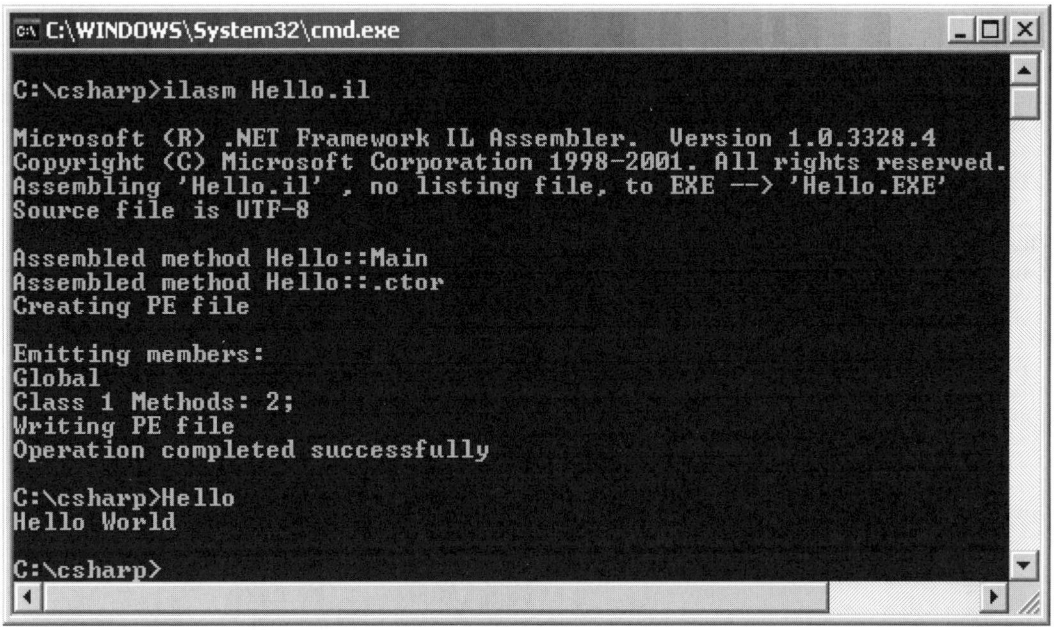

Figure 4.8: Assembling Using ILASM Tool

Using Runtime Debuggers

Any programmer, no matter how experienced, cannot create complex programs without any errors on the first attempt! Although syntax errors are reported at the compiler level, the compiler cannot detect and report more complex runtime errors. To determine the bugs of a program at runtime, we use *debuggers*. The .NET Framework provides two: CorDbg, the command-line runtime debugger, and DbgCLR, the Windows-based debugger. Both debuggers can be used only to debug managed code.

Debugging with CorDbg

The CorDbg debugger runs on the command line. Although CorDbg actually is more suitable for third-party tool developers and expert users, let's briefly explore use of this tool by debugging the code for the JustButton class defined in Listing 4.2.

Listing 4.2—JustButton Class (JustButton.cs)

```
using System;
using System.Windows.Forms;

public class JustButton:Form
{
  private Button oneButton;

  public JustButton()
  {
    oneButton = new Button();
    oneButton.Text="Click Me!";
    oneButton.Dock= DockStyle.Bottom;
    oneButton.Click+= new System.EventHandler(Button_Clicked);
    this.Controls.Add(oneButton);
  }

  protected void Button_Clicked(object sender, EventArgs e)
  {
    MessageBox.Show("The Button was Clicked!!");
```

```
    }

    [STAThread]
    public static void Main()
    {
        Application.Run(new JustButton());
    }
}
```

JustButton is a simple Windows form application that contains a single button. When you click the Click Me! button in the JustButton form, a message box (shown in Figure 4.9) is displayed.

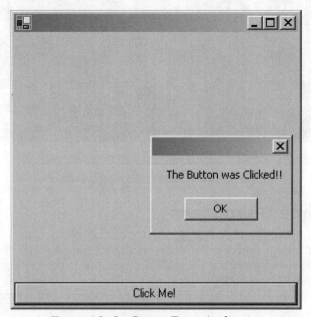

Figure 4.9: JustButton Form Application

Compile this class into a Windows application using the following command-line compilation string:

```
csc /debug+ /t:winexe JustButton.cs
```

Be sure use the /debug+ directive because it makes the compiler emit extra debugging information in a file called <filename>.pdb.

Once you compile the file, the next step is to debug this small program. Start up the command prompt window and navigate to the directory where you have compiled the above application. Now start the debugger by running the command CorDbg at the command prompt. This brings up the (CorDbg) command prompt. Use the CorDbg command called run JustButton to start debugging the application and load the debugging information from the *.pdb files. You will encounter errors if you don't have a corresponding *.pdb file for the referenced assemblies, but these errors can be ignored. Figure 4.10 shows a warning that CorDbg couldn't load symbols for mscorlib.dll and few other DLLs. Also shown in the figure is the line of source code where the debugger halted— Application.Run(new JustButton());.

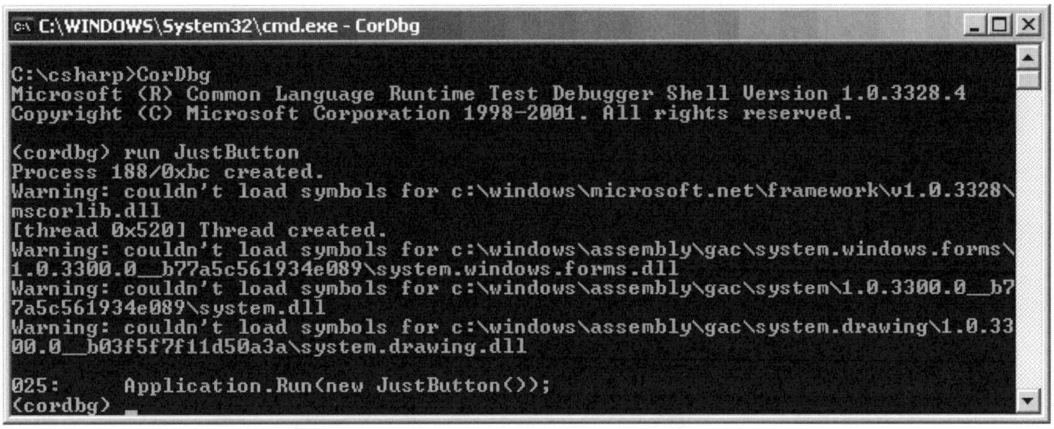

Figure 4.10: CorDbg Debugger

You can use commands such as *ap* to view the application domains and *pro* to view the current managed processes running.

To set a breakpoint, use the command *b* and specify the line number (in this example, the command *b 19* sets the breakpoint on the 19th line of the source code). The debugger shows that the breakpoint has been set within the Button_Clicked method. Use the *cont* command to continue running the application. Once the application shows, click the Click Me! button and switch to the debugger window.

As shown in Figure 4.11, the JustButton application breaks at line 19 and the source code is shown in CorDbg.

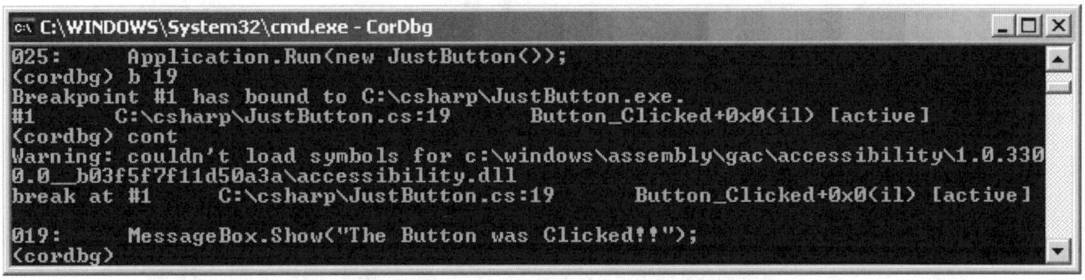

Figure 4.11: Breakpoint for JustButton Application

If you want to view the source code of a particular line, use the *sh* command and specify the line number (for the JustButton example, type *sh 18*). The selected line is marked with an asterisk (*), as shown in Figure 4.12.

```
C:\WINDOWS\System32\cmd.exe - CorDbg                          _ □ x
019:      MessageBox.Show("The Button was Clicked!!");
(cordbg) sh 18
001: using System;
002: using System.Windows.Forms;
003:
004: public class JustButton:Form
005: {
006:    private Button oneButton;
007:
008:    public JustButton()
009:    {
010:      oneButton = new Button();
011:      oneButton.Text="Click Me!";
012:      oneButton.Dock= DockStyle.Bottom;
013:      oneButton.Click+= new System.EventHandler(Button_Clicked);
014:      this.Controls.Add(oneButton);
015:    }
016:
017:    protected void Button_Clicked(object sender, EventArgs e)
018:    {
019:*     MessageBox.Show("The Button was Clicked!!");
020:    }
021:
022:    [STAThread]
023:    public static void Main()
024:    {
025:      Application.Run(new JustButton());
026:    }
027: }
(cordbg)
```

Figure 4.12: Viewing the Source Code with sh

To view the values of any of the variables, you can use the print <variable name> command. For example, to view the button instance, try using the *print sender* command, which lists the various properties of the button that raised this event (see Figure 4.13).

```
C:\WINDOWS\System32\cmd.exe - CorDbg                          _ □ x
(cordbg) print sender
sender=(0x00c26cf0) <System.Windows.Forms.Button>
  dialogResult=<System.Windows.Forms.DialogResult>
  isDefault=true
  inButtonUp=true
  mouseOver=true
  mouseDown=false
  mousePressed=false
  flatStyle=<System.Windows.Forms.FlatStyle>
  imageAlign=<System.Drawing.ContentAlignment>
  textAlign=<System.Drawing.ContentAlignment>
  imageIndex=0xffffffff
  imageList=<null>
  image=<null>
  currentlyAnimating=false
  window=(0x00c26d78) <ControlNativeWindow>
  parent=(0x00c25584) <JustButton>
  createParams=(0x00c26dc8) <System.Windows.Forms.CreateParams>
  x=0x00000000
  y=0x000000fa
  width=0x00000124
  height=0x00000017
  clientWidth=0x00000124
  clientHeight=0x00000017
  state=0x0902400f
  controlStyle=<System.Windows.Forms.ControlStyles>
  tabIndex=0x00000000
  text=(0x00c25668) "Click Me!"
  layoutSuspendCount=0x00
  propertyStore=(0x00c26d68) <System.Windows.Forms.PropertyStore>
  trackMouseEvent=(0x00c2f2b8) <TRACKMOUSEEVENT>
  updateCount=0x0000
  bitsPerPixel=0x0000
  site=<null>
  events=(0x00c26e08) <System.ComponentModel.EventHandlerList>
  __identity=<null>
(cordbg)
```

Figure 4.13: List of Property Values of the Button Instance After Using Print

To continue running the application, you can use the cont command, which displays the message box. Now every time you press the Click Me! button, the debugger automatically breaks at line 19. If you want to remove the breakpoint, you may do so in one of two ways. You can use del command to remove *all* the breakpoints; or, to remove a specific breakpoint, you may first use the break command to list all existing breakpoints along with their ID numbers and then use del <break id>, specifying the ID number of the breakpoint you wish to remove. Finally, to end debugging, use the *ex* command and exit the debugger.

Debugging with DbgCLR

The DbgCLR graphical user interface debugger is a downgraded version of the Visual Studio .NET debugger. It hosts the same interface and debugging methods but cannot compile applications or be used to write applications, whereas VS.NET can do all of the above and much more. You can find DbgCLR within the <drive>:\Program Files\Microsoft Visual Studio .NET\FrameworkSDK\GuiDebug directory. Run the tool and select the application to debug from the Debug menu's Program to Debug dialog box. Next, use the Open dialog box from the File menu to open the source code for debugging. Then you can set breakpoints in the source code and finally choose Run from the Debug menu to start debugging.

Because the rest of the debugging process with DbgCLR is identical to debugging with VS.NET, it is covered in the VS.NET debugger discussion that follows.

Using the Visual Studio .NET Debugger

The Visual Studio .NET debugger works best while debugging applications created in VS.NET. If you use it to debug other applications, its functionality is very similar to the DbgCLR tool. With the VS.NET debugger, you can debug all kinds of applications—console applications, library DLLs, Windows forms, Web forms, and Web services.

For a short look at how the debugger works, build the JustButton class in VS.NET, which is similar to the class built in the previous JustButton example. You can find the necessary VS.NET project file for this example in the downloadable code. In VS.NET, choose Open→Project from the File menu and select the JustButton project to open the project. This brings up the screen pictured in Figure 4.14.

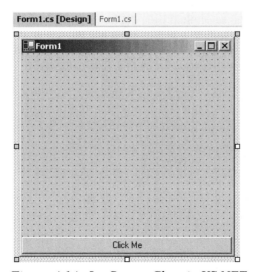

Figure 4.14: JustButton Class in VS.NET

Once you have the class ready, switch to the code view by either pressing the F7 shortcut key or selecting View→Code from the View menu. In code view, you have several ways to add breakpoints. You can click in the left margin alongside the line number; you can position the cursor on the line and press the F9 shortcut key; or you can press Ctrl+B to bring up a dialog box that helps you set advanced breakpoint options. Set a breakpoint on line 92 of the JustButton example, as shown in Figure 4.15.

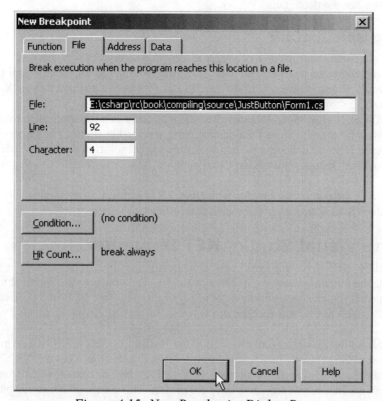

Figure 4.15: New Breakpoint Dialog Box

Once your breakpoints are set, select Start from the Debug menu. VS.NET automatically compiles the application and runs it. As soon as a breakpoint is reached, the application stops and you can view the details of the application in VS.NET. In this example, you must click the Click Me button so VS.NET will show the breakpoint you set on line 92 (Figure 4.16).

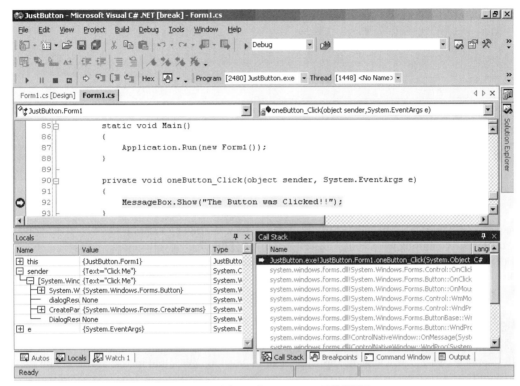

Figure 4.16: Debugging in VS.NET

As the figure shows, the VS.NET brings up a Locals window that lists all the method's variables in the local scope and their values at runtime. It is much easier to examine the values of different variables from the VS.NET debugger than from the CorDbg tool. From the Locals window, if you double-click an entry in the Value column and manually enter a value for a variable, the change is reflected immediately. Also shown in the figure is the Call Stack window, which displays the complete call stack for the application.

To continue running the application, you can choose Debug→Continue. You can also use functions such as Step Into, Step Over, or Step Out from the Debug menu to proceed with debugging line by line, to step over the breakpoint, or to step out of the breakpoint method, respectively. Once you finish debugging your application, select Stop Debugging from the Debug menu.

Summary

You may choose from many C# compiler options to compile your applications. ILDASM is a very useful tool that can be used to view the metadata of an assembly and disassemble an assembly into IL code. The ILASM tool can be used to compile MSIL code into a .NET assembly.

The .NET SDK provides a host of tools that support cross-language debugging, including the command-line debugger, CorDbg, and the Windows-based debugger, DbgCLR. The debugger included with Visual Studio .NET is equally powerful and easy to use.

The next chapter covers the details of the C# language so you can put the compiler and debugger to good use.

Chapter 5:
C# Language Programming

Introduction to C#

Chapter 3 contained a basic example of the classic "Hello World" application in C#, and Chapter 4 covered basic compiling and debugging features in C#. This chapter concentrates on C# language programming. First, it covers the language's basic elements, such as data types, operators, variables, statements, control flow, structures, and classes, followed by more complex features such as arrays, delegates, events, attributes, inheritance, overloading, indexers, and enumerators.

Definition

Microsoft touts its new, object-oriented language, C#, as the best language for writing Microsoft .NET applications. C# provides the rapid application development found in Visual Basic with the power of C++. C# syntax is similar to C++ syntax. Some experts also say that C# is Microsoft's answer to Sun Microsystems' Java and Borland's Delphi.

Revision of "Hello World"

Listing 5.1 provides another quick look at the classic "Hello World" application from Chapter 3.

Listing 5.1—HelloWorld.cs, Hello World Example

```
using System;
class HelloWorld
{
    static void Main()
    {
        Console.WriteLine("Hello, World");
        Console.WriteLine("Press any key to continue");
         Console.ReadLine();
    }
}
```

You can copy the code in Listing 5.1 into any editor such as Notepad and save the file as HelloWorld.cs. To compile the program, type the following at the command line:

```
csc HelloWorld.cs
```

Then run the program by typing HelloWorld at command line. The program output is shown in Figure 5.1.

Figure 5.1: Hello World Example Output

As discussed in Chapters 3 and 4, using the System statement makes the system namespace and its classes available in the program. The class statement followed by the name of the class defines a new class. Every program should have at least one Main method, which is the entry point of the application.

The System.Console class defines functionality to read from and write to the system console. The Console.WriteLine method writes a string to the console.

Object Class and Types

In .NET, the Object class is the root of all types. All types are implicitly derived from this class so they have access to the methods defined in the Object class. These methods are described in the Table 5.1.

Method	Description
Equals	Compares whether two object instances are equal. Returns true if two objects are equal; otherwise, returns false.
ReferenceEquals	Compares two object instances. Returns true if both are same instances; otherwise, returns false.
GetHashCode	Returns a hash code for the object.
GetType	Returns a Type object, which holds the types of current instance.
ToString	Converts an instance to a string type and returns a String object.

Table 5.1: The Object Class Methods and Their Descriptions

Type Information

The GetType method of the Object class returns a Type object. The Type class is useful when you need to know the internal details of a class such as the type of the class, its attributes, methods, properties, globally unique identifier, name, and fullname. Listing 5.2 demonstrates use of the GetType method.

Listing 5.2—Type Information Example

```
AClass cls1 = new AClass();
BClass cls2 = new BClass();

Type type1 = cls1.GetType();
Type type2 = cls2.GetType();

Console.WriteLine(type1.BaseType);
Console.WriteLine(type1.Name);
Console.WriteLine(type1.FullName);
Console.WriteLine(type1.Namespace);
```

You can use many other methods (GetFields, GetEvents, GetInterfaces, etc.) and properties to obtain more information about an object.

Comparing Two Objects

The Object class's Equals and ReferenceEquals methods can be used to compare two objects and their instances, respectively. Listing 5.3 shows one such use of the Equals method.

Listing 5.3—Compare.cs, Compare Two Objects Example

```csharp
using System;

// Define A Class
public class AClass : Object
{
        private void AMethod()
        {
                Console.WriteLine("A method" );
        }
}

// Define B Class
public class BClass : AClass
{
        private void BMethod()
        {
                Console.WriteLine("B method" );
        }
}

public class Test
{
        public static void Main()
        {
                AClass cls1 = new AClass();
                BClass cls2 = new BClass();

                string str1 = "Test";
                string str2 = "Test";

                Console.WriteLine(Object.Equals(cls1, cls2));
                Console.WriteLine(Object.Equals(str1, str2));
        Console.WriteLine("Press any key to continue");
        Console.ReadLine();

        }
}
```

Figure 5.2 shows the result of the program in Listing 5.3.

Figure 5.2: Screen Generated by Listing 5.3.

You use ReferenceEquals in the same manner, as shown:

```
Console.WriteLine(Object.ReferenceEquals(obj1, obj2));
```

Convert to a String Type

The ToString method of the Object class converts a type to a string type. Because converting to a string type is a very common programming practice, Microsoft defined the ToString method in the Object class, thus making it available to each type in the .NET world through inheritance. The example code in Listing 5.4 converts an integer type and a floating-point number type to a string type.

Listing 5.4—ToString.cs, Convert to String Example

```
using System;

public class FloatTest
{
  public static void Main()
  {
        int i = 12;
        float flt = 12.005f;

        Console.WriteLine(i.ToString());
        Console.WriteLine(flt.ToString());
  }
}
```

Hash Code

You don't use a hash code in regular programming practices, but it's useful if you want to use a type in hashing algorithms such as a hash table. A hash table provides a quick lookup, much like a dictionary. Each member of the hash table has a key value and the object can be referenced by using the key. All members of a class have a memory area defined in the hash table of that class. Members with different names can have the same values but different hash code.

By using the method GetHashCode, .NET gives you the flexibility to access the hash code of an object directly and work with it. A derived class can override this method. It's not necessary to return the same hash code for two objects referencing the same value.

Types in C#

There are two kinds of types in C#: *reference* types, which denote a memory location of the actual data, and *value* types, which reference the actual data. For example, if you define a reference type called aType, it would hold an address of memory where the actual data would be stored. If you define aType as a value type, it would contain the actual value, with no indication of the memory address where the value is stored.

Reference and value types differ in some important ways that are summarized in Table 5.2.

	Reference Types	**Value Types**
Contents of variable	Reference to actual data	Actual data
Location	Heap (global) memory	Data stack
Initialization	Null	0, 0.0, ", "" (Zero , Empty Character, Empty String)
Effect of the = operator	Copies the memory location address or reference	Copies the actual value that the source stores into the destination

Table 5.2: Reference and Value Types

Value types include simple (char, int, bool, etc.), enum, and struct types; reference types include class, interface, delegate, and array types. Let's explore these types in more detail.

Value Types

Value types are declared by using their default constructors. In most cases, you use the new keyword to call the default constructor of a value type; but for some simple types, you don't even have to call the new keyword.

The default constuctor of value types returns a zero-intialized instance, so you don't have to intialize a type when you define it. For example, the output value of both int1 and int2 in Listing 5.5 is 0.

Listing 5.5—ValueTypeTest.cs, Value Types Example

```
using System;

public class ValueTypeTest
{
        public static void Main()
        {
                // integer int1 and int2 initialization with 0
                int int1 = 0;
                int int2 = new int();

                Console.WriteLine(int1.ToString());
                Console.WriteLine(int2.ToString());

        }
}
```

The value types can be categorized as simple types, struct types, and enum types.

Simple Types

Simple value types include the traditional simple types listed in Table 5.3.

C# Type Alias	CLS Type	Size (bits)	Suffix	Description	Range
sbyte	SByte	8		signed byte	–128 to 127
byte	Byte	8		unsigned byte	0 to 255
short	Int16	16		short integer	-32,768 to 32,767
ushort	UInt16	16		unsigned short integer	0 to 65535
int	Int32	32		integer	-2,147,483,648 to 2,147,483,647
uint	UInt32	32	u	unsigned integer	0 to 4,294,967,295
long	Int64	64	L	long integer	–9,223,372,036,854,775,808 to 9,223,372,036,854,775,807
ulong	UInt64	64		unsigned long integer	0 to 18,446,744,073,709,551,615
char	Char	16		Unicode character	any valid character (e.g., 'a', '*', '\x0058' [hexadecimal], or '\u0058' [Unicode])
float	Single	32	F	floating-point number	$\pm 1.5 \times 10^{-45}$ to $\pm 3.4 \times 10^{38}$
double	Double	64	d	double floating-point number	Range $\pm 5.0 \times 10^{-324}$ to $\pm 1.7 \times 10^{308}$
bool	Boolean	1		logical true/false value	true/false
decimal	Decimal	128	m	used for financial and monetary calculations	from approximately 1.0×10^{-28} to 7.9×10^{28} with 28 to 29 significant digits
bool	Boolean	true or false		used to represent true or false values	

Table 5.3: Value Types

Simple types have a reserved keyword corresponding to one class of Common Language Specification (CLS) type defined in the System class. For example, keyword int represents System.Int32 type, and keyword long represents System.Int64 type. You can use either the C# shorthand-type keywords or the direct CLS types.

Note that you use suffixes for explicit type determination on demand. If you do that appropriately (as shown), you avoid compiler-selected automatic type conversions.

```
double dblMyValue1 = 3.14d;
```

When defining a variable and assigning a value to it, use the *m* suffix (as shown) to denote a decimal value:

```
decimal decMyValue2 = 1.234567890m;
```

If you omit the *m*, the variable will be treated as type double by the compiler before it is assigned.

Structs

The struct, another kind of value type, can declare constructors, constants, fields, methods, properties, indexers, operators, and nested types. The main idea of using a struct is to create lightweight objects similar to a class. You can conserve memory using a struct because no additional references are created, as is needed in the case of class objects. When declaring arrays containing thousands of objects, this makes quite a difference in terms of resources.

Listing 5.6—Struct.cs, Struct Example

```
//example struct
using System;

struct StdRecord
{
        public string stdName;
        public string stdAddress;
        public int stdID;
}

class Test
{
        public static void Main()
        {
                StdRecord rec;
                rec.stdName = "FirstName";
                rec.stdName = "LastName";

                rec.stdAddress = "Bank Street, NY";
                rec.stdID = 12794;

                Console.WriteLine("Student Name :" +rec.stdName);
                Console.WriteLine("Student Address :" +rec.stdAddress);
                Console.WriteLine("Student ID :" +rec.stdID);
        }
}
```

The main use of struct types is to create your own data types. For example, the code in Listing 5.6 is used to generate a student record type containing a student name, address, and ID, as displayed in Figure 5.3.

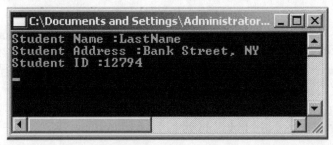

Figure 5.3: Display Generated by Listing 5.6

Enum Types

The enum type is a set of named enumerated constants. Enums are generally used to give a meaningful name to a set of commonly used numeric values. Days in a week or months in a year are two suitable examples for the enumerations shown here.

```
enum WeekDays {Sun, Mon, Tue, Wed, Thur, Fri, Sat};
enum YearMonths {Jan, Feb, Mar, Apr, May, Jun, Jul, Aug, Sep, Oct, Nov, Dec};
```

Enum types are limited to long, int, short, and byte; the compiler does not recognize any other enum type. The default value is int. Note that you cannot convert basic types to enum types or vice versa. You have to cast them explicitly. Examples of the enum type follow:

```
// Sun is 0, Mon is 1, Tue is 2, Tue is 3 and so on.
enum WeekDays { Sun, Mon, Tue, Wed, Thu, Fri, Sat};

// Sun is 5, Mon is 6, Tue is 7, Wed is 8 and so on.
enum WeekDays { Sun=5, Mon, Tue, Wed, Thu, Fri, Sat };

// Sun is 5, Mon is 9, Tue is 6, Wed is 0 and so on.
enum WeekDays { Sun =5, Mon =9, Tue =6, Wed=0};
```

Reference Types

A *reference type* is a reference to an instance of the type. In other words, a reference type is a memory address location that holds the actual value is stored. It is possible to have two variables holding the same memory address pointing to the same data. The main reference types are class, array, interface, delegate, and event types. Let's take a quick look at these types before exploring them in greater detail later in this chapter.

Class Type

The class type is used to represent real-life entities in object-oriented programming. A class can have members in the form of methods, properties, indexers, events, and delegates. You always declare and define all code fragments inside a class. Object and String are classes provided by the .NET framework. Listing 5.7 contains a simple example of class types.

Listing 5.7—Class Types Example

```
// Define A Class
public class AClass : Object
{
        public void AMethod()
        {
                Console.WriteLine("A method" );
        }
}
```

You use the class keyword to create a class type. You can add methods, properties, indexers, delegates, and events to the class, as you'll see later in this chapter.

You can create an instance of a class type by using the operator new and then access the class type's public members by using the dot (.) operator used in Listing 5.8. These class-related concepts also warrant discussion in more detail later.

Listing 5.8—ClassType.cs, Class Types Example 2

```
using System;

// Define A Class
public class AClass : Object
{
        public void AMethod()
        {
                Console.WriteLine("A method" );
        }
}

// Define B Class
public class BClass : AClass
{
        public void BMethod()
        {
                Console.WriteLine("B method" );
```

```
        }
}

public class ValueTypeTest
{
        public static void Main()
        {
                AClass cls1 = new AClass();
                BClass cls2 = new BClass();

                cls1.AMethod();
                cls2.BMethod();

        }
}
```

Figure 5.4 contains the screen output generated from the code in Listing 5.8.

Figure 5.4: Screen Output from Listing 5.8.

Interface Type

An interface is a pure, virtual abstract class, useful for sharing functionality between similar classes. An interface defines a contract for the implementers of the interface; in other words, classes that implement an interface accept responsibility for defining the interface method body. You cannot instantiate an interface object. A class or struct that implements an interface must adhere to its contract. An interface may inherit from multiple base interfaces, and a class or struct may implement multiple interfaces.

Interfaces can contain methods, properties, events, and indexers only. The interface itself does not provide implementations for the members that it defines. The interface merely specifies the members that must be supplied by classes or interfaces that implement this interface. In fact, defining the methods in interfaces will cause a compile-time error. When you define the interface methods in a class, the method signature should be the same as the method declaration in the interface.

Listing 5.9 illustrates the functionality of interfaces through the ICopyable interface.

Listing 5.9—Interface ICopyable Example

```
using System;
interface ICopyable
{
    Object Copy(); // returns a reference to a copy of the object
}

class SomeClass : ICopyable
{
        Int32 i;
        public SomeClass (Int32 i)
          {
            this.i = i;
          }
        public Object Copy()
```

```
        {
          return new SomeClass (i);
        }
}

class ExampleApp
{
        static void Main()
        {
          SomeClass cls1 = new SomeClass (19);
          SomeClass cls2 = (SomeClass) cls1.Copy();
        // note cast necessary
      }
}
```

Delegate Type

A delegate type encapsulates a method with a certain signature. Delegates, the type-safe and secure version of function pointers, are commonly used for the implementation of callback functionality. This is a new feature. A common usage of the delegate type is class events. Delegates allow you to specify what the function you call looks like without having to specify which function to call. The declaration for a delegate looks just like the declaration for a function, except that you declare the signature of functions that this delegate can reference.

In the delegate application in Listing 5.10, the class MsgClass contains no specifics about the implementation of the Messenger function besides the function signature.

The class ExampleApplication can "delegate" the Messenger functionality to the designated method at runtime.

Listing 5.10—Delegate.cs, Delegate Example

```
// example delegate application

using System;

public class MsgClass
{
   public delegate void Messenger(string message);

   public void MessageProcess(Messenger myMessenger)
   {
      if (myMessenger!= null)
         myMessenger ("MessageProcess () begin");
      // other stuff here...
      if (myMessenger!= null)
         myMessenger ("MessageProcess () end");
   }
}

class ExampleApplication
{
   static void Sender(string s)

   {
      Console.WriteLine(s);
   }

   public static void Main()
   {
      MsgClass myMsgClass = new MsgClass ();

      MsgClass.Messenger msg = new MsgClass.Messenger (Sender);
```

```
        myMsgClass.MessageProcess (msg);
    }
}
```

The screen output of Listing 5.10 appears in Figure 5.5.

Figure 5.5: Screen Output from Listing 5.10

Event Type

The event keyword allows you to specify a delegate to be called upon the occurrence of a particular event in your code. Listing 5.11 provides an example of this use of an event type. The delegate can have one or more associated methods to call when your code indicates the event has occurred. An event in one program can be made available to other programs that target the .NET runtime. Properties and events, which are central to component-based programming, are supported directly by the .NET framework.

Listing 5.11—Event.cs, Event Example

```
// example event application
using System;

public delegate void MyDelegate();    // delegate declaration

public interface IFire
{
    event MyDelegate MyEvent;
    void FireAway();
}

public class MyClass: IFire
{
    public event MyDelegate MyEvent;

    public void FireAway()
    {
        if (MyEvent != null)
            MyEvent();
    }
}

public class MainClass
{
    static private void f()
    {
        Console.WriteLine("This is called when the event fires.");
    }

    static public void Main ()
    {
        IFire ifire = new MyClass();

        ifire.MyEvent += new MyDelegate(f);
        ifire.FireAway();
    }
}
```

Figure 5.6 contains the output generated by the event type example in Listing 5.11.

Figure 5.6: Screen Output from Listing 5.11

Array Type

An array type is a sequential set containing an indexed list of objects. Arrays can also contain an ordered set of values. All of the elements must be of the same base type. An array can be one-dimensional or multidimensional. The two types of multidimensional arrays, jagged and rectangular, are covered in Chapter 20.

In C#, the lower index of an array starts with 0 and the upper index is the number of items minus one. You can even make an array of structures or your custom data types, as Listing 5.12 illustrates.

Listing 5.12—Array Example

```
Int32[] MyIntArray = new Int32[]{1,2,3};
Int32 intMyValue = MyIntArray[2];
// intMyValue stores 3 after this line
```

You can also declare various arrays such as those shown in Listing 5.13.

Listing 5.13—Multidimensional Array Example

```
Int16[,] myIntArray1 = {{0,1}, {2,3}, {4,5}}; // 3 x 2 multidimensional array
Int16[,] myIntArray2 = new int[5,3]; // 5 x 3 array with empty elements
Int16 intVar3 = 5;
Int16[] myIntArray3 = new int[intVar3]; // variable-sized array initialization
```

The static function below uses the static method Clear to clear all the numbers in the array, starting from 0 through the length of the array.

```
System.Array.Clear(MyIntArray,  0,  MyIntArray.Length);
```

Type Conversions

Conversion allows you to treat one type as another. For example, storing an integer value in a long variable constitutes conversion from integer to a long. C# supports limited implicit conversions as well as explicit conversions.

With implicit conversions, you pass a type to another type without losing any data. Conversion from short to long—or from int to long, in the case that follows—is an example of implicit conversion.

```
int num1 = 34;
long num2 = a;
```

Implicit conversion is only possible when you pass a small-range type to a big-range type. A long data type can hold short and int values with no problem, but the reverse is not true without risking data loss. Some of the implicit conversions are as follows:

- From sbyte to short, int, long, float, double, or decimal.
- From byte to short, ushort, int, uint, long, ulong, float, double, or decimal.
- From short to int, long, float, double, or decimal.
- From ushort to int, uint, long, ulong, float, double, or decimal.
- From int to long, float, double, or decimal.
- From uint to long, ulong, float, double, or decimal.
- From long to float, double, or decimal.
- From ulong to float, double, or decimal.
- From char to ushort, int, uint, long, ulong, float, double, or decimal.
- From float to double.

In explicit conversions, you must cast a type with another type to pass data between them. For example, conversion from long to int is handled explicitly, as follows:

```
long num1 = 3443;
int num2 = (int) a;
```

Some possible explicit conversions are as follows:

- From sbyte to byte, ushort, uint, ulong, or char.
- From byte to sbyte or char.
- From short to sbyte, byte, ushort, uint, ulong, or char.
- From ushort to sbyte, byte, short, or char.
- From int to sbyte, byte, short, ushort, uint, ulong, or char.
- From uint to sbyte, byte, short, ushort, int, or char.
- From long to sbyte, byte, short, ushort, int, uint, ulong, or char.
- From ulong to sbyte, byte, short, ushort, int, uint, long, or char.
- From char to sbyte, byte, or short.
- From float to sbyte, byte, short, ushort, int, uint, long, ulong, char, or decimal.
- From double to sbyte, byte, short, ushort, int, uint, long, ulong, char, float, or decimal.
- From decimal to sbyte, byte, short, ushort, int, uint, long, ulong, char, float, or double.

However, prudent testing is always advisable to determine whether a conversion will cause loss of data or the unexpected conversion of values.

Boxing and Unboxing

The term *boxing* describes the process of converting a value type into a reference type. The following conversion is an example of boxing, which is always an implicit conversion.

```
int int1 = 34;
Object obj = int1;
```

With the preceding example, you could output these variables:

```
Console.WriteLine(int1.ToString());
Console.WriteLine(obj.ToString());
```

The value of both int1 and obj is 34.

When *unboxing* (the reverse process of boxing), you convert a reference type to a value type, as in the following example.

```
Object obj = 43;
```

```
int i = (int)obj;
```

From the example, you can output these variables:

```
Console.WriteLine(i.ToString());
Console.WriteLine(obj.ToString());
```

Variables

A *variable* is a programming unit that stores transient data during execution of code. Variables are used in programming for calculating and storing values and for reusability. When a class is loaded, all static fields are initialized to their default values; and when an instance of a class is created, all instance fields are initialized to their default values. It is not possible to observe the value of a field before this default initialization has occurred.

Defining Variables

Variables represent storage locations. Every variable has a type that determines what values the variable can store. C# is a type-safe language, so the C# compiler guarantees that values stored in variables are always of the appropriate type. The value of a variable can be changed through assignment or through use of the ++ and -- operators.

A variable must have a value assigned to it before that value can be obtained. A variable that is assigned initially at declaration has a well-defined initial value and is always considered definitely assigned. An initially unassigned variable has no initial value. For an initially unassigned variable to be considered definitely assigned at a certain location, an assignment to the variable must occur in every possible execution path leading to that location.

As you've already learned from this chapter, variables come in two types: value types, which directly contain the actual data in a variable; and reference types, in which the variable stores a reference to the actual data.

With value types, the variables each have their own copy of the data, and it is not possible for operations on one value type variable to affect another.

With reference types, multiple variables can reference the same object; thus, it is possible for operations on one reference type variable to affect the object referenced by another variable.

Static variables, instance variables of class instances, and array elements are automatically initialized to their default values.

For a variable of type value, the default value is the same as the value computed by the value-type's default constructor. For a variable of type reference, the default value is null.

Initialization to default values is typically done by having the memory manager or garbage collector initialize memory to all-bits-zero before allocating it for use. For this reason, it is convenient for an implementation to use all-bits-zero to represent the null reference.

Variable Scope

All variables have a visibility scope that affects how you access them within the code segments.

Local variables are declared and initialized inside a function block, and you do not specify a modifier. The variable is created on the stack and destroyed immediately after processing exits the block, as indicated in Listing 5.14.

Listing 5.14—Variable Scope Example

```
void Myfunc(int param1)
{
  // localint1 is created on the stack
  // and destroyed immediately after returning
  int localint1 = 5;
}
```

Public variables are declared inside the class block and allow you to access the variable from within other classes with no limitations.

When a field declaration includes a static modifier, the fields introduced by the declaration are static fields. When no static modifier is present, the fields introduced are instance fields.

A static field identifies exactly one storage location. No matter how many instances of a class are created, only one copy of a static field is created. A static field comes into existence when the type in which it is declared is loaded, and it ceases to exist when that type is unloaded.

Every instance of a class contains a separate copy of all instance fields of the class. An instance field comes into existence when a new instance of its class is created, and it ceases to exist when there are no references to that instance and the destructor of the instance has executed.

So if you want to use the static function Write of the Console class, you can code it using absolute reference (as in the first example that follows) or relative reference (as in the second example):

```
System.Console.Write("Hello World"); // absolute referring

using System; // defined once in the very beginning of the code segment
Console.Write("Hello World"); // relative referring
```

Static members are like global members in premature development languages. However, they provide a higher level of encapsulation because they reside in classes and namespaces. Static members are classwide members in that they are shared by and accessible to all objects of that class, because static variables and static functions do not need to be initialized. Static functions are initialized only when the class is defined and called either by using a directive or by directly invoking it through its namespace. Have you noticed the syntax of the Console.Write function? Since the Console namespace has a static Write function, we do not need to create a Console object.

To create an instance of the Console class, we would have used the code in Listing 5.15.

Listing 5.15—Console Class Usage

```
// the following code snippet is completely useless
// static functions save us
// from an unnecessary temporary object creation
Console myConsole = new Console();
myConsole.Write("I am tough enough...");
```

This code is equivalent to the following:

```
Console.Write("I am tough enough...");
```

When a field declaration includes a read-only modifier, assignments to the field introduced by the declaration can only occur as part of the declaration or in a constructor in the same class. The constants section has an example to illustrate appropriate usage of the const and static read-only modifiers.

Variable Accessibility

Access modifiers define the level of access that certain code has to particular class members, such as methods and properties. You must apply the desired access modifier to each member; otherwise, the default access type is implied.

You can apply one of the following class member access modifiers:

- **public**—access not limited
- **protected internal**—access limited to this program or types derived from the containing class
- **protected**—access limited to the containing class or types derived from the containing class
- **internal**—access limited to this program
- **private**—access limited to the containing type

Please refer to the C# Language Specification for more details and recent updates to the C# language (http://msdn.microsoft.com/net/ecma/).

When a member declaration does not include any access modifiers, the context in which the declaration takes place determines the accessibility declared by default. In declaring accessibility, you should keep the following points in mind:

- Namespaces implicitly have public accessibility declared. No access modifiers are allowed on namespace declarations.
- Types declared in compilation units or namespaces can have public or internal accessibility declared but default to internal accessibility.
- Class members can have any of the five kinds of declared accessibility but default to private accessibility. Note that a type declared as a member of a class can have any of the five kinds of declared accessibility, whereas a type declared as a member of a namespace can have only public or internal accessibility declared.
- Struct members can have public, internal, or private accessibility declared, and they default to private accessibility. Struct members cannot have protected or protected internal accessibility. Note that a type declared as a member of a struct can have public, internal, or private accessibility declared, whereas a type declared as a member of a namespace can have only public or internal accessibility declared.
- Interface members implicitly have public accessibility declared. No access modifiers are allowed on interface member declarations.
- Enumeration members implicitly have public accessibility declared. No access modifiers are allowed on enumeration member declarations.

Let's look at an example (Listing 5.16) in order to comprehend some of these concepts, which are the bricks and mortar of object-oriented programming. You will improve your accessibility design skills after following some of these programming practices. You should initially declare most of your object variables (nonstatic) and class variables (static) to have private accessibility. If you need access to the variables from other objects, then provide public methods or properties to expose them.

Listing 5.16—Variable Accessibility Example 1

```
public class A1
{
   public static int X;
   internal static int Y;
   private static int Z;
}

public class A2
{
   public int X;
   internal int Y;
   private int Z;
}
```

Let's examine the accessibility details of each element in Listing 5.16:

- The accessibility of A1 and A1.X is unlimited.
- The accessibility of A1.Z is limited to the program context of class A1.
- The accessibility of A1.Y is limited to the program context of the containing program.

The accessibility of a member is never larger than that of a containing type. For example, even though all X members here and in Listing 5.16 have publicly declared accessibility, all A.X members have accessibility domains that are constrained by a containing type.

Let's look at another, more complex example in Listing 5.17.

Listing 5.17—Variable Accessibility Example 2

```
internal class B1
{
   public static int X;
   internal static int Y;
   private static int Z;

   public class C1
   {
      public static int X;
      internal static int Y;
      private static int Z;
   }

   private class D1
   {
      public static int X;
      internal static int Y;
      private static int Z;
   }

}

internal class B2
{
   public int X;
   internal int Y;
   private int Z;

   public class C2
   {
      public int X;
      internal int Y;
      private int Z;
   }
```

```
   private class D2
   {
      public int X;
      internal int Y;
      private int Z;
   }

}
```

Let's examine the accessibility details of each element in Listing 5.17:

- The accessibility of B1, B1.X, B1.Y, B1.C1, B1.C1.X, and B1.C1.Y is limited to the program text of the containing program.
- The accessibility of B1.Z and B1.D1 is limited to the program text of B1, including the program text of B1.C and B1.D.
- The accessibility of B1.C1.Z is limited to the program text of B1.C1.
- The accessibility of B1.D1.X, B1.D1.Y, and B1.D1.Z is limited to the program text of B1.D1.

The A1, B1, C1, and D1 classes all contain static members, so there is no need to declare objects of each relevant class to access their class members. However, note that you cannot access private and protected members this way.

A2, B2, C2, and D2 classes have ordinary members. Thus, the same rules apply for static members as above, but you have to create concrete class objects instead.

Constants

A *constant* is a variable modifier that represents a constant value, a value that can be computed at compile-time. A constant declaration introduces one or more constants of a given type.

A constant declaration can declare multiple constants (as in Listing 5.18) in a process that is equivalent to multiple declarations of single constants with the same attributes, modifiers, and type.

Listing 5.18—Constants Example 1

```
class A
{
   public const int X = 1, Y = 2, Z = 3;
}

class B
{
   public const int X = 1;
   public const int Y = 2;
   public const int Z = 3;
}
```

Evaluating constant values in complex class hierarchies can be a bit confusing and warrants closer examination.

The declaration of constants can depend on other constants within the same program (see Listing 5.19) as long as the dependencies are not of a circular nature. The .NET framework automatically arranges constant declarations to evaluate the declarations in the appropriate order.

Listing 5.19—Constants Example 2

```
class A
{
   public const int X = B.Z + 1;
   public const int Y = 10;
}
class B
{
   public const int Z = A.Y + 1;
}
```

In this example, the compiler first evaluates Y, then Z, and finally X, producing the values 10, 11, and 12. Constant declarations may depend on constants from other programs, but such dependencies are only possible in one direction. Referring to the example above, if A and B were declared in separate programs, it would be possible for A.X to depend on B.Z; however, B.Z could not then depend on A.Y.

A static read-only field is useful when a symbolic name for a constant value is desired—for example, when the type of the value is not permitted in a constant declaration or when the value cannot be computed at compile-time. Constants and read-only fields have different binary versioning semantics. When an expression references a constant, the value of the constant is obtained at compile-time. When an expression references a read-only field, the value of the field is not obtained until runtime.

Listings 5.20, 5.21, and 5.22 present a solid example of the difference between const and read-only in real-world applications.

Listing 5.20—ConstOut.cs , Constant Usage Example

```
using System;

public class A
{
    public const int X = 123;
}
```

The code in Listing 5.20 is compiled with `csc /t:library /out:A.dll ConstOut.cs`.

Listing 5.21—ReadOnlyOut.cs, ReadOnly Usage Example

```
using System;

public class B
{
    public static readonly int X = 123;
}
```

This code is compiled with csc /t:library /out:B.dll ReadOnlyOut.cs.

Listing 5.22—ReadOnlyConst.cs, ReadOnly Const User Class Example

```
using System;
public class MyTest
{
    public static void Main()
    {
        Console.WriteLine("A.X value = {0}", A.X);
        Console.WriteLine("B.X value = {0}", B.X);
    }
}
```

The code in the preceding listing is compiled with *csc /r:A.dll /r:B.dll ReadOnlyConst.cs.*

The code in these three examples produces the display shown in Figure 5.7.

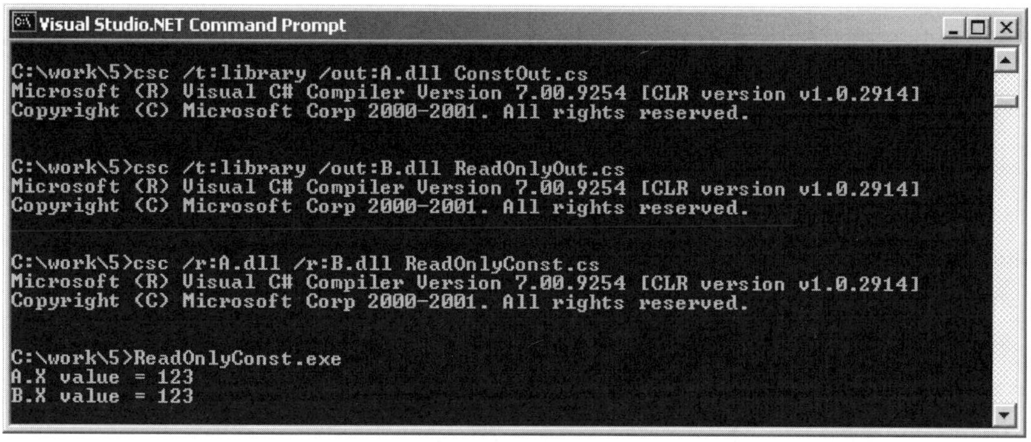

```
Visual Studio.NET Command Prompt                                    _ □ ×

C:\work\5>csc /t:library /out:A.dll ConstOut.cs
Microsoft (R) Visual C# Compiler Version 7.00.9254 [CLR version v1.0.2914]
Copyright (C) Microsoft Corp 2000-2001. All rights reserved.

C:\work\5>csc /t:library /out:B.dll ReadOnlyOut.cs
Microsoft (R) Visual C# Compiler Version 7.00.9254 [CLR version v1.0.2914]
Copyright (C) Microsoft Corp 2000-2001. All rights reserved.

C:\work\5>csc /r:A.dll /r:B.dll ReadOnlyConst.cs
Microsoft (R) Visual C# Compiler Version 7.00.9254 [CLR version v1.0.2914]
Copyright (C) Microsoft Corp 2000-2001. All rights reserved.

C:\work\5>ReadOnlyConst.exe
A.X value = 123
B.X value = 123
```

Figure 5.7: Screen Output Generated from Listings 5.20, 5.21, and 5.22

If you modify X in ConstOut.cs, then you have to compile both ConstOut.cs and ReadOnlyConst.cs consecutively. But if you modify X in ReadOnlyOut.cs, then you only need to compile ReadOnlyOut.cs; there is no need to recompile MyTest.cs. However, the execution speed of const is better than that of the static read-only.

Expressions and Operators

An *expression*, constructed of a sequence of operators and operands, specifies computation of a value or designates a variable or constant. The operators of an expression indicate which operations to apply to the operands. Examples of operators include +, -, *, /, and new. Examples of operands include literals, fields, local variables, and expressions.

Most of the constructs that involve an expression ultimately require the expression to denote a value. In such cases, an error occurs if the actual expression denotes a namespace, a type, a method group, or nothing. However, if the expression denotes a property access, an indexer access, or a variable, the value of the property, indexer, or variable is implicitly substituted.

The C# Language Specification includes just three types of operators:

- *Unary operators* take one operand and use either prefix notation (such as –x) or postfix notation (such as x++).
- *Binary operators* take two operands and use infix notation (such as x + y).
- The lone *ternary operator* (?:) takes three operands and uses infix notation (such as c? x: y).

Certain operators can be overloaded. Operator overloading permits user-defined operator implementations to be specified for operations where one or both of the operands are of a user-defined class or struct type.

The order of evaluation of operators in an expression is determined by the precedence and associativity of the operators. When an expression contains multiple operators, the precedence of the operators controls the order in which the individual operators are evaluated. For example, the expression $x + y * z$ is evaluated as $x + (y * z)$ because the * operator has higher precedence than the + operator.

Table 5.4 lists all operators, grouped by category and presented in order of precedence, from highest to lowest.

Category	Operators
Primary	`x.y  f(x)  a[x]  x++  x--  new typeof` `checked  unchecked`
Unary	`+  -  !  ~  ++x  --x  (T)x`
Multiplicative	`*  /  %`
Additive	`+  -`
Shift	`<<  >>`
Relational and type testing	`<  >  <=  >=  is  as`
Equality	`==  !=`
Logical	`AND &`
Logical	`XOR ^`
Logical	`OR |`
Conditional	`AND &&`
Conditional	`OR ||`
Conditional	`?:`
Assignment	`=  *=  /=  %=  +=  -=  <<=  >>=  &=  ^=` `|=`

Table 5.4: Operator Priority

The precedence of an operator is established by the definition of its associated grammar production in the C# Language Specification (http://msdn.microsoft.com/net/ecma/). For example, an additive expression consists of a sequence of multiplicative expressions separated by + or − operators, thus giving the + and - operators lower precedence than the *, /, and % operators.

When an operand occurs between two operators with the same precedence, the associativity of the operators controls the order in which the operations are performed.

Except for the assignment operators, all binary operators are left-associative, meaning that operations are performed from left to right. For example, $x + y + z$ is evaluated as $(x + y) + z$. The assignment operators and the conditional operator *(?:)* are right-associative, meaning that operations are performed from right to left. For example, $x = y = z$ is evaluated as $x = (y = z)$.

The evaluation of operands is separate from and unrelated to operator precedence. Operands in an expression are evaluated from left to right. Consider the following expression:

```
F(i) + G(i++) * H(i)
```

In this example, method F is called using the old value of i; then method G is called with the old value of i (in this case, the post-increment operator was used); and, finally, method H is called with the new value of i.

Control Statements

Control statements give you additional means to control the processing within the applications you develop. This section explores the syntax and function of the if, switch, do-while, for, foreach, goto, break, continue, and return statements.

If-then-else

The if statement has three forms: single selection, if-then-else selection, and multicase selection. Listing 5.23 contains an example of each form.

Listing 5.23—If-Else-ElseIf Example 1

```
//single selection
 if(i > 0)
  Console.WriteLine("The number {0} is positive", i);

 //if-then-else selection
 if(i > 0)
  Console.WriteLine("The number {0} is positive", i);
 else
  Console.WriteLine("The number {0} is not positive", i);

 //multicase selection
 if(i == 0)
  Console.WriteLine("The number is zero");
 else if(i > 0)
  Console.WriteLine("The number {0} is positive",i);
 else
  Console.WriteLine("The number {0} is negative",i);

The variable i is the object of evaluation here. The expression in an if statement
must resolve to a boolean value type.

// Compiler Error
if(1)
   Console.WriteLine("The if statement executed");
```

When the C# compiler compiles the preceding code, it generates the error "Constant value 1 cannot be converted to bool."

Listing 5.24 shows how *conditional or* (||) and *conditional and* (&&) operators are used in the same manner.

Listing 5.24—If-Then-Else Example 2

```
//Leap year
int year = 1974;
if((year % 4 == 0 && year % 100 != 0) || year % 400 == 0 )
   Console.WriteLine("The year {0} is leap year ",year);
else
   Console.WriteLine("The year {0} is not leap year ",year);
```

Switch

From the example in Listing 5.25, you can see that the switch statement is similar to an if-else if-else if-else form of an if statement.

Listing 5.25—Switch Example 1

```
int i = 1;
switch(i)
{
case 1 :
    Console.WriteLine("one");
    break;
default :
    Console.WriteLine("default");
    break;
}
```

If you try to compile this code without putting the break statement in case 1, the compiler raises the error "Control cannot fall through from one case label."

The switch expression can evaluate to the following types: sbyte, byte, short, ushort, int, uint, long, ulong, char, string, and enum. Thus, the C# compiler can compile the code in Listing 5.26 without generating an error.

Listing 5.26—Switch Example 2

```
    string day = "Monday";
Console.WriteLine("enter the day :");
day = Console.ReadLine();

switch(day)
{
case "Mon" :
    break;
case "Monday" :
    Console.WriteLine("day is Monday: go to work");
    break;
default :
    Console.WriteLine("default");
    break;
}


switch (strVal1)
{
    case "reason1":
        goto case "reason2"; // this is a jump to mimic fall-through…
    case "reason2":
        intOption = 2;
        break;
    case "reason 3":
        intOption = 3;
        break;
    case "reason 4":
        intOption = 4;
        break;
    case "reason 5":
        intOption = 5;
        break;
    default:
        intOption = 9;
        break;
}
```
Do-While
The while loop allows the user to repeat a section of code until a guard condition
is met. Listing 5.27 presents a simple while loop designed to find out the number
of digits in a given value.

Listing 5.27—While Example

```
//find out the number of digits in a given number
int i = 123;
int count = 0;
int n = i;

//while loop may execute zero times
while(i > 0)
{
  ++count;
  i = i/10;
}

Console.WriteLine("Number {0} contains {1} digits.",n,count);
```

For a given number i = 123, the loop will execute three times. Hence the value of the count is three at the end of the while loop.

This example has one logical flaw. If the value of i is 0, the output of the code will be "Number 0 contains 0 digits." Actually, the number 0 contains one digit. Because the condition of the while loop i > 0 is false from the beginning for the value i = 0, the while loop does not even execute one time and the count will be zero. Listing 5.28 presents a solution.

Listing 5.28—Do Example

```
//find out the number of digits in a given number

int i = 0;
int count = 0;
int n = i;

do
{
  ++count;
  i = i/10;
}while(i > 0);

Console.WriteLine("Number {0} contains {1} digits.", n, count);
```

The do-while construct checks the condition at the end of the loop. Therefore, the do-while loop executes at least once even though the condition to be checked is false from the beginning.

For

The for loop is useful when you know how many times the loop needs to execute. An example of a for statement is presented in Listing 5.29.

Listing 5.29—For Example 1

```
for (int i=0; i<3; i++)
  a(i) = "test";

for( string strServer = Console.ReadLine();
     strServer != "q" && strServer !="quit";
     strServer = Console.ReadLine() )
{
  Console.WriteLine(strServer);
}
```

Listing 5.30 shows the use of a for loop with the added functionality of break and continue statements.

Listing 5.30—For Example 2

```
//For loop with break and continue statements
for(int i = 0 ; i < 20 ; ++i)
{
  if(i == 10)
        break;
  if(i == 5)
        continue;
  Console.WriteLine(i);
}
```

The output of the code in the listing is as follows:

```
0
1
2
3
4
6
7
8
9
```

When i becomes 5, the loop skips over the remaining statements in the loop and goes back to the postloop action. Thus, 5 is omitted from the output. When i becomes 10, the program will break out of the loop.

ForEach

The foreach statement allows the iteration of processing over the elements in arrays and collections. Listing 5.31 contains a simple example.

Listing 5.31—ForEach Example 1

```
//foreach loop
string[] a = {"Chirag","Bhargav","Tejas"};

foreach(string b in a)
        Console.WriteLine(b);
```

Within the foreach loop parentheses, the expression consists of two parts separated by the keyword in. To the right of in is the collection, and to the left is the variable with the type identifier matching whatever type the collection returns.

Listing 5.32 presents a slightly more complex version of the foreach loop.

Listing 5.32—ForEach Example 2

```
Int16[] intNumbers = {4, 5, 6, 1, 2, 3, -2, -1, 0};
foreach (Int16  i  in  intNumbers)
{
    System.Console.WriteLine(i);
}
```

Each iteration queries the collection for a new value for i. As long as the collection intNumbers returns a value, the value is put into the variable i and the loop will continue. When the collection is fully traversed, the loop will terminate.

GoTo

You can use the goto statement to jump to a specific segment of code, as shown in Listing 5.33. You can also use goto for jumping to switch cases and default labels inside switch blocks. You should avoid the overuse of goto because code becomes difficult to read and maintain if you have many goto jumps within your code.

Listing 5.33—GoTo Example

```
label1:;
//...
if(x == 0 )
        goto label1;
//...
```

Break

The break statement, used within for, while, and do-while blocks, causes processing to exit the innermost loop immediately. When a break statement is used, the code jumps to the next line following the loop block, as you'll see in Listing 5.34.

Listing 5.34—Break Example

```
while(true)
{
 //...
 if(x == 0)
   break;
 //...
}
Console.WriteLine("break");
```

Continue

The continue statement (shown in Listing 5.35) is used to jump to the end of the loop immediately and process the next iteration of the loop.

Listing 5.35—Continue Example

```
int x = 0;

while(true)
{
 //...
 if(x == 0)
  {
    x=5;
    continue;
  }
 //...
 if( x == 5)
Console.WriteLine("continue");
 //...
}
```

Return

The return statement is used to prematurely return from a method. The return statement can return empty or with a value on the stack, depending upon the return value definition in the method (Listing 5.36 shows both). Void methods do not require a return value. For other functions, you need to return an appropriate value of the type you declared in the method signature.

Listing 5.36—Return Example

```
void MyFunc1()
{
  // ...
  if(x == 1)
    return;
  // ...
}

int MyFunc2()
{
  // ...
  if(x == 2)
    return 1919;
  // ...
}
```

Namespaces and Assemblies

Assemblies are for physical scope and namespaces are for logical scope, so namespaces can be expanded over assemblies but the converse is not possible.

The namespace keyword is used to declare a scope. This namespace scope lets you organize code and gives you a way to create globally unique types.

Even if you do not explicitly declare one, a default namespace is created. This unnamed namespace, sometimes called the global namespace, is present in every file. Any identifier in the global namespace is available for use in a named namespace.

Namespaces are hierarchical. They implicitly have public access, which you cannot modify.

It is possible to define a namespace in two or more declarations. For example, the code in Listing 5.37 defines both classes as part of namespace MyCompany.

Listing 5.37—NameSpace.cs, Namespaces Example

```
using System;

// recurring namespaces
namespace MyCompany.Proj1
{
    class MyClass
    {
    }
}

namespace MyCompany.Proj1
{
    class MyClass1
    {
    }
}

//nested namespaces
namespace SomeNameSpace
{
    public class MyClass
    {
      public static void Main()
      {
        Nested.NestedNameSpaceClass.SayHello();
      }
```

```
    }

namespace Nested    // a nested namespace
{
   public class NestedNameSpaceClass
   {
      public static void SayHello()
      {
         Console.WriteLine("Hello");
      }
   }
}
}
```

The code listing generates the screen output in Figure 5.8.

Figure 5.8: Screen Output from Listing 5.37

C# programs are organized using namespaces, which serve as both an internal organization system for a program and an external organization system—that is, a way of presenting program elements that are exposed to other programs.

C# also enables the definition and use of aliases. Such aliases can be useful in situations in which name collisions occur between two libraries, or when a few types from a much larger namespace are being used. Listing 5.38 presents code from the preceding example, rewritten to use aliases.

Listing 5.38—NameSpace Assignment Example

```
using MessageSource = Microsoft.CSharp.Introduction.HelloMessage;
class Hello
{
      static void Main() {
             MessageSource m = new MessageSource();
             System.Console.WriteLine(m.GetMessage());
      }
}
```

An assembly is everything that comprises a .NET application. It is the unit of deployment for the Microsoft .NET framework and takes the form of an executable (.exe) file or dynamic-link library (DLL). What makes assemblies different from .exe files or DLLs in earlier versions of Windows is that assemblies contain within them all the information that you would find in a type library along with information about everything else that is necessary to use the application or component.

One of the primary goals of assemblies is versioning. Specifically, assemblies provide a means for developers to specify version rules between different software components and to have those rules enforced at runtime.

Because assemblies are the building blocks of applications, they are the logical point for specifying and enforcing version information. Each assembly has a specific version number as part of its identity.

Struct and Class Differences

The section of this chapter that deals with types introduced the class and struct keywords, and other topics in the chapter illustrate class and struct concepts such as attributes, member variables, member functions, constructors, and destructors. Even with that background information, people often confuse the concepts of class and struct. However, each keyword has distinct uses.

A *class* is a data structure that contains data members (e.g., constants and fields), function members (e.g., methods, properties, indexers, events, operators, instance constructors, static constructors, and destructors), and nested types. Class types support inheritance.

Struct data types are similar to classes: they represent data structures that can contain data members and function members. Unlike classes, structs are value types and do not require heap allocation. They are always created on the stack. A variable of a type struct directly contains the data of the struct, whereas a variable of a type class contains a reference to the data.

Struct data types are particularly useful for small data structures that have value semantics. Complex numbers, points in a coordinate system, or key-value pairs in a dictionary are all good examples of structs. Structs should have few data members. They do not require use of inheritance or referential identity, and they can be conveniently implemented using value semantics where assignment copies the value instead of the reference.

The simple types provided by C#, such as int, double, and bool, are in fact all struct types. Just as these predefined types are structs, so is it possible to use structs and operator overloading to implement new "primitive" types in the C# language.

Delegates and Events

A delegate is a class that can hold a reference to a method. Unlike other classes, a delegate class has a signature, and it can hold references only to methods that match its signature. A delegate is thus equivalent to a type-safe function pointer or a callback. Although delegates have other uses, the discussion here focuses on the event-handling functionality of delegates.

Events in C# are handled by delegates, which serve as a mechanism that defines one or more callback functions to process events.

An event is a message sent by an object to signal the occurrence of an action. The action could arise from user interaction, such as a mouse click, or could be triggered by some other program logic. The object that triggers the event is called the event sender. The object that captures the event and responds to it is called the event receiver.

In event communication, the event sender class does not know which object or method will handle the events it raises. It merely functions as an intermediary or pointer-like mechanism between the source and the receiver, as illustrated in Listing 5.47. The .NET framework defines a special type delegate that serves as a function pointer.

Listing 5.47—DelegateEvent.cs, Delegates and Events Example

```
using System;

public class MyEvt
{
    public delegate void t(Object sender, MyArgs e);
    // declare a delegate

    public event t tEvt; //declares an event for the delegate
```

```
      public void mm()
      { //function that will raise the callback
        MyArgs r = new MyArgs();
        tEvt(this, r); //calling the client code
      }
      public MyEvt()
      {
      }
}

//arguments for the callback
public class MyArgs:EventArgs
{
    public MyArgs()
    {
    }
}

public class MyEvtClient
{
      MyEvt oo;

      public MyEvtClient()
      {
            this.oo = new MyEvt();
            this.oo.tEvt += new MyEvt.t(oo_tt);
      }

      public static void Main (String [] args)
      {
            MyEvtClient cc = new MyEvtClient();
            cc.oo.mm();
      }

      //this code will be called from the server
      public void oo_tt(object sender, MyArgs e)
      {
            Console.WriteLine("yes");
      }
}
```

Figure 5.10 contains the output of the code in Listing 5.47.

Figure 5.10: Screen Output Generated from Listing 5.47

Attributes

C# provides a mechanism for defining declarative tags, called *attributes*, which you can place on certain entities in your source code to specify additional information. The information that attributes contain can be retrieved at runtime through reflection. You can use predefined attributes, or you can define your own custom attributes.

One very powerful predefined attribute is DllImport, which allows you to bring in existing Windows dynamic-link libraries to utilize software development kit functionality.

```
[DllImport("winmm.dll ")]
```

Another useful attribute is the conditional attribute (see Listing 5.48), which works just like #ifdef but looks a little better.

Listing 5.48—Attributes Example

```
[Conditional("_DEBUG")]
void DumpDebugInfo()
{
   System.Console.WriteLine(MyErrors);
}
```

Listing 5.49 shows what a custom attribute looks like.

Listing 5.49—Attribute.cs, Custom Attributes Example

```
// Example Custom Attribute
using System;
[AttributeUsage(AttributeTargets.Class|AttributeTargets.Struct,
   AllowMultiple=true)]
public class Writer : Attribute
{
   public Writer(string name)
   {
      this.name = name; version = 1.0;
   }
   public double version;
   string name;
   public string GetName()
   {
      return name;
   }
}

[Writer("Mehmet Akif Ersoy")]
class FirstClass
{
   /*...*/
}

class SecondClass  // no Writer attribute
{
   /*...*/
}

[Writer("Mehmet Akif Ersoy"), Writer("Necip Fazil Kisakurek", version=1.1)]
class Steerage
{
   /*...*/
}

class WriterInfo
{
   public static void Main()
   {
      PrintWriterInfo(typeof(FirstClass));
      PrintWriterInfo(typeof(SecondClass));
      PrintWriterInfo(typeof(Steerage));
   }
   public static void PrintWriterInfo(Type t)
   {
      Console.WriteLine("Writer information for {0}", t);
      Attribute[] attrs = Attribute.GetCustomAttributes(t);
```

```
      foreach(Attribute attr in attrs)
      {
         if (attr is Writer)
         {
            Writer a = (Writer)attr;
            Console.WriteLine("   {0}, version {1:f}",
a.GetName(), a.version);
         }
      }
   }
}
```

Figure 5.11 shows the screen output generated by this code.

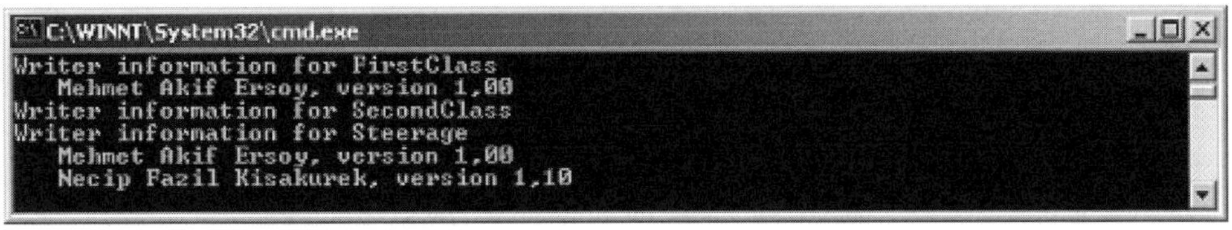

Figure 5.11: Screen Output Generated from Listing 5.49

Inheritance

Inheritance is a relationship that defines one entity in terms of another. Class inheritance defines a new class in terms of one parent class or one or more interfaces. The new class inherits its interface and implementation from its parent class and method signatures. The new class is called a subclass or a derived class.

Class inheritance combines interface inheritance and implementation inheritance. *Interface inheritance* defines a new interface in terms of one or more existing interfaces. *Implementation inheritance* defines a new implementation in terms of one or more existing implementations.

Classes in C# support only single inheritance, and Object is the ultimate base class for all classes. The classes shown in earlier examples all implicitly derive from Object.

Access modifiers in a classes members give different levels of access to derived classes. Below is a table that describes the access a child class has to the members of the inherited class depending upon the access modifier.

access-specifier: public

Parent class access modifier	Access in child class
public	accessible
protected	accessible
private	not accessible

Table 5.6: Access-Specifier Members and inheritance scope

C# only makes use of public inheritance, meaning that you cannot specify an inheritance modifier in C#. (Refer to the C# Language Specification, available at http://msdn.microsoft.com/net/ecma/, for more details and recent updates to the C# language.) Listing 5.50 shows an example of a class deriving inheritance with public access specified.

Listing 5.50—Inheritance Example 1

```
using System;
class A    // derived from object behind the scenes
{
    public void F() { Console.WriteLine("A.F"); }
}


class B: A    // B inherits A
{
    public void G() { Console.WriteLine("B.G"); }
}

class Test
{
    static void Main() {
        B b = new B();
        b.F();            // Inherited from A
        b.G();            // Introduced in B

        A a = b;            // Treat a B as an A, polymorphic access
        a.F();
    }
}
```

Listing 5.51 presents another inheritance example, this time with protected access specified.

Listing 5.51—Inheritance Example 2

```
// example1 protected

class A
{
    protected int x = 123;
}

class B : A
{
    void F()
    {
        A a = new A();
        B b = new B();
        a.x = 10;    // Error
        b.x = 10;    // OK
    }
}
```

Listing 5.52 shows another example of private inheritance that enables direct access to protected members.

Listing 5.52—Protected.cs, Protected Modifier Example

```
// example2 protected
using System;

class MyClass
{
    protected int x;
    protected int y;
}

class MyDerivedC: MyClass //private inheritance
{
    public static void Main()
    {
```

```
        MyDerivedC mC = new MyDerivedC();

        // Direct access to protected members:
        mC.x = 10;
        mC.y = 15;
        Console.WriteLine("x = {0}, y = {1}", mC.x, mC.y);
    }
}
```

Figure 5.12 contains the resulting screen output.

Figure 5.12: Screen Output Generated from Listing 5.52

Polymorphism

Polymorphism is the ability to define a method or property in a set of derived classes with matching method signatures but provide different implementations and then distinguish the objects' matching interface from one another at runtime when you call the method on the base class.

From within the derived class that has an override method, you still can access the overridden base method that has the same name by using the base keyword. For example, if you have a virtual method MyMethod() and an override method on a derived class, you can access the virtual method from the derived class by using the call base.MyMethod(). Listing 5.53 illustrates this concept.

Listing 5.53—Polymorphism.cs, Polymorphism Example

```
// notice the comments/warnings in the Main
// calling overridden methods from the base class

using System;

class TestClass
{
    public class Square
    {
        public double x;

        // Constructor:
        public Square(double x)
        {
            this.x = x;
        }

        public virtual double Area()
        {
            return x*x;
        }
    }

    class Cube: Square
    {
        // Constructor:
        public Cube(double x): base(x)
```

```
        {
        }

    // Calling the Area base method:
    public override double Area()
    {
        return (6*(base.Area()));
    }
}

 public static void MyFormat (IFormattable value, string formatString)
 {
     Console.WriteLine ("{0}\t{1}", formatString, value.ToString (formatString,
null));
 }

public static void Main()
{
    double x = 5.2;
    Square s = new Square(x);
    Square c = new Cube(x); // This is OK, polymorphic
    // a base reference can refer to the derived object

     Console.Write("Area of Square = ");
     MyFormat(s.Area(), "n");

    Console.Write("Area of Cube = ");
     MyFormat(c.Area(), "n");

    // ERROR: Cube q = new Square(x);
    // Cannot implicitly convert type 'TestClass.Square' to 'TestClass.Cube'

    Cube q1 = (Cube) c; // This is OK, polymorphic
    Console.Write("Area of Cube again = ");
     MyFormat(q1.Area(), "n");

    // try uncommenting the following line and see if it works
    // Cube q2 = (Cube) new Square(x);
   // This compiles but is this OK? NO!

    //Runtime Exception occurs here: System.InvalidCastException:
    //An exception of type System.InvalidCastException was thrown.

    // A derived reference should not be transformed from base object,
    // since the orphaned parts may occur in the derived.
    // Cube constructors those may be necessary had not worked up to now for q2.
    // C# compiles code but gives an exception during runtime
}
}
```

Figure 5.13 contains the resulting screen output.

```
C:\WINNT\System32\cmd.exe                                    _ □ ×

C:\work>test1
Area of Square = n        27,04
Area of Cube = n          162,24
Area of Cube again = n    162,24

C:\work>_
```

Figure 5.13: Screen Output Generated from Listing 5.53

Overloading

C# allows user-defined types to overload operators by defining static member functions using the operator keyword. The operator keyword is used to declare an operator in a class or struct declaration. Not all operators can be overloaded, and some that can be overloaded have certain restrictions, as listed in Table 5.7.

Operators	Overloadable
Unary operators +, -, !, ~, ++, —, true, false	Yes
Binary operators +, -, *, /, %, &, |, ^, <<, >>	Yes
Comparison operators ==, !=, <, >, <=, >=	Yes, in pairs (e.g., if < is overloaded, > must be too, and vice versa. Note that if you overload == or !+, you must override the Object.Equals and Object.GetHashCode functions.)
Conditional logical operators &&, ||	No, but they are evaluated using & and |, which can be overloaded
Array-indexing operators []	No, but you can define indexers
Cast operator ()	No, but you can define new conversion operators
Assignment operators +=, -=, *=, /=, %=, &=, |=, ^=, <<=, >>=	No, but +=, for example, is evaluated using +, which can be overloaded
Miscellaneous operators =, ., ?:, ->, new, is, sizeof, typeof	No

Table 5.7: Operator Overloading

Listing 5.54 illustrates overloading on complex numbers.

Listing 5.54—OpOverload.cs, Operator Overloading Example

```
// operator overloading your custom classes in C#
// OperatorOverloading Complex Numbers

using System;

 public class Complex
 {
    public int real = 0;
    public int imaginary = 0;

    public Complex(int real, int imaginary)
    {
       this.real = real;
       this.imaginary = imaginary;
    }

    public static Complex operator +(Complex c1, Complex c2)
    {
       return new Complex(c1.real + c2.real, c1.imaginary + c2.imaginary);
    }

    public static void Main()
```

```
    {
        Complex num1 = new Complex(2,3);
        Complex num2 = new Complex(3,4);

        Complex sum = num1 + num2;

        Console.WriteLine("Real: {0}", sum.real);
        Console.WriteLine("Imaginary: {0}", sum.imaginary);
    }
}
```

Figure 5.14 shows the resulting display.

Figure 5.14: Screen Output Generated from Listing 5.54

Listing 5.55 presents a more sophisticated example of operator overloading.

Listing 5.55—SopOpOverload.cs, Sophisticated Operator Overloading Example

```
// operator overloading

using System;
class Rectangle
{
  private int iHeight;
  private int iWidth;

  public Rectangle()
  {
    Height=0;
    Width=0;
  }
  public Rectangle(int w,int h)
  {
    Width=w;
    Height=h;
  }

  public int Width
  {
    get
    {
      return iWidth;
    }
    set
    {
      iWidth=value;
    }
  }
  public int Height
  {
    get
    {
      return iHeight;
    }
```

```
  set
  {
    iHeight=value;
  }
}

public int Area
{
  get
  {
    return Height*Width;
  }
}

/* Overloading ==  */

public static bool operator==(Rectangle a,Rectangle b)
{
  return ((a.Height==b.Height)&&(a.Width==b.Width));
}

/* Overloading != */

public static bool operator!=(Rectangle a,Rectangle b)
{
  return !(a==b);
}

/* Overloading > */

public static bool operator>(Rectangle a,Rectangle b)
{
  return a.Area>b.Area;
}

/* Overloading < */
public static bool operator<(Rectangle a,Rectangle b)
{
  return !(a>b);
}

/* Overloading >= */

public static bool operator>=(Rectangle a,Rectangle b)
{
  return (a>b)||(a==b);
}

/* Overloading <= */

public static bool operator<=(Rectangle a,Rectangle b)
{
  return (a<b)||(a==b);
}

public override bool Equals(object o)
{
  return this.Equals(o);
}

public override int GetHashCode()
{
  return this.GetHashCode();
}

public override String ToString()
{
```

```
      return "Height=" + Height + ",Width=" + Width;
   }
   public static void Main()
   {
     Rectangle objRect1 =new Rectangle();
     Rectangle objRect2 =new Rectangle();
     Rectangle objRect3 =new Rectangle(10,15);
     objRect1.Height=15;
     objRect1.Width=10;
     objRect2.Height=25;
     objRect2.Width=10;
     Console.WriteLine("Rectangle#1 " + objRect1);
     Console.WriteLine("Rectangle#2 " + objRect2);
     Console.WriteLine("Rectangle#3 " + objRect3);

     if(objRect1==objRect2)
     {
       Console.WriteLine("Rectangle1 & Rectangle2 are Equal.");
     }
     else
     {
       if(objRect1>objRect2)
       {
         Console.WriteLine("Rectangle1 is greater than Rectangle2");
       }
       else
       {
         Console.WriteLine("Rectangle1 is lesser than Rectangle2");
       }
     }

     if(objRect1==objRect3)
     {
       Console.WriteLine("Rectangle1 & Rectangle3 are Equal.");
     }
     else
     {
       Console.WriteLine("Rectangle1 & Rectangle3 are not Equal.");
     }
   }
}
```

Figure 5.15 contains the screen output from this example.

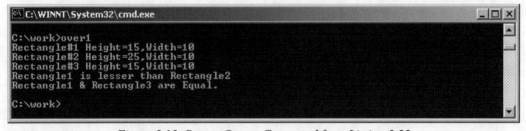

Figure 5.15: Screen Output Generated from Listing 5.55

Indexers

Indexers, another nifty feature of C#, are similar to the overloaded [] (array subscript) operator in C++. An indexer allows you to access a class instance in terms of a member array.

Please refer to C# Language Specification (http://msdn.microsoft.com/net/ecma/) for more details and recent updates to the C# language.

An indexer declaration may include a set of attributes; a new modifier; a valid combination of the public, private, protected, and internal access modifiers; and one of the virtual, override, or abstract modifiers.

The type of an indexer declaration specifies the element type of the indexer introduced by the declaration. Unless the indexer is an explicit interface member implementation, the type is followed by the keyword this. For an explicit interface member implementation, the type is followed by an interface type, a period (.), and the keyword this. Unlike other members, indexers do not have user-defined names.

The formal parameter list of an indexer corresponds to that of a method, with two differences: at least one parameter must be specified, and the ref and out parameter modifiers are not permitted.

The accessors specify the executable statements associated with reading and writing indexer elements.

Even though the syntax for accessing an indexer element is the same as that for an array element, an indexer element is not classified as a variable. Thus, it is not possible to pass an indexer element as a ref or out parameter.

It is an error for an indexer accessor to declare a local variable with the same name as an indexer parameter. With these differences in mind, all rules defined in apply to indexer accessors as well as property accessors.

Indexers and properties, although very similar in concept, differ in the following ways:

- A property is identified by its name whereas an indexer is identified by its signature.
- A property is accessed through a simple-name or a member-access whereas an indexer element is accessed through an element-access.
- A property can be a static member whereas an indexer is always an instance member.
- A get accessor of a property corresponds to a method with no parameters whereas a get accessor of an indexer corresponds to a method with the same formal parameter list as the indexer.
- A set accessor of a property corresponds to a method with a single parameter named value whereas a set accessor of an indexer corresponds to a method with the same formal parameter list as the indexer, plus an additional parameter named value.

To understand these concepts, refer to the code in Listing 5.56.

Listing 5.56—Indexer.cs, Indexer Example

```
// indexer example, to get DNS aliases for a given IPAddress

using System;
using System.Net;

class GetDNSaliases
  {
  string[] m_arrAlias;

  public void Fetch(string strHost)
    {
    IPHostEntry iphe = Dns.GetHostByAddress(strHost);
    m_arrAlias = iphe.Aliases ;
    }

  public string this[int nIndex] //indexer
```

```
  {
   get
   {
    return m_arrAlias[nIndex];
   }
  }

  public int Count // property
  {
   get { return m_arrAlias.GetUpperBound(0); }
  }
 }

 class MyApp
 {
  public static string str1;

  public static void Main()
  {
   GetDNSaliases myGetDNSaliases = new GetDNSaliases();
   do{
    try{
     Console.WriteLine(@"write a valid IP Address and press ENTER (to exit enter
 ""q"").");
      if( (str1 = Console.ReadLine()) == @"q")
       {
        break;
       }

     myGetDNSaliases.Fetch(str1);

     Int32 nCount = myGetDNSaliases.Count;
     Console.WriteLine("Found {1} aliases for IP {0}", str1, nCount);
     for (Int32 i=0; i < nCount; i++)
      {
        Console.WriteLine(myGetDNSaliases[i]);
      }
    }
    catch(Exception e)
    {
      Console.WriteLine("Exception occurred!{0}\r\n", e.ToString());
    }
    finally
    {
     //final code to be executed
    }
   } while(true);
  }
}
```

The code in this listing generates the display in Figure 5.16.

Figure 5.16: Screen Output Generated from Listing 5.56

Enumerators

As explained earlier, C# has a new iteration syntax called foreach. The foreach statement can only be applied to objects of classes that implement the IEnumerable interface. The IEnumerable interface exposes the enumerator, which supports a simple iteration over a collection. Enumerators are intended to be used only to read data in the collection and cannot be used to modify the underlying collection. The enumerator does not have exclusive access to the collection. To understand what happens in the background, consider the code snippet in Listing 5.57.

Listing 5.57—Enumerator Example 1

```
foreach(int i in a)
{
    Console.WriteLine(i);
}
```

This code functions just like the while loop used in Listing 5.58.

Listing 5.58—Enumerator Example 2

```
a = x.GetEnumerator();
while(a.MoveNext())
{
    Console.WriteLine(a.Current);
}
```

Please refer to the C# Language Specification (http://msdn.microsoft.com/net/ecma/) for more details and recent updates to the C# language.

Before entering the statement block, the compiler generates the code to call the method GetEnumerator of the object passed as the second parameter in the foreach statement. The GetEnumerator method must return an object, having a property named Current, of type similar to the first argument of the foreach statement. Also this object must have a MoveNext method of return type bool. This method informs the runtime when to terminate the loop.

When an enumerator is instantiated, it takes a snapshot of the current state of the collection. If changes are made to the collection, such as the addition, modification, or deletion of elements, the snapshot gets out of sync and the enumerator throws an InvalidOperationException. Two enumerators instantiated from the same collection simultaneously can have different snapshots of the collection.

If the enumerator is positioned before the first element in the collection or after the last element in the collection, the enumerator is in an invalid state. In that case, calling Current throws an exception.

The enumerator is positioned before the first element in the collection initially. The Reset function brings the enumerator back to this position. The MoveNext method must be called to advance the enumerator to the first element of the collection before reading the value of Current, after an enumerator is created or after a Reset. The Current property returns the same object until either MoveNext or Reset is called.

Once the end of the collection is passed, the enumerator is in an invalid state and calling MoveNext returns false. Calling Current throws an exception if the last call to MoveNext returned false.

With this information under your belt, you should insert your enumerating code inside a try-catch-finally block to prevent unexpected exits.

C# Preprocessor Directives

The C# preprocessor is a macro processor that the C# compiler automatically uses to transform your program before actual compilation. The C# preprocessor allows you to define macros, which are brief abbreviations for longer constructs.

A preprocessor directive must be the only instruction on a line. Preprocessing directives start with #, followed by an identifier that is the directive name. For example, #define is the directive. White space is allowed before and after the #.

The C# language's preprocessor directives are as follows:
- #define
- #if
- #else
- #elif
- #endif
- #undef
- #warning
- #error
- #line
- #region
- #endregion

The main uses of directives include conditional compilation, line control, error and warning reporting, and region and end region. Let's take a preliminary look at each.

Conditional compilation—Using special preprocessing directives, you can include or exclude parts of the program according to various conditions.

Line control—If you use a program to combine or rearrange source files into an intermediate file that is then compiled, you can use line control to inform the compiler where each source line originated.

Error and warning reporting—The directive #error causes the preprocessor to report a fatal error. The directive #warning is much like the directive #error, but it causes the preprocessor to issue a warning and continue preprocessing.

Region and end region—These new directives, not found in C and C++, allow you to specify a block of code that you can expand or collapse.

Before further explaining the meaning of each preprocessor directive, it's helpful to see how to define these directives. Listings 5.59 and 5.60 illustrate the two methods for defining directives: in your C# program and on the command line at compile-time.

Listing 5.59—Define1.cs, Define Example 1

```
#define TEST
using System;
public class MyClass
{
    public static void Main()
    {
        #if (TEST)
            Console.WriteLine("TEST is defined");
        #else
            Console.WriteLine("TEST is not defined");
```

```
        #endif
    }
}
```

This first example of directive defining produces the output in Figure 5.17.

Figure 5.17: Screen Output Generated from Listing 5.59

Illustrating the second means of defining preprocessor directives is the code in Listing 5.60, which you compile using the /define:TEST compiler option.

Listing 5.60—Define2.cs, Define Example 2

```
using System;
public class MyClass
{
    public static void Main()
    {
        #if (TEST)
            Console.WriteLine("TEST is defined");
        #else
            Console.WriteLine("TEST is not defined");
        #endif
    }
}
```

This code generates the output in Figure 5.18.

Figure 5.18: Screen Output Generated from Listing 5.60

#define Directive

The #define directive allows you to define a symbol that, when used as the expression passed to the #if directive, causes the expression to evaluate to true.

#undef Directive

The #undef directive allows you to undefine a symbol that, when used as the expression in an #if directive, causes the expression to evaluate to false.

For the #undef example in Listing 5.61, compile the code with the /D:DEBUG compiler option.

Listing 5.61—Undef.cs, Undef Example

```
#undef DEBUG
using System;
public class MyClass
{
    public static void Main()
    {
```

```
    #if DEBUG
        Console.WriteLine("DEBUG is defined");
    #else
        Console.WriteLine("DEBUG is not defined");
    #endif
  }
}
```

The code snippet produces the screen output shown in Figure 5.19.

Figure 5.19: Screen Output Generated from Listing 5.61

#if Directive

The #if directive allows you to conditionally choose to include code if the expression is true and in its simplest form consists of the following elements:

#if expression
controlled text
#endif /* expression */

The comment following the #endif is not required, but it is a good practice because it helps people match the #endif to the corresponding #if. Such comments should always be used, except in short conditionals that are not nested.

#else Directive

The #else directive can be added to a conditional directive to provide alternative text to be used if the condition is false. It consists of the following elements:

#if expression
text-if-true
#else /* Not expression */
text-if-false
#endif /* Not expression */

If the expression is nonzero and thus the text-if-true element is active, then #else acts like a failing conditional and the text-if-false element is ignored.

#elif Directive

Like #else, the #elif directive goes in the middle of an #if-#endif pair and subdivides it. It does not require a matching #endif of its own. Like #if, the #elif directive includes an expression to be tested.

The text following the #elif is processed only if the original #if condition fails and the #elif condition succeeds. More than one #elif can go in the same #if-#endif group. In the case of multiple #elif directives, the text after each successive #elif is processed only if all previous #elif directives have failed. You may use the #else directive after any number of #elif directives, but an #elif directive may not follow #else. Listing 5.62 illustrates the use of the #if-#elif-#else preprocessor structure.

Listing 5.62—ifelif.cs, If-Elif-Endif Example

```
#define DEBUG
#define VC_V6
using System;
public class MyClass
{
    public static void Main()
    {
        #if (DEBUG && !VC_V6)
            Console.WriteLine("DEBUG is defined");
        #elif (!DEBUG && VC_V6)
            Console.WriteLine("VC_V6 is defined");
        #elif (DEBUG && VC_V6)
            Console.WriteLine("DEBUG and VC_V6 are defined");
        #else
            Console.WriteLine("DEBUG and VC_V6 are not defined");
        #endif
    }
}
```

```
C:\WINNT\System32\cmd.exe
Microsoft (R) Visual C# Compiler Version 7.00.9254 [CLR version v1.0.2914]
Copyright (C) Microsoft Corp 2000-2001. All rights reserved.

C:\work>debug2
DEBUG and VC_V6 are defined

C:\work>
```

Figure 5.20: Screen Output Generated from Listing 5.62

#endif Directive

The #endif directive specifies the end of a conditional directive that begins with the #if directive.

#error Directive

The directive #error causes the preprocessor to report a fatal error. The tokens forming the rest of the line following #error are used as the error message.

Listing 5.63—Error.cs, Error Example

```
#define DEBUG
public class MyClass
{
    public static void Main()
    {
        #if DEBUG
        #error DEBUG is defined
    #endif
    }
}
```

Figure 5.21 contains the resulting output.

```
C:\WINNT\System32\cmd.exe                                           _ □ x
C:\work\5>csc 5.21.cs
Microsoft (R) Visual C# Compiler Version 7.00.9254 [CLR version v1.0.2914]
Copyright (C) Microsoft Corp 2000-2001. All rights reserved.

5.21.cs(7,14): error CS1029: #error: 'DEBUG is defined'
```

Figure 5.21: Screen Output Generated from Listing 5.63

#warning Directive

The directive #warning is much like the directive #error, but it causes the preprocessor to issue a warning and continue preprocessing. The tokens following #warning are used as the warning message. Listing 5.64 presents an example.

Listing 5.64—Warning.cs, Warning Example

```
#define DEBUG
public class MyClass
{
    public static void Main()
    {
        #if DEBUG
        #warning DEBUG is defined
    #endif
    }
}
```

The resulting screen output appears in Figure 5.22.

```
C:\WINNT\System32\cmd.exe                                           _ □ x
C:\work\5>csc 5.22.cs
Microsoft (R) Visual C# Compiler Version 7.00.9254 [CLR version v1.0.2914]
Copyright (C) Microsoft Corp 2000-2001. All rights reserved.

5.22.cs(7,16): warning CS1030: #warning: 'DEBUG is defined'
```

Figure 5.22: Screen Output of Listing 5.64

#line Directive

The #line directive (an example of which is shown in Listing 5.65) specifies the original line number and source file name for subsequent input in the current preprocessor input file.

Listing 5.65—Line.cs, Line Example

```
using System;
public class MyClass
{
 public static void Main()
 {
        #line 100 "abc.sc"    // change file name in the compiler output
        intt i;    // error will be reported on line 100, because of intt

/* abc.sc(100,3): error CS0246: The type or namespace name 'intt' could not be
        found (are you missing a using directive or an assembly reference?) */

 }
}
```

Screen output from this listing is shown in Figure 5.23.

Figure 5.23: Screen Output Generated from Listing 5.65

#region and #endregion Directives

The #region directive allows you to specify a block of code that you can expand or collapse when using the outlining feature of the Visual Studio Code Editor. Listing 5.66 illustrates the use of #region, paired with the #endregion directive, which marks the end of the block.

Listing 5.66—Region EndRegion Example

```
#region MyClass definition
public class MyClass
{
    public static void Main()
    {
    }
}
#endregion
```

Exception Handling

When you execute your programs, they may encounter errors to be handled. If errors are not handled, your process terminates and may even be unstable. Your processing is not safe unless you have mechanisms in place to handle these exceptions appropriately. Exception handling is covered in detail in chapter 7.

Method Parameter Types

C# supports three parameter-passing styles to class member methods: [in], ref, and out. All data types in C# are passed by reference, but their default behavior is handled differently depending upon whether they are a value or reference type. The [in] parameter style is the default for value types, so you do not have to explicitly define it in your method. In fact, defining it explicitly causes a compile error. The [in] parameter style indicates that the value type parameter being passed is not being altered upon returning from the method. Thus, the value of passed parameters of a value type, by default, cannot be changed.

For integral types and immutable classes such as strings, the C# [in] parameter type is similar to the C++ const type&. The [in] type has no effect on mutable classes—classes whose contents can be changed. The default behavior of references to mutable objects is handled as if the object was preceded with the ref keyword. In other words, with the [in] keyword, you can pass the value's address to the method, but the value itself cannot be changed. To make the value changeable, use the C# parameter type ref.

The C# ref parameter type works like the type& standard reference in C++. A reference parameter does not create a new storage location. Instead, it represents the same storage location as the variable given as the argument in the function member invocation. Thus, the value of a reference parameter is always the same as the underlying variable.

A variable must be assigned before it can be passed as a reference parameter in a function member invocation. Within a function member, a reference parameter is considered initially assigned. Within an instance method or instance accessor of a struct type, the this keyword behaves exactly as a reference parameter of the struct type.

The out parameter is for explicitly referencing a parameter that will be filled by the called method. It has no complement in C++, but in COM+ the distinction was made in order to fulfill thorough marshalling back from a method. An out parameter differs from the ref parameter in that the caller doesn't need to initialize the variable prior to calling the method. Instead, a reference to the object can be sent uninitialized and initialized by the called method and then returned after instantiation. As with the ref parameter, an output parameter does not create a new storage location. Instead, it represents the same storage location as the variable given as the argument in the function member invocation. Thus, the value of an output parameter is always contained in the underlying variable that was passed into the method. Note that although an output parameter need not be assigned a value when it is passed into a method, it must be assigned a value when it returns from a method, otherwise the compiler will give an error.

Because structs are value types, when an instance of one is passed to a method, a copy is created of the structure. You can use the out keyword with a struct parameter to prevent the creation of large temporary storage space of a structure on the stack. C# syntax encourages the return only of values or objects you really need and discourages the storage of temporary objects. This seems a sensible alternative to the C++ approach. In addition, the parameter distinction simplifies component programming for the developer.

Listing 5.68 provides an example of how to use the [in], ref, and out parameter modifiers.

Listing 5.68—Parameter1.cs, Parameter Modifiers Example 1

```
// example method parameter usage; in out ref
using System;

 public class ThirdFourthPower
 {
  public void XPower (Int32 intparam1, ref Int32 intparam2, out Int32 intparam3,
 out Int32 intparam4 )
   {
       intparam3 = intparam1 * intparam1 * intparam1;
       intparam2 = intparam1 * intparam1 * intparam1 * intparam1;
       // ERROR: you cannot use out parameters as a value, right value here
       // intparam2 = intparam3 * intparam1;
       intparam4 = intparam1 + intparam2 / intparam1; // notice operator
     // precedence
  }
 }

 class MathyApp
 {
  public static void Main()
  {
   ThirdFourthPower app1 = new ThirdFourthPower();

   Int32 nTriple1; // out parameters need not be initialized because filled in
 callee
   Int32 nTriplePlus2; // out
   Int32 nQuadruple = 0; // ref parameters must be initialized or assigned
   // otherwise you receive ERROR : Use of unassigned local variable nQuadruple
```

```
  app1.XPower( 3, ref nQuadruple, out nTriple1, out nTriplePlus2);

  Console.WriteLine("out1: {0}", nTriple1.ToString()); // out parameter,
                                                    // 27
  Console.WriteLine("ref: {0}", nQuadruple.ToString()); // ref parameter,
  // 81
  Console.WriteLine("out2: {0}", nTriplePlus2.ToString()); // out parameter
// 27

    // you should not use ref for returning values; use it if you really
    // need in-place change
    // note that in parameters are also references, but const, so you
    // cannot change them.
  }
}
```

The screen output of this code is given in Figure 5.25.

Figure 5.25: Screen Output Generated from Listing 5.68

Listing 5.69 presents a complete array example with out and ref parameters.

Listing 5.69—Parameter2.cs, Parameter Modifiers Example 2

```
// in & out & ref - passing arrays

using System;

class MyApp
{
    // out
    static public void FillArray(out int[] myArray)
    {
        // Initialize the array:
        myArray = new int[5] {1, 2, 3, 4, 5};
    }
    // ref
    public static void FillArray2(ref int[] arr)
    {
        // Create the array on demand:
        if (arr == null)
            arr = new int[10];
        // Otherwise fill the array:
        arr[0] = 19;
        arr[4] = 1919;
    }

    // implicit ref default for references, not in
    static public void WriteArray(int[] myArray)
    {

      // myArray[2] = 19; // CAVEAT: this is also valid
      Console.WriteLine("Array elements are:");
      for (int i = 0; i < myArray.Length; i++)
          Console.WriteLine(myArray[i]);
```

```
    }
    public static void Main()
    {
        int[] myArray; // Initialization is not required
        FillArray(out myArray);
        WriteArray(myArray);

        // Initialize the array:
        int[] myArray2 = {1,2,3,4,5};
        FillArray2(ref myArray2);
        WriteArray(myArray2);
    }
}
```

Figure 5.26 shows the output listing the array elements.

Figure 5.26: Screen Output Generated from Listing 5.69

Table 5.9 compares method parameter modifiers for none, [in], and ref derived from the tests.

Method Parameter Modifier ([in]/ref)	Status After the Method
ref string or any other value type	Changed
string or any other value type without modifier–immutable (implicit [in])	read-only, not changed
ref anyobject—reference type (mutable)	Changed
anyobject without modifier—reference type–mutable (implicit [ref])	Changed

Table 5.9: Method Parameter Modifiers

Listing 5.70 contains a third example of the use of parameter modifiers.

Listing 5.70—Parameter3.cs, Parameter Modifiers Example 3

```
using System;

public class SomeItems {
    public int One;
    public string Two;
}

public class App
{
 public int m_three = 5;
        public int methodTwo(SomeItems  o, string s)
```

```
        {
            o.One = m_three;
            s = "BlaBla";
            return 0;
        }

    public int methodTwo2(SomeItems   o)
        {
            o.One = m_three;
            o.Two = "Is Gone";
            return 0;
        }

        public static void Main( string[] args)
        {
            App  _a = new App( );
            SomeItems si = new SomeItems();
            si.One = 1;
            si.Two = "Goodbye string";
            Console.WriteLine( "Before = {0} - {1}", si.One, si.Two);
            _a.methodTwo(si, si.Two);
            Console.WriteLine( "After = {0} - {1}", si.One, si.Two);
            _a.methodTwo2(si);
            Console.WriteLine( "After = {0} - {1}", si.One, si.Two);
            return;
        }
}
```

Figure 5.27 contains output from this code listing.

Figure 5.27: Screen Output Generated from Listing 5.70

Please refer to C# Language Specification (http://msdn.microsoft.com/net/ecma/) for more details and recent updates to the C# language.

The params keyword allows you specify a method parameter that takes an argument where the number of arguments is variable.

Only one params keyword is permitted in a method declaration, and no additional parameters can follow the params keyword.

Listing 5.71—Params.cs, Params Example

```
//params keyword

using System;
public class MyClass
{

    public static void UseParams(params int[] list)
    {
        for ( int i = 0 ; i < list.Length ; i++ )
            Console.WriteLine(list[i]);
        Console.WriteLine();
    }
```

```
public static void UseParams2(params object[] list)
{
   for ( int i = 0 ; i < list.Length ; i++ )
      Console.WriteLine((object)list[i]);
   Console.WriteLine();
}

public static void Main()
{
   UseParams(1, 2, 3);
   UseParams2(1, 'a', "test");

   int[] myarray = new int[3] {10,11,12};
   UseParams(myarray);
}
}
```

Figure 5.28 contains the output generated by this listing.

Figure 5.28: Screen Output Generated from Listing 5.71

Garbage Collection

In C#, the deallocation or freeing of resources consumed by created instances occurs automatically on a system-determined schedule by an intelligent mechanism known as garbage collection. The Garbage Collector (GC) is like a sweeper fish in an aquarium. If you drop more food than the other fish can cat, the sweeper fish consumes the remaining food without leaving any behind.

The convenience and usefulness of GC has been evident since Java. In C++ Builder, Borland introduced a similar mechanism that makes every allocation owned by some parent—a kind of owned object pattern in which a button must belong a form, for example. When the form is destroyed, so is the button. Borland's Visual Component Library (VCL) implements this by forcing a common base class of all components so you can utilize polymorphism.

The GC in C# improves on the concept because it does not reduce the system's performance until really needed. It is smarter than other garbage collectors currently on the market. You can overcome the disadvantages of CG's nondeterministic behavior by using destructors (dtors) and finalizers. You can allocate member instances with constructors (ctors). Let's explore some important aspects of garbage collecting in .NET.

In C#, most of the time, you do not need to code destructors or finalizers because you can trust GC to clean up for you with dtors. These functions are called implicitly by the C# runtime system's garbage collector.

If explicit deterministic deallocation of objects is important in class and inheritance hierarchy, make sure your classes inherit the `IDisposable` interface and implement the Dispose function. You can call this function anytime to finalize an object and release the resources you want to free.

Listing 5.72 illustrates the concept of garbage collection in C#.

Listing 5.72—GC Example

```
class X
{
// implicit dtor ~X()
// created for you automatically by C#
}

class Y
    {
    ~Y() // explicit dtor, same as Finalize
        {
        // ...
        }
    }

//verbose syntax:

class Z
    {
    protected override void Finalize() //verbose explicit dtor, same as ~
        {
        // ...
        // implicit call to base.Finalize();
        }
    }
```

Indeed, if you look at the intermediate language (IL) generated for each .NET Framework instruction via ildasm.exe (Intermediate Language Disassembler), you'll find that the C# compiler emits the name ~Y (destructor in Listing 5.72 above) as Finalize.

X's implicit call to base.Finalize is mysterious. In C++, destructors for derived objects destroy their base-class subobjects automatically. By contrast, C# finalizers don't intrinsically call other finalizers, including base-class finalizers. Nonetheless, you often want to finalize both a derived object and its base class in the same call. Furthermore, every C# class you write has exactly one base class, even if that base class is implicitly System.Object.

When you exit the program, you can make the System.GC methods force the GC to schedule the implicit finalizer call, then wait for that call to complete, as shown.

```
System.GC.Collect();
System.GC.WaitForPendingFinalizers();
```

You can also call System.GC.SuppressFinalize to prevent the garbage collector from implicitly invoking the finalizer a second time.

Do not directly call your base class Finalize method. It is called automatically from your destructor.

Destructors and object.Finalize cannot be called directly. Consider calling IDisposable.Dispose, if available.

To explicitly destroy the object, you should call System.GC.SuppressFinalize immediately to prevent multiple object deallocation by the GC:

```
System.GC.SuppressFinalize(anyInstance);
```

Your C# common program structure can resemble that in Listing 5.73 if, in fact, you want to provide your own finalizers. If the order of destruction is important, you should store in a dequeue or a stack the order of the objects created for which dispose/finalize will be called.

Listing 5.73—Dtor.cs, Destructors Example

```csharp
// example: explicit destruction/finalize

using System;

class MyClass : IDisposable
    {
    public MyClass() //default ctor
        {
          this.iNumber = 0;
          System.Console.WriteLine("ctor:MyClass {0}", iNumber);
        }
    public MyClass(Int32 iNumber) // specialized ctor
        {
          this.iNumber = iNumber;
          System.Console.WriteLine("ctor:MyClass {0}", iNumber);
        }
    ~MyClass() // dtor or finalize
        {
                System.Console.WriteLine("dtor:~MyClass {0}", iNumber);
        }
    public void Dispose() // helper finalize function
        {
                // here you can free the resources you allocated explicitly
          System.GC.SuppressFinalize(this);
        }
    private int iNumber;
    }

class main
    {
    static void Main()
        {
          MyClass myClass1 = new MyClass();
          MyClass myClass2 = new MyClass(19);
          myClass1.Dispose(); // myClass1 is explicitly exposed.
          System.GC.Collect();
          System.GC.WaitForPendingFinalizers();
          // myClass2 is implicitly exposed by GC.
        }
    }
```

Figure 5.29 shows the order in which Listing 5.73 implements the ctors and dtors.

Figure 5.29: Screen Output Generated from Listing 5.73

The ctors and dtors have a specific order of execution for chained, derived classes. This order can be crucial for the appropriate allocation and release of resources. Let's assume the following simple class architecture:

```
class A{} // base
classB:A{} // B inherits A
class C:B{} // C inherits B
```

When you create a C object with the following specification, the ctors are invoked in order of A, then B, and then C (base to be derived).

```
C c = new C();
```

Then, if you call dtor/Finalize explicitly, the dtors should be invoked in order of C, then B, and then A (derived to base).

Since GC handles the deallocation for you behind the scenes, the sequence of object destruction is controlled by the GC—that is, objects can be destroyed in a random order such as A, then C, and then B. Beware of this behavior, which sometimes creates problems by prematurely releasing required resources in the parent classes even if they are needed by the derived classes.

Fields and Properties

Fields are ordinary member variables or member instances of a class. *Properties* are an abstraction to get and set their values. Properties are also called accessors because they offer a way to change and retrieve a field if you expose a field in the class as private. Generally, you should declare your member variables private, then declare or define properties for them.

There are three obvious reasons for the necessity of properties in C#.

You can delay the creation of actual reference fields until you use them, which saves resources. You can differentiate the representation and actual storage. Representation is implemented via properties and storage is implemented via fields. You can check constraints when setting and getting properties. If the value is not suitable, you do not store the data in the field and a type-safety error is returned. This really provides 100% type-safe accessors on demand.

Properties afford you the advantage of more elegant syntax along with the robustness and better encapsulation of accessor methods. The syntax for implementing a property in C#, along with a constructor and a destructor and using the property, is shown in the Age property in Listing 5.74.

Listing 5.74—CtorDtor.cs, Constructor Destructor Example

```
// example property, ctor, dtor, exception

using System;

public class Individual
{
Int32 age; // note that this is private
// we could do this instead, more explicit
// private Int32 age;
// the default specifiers are all private!!!
public Individual (Int32 age) { // constructor, ctor
      this.age = age; // this object, just for more clarity
   }

 ~ Individual () { // destructor
```

```
        age = 0;
    }

    public Int32 Age { // public property
        get {
            return age;
        }
        set {              // validating value
            if (value > 0 && value < 200) {
                age = value;
            }
            else {        // throw exception if invalid value
                throw new ArgumentException("not between 1 and 150 ?");
            }
        }
    }
}

class TestIndividual {
    public static void Main()
    {
      try
      {
      Individual  Jabbar = new  Individual (27);
       Console.WriteLine("This year, Jabbar was {0} years old", Jabbar.Age);
       Jabbar.Age++;        // uses both get and set to do increment
       Console.WriteLine("Next year, Jabbar will be {0} years old", Jabbar.Age);
       }
       catch(ArgumentException e)
       {
         // catches this specific type and derived types
         // uses Exception.ToString()
Console.WriteLine("{0} Caught exception #1.", e);
       }
     }
}
```

The resulting output is shown in Figure 5.30.

Figure 5.30: Screen Output Generated from Listing 5.74

The pseudocode in Listing 5.75 presents a read-only property example that defers resource allocation with the help of properties.

Listing 5.75—Properties Example

```
// example property pseudocode, delayed resource allocation
// you allocate resources only when you really need them

// class 1
class MyReader
{
  // prop1 - property
}

// class 2
class MyWriter
{
```

```csharp
   // prop2 - property
   // prop3 - property
}

public class ExamplePropertyImplementation
{
   private static MyReader reader;
   private static MyWriter writer;
   private static MyWriter error;

   // public property
   public static MyReader prop1 {
      get {
         if (reader == null) {
            reader = new Reader();
         }
         return reader;
      }
   }

   // public property
   public static MyWriter prop2 {
      get {
         if (writer == null) {
            writer = new MyWriter();
         }
         return writer;
      }
   }

   // public property
   public static MyWriter prop3 {
      get {
         if (error == null) {
            error = new Writer();
         }
         return error;
      }
   }
}
```

By exposing these members as properties, the class can delay their initialization until they are actually used. Thus, if the application makes no reference to the prop2 and prop3 properties, no objects are created for those objects.

Runtime Type Information (Reflection)

Reflection is the sole mechanism of discovering class information at runtime. You can create instances of classes on the fly at runtime using Reflection namespace members, which is similar to the optional Runtime Type Information mechanism in C++.

The ability to list a type's members is a great way to quickly discover which elements are available. It is an important tool for reporting on your system as well as assisting in the development of user documentation. Using the Reflection namespace, you can control what kind of members you want to show to your users, as well as other information (such as the visibility of a particular method). You can also get information on all of the members in a class or specify only certain subsets (such as methods or fields). Also you can use this neat feature when documenting class hierarchy.

Listing 5.76—Reflection.cs, Reflection Example

```csharp
// example object creation factory

using System;
```

```csharp
using System.Reflection;

// simple class
class MyClass
{
    public static int x = 0;

    public void prompt(string param1)
    {
        Console.WriteLine("MyClass… " + param1);
    }

    public static void prompt2()
    {
        Console.WriteLine("Here is a message from prompt2.");
    }

}

class TheApp {
    public static void Main()
    {
        // create the Type object
        Type type1 = typeof(MyClass);
        //or
        // Type type1 = Type.GetType("MyClass");

        // create an instance of that type
        Object o = Activator.CreateInstance(type1);
        ((MyClass) o).prompt("hello1");

        // declare and populate the arrays to hold the information...
        FieldInfo [] fi = type1.GetFields (BindingFlags.Default |
            BindingFlags.Static |
            BindingFlags.NonPublic | BindingFlags.Public);        // fields

        MethodInfo [] mi = type1.GetMethods (BindingFlags.Default |
        BindingFlags.Static |
                    BindingFlags.NonPublic | BindingFlags.Public);     // methods


        // iterate through all the method members
        foreach (MethodInfo m in mi)
        {
            Console.WriteLine(m);
        }

        // iterate through all the field members
        foreach (FieldInfo f in fi)
        {
            Console.WriteLine(f);
        }

        object[] argValues = new object [] {"Hello2"};
        String [] argNames = new String [] {"param1"};
        // call the requested method with filled parameters
        type1.InvokeMember("prompt", BindingFlags.Default |
        BindingFlags.InvokeMethod,
            null, o, argValues, null, null, argNames);
    }
}
```

Figure 5.31 contains the resulting output.

Figure 5.31: Screen Output Generated from Listing 5.76

The reflection mechanism is also useful when developing applications that use third-party COM+ components at your site or in the market because you can use Reflection to accomplish late binding to COM objects via the IDispatch interface.

Method Signatures

Methods, constructors, indexers, and operators are characterized by their signatures. A signature makes a method look unique to the C# compiler. The method name and the type and order of parameters all contribute to the uniqueness of signatures.

Signatures enable the overloading mechanism of members in classes, structs, and interfaces.

A method signature consists of the name of the method and the type and kind, such as value or reference. A method signature does not include the return type, nor does it include the params modifier that may be specified for the last parameter.

A constructor signature consists of the type and kind, such as value or reference. A constructor signature does not include the params modifier that may be specified for the last parameter.

An indexer signature consists of the type. An indexer signature does not include the element type.

An operator signature consists of the name of the operator and the type. An operator signature does not include the result type.

Listing 5.77 illustrates the signature concept.

Listing 5.77—Signatures Example

```
class MyClass
{
   void MyFunc();                        // MyFunc ()
   void MyFunc (int x);                  // MyFunc (int)
   void MyFunc (ref int x);              // MyFunc (ref int)
   void MyFunc (out int x);              // MyFunc (out int)
   void MyFunc (int x, int y);           // MyFunc (int, int)
   int MyFunc (string s);                // MyFunc (string)
   int MyFunc (int x);                   // MyFunc (int)
   void MyFunc (string[] a);             // MyFunc (string[])
   void MyFunc (params string[] a);      // MyFunc (string[])
}
```

The ref and out parameter modifiers are part of a signature. MyFunc(int), MyFunc(ref int), and MyFunc(out int) are all unique signatures. The return type and the params modifier are not part of a signature, and it is not possible to overload based solely on return type or on the inclusion or exclusion of the params modifier.

Notice that there are some errors for the methods that contain duplicate signatures like MyFunc(int) and MyFunc(string[]) whose multiple signatures differ only by return type.

Summary

This chapter explored the syntax and semantics of the C# language. This modern, type-safe, object-oriented programming language enables programmers to quickly and easily build solutions for the Microsoft .NET platform. C# is very powerful and simple for building interoperable, scaleable, robust local and networked applications. The .NET framework classes and data types are common to all of the .NET languages not only for VC#.NET but also for VB.NET, VC++.NET, and more.

Let's reiterate some benefits of the C# language.

- Because C# is object-oriented, it supports data encapsulation, inheritance, polymorphism, and interfaces.
- C# does not allow unsafe casts, such as converting a double value type to a boolean value type. Primitive value types are initialized to zeros and reference types (objects and classes) are initialized to null by the compiler automatically. Arrays are zero-base indexed, and their bounds are checked. Overflow of value or reference types is checked by the Common Language Infrastructure.
- C# includes built-in support to turn any component into a Web Service very easily. These Web Services, which are covered in detail in the chapters addressing the Simple Object Access Protocol and the ASP.NET, can be invoked over the Internet from any application running on any platform.
- .NET has introduced assemblies that are self-describing by means of their manifest. The manifest establishes the assembly identity, version, culture, digital signature, and more.
- Assemblies need not be registered anywhere.
- C# includes native support for applications based on COM+ and Windows.
- Because C# works on .NET, it inherits features such as automatic memory management and garbage collection.
- C# is smart—for example, integer values of 0 and 1 are no longer accepted as Boolean values. Boolean values are pure true or false values in C#, so you will face errors if you confuse the = operator and the == operator inside if-then-else statements. (The == operator is often mistakenly used for assignment operations and the = operator is mistakenly used for comparison operations.)

Chapter 6:
System I/O and Streams

Introduction

A software system has three major components: input, output, and processing, as shown in Figure 6.1.

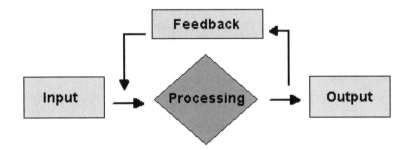

Figure 6.1: Software System Components

The *input* part of the system is responsible for accepting data in the form of bytes, streams, binary data, or strings from input devices such as keyboards, mouses, pads, or other media. In the *processing* component of a software system, you apply your logic on the data to produce some information. The *output* part of the system displays processed data through devices such as monitors or printers.

Input/output (I/O) is an important consideration when you design a system or computer application. All software applications must control input and output in some manner.

The .NET Framework provides a rich application program interface (API) to work with the system I/O. This API resides in the System.IO namespace.

Overview of System.IO Namespace

In the .NET Framework, the System.IO namespace defines classes for reading and writing files and data streams. The System.IO namespace, which resides in the mscorlib.dll assembly, provides classes for working with the system I/O and with streams.

The main functionality of the System.IO namespaces in .NET includes the following features:

- **Accessing Buffer**—The .NET Framework defines classes for reading and writing bytes, multibytes, binary data, strings, and character data with the help of StreamReader,

StreamWriter, BinaryReader, BinaryWriter, StringReader, and StringWriter classes. The FileStream class can be used for random file access.

- **File and Directory Operations**—The classes in the System.IO namespaces provide functionality for creation, deletion, and manipulation of files and directories. You can use the File, FileInfo and the Directory, DirectoryInfo classes to do most of your file and directory manipulations. The FileSystemWatcher class is used to monitor the file system.
- **Performance Optimization**—The MemoryStream and the BufferStream classes enhance the performance of read/write operations by storing data in memory.

System I/O

The Console Class

The Console class from the System namespace helps you with system I/O to the command prompt window or console (remember the Hello C# example). The System.IO namespace contains classes like BinaryReader/BinaryWriter, StreamReader/StreamWriter, and FileStream to process streams of different kinds. All these classes are contained within the mscorlib.dll assembly.

The Console class provides access to the three standard streams—standard input, standard output, and standard error—by way of Console.In, Console.Out, and Console.Error, respectively.

System Output

The Console class has two methods, Write and WriteLine, to display output to the console. The distinction between these two methods is that the WriteLine method adds a line terminator after the output so you don't have to manually add the /n character to go to the next console line. Java programmers can map this method to the System.out.println method.

Note: Even though Console.Out is the output stream, you can omit the Out. In other words, the simplified Console.Write/Console.WriteLine generates the same output as Console.Out.Write/ Console.Out.WriteLine, with less typing!

Both methods are overloaded to take a variety of primitive data types such as int, float, char, long, double, uint, ulong, and string, as well as other parameters such as object and char[].

If you are passing a class containing data other than the primitive types, then that class's ToString method is called and printed on the screen. If the class does not have an implementation of the ToString method, then the object class's ToString method is called (because all classes in C# are derived from the object class).

Let's look at an example of overriding the ToString method. Note that compiling program in Listing 6.1 will generate the warning *The private field 'OneMem.i' is never used*. You can ignore this warning.

Listing 6.1—Example of Overriding ToString()

```
using System ;
public class OneMem
{
   int i=10 ;
}
public class OneOver
{
   int i=10 ;
   public override string ToString()
   {
```

```
      return i.ToString();
  }
}
public class OneUser
{
  public static void Main()
  {
    OneMem F = new OneMem() ;
    OneOver B = new OneOver() ;
    Console.WriteLine(F) ; //This will print "OneMem"
    Console.WriteLine(B) ; //This will print "10"
  }
}
```

In Listing 6.1, the classes OneMem and OneOver have just one integer field each, but OneOver also overrides the ToString method to return the value of the integer field. In the class OneUser, when the WriteLine method is called upon instance F of the OneMem class (which has no implementation of the ToString method), the Object class's ToString method is called. The Object class's ToString method prints the name of the class OneMem. On the other hand, when WriteLine is called on instance B, it uses the overridden ToString method of the OneOver class. In this particular implementation, the ToString method prints the value of the integer field.

There is one more overloaded style of these methods, which takes a format string and three objects as input parameters (although four objects are supported, it is not Common Language Specification compliant). This overloaded method gives you control over the format of the string representation of the objects written to the console.

In Listing 6.2, *"The sum of {0} and {1} is {2}"* is the format string. The brackets {0}, {1}, and {2} are replaced by the values from the variables, which come after the format string in serial order. Here, {0} is replaced by the value of i, {1} by the value of j, and {2} by the value of z.

Listing 6.2—Example of Using a Format String

```
using System ;
public class FormatOut
{
  public static void Main()
  {
    int i =10 ;
    int j = 5 ;
    int z = i+j ;
    Console.Write("The sum of {0} and {1} is {2}" , i, j, z);
    //This will print
    //The sum of 10 and 5 is 15
  }
}
```

System Input

Console.In, which provides the standard input stream, has two methods for taking input from the console: the Read and ReadLine methods. The Read method reads one character at a time from the console whereas the ReadLine method, as its name suggests, reads a line off the console. Just as in system output, in system input you can also omit the In and use Console.Read/Console.ReadLine instead of Console.In.Read/Console.In.ReadLine.

The Read method reads a single character and returns an integer value, which represents the Unicode value of the character. The Read method does not return a Unicode value until the line is terminated by pressing the ENTER key. If there are no more characters to be read, it returns -1. Hence, if a user types more characters on the console before pressing ENTER, the first call to the

Read method returns only the first character; and rest of the characters can be read with subsequent calls of the Read method.

Note: Pressing ENTER actually adds two characters at the end of the line: a carriage return (/r) and a line feed (/n). If you employ a loop using successive calls of the Read method, be sure to read the carriage return and line feed pair (with two additional reads) before the next Read call; otherwise, the next call will return /r instead of the user input.

The ReadLine method returns a string after reading a line from the console. A line ends with the first occurrence of a line terminator, such as /r or /n. In the case of ReadLine, the string returned does not contain the line terminator. If end of input is reached, then a null value is returned.

The example in Listing 6.3, although very simple, highlights some of the important features of system I/O. The purpose of the program is to display the number of words in a string that a user has entered.

Listing 6.3—Example of Reading Character Input from the Console

```
using System;
public class WordCount
{
  public static void Main()
  {
    Console.WriteLine("Welcome to the Word Count Program") ;
    bool con = true ;
    while(con)
    {
      Console.Write("Enter a String :") ;
      //Read a string from the user
      string original = Console.ReadLine() ;
      //Remove any white spaces at the end of the sentence
      string trimmed =original.Trim();
      char[] sp = {' '};
      //Split the string at every occurrence of a white space
      string[] str = trimmed.Split(sp) ;
      //Print the word count using a formatted string
      Console.WriteLine("The word count is {0} for the string
      \"{1}\" ", str.Length, original);
      //Leave one line blank on the screen
      Console.WriteLine();
      //Ask the user if he wants to continue
      Console.Write("Do you want to continue [n]?");
      //Read a single character 'y' or 'n' or 'N'
      int ans = Console.Read();
      //Read the carriage return '/r'
      int carriage= Console.Read();
      //Console.WriteLine("The value of carriage is "+carriage) ;
      //13
      //Read the line feed '/n'
      int linefeed= Console.Read();
      //Console.WriteLine("The value of h is "+linefeed) ;//10
      //Check if the user has put 'n' or 'N'
      //We use the Unicode value for the characters 'n' and 'N'
      if(ans==110||ans==78)
      {
        //Set the bool variable to false so we exit the loop
        con=false ;
      }
    }
    Console.WriteLine("Thank you for using my program !") ;
    Console.WriteLine("Press Enter to exit") ;
    //Wait for the user to press Enter to exit
    Console.ReadLine();
```

```
    }
}
```

The Main method of class WordCount (shown in Listing 6.3) takes a sentence as input from the user. Then it removes any trailing white spaces at the end of the sentence and finally breaks up the sentence into an array of strings using the Split method of the String class. The length of this array denotes the number of words in the sentence on the console.

Next, the user is given an option to continue or quit the program. A single character is read off the console and checked for its value. User input of 'n' or 'N' indicates a need to discontinue the while loop. We then set the condition flag to false, which causes the program to exit the loop .

You might note, as previously mentioned, the use of two Read methods after reading the input for the user to continue. This is due to the fact that the Read method returns when the ENTER key is pressed. Pressing ENTER has two effects: (1) the Read method returns, and (2) a carriage return (/r) and a line feed (/n) are appended to the console. Therefore, you read these two characters from the console input stream before calling the next ReadLine method.

As an aside, here's an observation and a handy tip. Many new programmers wonder why clicking on the console application from Windows Explorer causes the console screen to close quickly before they can see any output on the console screen. The solution to this problem is simple. Just place a ReadLine statement at the end of your code; the next time you run your program, the console screen does not close until ENTER is pressed.

System Error

System.Error is used to display error messages on the console. It also uses the Write and the WriteLine methods. You might wonder why you would use a separate stream to display errors if you can display errors using Console.Out. When you develop applications that use the SetOut method of the Console class to redirect the output of Console.Out to some other stream, then errors also need to be redirected to a separate stream. The Console.Error class provides a means of accomplishing this. Suppose you create an installer application that runs on the command line. You want the log file to record the success or failure of the component being installed, so you redirect Console.Out to a stream that writes to a log file. Thus, the user sees no output on the console. However, some missing files cause an exception to be thrown and you want to inform the user about it. You use the Console.Error stream to notify the user of the missing files on the console screen.

You might also wonder why you need the In and Out classes at all if you don't need to specify the In or Out during input or output. In and Out allow you to differentiate between different streams when you use the System.Error class. Because the Error stream uses the same methods as those of the Output stream, it's better to use the full name of the Output stream in such cases.

Files and Directories

Under Windows, the file system is divided into files and directories (or folders). Files are the actual files of data, while directories are repositories for logical placement of files on your system. Under the System.IO namespace, the common language runtime (CLR) has the classes File, FileInfo, Directory, and DirectoryInfo to deal with files and directories.

File and FileInfo Classes

The basic functionality of both the File class and FileInfo class is the same. It differs only in that the File class provides static methods to deal with files whereas the FileInfo class provides instance methods to deal with files. The choice belongs to the programmer. Table 6.1 below shows a side-by-side comparison of the two file manipulation class methods:

File Class (Static Methods)	FileInfo Class	Use
Copy	CopyTo	Copy a file to a destination path.
Create	Create	Create a file.
Delete	Delete	Delete the file.
Exists	Exists (property)	Check whether the file exists. Note: The File class implements a method Exists while the FileInfo class implements Exists as a property.
Move	MoveTo	Move the file to a destination path.
Open	Open	Open a FileStream to the file.

Table 6.1: File and FileInfo class members

The FileInfo class has a single constructor that takes a single parameter of a string containing the path to the file. The path to the file can be a fully qualified path or a relative one. The file need not exist when you make a FileInfo object, so making FileInfo objects is as simple as the code shown in Listing 6.4.

Listing 6.4—Example of Constructing a FileInfo Object

```
FileInfo f1 = new FileInfo("c:\\temp\\readme.txt");  //Fully qualified path
FileInfo f2 = new FileInfo("\\db\\myData.xml");   //Relational path
FileInfo f3 = new FileInfo(@"\db\myData.xml") ;
//Use of a verbatim string literal
```

You can use the *at* symbol (@) to define a verbatim string that does not need to have an escape sequence in it, making it easier to read.

Some of the important properties of the FileInfo class are Attributes, CreationTime, DirectoryName, Exists, FullName, Length, and Name.

Since the File class consists of static methods, you can perform many of the necessary file functions without creating an instance of the file, as shown in Listing 6.5.

Listing 6.5—Example of Using Static File Methods

```
File.Copy(@"c:\temp\readme.txt",@"d:\temp\readme.txt");//Copy a file
File.Create(@"C:\temp\newdoc.txt");//Create a file
File.Delete(@"C:\temp\readme.txt");//Delete a file
File.Move(@"d:\temp\readme.txt" , @"c:\temp\readme.txt");//Move a file
```

Directory and DirectoryInfo Classes

The Directory and DirectoryInfo classes are used to perform various operations on directories such as Create, Move, Delete, and Enumerate. The functional distinction between these classes is the same as that between the File and FileInfo classes: the Directory class provides static methods whereas the DirectoryInfo class provides instance methods to deal with directories. Below, Table 6.2 compares these directory classes.

Directory Class (static methods)	DirectoryInfo Class	Use
CreateDirectory	Create	Create a directory.
Delete	Delete	Delete a directory.
Exists	Exists (property)	Check whether a directory exists. Note: The Directory class implements a method Exists while the DirectoryInfo class implements Exists as a property.
Move	MoveTo	Move a directory to the destination path.
GetDirectories	GetDirectories	Get subdirectories within a directory.
GetFiles	GetFiles	Get files within a directory.
GetDirectoryRoot	Root (property)	Get the root of a directory. Note: DirectoryInfo class implements Root as a property.
GetLogicalDrives		Get the logical drives available. Note: There is no corresponding DirectoryInfo class member.
GetParent	Parent (property)	Get the parent directory. Note: DirectoryInfo class implements Parent as a property.

Table 6.2: Directory and DirectoryInfo class members

Like the FileInfo class, the DirectoryInfo class also has a single constructor that takes either the full path or relative path to the directory as the input parameter:

```
DirectoryInfo d1 = new DirectoryInfo(@"c:\temp") ; //Make a directory object
```

Some important properties of the DirectoryInfo class, such as CreationTime, Exists, FullName, LastAccessTime, LastWriteTime, Name, Parent, and Root, work as their names suggest. For example, CreationTime shows the creation time of the directory. FullName is the full qualified path of the directory, while Name is just the relative folder name without the path (e.g., a directory with the FullName of *c:\My Project\test* would have a Name of *test*).

FileSystemWatcher Class

Another very useful class, FileSystemWatcher, acts as a watchdog for file system changes and raises an event when a change occurs. You must specify a directory to be monitored. The class can monitor changes to subdirectories and files within the specified directory. If you have Windows 2000, you can even monitor a remote system for changes. (Only remote machines running Windows NT or Windows 2000 are supported at present.) The option to monitor files with specific extensions can be set using the Filter property of the FileSystemWatcher class. You can also fine-tune FileSystemWatcher to monitor any change in file Attributes, LastAccess, LastWrite, Security, and Size data.

The FileSystemWatcher class raises the events described in Table 6.3.

Event Name	Use
Changed	Fired when a file or directory in the watched path is changed
Created	Fired when a file or directory in the watched path is created
Deleted	Fired when a file or directory in the watched path is deleted
Error	Fired when the internal buffer overflows due to many changes made over a short time, particularly when the buffer size is small
Renamed	Fired when a file or directory in the watched path is renamed

Table 6.3: FileSystemWatcher events

Listing 6.6 illustrates the use of the FileSystemWatcher class to capture changes to files and directories and report them on the console screen.

Listing 6.6—Using the FileSystemWatcher Class

```
using System;
using System.IO;
public class FileWatcher
{
  public static void Main(string[] args)
  {
    // If a directory is not specified, exit program.
    if(args.Length != 1)
    {
      // Display the proper way to call the program.
      Console.WriteLine("Usage: FileWatcher.exe <directory>");
      return;
    }
    try
    {
      // Create a new FileSystemWatcher and set its properties.
      FileSystemWatcher watcher = new FileSystemWatcher();
      watcher.Path = args[0];
      // Watch both files and subdirectories.
      watcher.IncludeSubdirectories = true;
      // Watch for all changes specified in the NotifyFilters
      //enumeration.
      watcher.NotifyFilter =   NotifyFilters.Attributes |
                               NotifyFilters.CreationTime |
                               NotifyFilters.DirectoryName |
                               NotifyFilters.FileName |
                               NotifyFilters.LastAccess |
                               NotifyFilters.LastWrite |
                               NotifyFilters.Security |
                               NotifyFilters.Size;
      // Watch all files.
      watcher.Filter = "*.*";
      // Add event handlers.
      watcher.Changed+=new FileSystemEventHandler(OnChanged);
      watcher.Created+=new FileSystemEventHandler(OnChanged);
      watcher.Deleted+=new FileSystemEventHandler(OnChanged);
      watcher.Renamed+=new RenamedEventHandler(OnRenamed);
      //Start monitoring.
      watcher.EnableRaisingEvents=true;
      //Do some changes now to the directory.
      //Create a DirectoryInfo object.
      DirectoryInfo d1 = new DirectoryInfo(args[0]);
      //Create a new subdirectory.
      d1.CreateSubdirectory("mydir") ;
      //Create some subdirectories.
      d1.CreateSubdirectory("mydir1\\mydir2\\mydir3") ;
      //Move the subdirectory "mydir3 " to "mydir\mydir3"
```

```
      Directory.Move(d1.FullName+"\\mydir1\\mydir2\\mydir3",
                     d1.FullName+"\\mydir\\mydir3") ;
      //Check if subdirectory "mydir1" exists.
      if(Directory.Exists(d1.FullName+"\\mydir1"))
      {
        //Delete the directory "mydir1"
        //I have also passed 'true' to allow recursive deletion of
        //any subdirectories or files in the directory "mydir1"
        Directory.Delete(d1.FullName+"\\mydir1", true);
      }
      //Get an array of all directories in the given path.
      DirectoryInfo[] d2 =d1.GetDirectories();
      //Iterate over all directories in the d2 array.
      foreach (DirectoryInfo d in d2)
      {
        if(d.Name=="mydir")
        {
          //If "mydir" directory is found then delete it recursively.
          Directory.Delete(d.FullName, true) ;
        }
      }
      // Wait for user to quit program.
      Console.WriteLine("Press \'q\' to quit the sample.");
      Console.WriteLine();
      //Make an infinite loop till 'q' is pressed.
      while(Console.Read()!='q');
    }
    catch(IOException e)
    {
      Console.WriteLine("A Exception Occurred :"+e) ;
    }
    catch(Exception oe)
    {
      Console.WriteLine("An Exception Occurred :"+oe) ;
    }
  }
  // Define the event handlers.
  public static void OnChanged(object source, FileSystemEventArgs e)
  {
    // Specify what is done when a file is changed.
    Console.WriteLine("{0}, with path {1} has been
                       {2}",e.Name,e.FullPath, e.ChangeType);
  }
  public static void OnRenamed(object source, RenamedEventArgs e)
  {
    // Specify what is done when a file is renamed.
    Console.WriteLine(" {0} renamed to {1}", e.OldFullPath,e.FullPath);
  }
}
```

The code starts with the parameter obtained from the user in the form of a path to a directory. Then it creates a FileSystemWatcher instance to monitor all changes in files and directories. Once the FileSystemWatcher is enabled, we are ready to make some changes. In this example, a file and few directories are created and later deleted. Figure 6.2 contains the output displayed on the console screen.

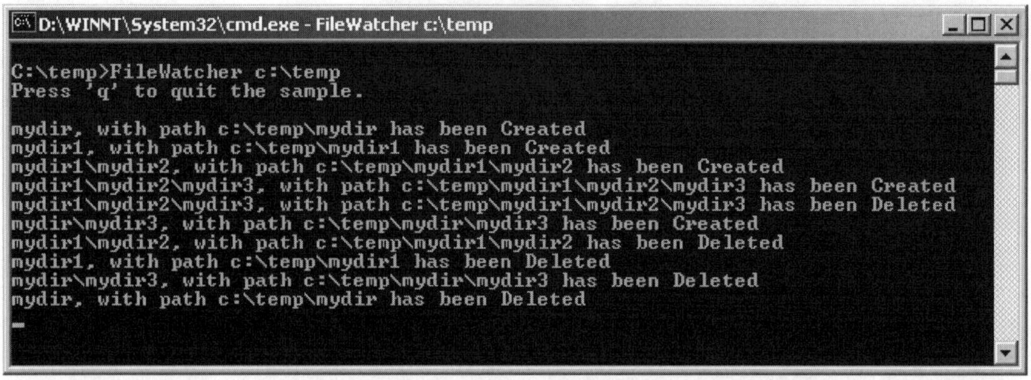

Figure 6.2: Output of the FileWatcher class

As you can see, the `FileSystemWatcher` captured every change made. If you start Windows Explorer and browse the directory you have provided as the parameter, you will find that every change you make in Explorer is reflected in the console. Since input is obtained from the user, chances are high that invalid arguments could raise exceptions; therefore, all the file manipulation code is placed within the try-catch block.

IOException Class

The IOException class is the base class for exceptions under the System.IO namespace. All other exceptions under this namespace—DirectoryNotFoundException, EndOfStreamException, FileNotFoundException, and FileLoadException—derive from the IOException class. I/O operations deal with various resources like hard disk, floppy disk, and network sockets, which have a greater chance of failing. Therefore, you should always encapsulate your I/O code within the try-catch block to intercept any exceptions that might occur.

Streams

Whether they contain water or data, streams evoke an image of efficient flow. Suppose you have to transfer water from one tank to another. You could repeatedly fill a bucket with water from one tank and empty it into the other tank. However, if you simply use a pipe to join the two tanks and let the water flow as a stream, your work becomes very fast and easy!

The same concept applies to the flow of data. Streams in C# allow you to carry data from one point to another quickly and efficiently. The data transfer can take place between files, sockets, objects, or even other streams.

Streams in CLR come in three forms: streams that read and write bytes, streams that read and write characters, and a stream to read and write primitive types. Table 6.4 lists the types of streams.

Byte Streams	Character Streams	Primitive Type Stream
Stream	TextReader/TextWriter	BinaryReader/BinaryWriter
FileStream	StreamReader/StreamWriter	
MemoryStream	StringReader/StringWriter	
BufferedStream		

Table 6.4: Streams in .NET

Byte Streams

Byte streams comprise classes that treat data in the stream as bytes. These streams are most useful when you work with data that is not in a format readable by humans.

Stream Class

In the CLR, the Stream class provides the base for other byte stream classes. If you want to implement your own byte-stream class, you have to override the Stream class, which is an abstract class. Table 6.5 highlights some of the properties of a stream.

Property	Use
CanRead	Indicates whether the stream supports reading.
CanSeek	Indicates whether the stream supports seeking (used for random access)
CanWrite	Indicates whether the stream supports writing.
Length	Returns the length of the stream.
Position	Returns the current position of the cursor in the stream.

Table 6.5: Some Important Properties of a Stream

The Stream class provides support for both synchronous and asynchronous reading and writing of data through the methods outlined in Table 6.6.

Method	Use
BeginRead	Starts an asynchronous read
BeginWrite	Starts an asynchronous write
EndRead	Ends an asynchronous read
EndWrite	Ends an asynchronous write

Table 6.6: Some Methods for Asynchronous Reads and Writes

Table 6.7 lists other methods you can use with the Stream class. Note that you should always call the Close method explicitly rather than depend upon the Garbage Collector (GC) to free any resources used by the stream.

Method	Use
Close	Closes the stream and frees up any resources
Flush	Flushes the current buffer to the file and then clears the buffer
Read	Reads the specified number of bytes into the buffer and increments the current position accordingly
ReadByte	Reads a single byte from the stream
Seek	Seeks to a specified position within the current stream
Write	Writes the specified number bytes from the buffer and increments the current position accordingly
WriteByte	Writes a single byte to the stream

Table 6.7: Other Useful Methods

FileStream

The FileStream class extends the Stream class and provides access to the standard input, output, and error streams for files. It is used extensively when dealing with file I/O. It implements all the methods and properties of the Stream class. FileStream implements two new methods: Lock and Unlock. Lock is used to lock up the underlying file exclusively for the current process, whereas Unlock frees this lock. Random access to files is also provided in this stream.

Nine overloaded constructors help you gain finer control over the file states. The constructor most commonly used, shown in Listing 6.7, helps set the various access permissions and creation states on the file through the use of the FileMode, FileAccess, and FileShare enumerations.

Listing 6.7—FileStream Constructor

```
public FileStream(string path,
                  FileMode mode,
                  FileAccess access,
                  FileShare share)
```

FileMode Enumeration

The FileMode enumeration helps you the set the mode in which you want to open the file. You can use these modes to set your file up for appending or overwriting or initial creation, as detailed in Table 6.8.

Enumeration	Use
Append	Opens a file, if it exists, and seeks to the end of file; if file does not exist, creates a new file.
Create	Creates a new file, overwriting the previous file, if it exists
CreateNew	Creates a new file
Open	Opens an existing file
OpenOrCreate	Opens the file, if it exists, or creates a new one
Truncate	Opens an existing file and truncates its size to zero bytes

Table 6.8: Enumeration FileMode

Note that the Append mode can only be used when FileAccess.Write permission (described next) is set.

FileAccess Enumeration

With the FileAccess enumerations described in Table 6.9, you can set the mode of access to a file. It's never good to authorize more access than needed—or less access than needed, for that matter. Choose Read when you intend to read from a file and Write when you write to a file. Remember, though, that if you specify Read access and later try to write to the file, an exception will be raised. The same applies when you specify Write access and try to read the file later.

Enumeration	Use
Read	Allows you to only read from the file
ReadWrite	Allows you to read and write to a file
Write	Allows you to only write to a file

Table 6.9: Enumeration FileAccess

FileShare Enumeration

The FileShare enumeration, detailed in Table 6.10, is very important if you wish to share your file with other processes. For example, suppose you have an XML file acting as a database file for an ASP.NET application. If you don't specify the FileAccess enumeration, only one user can read from the XML database file at a time; other concurrent users encounter an error when accessing the database because the FileShare.None enumeration is implemented by default.

Enumeration	Use
None	Gains exclusive access to the file; no other process can access the file until it is closed and reopened
Read	Allows subsequent opening of the file but for read-only purposes
ReadWrite	Allows subsequent opening of file for reading and writing
Write	Allows subsequent opening of file for write-only purposes

Table 6.10: Enumeration FileShare

The short example in Listing 6.8 demonstrates how you can work with the FileStream class.

Listing 6.8—FileStream Reading and Writing Example

```csharp
using System;
using System.IO;
public class FileCopy
{
  public static void Main(string[] args)
  {
    if(args.Length<2)
    {
      //Show usage information if incorrect number
      //of parameters has been entered
      Console.WriteLine("Usage: FileCopy <SourceFile>
                    <DestinationFile>");
      return;
    }
    try
    {
        //Open a FileStream to the source file
        FileStream fin = new FileStream(args[0], FileMode.Open,
                    FileAccess.Read, FileShare.Read);
        //Open a FileStream to the destination file
        FileStream fout = new FileStream(args[1],FileMode.OpenOrCreate,
                                    FileAccess.Write, FileShare.None);
        //Create a byte array to act as a buffer
        Byte[] buffer = new Byte[32];
        Console.WriteLine("File Copy Started");
        //Loop until end of file is not reached
        while(fin.Position!=fin.Length)
        {
          //Read from the source file
            //The Read method returns the number of bytes read
            int n=  fin.Read(buffer,0,buffer.Length) ;
            //Write the contents of the buffer to the destination file
            fout.Write(buffer,0,n) ;
        }
        //Flush the contents of the buffer to the file
        fout.Flush();
        //Close the streams and free the resources
        fin.Close();
        fout.Close();
        Console.WriteLine("File Copy Ended");
```

```
    }
        catch(IOException e)
        {
          //Catch a IOException
          Console.WriteLine("An IOException Occurred :"+e);
        }
        catch(Exception oe)
        {
          //Catch any other exception that occurs
          Console.WriteLine("An Exception Occurred :"+oe);
        }
    }
}
```

Similar to the copy command used in MS-DOS, this example takes two user-supplied parameters: source file and destination file. The program then opens a FileStream on the source file and reads it into the buffer. The contents of the buffer are written to the destination file.

BufferedStream Class

The BufferedStream class also extends the Stream class. *Buffers*, or cached blocks of data in memory, provide speed and stability to the process of reading or writing because they prevent numerous calls to the operating system. Buffered streams are used in conjunction with other streams to provide better read/write performance. The BufferedStream class can be used to either read data or write data but it cannot be used to perform both read and write operations together. The class has been optimized so that it maintains a suitable buffer at all times. When a buffer is not required, instead of slowing down the process, the class does not allocate any space in memory. File streams are already buffered and therefore a buffered stream is generally used to buffer network streams used in networking applications.

MemoryStream Class

A memory stream is created from an array of unsigned bytes rather than from a file or other stream. Memory streams are used as temporary, in-memory storage (temporary buffers) in lieu of creating temporary files. This stream is highly optimized for speed since the data is stored in memory and the processor can easily access it. Memory streams should be used to store frequently accessed data.

The Read and Write methods of the MemoryStream class read and write from an internal buffer that is created when the memory stream is created. The example shown in Listing 6.9 uses the MemoryStream class to add a custom signature at the end of the specified file.

Listing 6.9—MemoryStream Reading and Writing Example

```
using System;
using System.IO;
using System.Text;
public class MemStream
{
  public static void Main(string[] args)
  {
    //Check the number or arguments
    if(args.Length<1)
    {
      Console.WriteLine("Usage: MemStream <sourcefile>");
      return;
    }
    try
    {
        //Get the current date
        DateTime dt = DateTime.Now;
        string tag ="This file was signed on "+dt.ToShortDateString();
```

```
        //Get a byte array from the string
        byte[] tagarray = System.Text.Encoding.ASCII.GetBytes(
                                    tag.ToCharArray());
        //Construct a memory stream with the byte
        //array as a parameter
        MemoryStream mstream= new MemoryStream(tagarray);
        //Open a FileStream on the source file
        FileStream fout = new FileStream(args[0],FileMode.Open,
                                    FileAccess.Write);
        //Seek to the end of the file
        fout.Seek(0,SeekOrigin.End);
        Byte[] buffer = new Byte[tagarray.Length];
        Console.WriteLine("Starting to write signature");
        //Read the contents of the MemoryStream into a buffer
        int n = mstream.Read(buffer,0,buffer.Length);
        //Write the buffer to the file
        fout.Write(buffer,0,n);
        //Close the streams
        mstream.Close();
        fout.Close();
        Console.WriteLine("Signature Written");
      }
      catch(IOException e)
      {
        Console.WriteLine("An IO Exception Occurred :"+e);
      }
      catch(Exception oe)
      {
        Console.WriteLine("An Exception Occurred :"+oe);
      }
  }
}
```

In this example, a MemoryStream object is created and a byte array–containing signature is stored in the memory stream's buffer. Then a file stream is opened on the source file and the Seek method is used to seek to the end of the file. Once positioned at the end of the file, the code gets the contents of the memory stream and writes the contents to the file stream.

Character Streams

Character streams treat data as a stream of characters. These streams are most useful if they contain data in a format readable by humans.

TextReader and TextWriter Classes

Like the abstract Stream class, which provides the base of all byte streams, the abstract TextReader and TextWriter classes provide the base for all character streams. These classes are used to read and write a sequential stream of Unicode characters. Since these classes read and write characters, streams extending these classes can do specific encoding for localization purposes. TextReader and TextWriter do not provide random access. Table 6.11 lists some of the methods used with the TextReader class, and Table 6.12 lists methods to be used with TextWriter.

Method	Use
Synchronized	Marks the method as thread safe; a static method
Close	Closes the stream and frees the resources
Peek	Reads the next character from the stream without moving the current position in the stream
Read	Reads a character or a character array from the data source
ReadBlock	Reads maximum amount of characters from the data source and stores it in a buffer
ReadLine	Reads a single line from the data source
ReadToEnd	Reads the full contents of the data source

Table 6.11: Some Methods of the TextReader Class

Method	Use
Close	Closes the stream and frees the resources
Flush	Flushes the contents of the buffer and clears the buffer
Write	Writes the string representation of various data types
WriteLine	Writes a string followed by a line terminator

Table 6.12: Some Methods of the TextWriter Class

StreamReader and StreamWriter Classes

The StreamReader and StreamWriter classes extend the TextReader and TextWriter classes to provide the most widely used stream for writing textual data. In addition, these classes are encoding sensitive and can be used to read and write text in different encoded formats. By default, the encoding used is UTF8. Since these classes override the TextReader and TextWriter classes, all the underlying methods are the same as those listed in Tables 6.11 and 6.12. The StreamRW class shown in Listing 6.10 uses StreamReader and StreamWriter to read and write a profile from a text file.

Listing 6.10—StreamReader and StreamWriter Example

```
using System;
using System.IO;
public class StreamRW
{
  //Constructor
  public StreamRW()
  {
    //Call the Writer Method
    Writer();
    //Call the Reader Method
    Reader();
  }
  public static void Main()
  {
    StreamRW srw = new StreamRW();
  }
  //Writer Method
  private void Writer()
  {
    try
    {
```

```
             //Open or create a new file called "urprofile.txt"
             FileInfo f1 = new FileInfo("urprofile.txt");

        //Get a StreamWriter for the file
          StreamWriter sw = f1.CreateText();
          Console.WriteLine("Welcome to the profile program") ;
          Console.Write("Name :") ;

          //Get the name from the console
          string name = Console.ReadLine();
          //Write to file
          sw.WriteLine("Name :"+name) ;
          Console.Write("Country :") ;
          string country = Console.ReadLine();
          //Write to file
          sw.WriteLine("Country :"+country) ;
          Console.Write("Age :") ;
          string age =Console.ReadLine();
          //Write to file
          sw.WriteLine("Age :"+age) ;
          Console.WriteLine("Thank You");
          Console.WriteLine("Information Saved!") ;
          Console.WriteLine();
          //Close the writer and file
          sw.Close();
      }
      catch(IOException e)
      {
          Console.WriteLine("An IO Exception Occurred :"+e);
      }
  }
  private void Reader()
  {
    try
    {
          //Open the file
          FileInfo f2 = new FileInfo("urprofile.txt") ;
          //Get the StreamReader
          StreamReader sr = f2.OpenText();
          Console.WriteLine("Reading profile from file") ;
          //Peek to see if the next character exists
          while(sr.Peek()>-1)
          {
            //Read a line from the file and display it on the
            //console
            Console.WriteLine(sr.ReadLine());
          }
          Console.WriteLine("Data Read Complete!") ;
          //Close the file
          sr.Close();
      }
      catch(IOException e)
      {
          Console.WriteLine("A Error Occurred :"+e);
      }
  }
}
```

In this example, two methods—Writer and Reader—are called from the constructor. The Writer method opens file urprofile.txt and gets a StreamWriter for the file. Input from the console screen is saved to the file and the file is closed. The Reader method opens up the file again and gets a StreamReader. Data is then read from the file line by line and displayed on the console. Finally, the file is closed.

StringReader and StringWriter Classes

The StringReader and StringWriter classes, also derived from TextReader and TextWriter, are mainly used to manipulate strings rather than files. The StringReader class is built from a string and provides methods Read and ReadLine to read parts of that string. The StringWriter class is used to write to a StringBuilder class (from the System.Text namespace). Since strings in C# are immutable, the StringBuilder class is used to build a string efficiently. StringWriter provides methods like Write and WriteLine to write to the StringBuilder object. Use these streams if you are dealing with many string manipulations (e.g., a text-to-HTML parser). The StringRW class in Listing 6.11 is similar to the StreamRW class shown in Listing 6.10, except that it uses the StringReader and StringWriter classes.

Listing 6.11—StringReader and StringWriter Example

```
using System;
using System.IO;
using System.Text;
public class StringRW
{
  StringBuilder sb = new StringBuilder();
  public StringRW()
  {
    //Call the Writer Method
    Writer();
    //Call the Reader Method
    Reader();
  }
  public static void Main()
  {
    StringRW srw = new StringRW();
  }
  //Writer Method
  private void Writer()
  {
    StringWriter sw = new StringWriter(sb);
    Console.WriteLine("Welcome to the Profile Program");
    Console.Write("Name :") ;
    //Get the name from the console
    string name = Console.ReadLine();
    //Write to StringBuilder
    sw.WriteLine("Name :"+name);
    Console.Write("Country :");
    string country = Console.ReadLine();
    //Write to StringBuilder
    sw.WriteLine("Country :"+country) ;
        Console.Write("Age :") ;
        string age =Console.ReadLine();
        //Write to StringBuilder
        sw.WriteLine("Age :"+age) ;
        Console.WriteLine("Thank You");
        Console.WriteLine("Information Saved!") ;
        Console.WriteLine();
        //Close the stream
        sw.Flush();
        sw.Close();
  }
  private void Reader()
  {
        StringReader sr = new StringReader(sb.ToString());
        Console.WriteLine("Reading Profile") ;
        //Peek to see if the next character exists
        while(sr.Peek()>-1)
        {
          //Read a line from the string and display it on the
          //console
```

```
        Console.WriteLine(sr.ReadLine());
    }
    Console.WriteLine("Data Read Complete!") ;
    //Close the string
    sr.Close();
  }
}
```

Instead of using a file as a data source (as in the StreamRW class in Listing 6.10), this example uses a StringBuilder object to store the input from the user in the Writer method using the StringWriter class. Later, in the Reader method, the example uses the StringReader class to read from the string, which was built in the Writer method.

Primitive Type Stream

Primitive type streams serialize the primitive data types into their native formats. These streams are used when you want to store and retrieve data directly in the form of primitive data types like int, double, char, and byte.

BinaryReader and BinaryWriter Classes

These classes are used to read and write primitive data types and strings. If you deal only with primitive types, this is the best stream to use. Remember that this data is not easily readable by a human eyeing its contents since the data is read in its binary form.

Table 6.13 lists some of the read and write methods.

BinaryReader	BinaryWriter	Data Type
Read	Write(byte[], int, int)	Buffer of bytes
ReadBoolean	Write(boolean)	Boolean
ReadByte	Write(byte)	Byte
ReadBytes	Write(byte[])	Byte array
ReadChar	Write(char)	Char
ReadChars	Write(char[])	Char array
ReadDouble	Write(double)	Double
ReadInt16	Write(Int16)	Int16
ReadInt32	Write(Int32)	Int32
ReadInt64	Write(Int64)	Int64
ReadSingle	Write(single)	Single
ReadString	Write(string)	String

Table 6.13: Some Methods of the BinaryReader and BinaryWriter Classes

The BinStream class shown in Listing 6.12 is again similar to the StreamRW class from Listing 6.10, with the distinction that the user profile here is stored in binary format.

Listing 6.12—BinaryReader and BinaryWriter Example

```
using System;
using System.IO ;
public class BinStream
{
```

```
public BinStream()
{
  Writer();
      Reader();
}
public static void Main()
{
  BinStream bs = new BinStream();
}
private void Writer()
{
  try
  {
    Console.Out.WriteLine("Preparing to Write ...") ;
        //Open a FileStream on the file "aboutme"
        FileStream fout = new        FileStream("aboutme.txt",FileMode.OpenOrCreate,
                                    FileAccess.Write, FileShare.ReadWrite) ;

        //Create a BinaryWriter from the FileStream
        BinaryWriter bw = new BinaryWriter(fout) ;
        //Create some arbitrary variables
        string name = "Saurabh" ;
        int age = 20 ;
        double height = 5.11 ;
        bool single = true;
        char gender = 'M';
        //Write the values to file
        bw.Write(name);
        bw.Write(age);
        bw.Write(height) ;
        bw.Write(single) ;
        bw.Write(gender);
        //Close the file and free resources
        bw.Close();
        Console.WriteLine("Data Written!") ;
    Console.WriteLine();
    }
    catch(IOException e)
    {
        Console.WriteLine("An IO Exception Occurred :"+e);
    }
}
private void Reader()
{
  try
  {
    Console.WriteLine("Preparing to Read ...") ;
        //Open a FileStream in Read mode
        FileStream fin = new FileStream("aboutme.txt", FileMode.Open,
                        FileAccess.Read, FileShare.ReadWrite) ;
        //Create a BinaryReader from the FileStream
        BinaryReader br = new BinaryReader(fin) ;
        //Seek to the start of the file
        br.BaseStream.Seek(0,SeekOrigin.Begin);
        //Read from the file and store the values to the variables

        string name = br.ReadString();
        int age = br.ReadInt32() ;
        double height = br.ReadDouble() ;
        bool single = br.ReadBoolean();
        char gender = br.ReadChar();
        //Display the data on the console
        Console.WriteLine("Name :"+name);
        Console.WriteLine("Age :"+age);
        Console.WriteLine("Height :"+height) ;
        Console.WriteLine("Single? :"+single) ;
        Console.WriteLine("Gender M/F:"+gender);
```

```
        //Close the stream and free the resources
        br.Close();
        Console.WriteLine("Data Read!") ;
      }
      catch(IOException e)
      {
        Console.WriteLine("An IO Exception Occurred :"+e) ;
      }
   }
}
```

This example has defined a class called BinStream that has two methods: Writer and Reader. The Writer method creates a FileStream object on the file called aboutme.txt and then creates a BinaryWriter from the FileStream object. Then some primitive variables are written to the file using the Write method from the BinaryWriter class. Finally, the BinaryWriter is closed. The Reader method creates a FileStream object on the file previously written (aboutme.txt) in Read mode. A BinaryReader class is instantiated using the FileStream object. The different overloads of the Read method of the BinaryReader class are used to read different primitive data types from the file. Finally, the read values are displayed on the console and the stream is closed.

Summary

The three major components of a software system are input, processing, and output. The standard input stream (Console.In), standard output stream (Console.Out), and standard error stream (Console.Error) from the System namespace are used by console applications to interact with the user.

The classes under the System.IO namespace enable you to perform file and directory operations as well as manipulate the contents of files with the help of various streams. The File and FileInfo classes help you to perform common operations on files like open, create, move, and delete, whereas the Directory and DirectoryInfo classes allow you to perform similar tasks on directories. Changes made to the file system can be monitored with the help of the FileSystemWatcher class.

There are three basic kinds of streams to manipulate files: byte-based streams (deriving from the Stream class), character-based streams (deriving from the TextReader and TextWriter classes), and streams to manipulate primitive data types (the BinaryReader and BinaryWriter classes).

As with all classes in .NET, we need a way of handling exceptions if and when they do occur. In the next chapter we will describe how to deal with exception handling in C#.

Chapter 7:
Exception Handling

Introduction

Exception handling is crucial since the robustness of software depends on how effectively a program deals with exceptions. If you have ever developed software, you realize that code requires intensive exception handling. Even well-written lines of code fail and cause errors, so there must be a mechanism to capture and deal with such failures. Like C++ and Java, C# provides exception handling. So for you, exception handling is a matter of planning for the handling of failures.

Why Exception Handling?

Let's assume that your program doesn't have an exception-handling mechanism. What would happen if it tries to access a floppy drive that doesn't contain a disk? Similarly, if you have a lot of open applications, will the program be able to handle an "out of memory" error? In these cases, there is nothing a program can do to prevent these errors from occurring—they're out of its control. These are examples of an abnormal execution of an application.

Have you ever received a divide-by-zero error, a stack-overflow error, or a type-mismatch error? These errors occur when a calling program makes mistakes in passing arguments or when it does not check error conditions—in other words, erroneous execution. When these kinds of errors occur, the program should be able to capture the error and exit gracefully or continue normally. As in the floppy disk example, the program could capture the error and ask the user to retry the operation. These examples show why the exception handling mechanism is so important to software developers.

Exception Handling in C#

Exception handling in C# provides a uniform, structured, and type-safe way of handling errors. (We will see the details of these features later in this chapter.) The exception mechanism in C# is very similar to the one in C++, including these notable features:

- All exceptions are derived from System.Exception, allowing type-safe handling of exceptions.
- Well-defined exception classes exist for system-level errors—such as overflow, divide-by-zero, and null dereferences—which are treated on par with application-level errors.
- C# contains inner exceptions. When a new exception is thrown from an existing exception, the new exception's inner exception can carry the existing exception.
- Checked and unchecked statements are used to control overflow checking.
- An exception raised in VB.NET but handled in a C# program is handled in the same way as one raised in C# but handled in VB.NET. There is a uniform way of handling errors.

C# provides a structured way of handling errors: the block of code where errors are expected is guarded by try-catch blocks where exceptions are handled. (Try-catch and block statements will be covered in more detail in the following sections.)

System.Exception Overview

System.Exception represents errors that occur during application execution. This is the base class for all exceptions in C#, so any other type of exception must be derived from it. When an error occurs, either the system or the currently executing application reports it by throwing an exception containing information about the error. The Exception class is present in the System namespace and in the assembly mscorlib.dll.

Some Important Properties of Exception class

In this section we'll focus on properties of the Exception class that we can use in the application for exception handling. The Exception class properties below will make understanding exceptions easier.

StackTrace

This StackTrace property can be used to determine where the error occurred. Examples in the following sections use the StackTrace property to display the location of the error in the code.

Message

The Message property returns a description of the error's cause. Examples in the following sections use the Message property to display a description of error message to the user.

InnerException

The InnerException property can be used to create and preserve a series of exceptions during exception handling. When there are series of exceptions, the most current exception can be used to obtain the prior exception through the InnerException property.

HelpLink

The HelpLink property can hold a URL to a help file that provides extensive information about the cause of an exception.

Exceptions Inherited from Exception Class

The .NET framework defines area-related exception classes, which are all derived from the Exception class. The main purpose of these classes is to handle specific type of exceptions. Table 7.1 briefly defines some of these classes. We'll see more detail on these classes in their related chapters.

Exception Type	Description
Exception	This is the main class for all exceptions in the .NET framework.
AmbiguousMatchException	This represents the error that occurs when binding to a method or retrieving custom attributes results in more than one item matching the specified criteria.
ArgumentException	This occurs when an argument passed to a method is invalid.
ArgumentNullException	This is thrown when a null reference is passed to a method which cannot not accept it.
ArgumentOutOfRangeException	This is thrown when an argument passed to a method is invalid because it is outside the allowable range of values as specified by the method.
AppDomainUnloadedException	This occurs when unloaded application domain is tried to be accessed.
ArithmeticException	This is thrown for errors caused by an arithmetic operation.
ArrayTypeMismatchException	This is thrown when an attempt is made to store an element of the wrong type in an array.
BadImageFormatException	This is thrown when an attempt is made to load a Assembly from a file with an invalid file image.
CannotUnloadAppDomainException	This is thrown when an attempt to unload an application domain fails.
ConfigurationException	This is thrown if there is an error in a configuration settings.
ContextMarshalException	This is thrown if marshalling an object across a context boundary fails.
CryptographicException	This is thrown if there is an error occurred during a cryptographic operation.
DataException	This is thrown if ADO.NET components generates errors.
DivideByZeroException	This is thrown when an error caused by an attempt to divide a number by zero.
ExecutionEngineException	This is thrown if there is an internal error in the execution engine.
ExternalException	This is the main exception for all COM interop exceptions.
FileNotFoundException	This is thrown when a file path argument specifies a file that does not exist.
FormatException	This is thrown when the format of an argument does not meet the parameter specifications.
IndexOutOfRangeException	This is thrown when you attempt to access an element of an array with an index that is outside the bounds of the array.
InvalidCastException	This is thrown when an explicit conversion fails because the source type cannot be converted to the destination type.

Exception Type	Description
InvalidOperationException	This is thrown when an operation cannot be performed.
InvalidProgramException	This exception is thrown by the system when a compiler emits incorrect IL or metadata.
LicenseException	This is thrown when a .NET component cannot be granted license.
MemberAccessException	This is typically thrown by the system when members in a class library have been changed or removed.
NotImplementedException	This is thrown when you request a method or operation which is not implemented.
NotSupportedException	This is thrown when *element* does not represent a constructor, method, property, event, type, or field member.
NullReferenceException	This is thrown when there is an attempt to dereference a null object reference.
OleDbException	This exception is thrown when an managed OLE-DB provider returns an error.
OutOfMemoryException	This is thrown when insufficient memory prevents the current memory allocation from succeeding.
OverflowException	This is thrown when result of an arithmetic operation is too large to be represented by the destination type.
RankException	This is thrown when an array with an incorrect number of dimensions is passed to a method.
RegistrationException	This is thrown when a registration error is detected.
RemotingException	This is thrown when there is an error occurred during remoting process.
SecurityException	This exception is thrown when a security-related error occurs.
ServicedComponentException	This is thrown if an error is occurred in a serviced component.
ServerException	This is thrown when the client connects to non-.NET framework applications which cannot throw exceptions.
SerializationException	This is thrown when an error occurs during serialization or deserialization.
SqlException	This is thrown when SQL Server returns error in the process of data access.
SqlTypeException	This is the main exception for Sql Types.
StackOverflowException	This is thrown when the execution stack overflows due to too many method calls.
SynchronizationLockException	This is thrown when the method is invoked by a caller that does not own that lock.
ThreadAbortException	This is thrown when a call is made to System.Threading.Thread.Abort.
ThreadInterruptedException	This is thrown when a Thread is interrupted.
ThreadStateException	This is thrown when a method is invoked on a Thread and the thread is in a

Exception Type	Description
	System.Threading.Thread.ThreadState that is invalid for the method.
TimeoutException	This is thrown when time has expired.
TypeInitializationException	This is thrown is thrown inside the static constructor of a type.
TypeLoadException	This is thrown when the system cannot load a Type.
TypeUnloadedException	This is thrown when there is an attempt to access a Type that has been unloaded.
UnauthorizedAccessException	This is thrown when an I/O operation cannot be performed because of incompatible file access levels.
VerificationException	This is thrown when the security system requires code to be type-safe and the verification process is unable to verify that the code is type-safe.
WarningException	This is an exception which is handled as a warning instead of an error.
XmlSyntaxException	This is thrown when syntax error occurs in XML parsing.
XmlSchemaException	This is thrown when there is an error in schema of XML.
XsltException	This is thrown when an error occurs while processing an XSL transform.

Table7.1: Commonly Used Exceptions

Exception Class Constructors

All derived classes must provide these Exception class constructors:

```
Exception()
Exception(string)
Exception(string,Exception)
```

In the last constructor, the argument of type Exception is for the InnerException, which will be explained in detail later in this chapter. The string passed is the error message, which can be obtained through the Message property after construction.

Exception Statements in C#

C# supports structured exception handling similar to that seen in C++. In structured exception handling, you write code surrounded by blocks. If an exception occurs, the block throws the execution control to a predefined handled code. The try, catch, finally statements define these blocks. In other words, if an application handles exceptions that occur during the execution of a block of application code, the code must be placed within a try statement. Application code within a try statement is a try block. Application code that handles exceptions thrown by a try block is placed within a catch statement and is called a catch block. In a try block, you define the code you want to execute and protect from any possible errors. The catch block defines the handlers for the exception. The finally block is used to free resources allocated in the try block.

The try statement provides a mechanism to capture exceptions in a block of code and a mechanism to execute blocks of code both under normal circumstances and when an exception occurs.

You can define a try statement in a few different forms:

- try-catch
- try-finally
- try-catch-finally

Let's discuss each one of them below.

Try-Catch

In try-catch, a try block is followed by one or more catch blocks. You basically surround the block of code where you expect an error to occur with the try statement followed by one or more catch blocks to handle one or more types of exceptions. Let's look at the example in Listing 7.1 to understand it better:

Listing 7.1—Exception1.cs, Try-Catch Example

```
using System;
using System.Text;
        public class LearnAboutTryCatch1
        {

                public static void GenerateException(Int32 arg1,Int32 arg2)
                {
                        Int32 result1;
                        result1=0;
                        try
                        {
                                //BLOCK OF CODE WHERE ERRORS ARE EXPECTED

                                //division
                                result1=arg1/arg2;
                                Console.WriteLine(result1);


                        }
        catch   (System.DivideByZeroException e)
        {

                                //HANDLE THE ERROR
//StackTrace gives us the location of error as string
                        Console.WriteLine(String.Concat(e.Message,e.StackTrace));

//e.Message: gives the error message in this case,
//Attempted to divide by zero.

//e.Stacktrace: gives the location of the error in text
//form. In this case at
//LearnAboutTryCatch1.GenerateDivideByZeroError(Int32
//                 Numerator,Int32 Denominator)
//in this case the output would be
//Attempted to divide by zero. at
//LearnAboutTryCatch1.GenerateDivideByZeroError(
//                     Int32 Numerator,Int32 Denominator)
                        }
                }
                public static void Main()
                {
                        GenerateException (6,0);
                }
        }
```

First we create the class LearnAboutTryCatch1, which has the method GenerateException that divides two numbers. The block of code where we would expect errors—in this case, the division operation—is surrounded by the try clause. The try clause is followed by a catch statement, which has an argument of type System.DivideByZeroException to catch divide-by-zero errors. If you divide a number by zero, this causes a divide-by-zero exception.

You have to handle all of the exceptions inside the catch clause. In this example, the block of code inside the catch clause writes a message to console. Note that we have concatenated the Message property and the StackTrace property of the exception to generate the message. The Message property gives the actual error message, and the StackTrace gives the location of the actual error. Finally in the Main() method, we call the function by passing 6 and 0 to generate a divide-by-zero error. Now, in Listing 7.2, we will modify the code above to illustrate how to use multiple catch statements:

Listing 7.2—Exception2.cs, Second Exception Example

```
using System;
using System.Text;
public class LearnAboutTryCatch2
        {

        public static void GenerateException(Int32 arg1,Int32 arg2)
               {

                        Int32 result1=0;
                        Int32 result2=0;

                        try
                        {
                                //BLOCK OF CODE WHERE ERRORS ARE EXPECTED

                                //division
                                result1=arg1/arg2;

                                //multiplication
                                result2=arg1*arg2;

                                Console.WriteLine(result1);
                                Console.WriteLine(result2);

                        }
                        catch  (System.DivideByZeroException e)
                        {

                        //HANDLE THE ERROR
                        //StackTrace gives us the location of error as
                        // string
                        Console.WriteLine(
                         String.Concat(e.Message,e.StackTrace));

                        //e.Message: gives the error message, in this
                        // case, Attempted to divide by zero.
                        //e.Stacktrace: gives the location of the error
                        //in text form. In this case at
                        // LearnAboutTryCatch1.GenerateDivideByZeroError(
                        //          Int32 Numerator,Int32 Denominator)
                        //in this case the output would be
                        //Attempted to divide by zero. at
                        //LearnAboutTryCatch1.GenerateDivideByZeroError(
                        //          Int32 Numerator,Int32 Denominator)
                        }
                        catch(System.OverflowException e)
```

```
        {
                //HANDLE THE ERROR
          //StackTrace gives us the location of error as
          //  string
          Console.WriteLine(
            String.Concat(e.Message,e.StackTrace));

          //e.Message: gives the error message in this case,
          //e.Stacktrace: gives the location of the
          // error in text form.
          }
    }

    public static void Main()
    {
            GenerateException(6,0);
            GenerateException(999999999,999999999);
    }
  }
```

Figure 7.2 shows the output of Listing 7.2 in the console. Note that it shows the
divide by zero error and its location in the code.

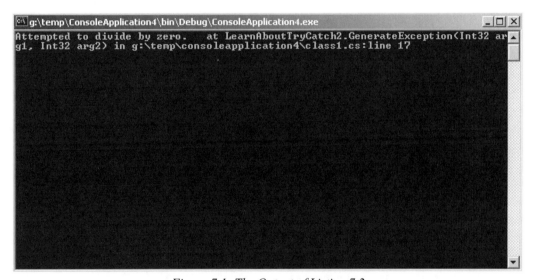

Figure 7.1: The Output of Listing 7.2

We have added a multiplication operation inside the GenerateException function, and we have also
added one more catch clause to handle System.OverflowException, which could result from
multiplying two big numbers. For example, if the resulting value of the multiplication is bigger than
what an Int32 type can hold, we would expect to get an overflow exception—so we have to add one
catch block for each exception. Hence, this example, Listing 7.2, demonstrates how to handle more
than one type of exception.

Assume that we have passed 999999999 as arg1 and 999999999 as arg2 to the GenerateException
method. Note that result2 is Int32 type, and when we multiply 999999999 and 999999999, we get a
stack overflow error.

Compile the code as usual with the following command:

```
csc LearnAboutTryCatch2.cs.
```

```
Once you run LearnAboutTryCatch2.exe, you would expect that both the divide-by-zero
and the overflow exceptions would be thrown. However, you would be surprised to
know that only the divide-by-zero exception is raised and not the overflow
exception because  result1=arg1/arg2; code comes first.
```

What if you want to change this behavior? This leads us to the next important concept, checked and unchecked statements in C#.

The different ways of controlling overflow behavior are listed below:

- Set the compiler option to checked+ or checked–
- Add the checked statement and unchecked statement to your code

Compiler options apply to the application level whereas checked and unchecked statements can apply to specific blocks of code. Checked and unchecked statements always override the compiler options, so if you have compiled with the checked+ option and have a block of code surrounded by an unchecked statement, the overflow exception will not be raised for any overflow conditions within the unchecked block. Similarly, if you have compiled with the checked– option and have a block of code surrounded by the checked statement, the overflow exception would be raised for any overflow conditions within the checked block of code. Listing 7.3 shows what the code looks like after adding the checked statement.

Listing 7.3—Exception3.cs, Checked-Unchecked Example

```csharp
using System;
using System.Text;
public class LearnAboutTryCatch1
{

public static void GenerateException(Int32 arg1,Int32 arg2)
    {

            Int32 result1=0;
            Int32 result2=0;

        try
        {
            //BLOCK OF CODE WHERE ERRORS ARE EXPECTED
            //division

            result1=arg1/arg2;

                    //multiplication

        checked
            {
                    result2=arg1*arg2;
            }

            Console.WriteLine(result1);
            Console.WriteLine(result2);

            }
        catch  (System.DivideByZeroException e)
            {

            //HANDLE THE ERROR
            //StackTrace gives us the location of error
            // as string
            //e.Message: gives the error message in this
                Console.WriteLine(String.Concat(e.Message,
                                        e.StackTrace));
```

```
            //  case, Attempted to divide by zero.
            //e.Stacktrace: gives the location of the error
            // in text form. In this case at
            // LearnAboutTryCatch1.GenerateDivideByZeroError(
            //              Int32 Numerator,Int32 Denominator)
            //in this case the output would be
            //Attempted to divide by zero. at
            // LearnAboutTryCatch1.GenerateDivideByZeroError(
            // Int32 Numerator,Int32 Denominator)


                    }
            catch(System.OverflowException e)
            {
            //HANDLE THE ERROR
             //StackTrace gives us the location of error as
             //string.
             //e.Message: gives the error message in this
             // case,
             //e.Stacktrace: gives the location of the error
            // in text form.

            Console.WriteLine(String.Concat(e.Message,
                    e.StackTrace));


            }


        }

        public static void Main()
        {
            GenerateException(6,0);
            GenerateException(999999999,999999999);
        }
    }
```

Figure 7.2 illustrates the output of the overflow exception to the console resulting from using the checked keyword in Listing 7.3.

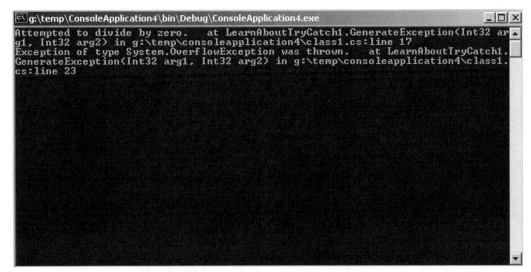

Figure 7.2: Output of Listing 7.3

The code in Listing 7.3 would raise both exceptions: the divide-by-zero exception and the overflow exception. We leave it to you as an exercise to play with different combinations of compiler options, as well as checked and unchecked statements.

Now, let's say we want to capture all other exceptions other than the specific exceptions described here (DivideByZeroException and OverflowException). To do that we have to add another catch statement with the argument of type System.Exception. By adding the System.Exception, the code now will look like Listing 7.4. Pay specific attention to the place where we insert the catch statement.

Listing 7.4—Exception4.cs, General Exception Example

```
using System;
using System.Text;
      public class LearnAboutTryCatch1
      {

            public static void GenerateException(Int32 arg1,Int32 arg2)
            {

                  Int32 result1=0;
                  Int32 result2=0;

                  try
                  {
                        //BLOCK OF CODE WHERE ERRORS ARE EXPECTED

                        //division
                        result1=arg1/arg2;

                        //multiplication
                        checked
                        {
                              result2=arg1*arg2;
                        }

                        Console.WriteLine(result1);
                        Console.WriteLine(result2);

                  } catch  (System.Exception e)
                  {

                        //HANDLE THE ERROR
                  //StackTrace gives us the location of error as string
                  //e.Message: gives the error message.
                  //e.Stacktrace: gives the location of the error in text
                  //form.

                   Console.WriteLine(String.Concat(e.Message,e.StackTrace));

                  }
                  catch  (System.DivideByZeroException e)
                  {

                  //HANDLE THE ERROR
                  //StackTrace gives us the location of error as string
                  //e.Message: gives the error message, in this
                  // case, Attempted to divide by zero.

                   Console.WriteLine(String.Concat(e.Message,e.StackTrace));

            //e.Stacktrace: gives the location of the error in text form. In
```

```
        // this case at LearnAboutTryCatch1.GenerateDivideByZeroError(
        //  Int32 Numerator,Int32 Denominator)
        //in this case the output would be
        //Attempted to divide by zero. at
        // LearnAboutTryCatch1.GenerateDivideByZeroError(
        //          Int32 Numerator,Int32 Denominator)


            }
        catch(System. OverflowException e)
        {
                //HANDLE THE ERROR

        //stackTrace gives us the location of error as string
        //e.Message: gives the error message in this case,
        //e.Stacktrace: gives the location of the error in text
        // form.

            Console.WriteLine(String.Concat(e.Message, e.StackTrace));
            }


    }

    public static void Main()
    {
        GenerateException(6,0);
        GenerateException(999999999,999999999);
    }
}
```

The compiler would not let you compile the code in Listing 7.4. Instead, it would give you the following error message: "A previous catch clause already catches all exceptions of this or a super type ('System.Exception')." The lesson to learn is *you have to first catch specific exceptions and then catch the general exception* (System.Exception*). We leave it as an exercise for you to change the code above to fix the order of catching exceptions.

As shown in Listing 7.5, there are two ways to catch a general System.Exception. In the first case you would capture the exception and get all the information about it from the Exception parameter. However, in the second code block you would not have access to that information.

Listing 7.5—Try-Catch Syntax

```
try
{
}
catch(Exception e)
{
}
and

try
{
}
catch
{
}
```

Try-Catch-Finally

If you are interested in executing a certain block of code irrespective of whether an exception occurs or not—and still worry about catching an exception—you might use the try-catch-finally block. Even if a goto statement is present in a try block, the control gets transferred to the label in the goto statement, only after executing the finally block. Listing 7.6 illustrates the structure of the finally block.

Listing 7.6—Try-Catch-Finally Syntax

```
try
{
 //Even if a goto statement were here
 //control gets transferred to the statement identified  in
 //goto statement only after executing the finally block.

}
catch
{
   //Catch the exception
}
finally
{
//this block of code will always get executed whether an
// exception occurs or not as long as there are no exceptions
// within this block itself. If an Exception is thrown here
// some outer try block should handle it
//Any Clean up code goes here. Especially to release any
//system resources such as file handles and network
 //connections
}
```

Let's go through an example so that we can better understand the purpose of the finally block. Listing 7.7 illustrates the use of the finally block to clean up file states.

Listing 7.7—Exception7.cs, TestFinally

```
namespace TestFinally
{
    using System;
    using System.IO;
    /// <summary>
    ///     Summary description for TestFinally.
    /// </summary>
    public class TestFinally
    {
        public TestFinally()
        {
            //
            // TODO: Add Constructor Logic here
            //
            }

            public static void Main()
            {
                    StreamReader sr1=null;
                    StreamWriter sw1=null;
                    try
                    {
                     System.Console.WriteLine("In try block");
                     //Open  files
                    sr1= new StreamReader(File.Open("Test1.txt",
                              System.IO.FileMode.Open));
                    sw1= new StreamWriter(File.Open("Test2.txt",
                            System.IO.FileMode.Append,
                            FileAccess.Write));

                    while(sr1.Peek()!=-1)
                    {
                            sw1.WriteLine(sr1.ReadLine());
```

```
            }

        goto MyLabel;

        }
        catch(Exception e)
{
                Console.WriteLine(String.Concat(e.Message,
                e.StackTrace));
        }
        finally
        {
                //Int32 j ;
                //j=0;
                //j=j/5;

        //If an Exception is thrown here some outer
        //try block should handle it. The finally block
        // will not be completely executed

        Console.WriteLine("In finally block");

        //we need to make sure that Close method of the
        //Streamreader sr1 or StreamWriter sw1
        //is called irrespective of whether an exception
        // occurs or not
        //to release any system resources associated with
        //the reader or writer

        if (sr1!=null)
        {
        sr1.Close();
        }
        if(sw1!=null)
        {
                sw1.Close();
        }

        }
        MyLabel:
                Console.WriteLine("In Mylabel");

    // note: the following statements are not allowed
    //inside a finally block:
    //return, goto, break and continue

        }
    }
}
```

In Listing 7.7, inside the Main method, we opened two files. First we opened Test1.txt using a StreamReader object by passing a FileStream object returned by the File.Open method, and then we opened Test2.txt through a StreamWriter object by passing a FileStream object returned by the File.Open method. The intention here is to copy lines of Test1.txt and append them to Test2.txt. If the code in the try block executes successfully, we want to close StreamReader sr1 and StreamWriter sw1 so that system resources associated with the reader/writer are released.

If Test1.txt opens successfully but for some reason there is an exception thrown while opening Test2.txt, we still want to close the stream associated with Test1.txt. So in this example we haveadded the close methods in the finally code block so that they can be positively executed. We are checking for a null value because if none of the files is opened, we would get a null-dereferencing exception in the finally block.

We have also added a goto statement and a label to show that the label is executed only after executing the finally block.

If one of the two files is not opened successfully, the output would look like figure 7.3.. The exceptions are written out to the console from the catch block and the finally block is entered to clean up the files.

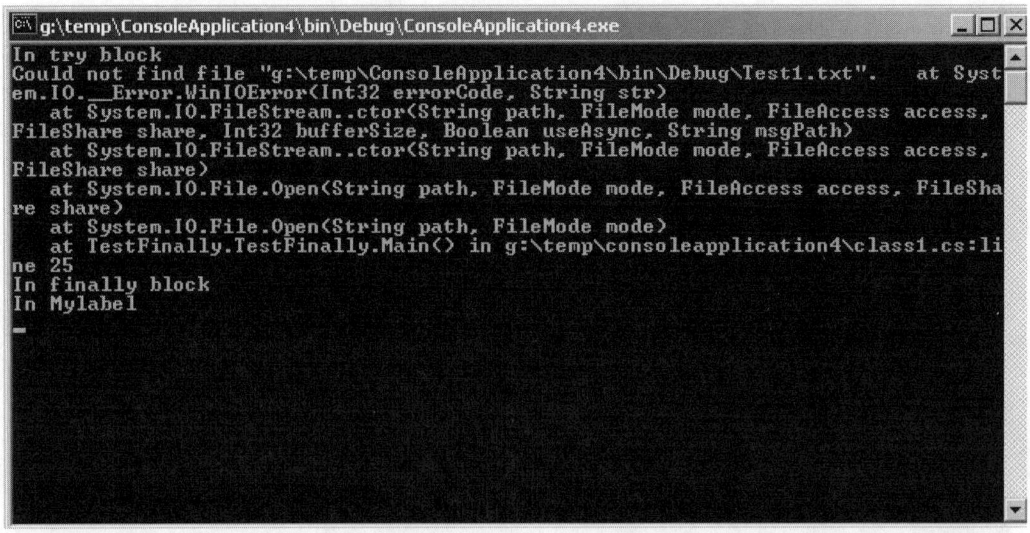

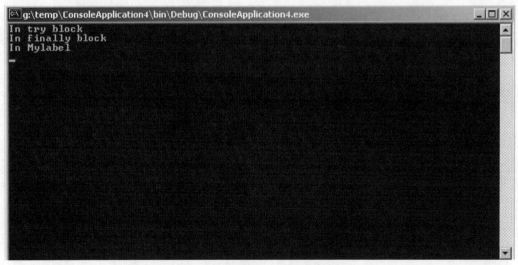

Figure 7.3: Output of Listing 7.7

If the two files are opened successfully, the output would look like figure 7.4Note that the finally block is entered regardless of whether or not an exception is thrown and the files are closed.

Figure 7.4: Output of Listing 7.7

The only time a finally block will not get executed completely is if an exception occurs in the finally block.

Note: goto, break, continue, and return statements inside a finally block clause cause an error.

Try-Finally

If you are interested in executing a certain block of code irrespective of whether an exception occurs and you do not worry about catching an exception, then you'll likely want to use the try-finally statement. However, we do not recommend using this statement because you will not be able to see what the exception is about. Instead, you should use the try-catch-finally statement. Listing 7.8 shows the structure of the Try-Finally block:

Listing 7.8—Try-Finally Syntax

```
try
        {
        //Even if a goto statement were here
        //control gets transferred to the statement identified  in
        //goto  statement only after executing the finally block.

        }
finally
        {
        // This block of code will always get executed
        // whether an exception occurs or not
        // Any cleanup code  goes here,
        // especially to release any system resources
        // such as file handles and network connections
        }
```

First the try block is executed, and then the finally block is executed, irrespective of whether an exception occurs or not. Even if a goto statement is present in the try block, the control gets transferred to the label in the goto statement only after executing the finally block.

Throw Statement

All along we have been talking about catching exceptions, but you may have been wondering who is throwing them or how you can throw one yourself. If an exception occurs during the evaluation of an expression, the language runtime automatically throws the appropriate exception. If an exception must be thrown programmatically, you would use the throw statement. Listing 7.9 gives an example of using the throw statement.

Listing 7.9—Exception9.cs, Throw Example

```
using System;

public class ThrowTest
{

  public static void fn(Int32 age)
  {
  if(age<0)
   {
        // throw an argument out of range exception if the age is
        // less than zero.

        throw new ArgumentOutOfRangeException("Age Cannot Be Negative ");
   }
  }

  public static void Main()
  {
        try
        {
         fn(-10);
        }
        catch(Exception e)
```

```
        {
            Console.WriteLine(String.Concat(e.StackTrace,e.Message));
        }
    }
}
```

Figure 7.5 below shows the result of throwing the argument out of range exception and displaying it in the catch block:

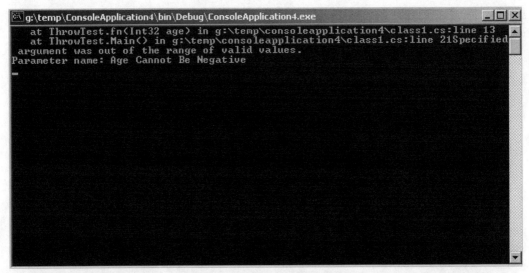

Figure 7.5: Output of Listing 7.9

In this example we have a function called fn, which takes age as an argument. In this function we check if the age is a negative value, and if so, throw ArgumentOutOfRangeException. As you can see, throwing an exception is a fairly simple task.

Let's modify this example, as shown in Listing 7.10.

Listing 7.10—Exception10.cs

```
using System;

public class ThrowTest{

public static void fn(Int32 age)
{
        if(age<0)
        {
                throw new ArgumentOutOfRangeException(
                  "Age Can Not Be Negative ");
        }
}


public static void Main()
{
 try
 {
        try
        {
          fn(-10);
        }
        catch(Exception e)
        {
```

```
            Console.WriteLine(String.Concat(e.StackTrace,e.Message));
                        throw;                        }
      // or we could also have called throw e ;


      }
}
catch(Exception e)
  {
        Console.WriteLine("In the outer catch");
        Console.WriteLine(String.Concat(e.StackTrace,e.Message));

        // Executing this statement would cause a
        //  NullreferenceException


        //Console.WriteLine(e.InnerException.Message);
  }


 }


}
```

In Listing 7.10 we add a throw statement in the catch block—basically rethrowing System.Exception—causing the same exception to occur in the catch clause. So, if we have one more try block outside the inner try block, the outer try-catch block catches the exception.

The output for the program in Listing 7.10 is shown in Figure 7.6.

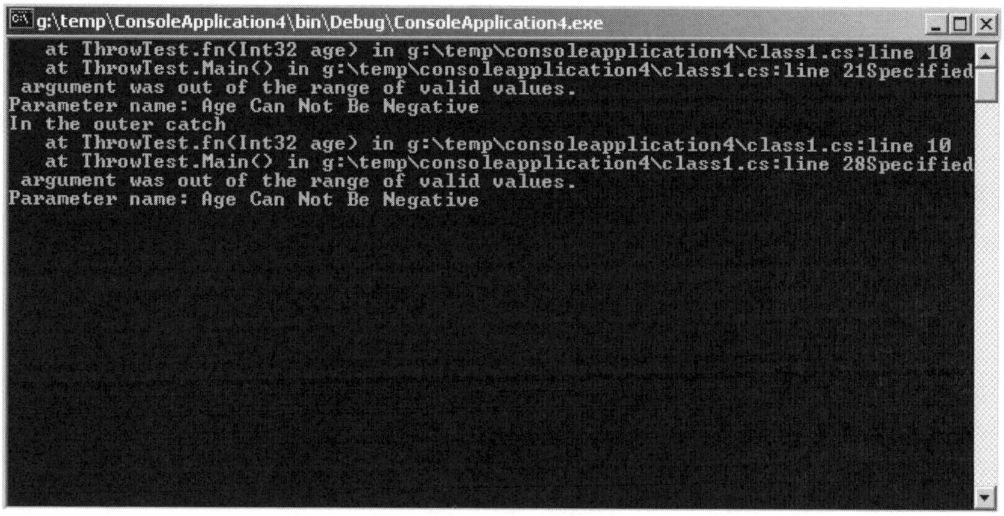

Figure 7.6: Output of Listing 7.10

One last thing about the throw statement: you will never need to throw system exceptions such as IndexOutOfRange or NullReferenceException, which are thrown normally by the runtime. The .NET framework developer specification requires that you don't throw these exceptions programmatically. However, if you *really* wanted to do it, you could write a piece of code that throws these exceptions programmatically and compiles and executes successfully.

Creating Your Own Exception Classes

To create your own exception class, the .NET framework requires you to derive your class from the System.Exception class and recommends that you implement all the constructors that are implemented by the base class. Here are some important recommendations:

- Give a meaningful name to your Exception class and end it with *Exception*.
- Do not develop a new Exception class unless there is a scenario for developers needing the class.
- Throw the most specific exception possible.
- Give meaningful messages.
- Do use InnerExceptions.
- When wrong arguments are passed, throw an ArgumentException or a subclass of it (e.g., ArgumentNullException), if necessary.

Let's go ahead and create an exception called MyException. The code and test for the exception are shown in Listing 7.11. Output is shown in Figure 7.7.

Listing 7.11—Exception11.cs

```csharp
using System;
public class MyException:Exception
{

//Constructors. It is recommended that at least all the
//constructors of
        //base class Exception are implemented
        public MyException():base() {}
        public MyException(string message):base(message) {}
        public MyException(string message,Exception e):base(message,e) {}

        //If there is extra error information that needs to be captured
        //create properties for them.
        private string strExtraInfo;
        public string ExtraErrorInfo
        {
                get
                {
                        return strExtraInfo;
                }
                set
                {
                        strExtraInfo=value;
                }
        }
}
public class TestMyException
{
        public static void Main()
        {
                try
                {
                        MyException m;
                        m=new MyException("My Exception Occured");
                        m.ExtraErrorInfo="My Extra Error Information";
                        throw m;
                }catch(MyException e)
                {
                        Console.WriteLine(String.Concat(e.StackTrace,e.Message));
                        Console.WriteLine(e.ExtraErrorInfo);
                }
        }
}
```

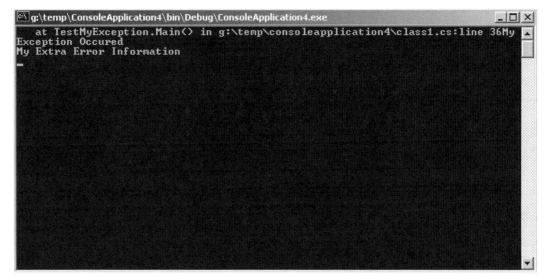

Figure 7.7: Output of Listing 7.11

In Listing 7.11 we create the MyException class, which is derived from the System.Exception class. As the code shows, all constructors simply call the base class constructors—the typical way to implement constructors. We also create a property called ExtraErrorInfo, which can be used to store any other extra error information. The reason you would create your own exception type is so the program catching this exception can take a specific action. You could also add your own properties to give any extra error information.

Propagation of Exceptions

Whenever an exception occurs in a try block, the corresponding catch blocks are checked to see if they can catch the exception. If no matching exception is found—even if a finally block is executed—the exception is propagated to a higher-level try block. This process repeats until the exception is caught—but if it is not caught, the program execution comes to an end. In other words, if the top of the call stack is reached without finding a catch block handling the exception, the default exception handler handles it and then the application terminates. If an exception is thrown from inside a catch clause—when any finally block is present—the finally block is executed, and the exception is propagated to higher-level exceptions. Similarly, if an exception is thrown from within a finally block, this exception is propagated to a higher-level try clause.

Listing 7.12 demonstrates propagation of exceptions.

Listing 7.12—Exception12.cs

```
using System;
public class TestPropagation
{
        public static void Main()
        {
                try //3
                {
                        try //2
                        {
                                try //1
                                {
                                        throw new ArgumentException();
                                }
                                catch(NullReferenceException e) //1
```

```
                                    {
                                            Console.WriteLine("Inside catch 1");
                                    }
                                finally //1
                                {
                                    Console.WriteLine("Inside finally 1");
                                }  //1

                        }
                        catch(NullReferenceException e)//2
                        {
                                Console.WriteLine("Inside catch 2");
                        }
                        finally //2
                        {
                                Console.WriteLine("Inside finally 2");
                        } //2
                }
                catch(Exception  e) //3
                {
                    //try catching some other Exception instead
                  //of general Exception and ArgumentException
                //Program would throw unhandled System.ArgumentException: value
                //does not fall within the expected range

                    Console.WriteLine("Inside catch 3");

                }
                finally  //3
                {
                        Console.WriteLine("Inside finally 3");
                }//3

        }
}
```

The output of the program in Listing 7.12 is shown in Figure 7.8.

Figure 7.8: Output of Listing 7.12

Let's explain Listing 7.12 step by step. Let's start with try 1:

```
try //1
{
        throw new ArgumentException();
}
catch(NullReferenceException e) //1
{
        Console.WriteLine("Inside catch 1");
}
finally //1
{
        Console.WriteLine("Inside finally 1");
}   //1
```

In the try block above, we throw a new ArgumentException, and the catch statement only checks NullReferenceException. Therefore, we are not able to catch ArgumentException. Because of that, the first thing to display in the console is the line *Inside finally 1*.

```
catch(NullReferenceException e)//2
{
        Console.WriteLine("Inside catch 2");
}
finally //2
{
        Console.WriteLine("Inside finally 2");
} //2
```

In the second catch statement, we again check the NullReferenceException. However, we already know that we throw ArgumentException in the first try code block. Therefore, we are again not able to catch the ArgumentException. Because of that, the console will display *Inside finally 2*.

```
catch(Exception  e) //3
{
        Console.WriteLine("Inside catch 3");
}
finally//3
{
Console.WriteLine("Inside finally 3");
}//3
```

At last, in the third catch statement, we check the exception. Therefore, we are able to catch the ArgumentException because Exception is the base class for ArgumentException. The next thing to display in the console is *Inside catch 3* and then *Inside finally 3*.

InnerException

The InnerException is a property of an exception. When there are series of exceptions, the most current exception can obtain the prior exception in the InnerException property.

Let us say we have an exception inside a try block throwing an ArgumentException and the catch clause catches it and writes it to a file. However, if the file path is not found, FileNotFoundException is thrown. Let's say that the outside try block catches this exception, but how about the actual ArgumentException that was thrown? Is it lost? No, the InnerException property contains the actual exception. This is the reason for the existence of an InnerException property for any exception.

The following example, Listing 7.13, demonstrates the concept of checking the inner exception.

Listing 7.13—Exception13.cs, InnerException Example

```
using System;
```

```
using System.IO;
public class TestInnerException
{
        public static void Main()
        {
                try
                {
                        try
                        {
                                throw new ArgumentException();
                        }
                        catch(ArgumentException e)
                        {
                         //make sure this path does not exist
                          if (File.Exists("\\Bigsky\\log.txt")==false)
                            {
                                throw new FileNotFoundException("File Not found when
                                    trying to write argument exception to the file",e);

                            }

                        }

                }
                catch(Exception e)
                {
                   Console.WriteLine(String.Concat(e.StackTrace,e.Message));
                   if (e.InnerException!=null)
                        {
                                Console.WriteLine("Inner Exception");
                                Console.WriteLine(String.Concat(
                                        e.InnerException.StackTrace,
                                        e.InnerException.Message));
                        }
                }
        }
}
```

Let's explain what happens in Listing 7.13: As you can see below, in the inner try code block we throw ArgumentException. The inner catch statement will then catch ArgumentException.

```
catch(ArgumentException e)
{
  //make sure this path does not exist
  if (File.Exists("\\Bigsky\\log.txt")==false)
  {
   throw new FileNotFoundException("File Not found when trying to write argument
     exception to the file",e);
  }
}
```

The Exists method of the File class is used to check if the file exists. If the file does not exist, we again throw a new FileNotFoundException with the user-entered exception message. The outer catch will catch the inner exception. The code below is the outer catch block, which we'll explain step by step:

```
catch(Exception e)
{
   Console.WriteLine(String.Concat(e.StackTrace,e.Message));
   if (e.InnerException!=null)
   {
       Console.WriteLine("Inner Exception");
     Console.WriteLine(String.Concat(e.InnerException.StackTrace,
       e.InnerException.Message));
   }
```

```
}
```

The first step is to display e.StackTrace and e.Message in the console:

```
Console.WriteLine(String.Concat(e.StackTrace,e.Message));
```

The e.StackTrace property gives us the location of the error and has the value of *at TestInnerException.Main() in g:\temp\consoleapplication4\class1.cs:line 18.*

The e.Message property will have the value of File Not found when trying to write argument exception to the file.

After that we check if the InnerException is null or not. If it is not null, we can display InnerException.StackTrace and InnerException.Message in the console:

```
if (e.InnerException!=null)
    {
        Console.WriteLine("Inner Exception");
        Console.WriteLine(String.Concat(e.InnerException.StackTrace,
        e.InnerException.Message));
    }
```

The e.InnerException.StackTrace property will have the value of *at TestInnerException.Main() in g:\temp\consoleapplication4\class1.cs:line 11.*

The e.InnerException.Message property will have the value of *Value does not fall within the expected range.*

Figure 7.9 shows the output of the code in Listing 7.13.

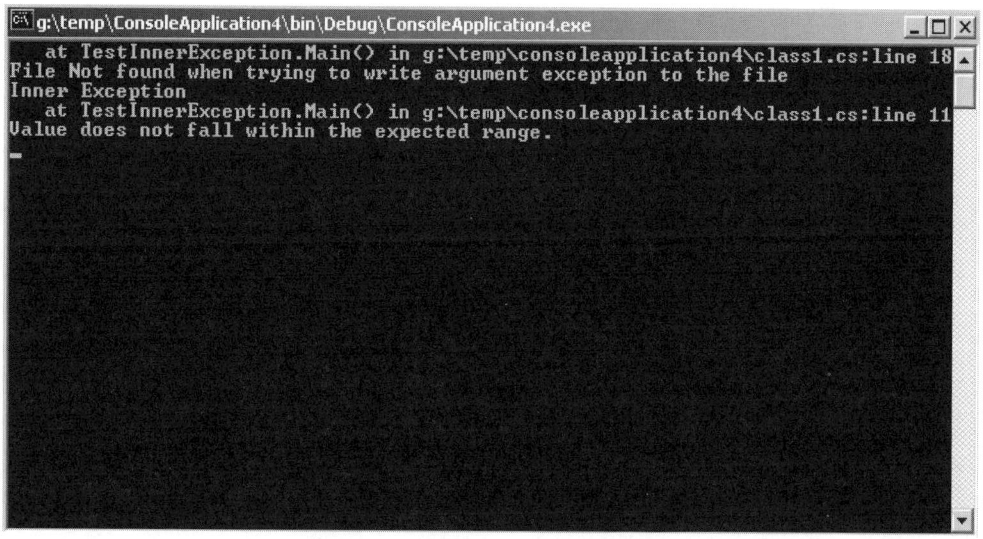

Figure 7.9: Output of Listing 7.13

Summary

Being a modern object-oriented language, C# provides a convenient mechanism to handle exceptions. Exception handling is crucial since the robustness of software depends on how effectively it deals with exceptions. If you have ever developed software in the past, you realize that software development requires intensive exception handling, so it is recommended that you have a thorough understanding of the topics covered in this chapter before delving deeply into further programming.

The next chapter in this book will introduce you to the powerful Visual Studio IDE for developing .NET applications in C#. Reading this chapter will greatly ease your programming experience in working with .NET.

Chapter 8:
Visual Studio .NET IDE

Introduction

The latest release of Visual Studio Suite from Microsoft is called Visual Studio .NET (VS.NET). In the previous versions of Visual Studio there were separate IDEs like VC++, Visual Basic, and Visual Interdev for working with different languages and applications. In this release, integration is the key premise and VS.NET packs a handful of goodies in one IDE. Now available are a Web browser, a multilanguage development environment, a Web application development environment, a multilanguage debugger, an XML editor, and more—all integrated into the IDE!

The extensive customization capabilities in VS.NET let the IDE adapt itself to the developer's needs rather than requiring the developer to adapt to the IDE. Users of previous versions of Visual Studio will find the IDE familiar, but once they sit down to actually build applications, they will find VS.NET far more powerful. Currently there are quite a few different versions of VS.NET available—including professional, enterprise, and single-language versions. Since the professional version is most readily available, we'll describe its features in this chapter.

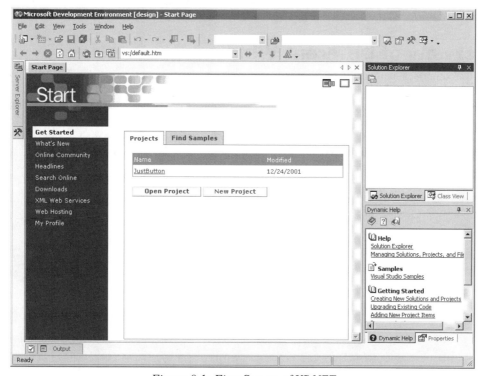

Figure 8.1: First Screen of VS.NET

Tour of Visual Studio .NET

Figure 8.1 shows the VS.NET Start Page, where you can customize the IDE according to your needs and find information on .NET. For example, developers who had been using Visual Studio 6 can easily choose their profile from the My Profile link so that keyboard shortcuts remain the same.

These are Start Page links:

- *Get Started* shows your latest projects. You can open an existing project or create a new one.
- *What's New* provides easy access to .NET: new products, Microsoft supported languages, and partner add-ins. This page also provides the latest updates and service packs for VS.NET.
- *Online Community* allows you to access public newsgroups run by Microsoft, which are good sources of support and knowledge. You'll need an external newsgroup reader like Outlook Express.
- *Headlines* allows you to browse the MSDN online library without leaving the IDE. The library is a very good source of up-to-date developer information, as well as comprehensive examples from Microsoft.
- *Search Online* allows you to search the extensive MSDN online library.
- *Downloads* gives you access to free downloads available from Microsoft and also to code samples available on MSDN Online.
- *XML Web Services* allows you to search the UDDI directory hosted by Microsoft for XML Web Services.
- *Web Hosting* allows you to directly choose among several ASP.NET hosting solutions. You can sign-up and start working with your hosting service provider from the IDE.
- *My Profile* allows you to customize the IDE according to your needs.

Overview of Different Windows

VS.NET comprises many different windows that each serve a different purpose. In VS.NET you will find a couple of old windows that have migrated from older versions of Microsoft Tools—such as the Server Object in Visual Interdev, the Toolbox from Visual Basic, and the Properties window from Visual Basic. There are many new windows like Dynamic Help, Class View, and Object Browser, which were added in this version of Visual Studio. Below, Figure 8.2 shows the different views making up Visual Studio .NET, and Table 8.1 provides a description of each. We shall review each window in the pages that follow.

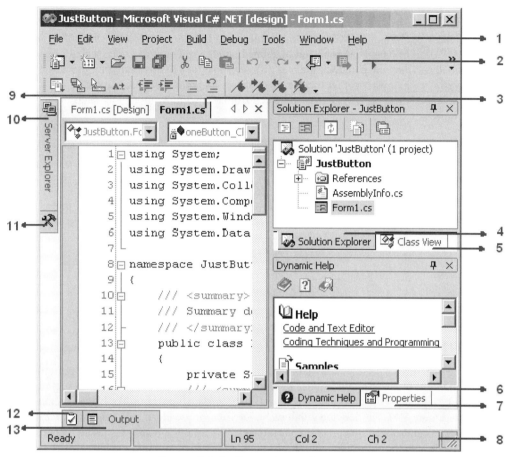

Figure 8.2: Different Parts of VS.NET

Index	Description
1	Menu Bar (File, Edit, View, Build, Project, Debug, Tools, Window, Help)
2	Toolbar
3	Code Editor Window
4	Solution Explorer Window
5	Class View Window
6	Dynamic Help Window
7	Properties Explorer Window
8	Status Bar
9	Windows Forms Designer Window
10	Server Explorer Window
11	Toolbox Window
12	Task List Window
13	Output Window

Table 8.1: Description of different parts of VS.NET IDE

Tabbed Windows

In VS.NET the Visual Studio 6 MDI (Multiple Document Interface) and SDI (Single Document Interface) IDE designs have been replaced by tabbed windows. You will notice that all the windows are now tabbed and that you can dock them at different positions by just dragging the tabs. Also you can group various windows together to save work space. Even the Code Editor and Windows Forms Designer are tabbed, making it very easy to switch from one window to another such as the window shown in Figure 8.3.

Figure 8.3: Tabbed Windows Grouped Together

Auto-Hide

One more new feature of these windows is auto-hide: the window hides as a vertical button on the side of the IDE until you drag your mouse over it. Then the window appears and stays up until you are done working with it. To auto-hide a window, click the small pushpin-like button on the window (as shown in Figure 8.4). To view the window, hover your mouse close to the title of the docked window. Once your work is done, move your mouse away from the window, and the window will auto-hide. To disable the auto-hide feature, just click on the pushpin button again. This is a very good feature and helps you save a lot of real-estate space for your Code Editor.

Push Pin Button

Figure 8.4: Push Pin Button

Windows Forms Designer

The Windows Forms Designer in VS.NET is the same as that of VB6 and allows you to design forms by dragging controls from the Toolbox and laying them out on a blank form. The only difference is that now Windows Forms Designer windows are also tabbed, so working with multiple Code and Designer windows becomes very easy. The Windows Forms Designer is used to build Windows forms quickly in a WYSIWYG (What You See Is What You Get) interface. Figure 8.5 shows the Windows Forms Designer.

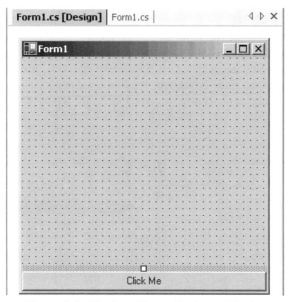

Figure 8.5: Windows Forms Designer Window

Code Editor

To view the Code Editor, either press the F7 key or select View Menu→Code. At first sight the Code Editor looks similar to that of previous versions of Visual Studio, but there have been a significant number of changes to the Code Editor in VS.NET, some of which are listed below.

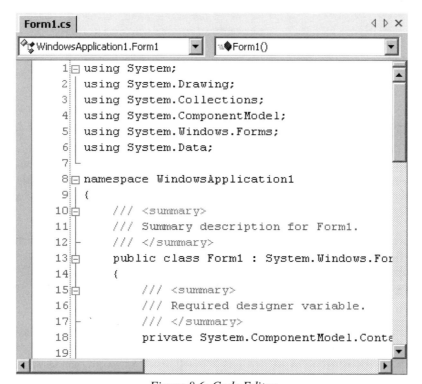

Figure 8.6: Code Editor

Code Navigation Boxes

At the very top of the Code Editor you will find two dropdown list boxes. These boxes help you navigate to different parts of the code file currently open. The right box contains a list of all methods in the code, while the left box contains a list of all classes in the code. Just select the method name from the dropdown list, and the Code Editor will scroll to that method. This is a very handy feature if you are working with many methods in your code. Figure 8.7 depicts the list of default properties and methods inserted by VS.NET while making a Windows forms project.

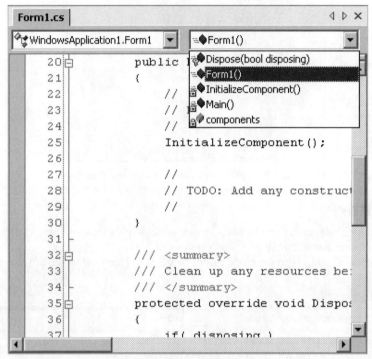

Figure 8.7: Code Navigator Boxes

Breakpoint, Bookmarks, and Shortcut Margin

To the left of the code window is a gray margin, which can be used to set debugging breakpoints, bookmarks, and Task List shortcuts. Breakpoints are used to halt the application execution while the application is running in debug mode. To add a breakpoint, just click in the gray margin next to the line you want to set as the breakpoint. A red circle will appear next to the line indicating a breakpoint (see line 19 in Figure 8.8).

Bookmarks are used to quickly navigate a large code file. To set bookmarks and shortcuts, go to Edit Menu→Bookmarks→Toggle Bookmark, or press Ctrl+K twice (see line 26 in Figure 8.8). Once the bookmarks are set, you can quickly navigate through them using Ctrl+K followed by Ctrl+N to move to the next bookmark or Ctrl+K followed by Ctrl+P to move to previous bookmark.

Task List shortcuts are very useful when a team of developers is working on the same project. Creating a Task List shortcut adds a new entry in the Task List window, where you can insert additional comments relating to the shortcut that you would like to share with the other developers. Select Edit Menu→Bookmarks→Add Task List Shortcut to add a new shortcut (see line 21 in Figure 8.8).

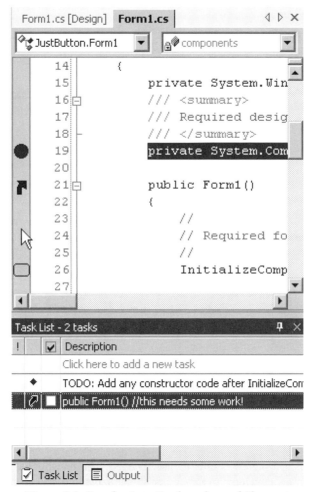

Figure 8.8: Breakpoints, Bookmarks, and Shortcuts

Code Outlining

Code outlining is another new feature to help developers navigate through large chunks of code. In the Code Editor just after the gray margin you will find a gray line running through the code marked at points with plus and minus signs. A minus sign precedes every block of code or comments.

To hide a block, click the minus sign, and the block becomes a single line containing the block heading preceded by a plus sign. If you hide the contents of a method, the whole method block reduces to just the method definition, along with the plus sign. To unhide the method block, click on the plus sign, and the code block expands.

If you are working with multiple methods, this feature can be a great time-saver since you don't spend so much time scrolling up and down looking for methods.

You can also define blocks of code using the #region and #endregion directives, allowing you to collapse and expand those block regions. You can turn off this outline feature by going to Edit Menu→Outlining→Stop Outlining. In Figure 8.9 we have defined a custom block region, Some Methods. Here, the InitializeComponent method is collapsed, showing only the method definition.

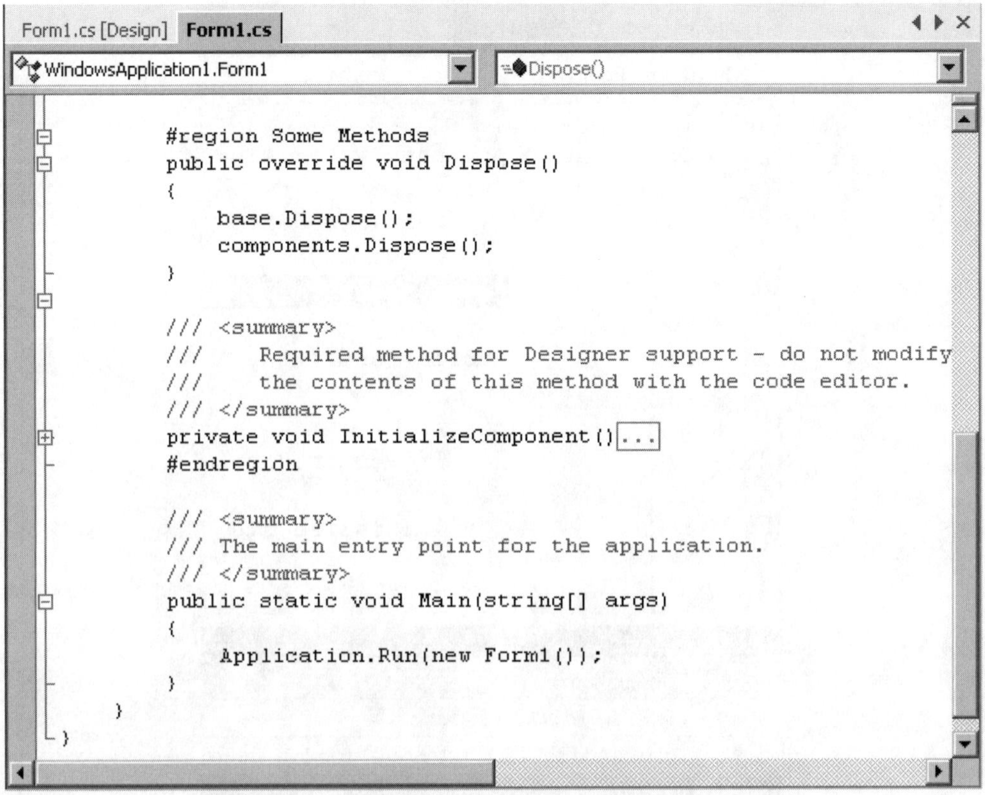

Figure 8.9: Code Outlining

IntelliSense

One of the best features of VS.NET is IntelliSense. The .NET Framework has so many base classes
that it is impossible for any developer to remember all class, method, and property names.
IntelliSense makes code writing easy by listing a class's methods or properties as you type.
IntelliSense can also list method parameters and overloaded methods. The Code Editor supports
four main types of IntelliSense, which are enabled/disabled from Edit Menu→IntelliSense: List
Members, Parameter Info, Quick Info, and Complete Word.

List Members. If you type an object name followed by a period (the scope operator), a box will pop
up containing the list of all properties and methods supported by that class. In Figure 8.10, the pop-
up box shows all possible properties and methods that can be used by the instance of the class.
When the box pops up, you can either use your mouse to select the right method or property or use
the arrow keys to navigate to the right member and select it by pressing Enter.

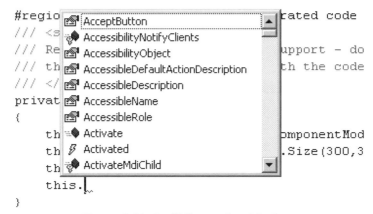

Figure 8.10: IntelliSense—List Members

Parameter Info. When you write methods in the Code Editor, a box will pop up containing the list of parameters supported by that method's various overloads. In Figure 8.11, the pop-up box shows the list of parameters that can be passed to the System.Drawing.Size() constructor. Click on the small black arrows within the box or use the up and down arrow keys to cycle through the various overloaded options available for the method.

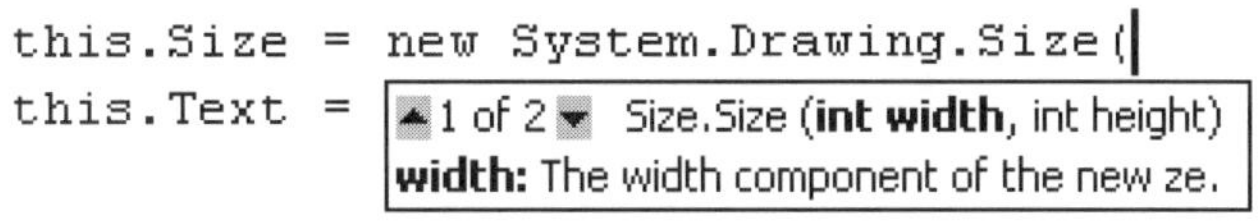

```
this.Size = new System.Drawing.Size(|
this.Text =   ▲ 1 of 2 ▼  Size.Size (int width, int height)
              width: The width component of the new ze.
```

Figure 8.11: IntelliSense—Parameter Info

Quick Info. In the Code Editor, when you move your cursor over some code, a box will pop up giving you information about the item under the cursor. Figure 8.12 shows the box that appears when the mouse is positioned over the property this.Text in the Code Editor.

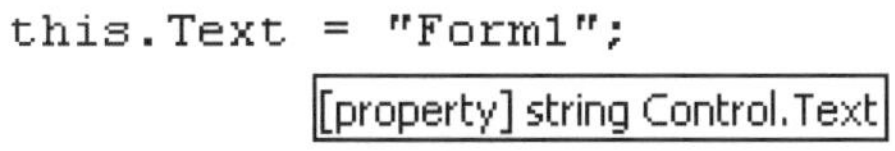

```
this.Text = "Form1";
          [property] string Control.Text
```

Figure 8.12: IntelliSense—Quick Info

Complete Word. As the name suggests, this IntelliSense feature helps you to complete words. For example, if you are writing the definition of the while-for or for-each loop, IntelliSense automatically adds the necessary brackets for you.

IntelliSense also checks the code while you are typing and underlines mistakes with a squiggly red line. For example, IntelliSense detects syntax errors like omitted enclosing quotes, enclosing brackets, and terminating semicolons.

Toolbox Window

VS.NET enables rapid application development (RAD) in all languages supported on the .NET platform. VS.NET has adopted Visual Basic's Toolbox, presenting you with its list of components, dividing them into four different groups: Windows Forms, Components, Data, and General (all shown in Figure 8.13). To access components under a tab, just click the tab's title box and the components will be displayed. The Toolbox changes the group tabs according to the type of application currently active in the main designer window.

Figure 8.13 shows the Toolbox tab for creating Windows forms applications. If you were designing a Web application or writing an XML schema, the Toolbox would change its group tabs accordingly. When the components list is very long, a small black arrow appears at the end of the list, letting you scroll through it.

Figure 8.13: Toolbox Window

There are a couple of ways to add components from the Toolbox to your project:

- Drag the components from the Toolbox to the Forms Designer window.
- Click on the component in the Toolbox and then click on the Forms Designer window.
- Double-click the component in the Toolbox.

Clipboard Ring Tab

The Clipboard Ring tab comes from Microsoft Office 2000 and shows up in the Toolbox window when you are working with the Code Editor. The Clipboard Ring tab stores up to 15 text items that you either cut or copy from the VS.NET IDE. If you have a lot of code duplication or remodeling, then this is the perfect feature for you. You can cycle through all the items using the Ctrl-Shift-V key combination. Figure 8.14 shows the Clipboard Ring tab.

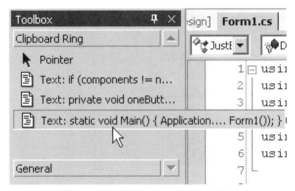

Figure 8.14: Clipboard Ring Tab

General Tab

The General tab can be used to store custom pieces of text and code. To place code there, select it in the code window and drag it to the General tab on the Toolbox. Now you can use that code anywhere and in any project by just dragging it from the General tab to your code window. The code stays even after you shut down VS.NET.

Let's take an example: Many companies require developers to add custom copyright information at the start of very code page. To do this in VS.NET, just write the information once and then select and drag it to the General tab. Now, at the beginning of every new project, just drag the copyright information from the General tab to your code window to add the copyright information. This will definitely save you a lot of time.

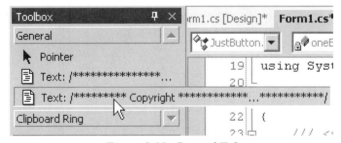

Figure 8.15: General Tab

Adding a Custom Tab

To add your own tab to the Toolbox, right-click the Toolbox and select Add Tab. A textbox appears at the end of the Toolbox; fill in the name of your tab and press Enter. Now you can add to it custom components, pieces of text, or your most frequently used components. For example, you can use this option to create a Favorite Components tab, as shown in Figure 8.16.

Figure 8.16: Add a New Tab

Deleting/Renaming a Tab

To delete or rename a tab, right-click on the tab and select Delete Tab or Rename Tab, respectively.

Customizing Components on a Tab

To add or remove components from the tab, right-click the Toolbox and select Customize Toolbox. The dialog that pops up allows you to add or remove both COM components and .NET components.

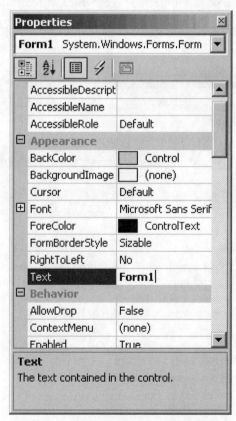

Figure 8.17: Properties Window

Properties Window

The Properties window lets you view and change design-time properties of your components, forms, and documents. When you select a document, component, or form from the Designer window, the Properties window will display its corresponding properties. Figure 8.17 displays the properties of a Windows form that was selected in the Windows Forms Designer window.

The dropdown list at the beginning of the Properties window lets you choose different components, documents, or forms that are placed in the Designer window.

The Properties window can also be used to wire-up event handlers for the selected component. To edit an event handler, click on the yellow lightning-bolt-like button (shown in Figure 8.18) to get a list of all events supported by the selected component. To write an event handler, fill in the name of the method that will contain the event-handling code against the name of the event and press Enter. VS.NET will automatically wire-up the event and present the Code Editor window with the signature for the event-handling method.

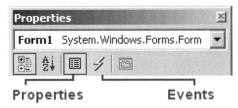

Figure 8.18: Properties and Events Buttons on the Properties Window

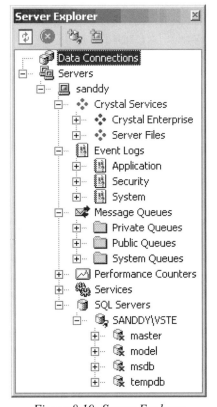

Figure 8.19: Server Explorer

Server Explorer

The Server Explorer has been extended from Visual Interdev's Server Object. It is a very powerful and useful tool for enterprise developers, providing one-stop access and management of all resources on your server, as well as other servers on the network. You can directly drag and drop resources to your project from the Server Explorer, and VS.NET does all the necessary plumbing for you to access the resource.

The Server Explorer fully integrates with SQL Server, letting you view, create, edit, and delete tables, data, stored procedures, triggers, functions, views, and database diagrams/relationships. From Server Explorer, you can also manage various other server resources, like event logs and MSMQ message queues without leaving the IDE.

Connect to a Server

In VS.NET, to add the resources of a new server, click on Connect to Server (the small computer with a plus sign) in the Solution Explorer. As shown in Figure 8.20, a dialog pops up asking you the path of the new server. If you have proper rights to access the server, the Server Explorer will connect to the specified server and add its resources.

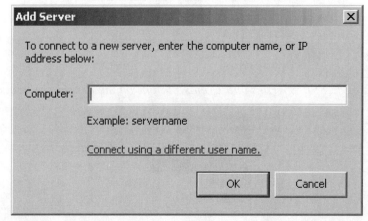

Figure 8.20: Connect to Server Dialog in the Server Explorer

Connect to a Database

If you want to use a database other than SQL Server in your VS.NET project, choose Connect to Database (the small yellow cylinder with a plus sign) in the Server Explorer to connect to the database. The Data Link Properties dialog that pops up (Figure 8.21) allows you to choose the database and the provider. Once you add the data connection, you can directly drop tables into your project from the Server Explorer, and VS.NET will create all necessary plumbing to connect to the database.

Data Link Properties

Provider | Connection | Advanced | All

Specify the following to connect to Oracle data:

1. Enter a server name:

2. Enter information to log on to the database:

User name:

Password:

☐ Blank password   ☐ Allow saving password

Test Connection

OK   Cancel   Help

Figure 8.21: Connect to Database Dialog

Solution Explorer

In VS.NET all projects and resources needed to build an application are grouped as solutions. While projects are the actual building blocks of an application, solutions are logical heads and can contain one or more projects or miscellaneous files. You can manage solutions and projects from the Solution Explorer, shown in Figure 8.22.

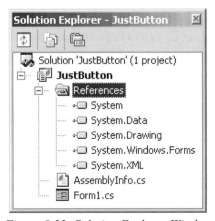

Solution Explorer - JustButton

Solution 'JustButton' (1 project)
- JustButton
  - References
    - System
    - System.Data
    - System.Drawing
    - System.Windows.Forms
    - System.XML
  - AssemblyInfo.cs
  - Form1.cs

Figure 8.22: Solution Explorer Window

Add Projects and Items

To add new projects to your solution, right-click the solution in the Solution Explorer and from the context menu choose Add→New Project/Existing Project, as shown in Figure 8.23. If you want to open a project from Visual Source Safe (VSS) choose File→Source Control→Open Project.

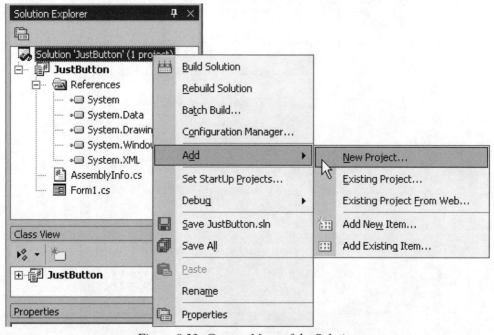

Figure 8.23: Context Menu of the Solution

Set as Startup Project

When you have multiple projects in your solution, you need to set one main project as the startup project. Every time you compile and run your solution, the application in the startup project will execute first. Generally you should make the main executable file the startup project.

To make a project the startup project, either right-click the Solutions tab in Solution Explorer and select Set as Startup Project or right-click the project and select Set as Startup Project. If you have multiple startup projects in your solution, you can modify the solution properties to specify the projects that will act as startup projects. To edit a solution's properties, right-click the solution in the Solution Explorer and choose select Properties from the context menu.

Solution Properties

The Solution Properties dialog, shown in Figure 8.24, allows you to set the dependencies of your project and the order of compilation—when you have multiple dependant projects in your solution. You can also configure the various compilation options for your projects.

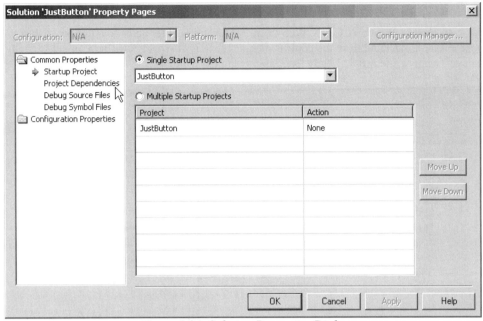

Figure 8.24: Solution Properties Dialog

Project Properties

Project properties can be accessed by right-clicking the target project in the Solution Explorer and selecting Properties. The Project Properties dialog helps you define your application's namespace, assembly name, and output file name, as shown in Figure 8.25. Also you can set various compiler options, like incremental build and optimize code, and set the output path to be used while building your project from VS.NET.

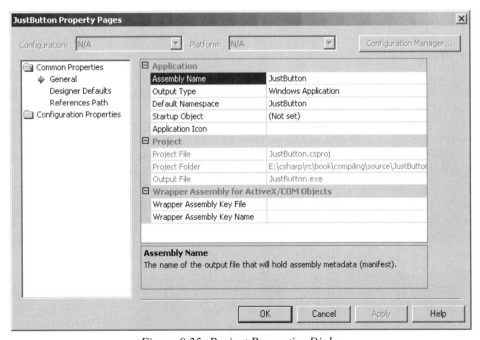

Figure 8.25: Project Properties Dialog

Add New Items to a Project

To add new classes, Windows forms, Web forms, and various other items to a project, right-click the appropriate project and from the context menu choose Add→Add New Item, or select the type of item you want to add if it's already listed in the context menu, as shown in Figure 8.26.

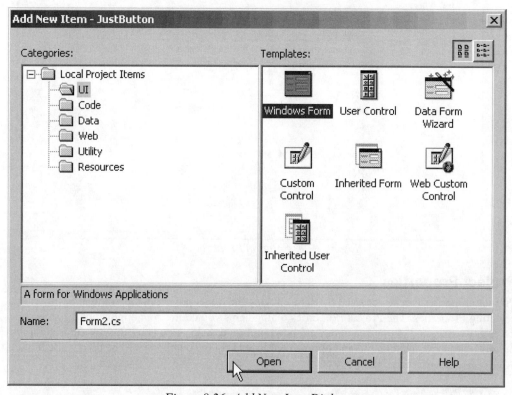

Figure 8.26: Add New Item Dialog

Add References

If you are using classes or namespaces not defined in your project, you need to reference the appropriate assemblies containing the metadata for those referenced classes. The References tab in Solution Explorer displays the list of assemblies that the project is currently referencing. When you create a new project, VS.NET automatically adds a few references to assemblies, like system.dll, system.xml.dll, and so on. To add references to other assemblies, right-click the References tab in Solution Explorer and choose Add References from the context menu. The Add Reference dialog, shown in Figure 8.27, allows you to choose the necessary assemblies to reference.

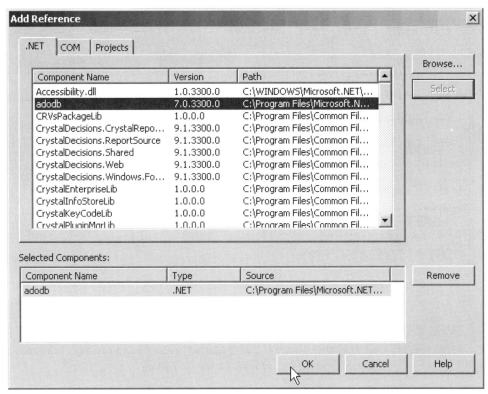

Figure 8.27: Add Reference Dialog

The Add Reference dialog allows you to add references to standard assemblies, COM objects, ActiveX controls, and assemblies contained in other projects in the same solution, or to browse and select a DLL library file containing the assembly.

Add Web Reference

If you are creating a client application that consumes a Web service, you have to add a Web reference to the Web service so that VS.NET can create the necessary plumbing. To add a Web reference, right-click the Project tab and select Add Web Reference from the context menu. The Add Web Reference dialog, shown in Figure 8.28, allows you to browse and find the Web service you require to consume in your client application. The dialog's right pane allows you to view the Web service's contract and documentation. You can also directly query the Microsoft UDDI (Universal Description, Discovery, and Integration) directory for Web services.

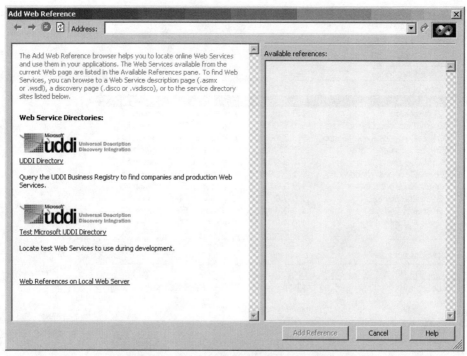

Figure 8.28: Add Web Reference Dialog

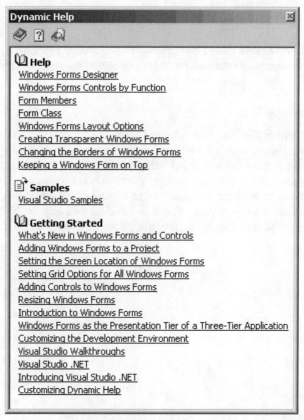

Figure 8.29: Dynamic Help Window

Dynamic Help Window

One new window added in VS.NET is Dynamic Help. As its name suggests, the Dynamic Help window updates its contents dynamically as you work on different parts of a project to provide context-sensitive help. The Dynamic Help window is very intelligent, updating itself with topics relating to the code you are writing. Figure 8.29 shows the Dynamic Help window when a Windows form is in focus in the Designer Window.

Class View Window

The Class View window allows you to view classes, enums, structs, methods, fields, and properties in the current project. The window also allows you to add new classes, methods, fields, properties, and indexers. As shown in Figure 8.30, to add a new class member, right-click the class entry and from the context menu select Add→Add Method/Add Field/Add Property/Add Indexer.

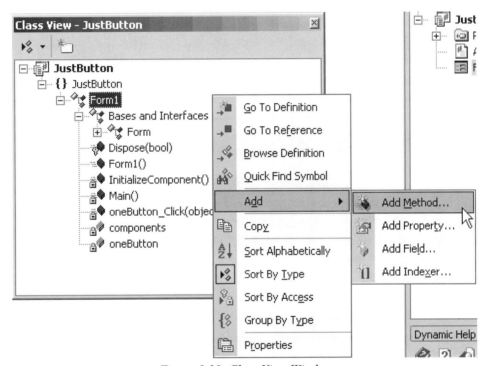

Figure 8.30: Class View Window

Output Window

VS.NET uses the Output window to display various status updates, such as a project's compilation success or error. Figure 8.31 shows a project's success on compilation, giving information about the project's build type (debug below), errors, and warnings. When you have multiple projects in your solution, you'll need to select the appropriate project from the Output window's dropdown list.

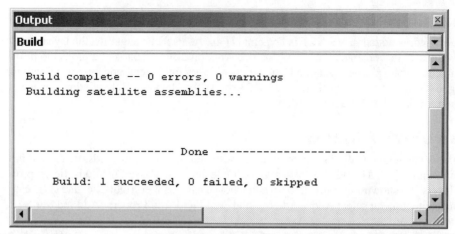

Figure 8.31: Output Window

Task List Window

You can use the Task List window to view and enter tasks for your project. The Task List in Figure 8.32 shows a few sample tasks. The first task was added automatically because of a compilation error.

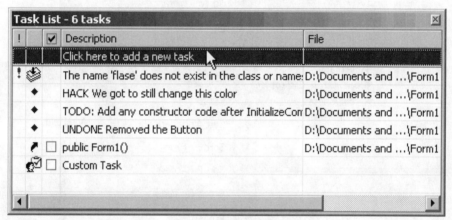

Figure 8.32: Task List Window

Double-clicking on any task will take you to the location in the Code Editor where the error occurred or where you have placed a comment or shortcut.

The next three tasks in Figure 8.32 were automatically added due to custom comments in the source code followed by the keywords TODO, HACK, or UNDONE (case is important), for example:

```
// HACK We have to still change this color
```

```
// TODO: Add any constructor code after InitializeComponent call
```

```
// UNDONE Removed the Button
```

You can also add bookmarks to your code by going to Edit→Bookmarks→Add Task List. The fifth task in Figure 8.32 is a task list shortcut to the Form1 Constructor.

Finally, the last task in Figure 8.32 is a custom user task. The solution stores separate tasks for each user. Task lists have lately gained popularity among developers because of the convenience they provide in collaboration by multiple developers.

Command Window

The Command window can be used to enter special VS.NET commands that help you execute various tasks in the IDE without going through the menus. The Command window also has IntelliSense: if you just type a character after the command prompt (>), you'll see a list of commands beginning with that character. Figure 8.33 shows the Command window, with a context menu showing all the commands that start with the word *Database* (To Bring up the Command window, go to View→Other Windows→Command Window or type Ctrl+Alt+A).

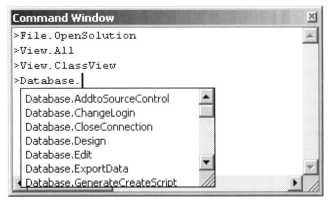

Figure 8.33: Command Window

Object Browser

The Object Browser offers viewing capabilities similar to those of the Class View window. The main difference is that the Object Browser's scope is wider, letting you view any assembly's namespaces, classes, enums, structs, methods, fields, properties, and indexers—details you may not know about.

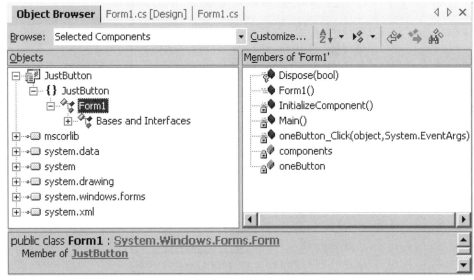

Figure 8.34: Object Browser

The Object Browser window is divided into three parts: The left pane gives access to namespaces and classes. The right pane shows the various namespaces and classes contained in the item selected in the left pane. The bottom pane provides a summary for the item selected in the left pane.

Figure 8.34 shows the JustButton project, along with many other assemblies. The right pane shows the properties, fields, and methods of the Form1 class. The bottom pane displays information about Form1 class.

Menus

VS.NET has various menus listing available commands. Some are fixed and contain commonly accessed commands, while others are context-sensitive and appear only in relevant cases. We will describe a few commonly used menus next.

File Menu

The File menu offers common commands for opening and creating new projects, files, and solutions. The Recent Files and Recent Projects submenus—a feature of Microsoft Office 2000—give you direct links to the files and projects you've most recently worked in. If you are using Source Control (which is not bundled with the current version of VS.NET), the Source Control submenu lets you can share your source code. Figure 8.35 shows the File menu in the IDE.

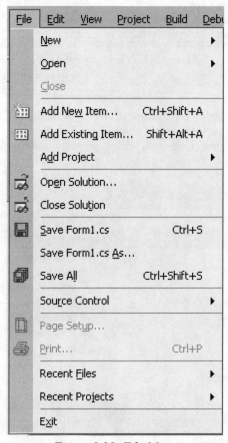

Figure 8.35: File Menu

Edit Menu

Besides the standard Cut, Copy, and Paste commands, the Edit menu includes some other useful commands. For example, commands under the Find and Replace submenu let you find or replace text—even in multiple files across multiple projects in the same solution. The Advanced submenu offers formatting commands—such as Tabify Selection, Untabify Selection, Make Uppercase, Make Lower Case—and other commands like Bookmarks, Outlining, and IntelliSense. Figure 8.36 shows the Edit menu and its corresponding items.

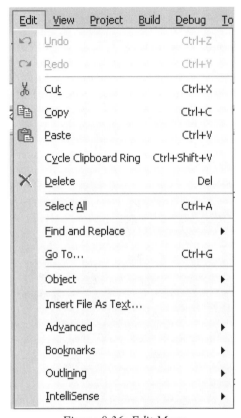

Figure 8.36: Edit Menu

View Menu

The View menu lets you show or hide various windows and toolbars, offering a huge list of toolbars (Figure 8.37) that you can view and customize. Two interesting new features are the Navigate Backward and Navigate Forward commands, letting you move through all windows you have visited in VS.NET. These commands also let you navigate through various portions of code you have visited in the Code Editor.

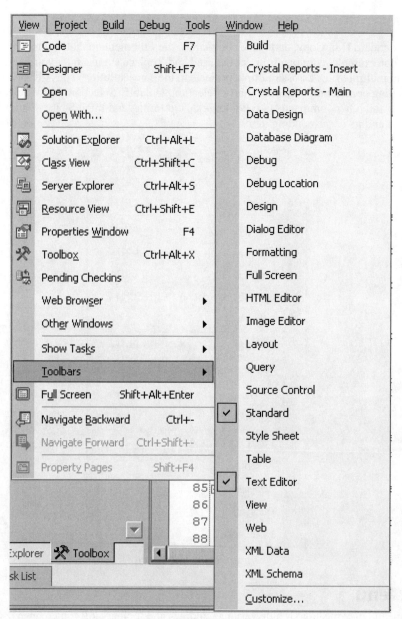

Figure 8.37: View Menu

Project Menu

The Project menu contains all commands relating to Projects and Solutions. Most commands listed here are also available in the context menu of Solution Explorer. Use the Add Reference and Add Web Reference commands to add references to your project's assemblies and Web Services. The Show All Files command shows all hidden files and folders in your solution. Figure 8.38 shows the Project menu with many of its useful features.

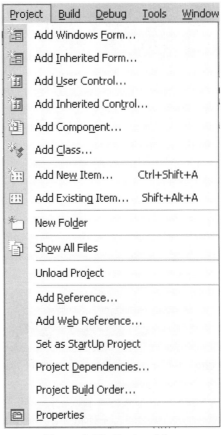

Figure 8.38: Project Menu

You can use the Unload Project command when you want to exclude a project while compiling your solution. This option is available only when you've selected the project in Solution Explorer.

The Project Dependencies command lets you set the build order used in compiling your solution. This option is available, of course, only when your solution has multiple projects. Figure 8.39 shows the Project Dependencies dialog, where we want to establish a dependency between two sample projects: JustButton and OnlyButton. To make JustButton depend upon OnlyButton, select the checkbox next to OnlyButton. Now during the solution's compilation, OnlyButton will compile first, followed by JustButton.

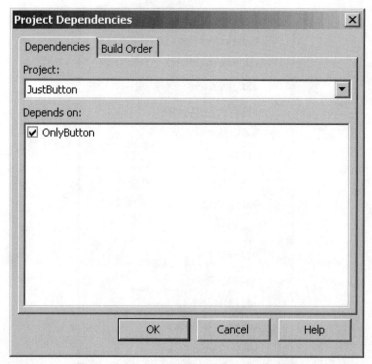

Figure 8.39: Project Dependencies Dialog

Build Menu

The Build menu, shown in Figure 8.40, contains commands used to build, or compile, a project or solution. This menu's contents change depending upon the number of projects in the solution and the project currently selected in Solution Explorer. Some commonly used tasks in this menu are described below.

This Build command performs a normal build on all projects and components in a solution. The Rebuild command first cleans all output windows, then logs and rebuilds all projects and components in a solution.

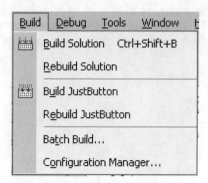

Figure 8.40: Build Menu

The Configuration Manager command gives you access to the Build Configuration dialog. In VS.NET every project by default has two build options: debug and release. The debug option generates additional debugging symbols used to debug the project during development. The release option generates code optimized for size and speed that should be used for final distribution to your clients.

In addition to debug and release, Configuration Manager lets you define your own build options. To customize settings for a build option, right-click the project in Solution Explorer and select Properties. In the Project Properties dialog you can customize compiler options used while building your project.

In Figure 8.41 we have defined a new build called myBuild using the <New…> option in the Active Solution Configuration. Figure 8.42 shows the Project Properties dialog, accessible from the Solution Explorer. Under the Configuration Properties heading, we have customized the myBuild build option. Our changes—like that to Optimize code—are displayed in boldface in the adjoining display panel. Now when we build the solution using the myBuild option, our custom compiler options will be used instead of the default compiler options.

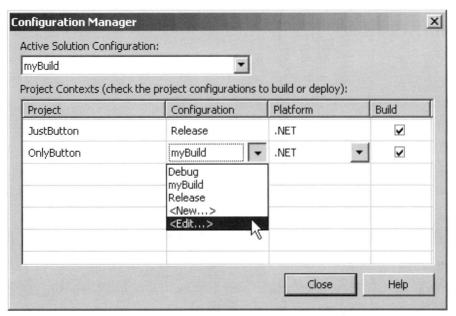

Figure 8.41: Configuration Manager Dialog

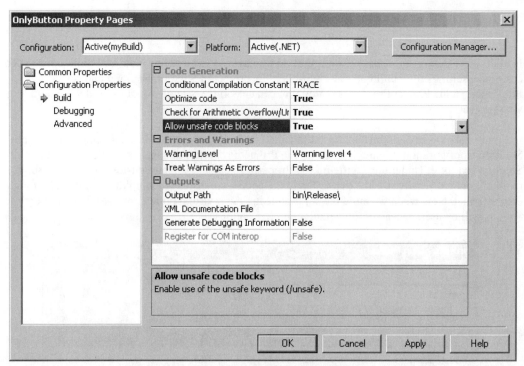

Figure 8.42: Project Properties Dialog

Use the Batch Build command from the Build menu to build multiple project build configurations. The Batch Build dialog lets you select the various builds to occur prior to the project build. Figure 8.43 shows the list of all customized build options for two projects in our solution.

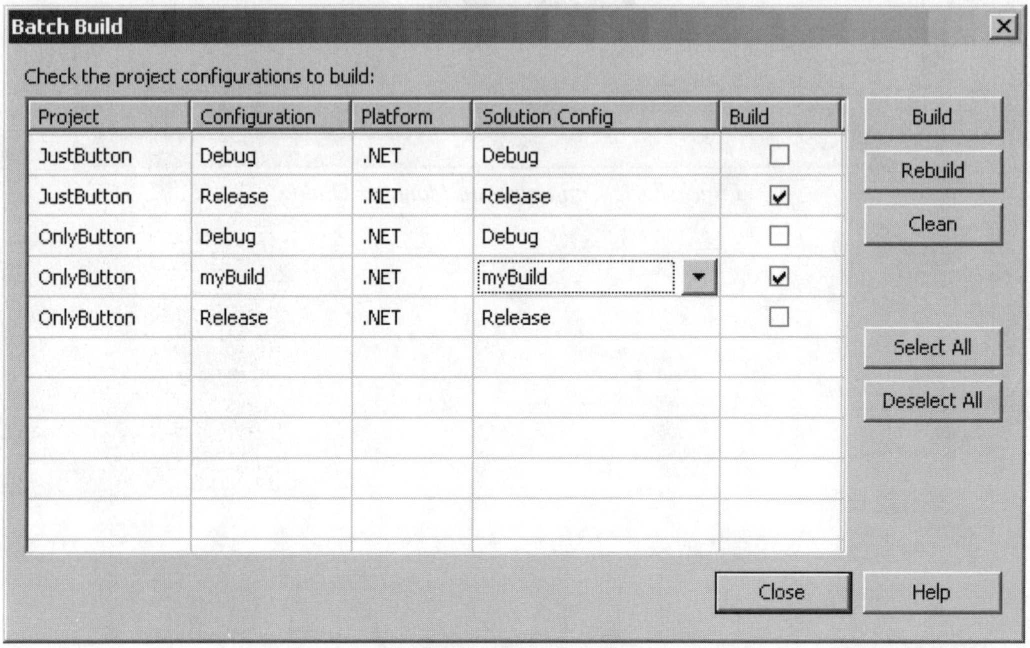

Figure 8.43: Batch Build Dialog

Debug Menu

From the Debug menu, shown in Figure 8.44, you can run and debug an application. The Start command starts a solution in debug mode, while the Start Without Debugging command starts a solution without debugging. The Step Into command steps inside methods when they are called, while the Step Over command steps over a method while debugging, not showing the method's internal steps. The Processes command debugs an application or process that is either currently running on your computer or running remotely.

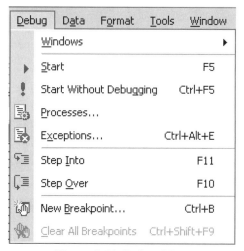

Figure 8.44: Debug Menu

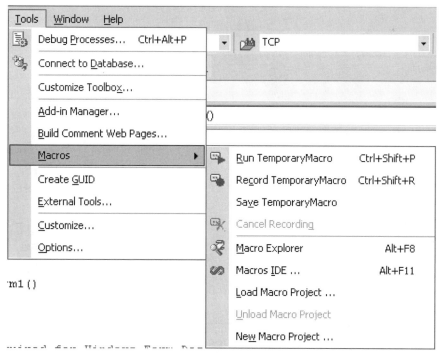

Figure 8.45: Tools Menu

Tools Menu

The Tools menu, shown in Figure 8.45, contains utility commands and commands for modifying the Toolbox window. The Connect to Database and Connect to Server commands are similar to those in Server Explorer. The Customize Toolbox command customizes the various tools available in the Toolbox window. The Add-in Manager command displays a list of registered VS.NET add-in controls. VS.NET has an extensive programming model that allows you to write tools that plug into the VS.NET interface. For example, Microsoft has an add-in called CodeSwap that allows developers to share or search for code snips from within VS.NET.

The Build Comment Web Pages command automatically generates a series of styled HTML files from the XML comments included in your C# code—letting you generate documentation for your code on the fly. Figure 8.46 shows the comments page generated for the JustButton Windows forms application.

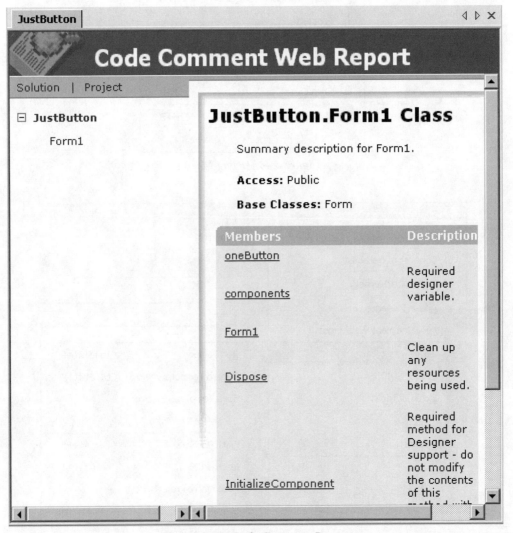

Figure 8.46: Code Comment Report

Macros are small programs you can write to automate certain tasks. The Macros submenu has commands that let you add, edit, and delete macros. The Macro Explorer provides access to all sample and user-written macros. At present, you can write macros only in Visual Basic .NET. Figure 8.47 shows the Macro Explorer with the Samples tab expanded.

Figure 8.47: Macro Explorer

The External Tools command is used to manage the list of external tools. The Customize command is used to customize toolbars. You can also make your own toolbar containing custom commands.

The Options command provides one-stop access to all customization options in VS.NET. From the Options dialog, you can customize everything from the colors used by the code editor to the style and behavior of windows.

The Options dialog is divided into two parts: the navigation tree view to the left and the page display view to the right. In the tree view, different setting options are grouped under different heads. Clicking on a subhead displays the properties for that subhead in the page display view on the right. Figure 8.48 displays the settings for Server Explorer.

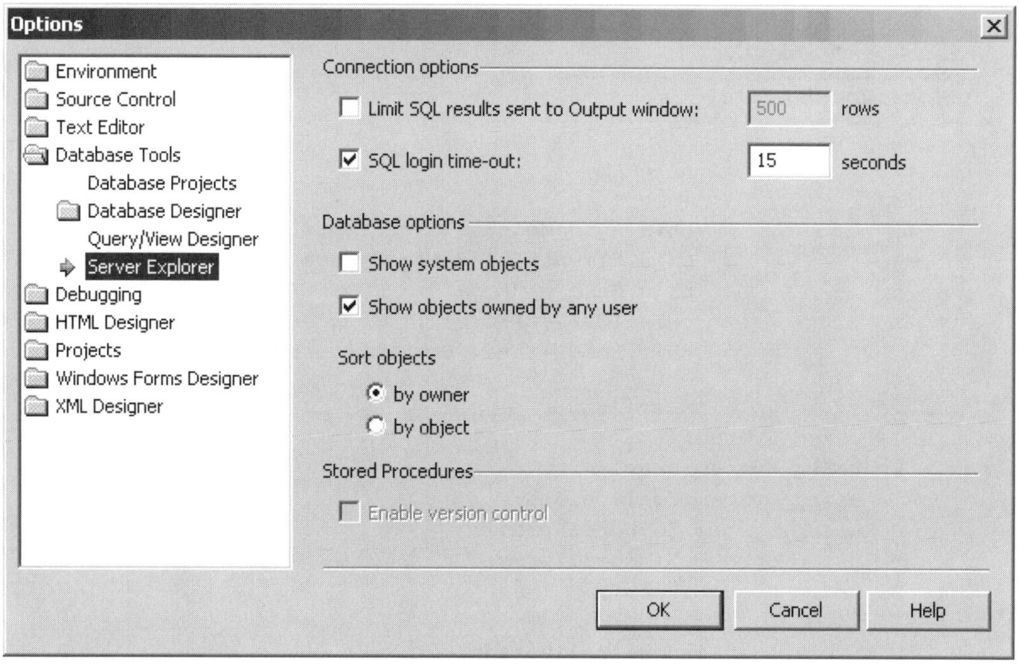

Figure 8.48: Options Dialog

Window Menu

The Window menu, shown in Figure 8.49, provides various commands for displaying windows. It also lists all open windows. The New Horizontal Tab Group and New Vertical Tab Group commands help you divide the main editor window into horizontal or vertical tabs for easier access to multiple windows.

Figure 8.49: Window Menu

```
Form1.cs [Design]  Form1.cs                                        ◁ ▷ ✕
WindowsApplication1.Form1              ▼   InitializeComponent()       ▼
    60            //
    61            // Form1
    62            //
    63            this.AutoScaleBaseSize = new System.Drawing.Si
    64            this.ClientSize = new System.Drawing.Size(292,
    65            this.Name = "Form1";
    66            this.Text = "Form1";
    67            this.Load += new System.EventHandler(this.pop)
    68
    1  using System;
    2  using System.Drawing;
    3  using System.Collections;
    4  using System.ComponentModel;
    5  using System.Windows.Forms;
    6  using System.Data;
    7
    8  namespace WindowsApplication1
    9  {
   10        //HACK We got to still change this color
```

Figure 8.50: Split Code Editor Window

One very useful command is the Split command, which splits a single Code Editor window into two horizontal windows. You can edit in either window, and the change is reflected in the other. This feature is very useful if you are working with two different methods from the same file at the same time. Figure 8.50 shows the Code Editor window split into two editors.

Help Menu

The Help menu, shown in Figure 8.51, provides links for help from Visual Studio Help or from the Web, including links to the Microsoft Web Site for customer feedback and technical support. The Check for Updates command identifies and installs new service packs and updates for VS.NET.

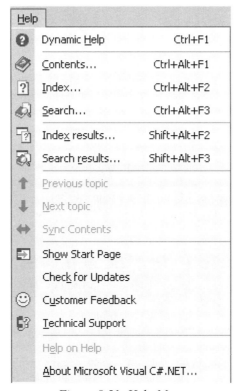

Figure 8.51: Help Menu

Customizing the IDE

We have already covered some customization options. We'll now summarize those options and then discuss a few other ways to customize the VS.NET IDE.

My Profile

The My Profile option is available from the VS.NET home page, which can be displayed from Help Menu→Show Start Page. My Profile allows you to customize the IDE's default behavior for such things as placement of windows and keyboard shortcuts. This is helpful for people migrating from earlier versions of Visual Studio, allowing them to continue using previous shortcuts and windows placements.

Help Filter

VS.NET has the ability to provide filtered help, displaying more accurate and relevant results. For example, you can filter help to display topics relating to only a particular language from the VS.NET Start Page. You can further modify each filter from the Edit Filter window, which is accessed from Help Menu→Edit Filters.

Tabbed and Auto-Hide Windows

All VS.NET windows, including the Code Editor and designer windows, are tabbed for easier access. You can drag and dock all windows to any location within the IDE. You can group multiple windows together to save space. Also, the new auto-hide feature lets you save space by hiding the window until you bring the cursor near it.

Toolbars

VS.NET is packed with toolbars. You can customize these toolbars or create your own from the Customize dialog, which can be accessed from Tools Menu→Customize. You can drag toolbars to a new location or leave them floating.

Options Dialog

In VS.NET you can do most customizations from the Options dialog, which is accessed from Tools Menu→Options. Among the many customizations are changing the color of the Code Editor, changing the behavior of the tabbed Main Editor window to MDI, and enabling line numbering in the code editor. If you are going to be working in VS.NET for a long time, it's a good idea to take a few moments to go through the various customization options available in the IDE.

Overview of Various Projects in VS.NET

VS.NET provides various ready-made templates to help you develop the different types of applications and libraries available in .NET. These templates write the basic framework code for you so that you can directly begin to develop your project. You can start a project using these templates from File Menu→New→Project. The New Project dialog, shown in Figure 8.52, lets you choose the type of project you want to build. In this dialog, you can select a template from a Project Types panel and enter the project name. You can also choose the location of the project directory. Clicking OK generates the code and puts you in the most logical design window for that particular project.

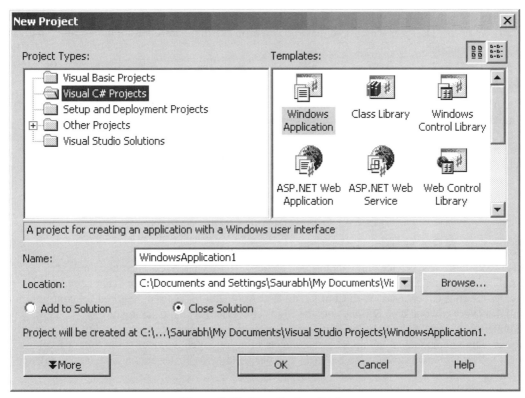

Figure 8.52: New Project Dialog

Visual C# Projects

Templates for building different kinds of applications in C# are grouped under the Visual C# Projects tab. There are 11 templates under this group to help you start the various kinds of projects.

1. Windows Application

The Windows Application template allows you to develop a Windows form. Choosing this template generates the initial Windows form application classes and brings up a Windows form in the Windows Forms Designer window. You can drag and drop components directly from the Toolbox window onto the Windows Forms Designer window to build your Windows form application. By default, VS.NET creates a project named WindowsApplication1 and a file named Form1.cs. The file contains a class Form1, which extends the System.Windows.Forms.Form class. Windows forms creation is covered in more detail in Chapter 9.

2. Class Library

The Class Library template should be used when you want to develop libraries (DLLs). The template creates a Class1.cs file under the ClassLibrary1 project. The Class1 class just contains an empty constructor.

3. Windows Control Library

The Windows Control Library template enables you to create your own custom Windows forms controls and compile them into a library (DLL). If you want to create your own controls, such as buttons and datagrids, then this template is for you. When you utilize this template, the Control1.cs file is created under the project WindowsControl1. The Control1.cs file contains the Control1 class, which extends the System.Windows.Forms.UserControl class. The control is also shown in the Windows Forms Designer window so that you can drop existing controls from the Toolbox to create your own composite control.

4. ASP.NET Web Application

The ASP.NET Web Application template is used to create ASP.NET Web applications. This template automatically creates the necessary virtual directory in the path given. It also creates the files Global.asax, Web.Config, and WebApplication1.vsdisco, required for configuration and discovery of your Web application, along with the file WebForm1.aspx. Clicking on the WebForm1.aspx file in the Solution Explorer opens up the Web Form Designer window, which allows you to create Web applications in a WYSIWYG interface. The Toolbox tabs also change accordingly to provide you with a rich set of Web controls. To access the CodeBehind file for the Web form, press the F7 key. ASP.NET is covered in Chapters 11 and 12.

5. ASP.NET Web Service

The ASP.NET Web Service template lets you create XML Web services. Just like the Web Application template, this template also creates the necessary virtual directory. The template also creates the files Global.asax, Web.Config, and WebApplication1.vsdisco, required for configuration and discovery of your Web Service, and the file WebService1.asmx. Clicking on WebService1.asmx in the Solution Explorer opens up the Web Service Designer. For functionality, you can drag components—such as database access for your Web Service—from Server Explorer or the Toolbox window into the Web Service Designer window. Web services are covered in greater detail in Chapter 13.

6. Web Control Library

The Web Control Library template lets you build your own ASP.NET Web control library. The template creates the WebControl1.cs file, containing the WebControl1 class, under the project WebControl1. The WebControl1 class extends the System.Web.UI.WebControls.WebControl class. This class contains the necessary attributes and methods so that you can create your own ASP.NET Web control.

7. Console Application

The Console Application template creates a console application—one that executes in the Console window. By default, it creates a project named ConsoleApplication1 and a file named Class1.cs. The Class1.cs file contains the Class1 class with an empty constructor and main method.

8. Windows Service

The Windows Service template is used to create an application as a Windows service that runs on Windows NT, Windows 2000, and Windows XP. It creates the file WinService1.cs under the project WindowsService1. The file contains the class WinService1, which extends the System.ServiceProcess.ServiceBase class. The WinService1 class also overrides the OnStart and OnStop methods. The template also opens up in design view so that you can directly drop components from the Server Explorer or the Toolbox. Chapter 17 covers creating Windows service in more detail.

9. Empty Project

The Empty Project template creates an empty project file. You can later add new or existing items to the project from Project Menu→Add New Item/Add Existing Item.

10. Empty Web Project

The Empty Web Project template creates an empty virtual directory and project file. You can later add new or existing items to your project from Project Menu→Add New Item/Add Existing Item.

11. New Project in Existing Folder

Use the New Project in Existing Folder template to create multiple projects that operate from the same directory. This template will be useful in cases when you want to host multiple Web applications in the same Web folder. It is also useful for situations where you have created several library assembly projects that depend upon a main startup application.

Summary

Visual Studio .NET is the latest version of Microsoft's Visual Studio suite. Integration is the key tenant of this IDE, and all the tools you require for developing applications on the .NET platform have been packed into a single IDE, making VS.NET a very powerful tool and currently the optimal tool for .NET programming. The extensive customization capabilities help you adopt the IDE according to your personal preferences. Getting yourself familiar with the VS.NET IDE will help you in the following chapters, where you will learn to build applications using VS.NET.

Chapter 9:
Windows Programming

In this chapter, you will learn the basics of the Windows Forms platform and how to write Windows applications using Windows forms and controls. The space allocated to this chapter prevents an exploration of every control in the System.Windows.Forms namespace, but the following key topics are discussed and should provide the reader an ample grounding with which to tackle any orphaned controls:

- Windows Forms and the advantages of using forms
- Developing Windows applications using Windows Forms
- The basics of the System.Windows.Forms namespace and its classes such as Form, Control, and other control classes
- Working with menus, toolbars, ToolTips, and status bars
- Working with dialog boxes
- Working with common dialog classes

Windows Forms

Windows Forms is a framework located in the System.Windows.Forms.dll assembly for building Windows applications in .NET based on a graphical user interface (GUI). Any language that supports the common language runtime (CLR) can use Windows Forms.

Why Windows Forms?

If you have programmed in Visual Basic (VB), you are probably familiar with forms. In VB, all windows are forms. Controls are placed on forms to develop GUI applications. Visual C++ developers will more likely be familiar with windows and dialogs rather than forms (CWnd and CDialog in Microsoft Foundation Classes [MFC]).

The Microsoft .NET Framework is designed to remedy this "forms versus windows" situation. All windows are forms, including dialog boxes. From all of this synergy, Microsoft coined the term *Windows form*. Now developers using any .NET-supported language have access to the same windowing classes, whether they work with C#, VB, C++, or any other .NET-compliant language. This *language independence* has been extended to support many more languages, including Cobol.

In addition to the preceding, the main benefits of Windows Forms are its ease of use, the standardization of the control hierarchy, and that it allows for rapid application development (RAD). Changing the colors and fonts of controls using MFC or Win32 can be a real headache. The .NET Framework has taken care of most such problems and inconveniences.

In addition, Windows Forms applications provide the following:

- Simple and flexible property support, modeled after VB

- Common control support, including support for font and color dialogs
- Support for Web Services
- Data-aware controls using ADO.NET
- ActiveX support
- GDI+ (Graphical Device Interface +), a better and richer graphics library, which supports alpha blending, texture brushes, advanced transformations, and rich text
- Metadata support

Writing Your First Windows Application

Most readers of this book are developers desiring to master C# in a Visual Studio .NET (VS.NET) environment, but VS.NET is not a mandatory tool. A Windows Forms application, indeed all applications, may be developed without using Visual Studio's integrated development environment (IDE). Simply use any text editor to write your code and save the file with a .cs extension. It may then be compiled from the command line, as discussed in Chapter 3. In this section we discuss how to write Windows Forms applications without VS.NET.

Our first Windows application is a simple one that creates a window. To create a Windows-based application, you derive a class from System.Windows.Forms.Form and call the default constructor, as illustrated in Listing 9.1. The Form class acts as a container for other controls.

Listing 9.1—First Console Windows Application

```
using System;
using System.Windows.Forms;

// Derive your class from the System.Windows.Forms.Form class
public class WinForm : Form
{
    public WinForm()
    {
    }

    static void Main(string[] args)
    {
        // Create a Form object
        WinForm myFrm = new WinForm();

         // Set the window title
        myFrm.Text = "My First Windows Application";

         // Pass form object
        Application.Run(myFrm);
    }
}
```

The window's title is set by the form's Text property. The static method Application.Run creates a standard message loop on the current thread. The program, as Figure 9.1 illustrates, creates an empty form with the title "My First Windows Application" in the caption bar.

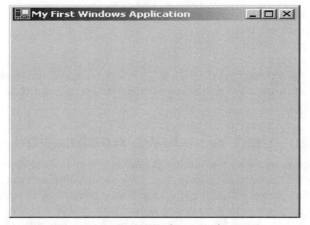

Figure 9.1: First Windows Application

In the Listing1-9App project you will find a file, compile.bat, that creates a Windows application, WinApp1.exe, from the following command line:

```
csc /target:exe /out:WinApp1.exe /reference:System.dll
/reference:System.Windows.Forms.dll class1.cs
```

As the command line now stands, a console window will appear prior to the GUI window. The reason lies in the "/target:" compiler option, which specifies a console application with the exe string. To display only the GUI window, change the option from exe to winexe. Also be aware that the /target: option can be abbreviated to /t:, as can the /reference option to /r:. To change the name of the executable program, simply change the name linked to the /out: compiler option.

The code in Listing 9.2 adds a button and a text box to the form and creates an event handler for the button. When a user clicks the button, an event is triggered that writes a string to the text box. A reference to the System.Windows.Forms.dll and System.Drawing.dll namespaces must be added before compiling the project.

As can be seen in Listing 9.2, we create a WinForm class derived from the Form class. After that, we create the Button and TextBox controls. We then set the button and text box properties such as Name, Text, BackgroundColor, ForegroundColor, and Size. The call to the Form.Controls.AddRange method takes an array of controls as a parameter and adds them to the form as indicated in the following code:

```
myFrm.Controls.AddRange(new System.Windows.Forms.Control[] {myFrm.textBox1,
myFrm.button1});
```

An event handler is also created for the Button control. The following code shows how to write a button click event handler for button1. The button1_Click method executes when the button is clicked.

```
myFrm.button1.Click += new System.EventHandler(myFrm.button1_Click);
```

Listing 9.2—Creating a Windows Application with Controls

```
using System;
using System.Windows.Forms;
using System.Drawing;

public class WinForm : Form
```

```
{
    private Button button1;
    private TextBox textBox1;
    public WinForm()
    {
    }

    static void Main(string[] args)
    {
    WinForm myFrm = new WinForm();

        // Create Button and TextBox objects
        myFrm.button1 = new System.Windows.Forms.Button();
        myFrm.textBox1 = new System.Windows.Forms.TextBox();

        // Setting the Button control Properties
        myFrm.button1.BackColor = System.Drawing.Color.Blue;
        myFrm.button1.ForeColor = System.Drawing.Color.Yellow;
        myFrm.button1.Location = new System.Drawing.Point(24, 40);
        myFrm.button1.Name = "button1";
        myFrm.button1.Size = new System.Drawing.Size(112, 32);
        myFrm.button1.TabIndex = 0;
        myFrm.button1.Text = "Click Me";

        // The button click event handler
        myFrm.button1.Click += new
                System.EventHandler(myFrm.button1_Click);

        // Setting the TextBox control Properties
        myFrm.textBox1.Location = new System.Drawing.Point(168, 48);
        myFrm.textBox1.Name = "textBox1";
        myFrm.textBox1.Size = new System.Drawing.Size(104, 20);
        myFrm.textBox1.TabIndex = 1;
        myFrm.textBox1.Text = "textBox1";

        // Setting the form Properties
        myFrm.AutoScaleBaseSize = new System.Drawing.Size(5, 13);
        myFrm.ClientSize = new System.Drawing.Size(292, 273);
        myFrm.Controls.AddRange(new System.Windows.Forms.Control[]
                {myFrm.textBox1, myFrm.button1});
        myFrm.Text = "My First Windows Application";
        myFrm.BackColor = Color.Red;
        myFrm.ForeColor = Color.Yellow;

        myFrm.ResumeLayout(false);
        Application.Run(myFrm);
    }

    // The button click event handler
    private void button1_Click(object sender, System.EventArgs e)
    {
        textBox1.Text = "Button is clicked";
    }
```

The result of compiling and running the code in Listing 9.2 appears in Figure 9.2, after the button has been clicked.

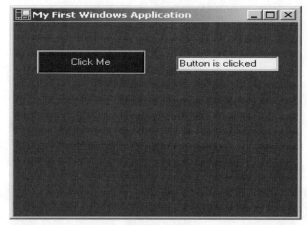

Figure 9.2: Creating a Windows Application with Controls

Creating a Windows Application in VS.NET

Now that you have seen how to create a Windows application from the command line, let's create a Windows application using the VS.NET wizard.

Creating a Skeleton of the Application

Select New→Project→Visual C# Projects→Windows Application from your VS .NET IDE (Figure 9.3).

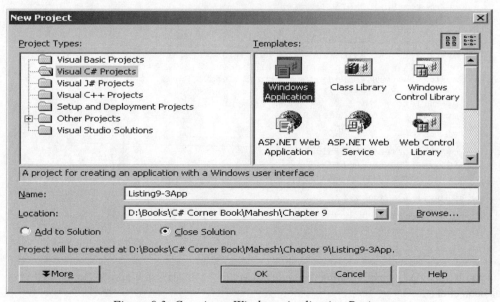

Figure 9.3: Creating a Windows Application Project

Press the OK button. The IDE takes you to the Design view of a form as in Figure 9.4.

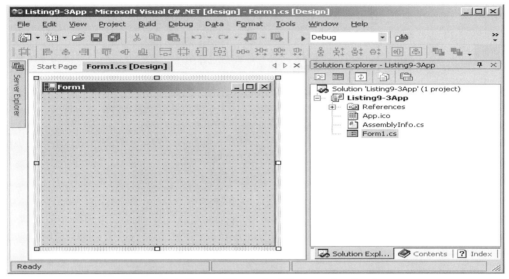

Figure 9.4: Design View of a Windows Application.

If the Solution Explorer is not visible, it can be opened from the View menu. The Solution Explorer (see Figure 9.5) provides a list of all available files in your project. The Form1.cs file contains the code for the form and its controls.

Figure 9.5: Available Classes in a Windows Application Project

To view the code added by the wizard, right-click on Form1.cs and select the View Code menu option as illustrated in Figure 9.6.

Figure 9.6: View Code Option

The code added by the wizard is discussed in the "Reviewing the Code" section.

Adding Controls

The next step is to add controls to the form. To open the toolbox, choose the View→ToolBox menu item as shown in Figure 9.7.

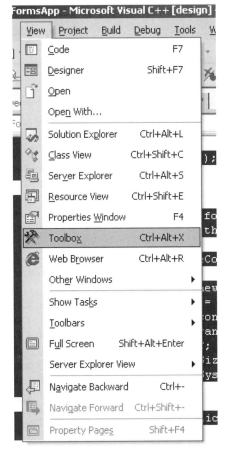

Figure 9.7: Toolbox Option

Figure 9.8: The Toolbox

The toolbox looks like that in Figure 9.8. To add controls to the form, drag a control from the toolbox onto the form and position it anywhere you want. Drag two Button controls and a TextBox, a Label, and a CheckBox control to the form and adjust them so that the form is similar to that shown in Figure 9.9.

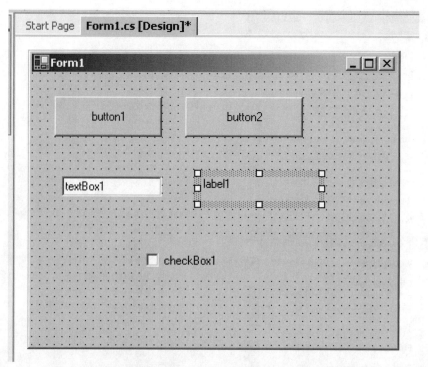

Figure 9.9: Controls on the form in design view

Set the properties of these controls by right-clicking the control and selecting the Properties menu option. The Properties window, shown in Figure 9.10, permits a developer to set design-time properties from within VS.NET. The property list varies, as would be expected, depending on the control type. The design-time values can be considered a control's default values, as they can be changed anytime during the program's execution. A property's value may be changed in two locations. If a value on the property page is altered, that change is reflected in the InitializeComponent method's code, and vice versa—a property's value modified in the code is mirrored on the property page by VS.NET.

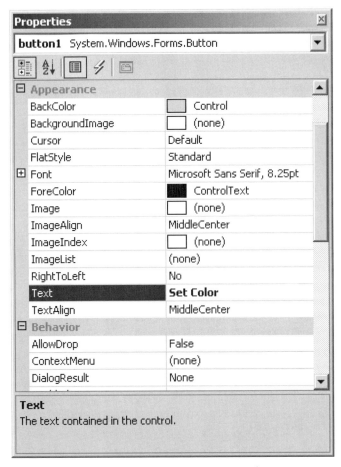

Figure 9.10: Properties Window

Set button1's Text property to *Set Color* and button2's property to *Set Font.*

Reviewing the Code

Now let's review the code that the Form Designer has written. You can view the code by right-clicking Form1.cs and choosing View Code. The code generated by the wizard appears in Listing 9.3. An instance of the form is created in the Main method as a parameter in the call to Application.Run().

<u>Listing 9.3—Code Added by the Wizard for the Windows Application</u>

```
using System;
using System.Drawing;
using System.Collections;
using System.ComponentModel;
using System.Windows.Forms;
using System.Data;

namespace Listing9_3App
{
  public class Form1 : System.Windows.Forms.Form
  {
    private System.Windows.Forms.Button button1;
    private System.Windows.Forms.Button button2;
    private System.Windows.Forms.TextBox textBox1;
```

```csharp
  private System.Windows.Forms.Label label1;
  private System.Windows.Forms.CheckBox checkBox1;
  private System.ComponentModel.Container components = null;

public Form1()
{
  InitializeComponent();
}

protected override void Dispose( bool disposing )
{
  if( disposing )
  {
    if (components != null)
    {
      components.Dispose();
    }
  }
  base.Dispose( disposing );
}

#region Windows Form Designer generated code
private void InitializeComponent()
{
  this.button1 = new System.Windows.Forms.Button();
  this.button2 = new System.Windows.Forms.Button();
  this.textBox1 = new System.Windows.Forms.TextBox();
  this.label1 = new System.Windows.Forms.Label();
  this.checkBox1 = new System.Windows.Forms.CheckBox();
  this.SuspendLayout();
  // button1
  this.button1.Location = new System.Drawing.Point(24, 24);
  this.button1.Name = "button1";
  this.button1.Size = new System.Drawing.Size(112, 40);
  this.button1.TabIndex = 0;
  this.button1.Text = "Set Color";
  // button2
  this.button2.Location = new System.Drawing.Point(160, 24);
  this.button2.Name = "button2";
  this.button2.Size = new System.Drawing.Size(120, 40);
  this.button2.TabIndex = 1;
  this.button2.Text = "Set Font";
  // textBox1
  this.textBox1.Location = new System.Drawing.Point(32, 104);
  this.textBox1.Name = "textBox1";
  this.textBox1.Size = new System.Drawing.Size(104, 20);
  this.textBox1.TabIndex = 2;
  this.textBox1.Text = "textBox1";
  // label1
  this.label1.Location = new System.Drawing.Point(176, 104);
  this.label1.Name = "label1";
  this.label1.Size = new System.Drawing.Size(120, 24);
  this.label1.TabIndex = 3;
  this.label1.Text = "label1";
  // checkBox1
  this.checkBox1.Location = new System.Drawing.Point(120, 168);
  this.checkBox1.Name = "checkBox1";
  this.checkBox1.Size = new System.Drawing.Size(176, 40);
  this.checkBox1.TabIndex = 4;
  this.checkBox1.Text = "checkBox1";
  // Form1
  this.AutoScaleBaseSize = new System.Drawing.Size(5, 13);
  this.ClientSize = new System.Drawing.Size(376, 273);
  this.Controls.AddRange(new System.Windows.Forms.Control[]
  { this.checkBox1, this.label1, this.textBox1,
            this.button2, this.button1});
  this.Name = "Form1";
```

```
      this.Text = "Form1";
      this.ResumeLayout(false);

    }
    #endregion

    [STAThread]
    static void Main()
    {
      Application.Run(new Form1());
    }
  }
}
```

The wizard creates a default namespace, Listing9_3App, that bears the same name as the project. It also adds references to various namespaces required by Windows Forms. Note that the Form1 class is derived from System.Windows.Forms.Form. The Dispose method performs any required cleanup of the resources and is called by the runtime when the application closes. The InitializeComponent method creates the Form and all its child controls. In Listing 9.3, the wizard sets the essential control properties and adds the controls to the form via the Controls.AddRange method.

The SuspendLayout and ResumeLayout methods, in the InitializeComponet method, should not be tampered with without a good reason. As the names imply, the methods suspend and resume a layout event, which is triggered whenever a child control must be repositioned or resized. If the layout events are not suspended during the initial window construction, the unnecessary number of events drastically slows the window's creation.

Adding an Event Handler

The last part of this tutorial involves adding an event handler for the Set Font and Set Color buttons. To create an event handler for a button, double-click the button. This generates the required code for a "click" event. Using this method for wiring up an event, the event handler method name will contain same name as the name of the button object. An alternative method is to use the control's Properties window and click the lightning bolt button as demonstrated in Figure 9.11.

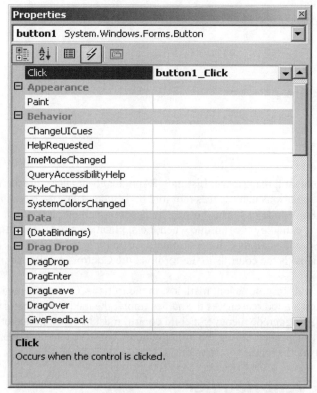

Figure 9.11: Adding an Event Handler for a Button

In Figure 9.11, the button1_Click method is the event handler for that button. If the control is deleted after creating an event handler, the handler method must be manually removed.

Next we create an event handler for button2. Listing 9.4 shows the button1 and button2 click event handlers' code. The button1_Click method uses the ColorDialog class to select a color and set the colors for all controls. The button2_Click method uses the FontDialog class to set the font of all the controls on the form.

Listing 9.4—Button Click Event Handler for Set Font and Set Color Buttons

```
private void button1_Click(object sender, System.EventArgs e)
{
    ColorDialog colorDlg = new ColorDialog();
    colorDlg.ShowDialog();
    textBox1.BackColor = colorDlg.Color;
    label1.BackColor = colorDlg.Color;
    checkBox1.BackColor = colorDlg.Color;
}

private void button2_Click(object sender, System.EventArgs e)
{
    FontDialog fntDlg = new FontDialog();
    fntDlg.ShowColor = true;
    if(fntDlg.ShowDialog() != DialogResult.Cancel )
    {
        textBox1.Font = fntDlg.Font ;
        textBox1.ForeColor = fntDlg.Color;
        label1.Font = fntDlg.Font ;
        label1.ForeColor = fntDlg.Color;
        checkBox1.Font = fntDlg.Font ;
```

```
        checkBox1.ForeColor = fntDlg.Color;
    }

}
```

Setting Properties at Runtime

We have just shown how to set a control's properties from the Properties window. You can also set the properties programmatically. For example, consider a button's color properties. The background and foreground colors of controls can be changed by using the BackColor and ForeColor properties. The same method for altering color applies to all control properties. They can be set both at design-time and runtime.

```
button1.BackColor = System.Drawing.Color.Blue;
```

The Font property of a control allows you to change the font of that control. The Font class of the System.Drawing namespace is used to create a new font. The following code demonstrates how to change the font of a button. Again, the same method for changing fonts applies to all controls.

```
button2.Font = new System.Drawing.Font ("Verdana", 10,
System.Drawing.FontStyle.Bold);
```

Building and Running the Project

To run the program press CTRL+F5 or click Start Without Debugging on the Debug menu as shown in Figure 9.12.

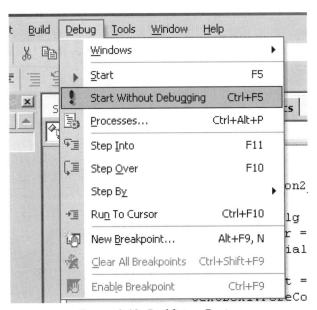

Figure 9.12: Building a Project

Now, run the project and click the Set Color and Set Font buttons. The Set Color button click sets the color of the controls, and the Set Font button sets the font of the controls. The Set Color button calls the ColorDialog class and lets you select a color, as you can see in Figure 9.13.

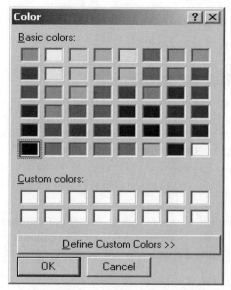

Figure 9.13: ColorDialog Dialog Box

The Set Font button event click calls the FontDialog class (see Figure 9.14) and allows the selection of a font as well as its color, style, and size.

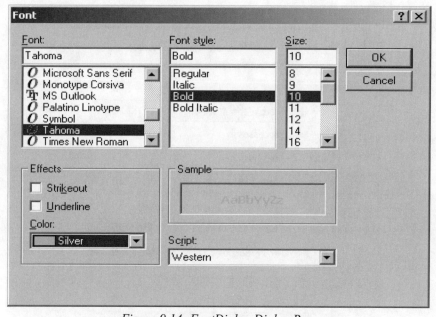

Figure 9.14: FontDialog Dialog Box

Figure 9.15 shows the application after the color and font have been set.

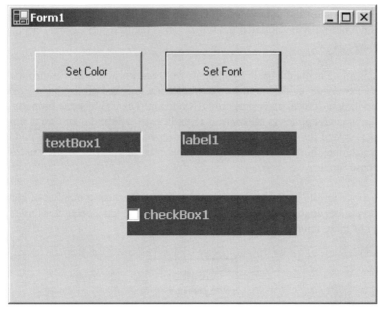

Figure 9.15: Windows Application Output After Setting Color and Font

The Windows.Forms Namespace: A Richer Library

Any application using Windows Forms relies on the System.Windows.Forms namespace, which contains more than 400 classes for windows, controls, and other objects. Table 9.1 describes some of the System.Windows.Forms namespace classes that we will explore..

Class	Description
Button, CheckBox, ComboBox, Label, ListBox, TextBox	Represent Windows controls according to their names. Each Windows control has a class corresponding to it.
Control	Implements the basic functionality for Windows controls. All control classes including the Form class are derived from the Control class.
FileDialog, FontDialog, ColorDialog, OpenFileDialog, SaveFileDialog, CommonDialog	Common dialog classes.
Form	Represents a window or dialog box.
ImageList	A control for a collection of images.
Menu, MainMenu, MenuItem, ContextMenu	Represents the menu functionality in Windows Forms.
MessageBox	A message box dialog.

Table 9.1: System.Windows.Forms Classes

Working with Controls

Consistency and adaptability are two often-undeclared but implicit software design goals. In an object-oriented world, a frequently employed mechanism to achieve these objectives is *inheritance*.

In the System.Windows.Forms namespace, all controls derive from the Control class. The raw Control class is not normally instantiated but rather forms the basis for further refining the user interface hierarchy.

The Control class implements the basic functionality of controls and, where appropriate, provides for members to be overridden. This approach promotes not only reusability but also standardization. This can be seen in two Control class properties, Name and Text. The Name property, the equivalent to a control ID in Win32, applies to all controls regardless of type and therefore is not declared "virtual," whereas a Text property implementation differs depending on the type and can be overridden. For example, Form.Text refers to the caption in the title bar, while TextBox.Text returns the user's keyboard input.

In addition to many controls directly deriving from the Control class, a number of classes act as intermediaries to collect controls into what loosely could be termed a behavioral unit. Figure 9.16 shows a number of these intermediate classes.

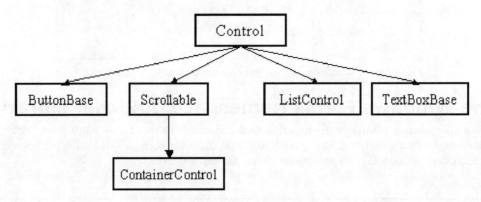

Figure 9.16: Intermediate Classes

The ButtonBase class, for instance, is the root of the Button, CheckBox, and RadioButton classes, which exhibit a similar behavior. The ButtonBase class handles common chores such as raising mouse and focus events. Other classes that use this method of control intercession will be pointed out as they arise.

Another gauge of consistency in the Windows.Forms namespace is its treatment of collections. While objects range from the general to the very specific, the means of accessing an object in a collection remains consistent throughout the namespace. Each collection in the namespace has an indexer, as well as identical methods to add and remove objects. The most commonly referenced collection is the nested Control.ControlCollection, accessible through the read-only property called Controls. This is a container for Control objects.

Some of the properties of the Control classes are defined in Table 9.2.

Property	Description
Text	The current text associated with a control or window.
ModifierKeys	Retrieves the current state of the modifier keys. Used to check the current state of the SHIFT, CTRL, and ALT keys.
MouseButtons	The current state of the mouse buttons such as left, right, and middle.
MousePosition	The current position of the mouse in screen coordinates.
Bottom, Top, Left, Right	Represents the bottom, top, left, and right coordinates of a control.
Bounds	Window coordinates of a control.
CanFocus, CanSelect	Indicate whether the control can receive focus or can be selected.
ClientRectangle, ClientSize	Represent the client rectangle and size of the client rectangle.
Controls	Represents a collection of child controls.
Enabled, Focused, Visible	Indicate whether the control is currently enabled, focused, or visible.
Handle	The HWND handle that this control is bound to. If the handle has not yet been created, this will force handle creation.
Height, Width	Represent the height and the width of a control.
Location	The location of the upper-left coordinate of a control with respect to the upper-left corner of its container.
Parent	The parent of a control.
Size	The size of a control.
TabIndex, TabStop	TabIndex is the tab index of a control. TabStop indicates whether the user can have the TAB key for this control.

Table 9.2: Control Class Properties

Some Control class methods are itemized in Table 9.3.

Method	Description
Focus	Sets focus to the control
Hide, Show	Hide and show the control by setting visible property
PointToScreen	Computes the location of the client point *p* in screen coordinates
PreProcessMessage	Called by the application's message loop to preprocess input messages before they are dispatched
RectangleToClient, RectangleToScreen	Location of the screen rectangle in client coordinates or screen coordinates
Refresh	Forces the control to invalidate and immediately repaint itself and any children
SetClientSizeCore	Sets the height and width of the client area of the control
Update	Forces the control to paint any currently invalid areas

Table 9.3: Control Class Methods

The Control class implements basic mouse and keyboard events, some of which are defined in Table 9.4.

Event	Description
Click, DoubleClick	Occur when the control is clicked and double-clicked
Enter	Occurs when the control is entered
GotFocus, LostFocus	Occur when the control receives or loses focus
KeyDown, KeyPress, KeyUp	Occur when a key is down, pressed, or up, accordingly
MouseDown, MouseEnter, MouseHover, MouseLeave, MouseMove, MouseUp, MouseWheel	Different mouse events that occur when the mouse button is down, the mouse enters the control, mouse is moved, mouse button is up, etc.
Move	Occurs when a control is moved
Resize	Occurs when a control is resized

Table 9.4: Control Class Events

Besides the methods defined in Table 9.4, there are overridable methods for raising events programmatically, such as OnClick, OnEnter, and OnKeyUp. When overriding any of these event-triggering methods, the base class's method *must* be called, so that any registered delegate receives the event.

Control Classes

Table 9.5 lists some of the common control classes.

Button	CheckBox	ComboBox	GroupBox	HscrollBar
ImageList	Label	LinkLabel	ListBox	ListView
Panel	PictureBox	ProgressBar	RadioButton	RichTextBox
Splitter	StatusBar	TabControl	TextBox	Timer
ToolBar	ToolTip	TrackBar	TreeView	VscrollBar

Table 9.5: Windows Forms Common Control Classes

As has been seen earlier, you can create these controls programmatically as well as from the VS.NET Form Designer. The Form Designer allows you to drag and drop controls from the toolbox onto a form. Here we will show you how to create a control manually and set its properties.

Creating a Control

Use a constructor to create an instance of a control. Most controls are constructed with a default constructor, that is, a constructor with no parameters. Here is an example of creating a Button control:

```
Button btn1 = new System.Windows.Forms.Button ();
```

Setting Properties

After creating the object, set the control's properties. The code in Listing 9.5 sets the button properties.

Listing 9.5—Setting the properties of a Button Control

```
btn1.ImageAlign = System.Drawing.ContentAlignment.TopLeft;
```

```
btn1.Dock = System.Windows.Forms.DockStyle.Left;
btn1.ForeColor = System.Drawing.Color.Red;
btn1.BackColor = System.Drawing.SystemColors.Desktop;
btn1.DialogResult = System.Windows.Forms.DialogResult.OK;
btn1.AllowDrop = true;
btn1.FlatStyle = System.Windows.Forms.FlatStyle.Flat;
btn1.Size = new System.Drawing.Size (336, 568);
btn1.TabIndex = 0;
btn1.Font = new System.Drawing.Font ("Verdana", 10, System.Drawing.FontStyle.Bold);
btn1.Text = "Click Me";
```

Once you have set the properties, you can write an event handler for the control. We discuss event handling in detail later in this chapter.

Understanding the Form Class

The main window of your Windows application is a form, derived from the ContainerControl class. A form is a representation of a window in .NET. You can use the Form class to create Single Document Interface (SDI), Multiple Document Interface (MDI), and dialog-based applications. The windows can be borderless, transparent, and floating. You can create an MDI form by setting the IsMDIContainer property to *true*. To make a form an MDI child, set the MdiParent property with a reference to the MDI container form. To display the child, the child form's Show method must be called or its Visible property set to *true*.

You can change the appearance, size, and color of a form by using the Properties window. You can use the Form class members to set properties or override event handler methods at runtime. The Form class contains properties and methods too numerous to completely itemize. Among the interesting ones are the following:

- *ControlBox.* A Boolean property that toggles the visibility of the minimize, maximize, and close buttons on the caption bar. The default value, *true,* displays the buttons. The buttons can be set individually, but only as to their being enabled or disabled.
- *KeyPreview.* A Boolean property that permits a form to intercept all keystrokes prior to the control that has focus. To implement this property, either a KeyPress, a KeyDown, or a KeyUp event handler must also be attached to the form. To prevent a text box from receiving the event, set the KeyXXXEventArgs.Handled property to *true.*
- *ShowInTaskbar.* A property that shows a window's caption bar text in the taskbar when set to *true.* The default value is *true.*
- *WndProc.* The .Net version of the Win32 default window procedure. The WndProc method has a Message structure as a parameter and returns *void.* A window procedure handles operating system notifications that an action, such as a mouse move, has taken place. Each window message, or notification, has a default behavior that is applied by the default window procedure if no action is taken by any of the previously called procedures in the window chain.

Table 9.6 describes some other members of the Form class.

Member	Description
ActiveForm	Gets the currently active form for this application
ActiveMDIChild	Gets the active MDI child window
AutoScroll	Gets or sets a value indicating whether the form implements autoscrolling
BackColor, ForeColor	Set and get the background and foreground colors
FormBorderStyle	Gets or sets the border style of the form
HelpButton	Gets or sets a value indicating whether a Help button is displayed in the title bar of the form
IsMDIChild	Gets a value indicating whether the form is an MDI child form
MaximizeBox, MinimizeBox	Get or set a value indicating whether the maximize and minimize buttons are displayed in the title bar of the form
MdiChildren	Gets an array of forms that represents the MDI child forms that are parented by this form
MdiParent	Indicates the MDI parent form of this form
Menu	Gets or sets the MainMenu that is displayed in the form
Modal	Gets a value indicating whether this form is displayed modally
Size	Gets or sets the size of the form
TopMost	Gets or sets a value indicating whether the form is displayed as the topmost form of your application
Visible	Gets or sets a value indicating whether the form is visible
Activate	Method to activate the form and give it focus
Close	Method that closes the form

Table 9.6: Form Class Members

Using the properties and methods of the Form class you can alter the appearance of the form. Listing 9.6 contains some samples that can change the appearance and functionality of the form.

Listing 9.6—Changing the appearance of the form

```
// Set the font of the form.
form1.Font = new System.Drawing.Font ("Verdana", 10,
System.Drawing.FontStyle.Bold);
// Make the Form transparent.
form1.Opacity = 0.50;
// Make the Form topmost.
form1.TopMost = true;

// Set the title bar text of the form.
form1.Text = "My Dialog Box";
// Display a help button on the form.
form1.HelpButton = true;

// Define the border style of the form to that of a dialog box.
form1.FormBorderStyle = FormBorderStyle.FixedDialog;
// Set the MaximizeBox to false to remove the maximize box.
form1.MaximizeBox = false;
// Display the form as a modal dialog box.
form1.ShowDialog();
```

Event Handling

Event handling is performed differently in .NET than it is in Visual C++. In Visual C++, each control is derived from CWnd and a message map handles any events. The message map concept doesn't exist in .NET. The Control class, or any derived class, has virtual functions, which can be overridden to raise an event. Therefore, a Form class can use any event handler in its hierarchy. For example, the Control class has many event methods including GotFocus, ControlRemoved, LostFocus, and MouseWheel. Table 9.7 lists some common event-handling methods.

Event Handler	Description
OnClick, OnDoubleClick	Raise the Click and DoubleClick event for button presses on the mouse.
OnDeactivate	Raises the Deactivate event when a form is deactivated.
OnKeyDown, OnKeyPress, OnKeyUp	Raise Key events from the keyboard.
OnMouseDown, OnMouseEnter, OnMouseHover, OnMouseLeave, OnMouseMove, OnMouseUp	Raise Mouse events.
OnMove	Raises the Move event when a control is moved.
OnPaint	Inheriting classes should override this method to handle this event. Call base class's OnPaint to send this event to any registered event listeners.
OnResize	Raises the Resize event when a control is resized.

Table 9.7: Windows Controls Events

To override the OnPaint method, for example, add the following method to your new form or control:

```
protected override void OnPaint(PaintEventArgs e) {
    // your code here
}
```

Adding Event Handlers at Design-Time

To attach events to a control at design-time, use the Properties window. Right-click the control and click the Properties menu item. Select the Events tab by pressing the lightening button at the top of the Properties window. Now, pick an event and type the corresponding function name. Alternatively, you could double-click in the field next to the event and VS.NET will choose a name for you. In Figure 9.17, we add a button click event handler as button1_Click.

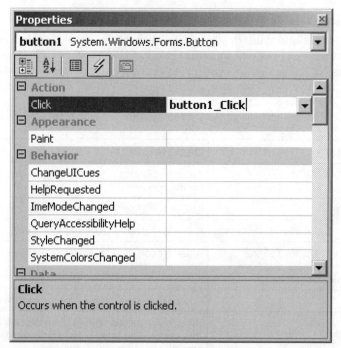

Figure 9.17: Adding an Event Handler Using the Properties Window

This action adds a delegate to the event, which looks like the following:

```
this.button1.Click += new System.EventHandler(this.button1_Click);
```

The event handler method takes the following form:

```
private void button1_Click(object sender, System.EventArgs e)
{
}
```

Now write whatever code, within the method, you wish to execute after the event takes place. You can use the "e" (event argument) parameter that is passed to retrieve any pertinent information about the event, such as which key was pressed. The sender parameter is the control that initiated the event, in this case, the button1 member.

Handling Mouse Events

The window in Figure 9.18 lists multiple mouse events. Event handlers can be generated simply by double-clicking the desired event.

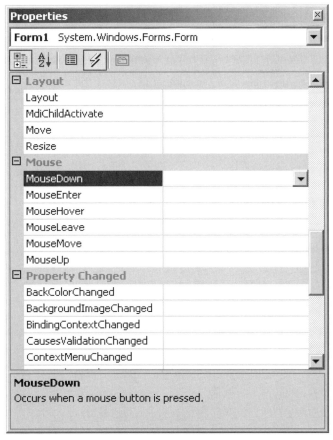

Figure 9.18: Mouse Events

To test the sample code that follows, create a Windows application and write the OnMouseDown and OnMouseMove event handlers in the InitializeComponent method.

```
this.MouseDown += new System.Windows.Forms.MouseEventHandler(this.OnMouseDown);

this.MouseMove += new System.Windows.Forms.MouseEventHandler(this.OnMouseMove);
```

The preceding code results in the OnMouseDown method being called if a mouse button is pressed and the OnMouseMove method being called whenever the mouse moves over the control, which in this case is the form.

To carry out some action after the mouse event occurs, we need to write the event handlers. The second parameter of the event handler method is a System.WinForms.MouseEventArgs object, which details the mouse's state. The MouseEventArgs' members are listed in Table 9.8.

Member	Description
Button	Indicates which mouse button was pressed: left, right, middle, or none
Clicks	Indicates the number of times the mouse button was pressed and released
Delta	Indicates a signed count of the number of detents the mouse wheel has rotated
X	The x coordinate of mouse click
Y	The y coordinate of mouse click

Table 9.8: MouseEventArgs Members

Listing 9.7 shows the event handler code for the MouseDown and MouseMove events.

Listing 9.7—Mouse Event Handlers

```
public void OnMouseDown(object sender, System.Windows.Forms.MouseEventArgs e)
{
        switch (e.Button)
        {
                case MouseButtons.Left:
                        MessageBox.Show(this,"Left Button Click");
                break;
                case MouseButtons.Right:
                MessageBox.Show(this,"Right Button Click" );
                break;
                case MouseButtons.Middle:
                break;
                default:
                break;
        }
}


private void OnMouseMove(object sender, System.Windows.Forms.MouseEventArgs e)
{
        this.Text = "Mouse Position:" +e.X.ToString() +","+ e.Y.ToString() ;
}
```

Figure 9.19 shows the output of Listing 9.7. A mouse click displays, in a message box, the mouse button clicked, while a mouse move shows the mouse's coordinates as the title of the form.

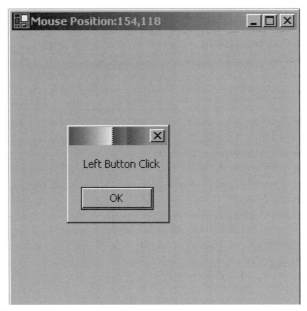

Figure 9.19: Handling Mouse Click and Mouse Move Events

Adding ToolTips to Windows Controls

Adding a ToolTip to a control is a simple matter of implementing the functionality provided by the ToolTip class. There are two steps to add a ToolTip to a control: first, create an instance of the ToolTip control; second, attach a control to the ToolTip object by calling the ToolTip.SetToolTip method. To activate the ToolTip, set the Active property to *true*. The following code adds a ToolTip to a button control:

```
ToolTip toolTip1 = new System.Windows.Forms.ToolTip();
toolTip1.SetToolTip (button1, "This is tooltip test");
toolTip1.Active = true;
```

Working with Menus

The MainMenu, MenuItem, and ContextMenu classes are controls that represent menu functionality. These classes are derived from the Menu class, an abstract, base class.

The Menu Class

Table 9.9 lists and describes some of the Menu class properties and methods.

Member	Description
Handle	Represents the Windows handle for the menu
IsParent	Represents whether a menu has items
MdiListItem	Represents a value indicating the menu item that is used to display a list of MDI child forms
MenuItems	Returns a collection of menu items associated with a menu
GetContextMenu	Returns the context menu that contains this menu
GetMainMenu	Returns the main menu that contains this menu
MergeMenu	Merges a menu item with the current menu
CloneMenu	Copies a menu

Table 9.9: Menu Class Members

The MenuItemCollection Class

The MenuItemCollection class represents the collection of MenuItem objects stored in the MainMenu or the ContextMenu. This class is used to count, add, or remove menu items from a menu. The MenuItemCollection properties and methods are defined in Table 9.10 and Table 9.11, respectively.

Property	Description
Count	Indicates the total number of MenuItem objects in the collection
Item	Indicates the MenuItem at the specified indexed location in the collection

Table 9.10: MenuItemCollection Class Properties

Method	Description
Add	Adds a new menu item to the collection
AddRange	Adds an array of menu items to the collection
Clear	Removes all menu items from the main menu
CopyTo	Copies the entire collection into an existing array at a specified location within an array
IndexOf	Returns the index of an item in the collection
Remove	Removes the specified menu item from the collection
RemoveAt	Removes a menu item at a specified index

Table 9.11: MenuItemCollection Methods

The MenuItem Class

The MenuItem class represents individual items displayed in a menu. To display menu items, you must add the menu item to a context menu or a main menu. The MenuItems property of the ContextMenu or MainMenu classes represents the collection of all the menu items. Table 9.12 defines some of the MenuItem properties.

Property	Description
BarBreak	Represents whether the menu item is placed on a new line or in a new column. Places a visible vertical bar before the item.
Break	Represents whether the menu item is placed on a new line or in a new column
Checked	Represents whether a check mark appears next to the text of a menu item
DefaultItem	Represents whether a menu item is the default menu item
Enabled	Represents a value indicating whether the menu item is enabled
Index	Represents the position of the menu item
MergeOrder	Represents the position of the menu item when it is merged with another
RadioCheck	Represents whether a menu item has a radio button
Shortcut	Represents the shortcut key for the menu item
ShowShortcut	Represents whether the shortcut key should be available next to the menu item
Text	Represents the text of a menu item
Visible	Represents whether a menu item is visible

Table 9.12: MenuItem Class Properties

Adding Menu Items to a Form

Menus can be created by dragging the MainMenu control from your toolbox and setting its properties and items. Double-clicking an item adds an event handler for that item. Menus can also be created programmatically. To do so, first create a MainMenu object and then create menu items using the MenuItem class and add the items to the main menu using the MainMenu.MenuItems.Add method. The MainMenu.MenuItems.Add method takes a MenuItem instance as a parameter. The source code in Listing 9.8 creates a menu and four menu items. Once done, the menu is added to the form.

Listing 9.8—Creating a Main Menu and Four Menu Items

```
public void CreateMenus()
{
    // Create a main menu
    MainMenu myMenu = new MainMenu();

    // Create menu items and set their properties
    MenuItem item1 = new MenuItem();
    MenuItem item2 = new MenuItem();
    MenuItem item3 = new MenuItem();
    MenuItem item4 = new MenuItem();

    item1.Text = "Create Database";
    item2.Text = "Open Database";
    item3.Text = "Help";
    item4.Text = "Exit";

    myMenu.MenuItems.Add(item1);
    myMenu.MenuItems.Add(item2);
    myMenu.MenuItems.Add(item3);
    myMenu.MenuItems.Add(item4);

    MenuItem generic = null;
    int             index = 0;

    generic = new MenuItem();
```

```
        generic.Text = "Table";
        generic.Click += new EventHandler( this.GenericClick);
        myMenu.MenuItems[1].MenuItems.Add( index++, generic);

        generic = new MenuItem();
        generic.Text = "Row";
        generic.Click += new EventHandler( this.GenericClick);
        myMenu.MenuItems[1].MenuItems.Add( index++, generic);

        generic = new MenuItem();
        generic.Text = "Column";
        generic.Click += new EventHandler( this.GenericClick);
        myMenu.MenuItems[1].MenuItems.Add( index++, generic);

    // Bind the MainMenu to Form
    Menu = myMenu;
}
```

To test this application, create a Windows application and call the CreateMenu method from the Form1_Load method. The output of Listing 9.8 is shown in Figure 9.20.

Figure 9.20: Adding Menus to a Form

Adding Events to Menu Items

Selection handlers can be added by using the click event of the MenuItem class. In the following code, you add a click event handler to the four menu items:

```
item1.Click += new System.EventHandler(this.item1Click);
item2.Click += new System.EventHandler(this.item2Click);
item3.Click += new System.EventHandler(this.item3Click);
item4.Click += new System.EventHandler(this.item4Click);
```

Listing 9.9 shows the code for the event handlers.

Listing 9.9—Click Event Handlers for Menu Items

```
private void item1Click(object sender, System.EventArgs e)
{
        MessageBox.Show("Create Database Menu Item");
}

private void item2Click(object sender, System.EventArgs e)
{
OpenFileDialog fdlg = new OpenFileDialog();

        fdlg.Title = "C# Corner Open File Dialog" ;
        fdlg.InitialDirectory = @"c:\" ;
        fdlg.Filter = "All files (*.*)|*.*|Access Database(*.mdb) files
(*.mdb)|*.mdb" ;
        fdlg.FilterIndex = 2 ;
        fdlg.RestoreDirectory = true ;
```

```
        if(fdlg.ShowDialog() == DialogResult.OK)
        {
                MessageBox.Show(fdlg.FileName.ToString()) ;
        }
}

private void item3Click(object sender, System.EventArgs e)
{
        MessageBox.Show("Help Menu Item");
}

private void item4Click(object sender, System.EventArgs e)
{
        this.Close();
}
```

Disabling Menu Items

Disabling a main menu disables all of its submenus. To disable a menu item at design-time, set the Enabled property to *false*. To disable menu items programmatically, set the menu item's Enabled property to *false:*

```
item3.Enabled = false;
```

Hiding Menu Items

All items of a menu are hidden if the main menu is hidden. To hide a menu at design-time, set the Visible property to *false*. To hide a menu item programmatically, set the Visible property to *false:*

```
item1.Visible = false;
```

Adding and Removing Menu Items Programmatically

Use the MenuItemCollection class's Add and Remove methods to add or remove an item in an existing context or main menu:

```
MenuItem miFile = mainMenu.MenuItems.Add("&Database Options");
miFile.MenuItems.Add(new MenuItem("&Open Database", new
EventHandler(this.FileOpen_Clicked), Shortcut.CtrlO));
```

Setting the Caption of Menu Items and Assigning a Shortcut Key

The Text property of MenuItem is used to set the caption of a menu item; the Shortcut property is used to set the shortcut:

```
menuItem1.Text = "&Open";
menuItem1.Shortcut = Shortcut.CtrlO;
menuItem1.ShowShortcut = true;
```

Adding Check Boxes and Radio Buttons to Menu Items

The Checked property of MenuItem adds a check box to a menu item:

```
menuItem3.Checked = true;
menuItem3.Checked = false;
```

The RadioCheck property replaces check boxes with radio buttons:

```
menuItem3.RadioCheck = true;
menuItem3.RadioCheck = false;
```

Adding Pop-Up Menus

The ContextMenu class provides pop-up menu functionality. A pop-up menu is displayed when the right mouse button is clicked. To construct a pop-up menu, create a ContextMenu object and attached it to the form via the Form.ContextMenu property. Menu items and event handlers are handled in the same manner as was demonstrated in previous sections.

To test the pop-up menu's functionality, create a Windows application and add the following members to the Form class. Call the CreatePopUpMenus method from the form's load event handler.

```
private ContextMenu popUpMenu = new System.Windows.Forms.ContextMenu();
private MenuItem item1 = new MenuItem();
private MenuItem item2 = new MenuItem();
private MenuItem item3 = new MenuItem();
```

The CreatePopUpMenus method creates and adds three items to the pop-up menu. The menu items' Text properties are set, and an event handler is attached to each. Listing 9.10 shows the CreatePopUpMenus method.

Listing 9.10—Creating Pop-Up Menus

```
public void CreatePopUpMenus()
{
        item1.Text = "Red";
        item1.Checked = true;
        item2.Text = "Blue";
        item3.Text = "Green";

        popUpMenu.MenuItems.Add(item1);
        popUpMenu.MenuItems.Add(item2);
        popUpMenu.MenuItems.Add(item3);

        item1.Click += new System.EventHandler(this.PopUp_Clicked);
        item2.Click += new System.EventHandler(this.PopUp_Clicked);
        item3.Click += new System.EventHandler(this.PopUp_Clicked);

        this.ContextMenu = popUpMenu;
}
```

The PopUp_Clicked method (see Listing 9.11) is the event handler for all the menu items. Using a single handler is possible because one menu item can be distinguished from another with an object comparison.

Listing 9.11—ContextMenu Click Event Handler

```
private void PopUp_Clicked(object sender, EventArgs e)
{
        if(sender == item1)
        {
          item1.Checked = true;
          item2.Checked = false;
          item3.Checked = false;
          textBox1.BackColor = Color.Red;
        }
        else if(sender == item2)
        {
          item1.Checked = false;
          item2.Checked = true;
          item3.Checked = false;
          textBox1.BackColor = Color.Blue;
        }
```

```
        else
        {
          item1.Checked = false;
          item2.Checked = false;
          item3.Checked = true;
          textBox1.BackColor = Color.Green;
        }
}
```

When you right-click on the form, the output looks like that shown in Figure 9.21. Clicking on a menu item changes the background color of the text box and checks the selected menu item.

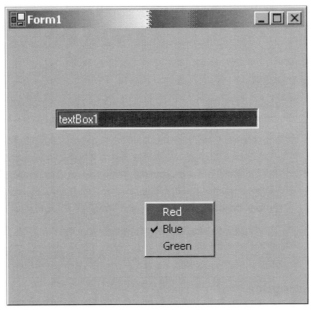

Figure 9.21: Context Menu Functionality

Working with Toolbars

The ToolBar class represents a ToolBar control in Windows Forms. A toolbar is a set of toolbar buttons that can appear as standard, toggle-style , or drop-down-style buttons. You can also assign images to the buttons.

The BorderStyle property of the ToolBar control represents the style of the border and is set with a BorderStyle enumeration. The BorderStyle enumeration has three members, defined in Table 9.13.

Member	Description
Fixed3D	A three-dimensional border
FixedSingle	A single-line border
None	No border

Table 9.13: BorderStyle Enumeration Members

See Table 9.14 for definitions of the ToolBar class properties.

Property	Description
Appearance	Determines the appearance of a toolbar and its buttons. The value is of the type ToolBar.Appearance, which has two members—Flat or Normal.
AutoSize	Represents whether a toolbar is autosize.
BorderStyle	Represents the border style of the toolbar.
Buttons	Represents the collection of buttons of a toolbar.
ButtonSize	Represents the size of buttons of a toolbar.
DropDownArrows	Represents whether drop-down buttons on a toolbar display *down* arrows.
ImageList	Represents the collection of images available to the toolbar's button controls.
ImageSize	Represents the size of the images in the image list assigned to the toolbar.
ImeMode	Represents the Input Method Editor (IME) mode supported by this control.
ShowToolTips	Represents whether the toolbar displays a ToolTip for each button.
TextAlign	Represents the alignment of text in relation to each image displayed on the toolbar's button controls.
Wrappable	Represents whether the toolbar buttons wrap to the next line if the toolbar becomes too small to display all the buttons on the same line.

Table 9.14: ToolBar Class Properties

The ToolBarButton class represents a toolbar button. Table 9.15 lists the ToolBarButton properties.

Property	Description
DropDownMenu	Represents whether the menu is to be displayed in the drop-down toolbar button
Enabled	Represents whether the button is enabled
ImageIndex	Represents the index value of the image assigned to the button
Parent	Returns the toolbar control that the toolbar button is assigned to
PartialPush	Represents whether a toggle-style toolbar button is partially pushed
Pushed	Represents whether a toggle-style toolbar button is currently in the pushed state
Rectangle	Returns the bounding rectangle for a toolbar button
Style	Represents the style of the toolbar button
Tag	Represents the object that contains data about the toolbar button
Text	Represents the text displayed on the toolbar button
ToolTipText	Represents the text that appears as a ToolTip for a control
Visible	Represents whether the toolbar button is visible

Table 9.15: ToolBarButton Class Properties

Creating a Toolbar and Toolbar Buttons

We have described the members of the ToolBar and ToolBarButton classes. Now we will see how to create toolbars and their buttons.

The simplest way to add a toolbar and buttons to a form is to drag the ToolBar control from the toolbox to the form and set its properties. The ToolBar.Buttons property (see Figure 9.22) is the collection of buttons displayed on the toolbar.

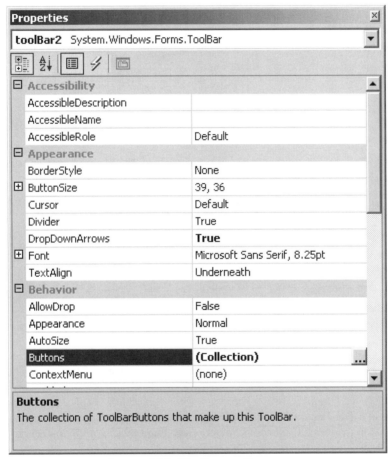

Figure 9.22: The Buttons Property

Clicking the Buttons property opens the ToolBarButton Collection Editor. From the editor toolbar buttons may be added or removed.

Using the ToolBarButton Collection Editor, add three buttons—File, Open, and Close—as in Figure 9.23. Toolbar button properties—such as Text and ToolTipText—can also be set.

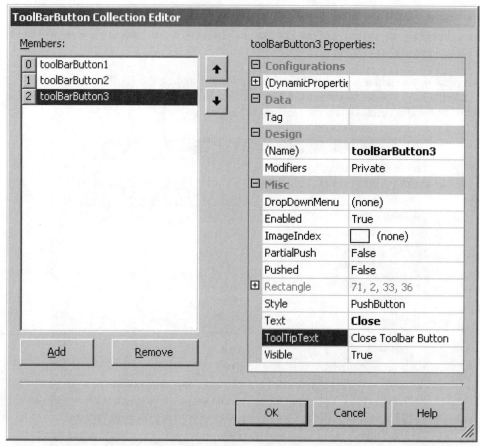

Figure 9.23: Adding Toolbar Buttons Using ToolBarButton Collection Editor

The ImageIndex property can be set from the ToolBarButton Collection Editor. Before setting the ImageIndex property, add an ImageList to the form and set the ImageList property of the ToolBar control.

To add images to a ToolBar control, add an ImageList control to the form by dragging the control from the toolbox to the form. The Images property (see Figure 9.24) of the ImageList control can be used to add images.

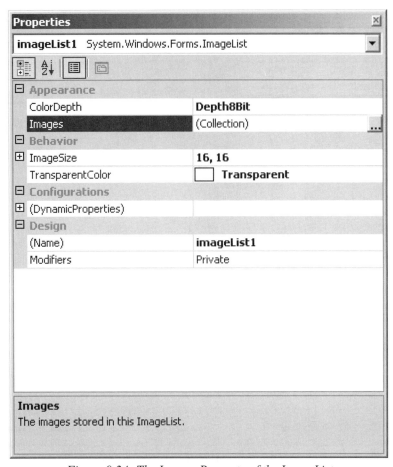

Figure 9.24: The Images Property of the ImageList

Clicking the Images property displays the Image Collection Editor. The Add and Remove buttons of the Image Collection Editor allow images to be inserted in or deleted from the collection. We add three images to the collection in Figure 9.25.

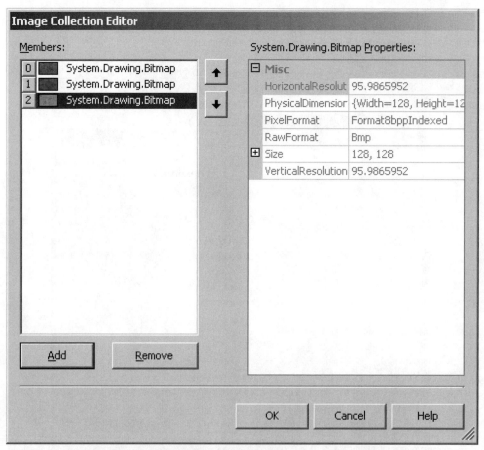

Figure 9.25: Image Collection Editor

The Add button of the Image Collection Editor allows you to browse images on a machine, as you can see from Figure 9.26.

Figure 9.26: Browsing Images from the Image Collection Editor

Now the ImageList property of the ToolBar control can be set to imageList1. See Figure 9.27.

Figure 9.27: Setting ImageList Property of ToolBar Control

Now select the Buttons property to launch the ToolBarButton Collection Editor, and then set the ImageIndex property to the desired bitmap for each toolbar button. The ImageIndex property (see Figure 9.28) displays a list of available images.

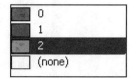

Figure 9.28: Images Available from the ImageList

Then set the toolbar buttons' ImageIndex property (see Figure 9.29) to 0, 1, and 2, respectively.

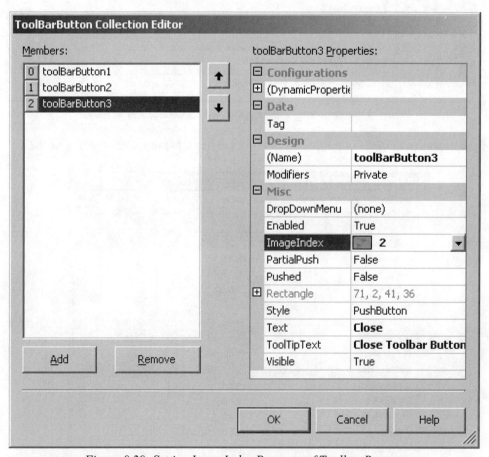

Figure 9.29: Setting ImageIndex Property of Toolbar Buttons

Now the form, with three toolbar buttons, looks like that in Figure 9.30.

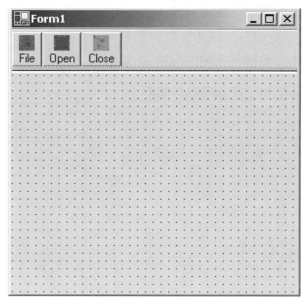

Figure 9.30: Form with Toolbar Buttons

Now add an event handler to the toolbar by double-clicking the toolbar control. To determine which button has been clicked, compare the ToolBarButtonClickEventArgs.Button property with the button objects, as demonstrated in Listing 9.12.

Listing 9.12—The Toolbar Button Click Event Handler

```
private void toolBar2_ButtonClick(object sender,
System.Windows.Forms.ToolBarButtonClickEventArgs e)
{
        if ( e.Button == toolBarButton1 )
        {
                MessageBox.Show( "Button1 Clicked ");
        }
        if ( e.Button == toolBarButton2 )
        {
                MessageBox.Show( "Button2 Clicked ");
        }
        if ( e.Button == toolBarButton3 )
        {
                MessageBox.Show( "Button3 Clicked ");
        }
}
```

Adding a Toolbar Dynamically

A toolbar and its toolbar buttons can be added easily by using the ToolBar and ToolBarButton classes. First, create a ToolBar and three ToolBarButton objects (see Listing 9.13).

Listing 9.13—Constructing Toolbars and Toolbar Buttons

```
private System.Windows.Forms.ToolBar toolBar2;
private System.Windows.Forms.ToolBarButton toolBarButton1;
private System.Windows.Forms.ToolBarButton toolBarButton2;
private System.Windows.Forms.ToolBarButton toolBarButton3;
private System.Windows.Forms.ImageList imageList1;

this.toolBar2 = new System.Windows.Forms.ToolBar();
this.toolBarButton1 = new System.Windows.Forms.ToolBarButton();
```

```
this.toolBarButton2 = new System.Windows.Forms.ToolBarButton();
this.toolBarButton3 = new System.Windows.Forms.ToolBarButton();
```

Now set the ToolBar and ToolBarButton properties (see Listing 9.14).

Listing 9.14—Setting Toolbar and Button Properties

```
this.toolBar2.DropDownArrows = true;
this.toolBar2.ImageList = this.imageList1;
this.toolBar2.Name = "toolBar2";
this.toolBar2.ShowToolTips = true;
this.toolBar2.Size = new System.Drawing.Size(292, 39);
this.toolBar2.TabIndex = 0;

this.toolBarButton1.ImageIndex = 0;
this.toolBarButton1.Text = "File";
this.toolBarButton1.ToolTipText = "File Toolbar Button";
// toolBarButton2
this.toolBarButton2.ImageIndex = 1;
this.toolBarButton2.Text = "Open";
this.toolBarButton2.ToolTipText = "Open Toolbar Button";
// toolBarButton3
this.toolBarButton3.ImageIndex = 2;
this.toolBarButton3.Text = "Close";
this.toolBarButton3.ToolTipText = "Close Toolbar Button";
```

The ToolBarCollection.Buttons.AddRange method adds the toolbar buttons to the toolbar:

```
this.toolBar2.Buttons.AddRange(new System.Windows.Forms.ToolBarButton[] {
this.toolBarButton1,
this.toolBarButton2,
this.toolBarButton3});
```

The ButtonClick event adds a click event handler to the toolbar:

```
this.toolBar2.ButtonClick += new
System.Windows.Forms.ToolBarButtonClickEventHandler(this.toolBar2_ButtonClick);
```

Finally, the toolbar control is added to the form with the Controls.AddRange method:

```
this.Controls.AddRange(new System.Windows.Forms.Control[] {
this.toolBar2});
```

Working with Status Bars

A status bar control is used to display the state of an application. As many panels as needed can be attached to a status bar. These panels can then display different types of information. The StatusBar class is used to create status bars, and the StatusBarPanel class creates the panels:

```
this.statusBar1 = new System.Windows.Forms.StatusBar();
StatusBarPanel pnl1 = new StatusBarPanel();
StatusBarPanel pnl2 = new StatusBarPanel();
```

A panel is added to a status bar by calling StatusBar.Panels.AddRange:

```
statusBar1.Panels.AddRange( new StatusBarPanel[] {pnl1, pnl2});
```
The Icon class inserts an image into the panel control:

```
Icon icon = new Icon(@"c:\mouse.ico");
pnl1.Icon = icon;
```

The source code in Listing 9.15 adds a status bar, with images, to a form. Note the setting of the ShowPanels property to *true,* which displays the panels. The default value of this property is *false.*

Listing 9.15—Adding a Status Bar to a Form

```
void AddStatusBar()
{
        StatusBar  statusBar1 = new System.Windows.Forms.StatusBar();

        statusBar1.ShowPanels = true;
        statusBar1.Location = new System.Drawing.Point(0, 253);
        statusBar1.Name = "statusBar1";
        statusBar1.Size = new System.Drawing.Size(292, 20);
        statusBar1.TabIndex = 0;
        statusBar1.Text = "statusBar1";

        StatusBarPanel pnl1 = new StatusBarPanel();
        StatusBarPanel pnl2 = new StatusBarPanel();

        pnl1.Text = "Panel 1";
        pnl1.Width = 32;
        pnl1.AutoSize = StatusBarPanelAutoSize.Spring;
        pnl2.Text = DateTime.Now.ToString();

        statusBar1.Panels.AddRange( new StatusBarPanel[] {pnl1, pnl2});

        Controls.Add(statusBar1);

}
```

The output of Listing 9.15 can be seen in Figure 9.31.

Figure 9.31: Output of the Status Bar Sample

Working with Dialog Boxes

A dialog box is simply a form with a few property settings that differ from the default Form values. In MFC, the CDialog class was inherited from the CWnd class. In .NET, a dialog box is a form with a three-dimensional border and no minimize or maximize buttons.

Creating a Dialog Box

Following are the steps to create a dialog box:

- Create a form.
- Set the FormBorderStyle property to FixedDialog.
- Set the ControlBox, MinimizeBox, and MaximizeBox properties to *false.*

A form can be displayed as a *modal* or a *modeless* dialog box. A modal dialog box is one that will not let the user click somewhere else until the dialog is closed. The modal dialog box traps all Windows events until it is dismissed.

Creating a Modal Dialog Box

To create a modal dialog box, you call the ShowDialog method:

```
Form myDlg = new Form1();
myDlg.ShowDialog();
```

Creating a Modeless Dialog Box

Calling the Show() method on a form creates a modeless dialog box:

```
Form myDlg = new MyDialog();
myDlg.Show();
```

A dialog box generally has some default buttons including OK, Cancel, Retry, Abort, Yes, No, and None. These values are defined in the DialogResult enumerator. See Table 9.16.

DialogResult Member Name	Description
Abort	The dialog box return value is Abort.
Cancel	The dialog box return value is Cancel.
Ignore	The dialog box return value is Ignore.
No	The dialog box return value is No.
None	Nothing is returned from the dialog box. This means that the modal dialog continues running.
OK	The dialog box return value is OK.
Retry	The dialog box return value is Retry.
Yes	The dialog box return value is Yes.

Table 9.16: The DialogResult Enumeration Members

Use the Form.DialogResult member to ascertain what button was clicked once the dialog is closed. The following source code shows you how to determine whether a Yes or No button is clicked.

```
if (myDlg.DialogResult == DialogResult.Yes)
    MessageBox.show("Yes button was clicked.");
else
    MessageBox.show("No button was clicked.");
```

If the dialog box does not contain these buttons, they can be set at runtime:

```
this.DialogResult = myDlg.Yes;
```

```
this.DialogResult = DialogResult.No;
```

Related to the DialogResult enumeration are the AcceptButton and CancelButton properties, which allow the user to terminate a dialog by striking the ENTER or ESC keys, respectively. The keys can be thought of as shortcuts for the OK and Cancel buttons, in that the user has the option of clicking the button or pressing the corresponding key. To set the CancelButton property, assign it a reference to an existing button and set that button's DialogResult property to DialogResult.Cancel. The same procedure, using a different button, is followed to set the AcceptButton property, with a dialog result value of DialogResult.OK. No event handlers are required, and the form's DialogResult will be mapped to the associated button's dialog result. While the preceding is true, beware that Visual Studio seems to want an event handler for the AcceptButton. It occasionally deletes a DialogResult.OK assignment, rendering the ENTER key and its button inoperable. A reasonable assumption for this behavior is that an OK termination will require some processing prior to the dialog closing and therefore needs an event handler.

Accessing the Parent Form of a Dialog

The parent form is the form that the dialog is launched from. Use the *this* reference and the ContainerControl.ParentForm to get the parent form of a dialog. For example, if you have a public member, a button1 variable, on the parent form and want to get its text, do the following:

```
string str = ((Form1)this.ParentForm).button1.Text;
```

Working with Common Dialog Classes

The CommonDialog class, an abstract class, is the root of the common Dialog classes. Any derived classes must implement the RunDialog method, which is invoked within ShowDialog(). Figure 9.32 shows the hierarchy diagram for common dialogs.

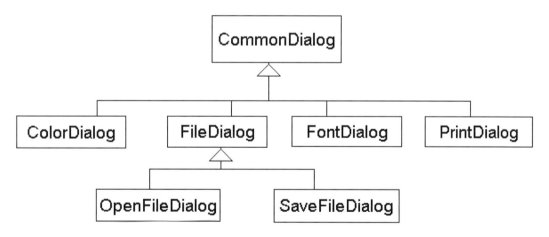

Figure 9.32: The Hierarchy Diagram of Common Dialogs

The FileDialog Class

FileDialog, also an abstract class, is the base class for OpenFileDialog and SaveFileDialog. Do not use this class directly, but access its members via other derived classes. Some of its useful members are listed in Table 9.17.

Property	Description
AddExtension	Indicates whether the dialog box automatically adds an extension to a file name if the user omits the extension
CheckFileExists	Indicates whether the dialog box displays a warning if the user specifies a file name that does not exist
CheckPathExists	Indicates whether the dialog box displays a warning if the user specifies a path that does not exist
DefaultExt	Indicates the default file extension
DereferenceLinks	Indicates whether the dialog box returns the location of the file referenced by the shortcut or whether it returns the location of the shortcut (.lnk)
FileName	Indicates a string containing the file name selected in the file dialog box
FileNames	A read-only property; indicates the file names of all selected files in the dialog box
Filter	Indicates the current file name filter string, which determines the choices that appear in the "Save as file type" or "Files of type" box in the dialog box
FilterIndex	Indicates the index of the filter currently selected in the file dialog box
InitialDirectory	Indicates the initial directory displayed by the file dialog box
RestoreDirectory	Indicates whether the dialog box restores the current directory before closing
ShowHelp	Indicates whether the Help button is displayed in the file dialog box
Title	Indicates the file dialog box title
ValidateNames	Indicates whether the dialog box accepts only valid Win32 file names

Table 9.17: FileDialog Properties

The OpenFileDialog Class

The OpenFileDialog class represents the Windows open file dialog, which can be used to browse a file. The OpenFileDialog class derives from FileDialog. The OpenFile method opens a file and returns a read-only stream.

The source code in Listing 9.16 uses the OpenFileDialog to browse files.

Listing 9.16—Browsing Files Using the OpenFileDialog

```
OpenFileDialog fdlg = new OpenFileDialog();
fdlg.Title = "C# Corner Open File Dialog" ;
fdlg.InitialDirectory = @"c:\" ;
fdlg.Filter = "Text files (*.txt)|*.txt|All files (*.*)|*.*";
fdlg.FilterIndex = 2 ;
fdlg.RestoreDirectory = true ;
if(fdlg.ShowDialog() == DialogResult.OK)
{
        string str = fdlg.FileName ;
}
```

The Title member sets the title of the dialog box. The Filter member defines the different types of files to display. Figure 9.33 shows the output of listing 9.12.

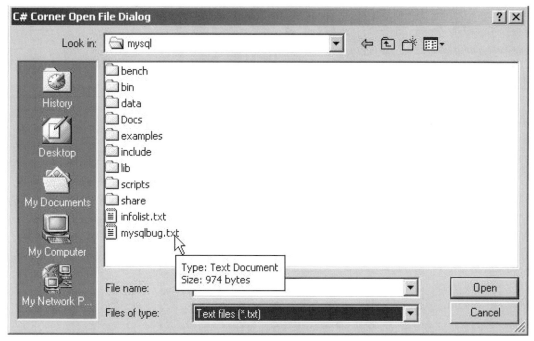

Figure 9.33: The Open File Dialog Box

The FileName member provides access to the name of the selected file.

The SaveFileDialog Class

The SaveFileDialog class represents a common dialog for saving files. Different options can be set for the way you wish to display file saving to the user. The source code in listing 9.17 uses the SaveFileDialog to browse and save files.

Listing 9.17—Using the SaveFileDialog

```
SaveFileDialog saveFileDlg = new SaveFileDialog();
saveFileDlg.Filter = "txt files (*.txt)|*.txt|All files (*.*)|*.*"  ;

if(saveFileDlg.ShowDialog() == DialogResult.OK)
{
        // save the file stuff here
}
```

The ColorDialog Class

The ColorDialog class does everything needed to choose a color. The ShowDialog method displays the dialog box for color selection. The Color property of the ColorDialog returns the currently selected color. The following source code calls the ColorDialog and then sets the text color of a text box control:

```
ColorDialog colorDlg = new ColorDialog();
colorDlg.ShowDialog();
textBox1.ForeColor = colorDlg.Color;
```

The color dialog box looks like that in Figure 9.34.

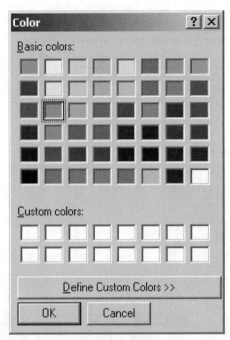

Figure 9.34: Color Dialog Box

The FontDialog Class

The FontDialog class can be used to pick a font. The ShowDialog method allows the selection of a font as well as its size, style, effects, and color. The Color and Font properties return the currently selected color and font. The font dialog box is shown in Figure 9.35.

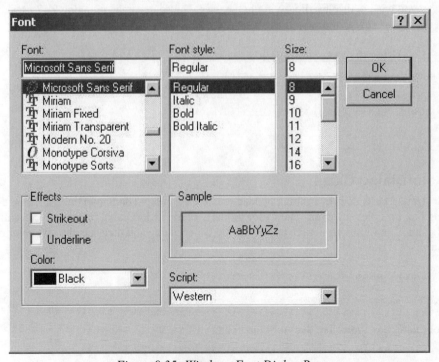

Figure 9.35: Windows Font Dialog Box

The source code in Listing 9.18 sets the selected font as the font of a text box.

Listing 9.18—Using the Windows Font Dialog

```
FontDialog fntDlg = new FontDialog();
fntDlg.ShowColor = true;
if(fntDlg.ShowDialog() != DialogResult.Cancel )
{
        textBox1.Font = fntDlg.Font ;
        textBox1.ForeColor = fntDlg.Color;
}
```

Working with Windows Controls

In this part of the chapter we investigate some commonly used Windows controls and how to work with them.

Button and TextBox Controls

The purpose of a button is to execute some event code when it is clicked. The Button class derives from the ButtonBase class.

The TextBox control is used to get keyboard input from the user. TextBox inherits the TextBoxBase class. Besides the functionality defined in the Control class, the TextBoxBase class defines properties and methods, as listed in Tables 9.18 and 9.19 respectively. The Text property of a text box is used to set its text.

Properties	Description	Example
Multiline	Supports multiple lines	textBox1.Multiline = true;
ScrollBars	Scroll bars	textBox1.ScrollBars = ScrollBars.Vertical;
AcceptReturn, AcceptTab	True or false; indicate whether a button accepts returns (ENTER key) and tabs	textBox1.AcceptsReturn = true; textBox1.AcceptsTab = true;
WordWrap	Wordwrap support	textBox1.WordWrap = true;
CanUndo	True or false; indicates whether previous operation can be undone	
AutoSize	Indicates whether text box is autosize based on the font size	textBox1.AutoSize = false;

Table 9.18: TextBoxBase Class Properties

Methods	Description	Example
Cut()	The save part of the cut and paste operation	textBox1.Cut();
Copy()	The save part of the copy and paste operation	textBox1.Copy();
Paste()	The paste part of the cut (or copy) and paste operation	textBox1.Paste();
Undo()	Undoes the last changes	textBox1.WordWrap = true;

ClearUndo()	Flushes the Undo buffer	if(textBox1.CanUndo == true)
		{
		    textBox1.Undo();
		    textBox1.ClearUndo();
		}

Table 9.19: TextBoxBase Class Methods

GroupBox Controls

A GroupBox control displays a frame around a group of controls with or without a caption. Generally, a group box is used to assemble radio buttons into a group. A number of techniques exist with which to add controls to a group box. Use the Add or AddRange methods or the Controls indexer property. Here are the steps to add radio buttons to a group box.

Step 1: Create a group box instance and radio button instances.

```
groupBox1 = new System.Windows.Forms.GroupBox();

radioButton1 = new System.Windows.Forms.RadioButton();
radioButton2 = new System.Windows.Forms.RadioButton();
radioButton3 = new System.Windows.Forms.RadioButton();
```

Step 2: Set the radio button properties and methods. (See the following section.)
Step 3: Add the radio buttons to a group box by using an Add method or an indexer.

```
groupBox1.Controls.Add(radioButton1);
groupBox1.Controls[groupBox1.Controls.Count] = radioButton2;
```

Step 4 (alternative to step 3): Add the radio buttons to the group box using the AddRange method.

```
groupBox1.Controls.AddRange(new System.Windows.Forms.Control[] {
this.radioButton1, this.radioButton2,this.radioButton3});
```

RadioButton and CheckBox Controls

Both the CheckBox and RadioButton controls, inherited from the ButtonBase class, provide a range of selection options. The functional difference between the two is that a checkbox self-toggles and its state is usually independent of other checkboxes, whereas a RadioButton's toggle-state usually depends on other radio buttons associated with it. Both return a Boolean value to denote selection—*true* indicates selected.

Step 1: Create an instance of the classes.

```
CheckBox checkBox1 = new System.Windows.Forms.CheckBox();
RadioButton radioButton1 = new System.Windows.Forms.RadioButton();
```

Step 2: Set the properties and methods of the controls.

```
this.checkBox1.Location = new System.Drawing.Point(8, 8);
this.checkBox1.Name = "checkBox1";
this.checkBox1.TabIndex = 1;
// The checkbox appears as a toggle button.
checkBox1.Appearance = Appearance.Button;
// Turn off the update of the display on the click of the control.
checkBox1.AutoCheck = false;
this.checkBox1.Text = "Circle";

this.radioButton1.Location = new System.Drawing.Point(8, 32);
this.radioButton1.Name = "radioButton1";
this.radioButton1.TabIndex = 4;
this.radioButton1.Text = "Red";
this.radioButton1.CheckedChanged += new
System.EventHandler(this.radioButton1_CheckedChanged);
```

Step 3: Add the controls to the form using the Controls.AddRange method. (Note: You use radio buttons through a GroupBox control and add the group box to the form.)

```
this.Controls.AddRange(new System.Windows.Forms.Control[] {
   this.button1, this.checkBox3, this.checkBox2, this.checkBox1,
this.groupBox1});
```

The Checked property determines whether a radio button has been selected. The AutoChecked property automatically selects and deselects the property. The Appearance property makes a check box look like a button. The same properties are also members of the RadioButton class.

```
if(radioButton1.Checked)
{
        // do something
}
else
{
        // do something else
}

if (checkBox1.Checked)
{
//      do something
}
else
{
        // do something else
}
```

An Example of Integrating Controls and Events

We will create a Windows application and add three check boxes and a group box with three radio buttons (Figure 9.36). A Draw button will also be added to the form. The Draw button renders graphical images based on the selection of the check boxes and radio buttons. The images are displayed based on the options selected.

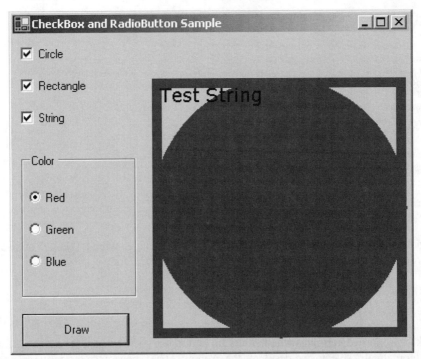

Figure 9.36: Check Box and Radio Button Sample

The Graphics object is employed to draw graphical objects in Listing 9.19. For an in-depth examination of the Graphics object, see Chapter 15, "GDI+ Programming."

Listing 9.19—Check Box and Radio Button Sample

```
private void button1_Click(object sender, System.EventArgs e)
{
        Graphics g = Graphics.FromHwnd(this.Handle);
        Pen pn = new Pen(Color.Blue, 10);
        SolidBrush br = new SolidBrush(Color.AliceBlue);
        Rectangle rc = new Rectangle(150, 50, 250, 250);

        if(radioButton1.Checked)
        {
                pn.Color = Color.Red;
                br.Color = Color.Red;
        }
        if(radioButton2.Checked)
        {
                pn.Color = Color.Green;
                br.Color = Color.Green;
        }
        if(radioButton3.Checked)
        {
                pn.Color = Color.Blue;
                br.Color = Color.Blue;
        }

        if (checkBox1.Checked)
        {
                g.FillEllipse(br, rc);
                g.DrawEllipse(pn, rc);
        }
        if (checkBox2.Checked)
        {
```

```
                g.DrawRectangle(pn, rc);
        }
        if (checkBox3.Checked)
        {
                g.DrawString("Test String", new Font("Verdana", 14), new
SolidBrush(Color.Black), rc);
        }

        pn.Dispose();
        br.Dispose();
}
```

ListBox and ListView Controls

The ListBox control, as well as its companion, the ComboBox control, derives from the ListControl class and represents a list of ordered items. The ListBox class supports single or multiple columns, in addition to single or multiple selection. The MultiColumn property provides multicolumn support. The SelectItem and SelectItems properties return the selected item(s). The Text property returns the string value of the selected item. The Items property returns a ListBox.ObjectCollection, which defines the methods and properties for manipulating the items in the list. Among the ObjectCollection methods are Add, AddRange, Clear, CopyTo, Insert, Remove, and RemoveAt. The Count property returns number of items in the collection. Listing 9.20 shows how to create a list box and add items to it.

Listing 9.20—Creating and Adding Items to a ListBox Control

```
private void CreateListBox()
{
        ListBox listBox1 = new ListBox();
        listBox1.Size = new System.Drawing.Size(400, 200);
        listBox1.Location = new System.Drawing.Point(10,10);
        this.Controls.Add(listBox1);
        listBox1.MultiColumn = true;
        listBox1.SelectionMode = SelectionMode.MultiExtended;

        listBox1.BeginUpdate();

        ListViewItem item1 = new ListViewItem();
        item1.Text = "Mahesh Chand";
        item1.BackColor = Color.Green;
        item1.Checked = true;

        int i = 23;
        float flt = 34.12f;

        listBox1.Items.Add(item1);
        listBox1.Items.Add("Testing Add Item");
        listBox1.Items.Add(i.ToString());
        listBox1.Items.Add(flt.ToString());

        listBox1.EndUpdate();
}
```

Another useful control, the ListView control, provides enhanced list box functionality.

The View property dictates how a list of items are displayed. The display options are details, list, and small and large icons. The Boolean CheckBox property displays a check box next to an item if set to *true*.

```
listViewCtrl.View = View.Details;
listViewCtrl.CheckBoxes = true;
```

The Columns property returns a ListView.ColumnHeaderCollection, which defines functionality to add, remove, count, and insert columns. Some of its methods are Add, AddRange, Remove, RemoveAt, Insert, and Clear. The Count property returns the number of columns. Other members of ListView are the Boolean GridLines property (which draws row and column lines) and MultiSelect property (which permits multiple selection). The BeginUpdate and EndUpdate methods prevent the redrawing of the control while items are added. The Clear method removes all items from the list. GetItemAt returns the item at the given index.

Adding Column Headers

To create a multicolumn list view, create instances of the ColumnHeader class:

```
private System.Windows.Forms.ColumnHeader NameCol;
this.NameCol = new System.Windows.Forms.ColumnHeader();
```

The following ColumnHeader properties set the name, width, and text alignment:

```
this.NameCol.Text = "Name";
this.NameCol.TextAlign = System.Windows.Forms.HorizontalAlignment.Center;
this.NameCol.Width = 150;
```

Once the properties are set, add the columns to the Columns collection using the AddRange method:

```
this.listViewCtrl.Columns.AddRange(new System.Windows.Forms.ColumnHeader[]
                   { this.NameCol} );
```

An Example of Populating a ListView

The source code in Listing 9.21 creates a multicolumn ListView control and adds data to it. The resulting output is shown in Figure 9.37. The CreateListViewControl method creates a list view, while the AddItemsToList method adds items to the control.

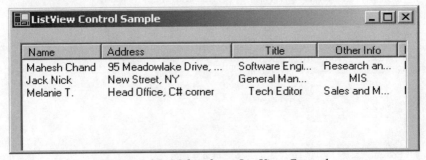

Figure 9.37: Multicolumn ListView Control

Listing 9.21—Multicolumn ListView Control Source Code

```
private System.ComponentModel.Container components = null;
private System.Windows.Forms.ListView listViewCtrl;
private System.Windows.Forms.ColumnHeader Address;
private System.Windows.Forms.ColumnHeader Title;
private System.Windows.Forms.ColumnHeader OtherInfo;
private System.Windows.Forms.ColumnHeader NameCol;
private System.Windows.Forms.ListBox listBox1;
private System.Windows.Forms.ColumnHeader LastCol;

private void Form1_Load(object sender, System.EventArgs e)
{
        CreateListViewControl();
        AddItemsToList();
```

```
        }

private void AddItemsToList()
{
        string[]                array = null;
        ListViewItem    item = null;
        array = new string[5];

        array[0] = "Mahesh Chand";
        array[1] = "95 Meadowlake Drive, DTown";
        array[2] = "Software Engineer";
        array[3] = "Research and Developmenet";
        array[4] = "Last Column";
        item = new ListViewItem(array);
        this.listViewCtrl.Items.Add(item);

        array[0] = "Jack Nick";
        array[1] = "New Street, NY";
        array[2] = "General Manager";
        array[3] = "MIS";
        array[4] = "";
        item = new ListViewItem(array);
        this.listViewCtrl.Items.Add(item);

        array[0] = "Melanie T.";
        array[1] = "Head Office, C# corner";
        array[2] = "Tech Editor";
        array[3] = "Sales and Marketing";
        array[4] = "Last Column";
        item = new ListViewItem(array);
        this.listViewCtrl.Items.Add(item);

}
private void CreateListViewControl()
{
        this.NameCol = new System.Windows.Forms.ColumnHeader();
        this.listViewCtrl = new System.Windows.Forms.ListView();
        this.Address = new System.Windows.Forms.ColumnHeader();
        this.Title = new System.Windows.Forms.ColumnHeader();
        this.OtherInfo = new System.Windows.Forms.ColumnHeader();
        this.LastCol = new System.Windows.Forms.ColumnHeader();

        this.NameCol.Text = "Name";
        this.NameCol.TextAlign = System.Windows.Forms.HorizontalAlignment.Center;
        this.NameCol.Width = 150;
        this.listViewCtrl.Columns.AddRange(new System.Windows.Forms.ColumnHeader[]
        { this.NameCol, this.Address, this.Title, this.OtherInfo, this.LastCol} );

        this.listViewCtrl.Location = new System.Drawing.Point(8, 16);
        this.listViewCtrl.Name = "listViewCtrl";
        this.listViewCtrl.Size = new System.Drawing.Size(400, 380);
        this.listViewCtrl.TabIndex = 0;
        this.listViewCtrl.View = System.Windows.Forms.View.Details;
        this.Address.Text = "Address";
        this.Address.Width = 100;

        this.Title.Text = "Title";
        this.Title.TextAlign = System.Windows.Forms.HorizontalAlignment.Center;
        this.Title.Width = 50;

        this.OtherInfo.Text = "Other Info";
        this.OtherInfo.TextAlign = System.Windows.Forms.HorizontalAlignment.Center;
        this.OtherInfo.Width = 50;

        this.LastCol.Text = "Last Column";
        this.LastCol.TextAlign = System.Windows.Forms.HorizontalAlignment.Center;
        this.LastCol.Width = 60;
```

```
    this.Controls.Add(this.listViewCtrl);
}
```

Summary

Windows Forms is a framework in Microsoft .NET with which to write GUI applications. The System.Windows.Forms namespace contains the classes for windows, dialog boxes, and controls. Before running a Windows application, you need to add a reference to the System.Windows.Forms assembly.

Writing Windows applications using Visual Studio is fairly easy. Simply drag a control to a form and set its properties at design-time. Then fill in the event handlers for these controls to provide the Window's functionality. The System.Windows.Forms.Form class represents a window or form in the .NET Framework.

The Controls class is the root of all controls and defines basic control functionality. There are three major steps involved in creating a control. First, create an object of the desired control; second, set its properties; and third, add the control to the form.

The Menu class and its derived classes provide menu functionality. The Menu class is the parent class for the MainMenu, ContextMenu, and MenuItem classes.

The abstract CommonDialog class and its derived classes provide the functionality for common dialogs such as the open file, save file, and print dialogs. Windows controls give your form life and allow the user to interact with their environment Each control is defined in a separate class and can be manipulated through their properties, methods, and events.

In this chapter, you learned to write Windows applications using Windows forms and controls. The next chapter demonstrates the power of ADO.NET and its components.

Chapter 10:
Database Programming Using ADO.NET

ADO.NET is an evolution of ActiveX Data Objects (ADO) and the previous version of ADO.NET called ADO+. If you have ever programmed any database application for Microsoft Windows, you are probably familiar with Microsoft Data Access Components (MDAC) used to connect to databases provided by Microsoft and various vendors. Microsoft provides many data access technologies, including open database connectivity (ODBC), Data Access Objects (DAO), OLE DB, and ADO. These technologies provide different means of accessing different data sources. Some are suitable for one kind of data source and some are suitable for others.

ODBC is suitable for relational data sources. There are two ways to use ODBC: through the ODBC application programming interface (API) and through ODBC wrapper classes. However, the ODBC API is tedious to program, and the ODBC wrapper classes (Microsoft foundation classes—MFCs—written in C++) aren't flexible enough for most work. The main advantage of ODBC is that it lets you work with various kinds of databases, as long as they have an associated ODBC driver. The ODBC drivers and ODBC administrator sit between the database and the application.

Another popular database technology for Windows is DAO. DAO is a set of OLE APIs designed to work only with databases supported by the Jet Database Engine, such as Access, Paradox, and SQL Server. DAO's advantage is that it is faster to develop with these databases. Its drawbacks are that the DAO API (OLE) is hard to implement and DAO is not geared for Data Sources outside the realm of the Jet Database Engine.

Microsoft then introduced OLE DB, a set of Component Object Model APIs that can access any kind of data source. Its drawback is that it too is hard to implement.

Microsoft next introduced ActiveX Data Objects (ADO). As a precursor to ADO.NET, it is much more than what its name indicates. Initially ADO was a nice wrapper around OLE DB, making development easier than using straight OLE DB API calls. The main advantage of ADO is that it is a hierarchy-free model, unlike both ODBC and DAO, where to connect to a table or recordset you have to go through the workspace to get to the connection and then through the connection to get to the database objects.

In one of our applications at an unnamed company,, we had to use both DAO and ODBC because DAO was not flexible enough and ODBC (MFCs) didn't support workspaces. Using both technologies, we had to install both, which incurred many complications and incompatibilities. Later, Microsoft came out with different versions of ODBC and DAO, which had to be constantly tracked in the configuration.

Even though ADO is the best solution, it still has some limitations. For example, it is designed for desktop client-server applications but not for Web applications. So, MDAC services are not convenient for working with XML—a real drawback when Web database access seems to be moving to XML.

Introduction to ADO.NET

The advent of .NET has brought a new database architecture: ADO.NET. Microsoft took care of drawbacks in previous technologies, coming up with a single solution, ADO+, now known as ADO.NET. All of ADO.NET's classes and architecture tie nicely into the .NET Framework. ADO.NET provides access to different types of data sources in n-tier, client-server, and XML application development.

Benefits of Using ADO.NET

Taking care of many of the problems and limitations of previous technologies, ADO.NET offers some rich advantages:

- Unlike previous database access technologies, ADO.NET is an open model. You can connect directly to a table without going through a class hierarchy.
- ADO.NET provides a unified data access model, which allows you to access all data the same way via DataSet objects.
- ADO.NET supports disconnected DataSets, which means your data gets cached and you don't have to reload it every time you want to manipulate it. This is a big advantage for Web applications since downloading and uploading data over the Web is tedious and consumes resources.
- ADO.NET provides a rich set of data-bound controls, which connect easily to a data source and can be utilized without writing a single line of code. Two of these data-bound controls are DataGrid and DataList.
- ADO.NET provides interoperability with ADO recordsets through DataSet objects.

ADO.NET Data Providers

ADO.NET data providers are namespaces that allow you to efficiently and quickly connect to different data sources and manipulate them. Data provider classes have different names and data sources, but all have the same symmetry and work in the same way as we will see later in the chapter. As of this writing, data providers exist for OLE DB, SQL Server, and ODBC. We anticipate data providers optimized for Oracle, Sybase, and other widely used databases: Microsoft provides incentives for companies to create their own custom data providers.

The *OLE DB data provider* acts as a kind of wrapper around the OLE DB API and uses it to access OLE DB data sources. All OLE DB data provider classes are named OleDb*xxx*—for example, OleDbConnection, OleDbCommand, and OleDbDataAdapter for the connection, command, and data adapter, respectively. We'll be talking about these classes in detail later in the chapter.

The *SQL data provider* is designed to work with SQL Server 7.0 or later. All SQL data provider classes are named Sql*xxx*—for example, SqlConnection, SqlCommand, and SqlDataAdapter for the connection, command, and data adapter, respectively.

The *ODBC data provider* is a separate addition to the .NET Framework. If you don't have the ODBC data provider on your machine, you may need to download it separately and install it. All ODBC data provider classes are named ODBC*xxx*—for example, ODBCConnection, ODBCCommand, ODBCDataAdapter.

The data providers are all contained in their own namespaces in .NET. ADO.NET offers two more useful namespaces, System.Data and System.Data.Common. Classes in these namespaces can be accessed by all data providers.

Table 10.1 defines ADO.NET namespaces and their classes.

Namespace	Description	Classes
System.Data	Basic classes for the ADO.NET architecture	DataRow, DataTable, DataSet, DataColumn, DataView
System.Data.OleDb	OleDb managed provider classes used to access data from OLE DB data sources: Jet database, XML file, MS Access	OleDbCommand, OleDbDataAdapter, OleDbDataReader, OleDbConnection, OleDbError
System.Data.Common	Classes shared by all data providers	DataAdapter, DataColumnMapping, DataTableMapping, DBDataAdapter, DbDataPermission
System.Data.SqlClient	SQLClient managed provider classes used to access data from SQL Server data sources	SqlCommand, SqlDataAdapter, SqlDataReader, SqlConnection, SqlError
System.Data.SqlTypes	Classes for the data types in SQL Server	SqlString, SqlDateTime, SqlInt32, SqlDouble, SqlLMoney, etc.
Microsoft.Data.Odbc	Classes for ODBC data sources	OdbcConnection, OdbcDataAdapter, OdbcCommand, OdbcDataReader

Table 10.1: ADO.NET Namespaces

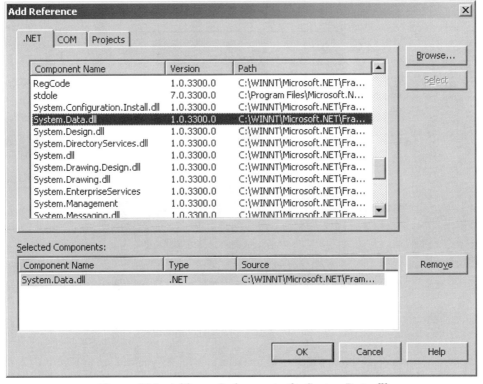

Figure 10.1: Adding a Reference to the System.Data.dll

Adding Namespace References to a Project

Before using ADO.NET, you must add references for the ADO.NET namespaces to your project. All ADO.NET namespace classes (except those for the ODBC data provider) are defined in the System.Data.dll assembly. You can add references to this assembly by using the Project→Add Reference menu option from VS.NET. As shown in Figure 10.1, select the Sytem.Data.dll assembly from the Add Reference dialog box and click the Select button.

After adding the ADO.NET reference, you need to call the namespaces in your application with the using directive. The namespaces for the OLE DB and SQL Server data providers are System.Data.OleDb and System.Data.Sql. To use these data providers, you need to add the following lines to your project.

```
using System.Data.SqlClient;
using System.Data.OleDb;
```

The ODBC data provider is available as an add-on to VS.NET. (If you don't have the ODBC data provider, you'll need to download the ODBC.NET SDK from the Microsoft site. You can also find links to downloads in the Downloads section of C# Corner: http://www.c-sharpcorner.com/downloads.asp). Unlike the OLE DB and the SQL Server data providers, the ODBC data provider is defined in the System.Data.Odbc namespace. You need to add this namespace reference if you are using the ODBC data provider classes to access ODBC data sources:

```
using Microsoft.Data.Odbc;
```

Understanding the ADO.NET Architecture

Figure 10.2 describes the architecture of the ADO.NET components.

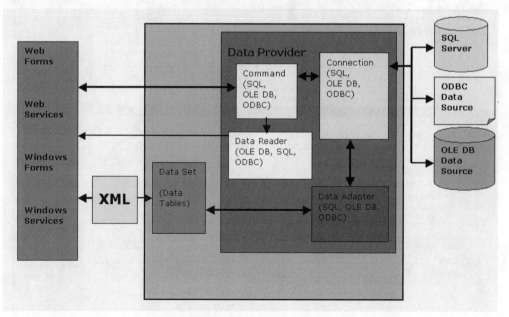

Figure 10.2: ADO.NET Architecture

The initial object is a connection, which talks to a data source. As you can see in Figure 10.2, the data adapter and command object get data from a data source through the connection. After setting up the connection, you can create a command object to execute SQL statements (INSERT,

UPDATE, DELETE) against the data source. The data adapter is a bridge between the data source and a data set, providing the Fill method, which fills a data set, and the Update method, which saves changes to the data source.

With the help of DataView and DataViewManager, a data set (represented by the DataSet object) can be used to bind data to data-bound controls. A data set is a collection of data tables, which are in-memory representations of database tables. A data set uses XML schemas to store and transfer data from one object to another.

The data reader (represented by SqlDataReader, OleDbDataReader, or OdbcDataReader for SQL, OLE DB, and ODBC data providers, respectively) is another useful component of ADO.NET. You can use it to read data from a data source by calling a command object's ExecuteReader method. (We'll talk more about data readers later in the chapter.)

As discussed earlier, ADO.NET provides data providers for many different kinds of data sources. All data providers define a hierarchical class model with one-to-one symmetry between classes and class architecture. Once you know how to work with one kind of data provider, you can use other data providers in almost the same way (except you would need to change the class name and the connection string). Table 10.3 lists the classes for OLE DB, SQL, and ODBC data providers.

Component	OLE DB data provider	SQL data provider	ODBC data provider
Connection	OleDbConnection	SqlConnection	OdbcConnection
Command	OleDbCommand	SqlCommand	OdbcCommand
Data adapter	OleDbDataAdapter	SqlDataAdapter	OdbcDataAdapter
Data reader	OleDbDataReader	SqlDataReader	OdbcDataReader
Transaction	OleDbTransaction	SqlTransaction	OdbcTransaction
Error	OleDbError	SqlError	OdbcError
Permission	OleDbPermission	SqlPermission	OdbcPermission
Parameter	OleDbParameter	SqlParameter	OdbcParameter
Exception	OleDbException	SqlException	OdbcException

Table 10.3: ADO.NET Classes for OLE DB, SQL, and ODBC Data Providers

As shown in Table 10.3, data providers have similar classes. Not only are names similar, but the classes also provide nearly the same methods and properties. For example, the OleDbConnection, SqlConnection, and OdbcConnection classes all provide Open and Close methods to open and close database connections.

The System.Data Namespaces

As discussed in the "ADO.NET Data Providers" section, the .NET base class library (also known as the BCL or the runtime class library) provides two common namespaces and a number of data-provider-related namespaces. The common namespaces are System.Data and System.Data.Common. The System.Data classes are independent of the data providers and can be used with or without them. For instance, DataTable is one of the classes in the System.Data namespace, and a DataTable object is an in-memory representation of a table. You can create a table programmatically and work with it to generate a DataSet, DataView, and DataViewManager and bind all of these objects to data-bound controls. There is no database involved in this case.

In the other case, you read data from a database and fill a DataSet using a DataAdapter and then generate a DataView and a DataViewManager for the DataSet. We will discuss these classes in more detail later in this chapter.

The System.Data namespace consists basically of ADO.NET component classes. Some of these classes are described in Table 10.4.

Class	Description
Constraint	Represents a constraint that can be applied to data column objects.
ConstraintCollection	Represents a collection of data table constraints.
ConstraintException	Represents the exception that is thrown when attempting an action that violates a constraint.
DataColumn	Represents a data table column schema.
DataColumnCollection	Represents a collection of data columns of a data table.
DataRelation	Represents a parent/child relationship between two data tables.
DataRelationCollection	Represents the collection of data relations of a data set.
DataRow	Represents a row of data in a data table.
DataRowCollection	Represents a collection of data rows.
DataRowView	Represents a customized view of a data row.
DataSet	Represents an in-memory cache of data.
DataTable	Represents one table of in-memory data.
DataTableCollection	Represents the collection of data tables.
DataView	Represents a data-bindable, customized view of a DataTable. A data view can be used for sorting, filtering, searching, editing, and navigation.
DataViewManager	Contains a default DataViewSettingCollection for each data table in a data set.
DataViewSetting	Represents the default settings for ApplyDefaultSort, DataViewManager, RowFilter, RowStateFilter, Sort, and Table for DataViews created from the DataViewManager.
TypedDataSetGenerator	Used to create a strongly typed DataSet.

Table 10.4: The System.Data Namespace Classes

Working with Different .NET Data Providers

There are two major differences in working with different data providers: different connection strings and slightly different class names (plus a few different methods and properties). The following example shows how to connect to all three data providers—SQL Server, OLE DB, and ODBC—when you already have a connection string available:

```
string str = connectionstring;
```

To work with the SQL data provider, you must import the System.Data.SqlClient namespace by adding the using directive:

```
using System.Data.SqlClient;
```

After that you can create a connection(or open an existing connection), and utilize other SqlClient classes:

```
SqlConnection con = new SqlConnection(connectionstring);
con.Open();
```

To work with the OLE DB data provider, you must import the System.Data.OleDb namespace by adding the using directive:

```
using System.Data.OleDb;
```

Afterwards, you can create a connection to your OLE DB provider or open an existing connection, and utilize the other available OLE DB classes:

```
OleDbConnection con = new OleDbConnection(connectionstring);
con.Open();
```

The ODBC data provider is defined in the Microsoft.Data.Odbc namespace, which you must import with the using directive:

```
using System.Data.Odbc;

OdbcConnection con = new OdbcConnection(connectionstring);
con.Open();
```

Most of the examples in this chapter are based on the SQL Server database. Toward the end of the chapter are some OLE DB and ODBC data provider examples, which show that once you know how to work with one data provider, you can work with them all.

Working with the Connections

Each data provider has a connection class: OleDbConnection, SqlConnection, and OdbcConnection are the connection classes for the OLE DB, SQL, and ODBC data providers, respectively.

Table 10.5 describes the SqlConnection class properties. The ConnectionString property represents a connection string, which may contain the SQL Server name, database name, user ID, and password. The Database and DataSource properties let you retrieve a database name and SQL Server name, respectively. Some of these properties, however, may not be available for other data providers. For instance, while the SqlConnection class provides the ServerVersion property, the OLE DB data provider connection class (OleDbConnection) does not.

Property	Description
ConnectionString	Represents the connection string. A connection string contains the data provider and data source names, with user ID, password, and other information.
ConnectionTimeout	Represents the time to wait while trying to establish a connection before terminating the attempt and generating an error.
Database	Represents the name of the current database.
DataSource	Represents the name of the instance of SQL Server to connect to.
PacketSize	Represents the size (in bytes) of network packets used to communicate with an instance of SQL Server.
ServerVersion	Represents the SQL Server version.
State	Represents the current state of the connection.
WorkstationId	Represents a string that identifies the database client.

Table 10.5: The SqlConnection Class Properties

The Open and Close methods open and close a connection with a data source. The ChangeDatabase method lets you change the connection to a different database. Table 10.6 briefly describes the SqlConnection class methods.

Method	Description
BeginTransaction	Begins a database transaction.
ChangeDatabase	Changes the current database.
Close	Closes a database connection.
CreateCommand	Creates and returns a SqlCommand.
Open	Opens a database connection

Table 10.6: The SqlConnection Class Methods

Create a Connection Programmatically

One way to create a connection is by using the default constructor with no parameters and afterward setting the ConnectionString property:

```
string str = "Data Source=localhost; Integrated Security=SSPI; Initial
Catalog=northwind";

SqlConnection con = new SqlConnection();
con.ConnectionString = str;
con.Open();
```

You can also create a connection by passing a connection string as a parameter of the constructor. The following source code uses the integrated security option as a security measure for connecting to the database:

```
string str = "Data Source=localhost; Integrated Security=SSPI; Initial
Catalog=northwind";
```

```
SqlConnection con = new SqlConnection(str);
con.Open();
```

In Windows 2000, the Security Support Provider Interface (SSPI) provides a uniform interface for using compliant authentication protocols. SSPI enables applications to access libraries containing common authentication and cryptographic data schemes, which lets an application avoid coding security options (checking user IDs and passwords).

The connection string can also have a user ID, a password, a workstation ID, and other options for connecting securely to the database. The following string uses the user ID *sa* and a null password to open a connection to the SQL Server database.

```
string str = "data source=(local);initial catalog=Northwind;persist security
info=False;user id" +
        "=sa;password=;workstation id=MCB;packet size=4096";

SqlConnection con = new SqlConnection(str);
con.Open();
```

The source code in Listing 10.1 shows how to open a connection. After opening the connection, the program displays the connection properties on the console.

Listing 10.1—Using Connection Object

```
using System;
using System.Data.SqlClient;

namespace ConnectionSamp
{
        class Class1
        {
                static void Main(string[] args)
                {
                // Create a connection string
                  string str = "Data Source=localhost; Integrated Security=SSPI;
                     Initial Catalog=northwind";

                SqlConnection con = new SqlConnection(str);
                con.Open();

                SqlCommand cmd = con.CreateCommand();

                Console.WriteLine("Data Source :"+ con.DataSource.ToString() );
                Console.WriteLine("Database :"+ con.Database.ToString() );
                Console.WriteLine("State :"+  con.State.ToString() );
                Console.WriteLine("Connection String :"+
                 con.ConnectionString.ToString() );
                Console.WriteLine("TimeOut :"+ con.ConnectionTimeout.ToString());
                con.Close();


                }
        }
}
```

The output of Listing 10.1 looks like Figure 10.3.

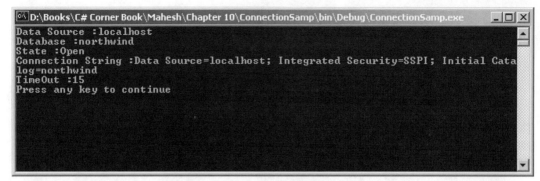

Figure 10.3: Output of Listing 10.1

Create a Connection Using VS.NET

If you are developing Windows form or Web form applications, you can add a connection object by simply dragging a SqlConnection (or OleDbConnection or OdbcConnection) from the Toolbox→Data tab to the forms, as shown in Figure 10.4.

Figure 10.4: Adding SqlConnection from the Toolbox

After adding a connection from the Toolbox, you will want to bring up the Properties window by right-clicking on SqlConnection in the Designer window and selecting the Properties menu item. The Properties window of SqlConnection looks like Figure 10.5. In the Properties window, you can set the SqlConnection object's various properties. If you click on the ConnectionString property, it launches the Server Explorer to create a new connection.

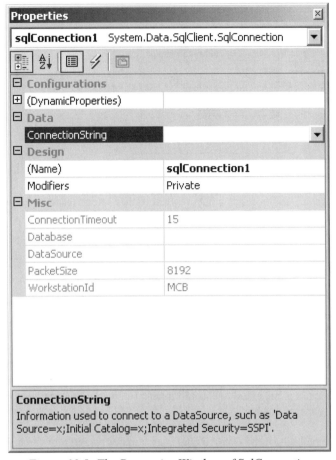

Figure 10.5: The Properties Window of SqlConnection

The Server Explorer can be used to create a new connection and manage database servers. We'll discuss the Server Explorer later in this chapter.

Working with Data Adapters

A data adapter sits between a data source and a DataSet object and provides communication between them. Each data provider has a data adapter class. Here are the classes for the SQL, OLE DB, and ODBC data providers:

- SqlDataAdapter: Data adapter for SQL Server 7.0 or later
- OleDbDataAdapter: Data adapter for OLE DB data sources
- OdbcDataAdapter: Data adapter for ODBC data sources

Actually, there is no direct communication between a data adapter and a Connection object. A data adapter communicates with a Connection object through Command objects. A Command object actually has a direct connection with the Connection object through its Connection property. The diagram in Figure 10.7 shows the relationship between a data set, data adapter, connection, and data source.

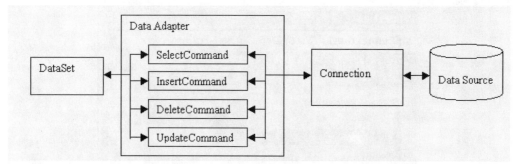

Figure 10.7: Relationship Between a Data Set, Data Adapter, Connection, and Data Source

As Figure 10.7 shows, a DataSet sends a data request (either select, insert, update, or delete) to a data adapter. A data adapter uses its command properties based on the requirement, executes the SQL statements, finally returns the desired data.

The data adapter bridges the data set and data source with two main methods: The Fill method of a data adapter fills a data set from the data source through the connection. The Update method of a data adapter saves changes from the data set to a data source through the connection.

DataAdapter Members

All the data providers' data adapter classes(SqlDataAdapter, OleDbDataAdapter, and OdbcDataAdapter classes) contain the same properties, fields and methods. All data adapter classes are derived from the DbDataAdapter class which in turn are derived from the DataAdapter class. The DbDataAdapter class is the class you would inherit to create your own custom DataAdapter (not covered in the scope of this book).

The Fill and Update methods of the DataAdapter play a major role in transferring data between a data set and a data source. The FillSchema method adds a DataTable to a DataSet and configures the schema of the DataSet to match the data source's schema.

The DataAdapter also has four command properties: DeleteCommand, InsertCommand, SelectCommand, and UpdateCommand. These properties set the SQL queries, which are executed during the call to the Update or Fill method. Later we'll see how you can set these properties.

TableMappings

The TableMapping class, defined in the System.Data namespace, represents a table mapping. The TableMappings property of a data adapter is useful when DataSet table names are different from the names picked up from the data source. By default, a DataSet's members are table names and column names. For instance, if a DataSet has two tables, A and B, you can access those tables by using their names in the DataSet's Tables property. Similarly, you can access a table's columns by using actual column names in the database table.

What if you don't want to use original table and column names in your program? This is where table and column mappings are helpful. A DataSet's original table is called the source table, and the mapped table is called the data set table. The DataSet's SourceTable property represents the original table name, and the DataSetTable property represents the mapped table name. You can use the DataTableMapping class to map aliases between the source and data set table names and the DataColumnMapping class to map data column names from the source table to the data set table. The ColumnMappings property is contained in the DataTableMapping class and returns the

DataColumnMappingCollection class object, which contains a DataColumnMapping object for each column in the table.

Creating Data Adapters

You can create data adapters either programmatically or by using the VS.NET IDE. We'll discuss the VS.NET IDE in more detail later, but here we'll concentrate on creating data adapters programmatically.

You can create a data adapter by passing a SQL statement and connection object as the first and second arguments of the data adapter constructor. The source code in Listing 10.2 creates a data adapter. We first create and open a connection, passing it a connection string. Then we create the data adapter, passing it a SQL Select statement and a connection object.

Listing 10.2—Creating a Data Adapter

```
// Create a connection and SQL strings
string str = "Data Source=localhost; Integrated Security=SSPI; Initial
Catalog=northwind";
string stmt = "SELECT * FROM Customers";

// Create a connection and open it
SqlConnection con = new SqlConnection(str);
con.Open();

// Create a data adapter
SqlDataAdapter adapter = new SqlDataAdapter(stmt, con);
```

Using Data Adapters

The source code in Listing 10.3 creates a data adapter and calls its Fill method to fill data to a data set. It then binds the default view of the data set to a data grid control. The data grid control is as the name suggests, a grid control filled with data. The columns of the grid are mapped to the columns of the database and the rows of the grid are mapped to rows of data in the database. Binding to the data grid control allows you to display the rows of data from the data set inside this control.

To test this application, create a Windows application and add a data grid control to the form. You can add a data grid in the VS.NET IDE by dragging the data grid control from the Toolbox to the form. Afterward, write the code in Listing 10.3 into the form's form_load event handler.

Listing 10.3—Accessing Data Using Data Adapter from a SQL Server Database

```
private void Form1_Load(object sender, System.EventArgs e)
{
      // Create a connection and SQL strings
      string str = "Data Source=localhost; Integrated Security=SSPI;
   Initial Catalog=northwind";
      string stmt = "SELECT * FROM Customers";

      // Create a connection and open it
      SqlConnection con = new SqlConnection(str);
      con.Open();

      // Create a data adapter
      SqlDataAdapter adapter = new SqlDataAdapter(stmt, con);

      // Create a data set and fill it by calling Fill method
      // of data adapter

      DataSet ds = new DataSet("Cust");
      adapter.Fill(ds, "customers");
```

```
    // Attach data set's default view to the data grid control
    dataGrid1.DataSource = ds.DefaultViewManager;

    // Close connection
    con.Close();
}
```

The output of Listing 10.3 looks like Figure 10.8.

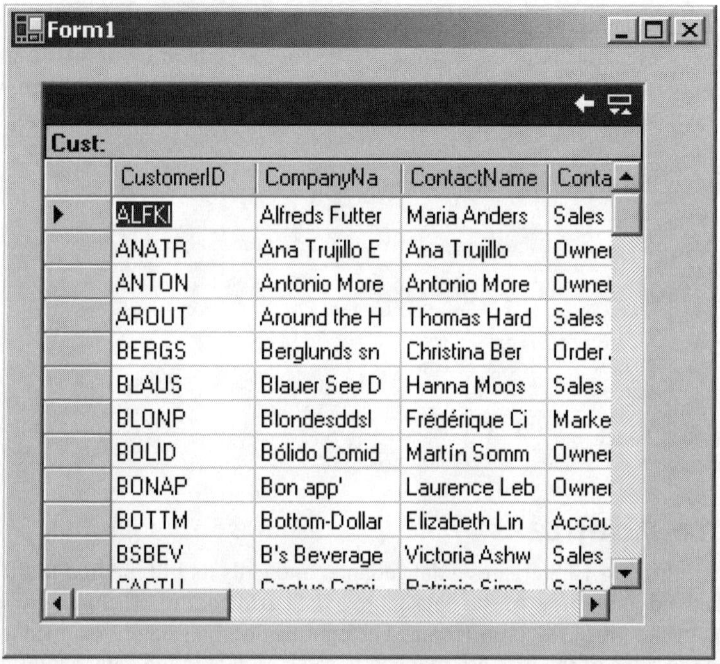

Figure 10.8: Filling Data in a Data Grid Using a Data Adapter

Understanding a Data Reader

A data reader provides a forward-only data stream of rows from a data source. The OleDbDataReader, SqlDataReader, and OdbcDataReader classes represent the data readers for OLE DB, SQL, and ODBC data providers, respectively.

You create a data reader by calling the command object's ExecuteReader method. The ExecuteReader method returns a data reader object. The following code example calls ExecuteReader on the SqlCommand object, which returns a SqlDataReader object:

```
// Create a command
SqlCommand cmd = new SqlCommand(stmt, con);

// Call ExecuteReader
SqlDataReader reader  = cmd.ExecuteReader();
```

A data reader's Read method can be used to read each row in a database table until the last record. You can access individual column data from a data reader either by passing the index of a table column or by passing the column name or the column index (starting with 0), as you can see from the following code snippet:

```
while (reader.Read())
```

```
{
        Console.WriteLine(reader[0].ToString());
        Console.Write(reader[1].ToString());
        Console.Write(reader[2].ToString());
        Console.WriteLine();
}
```

After all the reading is done, you should call the Close method of the data reader to close the data reader and free all resources consumed by the reader:

```
// Close reader and connection
reader.Close();
```

The data reader also implements dozens of Get*xxx* methods, which return values from the data source in native format. For example `GetChar(0)` returns a character from the first column of the current row.

The SqlReader also has some useful properties associated with it. For example FieldCount, gets the number of columns in a row of data. The Item property allows you to retrieve the data from a particular column in the current row. Table 10.6 describes some of the SqlDataReader class properties.

Property	Description
Depth	Represents the depth of nesting for the current row.
FieldCount	Returns the number of columns in the current row.
IsClosed	Returns a value indicating whether the data reader is closed.
Item	Returns the value of a column in its native format.
RecordsAffected	Returns the number of rows affected by execution of the Transact-SQL statement.

Table 10.6: The SqlDataReader Class Properties

We will see a more complete example of a data reader later in this chapter.

Understanding Command and CommandBuilder

A command represents a SQL statement or stored procedure that can be executed against a data source. The OleDbCommand, SqlCommand, and OdbcCommand classes represent the Command object for OLE DB, SQL, and ODBC data providers, respectively.

Creating a Command Object

You can create a command object using different constructors provided by the class. You can pass a connection and a SQL string as two parameters of the constructor. For example, the following code shows you how to create a SqlCommand object where stmt is a SQL string:

```
SqlConnection con = new SqlConnection(str);
con.Open();

// Create a command
SqlCommand cmd = new SqlCommand(stmt, con);
```

You can also create a command object by using the default constructor and then use the command object's properties to set a connection and appropriate SQL statement. The following source code creates a SqlCommand object and sets its Connection, CommandText, and CommandType properties.

```
SqlCommand cmd = new SqlCommand();
cmd.Connection = con;
cmd.CommandType = CommandType.Text;
cmd.CommandText = "stmt";
```

You can also execute stored procedures using the command object. To execute stored procedures, you need to set the CommandType property as CommandType.StoredProcedure and set the CommandText property as a stored procedure name. The following source code executes the CustOrderHist stored procedure available in the SQL Server Northwind database:

```
SqlCommand cmd = new SqlCommand();
cmd.Connection = con;
cmd.CommandType = CommandType.StoredProcedure;
cmd.CommandText = "CustOrderHist";
```

The complete source code is discussed later in this chapter.

Command Object Properties and Methods

Before we write any program, let's take a look at command properties and methods. Table 10.6 lists properties of the SqlCommand class. The CommandText property holds a SqlStatement, table name, or stored procedure. The CommandType property tells what type of command is being used—a SQL statement, stored procedure, or direct reading from a table.

Property	Description
CommandText	Represents the SQL statement or stored procedure.
CommandTimeout	Represents the wait time before terminating the attempt to execute a command and generating an error.
CommandType	Represents the type of command. The value can be StoredProcedure, Text, or TableDirect.
Connection	Represents the connection attached to the command.
DesignTimeVisible	Represents whether the command object should be visible in a Windows Forms Designer control.
Parameters	Returns the SqlParameterCollection.
Transaction	Represents the transaction in which the SqlCommand executes.
UpdatedRowSource	Represents how command results are applied to the DataRow when used by the Update method of the DbDataAdapter.

Table 10.6: The SqlCommand Class Properties

The SqlCommand methods are described in Table 10.7. Methods such as ExecuteReader, ExecuteNonQuery, and ExecuteScalar help you to execute SQL commands directly on the database.

Method	Description
Cancel	Attempts to cancel the execution of a SqlCommand.
ExecuteNonQuery	Executes a SQL statement and returns the number of rows affected.
ExecuteReader	Executes a statement and returns data in a data reader.
ExecuteScalar	Executes the query and returns only the first column of the first row in the resultset returned by the query.
ExecuteXmlReader	Executes a SQL statement and returns data in XmlReader.

Table 10.7: The SqlCommand Class Methods

Reading Data Using a Command Object

The source code in Listing 10.4 creates a command object and calls ExecuteReader, which returns data in a SqlDataReader object. To test this application, create a Windows application, add a List Box control to the form, and write the code in Listing 10.4 on the form load event handler.

Listing 10.4—Reading Data Using SqlCommand

```
private void Form1_Load(object sender, System.EventArgs e)
{
        // Create a connection and SQL strings
        string str = "Data Source=localhost;" +
        "Integrated Security=SSPI; Initial Catalog=northwind";
        string stmt = "SELECT * FROM Customers";
        string str1 = "";

        // Create a connection and open it
        SqlConnection con = new SqlConnection(str);
        con.Open();

        // Create a command
        SqlCommand cmd = new SqlCommand(stmt, con);

        // Call ExecuteReader
        SqlDataReader reader  = cmd.ExecuteReader();
        while (reader.Read())
        {
                str1 = reader[0].ToString();
                str1 += ", ";
                str1 += reader[1].ToString();
                str1 += ", ";
                str1 += reader[2].ToString();

                // Add data to the list box control
                listBox1.Items.Add(str1);
        }

        // Close the reader and connection
        reader.Close();
        con.Close();
}
```

The output of Listing 10.4 looks like Figure 10.9.

Figure 10.9: Viewing Data in a List Box Control from a Data Reader

You can also execute stored procedures using the command object by setting a few of its properties and calling ExecuteReader. To execute a stored procedure, you need to set the CommandType property as CommandType.StoredProcedure, and the CommandText property as the name of the stored procedure. If a stored procedure takes any parameters, you also need to add parameterss to the command object.

As you can see in Listing 10.5, we execute stored procedure CustOrderHist of the Northwind SQL Server database, which requires a parameter of type CustomerID. In Listing 10.5, we create a command object and set its properties. After that we create a SqlParameter and add it to the command. After that we call ExecuteReader and read the data.

SqlCommand also provides method ExecuteXmlReader, which returns an object of type XmlReader. XmlReader provides methods to treat data as an XML document. XmlReader is described in more detail in the chapter on XML in .NET.

Listing 10.5—Executing a Stored Procedure Using SqlCommand

```
private void Form1_Load(object sender, System.EventArgs e)
{
      // Create a connection and SQL strings
      string str = "Data Source=localhost;" +
            "Integrated Security=SSPI; Initial Catalog=northwind";

      SqlConnection con = new SqlConnection(str);

      try
      {
            // Create a connection and open it

            con.Open();
            // Create a command. Set CommandType as stored procedure,
            // Set CommandText as stored procedure name
            SqlCommand cmd = new SqlCommand();
            cmd.Connection = con;
            cmd.CommandType = CommandType.StoredProcedure;
            cmd.CommandText = "CustOrderHist";
```

```csharp
                // Create a parameter and add it to the command
                SqlParameter parm1 = cmd.Parameters.Add("@CustomerID",
                 SqlDbType.NChar, 20);
                parm1.Value = "BLONP";


                // Call ExecuteReader
                SqlDataReader reader = cmd.ExecuteReader();

                while (reader.Read())
                {
                        // Add data to the list box control
                        listBox1.Items.Add(reader[0].ToString());
                }

                // Close reader
                reader.Close();

        }
        catch(SqlException exp)
        {
                MessageBox.Show( exp.Message.ToString() );
        }
        finally
        {
                con.Close();
        }
}
```

The output of Listing 10.5 looks like Figure 10.10.

Figure 10.10: Executing a Stored Procedure Using SqlCommand

Adding, Updating, and Deleting Data Using a Command Object

You can execute all kinds of SQL statements using a command object. The ExecuteNonQuery method of SqlCommand is used to execute SQL statements that don't return any data. Examples of nonquery SQL statements are INSERT, UPDATE, and DELETE. The source code in Listing 10.6 adds data to the Categories table of the Northwind database using the INSERT statement. After that we use UPDATE and DELETE statements to update and delete the newly added row. As you can see from Listing 10.6, we just create a command object, assign it a SQL statement, and call the ExecuteNonQuery method to execute the SQL statement.

Listing 10.6—Adding, Updating, and Deleting Data Using SqlCommand

```
// Create a connection and SQL strings
string str = "Data Source=localhost;" +
       "Integrated Security=SSPI; Initial Catalog=northwind";
SqlConnection con = new SqlConnection(str);

try
{
       // Create a command
       SqlCommand cmd = new SqlCommand();
       cmd.Connection = con;
       cmd.CommandType = CommandType.Text;

       // Construct an INSERT SQL statement
       string stmt = "INSERT INTO Categories(CategoryName, Description)"+ "VALUES
              ('NewCat', 'This is new Category')" ;

       // Execute the statement
       con.Open();
       cmd.CommandText = stmt;
       cmd.ExecuteNonQuery();
       MessageBox.Show("INSERT Executed");
       con.Close();

       // Construct an UPDATE SQL statement
       stmt = "UPDATE Categories SET Description = 'Old Category' WHERE "+
              "CategoryName = 'NewCat' ";

       // Execute the statement
       con.Open();
       cmd.CommandText = stmt;
       cmd.ExecuteNonQuery();
       MessageBox.Show("UPDATE Executed");
       con.Close();

       // Construct a DELETE SQL statement
       stmt = "DELETE FROM Categories WHERE CategoryName = 'NewCat' ";
       // Execute the statement
       con.Open();
       cmd.CommandText = stmt;
       cmd.ExecuteNonQuery();
       MessageBox.Show("DELETE Executed");
       con.Close();

}
catch(SqlException exp)
{
       MessageBox.Show( exp.Message.ToString() );
}
```

Using Command Builder

To give the data adapter a way to execute final changes made to a data set into the database when calling the Update method, you need to assign its command properties to SQL statements (UPDATE, INSERT, DELETE). You can use the Command Builder to automatically generate these SQL statements at runtime by utilizing the value of the DataAdapter's SelectCommand property (a string containing the query).

To use a Command Builder object, you need to first construct a data adapter and attach it to the Command Builder object. In this way, the Command Builder listens when any changes are made to the data adapter. If you change the data adapter SELECT statement contained in the SelectCommand or the connection to the DataAdapter, you will need to call the RefreshSchema method of the Command Builder in order to update it using these latest command changes.

The source code in Listing 10.7 shows you how to use a SqlCommandBuilder to work with a SqlDataAdapter. To test this example, create a Windows application and drag a data grid control to the form and write the code in Listing 10.7 on the form load event.

Listing 10.7—Using the SqlCommandBuilder Class

```
// Create a connection and SQL strings
string str = "Data Source=localhost;" +
        "Integrated Security=SSPI; Initial Catalog=northwind";

SqlConnection con = new SqlConnection(str);

try
{
        string stmt = "SELECT * FROM Categories";
        // Create a data adapter
        SqlDataAdapter adapter = new SqlDataAdapter();
        adapter.SelectCommand = new SqlCommand(stmt, con);
        // Construct a command builder
        SqlCommandBuilder builder = new SqlCommandBuilder(adapter);

        con.Open();
        // Create a data set and call data adapter's fill method
        // to fill data to it
        DataSet ds = new DataSet();
        adapter.Fill(ds, "Categories");

        //Get the data table attached with the data set
        // And create a new row
        DataTable table = ds.Tables["Categories"];
        DataRow row1= table.NewRow();

        // set values of the new row and add it to the data table
        row1["CategoryName"] = "NewCategory";
        row1["Description"] = "New Description";
        table.Rows.Add(row1);

        //Update the data set
        adapter.Update(ds, "Categories");
        // Bind the data source to the data grid
        dataGrid1.DataSource = ds.DefaultViewManager;

}
catch(SqlException exp)
{
        MessageBox.Show( exp.Message.ToString() );
}
finally
{
```

```
        con.Close();
}
```

In Listing 10.7, we used the DataTable and DataRow classes to add data to a data set. The DataTable.Rows.Add method is used to add a row to a data table. We will discuss the DataTable, DataRow, and DataColumn objects in more detail in the next section.

The output of Listing 10.7 looks like Figure 10.11.

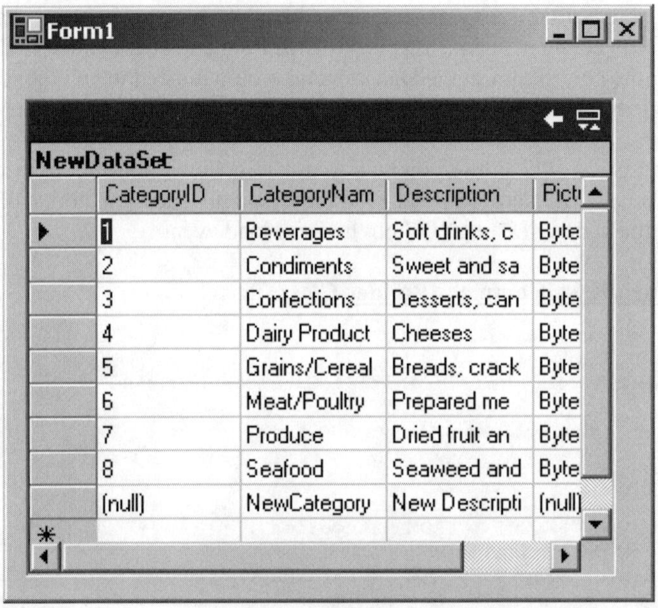

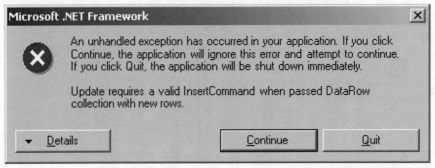

Figure 10.11: The Output of Listing 10.7

To demonstrate what happens if you call Update on the DataAdapter without using the Command Builder to create the SQL nonquery statements, comment out the following line in Listing 10.7. You should get an exception, which looks like Figure 10.12.

```
// SqlCommandBuilder builder = new SqlCommandBuilder(adapter);
```

Figure 10.12: Exception When Adding Data to a Data Adapter Without Constructing the Command Builder

The DataTable, DataRows, and DataColumn Objects

A DataSet object is a collection of DataTable objects. A DataTable object is an in-memory representation of a database table. A DataTable is a collection of DataRow and DataColumn objects. A DataColumn object represents a column of a DataTable, and a DataRow object represents a row of a DataTable.

Understanding a DataTable Object

A DataTable is a collection of DataRow and DataColumn objects. The schema of a DataTable is a collection of DataColumn objects. The DataColumnCollection properties represent a collection of DataColumns of a DataTable. The DataTable.Columns.Add method is used to add a DataColumn to a DataTable.

The DataRow object represents a row in a DataTable. The DataRowCollection represents a collection of DataRows of a DataTable. The DataTable.Rows.Add method is used to add a DataRow to a DataTable.

You can create parent-child (or master-detail) relationships between tables using one or more related columns in the tables using the DataRelation object. The DataTable contains two sets of DataRelationCollections. It contains a ParentRelations representing the relations to the parent DataTables, and ChildRelations, which points to the child tables related to the DataTable.

DataTable Members

The DataTable class defines many methods and properties. In this section, we will see some of the more commonly used ones. Some DataTable properties that you may recognize as having equivalent representations in the database are Constraints, Rows, Columns, and DefaultView.

Table 10.10 defines DataTable properties.

Property	Description
Columns	Returns the collection of columns that belongs to this data table.
Constraints	Returns the collection of constraints maintained by this data table.
DataSet	Returns the DataSet that this data table belongs to.
DefaultView	Returns a customized view of the table, which may include a filtered view or a cursor position.
Rows	Returns the collection of rows that belong to this data table.
TableName	Represents the name of the data table.

Table 10.10: DataTable Class Properties

Understanding a DataColumn Object

A DataColumn object represents a column schema of a DataTable. You can create a DataColumn object by using its constructors. After creating a DataColumn, you set its properties and add it to DataTable.

A DataColumn has properties common to schema information, such as ColumnName, DataType, AllowDBNull, and DefaultValue. The DataColumn class properties are listed in Table 10.8.

Property	Description
AllowDBNull	Represents if null values are allowed in a column or not.
AutoIncrement	Represents if a column automatically increments the value of the column for new rows added to the table.
AutoIncrementSeed	Represents the starting value for a column that has its AutoIncrement property set to true.
AutoIncrementStep	Gets or sets the increment used by a column with its AutoIncrement property set to true.
Caption	Represents the caption for the column.
ColumnMapping	Represents the MappingType of a column.
ColumnName	Represents the name of a column.
DataType	Represents type of data stored in a column.
DefaultValue	Represents the default value for a column when creating new rows.
Expression	Represents the expression used to filter rows, calculate the values in a column, or create an aggregate column.
ExtendedProperties	Represents the collection of custom user information.
MaxLength	Represents the maximum length of a text column.
Namespace	Represents the namespace of the DataColumn.
Ordinal	Returns the position of the column in the DataColumnCollection collection.
Prefix	Represents an XML prefix that aliases the namespace of the DataTable.
ReadOnly	Represents if the column allows changes once a row has been added to the table.
Table	Returns the DataTable to which the column belongs to.
Unique	Represents if the values in each row of the column must be unique.

Table 10.8: The DataColumn Class Properties

Understanding a DataRow Object

A DataRow object represents a row of a DataTable. You can create a DataRow using the DataRow class constructors. After that you call the DataTable.Rows.Add method to add a row to a DataTable.

You can also edit and delete a DataRow's contents. You use the BeginEdit and EndEdit methods of DataRow before and after editing the contents of a DataRow. The Delete method of DataRow deletes the row of data in memory. Table 10.9 describes some of the DataRow class methods.

Method	Description
AcceptChanges	Commits all the changes made to this row since the last time AcceptChanges was called.
BeginEdit	Starts an edit operation on a DataRow object.
CancelEdit	Cancels the current edit on the row.
Delete	Deletes the DataRow.
EndEdit	Stops the edit occurring on the row.
HasVersion	Returns a value indicating whether a specified version exists.
RejectChanges	Rejects all changes made to the row since AcceptChanges was last called.

Table 10.9: The DataRow Class Methods

Creating a DataTable

Although the DataSet will create DataTables for you when you fill it, you can create a DataTable dynamically using the DataTable class constructor. After creating an object of DataTable class, you can create table columns using the DataColumn class to construct the DataTable's schema. The DataColumn class defines a column data type and other properties. After creating a DataColumn and setting its properties, you can then call the DataTable.Columns.Add method, which takes a single parameter of DataColumn type and adds a column to DataTable.

The source code in Listing 10.8 creates a DataTable with three columns: ID, Name, and Address.

Listing 10.8—Using DataTable to Create a Table Schema

```
// Create a data table
DataTable table = new DataTable("TestTable");

// Create a data column
DataColumn dc = new DataColumn();
dc.DataType = System.Type.GetType("System.Int32");
dc.ColumnName = "ID";
dc.Unique = true;
// Add column to DataTable
table.Columns.Add(dc);

// Create Name column
dc = new DataColumn();
dc.DataType = System.Type.GetType("System.String");
dc.ColumnName = "Name";
// Add column to DataTable
table.Columns.Add(dc);

// Create Address column
dc = new DataColumn();
dc.DataType = System.Type.GetType("System.String");
dc.ColumnName = "Address";
// Add column to DataTable
table.Columns.Add(dc);
```

Adding Rows to a DataTable

After creating a table schema, the next step is to add data to it. DataRow is used to add rows to a DataTable. To add rows to a DataTable, you call the NewRow method of DataTable, which then returns a DataRow. Once you have a DataRow object, you can set the properties of the DataRow and then call the DataTable.Rows.Add method, which takes a DataRow as a parameter to add a row to DataTable.

The source code in Listing 10.9 adds three rows to a DataTable.

Listing 10.9—Adding Rows to a DataTable

```
// Adding three rows to the table
DataRow row = table.NewRow();
row[0] = 1;
row[1] = "Lofer";
row[2] = "30th Street, PA Avenue, NY";
table.Rows.Add(row);

row = table.NewRow();
row[0] = 2;
row[1] = "Penelope";
row[2] = "Super Market Avem London, UK";
table.Rows.Add(row);

row = table.NewRow();
row[0] = 3;
row[1] = "Robyn";
row[2] = "Kruse House, Jacksonville, FL";
table.Rows.Add(row);
```

Binding a DataTable to a DataGrid

After creating a DataTable you can bind it to a DataGrid control. To test this, we create a Windows application, add a DataGrid control to the form by dragging it from the Toolbox, and write the code shown in Listing 10.10 on the form load. As you can see from Listing 10.10, we set the DataGrid's DataSource property equal to the DataTable.DefaultView. The DefaultView is a particular view in memory of the DataTable. We will talk more about DataViews later in this chapter. Setting the DataView to the DataSource of the DataGrid tells the grid how the data should look in each row, as far as sorting and filtering are concerned.

Listing 10.10—Binding a DataTable to a DataGrid

```
private void Form1_Load(object sender, System.EventArgs e)
{
        // Create a data table
        DataTable table = new DataTable("TestTable");

        // Create a data column
        DataColumn dc = new DataColumn();
        dc.DataType = System.Type.GetType("System.Int32");
        dc.ColumnName = "ID";
        dc.Unique = true;
        // Add column to DataTable
        table.Columns.Add(dc);

        // Create Name column
        dc = new DataColumn();
        dc.DataType = System.Type.GetType("System.String");
        dc.ColumnName = "Name";
        // Add column to DataTable
        table.Columns.Add(dc);

        // Create Address column
        dc = new DataColumn();
        dc.DataType = System.Type.GetType("System.String");
        dc.ColumnName = "Address";
```

```
// Add column to DataTable
table.Columns.Add(dc);


// Adding three rows to the table
DataRow row = table.NewRow();
row[0] = 1;
row[1] = "Lofer";
row[2] = "30th Street, PA Avenue, NY";
table.Rows.Add(row);
row = table.NewRow();
row[0] = 2;
row[1] = "Penelope";
row[2] = "Super Market Avem London, UK";
table.Rows.Add(row);

row = table.NewRow();
row[0] = 3;
row[1] = "Robyn";
row[2] = "Kruse House, Jacksonville, FL";
table.Rows.Add(row);


// Bind DataTable to DataGrid
dataGrid1.DataSource = table.DefaultView;
}
```

The output of Listing 10.10 looks like Figure 10.13.

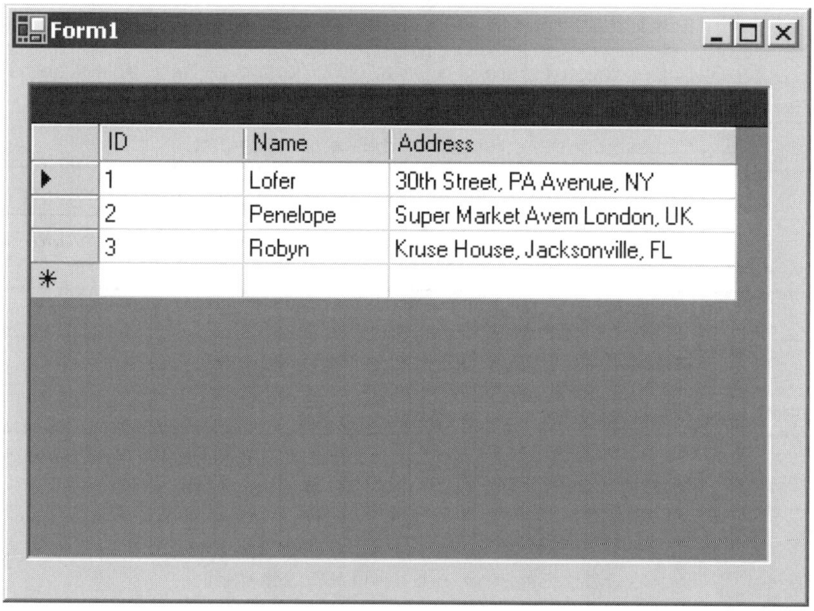

Figure 10.13: Output of Listing 10.10

Understanding a DataSet

A DataSet is a collection of tables, which may have relationships among one another and contain constraints. A DataSet plays a major role during data transfer between a data source and a .NET application. It sits in the application and receives and sends data to the data source via the data adapter. As previously mentioned, the Fill method of the data adapter fills data from a data source into a DataSet. The Update method of the data adapter reads the state of the DataSet and executes SQL statements on the data source based on how the DataSet has changed.

A DataSet's data and schema can be represented in XML format using such methods as GetXML and GetXMLSchema. The DataSet class provides methods ReadXml and ReadXmlSchema that let you read XML documents into a DataSet and also methods WriteXml and WriteXmlSchema that let you store data contained in the DataSet into XML documents.

Tables 10.11 and 10.12 describe DataSet class properties and methods, respectively.

Property	Description
DataSetName	Represents the name of a DataSet.
DefaultViewManager	Returns the custom view of the data of a DataSet, which can be bound to data-bound controls.
Relations	Returns a collection of relations of a DataTable.
Tables	Returns the collection of tables contained in a DataSet.

Table 10.11: DataSet Properties

Method	Description
AcceptChanges	Saves all the changes made to a DataSet since it was loaded or since the last time AcceptChanges was called.
Clear	Removes all rows of a DataSet.
Clone	Copies the structure of a DataSet, including all DataTable schemas, relations, and constraints. Does not copy any data.
Copy	Copies both the structure and data of a DataSet.
GetXml	Returns the XML representation of the data stored in a DataSet.
GetXmlSchema	Returns the XSD schema for the XML representation of the data stored in the DataSet.
Merge	Merges two data sets.
ReadXml	Reads an XML schema and data into a DataSet.
ReadXmlSchema	Reads an XML schema into a DataSet.
Reset	Resets the DataSet to its original state. Subclasses should override Reset to restore a DataSet to its original state.
WriteXml	Writes XML data, and optionally the schema, from a DataSet.
WriteXmlSchema	Writes a DataSet structure as an XML schema.

Table 10.12: DataSet Methods

Using a DataSet to Read Data

A DataSet's DefaultViewManager property represents the custom view of each DataTable in the DataSet. These data views can be bound directly to a data-bound control using the DataSource property.

You can create a DataSet using the constructor, which takes either an argument of the name of the DataSet or no arguments at all. For example, the following source code first creates a DataSet without a name, then creates one with a name.

```
DataSet ds1 = new DataSet();
DataSet ds2 = new DataSet("OurDataSet");
```

The DataSet name is required for an XML representation of a DataSet. The name of the DataSet is an XML document element, which is the root element in the DataSet schema definition. (We will talk more about XML in Chapter 14).

The source code in Listing 10.11 reads data from the SQL Server Northwind database and fills data into a DataSet. To test this application, create a Windows application, drag a DataGrid control to the form, and write code shown in Listing 10.11 on the form load event.

As shown in Listing 10.11, we first create a connection and data adapter and then call the Fill method of the data adapter (using SqlDataAdapter). Afterwards, we set the DataSource property of the DataGrid to the DataSet.DefaultViewManager.

Listing 10.11—Using a DataSet to Read Data from a Data Source

```
private void Form1_Load(object sender, System.EventArgs e)
{
        // Create a connection and SQL strings
        string str = "Data Source=localhost;" +
                "Integrated Security=SSPI; Initial Catalog=northwind";
        SqlConnection con = new SqlConnection();
        con.ConnectionString = str;
        con.Open();

        // Create a data adapter
        string stmt = "SELECT * FROM Employees";
        SqlDataAdapter adapter = new SqlDataAdapter(stmt, con);
        // Create a data set and call Fill method of data adapter
        DataSet ds = new DataSet("TestDS");
        adapter.Fill(ds, "Employees");

        // Bind data set to the DataGrid
        dataGrid1.DataSource = ds.DefaultViewManager;
}
```

The output of Listing 10.11 looks like Figure 10.14.

Reading and Writing XML Documents

The DataSet class provides four methods for reading and writing XML documents and schemas: ReadXml, ReadXmlSchema, WriteXml, and WriteXmlSchema. We will discuss XML and ADO.NET in more detail in Chapter 14, "XML.NET."

To give a bit more variety in utilizing namespaces, we will use the OLE DB data provider and Microsoft Access Northwind database for some of our examples.

To work with an OLE DB data provider, you must have one installed as a database on the system. The Microsoft .NET Framework SDK installs many OLE DB data providers, including those for Access, SQL Server, and Oracle OLE DB.

The connection string for an OLE DB data provider consists of a provider name, a data source name, a user ID, and a password. The following code shows the connection strings for Oracle, Microsoft Access, and Microsoft SQL Server databases:

```
Provider=MSDAORA; Data Source=ORACLE8i7; User ID=OLEDB; Password=OLEDB
Provider=Microsoft.Jet.OLEDB.4.0; Data Source=c:\bin\LocalAccess40.mdb;
Provider=SQLOLEDB; Data Source=OurSQLServer; Integrated Security=SSPI;
```

You can covert the OLE DB data provider examples to SQL or ODBC by just changing the connection string and data provider class name prefixes.

In the example below, we will write DataSet data to an XML file and read the XML file into a DataSet. Then we will bind the data to a data grid control. To test this application, create a Windows application and drag a DataGrid control to the form from the Toolbox. Also add two buttons and change their text properties to *Save Data as XML* and *Read XML,* respectively.

In the button1_Click event handler, we read the Northwind database's Employees table and save data into the file ds.xml, as shown in Listing 10.12.

Listing 10.12—Saving Data from an Access Database to an XML File

```
private void button1_Click(object sender, System.EventArgs e)
{
        string str = "Provider=Microsoft.Jet.OLEDB.4.0; Data
                      Source=c:\\Northwind.mdb";
        OleDbConnection con = new OleDbConnection(str);
        con.Open();
        // Create a data adapter
        string stmt = "SELECT * FROM Employees";
        OleDbDataAdapter adapter = new OleDbDataAdapter(stmt, con);
        // Create a data set and call Fill method of data adapter
        DataSet ds = new DataSet("TestDS");
        adapter.Fill(ds, "Employees");
        // Write data to an XML file
        ds.WriteXml("C:\\ds.xml");

        con.Close();
}
```

On button2_Click, we read the XML file, fill the DataSet with data using the ReadXml method of DataSet, and finally bind the DataSet to the DataGrid, as shown in Listing 10.13.

Listing 10.13—Reading an XML file in a DataSet

```
private void button2_Click(object sender, System.EventArgs e)
{
        // Create data set and read xml file
        DataSet ds = new DataSet();
        ds.ReadXml("C:\\ds.xml");
        // Bind DataSet to DataGrid
        dataGrid1.DataSource = ds.DefaultViewManager;
}
```

The output of our application looks like Figure 10.14. The *Save Data as XML* button saves data as an XML file, and the *Read XML* button loads data from an XML file into the DataGrid.

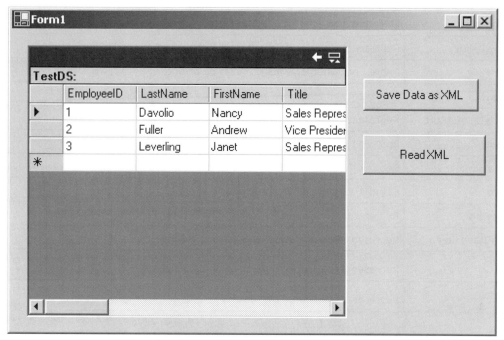

Figure 10.14: Reading and Writing XML Documents Using DataSet

DataView and DataViewManager

The DataView and DataViewManager classes provide you with a way to create different views of the data stored in a DataTable. You can bind both of these objects directly to data-bound controls. You can create different views of a DataTable by applying different sorting and filtering criteria and bind each view to different data-bound controls.

The DataViewManager represents a default view of a DataSet and contains a default DataViewSettingCollection for each DataTable in a DataSet. The DataSet property of the DataViewManager represents the DataSet attached to a particular DataViewManager. The DataViewSettings property represents the DataViewSettingCollection representing the view criteria for each DataTable. You can create a DataView from a DataViewManager by using the CreateDataView method, which takes a DataTable as an argument and returns a DataView object.

Using a DataView, you can apply the Sort and Filter members to sort and filter data. You can also search data in a DataView using its Find and FindRows methods. Tables 10.13 and 10.14 describe DataView properties and methods, respectively. Important properties include Sort, Filter, and RowStateFilter. Sort and Filter are strings representing sorting and filtering expressions. The RowStateFilter is an enumeration that allows you to apply filtering to the particular row state, such as selecting only deleted rows.

Property	Description
AllowDelete	Represents whether deletes are allowed or not.
AllowEdit	Represents whether edits are allowed or not..
AllowNew	Represents whether new row additions are allowed or not.
ApplyDefaultSort	Represents whether to use the default sort.
Count	Returns the number of records in a DataView.
DataViewManager	Returns the DataViewManager associated with this view.
Item	Returns a row of data from a specified table.
RowFilter	Represents the expression used to filter rows.
RowStateFilter	Represents the row state filter used in a DataView.
Sort	Represents the sort column or columns and sort order for the DataTable.
Table	Represents the source DataTable.

Table 10.13: DataView Class Properties

Some DataView methods are similar to DataTable methods because a DataView is like a snapshot of a DataTable. Delete and AddNew are two methods that operate on rows of the DataView. Find and FindRows let you zoom in on criteria in your DataView.

Method	Description
AddNew	Adds a new row to the DataView.
BeginInit	Starts the initialization of a DataView used on a form or used by another component.
CopyTo	Copies items into an array (for only Web forms interfaces).
Delete	Deletes a row at the specified index.
EndInit	Stops the initialization of a DataView that is used on a form or used by another component.
Find	Finds a row in the DataView by the specified sort key value.
FindRows	Returns an array of DataRowView objects whose columns match the specified sort key value.

Table 10.14: DataView Class Methods

The source code in Listing 10.14 shows usage of the DataViewManager and the DataView. As you can see, we open a connection, create a DataAdapter, create a DataSet, and fill it by applying the usual steps for getting data from the database into memory.

After that we programmatically create a new DataTable and add it to the DataSet, giving the DataSet two tables. Then we create two DataViews using the CreateDataView method of the DataViewManager. Once we have different DataViews, we can bind them with different data-bound controls. As you can see from our example, we bind our DataViews to the dataGrid1 and dataGrid2 DataGrid controls. The example also shows how you can apply sorts and filters on a DataView to search for or sort records. In this example, we use Northwind database's Customers table to read records, set the RowFilter as "Country = 'USA,'" and sort based on the City and PostalCode columns. The Sort property allows sorts in ascending (ASC) or descending (DESC) order.

Listing 10.14—Using DataView to Filter and Sort Data

```
private void Form1_Load(object sender, System.EventArgs e)
{
        // Create a connection string
        string str = "Provider=Microsoft.Jet.OLEDB.4.0;" +
                "Data Source=c:\\Northwind.mdb";

        // Create and open connection
        OleDbConnection con = new OleDbConnection(str);
        con.Open();

        // Create a data adapter
        string stmt = "SELECT * FROM Customers";
        OleDbDataAdapter adapter = new OleDbDataAdapter(stmt, con);

        // Create a data set and call Fill method of data adapter
        DataSet ds = new DataSet("TestDS");
        adapter.Fill(ds, "Customers");
        /* Create a DataTable programmatically
         * With three columns ID, Name and Address and add data to it */
        DataTable dt = new DataTable("OurTable");
        DataColumn col = new DataColumn();
        col.DataType = System.Type.GetType("System.Decimal");
        col.AllowDBNull = false;
        col.Caption = "ID";
        col.ColumnName = "ID";
        dt.Columns.Add(col);

        col = new DataColumn();
        col.DataType = System.Type.GetType("System.String");
        col.ColumnName = "Name";
        col.Caption = "Name";
    dt.Columns.Add(col);

        col = new DataColumn();
        col.DataType = System.Type.GetType("System.String");
        col.ColumnName = "Extra";
        col.Caption = "Extra";
        dt.Columns.Add(col);

        // Add data to the DataTable
        DataRow row = dt.NewRow();
        row[0] = 1001;
        row[1] = "John Pox";
        row[2] = "Lakewood Road, JaguarVille, LA";
        dt.Rows.Add(row);
        row = dt.NewRow();
        row[0] = 1002;
        row[1] = "Mr. Nixion";
        row[2] = "1234 Private Lane, HighLand, NJ";
        dt.Rows.Add(row);

        // Add new DataTable to the DataSet
        ds.Tables.Add(dt);

        // Get DataViewManager of DataSet
        DataViewManager views = ds.DefaultViewManager;


        // Create two DataView objects from DataViewManager
        DataView dv1 = views.CreateDataView(ds.Tables[0]);
```

```
    DataView dv2 = views.CreateDataView(ds.Tables[1]);
    // Look records for Country = USA
    // and sort them based on city and postal code
    dv1.RowFilter = "Country = 'USA'";
    dv1.Sort = "City, PostalCode ASC";

    // Bind dataview to the DataGrid
    dataGrid1.DataSource = dv1;
    dataGrid2.DataSource = dv2;

    // Close the connection
con.Close();
}
```

The output of Listing 10.14 looks like Figure 10.15.

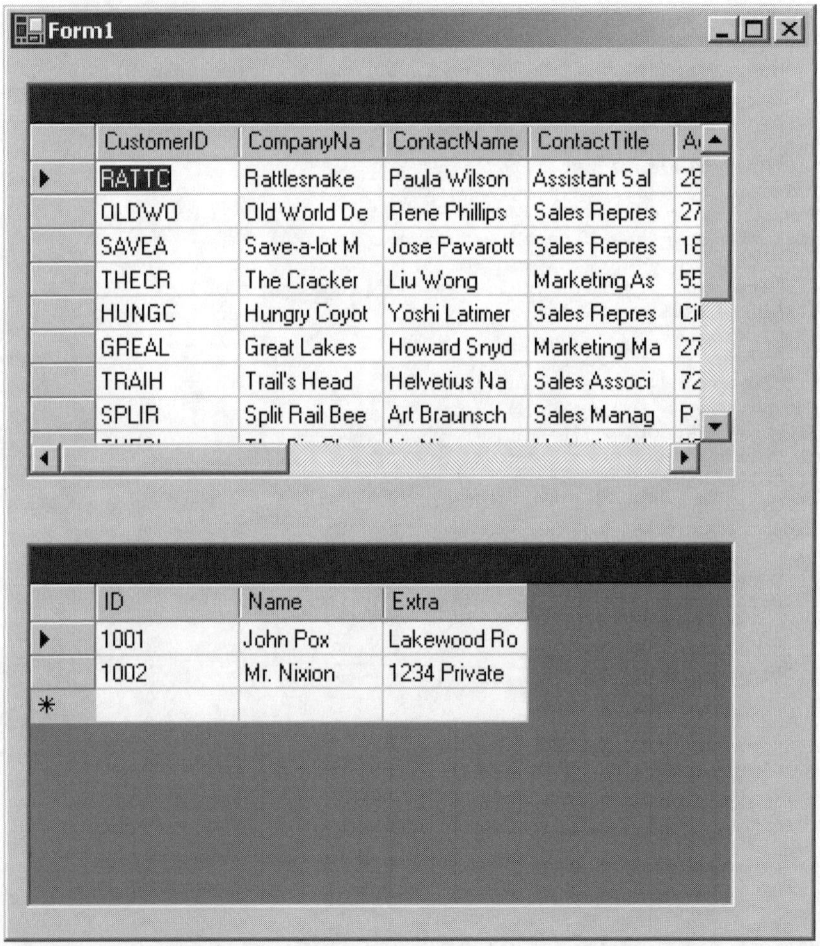

Figure 10.15: Using DataViewManager and DataView to View Data in Different Ways

The Server Explorer

Visual Studio .NET provides many wizards and tools for developing database applications while writing minimum code. So far in this chapter, we've seen how to programmatically work with ADO.NET components. We have not yet delved into some of the more powerful VS.NET features, such as wizards and utilities, which make database programming very easy for us developers.

Before writing database applications using these wizards, let's take a quick look at some of VS.NET's powerful tools. One database helper utility is the Server Explorer window, which allows you to create new database connections and view and manage data manually, just as you do from a database server. Using the Server Explorer, you can add, edit, and remove data and other database objects.

Open Server Explorer by clicking the View→Server Explorer menu item. As shown in Figure 10.16, Server Explorer has two root nodes: Data Connections and Servers. By default, the Data Connections node has no items. The Server node shows you all the available SQL Servers. You can expand the Servers node to see the contents of the servers and database objects. To view data of a database table or contents of database objects, just double-click on the object or right-click on the object to see more options.

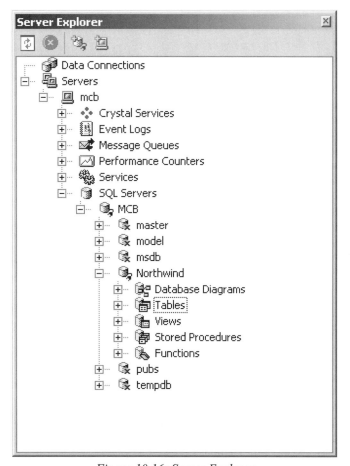

Figure 10.16: Server Explorer

To add a new connection, double-click on the Data Connections tree item. Right-Clicking and choosing the Add Connection option from the pop-up menu launches the Data Link Properties Wizard. On its first page, the Provider tab, you select the type of data provider from a list of all data source providers installed on your machine, including OLE DB, Jet OLE DB, or other data driver.

The second page is the Connection page, shown in Figure 10.17, which lets you create a database connection. If you selected the SQL Server option on the first page, this page shows you all available SQL Servers in a drop-down list. You can also enter a user ID and password and pick a database. The Test Connection button lets you make sure the connection is successful.

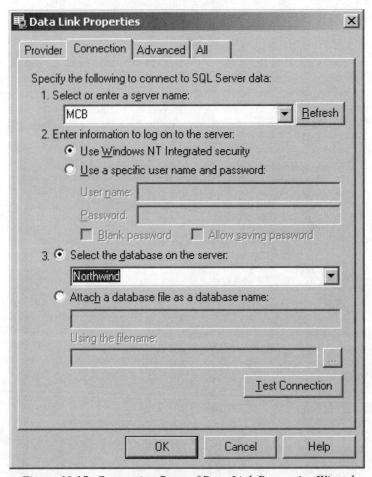

Figure 10.17: Connection Page of Data Link Properties Wizard

The Advanced page lets you set time-out and other permissions for the database. The All page shows you all properties of a data connection.

Now click the OK button to add the data connection to the Server Explorer. You can expand a database node to view database objects—including tables, views, stored procedures, and functions. You can view an object's data by double-clicking on the object or by right-clicking on the object and choosing the Retrieve Data From option.

Visual Data Components

One of the best features of database programming in .NET is design-time support of ADO.NET components. You can use these components from VS.NET by just dragging controls from the Toolbox and dropping them into the Windows or Web form; the IDE wizards write all the necessary code for you.

In this section we'll look at data components available under Toolbox→Data. With the wizard, working with data components is simple and easy. In many cases you do a series of drag and drops from the Toolbox or Server Explorer, write a few lines of code, and your application is ready to roll.

As shown in Figure 10.18, Toolbox→Data has these data components: DataSet, DataView, SqlConnection, SqlCommand, SqlDataAdapter, OleDbConnection, OleDbCommand, and OleDbDataAdapter.

Figure 10.18: Visual Data Components

You may not see ODBC data components in your Toolbox if you have not installed and added the ODBC data provider. We'll show you how to work with the ODBC data provider later in this chapter.

As you can see from Figure 10.18, the Toolbox contains the major ADO.NET classes we've used in this chapter so far. Connection, Command, DataAdapter, DataSet, and DataView are available as Windows controls. As we have discussed earlier, all data providers are utilized in the same way. In our sample, we will use a Microsoft Access 2000 database to show you how to take advantage of these components in the RAD IDE environment.

Adding a Data Adapter to a Form

There are different ways to add a data adapter to a form. The most obvious is by dragging and dropping a data adapter control from the Toolbox. When you do this, you'll be prompted to provide a connection to the database. Another way is to drag a database table or other object directly from the Server Explorer to the form. When you do this, Server Explorer will not ask you for any database setting because it figures out the connection and table query information from the hierarchy of data tables.

Writing a Database Application Using VS.NET

To better see VS.NET's features, let's create a database application: First, create a Windows application (see Chapter 9). Then drag a data adapter (SqlDataAdapter, OleDbDataAdapter, or OdbcDataAdapter) onto the form. We will use the Microsoft Access 2000 sample Northwind database for our applications, so we can use either OleDbDataAdapter or OdbcDataAdapter. In this case, we've chosen to use OleDbDataAdapter.

There are several ways to add a data adapter to a project. Two common ways are to drag a database object (table, stored procedure, view, or column) to the form from the Server Explorer or drag a data adapter directly from the Toolbox to the form.

Adding a Data Adapter Using Server Explorer

Adding a data adapter using Server Explorer is pretty easy: You open a data connection and expand its nodes until you reach the database tables. Then you drag a table from the Server Explorer to the form.

This adds a connection and a data adapter to the form and adds a SqlConnection, a SqlDataAdapter, and four SqlCommand objects to the project. After that, you can use the Data Adapter Configuration Wizard to generate a data set from this data adapter and use the data set to bind its data to to the data-bound controls.

Adding a Data Adapter from the Toolbox

Adding a data adapter from the Toolbox is also pretty easy: You drag a data adapter (SQL, OLE DB, or ODBC) from the Toolbox to the form.

To test these steps, let's create a Windows application and drag an OleDbDataAdapter from the Toolbox to the form. This adds OleDbDataAdapter and OleDbConnection objects to the project and launches the Data Adapter Configuration Wizard.

After the wizard's welcome page, the second page lets you pick a data connection from a drop-down list of those created using Server Explorer. If none exist, you can use the page's New Connection button. The drop-down list shows all data connections, no matter what data provider was used.

If you don't have a Microsoft Access 2000 data connection, click the New Connection button, launching the Data Link Properties Wizard. Now click its Provider tab and select the OLE DB provider. On the next page select the "C:\Northwind.mdb" database. (If it's not in your root directory, point it to the correct path.) Now click OK to return to the Data Adapter Configuration Wizard.

The next page of the wizard lets you choose the query type. For Access databases, only the Use SQL statements option is available. SQL Server databases also have options to create a new stored procedure or use an existing stored procedure.

The next page of the Configuration Wizard generates the SQL SELECT statement. This page has an Edit control, where you can either type your SQL SELECT statement or use the Query Builder button to generate one for you.

The Query Builder, shown in Figure 10.19, lets you select the tables used to generate a SQL SELECT statement. Select the table and click the Add button, adding as many as tables you want. Here, we add only the Customers table. Then, we select five columns for the query. A third pane shows the SELECT statement for these columns.

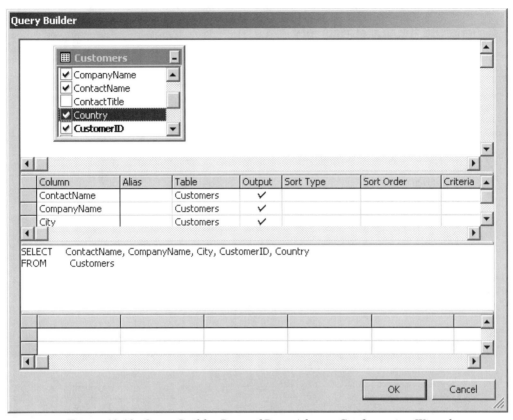

Figure 10.19: Query Builder Page of Data Adapter Configuration Wizard

Clicking OK sends you back to the Generate the SQL Statements page of the Data Adapter
Configuration Wizard, shown in Figure 10.20.

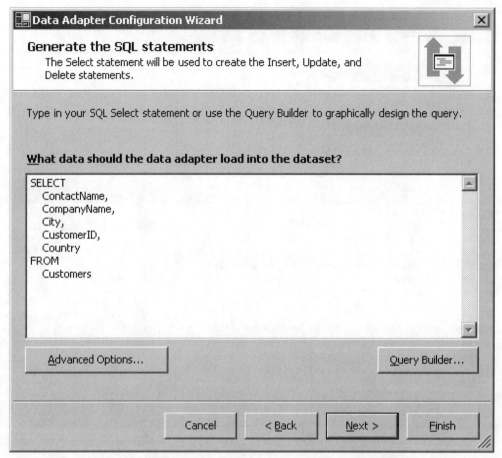

Figure 10.20: SQL Statement Generated by Query Builder

Clicking the Next button generates the SelectCommand and all nonquery command properties (InsertCommand, DeleteCommand, UpdateCommand) of the DataAdapter. The wizard uses the SELECT command you created in the Query Builder to generate the other SQL statements and table mappings. The View Wizard Results page shows what the Data Adapter Configuration Wizard has generated for you.

Setting DataAdapter Properties

As shown in Figure 10.21, if you want to change a DataAdapter's properties, you can open the Properties window by right-clicking on the DataAdapter graphic in the Designer view. Here you can change the DataAdapter's name, SQL statements, and other properties. For example, if you want to change the Insert SQL statement, just click on the InsertCommand and change the CommandText property.

Figure 10.21: InsertCommand of OleDbDataAdapter

Generating a DataSet and Other Options

There are two kinds of DataSet objects: typed and untyped. A typed DataSet is derived from the DataSet class and uses information in an XML schema file (an .xsd file) to generate a new class. The new generated class has members, which can be used to access a DataSet.

An untyped DataSet, however, has no corresponding built-in schema. So far in this chapter we've been using untyped DataSet objects.

The next step is to generate a DataSet from the OleDbDataAdapter we've created. The Properties window gives three options: Configure Data Adapter, Generate DataSet, and Preview Data. The Generate DataSet option, shown in Figure 10.22, generates a typed DataSet, which you can then use to work with a DataView and data-bound controls. The DataSet object's default name is DataSet1, which can be changed.

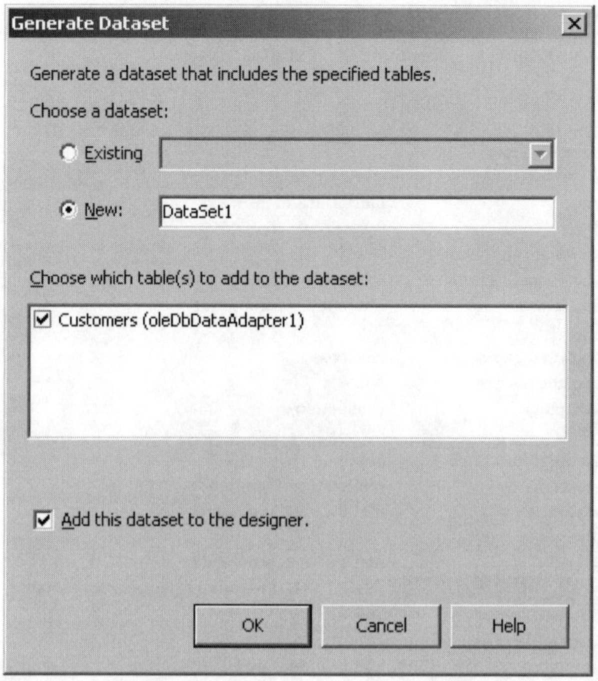

Figure 10.22: Generate DataSet Option of OleDbDataAdapter

To change some of DataSet1's properties, such as Locale and DataSetName, right-click on the DataSet appearing in the design view and select the Properties menu item.

The Preview Data option of a DataAdapter calls up what appears in Figure 10.23. Clicking the Fill Dataset button fills the DataGrid with the DataSet.

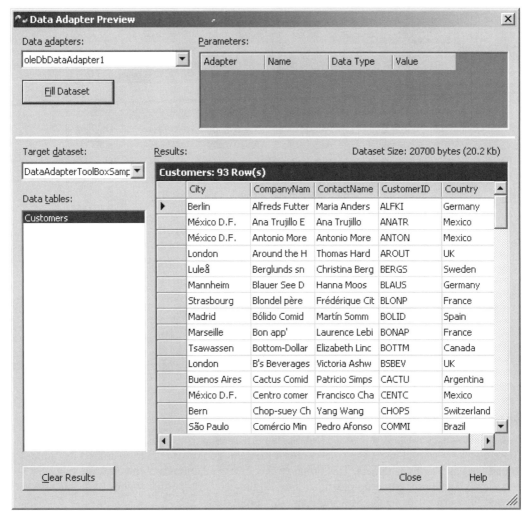

Figure 10.23: Data Adapter Preview

View Data Using DataSet

Now let's see how to use the DataSet in the application we just generated using the Generate DataSet option of the OleDbDataAdapter.

To test the DataSet1 class, add a DataGrid control to the form and set its DataSource property to the instance of DataSet1—dataSet11. You can either type *dataSet11* or use the DataSource property's drop-down combo and select *dataSet11* from the list.

Now write the single line of code shown in Listing 10.15 on the form load event. As you can see from the code, we only need to call the OleDbDataAdapter's Fill method to fill dataSet11 with data.

Listing 10.15—Using DataAdapter Generated DataSet to Fill Data to a DataGrid

```
private void Form1_Load(object sender, System.EventArgs e)
{
        oleDbDataAdapter1.Fill(dataSet11, "Customers");
}
```

Now if you run the application, the result looks like Figure 10.24.

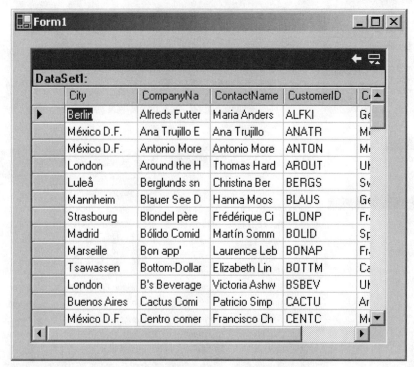

Figure 10.24: Output of Listing 10.15

Generating a DataView for the DataSet

You can also attach a DataView to the DataSet we just created using the Data Adapter Configuration Wizard. Drag a DataView control from the Toolbox to the form and set its Table property to dataSet11.Customers. This property becomes available when you click on the DataView's Table property drop-down list. From DataView's Properties window, you can also set sort and filter criteria using the Sort and RowFilter properties.

Now you can bind a DataView directly to a DataGrid control. Just set the DataSource property to the dataView1 object, which should be available in the DataSource property drop-down list.

Now, the last thing you need to do is call the Fill method of DataAdapter on the form load event:

```
oleDbDataAdapter1.Fill(dataSet11, "Customers");
```

If you want to set a filter and sort criteria on a DataView, go back to the DataView's Properties window and set the RowFilter property to "Country ='USA'"; the DataView will only return records with USA as the country. Setting the Sort property in the Properties window to "City ASC" will sort all records alphabetically based on the City column.

Working with an ODBC Data Provider

As we approach the end of this chapter, let's see how to use the ODBC data adapter to access ODBC data sources. With the ODBC.NET data provider you can access any data source that has an ODBC driver. As of this writing, the ODBC data provider is available as an add-on to VS.NET and can be downloaded from the Microsoft site (download links are available in the Downloads section of C# Corner's Web site, www.c-sharpcorner.com).

Adding ODBC Data Components

The ODBC data provider resides in the Microsoft.Data.Odbc.dll assembly and is defined in the Microsoft.Data.Odbc namespace. Before using the ODBC data provider, you need to add a reference for Microsoft.Data.Odbc.dll, which is installed in the C:\Program Files\Microsoft.NET\Odbc directory by default. You also need to import the Microsoft.Data.Odbc namespace into the project by using the following C# reference code:

```
using Microsoft.Data.Odbc;
```

To add a reference to this assembly, you can use the Add Reference option from the Solution Explorer and browse for the assembly, as shown in Figure 10.25.

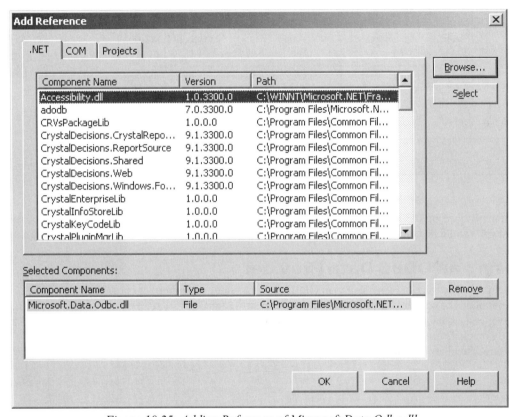

Figure 10.25: Adding Reference of Microsoft.Data.Odbc.dll

Clicking on the Browse button in the Add Reference dialog brings up a dialog for finding Microsoft.Data.Odbc.dll, which resides in Program Files under the Microsoft.NET directory.

Adding reference to the Microsoft.Data.Odbc.dll adds the Microsoft.Data.Odbc namespace to the project namespaces, which you can see by expanding Project→References in the Solution Explorer.

If the ODBC data components are not available in your Toolbox, you can add them by customizing the Toolbox. Right-click on Customize Toolbox, click on .NET Framework Components, and select ODBC components, as shown in Figure 10.31.

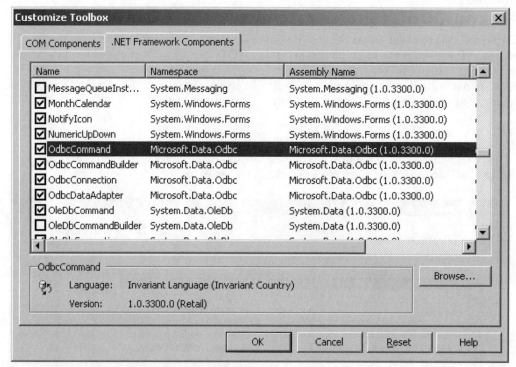

Figure 10.31: Adding ODBC Data Components

After customizing the Toolbox, the ODBC data components should be available from the Toolbox and you should be able to drag these controls from the Toolbox to forms.

Using an ODBC Data Provider

The main difference between using an ODBC data provider and other data providers is a slight variation in the connection string. The connection string for ODBC data providers takes an ODBC driver and a database, with the user ID and password being optional. The driver string contained in curly brackets can often be found by launching the ODBC Data Source Administrator from the Control Panel and looking at the names of the drivers, as shown in Figure 10.61.

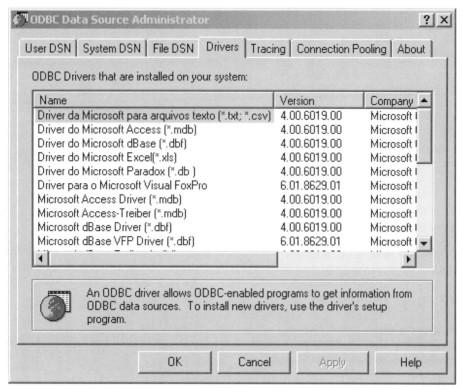

Figure 10.61: ODBC Data Source Administrator

For example, here is the ODBC connection string for Access:

```
"Driver={Microsoft Access Driver (*.mdb)};DBQ= Northwind.mdb"
```

And here is the string for SQL Server:

```
"DRIVER={SQL  Server};"+
"SERVER=localhost;UID=sa;PWD=;DATABASE=northwind;";
```

Once you know the connection string, you can write similar code for other data providers. For example, the following code shows you how to create an OdbcConnection:

```
// Create a connection and open it
string str = "Driver={Microsoft Access Driver (*.mdb)};DBQ= C:\\Northwind.mdb";
OdbcConnection  con = new OdbcConnection(str);
con.Open();
```

You can also use the ODBC Data Source Name (DSN) as a connection:

```
OdbcConnection  con = new OdbcConnection("DSN=ourDSN");
```

Listing 10.16 shows how to use the ODBC data provider to read the Microsoft Access 2000 Northwind database into a DataGrid.

Listing 10.16—Accessing the Microsoft Access 2000 Database Using ODBC Data Provider

```
private void Form1_Load(object sender, System.EventArgs e)
{
        // Create a connection and open it
```

```
string str = "Driver={Microsoft Access Driver (*.mdb)};DBQ=
  C:\\Northwind.mdb";

OdbcConnection  con = new OdbcConnection(str);
con.Open();

// Create a data adapter
OdbcDataAdapter adapter =
      new OdbcDataAdapter("SELECT * From Employees", con);

// Create and fill a DataSet
DataSet ds = new DataSet();
adapter.Fill(ds, "Employees");
dataGrid1.DataSource = ds.DefaultViewManager;
con.Close();
}
```

Summary

In this chapter you learned the basics of ADO.NET data providers and classes provided by the .NET class library. You learned how to use different data providers to access different data sources. Each data provider provides similar connection, data reader command, and data adapter classes, with similar members.

All data adapters share common classes, such as DataSet, DataView, DataTable, and DataViewManager. The DataSet object uses the data adapter's Fill method to fill data and the Update method to save data to a data source.

After examining the basic ADO.NET classes, you saw how to bind a DataSet with data-bound controls. In this chapter you also learned how to write database applications using VS.NET wizards and tools such as Server Explorer and the DataForm Wizard.

The ODBC data provider works like other data providers to access ODBC data sources. To access an ODBC data source, you must have an ODBC driver installed for that data source.

In the next chapter you will start to explore the basics of ASP.NET and how to write a simple ASP.NET application using C# and Visual Studio.NET.

Chapter 11:
An Introduction to ASP.NET

Introduction

ASP.NET is Microsoft's answer to dynamic server-side Web programming. ASP.NET differs drastically from its predecessor, ASP. ASP.NET is an integral part of the .NET Framework announced by Microsoft at the Professional Developer's Conference 2000. The .NET Framework is made up of features such as cross-language integration, cross-language exception handling, enhanced security, versioning and deployment support, a simplified model for component interaction, and debugging and profiling services. The preceding features make the .NET Framework and ASP.NET more robust.

History of Server-Side Web Programming

At the time the Internet was founded and during the time it was not widely used, most content on the Internet was available as static Hypertext Markup Language (HTML) pages. With the e-commerce boom a few years ago, dynamic server-side Web programming techniques started evolving. Programming based on the Common Gateway Interface specification was one of the famous server-side technologies available in those days. Next came Web development based on the Internet Server Application Programming Interface (ISAPI). This was the starting point for Microsoft to enter the Web-based technologies arena. ISAPI-based programming was not easy to use, so Microsoft revamped the ISAPI technology and created Internet Database Connector (IDC) programming. IDC programming works in a model of templates. Each IDC program has two files. The first file is an .idc file, which has data-specific information such as data source name, username, password, SQL query, and template file name (.htx file). The template file is an HTML template that needs to be used when rendering the output of the .HTX file. The IDC programming model was very easy compared with ISAPI programming. However, it lacked flexibility.

Birth of ASP

In early 1996 Microsoft introduced its first beta version (0.9) of the server-side Web programming technology called Active Server Pages (ASP), and it took the world by storm. ASP pages were simple, flexible, and powerful. It was at this time that ActiveX Data Objects (ADO) were also born.

Subsequent releases of ASP (such as ASP 2.0) and ADO ruled the Web development world. The Component Object Model (COM) and Microsoft Transaction Server (MTS) added more muscle to ASP. Moreover, Internet Information Server (IIS) 5.0, COM+, and ASP 3.0 added more stability and scalability to ASP-based applications.

What's Wrong with ASP?

Despite the ease with which ASP-based applications can be coded, ASP suffers from serious problems, some of which are as follows:

- ASP is a scripting language–based application, and it supports VBScript and JScript by default.
- VBScript and JScript are interpreted and loosely typed languages.
- Whenever a request comes to an ASP page, it will be interpreted, and ASP does not cache the code and reuse it again and again.
- The readability of ASP code is less than optimal because the inline ASP code (<% ... %>) is not manageable in large ASP pages.
- VBScript only supports the variant data type, and this causes significant performance problems for ASP pages.
- VBScript also is suboptimal in terms of error handling. In VBScript we have to use an On Error Resume Next statement and check the Err object after every line of execution.
- ASP is subpar with regard to code reuse technique, unless you use an include file. However, the include files also cause some problems. For example, in a large-scale ASP project, the include files are recursively included many times, and that causes a significant performance hit for ASP pages.
- Separation of code and content is not possible with ASP unless you are using the MSXML parser to generate the HTML using the Extensible Markup Language (XML) data and Extensible Stylesheet Language (XSL) style sheets inside ASP.
- The ASP session variables are not suitable for multiserver Web farms.
- Debugging and tracing ASP code is a nightmare.

Another of the major problems we face with ASP is called "DLL Hell." Custom COM components written in Visual Basic (VB), VC++, and so on can be used in ASP, and this causes many problems for ASP programmers. Let's assume you've already deployed a COM dynamic-link library (DLL) and you want to update the DLL with the newer version of the component. Guess what? You cannot unless you restart the machine. This problem might cause significant costs for a busy e-commerce site. Your best solution is to find out when there is the least amount of traffic, show a page saying the site is under maintenance, and put in place the newer version of the COM component. This actually is not an ASP problem, but ASP is significantly affected by it.

To overcome these problems Microsoft introduced a brand-new server-side Web programming technology called ASP.NET.

What Is ASP.NET?

ASP.NET is a new dynamic server-side Web programming technology based on the .NET platform. ASP.NET is not an upgrade of ASP 3.0 but rather a total rewrite from scratch to take advantage of the .NET platform. ASP.NET keeps all the good aspects of ASP (simplicity, flexibility, coding ease, etc.) and adds powerful features such as compiled code with C#, VB.NET, JScript.NET, or any other .NET-compliant language. ASP.NET also includes full-blown error-handling and debugging capabilities. We'll look at all the features in detail in the following sections.

Basic Differences

Before going further, let's examine the differences between ASP and ASP.NET. When a user requests an ASP page, the ASP.DLL interprets the ASP page, and the content is sent back to the client browser via IIS. This process happens every time a user requests this page (see Figure 11.1).

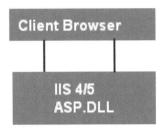

Figure 11.1: ASP Page-Processing Cycle

In contrast, when a user requests an ASP.NET page, if it is the first time, the language compiler (C#, VB.NET, or other language) will compile the page into an intermediate language (IL) such as Microsoft Intermediate Language (MSIL), and then the .NET Framework's Just-In-Time (JIT) compiler will compile the IL code into native code (see Figure 11.2).

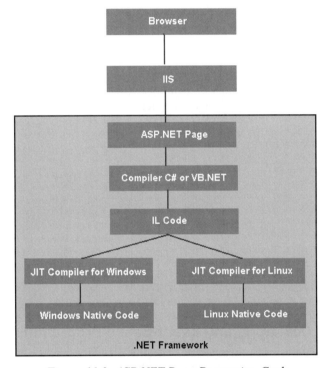

Figure 11.2: ASP.NET Page-Processing Cycle

After the native code is generated, the ASP.NET page will be executed within the context of the .NET Framework, and the result will be sent to the client browser. At the same time, the compiled code of the ASP.NET page will be cached, and the cached code will be used for subsequent calls to the ASP.NET page. The cached ASP.NET page is removed from the cache only when the ASP.NET page gets changed or when the caching time expires. This improves the performance of ASP.NET pages versus ASP pages, and this is the main difference between ASP and ASP.NET. The JIT compiler brings the advantage of platform-independent code. This is what makes ASP.NET superior to ASP.

Another big difference is that ASP uses loosely typed scripting languages such as VBScript or JScript to author the pages. ASP.NET is a compiled code, using strongly typed, fully compiled languages such as C#, VB.NET, C++ with Managed Extensions, and JScript.NET. (Yes, now JScript.NET is a fully compiled language.)

Advantages of ASP.NET

Language Independence

ASP.NET is a language-independent platform. We can use more than 20 languages to build ASP.NET pages. Out of those 20-plus languages, four—VB.NET, C#, JScript.NET, and C++ with Managed Extensions—are supported by Microsoft, and COBOL.NET, Perl.NET, and others are supported by third-party companies. Of these languages the most popular are VB.NET and C#.

Compiled Code

Whereas ASP is based on scripting languages and is always interpreted, ASP.NET moves into the domain of compiled code and strongly typed languages. Because of the compiled languages, ASP.NET uses true data types such as integers and strings rather than variants, as in ASP. For example:

```
int i = 0;
String S;
```

The compiled languages also bring better exception-handling techniques to ASP.NET. Now we can use the try-catch-finally statements to handle exceptions (see Listing 1.1).

Listing 11.1—Try-Catch-Finally Statement

```
try {
  ...;
}
catch(e) {
  ...;
}
finally {
  ...;
}
```

The .NET Framework takes care of the memory problems for ASP.NET using the Garbage Collection processes.

Drag-and-Drop Designing and Event-Based Programming

The main reason Visual Basic has been the language of choice for millions of programmers is drag-and-drop designing and event-based programming. ASP.NET brings the goodies of VB to Web programming—offering us, for example, drag-and-drop designing with ASP.NET Web Forms.

If you have programmed in Visual Basic, you should be familiar with VBX/OCX/ActiveX controls. ASP.NET similarly introduces the concept of server controls and events for each control.

Browser compatibility is a big headache for developers, and ASP.NET addresses browser compatibility issues. ASP.NET server controls can detect the browser type and spool browser-compatible code back.

ASP.NET is object-oriented in nature and supports the separation of code and content via the Page class.

Mobile Programming Support

ASP.NET not only addresses the desktop browser. It also supports mobile devices such as mobile phones and personal digital assistants (Palm, PocketPC, RIM (or Research In Motion) devices, etc.). The mobile devices support either WML (Wireless Markup Language), HTML 3.2, or the cHTML (Compact Hypertext Markup Language) of i-mode devices. ASP.NET can support all the mobile devices by spooling the content the devices require.

Disconnected Data Access

One of the main problems with the ASP and ADO combination is that ADO always maintains a live connection to the database. This creates significant overhead for the executing ASP page and the scalability of the ASP page. With ADO.NET, we can have disconnected data access, which improves the scalability of the ASP.NET application.

Session State

The ASP session state support is very limited and does not support multiserver Web farms. Therefore, if we want to scale out our ASP application using a Web farm, we cannot use ASP session objects. This all changes with ASP.NET. ASP.NET supports several session storage methods such as in-process (same as ASP), out-of-process (session state is maintained by a Windows Service), or in a SQL Server database. Both the out-of-process and SQL Server options support a Web farm.

Security Support

Whereas ASP supports only a handful of IIS authentication methods, ASP.NET supports a wide variety of security options including IIS/Windows authentication methods such as Basic authentication, Digest authentication, and Integrated Windows authentication and non-IIS authentication methods such as Forms-based authentication and Microsoft Passport authentication.

Tracing, Debugging, and Caching Support

Whereas ASP is wanting in terms of tracing and debugging support, ASP.NET provides Web server tools and classes to debug the ASP.NET pages. ASP.NET also provides excellent caching application programming interface classes to cache data including output caching, data caching, dependent caching, and fragment caching.

XML-Based Configuration File

In ASP the configuration information is stored in scattered places. For example, IIS settings are stored in the IIS Metabase (registry). If you use COM or COM+ components, all the information for those components are stored in the registry and in the COM+ Catalog, respectively. ASP.NET gives us a uniform way to store configuration information in XML-based files called web.config and machine.config. The configuration files are extendable so that we can add ASP.NET application-specific information to the configuration file and manipulate the settings from ASP.NET applications. For example, we may want to store the database connection string in the configuration file and retrieve it from the ASP.NET page before establishing a database connection.

XCopy Deployment

Unlike COM components, .NET components don't need to be registered in the Windows registry. All we have to do is compile the component, create a subfolder called BIN underneath the ASP.NET application folder, and copy the component (DLL file) into the BIN folder.

If you want to deploy your ASP.NET application in a multiserver Web farm, all you have to do is copy the ASP.NET application folder and paste it in the new server. That's all. No more registration of components and DLL Hell!

Hosting Options

ASP is an ISAPI application and heavily dependent on IIS. On the other hand, ASP.NET is based on the .NET Framework, and ASP.NET pages can be hosted outside of IIS using either a third-party Web server such as Apache or a command line .exe file.

Limitations of ASP.NET

ASP.NET has only a few limitations:

ASP.NET supports only one language per page. You can't mix and match more than one language in your ASP.NET page as you can in ASP. This is because ASP.NET pages are compiled, and there is no way you can break the ASP.NET page into multiple parts and compile with different compilers.

ASP.NET supports only one form tag per page. In ASP you can have as many HTML forms as you want, but that is not possible with ASP.NET. For example, in ASP you could have two forms: the first one generates the list of products and the other one does the search. However, you can simulate the same ASP effect in ASP.NET by calling different server-side event handlers to generate the list of products and do the searching.

Server Controls

In ASP we use HTML controls to construct the pages. ASP.NET introduces VB-like controls called server controls. The ASP.NET server controls fall into four major categories:

- HTML intrinsic controls
- ASP.NET Web server controls
- ASP.NET validation controls
- Mobile controls

HTML intrinsic controls are replicas of the standard HTML controls, and they provide the advantages of server controls. ASP.NET Web server controls are not just limited to the standard HTML controls; in addition, ASP.NET comes with a Calendar control, a DataGrid control, and more rich-featured controls. Validation controls focus on validating the user input with server-side or client-side code. Mobile controls, of course, address mobile devices. The great advantage of mobile controls is that they speak the markup language that a mobile device can understand with a single code base. For example, if a cellular phone understands only WML, mobile controls will then send WML back to the client and if a PDA understands only HTML 3.2, mobile controls will then send HTML 3.2 back to the client. Chapter 22 explains mobile controls more extensively.

ASP.NET also supports controls called user controls. User controls are like ASP "#include" files but have more functionality. We look at user controls in the next chapter.

Microsoft is shipping a suite of server controls called IE Web Controls. That suite offers many useful controls such as Tab Strip, Tree Control, and Toolbar Control. For more information about IE Web Controls visit http://www.asp.net.

Advantages of Server Controls

The following are a few of the advantages of server controls:

- Server controls can detect a browser's capabilities and spool content accordingly to the browser. For example, if a browser is able to render DHTML (or Dynamic HTML) content, server controls will spool DHTML content to the browser. If a browser is a low-level browser, server controls will spool HTML 3.2 back to the browser. This solves the biggest headache of browser compatibility for developers.
- Server controls can maintain (using HTML hidden controls) state during the form post back.
- Server controls expose events. They can expose events such as Click, Load, and so on. This gives programmers the flexibility of writing event-based code in ASP.NET.
- Server controls hide all the complexities involved in creating the presentation content and allow us to concentrate on the business problem. The next result would be less code to write because server controls do the rest. For example, if you want to show information in an HTML table, what you would do in ASP is run a loop and render the table using the Response.Write method with TR and TD tags. However, in ASP.NET all you have to do is place a DataGrid server control and bind it with the data source. That's it. You can display a table with just two lines of code.

Note that, as we have already discussed, ASP.NET is extensible, and the .NET Framework allows us to author custom server controls in any .NET-enabled language, such as C#, VB.NET, and so on.

HTML Intrinsic Controls

HTML intrinsic controls are ASP.NET's representation of the HTML controls. For example, the HTML text box control would look like this:

```
<input type="text" name="txtName">
```

If you want to make this an HTML intrinsic server control, change the name attribute of the input tag to *id* and add a new attribute called *runat* and set the value to *server* as shown:

```
<input type="text" id="txtName" runat="server">
```

With these minor changes, we have changed the plain HTML control to an ASP.NET HTML server control.

ASP.NET Web Server Controls

ASP.NET Web server controls are not limited to HTML controls; they go beyond HTML controls to create visually appealing and functional controls—for example, Calendar control. If you want to render a calendar in ASP, it'll take a lot of coding and debugging. In ASP.NET you can render a calendar with just one line of code:

```
<asp:Calendar runat="server" />
```

Wow! Just one line of code produces the calendar for us. All of the ASP.NET Web server controls are prefixed with the namespace *asp*.

Hello, World from ASP.NET!

Thus far we've explained what ASP.NET is and how it differs from its predecessor. Now let's see an example. We'll say "Hello, World!" from both ASP and ASP.NET. We'll then compare the differences.

First, let's write an ASP version of a "Hello, World!" page (see Listing 11.2).

Listing 11.2—ASP Version of "Hello, World!"

```
<html>
<head>
<title>Hello, World From ASP.NET</title>
</head>
<body>
<% Response.Write "Hello, World from ASP!" %>
</body>
</html>
```

Let's convert the same code into an ASP.NET page (see Listing 11.3).

Listing 11.3—ASP.NET Version of "Hello, World!"

```
<script language="C#" runat="server">
protected void Page_Load(object sender, EventArgs e){
    lblHello.Text = "Hello, World from ASP.NET!";
}
</script>
<html>
<head>
<title>Hello, World From ASP.NET</title>
</head>
<body>
<asp:Label id="lblHello" runat="server" />
</body>
</html>
```

Now we'll run the code. The screenshots in Figures 11.3 and 11.4 show the output of Listings 11.2 and 11.3.

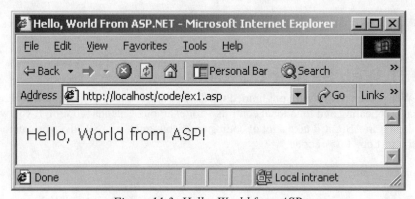

Figure 11.3: Hello, World from ASP

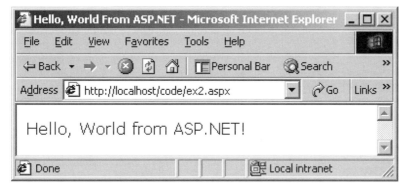

Figure 11.4: Hello, World from ASP.NET

Let's look at the differences one by one.

In the ASP version of the code, we have the standard HTML tags and the VBScript inline code that displays "Hello, World!" using the Response.Write command.

Now consider the ASP.NET code. First of all, we're declaring a <script> code block with the runat attribute as *server*. This is what defines the server-side code block. Whatever you write inside this code block will be executed at the server. We're declaring a function called Page_Load with few parameters. The Page_Load event will be executed when the ASP.NET page is called (for VB folks, it is similar to the Form_Load event in VB). In the Page_Load event, we have assigned the string "Hello, World from ASP.NET!" to an ASP.NET label control. (See Listing 11.4.)

Listing 11.4—Server Side Page_Load Event Handler

```
<script language="C#" runat="server">
protected void Page_Load(object sender, EventArgs e){
    lblHello.Text = "Hello, World from ASP.NET!";
}
</script>
```

If you notice, we've declared an ASP.NET label control inside the body tag and we're referencing the ASP.NET label control from the server side using its id attribute. Listing 11.5 shows the output generated by ASP.NET.

Listing 11.5—ASP.NET Page Output

```
<html>
<head>
<title>Hello, World From ASP.NET</title>
</head>
<body>
<span id="lblHello">Hello, World from ASP.NET!</span>
</body>
</html>
```

Notice that the label control has been transformed as the span tag, and the id attribute of the span tag holds the same id as the ASP.NET label control.

Hello, World from Visual Studio .NET!

Let's build the same code with Visual Studio .NET. Start Visual Studio .NET and click New Project. You'll see a dialog box (as shown in Figure 11.5). Select Visual C# Projects from the Project Types: tree node. From the right side panel select ASP.NET Web Application and name it

"HelloWorld." By default the project will be created in "http://localhost/HelloWorld." If you have any other server or directory preferences you can click the Browse button and locate your preferred place. Click OK now.

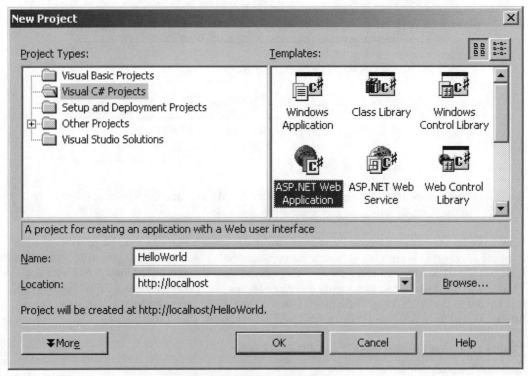

Figure 11.5: New Project Dialog Box

Visual Studio. NET will display a dialog box (shown in Figure 11.6) and try to create the ASP.NET Web application on your local host or your preferred IIS.

Figure 11.6: Create New Web Project Dialog Box

After the "HelloWorld" Web application has been created in IIS, you'll see the Visual Studio. NET development environment (shown in Figure 11.7).

If you are familiar with the Visual InterDev integrated development environment, you will find the Visual Studio .NET environment fairly similar to that.

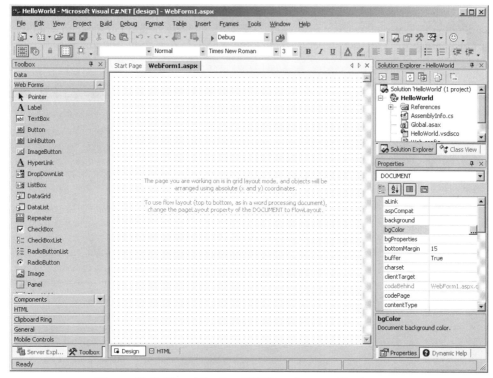

Figure 11.7: Visual Studio .NET Development Environment

On the left side are all the server controls that you can drag and drop into a Web form. On the right side is the solution explorer, and beneath that is the Properties window. In the center is your canvas, the Web form. Now you are pretty much ready to drag and drop the server controls into the Web form and start coding.

By default Visual Studio .NET names the Web form WebForm1.aspx. So let's change the name to HelloWorld.aspx by selecting the file WebForm1.aspx from the project explorer and changing the name from the Properties window or from the project explorer itself. Drag the Label control from the Web Forms toolbar and drop it into the Web form. You can also position the Label control as you want, and Visual Studio .NET will generate the necessary cascading style sheets for that control. Let's change the name of the Label control from label1 to lblHello to be in sync with our previous example and remove the string "Label" from the Text property (as shown in Figure 11.8).

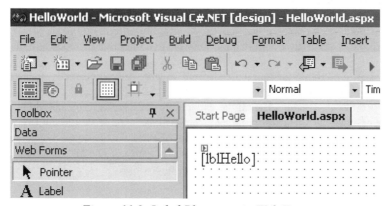

Figure 11.8: Label Placement in Web Form

Visual Studio .NET also allows you to go into the HTML view of the form design and edit the code if you are a hardcore HTML developer. Just click the HTML button at the bottom (as shown in Figure 11.9).

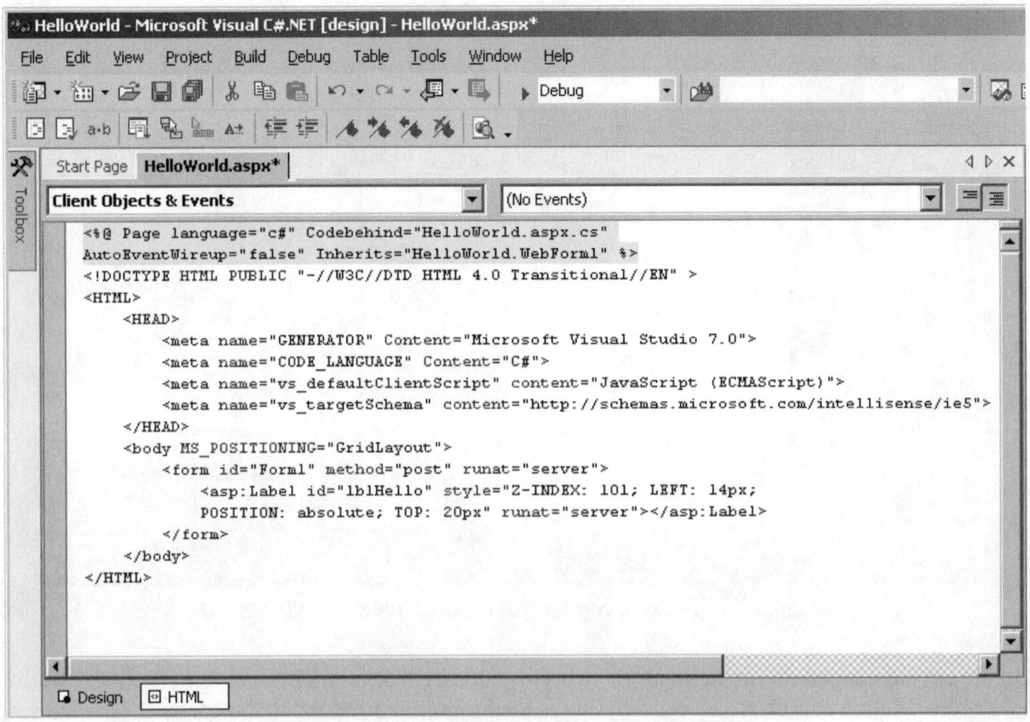

Figure 11.9: HTML View of the Web Form

Visual Studio .NET generates quite a bit of code for us. If you notice the first line of the code, we're specifying few attributes of the page:

```
<%@ Page language="c#" Codebehind="HelloWorld.aspx.cs"
AutoEventWireup="false" Inherits="HelloWorld.WebForm1" %>
```

Visual Studio .NET uses the technique called CodeBehind to separate code from content. What this means is that all your presentation elements, such as server controls, will remain in the .aspx file and all the code that you manipulate will remain in the .cs file.

In large implementations, a person other than the programmer might do the HTML design. In that scenario, this kind of CodeBehind will make it very easy to integrate the code and maintain it.

You can easily figure out what the language attribute means. As you correctly guessed, we're specifying the language that we're going to use for this ASP.NET page. The next attribute, CodeBehind, specifies from which file all the executable code for the page should be taken. The AutoEventWireup attribute specifies that the current ASP.NET page should not fire events such as Page_Load automatically. This is because the current ASP.NET page doesn't have any code in it and all the executable code resides in the file HelloWorld.aspx.cs. The last parameter, Inherits, specifies the class the current ASP.NET page should inherit from.

Now we've placed the label control on the Web form. Let's write the "Hello, World from ASP.NET!" code from the Page_Load event. By double-clicking in the Web form you can get into the code window (as shown in Figure 11.10).

```
Start Page | HelloWorld.aspx*  HelloWorld.aspx.cs* |
HelloWorld.WebForm1                          ▼    Page_Load(object sender,System.EventArgs e)

   using System.Web;
   using System.Web.SessionState;
   using System.Web.UI;
   using System.Web.UI.WebControls;
   using System.Web.UI.HtmlControls;

 namespace HelloWorld
 {
      /// <summary>
      /// Summary description for WebForm1.
      /// </summary>
      public class WebForm1 : System.Web.UI.Page
      {
           protected System.Web.UI.WebControls.Label lblHello;

           public WebForm1()
           {
                Page.Init += new System.EventHandler(Page_Init);
           }

           private void Page_Load(object sender, System.EventArgs e)
           {
                // Put user code to initialize the page here

           }

           private void Page_Init(object sender, EventArgs e)
           {
                //
                // CODEGEN: This call is required by the ASP.NET Web Form Designer.
                //
                InitializeComponent();
           }

           Web Form Designer generated code
      }
 }
```

Figure 11.10: Web Form Code Window

As you can see in Figure 11.10, Visual Studio .NET adds a namespace called HelloWorld and a class called WebForm1. The class WebForm1 inherits from the System.Web.UI.Page class. The System.Web.UI.Page class provides the entire infrastructure for the ASP.NET page and its events. Let's go to the Page_Load event and assign the string "Hello, World from ASP.NET!" to the Label control.

As mentioned in chapter 8, the neat thing about Visual Studio .NET is its "IntelliSense" feature. If you type the Label control's name you'll get all the relevant properties and method of the control (as shown in Figure 11.11).

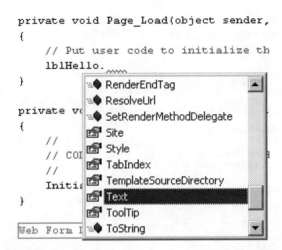

Figure 11.11: IntelliSense Feature of the Code Window

Here's a tip: C# is a case-sensitive language, unlike VB.NET, so you've got to be very careful when spelling the control name. The IntelliSense feature will work only if you type the control name correctly. If you want to see the control names, type "this" and a period, you'll get a list of properties and methods of the current Web form including the server controls.

Let's save our work and run the code by right-clicking on the file HelloWorld.aspx in the Solution Explorer menu and selecting the View in Browser option. You'll see the string "Hello, World from ASP.NET!" appear in the browser (as shown in Figure 11.12).

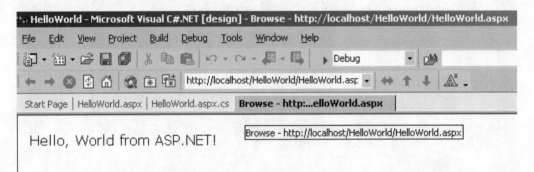

Figure 11.12: "Hello, World from ASP.NET!" from Visual Studio .NET

I'd like to point out a couple of other advantages of using server controls:

When we're using server controls, our code is strongly typed and will not break later. If we want to reference an HTML control such as an input element, we can reference it via the Response.QueryString method or Response.Form method. When we are using any of the Response object's methods we're trying to access an element inside the collection. If the element that we're trying to access is not found, the Response.QueryString method or Response.Form method will return an empty string and will not raise an exception. This is not good from a programmer's point of view. On the other hand, if we are using server controls, we're referencing the server control directly and we're not going to through a collection. Therefore, all the code that accesses the server control will be compiled at the design time, and if we are trying to access a server control that is not present in the ASP.NET page, we will get an error message at compilation. Let's look at the previous ASP.NET page and remove the Label server control declaration and execute the code. We'll get a compilation error message (as shown in Figure 11.13).

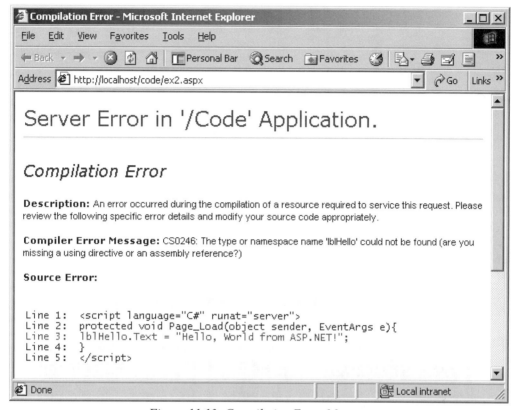

Figure 11.13: Compilation Error Message

Now you can't blame the ASP.NET page for not recognizing the control name for misspelled or undeclared controls. In addition, when you're using server controls, you can't give the same name to two controls. This prevents misbehavior of your application and helps you avoid debugging and tracing time.

Another big advantage we gain with server controls is in regard to placement of the content in the ASP.NET page. Look at both the ASP (see Listing 11.2) and ASP.NET (see Listing 11.3) versions of the code. We've embedded the ASP code to display "Hello, World from ASP!" inside the body tag. This means that we have to embed the ASP code wherever the string "Hello, World from ASP!" has to be placed. With ASP.NET, on the other hand, everything is based on the server controls. All we have to do is place the server controls in the proper presentation areas. Then we can manipulate the server controls from the code block. This gives us more readable and cleaner code. It also separates the code from the presentation elements.

ASP.NET Interactive Example

Let's look at an interactive example. We're going to accept the username and say hello to the user. The code is shown in Listing 11.6.

Listing 11.6— An Interactive Example

```
<script language="C#" runat="server">
void EnterBtn_Click(Object Src, EventArgs E) {
```

```
            lblHello.Text = "Hi " + txtName.Text + ", Welcome to ASP.NET!";
}
</script>
<html>
<head>
<title>Welcome to ASP.NET</title>
</head>
<body>
<form runat="server">
<b><asp:Label id="lblHello" runat="server" /></b> <br />
Enter your name: <asp:textbox id="txtName" runat=server/>
<asp:button text="Enter" Onclick="EnterBtn_Click" runat=server/>
</form>
</body>
</html>
```

We're starting the ASP.NET page with a server-side C# code block, and we've defined a custom event handler called EnterBtn_Click. Inside the body tab, we have a form tag and the runat attribute is set to *server*. Within the form tag are a label, a textbox, and a button control. In this example, we've used only ASP.NET Web server controls. When the button is clicked, we're calling the EnterBtn_Click server-side code.

Perhaps you are wondering why you need two sets of controls that do the same thing. The HTML intrinsic controls are great if you are migrating your ASP pages to ASP.NET pages. When you migrate the pages, all you need to do is insert runat="server" in all the HTML controls in your ASP page and add the id attribute with the same name as the HTML control.

Let's run the code and see how it looks in a Web browser (see Figures 11.14 and 11.15).

Figure 11.14: Accepting the Username

Click the Enter button now.

Figure 11.15: Greeting the User

There are no more submit and reset buttons to code. All you need to do is create a Button control, create a server-side event handler, and call the event handler from the Button control.

If you look at Figures 11.14 and 11.15 closely, you'll notice that we've entered the name "Srinivasa Sivakumar," and the name persisted after a post. This is because all the server controls maintain state by default. Let's see how the server controls maintain state. Let's open the source view of the page (see Listing 11.7).

Listing 11.7—ASP.NET Page Output

```
<html>
<head>
<title>Welcome to ASP.NET</title>
</head>
<body>
<form name="ctrl0" method="post" action="ex3.aspx" id="ctrl0">
<input type="hidden" name="__VIEWSTATE"
value="dDwxNzkwOTY3MjMyO3Q8O2w8aTwxPjs+O2w8dDw7bDxpPDE+Oz47bDx0PHA8cDxs
PFRleHQ7PjtsPEhpIFNyaW5pdmFzYSBTaXZha3VtYXIsIFdlbGNvbWUgdG8gQVNQLk5FVCE
7Pj47Pjs7Pjs+Pjs+"/>

<b><span id="lblHello">Hi Srinivasa Sivakumar, Welcome to ASP.NET!</span></b><br />
Enter your name: <input name="txtName" type="text" value="Srinivasa Sivakumar"
id="txtName" />
<input type="submit" name="ctrl1" value="Enter" />
</form>
</body>
</html>
```

Notice the form tag. In the ASP.NET code, we just declared the form tag with the runat attribute as *server.* But if you look at the code generated by ASP.NET, it adds all the necessary attributes such as name, method, action, and so on:

```
<form name="ctrl0" method="post" action="ex3.aspx" id="ctrl0">
```

The next line after the form tag is an HTML hidden control named _VIEWSTATE:

```
<input type="hidden" name="__VIEWSTATE"
value="dDwxNzkwOTY3MjMyO3Q8O2w8aTwxPjs+O2w8dDw7bDxpPDE+Oz47bDx0PHA8c
DxsPFRleHQ7PjtsPEhpIFNyaW5pdmFzYSBTaXZha3VtYXIsIFdlbGNvbWUgdG8gQVNQL
k5FVCE7Pj47Pjs7Pjs+Pjs+"/>
```

ASP.NET maintains the state for all the server controls in this hidden control.

Summary

In this chapter we started on the ASP.NET journey with a brief history of Web programming technologies and an explanation of how ASP.NET was born. Then we looked at what is missing from ASP.NET, the differences between ASP and ASP.NET, and the advantages and limitations of ASP.NET. Then we examined server controls and a "Hello, World" sample created with Notepad and Visual Studio .NET. We also saw how server controls maintain state.

ASP and ASP.NET applications can sit side by side in the same server and can be accessed in the same way. The only restriction is that they cannot share information such as session information. Still, ASP.NET is an excellent advancement from ASP, and we all will benefit from it. In the next chapter we will dive deeper into the advanced functionality provided by ASP.NET.

Chapter 12:
Advanced ASP.NET

Introduction

The last chapter introduced you to ASP.NET and explained how different it is from its predecessor, Active Server Pages (ASP). You learned some basic information about ASP.NET such as how it maintains its state. In this chapter we'll examine basic and advanced server controls, configuration files, session state information, and security settings. Let's get started.

HTML Server Controls

The Hypertext Markup Language (HTML) server controls are equivalent to their counterpart HTML controls. They reside in the System.Web.UI.HtmlControls namespace. Table 12.1 lists the HTML server controls.

HTML Server Control	Description
HtmlForm	Equivalent to the <form> tag in HTML; provides programmatic access to the HTML <form> tag from ASP.NET
HtmlInputText	Equivalent to the <input type="text"> tag in HTML
HtmlInputCheckBox	Equivalent to the <input type="checkbox"> tag in HTML
HtmlInputFile	Equivalent to the <input type="file"> tag in HTML
HtmlInputHidden	Equivalent to the <input type="hidden"> tag in HTML
HtmlInputImage	Equivalent to the <input type="image"> tag in HTML
HtmlInputRadioButton	Equivalent to the <input type="radio"> tag in HTML
HtmlInputButton	Equivalent to the <input type="button"> tag in HTML
HtmlButton	Equivalent to the <button> tag in HTML
HtmlSelect	Equivalent to the <select> tag in HTML
HtmlImage	Equivalent to the <image> tag in HTML
HtmlTextArea	Equivalent to the <textarea> tag in HTML
HtmlGenericControl	Gives access to the common HTML tags such as <body>, <div>, <span>, <font>, etc.
HtmlAnchor	Equivalent to the <a> or <anchor> tag in HTML

HTML Server Control	Description
HtmlTable	Equivalent to the <table> tag in HTML
HtmlTableCell	Equivalent to the <td> tag in HTML
HtmlTableRow	Equivalent to the <tr> tag in HTML

Table 12.1: ASP.NET HTML Server Controls

As you can see, the HTML server controls provide excellent interportability between them and the HTML controls. The HTML controls are of great help when you are converting ASP pages to ASP.NET pages.

Let's look at an example. Here we build a registration page using most of the HTML server controls. Figure 12.1 shows how the page will look. 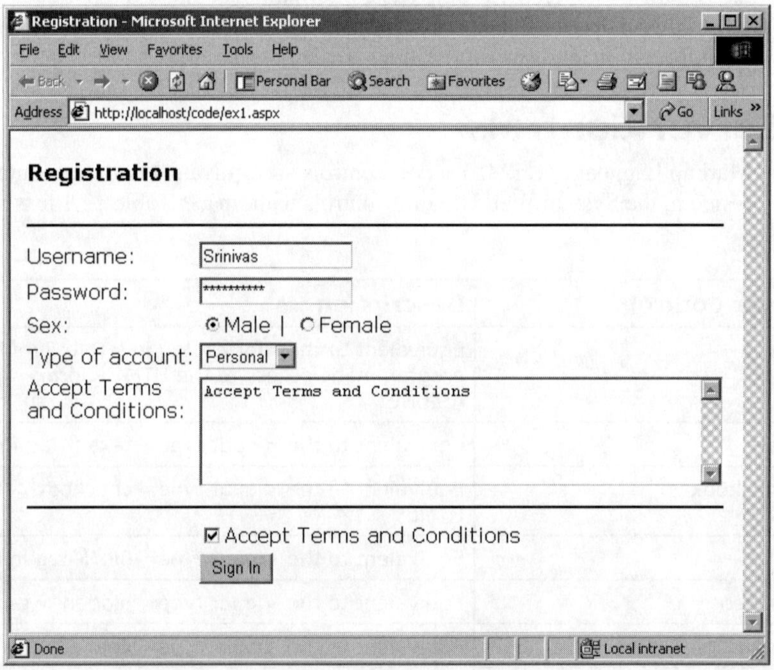

Figure 12.1: Registration Page

When the user submits the registration data, we'll display the values in a <div> tag. Figure 12.2 shows what the user-submitted data looks like. 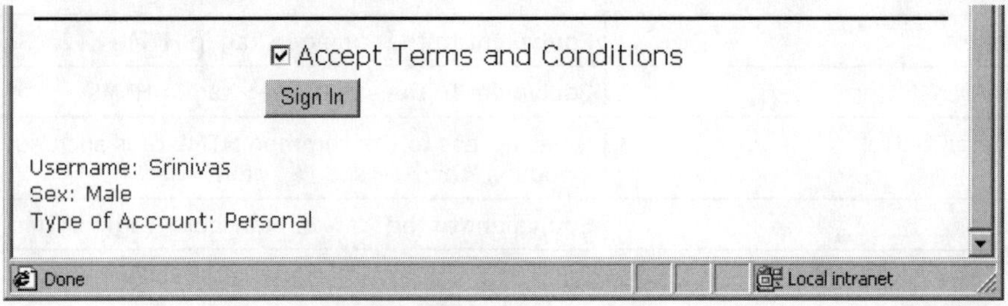

Figure 12.2: Registration Data

The server controls layout code appears in Listing 12.1. In that layout, we have a <form> tag—with *server* as the runat attribute—following the <body> tag. Then we define a table with two columns. The left-hand column displays the data label, and the right-hand column displays the HTML server controls to collect the user input. We use two HTML text controls for the user name and the password fields. We use HTML radio buttons for the user's sex, and we use a select list control for the type of account.

Listing 12.1—Registration Page

```
<html>
<head>
     <title>Registration</title>
</head>
<body>
<form id="frmFirst" runat="server">
<table border=0>
<tr>
     <td colspan=2><h3>Registration</h3></td>
</tr>
<tr>
     <td colspan=2><hr id="hr1" runat="server"/></td>
</tr>
     <td>Username:</td>
     <td><input type="text" runat="server" id="txtUsername"
maxlength="15" size="15" value="" /> </td>
</tr>
<tr>
     <td>Password: </td>
     <td><input type="password" runat="server" id="txtPassword"
         maxlength="15" size="15" value="" /> </td>
</tr>
<tr>
     <td>Confirmation Password: </td>
     <td><input type="password" runat="server" id="txtPassword1"
         maxlength="15" size="15" value="" /> </td>
</tr>
<tr>
     <td>Sex: </td>
     <td><input type="radio" runat="server" id="rdoMale" name="rdoSex"
         />Male | <input type="radio" runat="server" id="rdoFemale"
         name="rdoSex" />Female </td>
</tr>
<tr>
     <td>Type of account: </td>
     <td><select runat="server" id="selType">
         <option>Business</option>
         <option>Personal</option>
     </select>
</td>
</tr>
<tr>
     <td valign="top">Accept Terms <br />and Conditions: </td>
     <td><textarea runat="server" id="Trms" cols="50" rows="5">Accept
         Terms and Conditions</textarea></td>
</tr>
<tr>
     <td colspan=2><hr id="hr2" runat="server"/></td></tr>
     <td> </td>
     <td><input type="checkbox" runat="server" id="chkCondit" />Accept
         Terms and Conditions</td>
</tr>
<tr>
     <td> </td>
     <td><button runat="server" id="programmaticID"
OnServerClick="SignIn_OnClick">Sign In</button></td>
```

```
</tr>
</table><br />
<font size="2" color="Red">
    <div runat="server" id="divPostedValues" />
</font>
</form>
</body>
</html>
```

We use a text area control to display the terms-and-conditions information. Then we use a check box control to ensure that the user accepts the terms and conditions. We have a button control that accepts the registration data from the user and calls a server-side event handler called SignIn_OnClick by using the OnServerClick attribute. And lastly, we use a <div> tag to display the result. Also, notice that we have two horizontal lines (<hr /> tag) in the page with default attributes.

You should also note that when you don't add the runat="server" attribute to the HTML controls, these controls can't be accessed from ASP.NET server-side code.

Listing 12.2 shows the server-side code that we've added.

Listing 12.2—Server-Side Code

```
<script language="C#" runat="server">
protected void Page_Load(object sender, EventArgs e){
        //Change the Horizontal Line's color to black
        hr1.Attributes["color"]= "#000000";
        hr2.Attributes["color"]= "#000000";
}

void SingIn_OnClick(object Source, EventArgs e)
   {
        String strValues = "";

        //Check if the "terms and conditions"
        //checkbox is checked?
        if (chkCondit.Checked == true)
         {
          strValues = "Username: " + txtUsername.Value + "<br />";
          if (rdoMale.Checked == true){
          strValues = strValues + "Sex: Male <br />";
          }
          else
          {
            strValues = strValues + "Sex: Female <br />";
          }

          strValues = strValues + "Type of Account: " +
                            selType.Value + "<br />";

        //Display the results
          divPostedValues.InnerHtml= strValues;
        }
        else
        {
        //Display the error message
          divPostedValues.InnerHtml= "Please check the 'Accept Terms and Conditions'
                                  check box";
        }
    }
</script>
```

The server-side code block includes event handlers. The first one is the Page_Load event handler, in which we change the color of the horizontal lines to black.

```
hr1.Attributes["color"]= "#000000";
hr2.Attributes["color"]= "#000000";
```

We are using the Attributes collection of the <hr> tag and accessing the color element. In the SignIn_OnClick event handler we are checking whether the terms-and-conditions check box has been selected. If not, we display an error message or we concatenate the user data and display it in the <div> tag.

Optionally, we can raise events on the server side to perform some application-specific tasks. The OnServerClick and OnServerChange events are the two main events supported by HTML server controls, and we can write code to handle the events wherever necessary.

ASP.NET Web Server Controls

The ASP.NET Web server controls reside in the System.Web.UI.WebControls namespace and provide an alternative to the HTML server controls. The ASP.NET Web server controls are richer in functionality and follow the Extensible Markup Language (XML) syntax. They are listed in Table 12.2.

ASP.NET Web Server Control	Description	Example of Usage
TextBox	An input control	<asp:TextBox ... />
Label	A read-only control; will be rendered as a <span> tag at runtime	<asp:Label ... />
Button	An action control	<asp:Button ... />
CheckBox	An input control for multiple selections	<asp:CheckBox ... />
RadioButton	An input control for single selection from multiple choices	<asp:RadioButton ... />
ImageButton	An action control combined with an image; will be rendered as an <img> tag at runtime	<asp:ImageButton ... />
LinkButton	An action control that has the look of a hyperlink and the feel of a command button	<asp:LinkButton ... />
HyperLink	An action control; will be rendered as an <a> or <anchor> tag at runtime	<asp:HyperLink ... />
Image	An action control; will be rendered as an <img> tag at runtime	<asp:Image ... />
ListBox	An input control; will be rendered as a <select> tag	<asp:ListBox ... />
DropDownList	Creates a simple selection list; will be rendered as a <select> tag	<asp:DropDownList ... />
RadioButtonList	Can create a group of single-selection radio buttons	<asp:RadioButtonList ... />
DataList	A list control; provides excellent template-based customization for look and feel	<asp:DataList ... />

ASP.NET Web Server Control	Description	Example of Usage
DataGrid	A grid control (rendered as an HTML table); provides excellent template-based customization for look and feel	`<asp:DataGrid ... />`
Repeater	A template control; can be used with many other template-based controls	`<asp:Repeater ... />`
Table	Used to draw an HTML table at runtime	`<asp:Table ... />`
TableCell	Used to draw an HTML table cell (`<td>` tag) at runtime	`<asp:TableCell ... />`
TableRow	Used to draw an HTML table row (`<tr>` tag) at runtime	`<asp:TableRow ... />`
PlaceHolder	A container control; can be used to add a control dynamically at runtime	`<asp:PlaceHolder ... />`
Literal	Can be used to display static text; can be changed dynamically from the server side	`<asp:Literal ... />`
Panel	A container control; rendered as a `<div>` tag	`<asp:Panel ... />`
AdRotator	A special kind of control; spools an advertisement from an XML file	`<asp:AdRotator ... />`
Calendar	A special kind of control; displays a calendar with a wide variety of customization options	`<asp:Calendar ... />`
XML	An XML transformation control; takes an XML file and Extensible Stylesheet Language (XSL) style sheet to transform the content	Not applicable

Table 12.2: ASP.NET Web Server Controls

Common ASP.NET Web Server Control Properties

A few general properties are supported by all the ASP.NET Web server controls except the Literal, PlaceHolder, and XML controls. These properties allow us to completely customize a server control. Table 12.3 lists them.

Property	Description	Example of Usage
AccessKey	Assigns a shortcut to the control as with desktop controls (e.g., assign the Z key, and the user can press ALT+Z to access the server control); works only with Internet Explorer 4.0 and above.	`<asp:ControlName AccessKey="Y" ... />`
Attributes	Gives access to the attributes of the control (e.g., use to change the color of the control)	`ControlID.Attribute["bgcolor"] = "Black";`
BackColor	Changes the background color of the control	`<asp:ControlName BackColor="Gray" ... />`
BorderColor	Changes the border color of the control	`<asp:ControlName BorderColor="Gray" ... />`

Property	Description	Example of Usage
BorderWidth	Changes the border width of the control	`<asp:ControlName BorderWidth="1" ... />`
BorderStyle	Changes the border style of the control; possible values: NotSet, None, Dotted, Dashed, Solid, Double, Groove, Ridge, Inset, and Outset	`<asp:ControlName BorderStyle="Solid" ... />`
CssClass	Sets the CSS class name for the control	`<asp:ControlName CssClass="MyStyle" ... />`
Style	Sets the CSS style for the control	`<asp:ControlName Style="Font-face: verdana" ... />`
Enabled	Enables or disables the control	`<asp:ControlName Enabled="MyStyle" ... />`
Font	Sets the font properties for the control	`<asp:ControlName Font-Name="verdana" Font-size="2" ... />`
ForeColor	Sets the foreground color for the control	`<asp:ControlName ForeColor="White" ... />`
Height	Sets the height of the control	`<asp:ControlName Height="20" ... />`
TabIndex	Sets the tab index for the control	`<asp:ControlName TabIndex="3" ... />`
ToolTip	Sets the ToolTip text for the control	`<asp:ControlName ToolTip="Monthly Status Report" ... />`
Width	Sets the width for the control	`<asp:ControlName Width="640" ... />`

Table 12.3: Common Server Control Properties

Note that most of the properties in Table 12.3 generate CSS (cascading style sheets) code, and the CSS code may not work on Internet Explorer versions below 4.0.

Now let's look at the capabilities of each of the ASP.NET Web server controls.

Label, Literal, and Image Controls

The Label and Literal controls are read-only controls; they can be used to display static or dynamic text changed at runtime. The only difference between the Label and Literal controls is that the Label control allows one to specify a style to customize its look and feel. The Image control can be used to display images in the ASP.NET page. The sample code in Listing 12.3 employs all three controls.

Listing 12.3—Using the Label, Literal, and Image Controls

```csharp
<script language="C#" runat="server">
protected void Page_Load(object sender, EventArgs e){
        //Change the BackColor, Forecolor and
    //BorderColor of the label
        lbl.BackColor = System.Drawing.Color.Gray;
        lbl.ForeColor = System.Drawing.Color.White;
        lbl.BorderColor= System.Drawing.Color.Black;
```

```
}
</script>
<html>
<body>
<h3><font face="Verdana">Label, Literal and Image Example</font></h3>
<form runat=server>
<asp:Label id="lbl"  Text="Hello from Label!"
runat="server" /> <br /><br />
<asp:Literal id="ltrl" Text="Hello from Literal!"
runat="server" /> <br /><br />
<asp:Image id="img" runat="server" AlternateText="Goto C# Corner!"
 ImageAlign="left" ImageUrl="CSharpCorner.gif"/>
</form>
</body>
</html>
```

In the listing we change the background, foreground, and border color of the Label control from the Page_Load event.

TextBox Control

The TextBox control is an input control and can display a variety of controls such as an input text box or a text area control. The syntax of the TextBox control is shown in Listing 12.4.

Listing 12.4—Textbox Control Syntax

```
<asp:TextBox id=value
    AutoPostBack="True|False" Columns="characters"
    MaxLength="characters" Rows="rows" Text="text"
    TextMode="Single | Multiline | Password"
    Wrap="True|False" OnTextChanged="OnTextChangedMethod"
    runat="server"/>
```

The standard ID and runat attributes are applied to all the ASP.NET server controls. The TextBox control supports the OnTextChanged event; that event will be fired when we set the AutoPostBack attribute to *true*. See the example in Listing 12.5.

Listing 12.5—Using the Textbox Control

```
<script language="C#" runat="server">
void Text_Change(Object sender, EventArgs e) {
   Message.Text = txtChange.Text;
}
</script>
<html>
<body>
<h3><font face="Verdana">TextBox Example</font></h3>
<form runat=server>
       <asp:TextBox id="txtChange" AutoPostBack="True"
               OnTextChanged="Text_Change" runat="server"/> <br />
       Changed value: <asp:Label id="Message" runat="server"/>
</form>
</body>
</html>
```

When the user enters "ASP.NET" in the text box and tabs out, the event is fired and the text appears in the Label control. The screenshot in Figure 12.3 shows how this works.

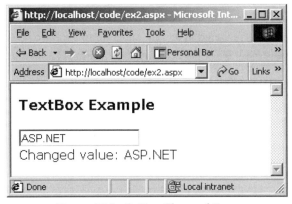

Figure 12.3: OnTextChanged Event

We can create a password control with TextBox by setting the TextMode attribute to Password. We can create a text area control by setting the TextMode attribute to Multiline. We can further customize the control's look and feel by setting the Rows and Columns attributes.

Note that whereas the HTML server controls expose the Value property to read the content of the control, the ASP.NET Web server controls provide the Text property to read the content.

Button, ImageButton, and LinkButton Controls

The Button control is an action control; it can be used to achieve an application-specific task. LinkButton is also an action control; it will be drawn as a hyperlink in the HTML page. The ImageButton control is an action button with an embedded image. The example in Listing 12.6 uses these controls.

Listing 12.6—Using the Button, ImageButton, and LinkButton Controls

```
<script language="C#" runat="server">
void Btn_Click(Object sender, EventArgs e) {
   //Do something
}
void ImgBtn_Click(Object sender, ImageClickEventArgs e) {
   //Do something
}
</script>
<html>
<body>
<h3><font face="Verdana">Button Example</font></h3>
<form runat=server>
Button: <asp:Button id="BtnClick" Text="Click Me!"
        OnClick="Btn_Click" runat="server"/> <br /> <br />
LinkButton: <asp:LinkButton id="LnkBtnClick" Text="Click Me!"
            OnClick="Btn_Click" runat="server"/> <br /> <br />
ImageButton: <asp:ImageButton ImageUrl="ClickMe.Gif"
             id="ImgBtnClick" Text="Click Me!"
             OnClick="ImgBtn_Click" runat="server"/>
</form>
</body>
</html>
```

The only difference between ImageButton and the other two controls is the second argument in the event method signature. The Button and LinkButton controls accept the second parameter as the class type EventArgs, and the ImageButton accepts it as the ImageClickEventArgs class.

HyperLink Control

The HyperLink control will be rendered as an <a> tag at runtime; it provides the flexibility of manipulating the <a> tag at runtime. Listing 12.7 shows a simple example.

Listing 12.7—Using the Hyperlink Control

```
<html>
<head>
</head>
<body>
<h3><font face="Verdana">HyperLink Control Example</font></h3>
<asp:HyperLink id="hyperLink1"
        NavigateUrl="http://www.c-sharpcorner.com"
        Text="Click here to visit C# Corner"
        Target="_new" runat="server" />
</body>
</html>
```

When a user clicks the hyperlink, the "C# Corner" site will be opened in a new browser window.

CheckBox and RadioButton Controls

The CheckBox control is an input control that allows multiple selections from available multiple options. On the other hand, RadioButton controls allow a single selection from multiple options. Listing 12.8 provides an example of these controls.

Listing 12.8—Using the CheckBox and RadioButton Controls

```
<html>
<body>
<h3><font face="Verdana">Button Example</font></h3>
<form runat=server>
<table border=0><tr valign="top" bgcolor="Silver">
<td>Operating Systems: </td>
<td>Processor: </td>
</tr>
<tr valign="top">
<td>
<asp:CheckBox id="chkWin95" Text="Windows 95"
   runat="server"/> <br />
   ...
<asp:CheckBox id="chkWinXp" Text="Windows XP"
   runat="server"/> <br /> <br />
</td>
<td>
<asp:RadioButton GroupName="Processor" id="Rd486"
   Text="486 DX2" runat="server"/> <br />
   ...
<asp:RadioButton GroupName="Processor" id="RdP4"
   Text="Pentium 4" runat="server"/>
</td></tr></table>
</form>
</body>
</html>
```

The code in Listing 12.8 creates five check boxes and five radio buttons. The radio buttons are grouped under one name—that is, they share the same group name.

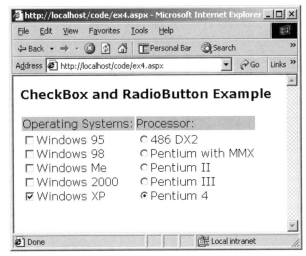

Figure 12.4: Check Boxes and Radio Buttons

Both the Checkbox and RadioButton controls can fire the OnCheckedChanged event when the selection is changed in the group. The AutoPostBack attribute enables this event handler to fire.

CheckBoxList and RadioButtonList Controls

The CheckBoxList and RadioButtonList controls provide the same functionality as their counterparts, the CheckBox and RadioButton controls. Their added advantage is that they can be dynamically populated from a data source such as an array or database object. These controls provide flexibility in displaying and designing the look and feel of a control by using the display mode with RepeatColumns, RepeatDirection, and RepeatLayout attributes. In addition, both controls can respond to the OnSelectedIndexChanged event.

Let's build a simple example. We will create a CheckBoxList control and a RadioButtonList control inside a table. We will set RepeatColumns="2", RepeatLayout="Table", and RepeatDirection="Vertical" for the CheckBoxList control. Then we will bind both list controls with a hash table in the Page_Load event. The code appears in Listing 12.9.

Listing 12.9—Using the CheckBoxList and RadioButtonList Controls

```
<%@ Import Namespace="System.Data" %>
<%@ Import Namespace="System.Data.OleDb" %>
<script language="C#" runat="server">
protected void Page_Load(object sender, EventArgs e){
        if (!Page.IsPostBack){
                //Declare a new HashTable and values
                Hashtable OS = new Hashtable(5);
                OS.Add("Windows 95", 1);
                OS.Add("Windows 98", 2);
                OS.Add("Windows Me", 3);
                OS.Add("Windows 2000", 4);
                OS.Add("Windows XP", 5);

                //Bind the Hashtable to the ListBox
                ChkOS.DataSource = OS;
                ChkOS.DataTextField="Key";
                ChkOS.DataValueField="Value";
                ChkOS.DataBind();

                //Declare a new HashTable and values
                Hashtable Pro = new Hashtable(5);
```

```
                Pro.Add("486 DX2", 1);
                Pro.Add("Pentium With MMX", 2);
                Pro.Add("Pentium II", 3);
                Pro.Add("Pentium III", 4);
                Pro.Add("Pentium 4", 5);

                //Bind the Hashtable to the ListBox
                Processor.DataSource = Pro;
                Processor.DataTextField="Key";
                Processor.DataValueField="Value";
                Processor.DataBind();
        }
}
void Btn_Click(Object sender, EventArgs e){
    String SelCnt= "";
    for (int i=0; i < ChkOS.Items.Count; i++) {
        if ( ChkOS.Items[i].Selected == true) {
            SelCnt += ChkOS.Items[i].Text + "<br />";
        }
    }
    Sel.Text = SelCnt;

    if (Processor.SelectedIndex > -1)
    SelPro.Text = Processor.SelectedItem.Text;
}
</script>
<html>
<body>
<h3><font face="Verdana">CheckBoxList and RadioButtonList Example</font></h3>
<form runat=server>
<table border=0><tr valign="top" bgcolor="Silver">
<td>Operating Systems: </td>
<td>Processor: </td>
</tr>
<tr valign="top">
<td>
<asp:CheckBoxList id="ChkOS" RepeatColumns="2" RepeatLayout="Table"
        RepeatDirection="Vertical" runat="server" />
</td>
<td>
<asp:RadioButtonList id="Processor" runat="server" />
</td></tr></table>
<asp:Button Text="Submit" id="cmdSubmit"
OnClick="Btn_Click" runat="server" /> <br /> <br/>
Selected Item (Processor): <asp:Label id="SelPro"
runat="server" /><br /><br />
Selected Items (OS): <br /><asp:Label id="Sel" runat="server" />
</form>
</body>
</html>
```

Figure 12.5 shows the output.

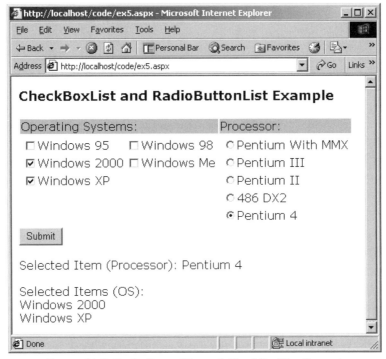

Figure 12.5: RadioButtonList and CheckBoxList Controls

When the Submit button is clicked, we call the Btn_Click event method from the code. The Btn_Click method runs a loop within the Items collection of the CheckBoxList control and checks each ListItem to see whether it is selected. If selected, it adds the ListItem's text to a string variable and displays the content of the string variable in a label control.

We're using the SelectedIndex property to make sure that something is selected. If that is the case, we use the Text property of the SelectedItem object to display the text of the selected item of the RadioButtonList and CheckBoxList controls.

ListBox and DropDownList Controls

The ListBox and DropDownList controls are very similar to the <select> tag in HTML. The only difference is that the ListBox control allows for multiple selections and can display more than one item, whereas the DropDownList control allows only a single selection. The ListBox and DropDownList controls support data binding from a database or a collection such as an array or hash table using the DataSource, DataTextField, and DataValueField attributes. The ListBox and DropDownList controls can respond to selection changes in the list with the OnSelectionIndexChanged event. The ListBox control can support single or multiple selections if you set the SelectionMode property to Single or Multiple.

The code in Listing 12.10 creates two list boxes—one a single-selection box and the other with multiple selection options and a drop-down list control.

Listing 12.10—Using the ListBox and DropDownList Controls

```
<script language="C#" runat="server">
protected void Page_Load(object sender, EventArgs e){
      if (!Page.IsPostBack){
            //Declare a new HashTable and values
            Hashtable OS = new Hashtable(5);
```

```
                 OS.Add("Windows 95", 1);
                 ...

                 //Bind the Hashtable to the ListBox
                 ...
                 LstOS.DataBind();

                 //Declare a new HashTable and values
                 Hashtable Pro = new Hashtable(5);
                 ...

                 //Bind the Hashtable to the ListBox
                 ...
                 LstProcessor.DataBind();

                 //Declare a new HashTable and values
                 Hashtable RAM = new Hashtable(5);
                 RAM.Add("32 MB", 1);
                 ...

                 //Bind the Hashtable to the ListBox
                 ...
                 lstRAM.DataBind();
          }
}
void Btn_Click(Object sender, EventArgs e){
    String SelCnt= "";
    for (int i=0; i < LstOS.Items.Count; i++) {
        if ( LstOS.Items[i].Selected == true) {
            SelCnt += LstOS.Items[i].Text + "<br />";
        }
    }
    Sel.Text = SelCnt;

    if (lstRAM.SelectedIndex > -1)
        SelRam.Text = lstRAM.SelectedItem.Text;

    if (LstProcessor.SelectedIndex > -1)
        SelPro.Text = LstProcessor.SelectedItem.Text;
}
</script>
<html>
<body>
<h3><font face="Verdana">ListBox Example</font></h3>
<form runat=server>
<b>RAM:</b> <asp:DropDownList id="lstRAM" runat="server" />
<table border=0><tr valign="top" bgcolor="Silver">
<td>Operating Systems</td>
<td>Processor</td>
</tr>
<tr valign="top">
<td>
<asp:ListBox id="LstOS" Rows="10"
    SelectionMode="Multiple" runat="server" />
</td>
<td>
<asp:ListBox id="LstProcessor"  Rows="10"
    SelectionMode="Single" runat="server" />
</td></tr></table>
<asp:Button Text="Submit" id="cmdSubmit" OnClick="Btn_Click" runat="server" /> <br
/> <br/>
Selected Item (RAM):
<asp:Label id="SelRam" runat="server" /><br /><br />
Selected Item (Processor):
<asp:Label id="SelPro" runat="server" /><br /><br />
Selected Items (OS): <br /><asp:Label id="Sel" runat="server" />
</form>
```

```
</body>
</html>
```

In the Page_Load event handler we declare two hash tables, and we bind two controls to the hash tables after adding some sample data to it. For the data binding, we set the DataSource attribute of the ListBox control to the hash table, and we use the DataTextField and DataValueField attributes to bind the columns. Finally, we call the DataBind method to bind the ListBox control to the data source. If you have used Visual Basic 6, you'll feel at home with the data-binding technique. We are following the same method as in our previous example when the Btn_Click event is called.

Table, TableCell, and TableRow Controls

We use the Table, TableCell, and TableRow controls for the dynamic manipulation of HTML tables at runtime. They are interpreted as <table>, <td>, and <tr> at runtime, respectively. The Table server control provides the same attributes as the HTML <table> tag, such as CellSpacing and CellPadding. On top of that, it provides a Rows collection that we use to enumerate all the rows in the table.

The TableRow control provides the standard attributes of a <tr> tag and a Cells collection that we use to enumerate the cells within a row. Let's look at an example. In Listing 12.11 we define a Table server control with two rows, each having two cells. Then we count the number of rows and the cells the control has from the Page_Load event.

Listing 12.11—Using the Table, TableCell, and TableRow Controls

```
<script language="C#" runat="server">
protected void Page_Load(object sender, EventArgs e){
        //Declare int's to count the rows and cells
        int iRows=0, iCells=0;

        //Read all the rows in the table
        foreach (TableRow  tr in tblGrow.Rows) {
                //Read all the Cells in the current row
                foreach (TableCell td in tr.Cells)
                        iCells ++;
                iRows ++;
        }

        //display the number of rows and the cells
        r.Text = iRows.ToString();
        c.Text = iCells.ToString();
}
</script>
<html>
<body>
<h3><font face="Verdana">Table, TableCell and TableRow Example</font></h3>
<form runat=server>
<asp:Table id="tblGrow" GridLines="Both" HorizontalAlign="Left"
        CellPadding="5" CellSpacing="0" runat="server">
    <asp:TableRow id="tr1" HorizontalAlign="Center"      VerticalAlign="Top"
runat="server">
            <asp:TableCell id="td1" HorizontalAlign="Left"
            VerticalAlign="Top" Wrap="True" runat="server">Cell 1
            </asp:TableCell>
            <asp:TableCell id="td2" HorizontalAlign="Left"
            VerticalAlign="Top" Wrap="True" runat="server">Cell 2
            </asp:TableCell>
    </asp:TableRow>
    <asp:TableRow id="tr2" HorizontalAlign="Center"
    VerticalAlign="Top" runat="server">
            <asp:TableCell id="td3" HorizontalAlign="Left"
```

```
                    VerticalAlign="Top" Wrap="True" runat="server">Cell 3
                    </asp:TableCell>
                    <asp:TableCell id="td4" HorizontalAlign="Left"
                    VerticalAlign="Top" Wrap="True" runat="server">Cell 4
                    </asp:TableCell>
            </asp:TableRow>
</asp:Table>
<b>Rows:</b> <asp:Label id="r" runat="server" /> <br />
<b>Cells:</b> <asp:Label id="c" runat="server" />
</form>
</body>
</html>
```

In the Page_Load event we use a for-each loop to enumerate all the rows in the table. Within the loop, we have one more for-each loop that enumerates all the cells in the current row. We use iRows and iCells variables to hold the count of rows and cells in the table, respectively, and we display the output in two label controls.

We can also use the Add method of Cells and Rows collections to add a new cell to the particular row and to add a new row to the table. See the example in Listing 12.12.

Listing 12.12—Manipulating the Table Control

```
<script language="C#" runat="server">
protected void Page_Load(object sender, EventArgs e){
        int iMaxRows=6, iMaxCells=3;
        //Create 6 rows
        for (int i=1; i<= iMaxRows; i++) {
                //Create a new TableRow object
                TableRow tblRow = new TableRow();
                //Create 3 cells
                for (int j=1; j<= iMaxCells; j++) {
                        //Create a new TableCell object
                        TableCell tblCell = new TableCell();
                        tblCell.Text = " Row= " + i + ", Cell= " + j;

                        //Append the new cell to the current row
                        tblRow.Cells.Add(tblCell);
                }
                //Append the new row to the table
                tblGrow.Rows.Add(tblRow);
        }
}
</script>
<html>
<body>
<h3><font face="Verdana">Dynamic Table Creation Example</font></h3>
<form runat=server>
<asp:Table id="tblGrow" GridLines="Both" HorizontalAlign="Left"
            CellPadding="5" CellSpacing="0" runat="server" />
</form>
</body>
</html>
```

In the Page_Load event we run an outer loop six times and an inner loop three times to create six rows and three cells. When a cell is created, we append the cell to the current row, and every row is appended to the table. Figure 12.6 shows the output.

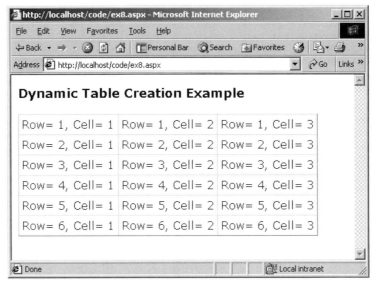

Figure 12.6: Dynamic Table Creation

DataList Control

The DataList control is similar to the ListBox control, but it has a variety of presentation capabilities and in-place editing capabilities. As an example we will build a data-bound DataList control that has editing capabilities. We will bind a hash table to the DataList control. The code appears in Listing 12.13.

Listing 12.13—Using the DataList Control

```
<html>
<script Language = "C#" runat="server">
void Page_Load(Object Sender, EventArgs e)
{
        //If the form is not posted back then
        //bind the data to the DataList control
        if (!IsPostBack) DataBind();
}
void DataBind()
{
        //Declare a new HashTable and values
        Hashtable OS = new Hashtable(5);
        ...

        //Bind the Hashtable to the DataList
        ...
        DataLst.DataBind();
}
void SelectDataList(Object source,DataListCommandEventArgs DlstArgs)
{
        //Make sure the Select button is clicked
        if (DlstArgs.CommandName == "Edit")
        {
                //Set the current items index as the SelectedIndex property
                DataLst.SelectedIndex = DlstArgs.Item.ItemIndex;
                //Rebind the controls
                DataBind();
                Msg.Text = "Selected!";
        }
}
```

```
void EditDataList(Object source, DataListCommandEventArgs DlstArgs)
{
        //Unselect the current row
        DataLst.SelectedIndex = -1;

        //Make the currnet item as editable
        DataLst.EditItemIndex = DlstArgs.Item.ItemIndex;
        //Rebind the controls
        DataBind();
        Msg.Text = "Ready for editing!";
}
void UpdateDataList(Object source, DataListCommandEventArgs DlstArgs)
{
        //Write code to Update
        Msg.Text = "Updating the Key = " +
                DataLst.DataKeys[DlstArgs.Item.ItemIndex];

        //Finish the edit process
        DataLst.EditItemIndex = -1;
        //Rebind the controls
        DataBind();
}

void DeleteDataList(Object source, DataListCommandEventArgs DlstArgs)
{
        //Write code to delete
        Msg.Text = "Deleting the Key = " +
                DataLst.DataKeys[DlstArgs.Item.ItemIndex];

        //Finish the edit process
        DataLst.EditItemIndex = -1;
        //Rebind the controls
        DataBind();
}

void CancelDataList(Object source, DataListCommandEventArgs DlstArgs)
{
        //Cancel the edit process
        DataLst.EditItemIndex = -1;
        //Rebind the controls
        DataBind();
        Msg.Text = "Cancelled the Update!";
}
</script>
<body>
    <form runat=server>
        <h3><font face="Verdana">DataList Example</font></h3>
            <asp:DataList id="DataLst" BorderColor="black"
                BorderWidth="1" CellPadding="3"
                Font-Name="Verdana" Font-Size="10pt" runat="server"
                SelectedItemStyle-BackColor="Navy"
                SelectedItemStyle-ForeColor="White"
                EditItemStyle-BackColor="Orange"
                EditItemStyle-ForeColor="Black"
        DataKeyField="Key"
                OnItemCommand="SelectDataList"
                OnEditCommand="EditDataList"
                OnUpdateCommand="UpdateDataList"
                OnDeleteCommand="DeleteDataList"
                OnCancelCommand="CancelDataList">

                <HeaderStyle BackColor="#808080"/>
                <HeaderStyle ForeColor="#FFFFFF"/>
                <AlternatingItemStyle BackColor="#C0C0C0"/>

                <HeaderTemplate>
                        <b>Hash Table Content</b>
```

```
        </HeaderTemplate>

        <ItemTemplate>
                <asp:LinkButton CommandName="Edit"
                Text="Select" runat="server" />
                <%# DataBinder.Eval(Container.DataItem, "Value") %>
        </ItemTemplate>

        <SelectedItemTemplate>
                <b>Key:</b> <%# DataBinder.Eval(Container.DataItem,
        "Key") %><br />
                <asp:LinkButton CommandName="Select" Text="Edit"
        runat="server" />
                Value: <%# DataBinder.Eval(Container.DataItem,
                "Value") %>
        </SelectedItemTemplate>

        <EditItemTemplate>
                <b>Key:</b> <%# DataBinder.Eval(Container.DataItem,
        "Key") %><br />
                <asp:LinkButton CommandName="Update" Text="Update"
        runat="server" />
                <asp:LinkButton CommandName="Delete" Text="Delete"
        runat="server" />
                <asp:LinkButton CommandName="Cancel" Text="Cancel"
        runat="server" /><br />
                Value: <asp:TextBox runat="server" id="txtValue"
        Text='<%# DataBinder.Eval(Container.DataItem,
        "Value") %>' size="20" />
        </EditItemTemplate>
        </asp:DataList>
        <font face="Verdana" color="Red" size="1">Message: <asp:Label
id="Msg" runat="server" /></font>
    </form>
</body>
</html>
```

If you look at the DataList control declaration, you will see that we define the style information for the data list as follows.

```
<asp:DataList id="DataLst" BorderColor="black" BorderWidth="1"
        CellPadding="3" Font-Name="Verdana" Font-Size="10pt"
        runat="server" SelectedItemStyle-BackColor="Navy"
        SelectedItemStyle-ForeColor="White"
        EditItemStyle-BackColor="Orange"
        EditItemStyle-ForeColor="Black"
```

Then we specify the DataKeyField for the data binding and editing.

```
        DataKeyField="Key"
```

Then we define the event functions for edit, delete, and so on.

```
        OnItemCommand="SelectDataList"
        OnEditCommand="EditDataList"
        OnUpdateCommand="UpdateDataList"
        OnDeleteCommand="DeleteDataList"
        OnCancelCommand="CancelDataList">
```

Then we define the style information for the data list header and alternative rows.

```
        <HeaderStyle BackColor="#808080"/>
        <HeaderStyle ForeColor="#FFFFFF"/>
        <AlternatingItemStyle BackColor="#C0C0C0"/>
```

Then we define the header template. The header template will display the string "Hash Table Content."

```
<HeaderTemplate>
        <b>Hash Table Content</b>
</HeaderTemplate>
```

Next we define the item template. That template will be used to generate the data list items. Every item in the data list will include a link button for row editing with the Select caption before the value of the DataList item. (Note that when an alternative row occurs in the data list, the style defined in the AlternativeItemStyle element will be used.)

```
<ItemTemplate>
        <asp:LinkButton CommandName="Edit" Text="Select"
        runat="server" />
        <%# DataBinder.Eval(Container.DataItem, "Value") %>
</ItemTemplate>
```

We define the SelectedItemTemplate, which will be used when the data list row is selected by clicking the Select link button. When a row is selected, the data list will display the Key value, the link button with the Edit caption, and the original hash table value.

```
<SelectedItemTemplate>
        <b>Key:</b><%# DataBinder.Eval(Container.DataItem, "Key") %><br/>
        <asp:LinkButton CommandName="Select" Text="Edit" runat="server"/>
        Value: <%# DataBinder.Eval(Container.DataItem, "Value") %>
</SelectedItemTemplate>
```

Then we define the EditItemTemplate, which will be used when the data list row is selected for editing by clicking the Edit link button. When a row is ready for editing, the data list will display the Key value; link buttons for updating, deleting, and canceling the edit operation; and the original hash table value in a text box.

```
<EditItemTemplate>
        <b>Key:</b><%# DataBinder.Eval(Container.DataItem, "Key") %><br/>
        <asp:LinkButton CommandName="Update" Text="Update"
            runat="server" />
        <asp:LinkButton CommandName="Delete" Text="Delete"
            runat="server" />
        <asp:LinkButton CommandName="Cancel" Text="Cancel"
            runat="server" /><br />
            Value: <asp:TextBox runat="server" id="txtValue"
            Text='<%# DataBinder.Eval(Container.DataItem,
            "Value") %>' size="20" />
</EditItemTemplate>
```

After the DataList declaration, we use a Label control to display the status messages. We define the event function for the data manipulation. Let's look at the functions one by one. In the Page_Load event, if the page is not posted back, we are binding the hash table to the DataList control.

```
void Page_Load(Object Sender, EventArgs e)
{
        //If the form is not posted back then
        //bind the data to the DataList control
        if (!IsPostBack) DataBind();
}

void DataBind()
{
```

```
        //Declare a new HashTable and values
        Hashtable OS = new Hashtable(5);
        OS.Add(1,"Windows 95");
        OS.Add(2,"Windows 98");
        OS.Add(3,"Windows Me");
        OS.Add(4,"Windows 2000");
        OS.Add(5,"Windows XP");

        //Bind the Hashtable to the DataList
        DataLst.DataSource = OS;
        DataLst.DataKeyField="Key";
        DataLst.DataBind();
}
```

Then we have the SelectDataList function, which will be called when a row is selected. In the function we check to make sure that this function is called by the "edit" command. If so, we set the SelectedIndex property of the DataList control to the current item from the ItemIndex collection and bind the data to the control again.

```
void SelectDataList(Object source, DataListCommandEventArgs DlstArgs)
{
        //Make sure the Select button is clicked
        if (DlstArgs.CommandName == "Edit")
        {
                //Set the current items index as the SelectedIndex property
                DataLst.SelectedIndex = DlstArgs.Item.ItemIndex;
                //Rebind the controls
                DataBind();
                Msg.Text = "Selected!";
        }
}
```

In the EditDataList function, we first set the SelectedIndex to −1, which will deselect the current row. Then we set the EditItemIndex property of the DataList control to the current item from the ItemIndex collection and bind the data to the control again.

```
void EditDataList(Object source, DataListCommandEventArgs DlstArgs)
{
        //Unselect the current row
        DataLst.SelectedIndex = -1;

        //Make the currnet item as editable
        DataLst.EditItemIndex = DlstArgs.Item.ItemIndex;
        //Rebind the controls
        DataBind();
        Msg.Text = "Ready for editing!";
}
```

In the UpdateDataList function, we call the DataLst.DataKeys [DlstArgs.Item.ItemIndex] to get the key for the current row. We're not doing any updates to the hash table in this code. In the real world, we might call a stored procedure or build a Structured Query Language (SQL) statement dynamically to update our database. Next, we set the EditItemIndex to −1, which will cancel the editing process.

```
void UpdateDataList(Object source, DataListCommandEventArgs DlstArgs)
{
        //Write code to Update
        Msg.Text = "Updating the Key = " +
        DataLst.DataKeys[DlstArgs.Item.ItemIndex];

        //Finish the edit process
        DataLst.EditItemIndex = -1;
```

```
        //Rebind the controls
        DataBind();
}
```

The DeleteDataList function is very similar to the previous one. We're not doing any deletes to the hash table in this code. In the real world, we might call a stored procedure or build an SQL statement dynamically to delete the row from the database.

```
void DeleteDataList(Object source, DataListCommandEventArgs DlstArgs)
{
        //Write code to delete
        Msg.Text = "Deleting the Key = " +
                        DataLst.DataKeys[DlstArgs.Item.ItemIndex];

        //Finish the edit process
        DataLst.EditItemIndex = -1;
        //Rebind the controls
        DataBind();
}
```

The CancelDataList function simply cancels the edit process by setting the EditItemIndex property to −1.

```
void CancelDataList(Object source, DataListCommandEventArgs DlstArgs)
{
        //Cancel the edit process
        DataLst.EditItemIndex = -1;
        //Rebind the controls
        DataBind();
        Msg.Text = "Cancelled the Update!";
}
```

Figure 12.7 shows the output in Internet Explorer 6 and Netscape 4.7.

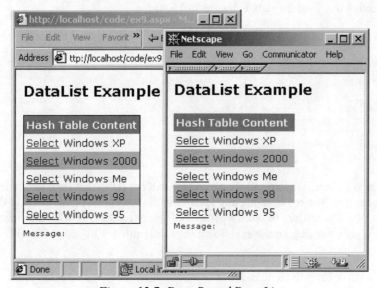

Figure 12.7: Data-Bound Data List

Clicking the Select button will cause the edit template to be called. The DataList will display the edit template as shown in Figure 12.8.

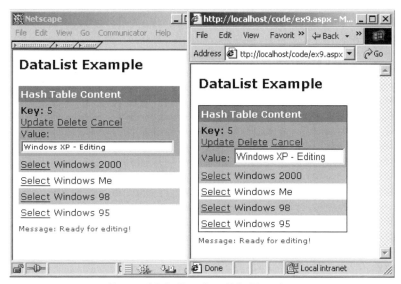

Figure 12.8: DataList Edit Template

When we click the Update button we'll see the updated message in the label control (see Figure 12.9).

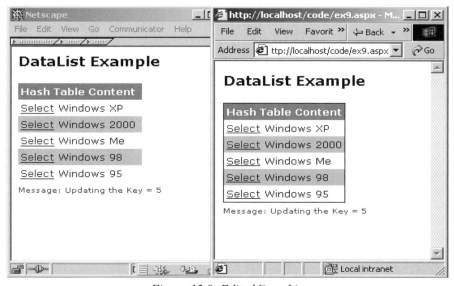

Figure 12.9: Edited Data List

DataGrid Control

The DataGrid control is one of the innovative controls that have been added to the Web server control family. This control renders a multicolumn data-bound table at runtime with such built-in functionalities as in-place editing, deleting, paging, sorting, and various presentation formats.

To learn to use the DataGrid control, we'll build a simple application that includes the paging and sorting features. We will build a DataTable object and add a list of operating systems from a string array. Then we'll create a DataView object from the DataTable and bind it with the DataGrid control. The DataTable and DataView objects are located in the System.Data namespace. So we have to include the namespace reference in the beginning of the ASP.NET page. The code is shown in Listing 12.14.

Listing 12.14—Using the DataGrid Control

```
<%@ Import Namespace= "System.Data" %>
<script Language = "C#" runat="server">
//Set the default sort order as OSID
string SortingField = "OSID";
void Page_Load(Object Sender, EventArgs e)
{
        if (!IsPostBack) DataBind();
}

void DataBind()
{
        String[] strAry = new String[28];

        strAry[0] = "DOS";
        ...
        strAry[27] = "Netware";

        DataTable objdt = new DataTable();
        DataRow objdr;

        objdt.Columns.Add(new DataColumn("OSID", typeof(Int32)));
        objdt.Columns.Add(new DataColumn("OSName", typeof(string)));

        for (int i = 0; i < 28; i++)
        {
                objdr = objdt.NewRow();
                objdr[0] = i;
                objdr[1] = strAry[i];
                objdt.Rows.Add(objdr);
        }

        //Build a new Dataview from the data table object
        DataView objdv = new DataView(objdt);

        //Sort the row
        objdv.Sort=SortingField;

        //Bind the Hashtable to the DataGrid
        DataGrd.DataSource = objdv;
        DataGrd.DataKeyField="OSID";
        DataGrd.DataBind();
}
void DoPaging(Object sender, DataGridPageChangedEventArgs e)
{
        // Set CurrentPageIndex to the page the user clicked.
        DataGrd.CurrentPageIndex = e.NewPageIndex;

        // Rebind the data.
        DataBind();
}
void Sort_Grid(Object sender, DataGridSortCommandEventArgs e)
{
        SortingField = e.SortExpression.ToString();
        DataBind();
}
</script>
<html>
<style>
 .DataStyle {font:x-small Verdana}
</style>
<body>
```

```
    <form runat=server>
      <h3><font face="Verdana">DataGrid Example</font></h3>
        <asp:DataGrid id="DataGrd" BorderColor="black" BorderWidth="1"
                CellPadding="3" AllowPaging="true" PageSize="10"
                AutoGenerateColumns="true" OnPageIndexChanged="DoPaging"
                AllowSorting="True" OnSortCommand="Sort_Grid"
                CssClass="DataStyle" runat="server">
        <HeaderStyle ForeColor="White" BackColor="Gray" />
        <ItemStyle BackColor="White" />
        <AlternatingItemStyle BackColor="#EFEFEF" />
        <PagerStyle Mode="NumericPages" HorizontalAlign="Right" />
        </asp:DataGrid>
    </form>
</body>
</html>
```

In Listing 12.14, we declare a page-level string variable called SortingField initialized with OSID.
We are going to use this variable to store the sorting field name; the default sort order is OSID.
Then we call the DataBind function from the Page_Load event.

```
//Set the default sort order as OSID
string SortingField = "OSID";
void Page_Load(Object Sender, EventArgs e)
{
        if (!IsPostBack) DataBind();
}
```

In the DataBind function, we declare a string array with a couple of operating system names.

```
        String[] strAry = new String[28];

        strAry[0] = "DOS";
        ...
        strAry[27] = "Netware";
```

Then we declare a DataTable object and define the structure with OSID and OSName fields. We run
a loop and add the OS values to the DataTable object. We set the sort key and create a DataView
object out of the DataTable object. Then we bind the DataView object to the DataGrid control.

```
        DataTable objdt = new DataTable();
        DataRow objdr;

        objdt.Columns.Add(new DataColumn("OSID", typeof(Int32)));
        objdt.Columns.Add(new DataColumn("OSName", typeof(string)));

        for (int i = 0; i < 28; i++)
        {
                objdr = objdt.NewRow();
                objdr[0] = i;
                objdr[1] = strAry[i];
                objdt.Rows.Add(objdr);
        }

        //Build a new Dataview from the data table object
        DataView objdv = new DataView(objdt);

        //Sort the row
        objdv.Sort=SortingField;

        //Bind the Hashtable to the DataGrid
        DataGrd.DataSource = objdv;
        DataGrd.DataKeyField="OSID";
        DataGrd.DataBind();
```

In the DataGrid declaration, we set the customized presentation of the control using the BorderColor, BorderWidth, CellPadding, CssClass, and AutoGenerateColumns = "true" properties.

```
BorderColor="black" BorderWidth="1" CellPadding="3"
CssClass="DataStyle" AutoGenerateColumns="true"
```

To enable the paging functionality we set AllowPaging to *true* and PageSize to 10. We call the function DoPaging in the case of the OnPageIndexChanged event being fired.

```
AllowPaging="true" PageSize="10" OnPageIndexChanged="DoPaging"
```

In the DoPaging function we set the CurrentPageIndex property to the page clicked by the user, and we rebind the data source to the DataGrid.

```
void DoPaging(Object sender, DataGridPageChangedEventArgs e)
{
        // Set CurrentPageIndex to the page the user clicked.
        DataGrd.CurrentPageIndex = e.NewPageIndex;
        // Rebind the data.
        DataBind();
}
```

Next we set AllowSorting to *true* and associate the OnSortCommand event with the function Sort_Grid. This gives us the sorting functionality of the DataGrid.

```
AllowSorting="True" OnSortCommand="Sort_Grid"
```

In the Sort_Grid function we get the sort field name from the event handler and store it in the page-level string variable; then we call the DataBind event to rebind the DataGrid to the data source.

```
void Sort_Grid(Object sender, DataGridSortCommandEventArgs e)
{
        SortingField = e.SortExpression.ToString();
        DataBind();
}
```

We define the header, item, alternative item, and paging templates.

```
<HeaderStyle ForeColor="White" BackColor="Gray" />
<ItemStyle BackColor="White" />
<AlternatingItemStyle BackColor="#EFEFEF" />
<PagerStyle Mode="NumericPages" HorizontalAlign="Right" />
```

Let's run the code and see the results (Figure 12.10).

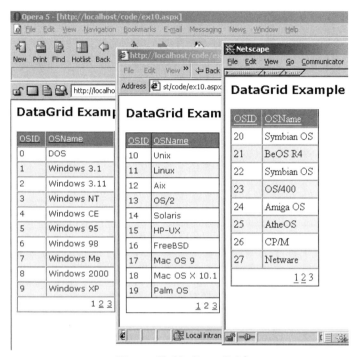

Figure 12.10: Data Grid

Repeater Control

The Repeater control allows us to create a custom layout and bind a data source to it. Unlike the DataGrid control, the repeater control doesn't provide any built-in style properties for customization. This gives the developer full control to customize the data presentation. Let's look at an example. In Listing 12.15 we bind a hash table to the Repeater control and display the hash table as a bulleted list.

Listing 12.15—Using the Repeater Control

```
<script language="C#" runat="server">
void Page_Load(Object Sender, EventArgs e) {
        if (!IsPostBack) DataBind();
}
void DataBind(){
        //Declare a new HashTable and values
        Hashtable OS = new Hashtable(5);
        ...
        //Bind the HashTable to the Repeater
        MyRep.DataSource = OS;
        MyRep.DataBind();
}
</script>
<html>
<head>
<style type="text/css">
        ul {font-face:verdana; font-size:10pt; font-weight:normal}
</style>
</head>
<body>
<form runat=server>
        <h3><font face="Verdana">Repeater Example</font></h3>
        <asp:Repeater id="MyRep" runat="server">
                <HeaderTemplate>
                        <ul>
```

```
            </HeaderTemplate>
            <ItemTemplate>
                    <li><%# DataBinder.Eval(Container.DataItem, "Key") %>
                    - <%# DataBinder.Eval(Container.DataItem, "Value")
            %></li>
            </ItemTemplate>
            <FooterTemplate>
                    </ul>
            </FooterTemplate>
        </asp:Repeater>
</form>
</body>
</html>
```

In the Page_Load event we call the DataBind function in which we bind the hash table to the Repeater control. In the Repeater control we define three templates: header, item, and footer. In the header template we use the <ul> tag to start the bulleted list. In the item template we use the <li> tag to build the bulleted list. We close the list in the footer template.

Note that, as an alternative, we could have used <table> tags to create a table output in this example.

PlaceHolder and Panel Controls

The PlaceHolder and Panel controls are both container controls to which other controls can be added dynamically at runtime. The only difference between them is that the PlaceHolder control doesn't support the common style properties. Let's look at an example of each.

To demonstrate the power of the Panel control, we will create a simple form that has places for a user name, password, and computer type. When the user's selection is PC, we'll dynamically customize the form display, showing the operating system options as "Windows Me," "Windows 2000," and "Windows XP." If the user selects Mac, we'll display the options as "Mac OS X 10.1" and "Mac OS 9." We will use the Visible property to flip the display to tailor the form dynamically. Yes, we can use the Visible property in the Web world, too. See the code in Listing 12.16.

Listing 12.16—Using Panel Control

```
<script language="C#" runat="server">
protected void OnRadioClick(object sender, EventArgs e)
{
        //If the PC radio button is
        //selected then
        if (RdoPC.Checked)
        {
                //Show the PC panel
                //and hide the Mac panel
                PnlPC.Visible=true;
                PnlMac.Visible=false;
        }
        else
        {
                //Show the Mac panel
                //and hide the PC panel
                PnlPC.Visible=false;
                PnlMac.Visible=true;
        }
}
</script>
<html>
<head>
</head>
<body>
<form id="frmFirst" runat="server">
```

```
<table border=0>
<tr>
<tr>
<td colspan=2><h3>Registration</h3></td>
</tr>
<tr>
<td colspan=2><hr id="hr1" runat="server"/></td>
</tr>
</tr><td>Username:</td>
<td><asp:TextBox id="txtusername" runat="server" /></td></tr>
<tr><td>Password: </td>
<td><asp:TextBox id="txtPwd" runat="server" TextMode="Password" /></td>
</tr>
<tr>
<td>Computer: </td>
<td><asp:RadioButton id="RdoPC" AutoPostBack="True" GroupName="Comp" Text="PC"
OnCheckedChanged="OnRadioClick" runat="server"/>
<asp:RadioButton id="RdoMac" AutoPostBack="True" GroupName="Comp" Text="Mac"
OnCheckedChanged="OnRadioClick" runat="server"/></td>
</tr>
<asp:Panel id="PnlPC" Visible="false" HorizontalAlign="Left" Wrap="True"
runat="server">
<tr><td>OS:</td>
<td><asp:RadioButton id="RdoMe" GroupName="OS" Text="Windows Me" runat="server"/>
<asp:RadioButton id="Rdo2000" GroupName="OS" Text="Windows 2000" runat="server"/>
<asp:RadioButton id="RdoXP" GroupName="OS" Text="Windows XP"
runat="server"/></td></tr>
</asp:Panel>
<asp:Panel id="PnlMac" Visible="false" HorizontalAlign="Left" Wrap="True"
runat="server">
<tr>
<td>OS:</td>
<td>
<asp:RadioButton id="RdoX" GroupName="MaxOS" Text="Mac OS X 10.1" runat="server"/>
<asp:RadioButton id="Rdo9" GroupName="MacOS" Text="Mac OS 9" runat="server"/></td>
</tr>
</asp:Panel>
</td></tr></table>
</form>
</body>
</html>
```

We call the OnRadioClick event function when the selection changes in the radio button. Figure 12.11 shows the output when the user selects either PC or Mac.

Figure 12.11: Panel Control

To demonstrate the power of the PlaceHolder control, we'll create a simple form that will have a Label, a TextBox, and a Button control at runtime. See Listing 12.17.

Listing 12.17—Power of the PlaceHolder Control

```
<script language="C#" runat="server">
void Page_Load(Object sender, EventArgs e)
{
        Label asplbl = new Label();
        asplbl.Text = "Your Name: ";
        MyPlaceHolder.Controls.Add(asplbl);

        TextBox asptxt = new TextBox();
        asptxt.Text = "Srinivasa Sivakumar";
        MyPlaceHolder.Controls.Add(asptxt);

        Button aspBtn = new Button();
        aspBtn.Text = "Submit";
        MyPlaceHolder.Controls.Add(aspBtn);
}
</script>
<html>
<body>
<h3><font face="Verdana">PlaceHolder Example</font></h3>
<form runat="server">
<asp:PlaceHolder id="MyPlaceHolder" runat="server"/>
</form>
</body>
</html>
```

In the Page_Load event we declare a label (asplbl) and set its text property to Your Name:. Then we use the Add method of the Controls collection, which adds the Label control to the PlaceHolder control. In the same way, we add the TextBox and Button controls to the PlaceHolder control at runtime. Figure 12.12 shows the output.

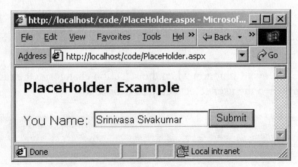

Figure 12.12: PlaceHolder Control

AdRotator Control

We use the AdRotator control to display advertisements on an ASP.NET page. To use the AdRotator control you need an XML file that contains all the advertisement-related data. At runtime the AdRotator control reads the XML file and spools advertisements from it. The AdRotator control also supports the event AdCreated. To illustrate the power of the AdRotator control, we'll create an advertisement campaign for all the online stockbrokers. Let's build the XML file (see Listing 12.18).

Listing 12.18—Ads.xml File

```
<Advertisements>
```

```
<Ad>
   <ImageUrl>ETrade.gif</ImageUrl>
   <NavigateUrl>http://www.etrade.com/</NavigateUrl>
   <AlternateText>ETrade</AlternateText>
   <Impressions>20</Impressions>
   <Keyword>Online Trading</Keyword>
</Ad>
...
<Ad>
   <ImageUrl>Ameri.gif</ImageUrl>
   <NavigateUrl>http://www.ameritrade.com/</NavigateUrl>
   <AlternateText>Ameritrade</AlternateText>
   <Impressions>20</Impressions>
   <Keyword>Online Trading</Keyword>
</Ad>
</Advertisements>
```

Each advertisement has an associated tag called <Ad> that includes advertisement-related information such as ImageUrl, NavigationUrl, AlternativeText, Impressions, and Keyword (see Table 12.4).

Tag	Description
ImageUrl	Specifies the URL for the advertisement image to be located for this advertisement.
NavigationUrl	Specifies to where the browser should be navigated when the user clicks on the advertisement.
AlternativeText	Text to be displayed in case the image is not available; alternatively, this will be included as the ToolTip for the advertisement image.
Impressions	Specifies the importance of the current advertisement—the higher the number, the more important the advertisement. Note: This value can't exceed 2,04,79,99,999.
Keyword	Categorizes the advertisements and allows filtering of advertisements based on this.

Table 12.4: AdRotator Contol Properties

See Listing 12.19 for the ASP.NET page that serves the advertisements.

Listing 12.19—Using the AdRotator Control

```
<script Language = "C#" runat="server">
void Ads_AdCreated(Object sender, AdCreatedEventArgs e)
{
   if (e.AdProperties["AlternateText"] != null)
   {
      // Display the Advt. info
      lblAddCap.Text = "Please visit our sponsor:" +
      (string)e.AdProperties["AlternateText"];
   }
}
</script>
<html>
<head>
<title>AdRotator Control</title>
</head>
<body>
<h3><font face="Verdana">AdRotator Example</font></h3>
<form runat="server">
```

```
<asp:AdRotator id="Ads" AdvertisementFile="Ads.xml" runat="server"
OnAdCreated="Ads_AdCreated" Target="_new"/><br />
<asp:Label id="lblAddCap" runat="server" Font-Name="Verdana" Font-Size="8pt" />
</form>
</body>
</html>
```

We place an AdRotator control on the page, and beneath it, we place a label control. We specify the source XML file for the AdRotator control and the event function for the OnAdCreated event. We also specify the target as "_new" to make sure that all the advertisements are opened in a new browser window. In the Ads_AdCreated event, we read the AlternativeText from the current advertisement and display it in the label control. Figure 12.13 shows the output in Internet Explorer 6, Opera 5, and Netscape 4.7 and 6.

Figure 12.13: AdRotator Control on Major Browsers

Calendar Control

The Calendar control is of great benefit to the development community. Listing 12.20 shows a simple example of its use.

Listing 12.20—Using the Calendar Control

```
<html>
<body>
<form runat="server">
<asp:Calendar id="Cal" runat="server" />
</form>
</body>
</html>
```

Our example adds a Calendar control to a ASP.NET page. The output is shown in Figure 12.14.

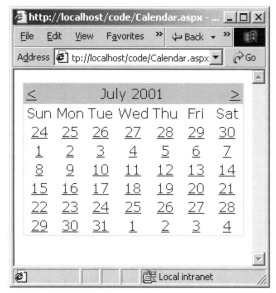

Figure 12.14: Simple Calendar Control

We can use numerous properties to customize the calendar's look and feel. The control supports the OnDayRender, OnSelectionChanged, and OnVisibleMonthChanged events.

The OnDayRender event occurs when a day is rendered on the calendar. The OnSelectionChanged event occurs when the selected day of the month is changed. The OnVisibleMonthChanged event occurs when the selected month is changed. Let's modify the preceding code and add some styles to it. We'll also fire the OnSelectionChanged event.

Listing 12.21—Customizing the Calendar Control

```
<script language="C#" runat="server">
protected void ShowSelectedDate(object sender, EventArgs e)
{
        lblDate.Text = "You've selected the date: " +
        Cal.SelectedDate.ToShortDateString();
}
</script>
<html>
<body>
<form runat="server">
<asp:Calendar id="Cal" runat="server"
        OnSelectionChanged="ShowSelectedDate" SelectionMode="Day"
        Font-Name="Verdana" Font-Size="12px" NextPrevFormat="ShortMonth"
        ShowGridLines="True" runat="server">

        <TodayDayStyle Font-Bold="True"/>
        <DayHeaderStyle Font-Bold="True"/>
        <TitleStyle BackColor="Navy" ForeColor="White" Font-Bold="True"/>

        <SelectedDayStyle BackColor="Red" Font-Bold="True"/>
        <NextPrevStyle ForeColor="White" Font-Size="10px"/>

</asp:Calendar><br />
<asp:Label id="lblDate" runat="server" Font-Name="Verdana" Font-Size="10pt" />
</form>
</body>
</html>
```

In Listing 12.21 we declare the Calendar control and the event function ShowSelectedDate associated with the OnSelectionChanged event. Then we set the SelectionMode to Day.

```
<asp:Calendar id="Cal" runat="server"
       OnSelectionChanged="ShowSelectedDate"
       SelectionMode="Day"
```

Next we customize the Calendar control's presentation.

```
Font-Name="Verdana" Font-Size="12px" NextPrevFormat="ShortMonth"
ShowGridLines="True" runat="server">

<TodayDayStyle Font-Bold="True"/>
<DayHeaderStyle Font-Bold="True"/>
<TitleStyle BackColor="Navy" ForeColor="White" Font-Bold="True"/>

<SelectedDayStyle BackColor="Red" Font-Bold="True"/>
<NextPrevStyle ForeColor="White" Font-Size="10px"/>
```

We add the font name and size and set the grid lines to *true*. We change today's date style to bold and the day headers to bold. We set the calendar's background to navy and foreground to white, and we set the selected date's background color to red. Figure 12.15 shows the new output.

Figure 12.15: Formatted Calendar Control

XML Control

The XML server control is an innovative control that makes a programmer's life easier. If you are an XML and XSL developer who loves to program with XML, you'll love this control. The XML server control simplifies the process of transforming an XML document into HTML or any other format.

Let's see an example. We will build a list of C# sites in an XML file, and we will author an XSL file to transform the XML data into a table. The source code for the XML, XSL, and ASP.NET files is shown in Listings 12.22, 12.23, and 12.24.

Listing 12.22—C# Site Listings

```
<?xml version="1.0"?>
<CSharpSites>
        <CSharpSite>
                <SiteName>C# Corner</SiteName>
                <URL>http://www.c-sharpcorner.com</URL>
        </CSharpSite>
         <CSharpSite>
                <SiteName>C# Today</SiteName>
                <URL>http://www.csharptoday.com</URL>
        </CSharpSite>
        ...
</CSharpSites>
```

Listing 12.23—XSL Transformation File

```
<?xml version="1.0"?>
<xsl:stylesheet xmlns:xsl="http://www.w3.org/1999/XSL/Transform" version="1.0">
        <xsl:template match="/">
                <table border="1" cellspacing="0" cellpadding="2"
                bordercolor="Gray">
                        <tr>
                                <th>C# Site Name</th>
                                <th>URL</th>
                        </tr>
                        <xsl:for-each select="//CSharpSite">
                        <tr class="BD">
                          <td><xsl:apply-templates select="SiteName" /></td>
                          <td><xsl:apply-templates select="URL" /></td>
                        </tr>
                        </xsl:for-each>
                </table>
        </xsl:template>
</xsl:stylesheet>
```

Listing 12.24—Using the XML Control

```
<html>
   <style type="text/css">
     th {font-face:verdana; font-size:10pt; font-weight:bold}
     tr {font-face:verdana; font-size:10pt; font-weight:normal}
   </style>
   <body>
     <asp:xml id="xmlSample" DocumentSource="sites.xml"
     TransformSource="sites.xsl" runat=server/>
   </body>
</html>
```

The XML server control is simple to use. It takes the XML file and the XSL transformation file as arguments and transforms the XML file. The result is shown in Figure 12.16.

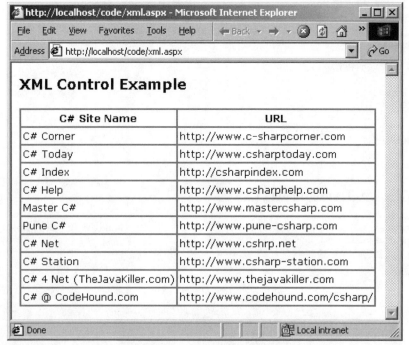

Figure 12.16: XML Control

Using Validation Server Controls

One of the main problems Web developers face is validating user input. Some prefer client-side validation and some prefer server-side validation. You might ask me, then, what the problem is. Well, if you support only client-side validation and a low-level browser that doesn't support JavaScript visits your site, your application will fail. Okay, then, you say, I'd like to use server-side validation. If you use server-side validation for all your controls, you add more stress to the server and you don't use the client-side capabilities. Where do you draw the line between server-side and client-side validation?

Don't worry—ASP.NET is here to help you. ASP.NET includes yet another innovative category of controls called validation controls. The beauty of validation controls is that they can detect the browser type and spool appropriate server-side or client-side code (JavaScript/DHTML) for validation. ASP.NET ships with six validation controls: RequiredFieldValidator, CompareValidator, RangeValidator, RegularExpressionValidator, CustomValidator, and ValidationSummary. These controls address all the validation requirements of an ASP.NET application.

RequiredFieldValidator Control

The most basic validation problem is ensuring that the user enters some data in the required form fields. The RequiredFieldValidator control helps us do that. We can customize the error message and the position of the message with this control. Let's look at the example in Listing 12.25.

Listing 12.25—Using the RequiredFieldValidator Control

```
<script language="C#" runat="server">
void OnSubmit(Object Sender, EventArgs e)
{
      if (Page.IsValid)
      {
            //Do something
```

```
            }
}
</script>
<html>
<head>
   <style type="text/css">
     tr {font-face:verdana; font-size:10pt; font-weight:normal}
   </style>
</head>
<body>
<form runat=server>
<h3><font face="Verdana">RequiredFieldValidator Example</font></h3>
<font size="-3" color="red">* - Marked fields are required.</font>
<hr color="black" size="1"/>
<table border=0>
        <tr>
        <td valign="top">User Name:</td>
        <td>
        <asp:TextBox id="txtUserName" runat=server />
        <font color="red">*</font><br />
        <asp:RequiredFieldValidator id="reqfldvldName" runat="server"
                ControlToValidate="txtUserName"
                Display="Dynamic">User Name is
                required!</asp:RequiredFieldValidator>
        </td>
        </tr>
</table>
<hr color="black" size="1"/>
<asp:Button Type="Submit" name="btnsub" onClick="OnSubmit" Text="Validate"
runat=server />
</form>
</body>
</html>
```

The ASP.NET page has a text box and a button control. When the button control is clicked, we are calling the event procedure OnSubmit on the server side. Before submitting the user name to the server, we want to make sure something has been entered in the text box field. Therefore, we place the RequiredFieldValidator control and a red asterisk next to the text box control. At the top of the page we tell the user that fields marked with a red asterisk are required fields.

```
        <font color="red">*</font><br />
        <asp:RequiredFieldValidator id="reqfldvldName" runat="server"
              ControlToValidate="txtUserName"
              Display="Dynamic">User Name is
              required!</asp:RequiredFieldValidator>
```

In the RequiredFieldValidator control we include "txtUserName" as the control to validate. This is how ASP.NET knows which control is to be validated. We then define an error message (*User Name is required!*) to be shown when this field is left blank. The ouput is shown in Figure 12.17.

Figure 12.17: RequiredFieldValidator Control

As you can see from the screenshot, the RequiredFieldValidator control triggers the validation and displays the error message that we have defined.

CompareValidator Control

We can use the CompareValidator control to validate the values in two controls. We find an excellent use of this control when we are comparing two password fields. The main properties are ControlToCompare, ValueToCompare, Type, and Operator to be used in the comparison.

Let's take the previous example and add the code in Listing 12.26 before closing the <table> tag to demonstrate the power of the CompareValidator control.

Listing 12.26—Using the CompareValidator Control

```
<tr>
<td>Password:</td>
<td><asp:TextBox TextMode=password id=txtPwd runat=server />
<font color="red">*</font><br />
<asp:RequiredFieldValidator id=reqfldvldPwd runat=server
        ControlToValidate = txtPwd
        Display = "Dynamic">Password is required!
</asp:RequiredFieldValidator></td>
</tr>
<tr>
<td>Confirm Password:</td>
<td><asp:TextBox TextMode=password id=txtConfirmpwd
runat=server /><font color="red">*</font><br />
<asp:CompareValidator id=cmpvldPwd runat=server
        ControlToValidate = txtConfirmpwd
        ControlToCompare = txtPwd
        Type = "String"
        Operator = "Equal"
        Display = "Dynamic">Password and Confirmation
        Password should match!
        </asp:CompareValidator></td>
</tr>
```

We are adding two more rows to the existing table. The first row has a text box control to accept a password from the user. Next to the password text box, we place a RequiredFieldValidator to make sure the user doesn't leave the password field blank. The next row also has a text box control to verify the password entered in the previous text box. Next to this password confirmation text box, we place a CompareValidator control to validate the content of both text boxes. In the CompareValidator control we declare the ControlToValidate as txtConfirmPwd and the ControlToCompare as txtPwd. This maps the two password text boxes to the CompareValidator control. Then we specify the data type both the controls hold (string) and the operator (equal) to be used when comparing the two controls. (The operator attribute supports the operators Equal, NotEqual, GreaterThan, GreaterThanEqual, LessThan, LessThanEqual, and DataTypeCheck.)

Then we include the custom error message to be used when the validation fails. Figure 12.18 shows what the output looks like when the validation fails.

Figure 12.18: CompareValidator Control

RangeValidator Control

The RangeValidator can be used to check whether the value in the server control is within a range of values. For example, when a user enters his or her age, we may want to validate that the age is between 18 and 80. This kind of checking can be done easily with this control.

The main attributes of the RangeValidator control are MaximumValue, MinimumValue, and ControlToValidate. The MaximumValue attribute holds the maximum value to be checked, and the MinimumValue attribute holds the minimum value. An example will help us understand this control a little better. Open the previous code example and add the code in Listing 12.27 to it before the </table> tag.

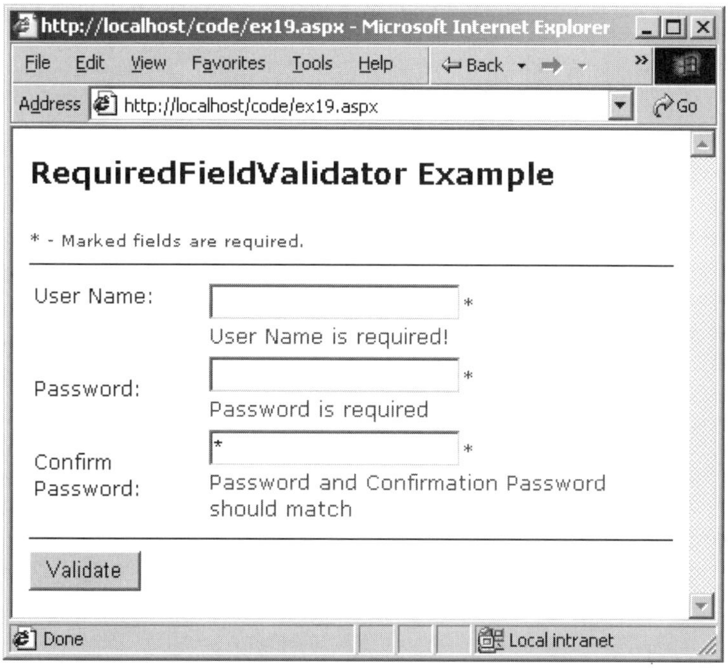

Listing 12.27—Using the RangeValidator Control

```
<tr>
<td valign="top">Age:</td>
        <td><asp:TextBox id=txtAge runat=server />
        <font color="red">*</font><br />
        <asp:RequiredFieldValidator id=reqfldvldAge runat=server
        ControlToValidate = txtAge
```

```
Display = "Dynamic">Age is required</asp:RequiredFieldValidator>
<asp:RangeValidator id=rngvldAge runat=server
ControlToValidate = txtAge MinimumValue = 18
MaximumValue = 100 Type="Integer" Display = "Dynamic">
Age must be between 18 and 100 </asp:RangeValidator>
</td>
</tr>
```

We are adding a new row to the table, and it's going to accept the user's age. For this field, we add two validation controls: RequiredFieldValidator and RangeValidator. The RequiredFieldValidator control will make sure the field is not left blank, and the RangeValidator control will ensure that the age entered is between 18 and 100. As you can see, we set the MinimumValue, MaximumValue, and Type attributes for the RangeValidator control. The output appears in Figure 12.19.

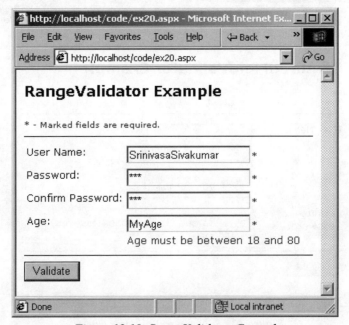

Figure 12.19: RangeValidator Control

Not only does the control validate that the age is between 18 and 80, but it also validates for invalid input such as "MyAge."

RegularExpressionValidator Control

The RegularExpressionValidator can be used to verify that the value in the server control complies with the rules specified in the regular expression. For example, validating the format of an e-mail address or a phone number is a function of the RegularExpressionValidator. The main attribute of the RegularExpressionValidator is ValidationExpression. That attribute includes the expression we will use to validate the user input. Open the previous example and add the code in Listing 12.28 before the </table> tag.

Listing 12.28—Using the RegularExpressionValidator Control

```
<tr>
<td valign="top">eMail Address:</td>
<td><asp:TextBox id=txtEmail runat=server />
<font color="red">*</font><br />
<asp:RequiredFieldValidator id=reqfldvldEmail runat=server
        ControlToValidate = txtEmail
```

```
                Display = "Dynamic">Email is required
                </asp:RequiredFieldValidator>
        <asp:RegularExpressionValidator id=regexpvldemail runat=server
                ControlToValidate = txtEmail
                ValidationExpression = "\w+\x40{1}\w{2,}\.{1}\w{2,}"
                Display = "Dynamic">Email must be of the format
                username@domain.com</asp:RegularExpressionValidator>
        </td>
        </tr>
```

The code adds one more row to the table, and that row will accept an e-mail address from the user. The e-mail address control has two validation controls associated with it: RequiredFieldValidator and RegularExpressionValidator. The RequiredFieldValidator makes sure the control is not left blank, and the RegularExpressionValidator validates the user input against a valid e-mail address. Figure 12.20 shows the output.

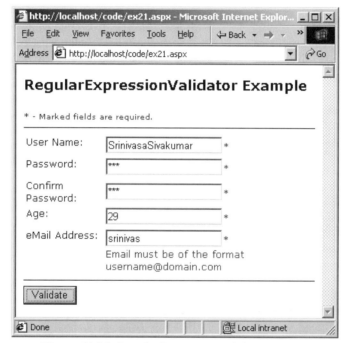

Figure 12.20: RegularExpressionValidator Control

CustomValidator Control

The CustomValidator control is the perfect solution if your validation requirement is not satisfied by any of the predefined validation controls that ship with ASP.NET. For example, you may want to check whether the typed user name has already been taken by another user. For that, you would have to go against a database or active directory or something else. This can't be done with the predefined set of validation controls. To overcome such a problem, ASP.NET ships with the CustomValidator control. The CustomValidator control supports client-side or server-side validation, or both. Open the previous example and add the code in Listing 12.29 after the RequiredFieldValidator for the user name field.

Listing 12.29—Using the CustomValidator Control

```
        <asp:CustomValidator id=custvldusrid runat=server
                controltovalidate="txtUserName"
                Display="Dynamic"
                OnServerValidate="UserNameCheck">
```

```
        UserID is already taken. Please choose a new one.
    </asp:CustomValidator>
```

Then add the C# code in Listing 12.30 to the server-side code block.

Listing 12.30—Using the CustomValidator Server-Side Code

```
void UserNameCheck(Object source, ServerValidateEventArgs args)
{
    //If the chosen username is "SrinivasaSivakumar"
    //then return false. Else return true. In the real
    //world example we'll check this against the database.
    if (args.Value == "SrinivasaSivakumar")
        args.IsValid = false;
    else
        args.IsValid = true;
}
```

The code adds a CustomValidator control to the user name field, and that control calls the server-side C# function called UserNameCheck. The UserNameCheck function checks whether the typed user name is "SrinivasaSivakumar." If so, it sends *false* back to the validator, which throws the error message shown in Figure 12.21.

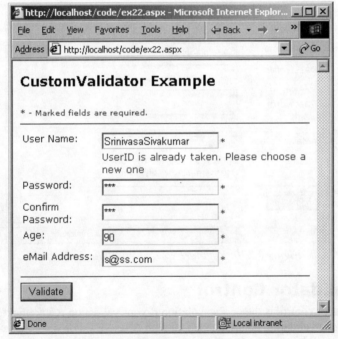

Figure 12.21: CustomValidator Control

ValidationSummary Control

The ValidationSummary control is used to gather all the validation messages in a single place instead of having them appear in each field. One requirement for the user is that the entire error message from the validation control should be placed in the ErrorMessage attribute of the control. Not in the way we placed the validation error messages in our previous examples (see Listing 12.31).

Listing 12.31—Using the ValidationSummary Control

```
<asp:RequiredFieldValidator id="reqfldvldName" runat="server"
      ControlToValidate="txtUserName"
      Display="Dynamic">User Name is required!
</asp:RequiredFieldValidator>
```

If we want to use the ValidationSummary control, we must place the validation error message as shown in Listing 12.32.

Listing 12.32—Configuring the Error Message

```
<asp:RequiredFieldValidator id="reqfldvldName" runat="server"
      ControlToValidate="txtUserName"
      ErrorMessage="User Name is required!"
      Display="Dynamic">?</asp:RequiredFieldValidator>
```

We put a question mark (?) in place of the error message, which alerts the user that there is a validation error at this field. The original error message will be displayed wherever we place the ValidationSummary control. Let's format our previous example in compliance with the ValidationSummary control's requirements. Then add the code in Listing 12.33 beneath the </h3> tag.

Listing 12.33—ValidationSummary Control

```
<font size="-3" color="red">* - Marked fields are required.<br />
? - Marked fields failed validation.</font>

<table border=1 cellpadding=2 bordercolor="black">
<tr><td><asp:ValidationSummary id=vldsmfrm Runat=server
      ForeColor="#CC3300"
      HeaderText="The following errors occurred while validating
      the input:" DisplayMode=BulletList  />
</td></tr>
</table>
```

The output appears in Figure 12.22.

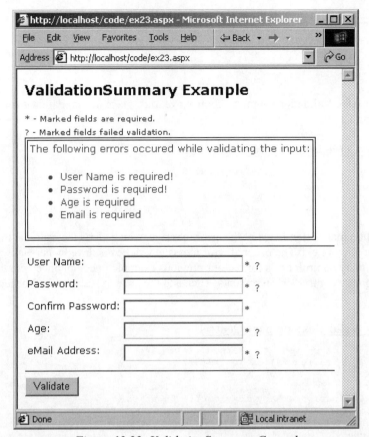

Figure 12.22: ValidationSummary Control

Note that the ValidationSummary control also supports the List and SingleParagraph display modes.

User Controls

User controls are similar to ASP include files, but they provide the flexibility of custom ASP.NET server controls. They can be altered dynamically and can expose properties and methods, things that are not possible with include files.

User controls are stored as .ascx files in ASP.NET. This is to ensure that the user controls can't be executed in stand-alone mode. The user controls can also expose properties, methods, and events. We can employ user controls to build common functionality for a Web site—such as header, footer, log-in page, and so on. Let's build a log-in user control. The code is shown in Listing 12.34.

Listing 12.34—Using the User Control

```
<script language="C#" runat="server">
  public String UserName {
    get { return txtUserName.Text; }
    set { txtUserName.Text = value; }
  }
  public String Password {
    get { return txtPwd.Text; }
  }
</script>
<table border=1 cellspacing=0 cellpadding=2 bordercolor="black"><tr>
        <td valign="top">User Name:</td>
```

```
        <td>
        <asp:TextBox id="txtUserName" runat=server />
        <font color="red">*</font><br />
        <asp:RequiredFieldValidator id="reqfldvldName" runat="server"
                ControlToValidate="txtUserName"
                Display="Dynamic">User Name is
                required!</asp:RequiredFieldValidator>
        </td>
</tr>
<tr>
        <td valign="top">Password:</td>
        <td><asp:TextBox TextMode=password id=txtPwd runat=server />
        <font color="red">*</font><br />
        <asp:RequiredFieldValidator id=reqfldvldPwd runat=server
                ControlToValidate = txtPwd
                Display = "Dynamic">Password is
                required!</asp:RequiredFieldValidator></td>
</tr>
</table>
```

With this code we create a log-in page layout with an HTML table, and we add two text boxes to accept the user name and password. We also add two RequiredFieldValidators to validate the input. In the C# code block we create a read-write property called UserName and a read-only property called Password. The read-write property allows us to set the value of the user name dynamically by reading a cookie, and this can be assigned to the user name text box. Let's use the log-in user control in an ASP.NET page. Listing 12.35 shows the code.

Listing 12.35—Registering the User Control

```
<%@ Register TagPrefix="Login" TagName="LoginForm" Src="Ex24.ascx" %>
<script language="C#" runat="server">
void OnSubmit(Object Sender, EventArgs e) {
        lblUN.Text = MyLogin.UserName;
        lblPW.Text = MyLogin.Password;
}
</script>
<html>
<head>
   <style type="text/css">
     tr {font-face:verdana; font-size:10pt; font-weight:normal}
   </style>
</head>
<body>
<form runat=server>
<h3><font face="Verdana">UserControl Example</font></h3>
<Login:LoginForm id="MyLogin" UserName="SrinivasaSivakumar" runat="server"/>
<br /><asp:Button id="btnLogin" Text="Login" onclick="OnSubmit" runat=server />
<hr color="black" />
Username: <asp:Label id="lblUN" runat="server" /></br>
Password: <asp:Label id="lblPW" runat="server" /></br>
</form>
</body>
</html>
```

First, we register the user control in the ASP.NET page with the register keyword.

```
<%@ Register TagPrefix="Login" TagName="LoginForm" Src="Ex24.ascx" %>
```

The register keyword includes the tag prefix, tag name, and source file name. The tag prefix and tag name will be used to declare the user control in the ASP.NET page. Then we place the user control in the ASP.NET page and pass the default user name "SrinivasaSivakumar."

```
<Login:LoginForm id="MyLogin" UserName="SrinivasaSivakumar" runat="server"/>
```

We are using a button control and two label controls to display the user name and password from the user control. The OnSubmit C# function will read the user name and the password from the user control and display it in the label controls. The output appears in Figure 12.23.

Figure 12.23: User Control

Note that user controls do have some restrictions; for example, <html>, <body>, or <form> tags can't be present. We can use the @Page directive on the user controls.

Configuration

In ASP all server- and application-specific information was stored in binary format in either the Internet Information Server (IIS) metabase or COM+ catalogs, or in both places. For example, the session timeout setting was stored in the IIS metabase. But in ASP.NET all the ASP.NET application- and server-specific configuration information is stored in an XML file.

Server Configuration

All ASP.NET server-specific information is stored in a file called machine.config stored in the following path:

```
(Drive):\WinNT\Microsoft.NET\Framework\(version)\Config\
```

The settings specified in this file will affect the entire server including all the ASP.NET applications hosted on the server.

Application Configuration

The application-specific information is stored in a file called web.config, which resides in the same folder as the ASP.NET application. The settings specified in the machine.config file can be overridden in the web.config file.

The advantage of the machine.config and web.config files is that all the ASP.NET application-specific information is stored in one place. Moreover, when we change machine.config or web.config, ASP.NET will reflect the changes immediately; there is no need to stop and start IIS as we did in ASP. We can also store application information such as a database connection string in the configuration file and we can later read the application specific information from the ASP.NET application.

Configuration File Format

The syntax for the configuration file is shown in Listing 12.36.

Listing 12.36—Configuration File Syntax

```
<?xml version="1.0" encoding="UTF-8"?>
<configuration>
  <[sectionGroup]>
    <[sectionSettings] attribute="[value]">
      <element attribute="[value]">
    </[sectionSettings]>
  </[sectionGroup]>
<configuration>
```

If we want to use Windows authentication, the web.config file will look like Listing 12.37.

Listing 12.37—Sample Configuration File for Windows Authentication

```
<?xml version="1.0" encoding="UTF-8"?>
<configuration>
      <system.web>
              <authentication mode="Windows" />
      </system.web>
</configuration>
```

We'll discuss Windows authentication later in this chapter.

Application-Specific Custom Configuration

We can also store application-specific custom configuration information. For example, we will store the database connection string in the web.config file and then retrieve the connection string from the ASP.NET file (see Listing 12.38).

Listing 12.38—Application-Specific Configuration Information

```
<configuration>
  <appSettings>
    <add key="DBConnStr"
         value="server=Win200Svr;uid=Sa;pwd=;database=ProdDB" />
  </appSettings>
</configuration>
```

We've stored the database connection string in the attribute DBConnStr. Let's read the connection string from the ASP.NET file and display it in a label control (see Listing 12.39).

Listing 12.39—Reading the Application-Specific Configuration Information

```
<%@ Import Namespace="System.Configuration" %>
<script language="C#" runat="server">
void Page_Load(Object Sender, EventArgs e) {
      lblConnStr.Text = ConfigurationSettings.AppSettings["DBConnStr"];
}
</script>
<html>
<body>
<form runat=server>
<h3><font face="Verdana">Custom configuration Example</font></h3>
DB Connection String: <asp:Label id="lblConnStr" runat="server" />
</form>
</body>
</html>
```

Session State

In ASP all session information was stored in the IIS memory pool. That led to some restrictions—for example, the ASP application could not be spanned to a multiserver Web farm. ASP.NET addresses this problem by providing three ways to store the session information.

In-process (default option): The in-process option is very similar to what we had in ASP. When we use in-process session, all the session information will be stored in local memory, and this can't be spanned across multiple servers.

Windows service: The Windows service option stores all the session state information in a Windows service. This can be on the same server or on a different server that can just maintain the session state information for a Web farm.

SQL Server: The SQL Server option provides the most reliable and scalable solution to maintain the session state information.

In-Process Session State

To implement in-process session state, we have to write the session state code in the web.config file. Then we can implement the session information in the ASP.NET pages. See Listings 12.40 and 12.41.

Listing 12.40—In-Process Session State Mode

```
<system.web>
        <sessionState mode="InProc" timeout="20" />
</system.web>
```

Listing 12.41—Session State Example

```
<script language="C#" runat="server">
void Page_Load(Object Sender, EventArgs e)
{
        if (!IsPostBack) Session["MyName"] = "Srinivasa Sivakumar";
}
void OnSubmit(Object Sender, EventArgs e)
{
        lblSession.Text = Session["MyName"].ToString();
}
</script>
<html>
<body>
<form runat=server>
<h3><font face="Verdana">Session Data Example</font></h3>
Session Data: <asp:Label id="lblSession" runat="server" />
<br /><asp:Button id="btnLogin" Text="Get Session Data" onclick="OnSubmit"
runat=server />
</form>
</body>
</html>
```

The web.config file instructs the ASP.NET runtime to store the session state information using the in-process methodology. In the ASP.NET page we assign the name "Srinivasa Sivakumar" in the session variable MyName. When the button is clicked, we are retrieving the session variable and displaying it in a label control.

Windows Service Session State

The Windows service session state requires ASP.NET State service on the server. Before using the Windows service session state, make sure that the ASP.NET State service is running. Then modify the web.config file as shown in Listing 12.42.

<u>**Listing 12.42—Session State configuration in Web.Config**</u>

```
<system.web>
            <sessionState mode="StateServer" timeout="20"
            stateConnectionString="tcpip=127.0.0.1:42424" />
</system.web>
```

We have changed the mode from InProc to StateServer, and we have specified the stateConnectionString with a TCP/IP address (127.0.0.1) and a port number (42424). The TCP/IP address 127.0.0.1 is the address for the local computer. If you are using a central server to maintain state, you can add the IP address of the central server here.

By default the port 42424 is used by the state server. If you want, you can change the port number in the registry at the following path:

```
HKEY_LOCAL_MACHINE/System/CurrentControlSet/Services/aspnet_state/Parameters/Port
```

Finally, we can use the previous example to store and retrieve the session information from the Windows service session state store.

SQL Server Session State

To store the session state on the SQL Server, we need to run the script InstallSqlState.sql. Remember the SQL Server–based session state is supported only in the Professional or Enterprise Edition of .NET Framework. The InstallSqlState.sql script creates a new database called ASPState to maintain the session information. Once the database is ready, we can configure the web.config file to use the SQL Server–based session state. The code is shown in Listing 12.43.

<u>**Listing 12.43—Storing Session state in SQL Server**</u>

```
<system.web>
  <sessionState mode="SQLServer" timeout="20"
  sqlConnectionString="data source=127.0.0.1;user id=sa;password=" />
</system.web>
```

We specify the mode as SQLServer, and we include the connection string for the SQL Server.

To uninstall the SQL Server session state database run the script UninstallSqlState.sql.

Security

Security is a key aspect of application development and deployment. Therefore, application security starts at the time of application design. ASP.NET offers built-in support for two new authentication methods (Forms authentication and Passport authentication) on top of the existing authentication methods supported by ASP (Basic, Digest, and Integrated Windows). Authentication is important in securing the application or personalizing it for a specific user.

The Basic, Digest, and Integrated Windows authentication methods are supported by ASP.NET with the help of IIS and the Windows operating system. Still, these authentication methods are in IIS territory, and we have to follow the very same steps that we used in ASP to set them up.

Basic Authentication

Let's see how we can use Basic authentication with ASP.NET. Create a folder called Basic in your favorite place and map it as an IIS virtual directory. Then right-click the virtual directory and select the Properties option from the shortcut menu. Then go to the Directory Security tab and click the Edit button. You'll see a dialog box like the one in Figure 12.24.

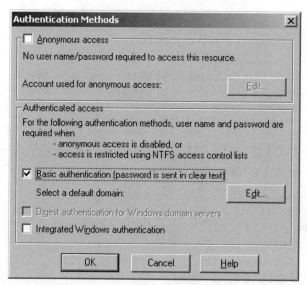

Figure 12.24: Authentication Options

Clear the *Anonymous access* and *Integrated Windows authentication* check boxes and click the *Basic authentication* check box. When you select it, you'll see one more dialog box that warns you that using the Basic authentication will send the user name and the password as clear text. Click Yes, click OK in the Authentication Methods dialog box, and click OK in the Basic Authentication dialog box. Let's create a web.config file to inform the ASP.NET that we're using the Windows authentication method (see Listing 12.44).

Listing 12.44—Windows Authentication Example

```
<configuration>
        <system.web>
                <authentication mode="Windows" />
        </system.web>
</configuration>
```

Note that the same web.config file will work for the Basic, Digest, and Integrated Windows authentication methods.

Now let's create an ASP.NET file to consume the Basic authentication (see Listing 12.45).

Listing 12.45—Using Basic Authentication

```
<script language="C#" runat="server">
void Page_Load(Object Sender, EventArgs e) {
        lblUsrName.Text = User.Identity.Name;
        lblAuthType.Text = User.Identity.AuthenticationType;
}
</script>
<html>
<body>
<form runat=server>
<h3><font face="Verdana">Authentication Example</font></h3>
User Name: <asp:Label id="lblUsrName" runat="server" /><br />
Authentication Type: <asp:Label id="lblAuthType" runat="server" />
</form>
```

```
</body>
</html>
```

In the Page_Load event we read the logged-in user information using the User object. The User object exposes the Identity property, and the Identity property exposes two more properties called Name and AuthenticationType. That's what we are using to the read the information in the Page_Load event.

When we log in to the Basic authentication virtual directory, the browser will prompt for user name and password as in Figure 12.25.

Figure 12.25: Basic Authentication Log-In Dialog Box

Once the log-in name and the password are verified against the Windows user account database, the control will go to the ASP.NET runtime and the default.aspx page will be served back. The page output is shown in Figure 12.26.

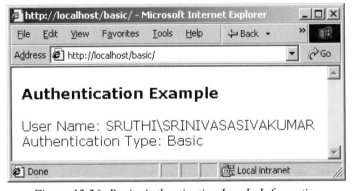

Figure 12.26: Basic Authentication Log-In Information

Forms Authentication

Forms authentication is a famous method used by many popular sites such as Amazon.com and Yahoo.com. The main advantage of Forms authentication is the absence of a messy pop-up dialog box to collect the user name and password; the log-in dialog box fits right into the site design. Another advantage is that the user name and password can be compared with any authority such as a database, XML file, or active directory. Forms authentication is based on cookies.

Implementing Forms authentication is simple. The method requires the web.config file, a log-in page, and the ASP.NET application. You set up the Forms authentication in the web.config file and you are all set to go. Let's look at an example. We will create a folder called Forms in your favorite place and map it as an IIS virtual directory. We'll create a web.config file to inform the ASP.NET that we're using the Forms authentication method (see Listing 12.46).

Listing 12.46—Configuring Forms Authentication

```
<configuration>
  <system.web>
    <authentication mode="Forms">
      <forms name=".CSharpAuth" loginUrl="login.aspx"
      protection="All" />
    </authentication>
  </system.web>
    <authorization>
      <deny user="?" />
    </authorization>
</configuration>
```

We specify the authentication mode as Forms and give a name—.CSharpAuth—to the cookie. In the loginUrl we specify the log-in page name where users will be transferred when they are not logged in. The protection tag specifies how the authentication cookie is to be protected.

Here's a tip: If you are hosting more then one ASP.NET application on the same IIS server, it's important to give each Forms authentication cookie a different name.

Let's create a log-in page where users can log in to the ASP.NET application using Forms authentication (see Listing 12.47).

Listing 12.47—Forms Authentication Log-In Page

```
<%@ Import Namespace="System.Web.Security " %>
<script language="C#" runat="server">
void OnLogIn(Object Sender, EventArgs e)
{
//Check Login
if (Page.IsValid)
    {
        if (txtEmail.Text == "SrinivasaSivakumar" &&
            txtPwd.Text == "CSharp")
                    FormsAuthentication.RedirectFromLoginPage
                            (txtEmail.Text,true);
        else
                lblLoginMsg.Text =
                    "Use SrinivasaSivakumar as user name
                     and password as CSharp. Please try again";
    }
}
</script>
<html>
<body>
<form runat=server>
<h3><font face="Verdana">Forms Authentication Example</font></h3>
User Name: <asp:textbox id="txtEmail" runat=server />
         <font size=2 color="red">*</font><br />
        <asp:RequiredFieldValidator  ControlToValidate="txtEmail"
        Display="Dynamic" runat=server
        ErrorMessage="Username can't be left blank." />
Password: <asp:textbox TextMode="Password" id="txtPwd" runat=server />
         <font size=2 color="red">*</font><br />
        <asp:RequiredFieldValidator  ControlToValidate="txtPwd"
        Display="Dynamic" runat=server
```

```
        ErrorMessage="Password can't be left blank." /><br/>
<asp:button  id="btnLogin"  Text="Login"  OnClick="OnLogIn"  runat=Server /><br />
<asp:Label id="lblLoginMsg" foreColor="red" runat=server />
</form>
</body>
</html>
```

In the login.aspx page, we include two text boxes to collect the user's name and password. We also include a RequiredFieldValidator to force the user to enter something. Then we have a button control with which to log in to the ASP.NET application. When the log-in button is clicked, we verify that the user name is "SrinivasaSivakumar" and the password is "CSharp." If the user name and password match, we call the RedirectFromLoginPage method of the FormsAuthentication class to transfer the user back to the previous page he or she was requesting. If the user name and password do not match, we display an error message. Now let's create an ASP.NET file to consume the Forms authentication (see Listing 12.48).

Listing 12.48—Using Forms Authentication

```
<script language="C#" runat="server">
void Page_Load(Object Sender, EventArgs e)
{
        lblUsrName.Text = User.Identity.Name;
        lblAuthType.Text = User.Identity.AuthenticationType;
}
void OnLogout(Object Sender, EventArgs e)
{
        //Do Logout
        FormsAuthentication.SignOut();
        Server.Transfer("login.aspx");
}
</script>
<html>
<body>
<form runat=server>
<h3><font face="Verdana">Authentication Example</font></h3>
User Name: <asp:Label id="lblUsrName" runat="server" /><br />
Authentication Type: <asp:Label id="lblAuthType" runat="server" /><br/>
<asp:Button id="btnLogin" Text="Logout" onclick="OnLogout" runat=server />
</form>
</body>
</html>
```

The default.aspx file is similar to the one we used for Basic authentication. But we have added a log-out button and have called the OnLogout function from the button control. When the log-out button is clicked, we call the SignOut method of the FormsAuthentication class, which will remove the authentication cookie from the user's computer. This forces the user to log in to the ASP.NET application again the next time.

When a user requests the default.aspx file, the ASP.NET runtime will check whether the user has the authentication cookie .CSharpAuth in the web.config file. If the cookie is present, the default.aspx page is served back. If the user doesn't have the cookie, ASP.NET will transfer the browser to the log-in page (login.aspx) defined in the web.config file. The output is shown in Figure 12.27.

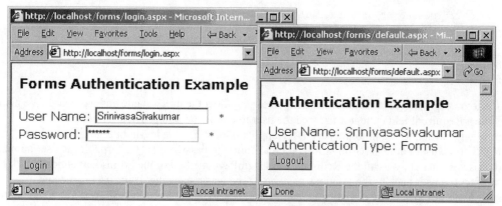

Figure 12.27: Log-In Page and Forms Authentication Information

Summary

In this chapter we've gone through a brief tour of ASP.NET and we've touched all the important topics of ASP.NET. Server controls will bring lots of excitement to the web development community and they reduce lot of work from the programmers when it comes to presenting data. Especially the DataGrid control can help us a lot in the way we present data and reduce our work significantly.

Then we've gone through a brief tour of advanced ASP.NET features and we've touched all the important topics of ASP.NET. The validation controls are excellent add-ons to the server side programming, and they make life easier for the web developers. The user controls, session state options and the forms authentication are very promising, and they can improve the quality of ASP.NET applications.

Chapter 13:
.NET Web Services

Introduction

Web services is the new buzzword in the technology market today. You may have heard of Web services and wondered what they are. This chapter explores the technical details of .NET Web services and how to build, consume, and deploy these Web services with .NET Framework and C#.

What Is a Web Service?

In simple terms *Web services* are distributed business components that can be invoked remotely across wires. Web services are not new to the computer world. We have been using them day in and day out without realizing it. For example, consider the scenario of a Distributed Component Object Model (DCOM) component or a common object request broker architecture (CORBA) component or a Java remote method invocation (RMI) being used over wire. They are actually services running on remote computers, and we access them via proprietary interfaces. You could then raise the question "How are Web services different from distributed components?"

Why Do We Need Web Services?

Actually, Web services are not different from distributed components. But a more platform-generic implementation such as hypertext transfer protocol (HTTP), Extensible Markup Language (XML), and Simple Object Access Protocol (SOAP) is used to discover, consume, and manipulate the Web services.

Let's use a real-world problem to better illustrate Web services. Consider, for example, a main corporate office and five satellite offices (as shown in Figure 13.1).

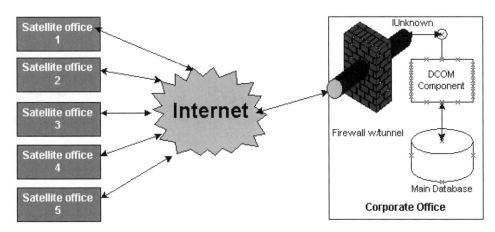

Figure 13.1: Distributed Computing Architecture

Each satellite office connects to the corporate office server and retrieves or updates data. In this scenario, when we are accessing the DCOM component via the Internet, we have to configure the corporate firewall to allow remote procedure calls (RPCs). That could introduce a security risk to the corporate network because DCOM cannot work on the started HTTP port 80 or SMTP port 25.

Most Internet systems work on standard ports Transmission Control Protocol (TCP) or User Datagram Protocol (UDP), and DCOM dynamically assigns the port address at runtime. By default, DCOM can use any port from 1024 to 65535 in the firewall, but it is not practical to open all these ports for the DCOM components. We can fix the dynamic port change problem by changing the post assignment for the DCOM applications in the registry (HKEY_LOCAL_MACHINE\Software\Microsoft\Rpc\Internet). But we still have to open a few nonstandard ports for DCOM RPC calls.

If we use other RPC-based technologies such as CORBA or Java RMI and then want to integrate our system with our partners or customers, should they also use the same technologies we use? If we are using DCOM for distributed computing, our customers cannot use Java or CORBA-based C++ because these technologies are not portable between each other. Although bridges are available to interpret the calls between the two, they are either very limited or inefficient.

The solution is an application model that will work on the truly distributed model, will be firewall friendly, and will not compromise the security of the existing infrastructure. Web services and the Simple Object Access Protocol (SOAP) address this issue. SOAP is an XML-based lightweight protocol, which can work on top of high-level protocols such as HTTP and HTTPS. With Web services and SOAP, all our calls go through HTTP/SOAP and we get data back in XML format over HTTP. We also discover the services offered by the Web services via Web Services Description Language (WSDL), an XML file format. We'll learn more about that later.

SOAP is based on a simple XML-RPC protocol developed by Dave Winer of UserLand. Microsoft, IBM, and others jointly submitted a proposal for SOAP for a distributed environment such as the Internet. Implementing SOAP is simple. The SOAP developers added a new multipurpose Internet mail extension (MIME) type (text/xml-SOAP) to manage the SOAP calls over HTTP.

Web Services Architecture

The Web services architecture (as shown in Figure 13.2) is very simple and matches the existing Web applications' architecture.

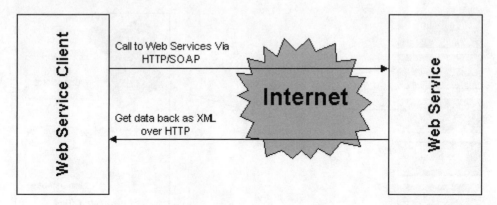

Figure 13.2: Web Service Architecture

The Web services speak the same language, HTTP, as the existing Web applications, and the SOAP protocol uses the HTTP transport layer to communicate. When we call a Web service from the Web client, we will make a SOAP call over the HTTP protocol. When the Web service receives the request, it will process the request and return SOAP/XML data to the client over the HTTP (no Java applets or ActiveX controls). The client will receive the XML data and display it. When we are using the HTTP layer to communicate, port 80 on the firewall is already open for the Web applications, and there are no new ports to be opened for Web services.

Web Services Components

When we refer to Web services we are referring to components such as the following:

- HTTP/Secure Sockets Layer (SSL)
- SOAP
- XML
- Universal Description, Discovery, and Integration (UDDI)
- Discovery Protocol (DISCO)
- WSDL
- Web service proxy

Figure 13.3 illustrates a typical way in which these components interact to implement Web services.

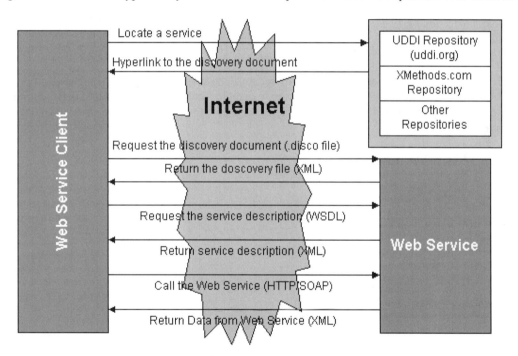

Figure 13.3: Web Service Components Architecture

When a Web service is deployed in a real-world situation, we have to register it with a discovering directory service such as UDDI.Org or Xmethods.com. When a Web client wants to access a Web service, it accesses the UDDI.Org's repository and finds the Web service it needs as a hyperlink to the discovery document.

When the user requests the discovery document (.disco file), the discovery document will return information about the Web service in XML format. Then the Web client reads the discovery document, finds the needed Web service, and requests the Web service description. The Web service will return the Web service description in XML format using WSDL. The Web service description includes the signature of the Web service, the arguments the Web service requires, and the return type of the Web service. Once the Web service signature is known, we can access the Web service via the Web service proxy and get the data back.

What Is a Proxy?

A *proxy* is a component that acts on behalf of the remote Web service. The proxy allows the remote Web service to be accessed via SOAP and takes care of all the plumbing beneath. The Web service client can use the proxy as a real object and access its properties and methods.

When we access a Web service via the proxy, the proxy converts our Web service call into a SOAP message and sends the SOAP request to the Web service. When the proxy receives the raw SOAP-based XML response back from the Web service, it converts the XML response to an object accessible by the client and returns the object to the client.

An Introduction to SOAP

SOAP is an XML-based protocol specification for invoking methods on remote servers, services, components, and objects. The SOAP specification also supports an XML vocabulary that is used for representing method parameters, return values, and exceptions. SOAP relies on HTTP 1.0 or greater, for communication between the client and the remote server. The firewalls can easily recognize SOAP packets on the basis of their content-type (text/xml-SOAP), and they can filter on the basis of the interface and method name exposed via HTTP headers.

Each SOAP request has an envelope and body section. The envelope includes the namespace reference for the SOAP message; the body section includes information about the SOAP call (other optional sections can be included in the SOAP message). Listing 13.1 contains a simple SOAP message.

Listing 13.1—SOAP Message Example

```
POST /SayHello.asmx HTTP/1.1
Host: www.Myserver.com
Content-Type: text/xml; charset="utf-8"
Content-Length: length
SOAPAction: "Some-URI"

<?xml version="1.0" encoding="utf-8"?>
<SOAP-ENV:Envelope
 xmlns:SOAP-ENV="http://schemas.xmlsoap.org/soap/envelope/"
 SOAP-ENV:encodingStyle="http://schemas.xmlsoap.org/soap/encoding/">
  <SOAP-ENV:Body soap:encodingStyle="http://schemas.xmlsoap.org/soap/encoding/">
     <m:SayHello xmlns:m="Some-URI">
         <YourName>Srinivasa Sivakumar</YourName>
     </m:SayHello>
  </SOAP-ENV:Body>
</SOAP-ENV:Envelope>
```

In this SOAP message we are accessing the file SayHello.asmx in the server www.MyServer.com, and the content type is set to text/xml. Because this call is a SOAP call, the <SOAP-ENV:Envelope tag opens the SOAP envelope, and the <SOAP-ENV:Body tag specifies the SOAP body.

The <m:SayHello specifies that we are accessing the method SayHello. The <YourName>Srinivasa Sivakumar</YourName> specifies that we are passing the value *Srinivasa Sivakumar* for the parameter YourName.

The SOAP message reply appears in Listing 13.2.

Listing 13.2—SOAP Message Reply

```
HTTP/1.1 200 OK
Content-Type: text/xml; charset="utf-8"
Content-Length: length

<?xml version="1.0" encoding="utf-8"?>
<SOAP-ENV:Envelope
  xmlns:SOAP-ENV="http://schemas.xmlsoap.org/soap/envelope/"
  SOAP-ENV:encodingStyle="http://schemas.xmlsoap.org/soap/encoding/">
  <SOAP-ENV:Body soap:encodingStyle="http://schemas.xmlsoap.org/soap/encoding/">
      <m:SayHelloResponse xmlns:m="Some-URI">
          <string>Hello Srinivasa Sivakumar</string>
      </m:SayHelloResponse>
  </SOAP-ENV:Body>
</SOAP-ENV:Envelope>
```

We are getting HTTP status code 200 and OK from the server. That means our call was successful. The reply type is XML because the content type is set as text/xml. The one noticeable change is in the body of the SOAP message. The tag <m:SayHello was replaced with <m:SayHelloResponse, and <string>Hello Srinivasa Sivakumar</string> was added to the SOAP body. SOAP always returns the response to the method call by adding "Response" to the section method name. For example, in the previous SOAP call, we called the method <m:SayHello and we received the reply as <m:SayHelloResponse. The name of the reply also changed to string, indicating that the method <m:SayHello returns string data.

SOAP 1.1 specifications were submitted to the World Wide Web Consortium in May of 2000. For more information about the SOAP specifications, go to http://www.w3.org/TR/2000/NOTE-SOAP-20000508/.

Hello, World Web Service

Let's step into the exciting world of Web services by writing a simple Web services application. Start your favorite editor (mine is still Notepad), and type the code shown in Listing 13.3.

Listing 13.3—Web Services Application

```
<%@ WebService Language="C#" Class="Hello" %>
using System.Web.Services;
public class Hello {
    [WebMethod]
    public string SayHello() {
            return "Hello, World from .NET Web Services!";
    }
}
```

Create a folder called Hello and save the code as SayHello.asmx. The Web services file should be saved with the asmx file extension; that is the way the .NET Framework identifies Web services.

We have defined the language we are going to use (C#) and the class name (Hello) using the @WebService directive. Then we set the reference to the class System.Web.Services. We defined a class (Hello) and a method (SayHello) inside the class. The SayHello method returns a string. We have also signed this method as WebMethod. This signature allows the method to be called as Web service.

Now our Web service is ready. Let's deploy it in Internet Information Server (IIS). Map the Hello folder as an IIS virtual directory and give access to the anonymous users. Now that our Web service is deployed, how do we access it? Let's take a simple approach. Start Internet Explorer (IE) and point it to http://localhost/hello/SayHello.asmx. Figure 13.4 is a screenshot of the output. (If you have deployed the Web service in a different location, access it from that location.)

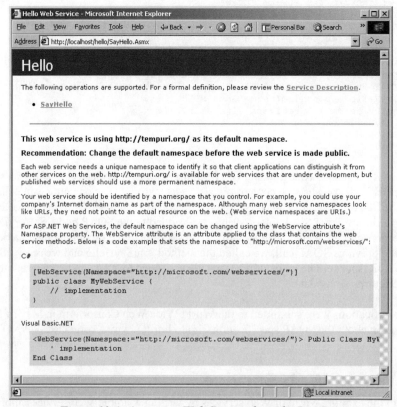

Figure 13.4: Accessing Web Service from the Browser

This instruction page tells us that we are using the default namespace references in our Web service and explains how to change the default namespace to a custom namespace. Do not worry about the namespaces right now. If you look at the top of the page, you will see two hyperlinks: Service Description and SayHello.

Click the Service Description link to see the WSDL contract for this Web service (as shown in Figure 13.5).

Figure 13.5: Web Services Description Language (WSDL)

The WSDL shown in the figure provides full information about the signature of the Web method, parameter for the Web method, return type, and access method. The element <s:element name="SayHello"> specifies the method name, the element <s:element name="SayHelloResponse"> specifies the return result tag, and the element <s:element minOccurs="1" maxOccurs="1" name="SayHelloResult" nillable="true" type="s:string" /> specifies the return type of the Web method as string.

Click the Back button of the browser to go back to the previous screen. Now click the SayHello link. The screen shown in Figure 13.6 will appear.

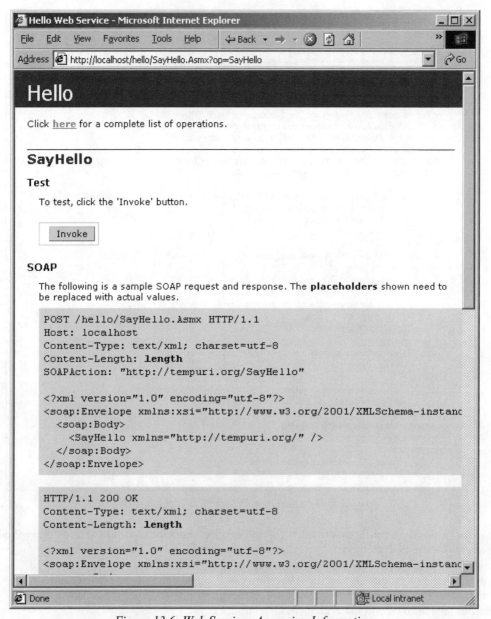

Figure 13.6: Web Services Accessing Information

This screenshot shows how the input and output calls will look when we use SOAP, HTTP Get, and HTTP Post to access the Web service. The Invoke button is at the top of the page. Click it to see the output shown in Figure 13.7.

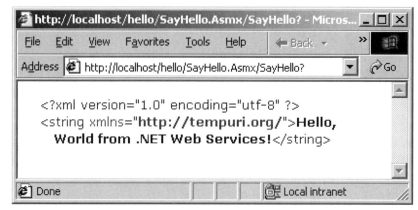

Figure 13.7: Web Services Output

Web services always return XML data; therefore, the first line shows the XML declaration. The next line shows the data returned by the Web service. The tag <string xmlns="http://tempuri.org/"> specifies the return type (string) of the Web service.

When we clicked the Invoke button, we accessed the Web service via the HTTP Get method. In the screen shown in Figure 13.6, right-click and select the View Source option. Look at the HTML source to see the following code in between the Invoke button:

```
<form target="_blank" action='http://localhost/hello/SayHello.asmx/SayHello'
method="GET">
        <input type="submit" value="Invoke" class="button">
</form>
```

We have a form tag. The action is set to the URL of the Web service, and the method is set to Get. We can access the Web service with HTTP POST by changing the method attribute to Post.

The Web service URL is always built as the location of the Web service (http://www.somewere.com/webservice.asmx) followed by a forward slash, the Web method name, a question mark, and parameters (if any) separated by an ampersand—for example, http://www.C-SharpCorner.com/WebService.asmx/ArticlesList?Sub=.NET&Page=1.

How do we access the Web service via SOAP? For that we have to build a proxy for the Web service, then we can use it with SOAP.

Web Services Inheritance

We can also write a Web service by inheriting from the WebService class. Let's see an example for this. Start your favorite editor, and type the code shown in Listing 13.4.

Listing 13.4—Web Service Inheritance

```
<%@ WebService Language="C#" Class="Hello" %>
using System.Web.Services;
public class Hello : WebService{
        [WebMethod]
        public string SayHelloToMe(string sName) {
                return "Hello " + sName +
                ", Welcome to the world of .NET Web Services!";
        }
}
```

Save the code as SayHelloToMe.asmx in the hello folder. In this example we have inherited our class Hello from the WebService class. Start IE and point it to http://localhost/hello/SayHelloToMe.asmx (see Figure 13.8).

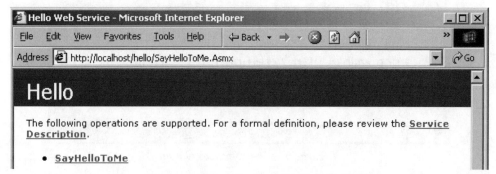

Figure 13.8:Access the "SayHelloToMe" Web Services

Click the SayHelloToMe link.

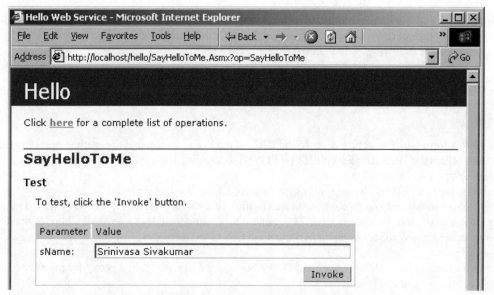

Figure 13.9: Access the "SayHelloToMe" Web Services

Enter your name in the Name parameter text box, and click the Invoke button (see Figure 13.9). You will see the result shown in Figure 13.10.

Figure 13.10:Web Services Output

Accessing Web Service via SOAP

Let's see how we can access Web services using SOAP. We have to build a proxy dynamic-link library (DLL) that can provide an object-oriented approach to Web services and interpret calls between our application and the Web service.

First, we have to build the Proxy class that can provide all the information about the Web service to the client application. We are going to use the WSDL command line utility to build it.

```
WSDL /l:CS /n:SayHelloNS /out:SayHelloToMe.CS
http://localhost/hello/SayHelloToMe.asmx?WSDL
```

The WSDL command line utility accepts a few command line parameters to build the Proxy class (see Table 13.1).

Command Line Switch	Description
/l:	The /l: specifies the language to be used when generating the Proxy class. We have specified C# (/l:CS) to be used when generating the Proxy class.
/n:	The /n: specifies the namespace for the Web service and we have specified the namespace as SayHelloNS.
/out:	The /out: specifies the output filename; in out example, it is the C# file SayHelloToMe.CS.
	The last parameter is the WSDL source. The WSDL file gives all the information about the Web service, how to contact it, and so on. When we pass the WSDL parameter to the ASMX file, it will generate the WSDL document to back and we will use it as our WSDL source.

Table 13.1: Command Line Description

When we use the WSDL command line utility, it will generate a C# Proxy class source code in the output file SayHelloToMe.CS. Listing 13.5 shows the Proxy class.

Listing 13.5—Proxy Class Example

```
//------------------------------------------------------------------//
<autogenerated>
//This code was generated by a tool.
//Runtime Version: 1.0.2914.16
//
```

```
//Changes to this file may cause incorrect behavior and will be lost if
//the code is regenerated.
// </autogenerated>
//----------------------------------------------------------------------
//
// This source code was auto-generated by wsdl, Version=1.0.2914.16.
//
namespace SayHelloNS {
    using System.Diagnostics;
    using System.Xml.Serialization;
    using System;
    using System.Web.Services.Protocols;
    using System.Web.Services;

    [System.Web.Services.WebServiceBindingAttribute(Name="HelloSoap",
    Namespace="http://tempuri.org/")]
    public class Hello :
    System.Web.Services.Protocols.SoapHttpClientProtocol {
        [System.Diagnostics.DebuggerStepThroughAttribute()]
        public Hello() {
            this.Url = "http://localhost/hello/SayHelloToMe.asmx";
        }
        [System.Diagnostics.DebuggerStepThroughAttribute()]
        [System.Web.Services.Protocols.SoapDocumentMethodAttribute(
        "http://tempuri.org/SayHelloToMe",
        Use=System.Web.Services.Description.SoapBindingUse.Literal,
        ParameterStyle=
        System.Web.Services.Protocols.SoapParameterStyle.Wrapped)]
        public string SayHelloToMe(string sName) {
        object[] results = this.Invoke("SayHelloToMe", new object[] {
                        sName});
            return ((string)(results[0]));
        }

        [System.Diagnostics.DebuggerStepThroughAttribute()]
        public System.IAsyncResult BeginSayHelloToMe(string sName,
        System.AsyncCallback callback, object asyncState) {
            return this.BeginInvoke("SayHelloToMe", new object[] {
            sName}, callback, asyncState);
        }

        [System.Diagnostics.DebuggerStepThroughAttribute()]
        public string EndSayHelloToMe(System.IAsyncResult asyncResult)
        {
            object[] results = this.EndInvoke(asyncResult);
            return ((string)(results[0]));
        }
    }
}
```

The C# Proxy class generated by the WSDL command line utility generated the namespace
SayHelloNS and the class Hello. The Hello class has three methods—SayHelloToMe,
BeginSayHelloToMe, and EndSayHelloToMe—and a default constructor. The Proxy class provides
us with synchronous and asynchronous access to the Web service. When we access the Web service
synchronously, the method SayHelloToMe will be used. For asynchronous access, the methods
BeginSayHelloToMe and EndSayHelloToMe will be used. For every asynchronous access, we need
begin and end methods, and that is what the Proxy class gives us.

If you look at the source .asmx file that we have coded, you will see we had only one method,
SayHelloToMe. The Proxy class generated two more methods.

Let's compile the C# Proxy class generated by the WSDL file with the C# command line compiler
and build the distributable Proxy class DLL file.

```
CSC /r:system.dll /r:System.Web.dll /r:System.Xml.dll /r:System.Web.Services.dll
/t:library
```

This command line compilation code will produce the SayHelloToMe.DLL file.

Web Service Client

Let's build an ASP.NET Web service client to access the Web service using SOAP. Create a new folder called HelloClient and a subfolder beneath it called bin. Copy the proxy DLL from the original place to the bin folder. That deploys the Web services proxy DLL at the client place. Notice that we did not register the DLL with the RegSvr32 file; there is no need to do so. All the .NET DLL have the metadata inside the DLL, and they do not have to be registered in the registry. Copying the DLL to the bin folder itself is enough.

Map the HelloClient folder as an IIS virtual directory, and give access to the anonymous users. Let's build an ASP.NET Web client.

Listing 13.6—Web Service Client

```
<%@ Import Namespace="SayHelloNS" %>
<html>
<head>
<style type="text/css">
    body {font-face:verdana; font-size:10pt; font-weight:normal}
</style>
</head>
<script language="C#" runat="server">
public void OnSubmit(Object sender, EventArgs E){
    Hello objWebSvc = new Hello();
    lblSayHelloToMe.Text = objWebSvc.SayHelloToMe(txtName.Text);
}
</script>
<body>
<h3>Web Service Client</h3>
<form runat="server">
    <asp:Textbox id="txtName" runat="server" />
    <asp:Button id="BtnSubmit" runat="server"
    OnClick="OnSubmit" Text="Say Hello To Me" />
    <hr color="black" />
<b>Result:</b><br /> <asp:Label id="lblSayHelloToMe" runat="server"/>
</form>
</body>
</html>
```

Save the code shown in Listing 13.6 as default.aspx file in the HelloClient folder. First, we are importing the namespace SayHelloNS, which is the custom namespace we used when compiling the Web services proxy file. This gives us access to the compiled Proxy class. In the ASP.NET file we have a text box, button, and label server controls. When the user enters his or her name and clicks the button control, the server side event function will be called OnSubmit.

In the OnSubmit function we have created an instance of the class Hello and called the method SayHelloToMe. We are passing the username entered in the text box as the argument to the method Call, and we are displaying the result in the label control. As you can see, the compiled Proxy class gives us object-oriented access to the Web service, and it takes care of all the plumbing it needs to do for the SOAP. Figure 13.11 shows the output.

Figure 13.11: ASP.NET Web Service Client

When we call the Web service using the proxy DLL, we are simply calling a method in an object with arguments. Under the hood, the proxy DLL makes a call to the Web service synchronously using SOAP and retrieves the result in SOAP/XML format. Then it rebuilds the XML result as an object and gives us access to the Web services result in an object-oriented way.

Building Web Services with Visual Studio .NET

Let's see how to build a Web service with Visual Studio .NET. Visual Studio .NET makes building a Web service painless. It takes care of building a proxy with WSDL with a few mouse clicks, and we do not have to get down to building Web services. We are going to build an insurance quote service that will take the age of the customer as input. If the customer's age is below 25, we will charge $700.50 for insurance; for all other customers we will charge $550.00.

Fire up Visual Studio .NET, and select a new project ASP.NET Web Service from the C# Projects tree node (as shown in figure 13.12).

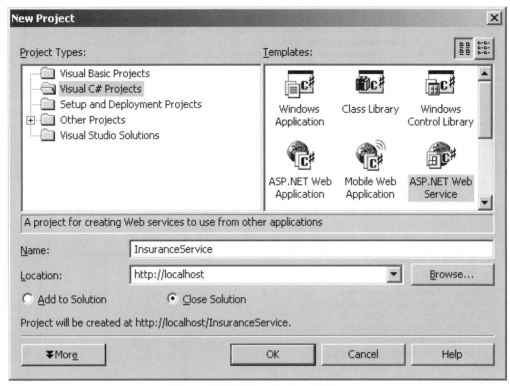

Figure 13.12: New Project Dialog

Name the project InsuranceService, and click OK. After you have clicked OK, a new dialog box will pop up and show that it is creating the ASP.NET Web service project (as shown in Figure 13.13).

Figure 13.13: Creating Project Dialog

Once the project is created, it will show the Main screen. Now select the Service1.asmx file from the Solutions Explorer and rename it InsService.asmx (as shown in Figure 13.1).

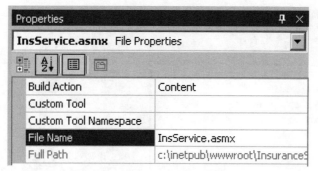

Figure 13.14: Property Dialog

Double-click the .asmx file to reach the Code window (as shown in Figure 13.15).

```
Start Page | InsService.asmx.cs [Design]  InsService.asmx.cs                          ◁ ▷ ×

InsuranceService.InsService                    ▼    Rate(int Age)                      ▼

using System;
using System.Collections;
using System.ComponentModel;
using System.Data;
using System.Diagnostics;
using System.Web;
using System.Web.Services;

namespace InsuranceService{
    /**/
    public class InsService : System.Web.Services.WebService{
        public InsService(){
            //CODEGEN: This call is required by the ASP.NET Web Services Designer
            InitializeComponent();
        }

        Component Designer generated code

        /// <summary>
        /// Clean up any resources being used.
        /// </summary>
        protected override void Dispose( bool disposing ){
        }

        [WebMethod]
        public double Rate(int Age){
            if (Age < 25)
                return 700.50;
            else
                return 550.00;
        }
    }
}
```

Figure 13.15: Code Window

Add the code in Listing 13.7 to the Code window.

__Listing 13.7—Rate WebMethod__

```
[WebMethod]
public double Rate(int Age){
      if (Age < 25)
            return 700.50;
      else
            return 550.00;
}
```

Now our Web service is ready. Next we have to build a client application that can access this Web service.

Discovering the Web Service

To build the client, we have to build a Proxy class for the Web service and compile it. We can do this easily with Visual Studio .NET. It takes care of all the plumbing work for us. Right-click on the references on the Solution Explorer, and select Add Web Reference from the Shortcut menu (as shown in Figure 13.16).

Figure 13.16: Adding Web Reference

A new dialog box will appear as shown in Figure 13.17.

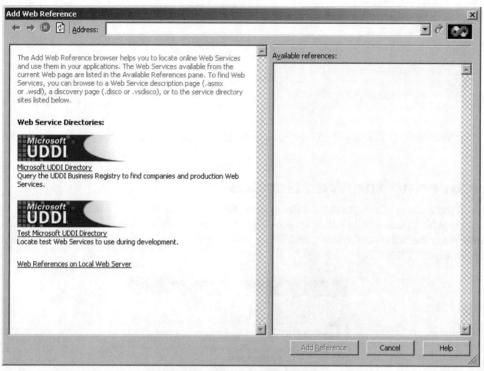

Figure 13.17: Add Web Reference Dialog

Click the Web References on Local Web Server link. The discovery document will appear on the left-side pane, and a list of available Web services from the local host and its discovery document will appear on the right-side pane (as shown in Figure 13.18).

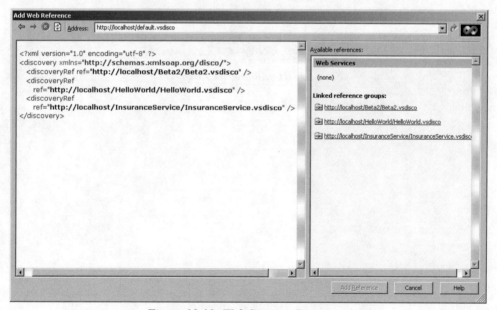

Figure 13.18: Web Services Discovery

Select the http://localhost/InsuranceService/InsuranceService.vsdicso from the left-side pane. You will see the URL for the WSDL file and the asmx file in the left and right pane (as shown in Figure 13.19).

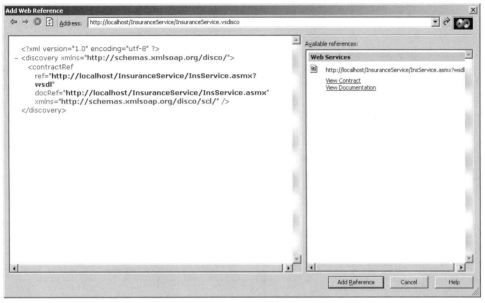

Figure 13.19: Insurance Web Service Information

Click the Add Reference button to add the Web reference to the Solution Explorer (as shown in Figure 13.20). This will build and compile the Proxy class and deploy the DLL as well.

Figure 13.20: Web Service Reference on Solution Explorer

Web Service Client

Let's build an ASP.NET Web client for the Web service with the Visual Studio .NET Integrated Development Environment . Right-click the project name in the Solution Explorer, and select Add

New Item. You will see a new dialog box. Select Web Form and give it the name WebServiceClient.aspx (as shown in Figure 13.21).

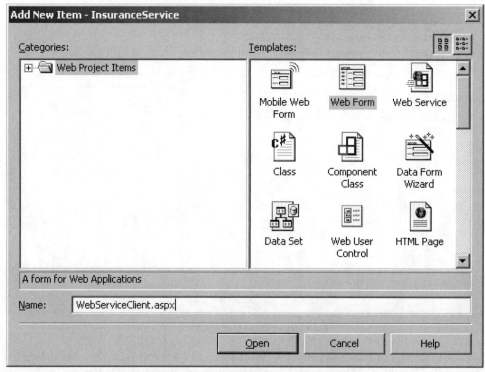

Figure 13.21: Add New Item Dialog

Let's add a label and change the text property to Age: Add a text box and button server controls, and change the text property of the button control to "Get Quote." Add one more label control, change the id property to "lblResult," and make the text property blank (as shown in Figure 13.22).

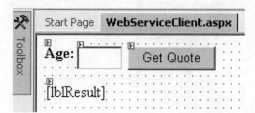

Figure 13.22: ASP.NET Web Form Design

Now double-click the button control, and add the code shown in Listing 13.8 to the click event of the button control.

Listing 13.8—Web Service Client Code

```
//Create a new Web service object of the type localhost.InsService
localhost.InsService objIns = new localhost.InsService();
//Parse the int from the text box.
int iAge = Int32.Parse(txtAge.Text);
//Send the age as a parameter to the Web service and display the
//result in the label control.
lblResult.Text = "Your insurance premium will be: " + objIns.Rate(iAge).ToString();
```

Save the changes to the WebServiceClient.aspx. Right-click the WebServiceClient.aspx file on the Solution Explorer, and select the Set As Start Page option on the Shortcut menu (as shown in Figure 13.23). This will make the WebServiceClient.aspx ASP.NET page the startup page when we run the solution.

Figure 13.23: Make the ASP.NET the Starting Page

Now press F5 from the keyboard to build the project and view it in the browser. The output for ages 20 and 26 is shown in Figure 13.23.

Figure 13.23: Web Service Output

Accessing Web Services Asynchronously

We can access Web services synchronously or asynchronously. The Proxy class supports both methods. So far in this chapter, we have accessed Web Services synchronously only. Let's see how we can access Web services asynchronously.

WebService Behaviors

The WebService behaviors are HTML components (.HTC file) that can be used in IE 5.0 or later to invoke remote Web service calls from client-side scripting using SOAP. The WebService behaviors are based on DHTML behaviors. We can use JavaScript from a Web page to invoke Web services asynchronously and use the return values in the client-side scripting. The WebService behavior hides all the complexities of the SOAP protocol from the developers and allows them to concentrate on the application-specific requirements.

When we are using the WebService behaviors, we have to include the webservice.htc file in the same folder as the Web service client application. For example, if we are using an HTML file to access the Web service, the webservice.htc should be present in the same folder as the HTML file. When the Client browser downloads the HTML file to access the Web service, the webservice.htc will be downloaded to the client behind the scenes.

You can download the webservice.htc file from the following URL:

http://msdn.microsoft.com/downloads/samples/internet/default.asp?url=/Downloads/samples/Internet/behaviors/library/webservice/default.asp

Let's look at a simple code example (see Listing 13.9).

Listing 13.9—Web Service Behavior Code

```
<html>
<head>
<title>Accessing the Web Services using WebService Behavior</title>
<script language="JavaScript">
<!--
//Get the result back in this variable
var Result;
function init(){
      //Specify the Web service to be used. In this example we are accessing
      //the SayHello Web service.
      HelloSvc.useService("http://localhost/Hello/SayHello.asmx?WSDL","Hello");
      //Store the Event handle in the result variable
   Result = HelloSvc.Hello.callService("SayHello");
}
function GetResult(){
   // if there was no error, and the call came from the call() in init()
   if((!event.result.error) && (Result == event.result.id)){
      // Show the Web services result
      msg.innerText = event.result.value;
   }
}
//-->
</script>
</head>
<body onload="init()">
<h3>Accessing the Web Services <br />using WebService Behavior</h3>
<form name="frm">
<div id="HelloSvc" style="behavior:url(webservice.htc)" onresult="GetResult()">
</div><hr color="black"/>
<b><div id="msg"></div></b>
```

```
</form>
</body>
</html>
```

We have two JavaScript functions (init and GetResults) in the <head> element and two <div> tags in the body in an HTML form element. The <div> tags and IDs are HelloSvc and msg, respectively. We are loading the Web Services behavior file (webservice.htc) by using the style element. We are also registering the event handler onresult with the JavaScript function GetResult. In the body tags' onload event we are calling the init function.

When the init function is called, it will use the useService method of the HelloSvc object (the <div> tag) to register the Web service using the WSDL URL as the first argument and the Web service name as the second argument. Then we are calling the Web service using the syntax objectname.webservicename.callService("WebMethod") [HelloSvc.Hello.callService("SayHello")] and storing the handle back in the Result variable.

When we receive the result from the Web service asynchronously, the JavaScript function Get Results will be called. We are checking that the result is not an error and that the event handle is equal to the event handle that we have already stored in the Result variable. If both conditions are true, we are displaying the Web service result in the <div> tag using the event.result.value object (as shown in Figure 13.25).

Figure 13.25: Web Service Output Using WebService Behavior

For more information about the WebService behavior, visit the following URLs at Microsoft Developers Network:

http://msdn.microsoft.com/library/default.asp?url=/workshop/author/webservice/overview.asp
http://msdn.microsoft.com/library/default.asp?url=/workshop/author/webservice/using.asp

Data Types

A Web service can return simple data types (integers, strings, enumerations), complex data types (structures; classes; arrays of simple data types, structures, or classes), and DataSets. Web services implement the XML serialization architecture to support the wide variety of data types and methods of serializing the data from server to client.

A Web service can also accept any of these data types as arguments. The arguments can be either by value or by reference when the SOAP protocol is used. When accessing the Web services using HTTP Get or Post, we are limited to using value types of arguments, and only standard data types and arrays of standard data types are supported.

Let's look at a simple Web service example that returns arrays of strings. Go to the Hello folder, create a new file called "ReturnStringArray.asmx," and paste the code shown in Listing 13.10.

Listing 13.10—Web Service Returning a String Array

```
<%@ WebService Language="C#" Class="ReturnStringArray" %>

using System;
using System.Web.Services;

public class ReturnStringArray : WebService{
        [WebMethod]
        public String[] GetOSStringArray() {
                //Load OS names into a String array
                String[] strOSAry = {"Windows XP", "Windows 2000",
                "Windows Me", "Windows 98", "Windows 95",
                "Windows 3.11", "Windows 3.1","DOS"};
                //OS String Array
                return strOSAry;
        }
}
```

We have created a class called ReturnStringArray and exposed a WebMethod called GetOSStringArray. The WebMethod returns simple string array back to the client. Let's access the Web service from the browser interface (as shown in Figure 13.26).

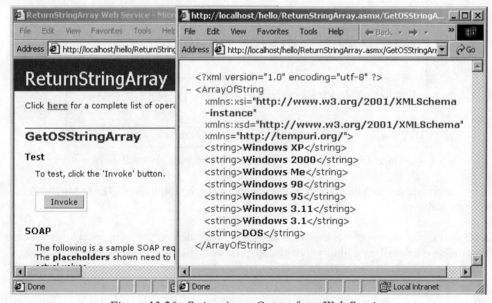

Figure 13.26: String Array Output from Web Service

Now that the Web service is working well, let's build a Proxy class and compile it into a DLL as shown in Listing 13.11.

Listing 13.11—Building Proxy

```
wsdl /l:CS /n:ReturnStringArrayNS /out:ReturnStringArray.cs
http://localhost/hello/ReturnStringArray.asmx?WSDL

CSC /r:system.dll /r:System.Web.dll /r:System.Xml.dll /r:System.Web.Services.dll
/t:library /out:ReturnStringArray.dll ReturnStringArray.cs
```

Let's copy the ReturnStringArray.DLL to the bin folder underneath the HelloClient folder. Let's build an ASP.NET Web client to access the ReturnStringArray Web service. Go to the HelloClient folder, create an ASP.NET page called StringArrayClient.aspx, and paste the code shown in Listing 13.12.

Listing 13.12—Web Service Client

```
<%@ Import Namespace="System" %>
<%@ Import Namespace="ReturnStringArrayNS" %>
<html>
<head>
<style type="text/css">
        body {font-face:verdana; font-size:10pt; font-weight:normal}
</style>
</head>
<script language="C#" runat="server">
protected void Page_Load(object sender, EventArgs e){
        //Create an object of the type ReturnStringArray
        ReturnStringArray objWebSvc = new ReturnStringArray();

        //Invoke the WebMethod and assign the result
        //into the Listbox server control
        LstOS.DataSource = objWebSvc.GetOSStringArray();
        LstOS.DataBind();
}
</script>
<body>
<h3>Web Service Client</h3>
<hr color="black" />
<form runat="server">
<b>String Array from web service:</b>
<asp:ListBox id="LstOS" Rows="9" SelectionMode="Single"
     runat="server" />
</form>
</body>
</html>
```

We have included the namespaces System for String array access and ReturnStringArrayNS for Web Service proxy access. Then we have added a ListBox server control to display the String array. In the Page_Load event we have created an object of Proxy class, accessed the WebMethod GetOSStringArray, and then bound the result into the ListBox control. Figure 13.27 shows a screenshot of the output.

Figure 13.27: String Array Output from Web Service

Web Service and WebMethod Attributes

Both the WebService declaration and the WebMethod declaration support a few attributes to give more descriptive information to Web service clients.

WebService Attributes

The WebService supports three main attributes—Name, Description, and Namespace—that are described in Table 13.2.

Attribute	Description
Name	Usually the name of the Web service will be the class name that we are defining for the Web service. This is the name that will be exposed to our clients as the name of the Web service and sometimes it is not client friendly. The Name attribute provides a meaningful name that can be used instead of the class name.
Description	The Description attribute gives descriptive information about the Web service.
Namespace	The default namespace used by the Web service is http://tempuri.org. This attribute allows us to customize the namespace.

Table 13.2: Description of Web Service Attributes

Let's use all three attributes in the SayHelloToMe Web service, which we have used in the past. Add the code shown in Listing 13.13 before the class declaration.

Listing 13.13—Customizing the Web Service

```
[WebService(
        Description="Description: Say Hello To Me Web Service",
        Namespace="http://www.SayHelloToMe.com/",
        Name="Name: Say Hello To Me WebService")]
]
public class Hello : WebService{
```

We have customized all three attributes of the Web service. Let's see how the output looks in the browser. Figure 13.28 shows the output before and after customization.

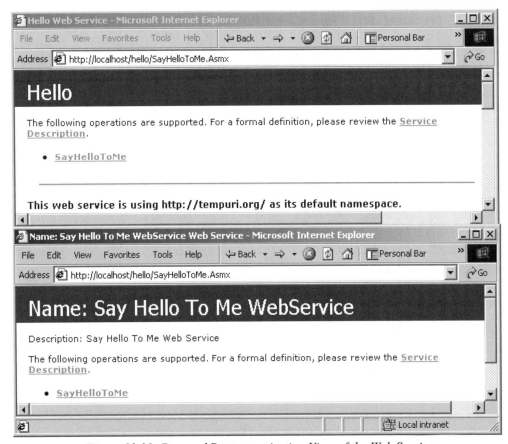

Figure 13.28: Pre- and Postcustomization View of the Web Service

We can see the difference. The name of the Web service is changed, and the description is showing. We also have a message in the precustomization version about changing the default namespace setting.

The WSDL for the Web service shows the namespace change in the document (see Figure 13.29).

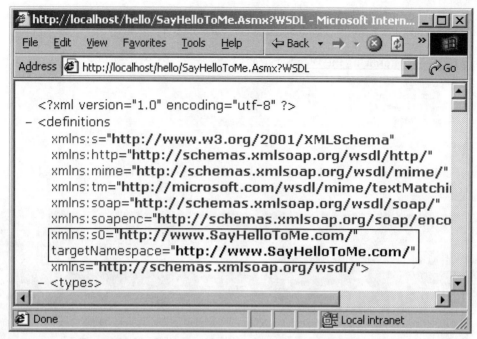

Figure 13.29: Customized Namespace in the WSDL Document

WebMethod Attributes

The WebMethod supports six attributes (described in Table 13.3) for customization. Some result in cosmetic changes to WebMethod and some result in functional changes.

Attribute	Description
Description	The Description attribute gives descriptive information about the WebMethod.
MessageName	When you have overloaded methods in the Web service, you can use the MessageName attribute to uniquely identify the methods. When you have the MessageName attribute, you can also use it to access the WebMethod.
TransactionOption	WebMethod can perform transactions using the TransactionOption attribute. The TransactionOption attribute supports Disabled, NotSupported, Supported, Required, and RequiresNew values. By default, Disabled is used for all WebMethods. *Only the Web service can initiate a transaction and a Web service cannot be part of another transaction. For example, if a transaction-enabled ASP.NET page calls the transaction-enabled Web service, ASP.NET will use its own transaction, and Web service will use its own transaction.*
EnableSession	The EnableSession attribute allows the Web service to maintain state. This is done through the HTTP cookies; more overheads will be added to the Web service.
CacheDuration	The CacheDuration attribute allows the WebMethod to cache its results

Attribute	Description
	for a certain number of seconds. When we set the CacheDuration attribute, Web service will cache the result for every combination. For example, if the WebMethod takes age as an argument and if we access the WebMethod with age 30 and 40, the WebMethod will cache the results for 30 and 40 separately. When another request with the age as 30 comes, WebMethod will serve the request from the cache.
BufferResponse	The BufferResponse attribute allows us to buffer the result and send the response at the end. If the WebMethod takes a long time to process, we should set the BufferResponse attribute to false. For smaller amounts of data, setting the BufferResponse attribute to true will scale well.

Table 13.3: Description of WebMethod Attributes

Let's try a quick example for the `WebMethod` attributes. We are going to build a stock quote Web service, and we will assign hard-code values for three stocks. Go to the Hello folder, create a new file called WebMethodAttributes.asmx, and paste the code shown in Listing 13.14 into it.

Listing 13.14—Customizing the WebMethod

```
<%@ WebService Language="C#" Class="Quote" %>
using System.Web.Services;

//
// We have customized the description, namespace,
// and the name of the Web service.
//
[WebService(
        Description="Stock Quote Web Service",
        Namespace="http://www.StockQuote.com/",
        Name="Stock Quote Web Service written in C# and .NET")]
public class Quote : WebService{
        //
        // We have customized the description and the MessageName of
        // the WebMethod. So this method can be accessed as StockQuote
        // or func_SQ. We have also enabled the session and set the caching
        // time to be one minute. We have also enabled the buffering
        // for the Web service.
        //
        [WebMethod(
        Description="The StockQuote WebMethod takes stock symbol as argument.",
        EnableSession=true,
        CacheDuration=60,
        MessageName="StockQuote",
        BufferResponse=true)]
        public string func_SQ(string sSymbol) {
         string rtnVal;
         if (sSymbol == "MSFT") //If Microsoft stock the value is 70.00
                    rtnVal = " 70.00";
         else if (sSymbol == "SUNW") //If Sun stock the value is 16.00
                    rtnVal = " 16.00";
         else if (sSymbol == "IBM") //If IBM stock the value is 105.00
                    rtnVal = " 105.00";
         else
                    rtnVal = " 0.00"; //If Others then 0.00

         //Add the timestamp to the reply.
         return sSymbol + " = " + rtnVal + " at " +
         System.DateTime.Now.ToString();
         }
 }
```

We have customized the description, the name, and the namespace for the Web service. We also customized the description for the WebMethod and MessageName for the method. In addition, we have enabled the session state for the WebMethod and cached the request for 60 seconds. We are buffering the WebMethod as well. Figure 13.30 shows how that looks in the browser.

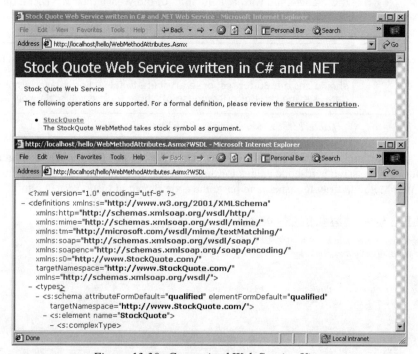

Figure 13.30: Customized Web Service View

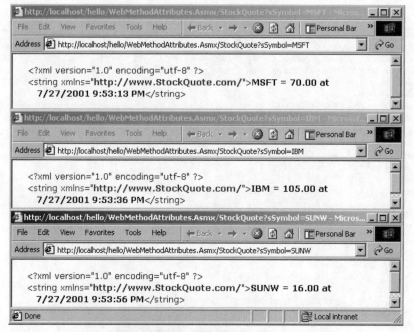

Figure 13.31: Web Service Output

We can see the name, the description of the Web service, and the WebMethod. We can see that the MessageName attribute changed the WebMethod name from func_SQ to StockQuote. Let's see the result for the stock quotes MSFT, IBM, and SUNW.

Figure 13.31 shows that we have three different timestamps for three different stock symbols. If we refresh the browser repeatedly, the timestamp will not change for 60 seconds because the WebMethod is cached for 60 seconds. The timestamp will be different for each stock symbol because the stock symbols are different and are in different cache locations. We can also see that the Namespace attribute of the Web service is in use.

Summary

Web services are a great advancement in the distributed computing architecture They provide significant flexibility when we are working with multiple types of platforms and tools. In this chapter we have learned many details about Web services, and how to build ASP.NET Web service with text editors and Visual Studio .NET. We have also seen the different data types we can pass with Web services and how to customize the look and feel of Web services with attributes. XML plays a large role in Web Services as well as other aspects of .NET. In the next chapter we will journey into some of the details of manipulating XML in the .NET framework.

Chapter 14:
XML.NET

XML.NET Model

In 1996, the World Wide Web Consortium (W3C) organized a working group tasked with creating a universal language for data on the Web. The result, a metalanguage called Extensible Markup Language (XML), allows users to design their own markup languages to form documents that use XML syntax and semantics. General use of the term *XML* refers to both the XML document and the XML language, if neither is specifically mentioned. XML is a public format and hence is not a proprietary format of any company.

XML enables a new generation of Web-based applications for viewing and manipulating data. It gives developers the power to deliver structured data from a wide variety of applications to the desktop for local computation and presentation. The .NET Framework offers libraries and solutions to utilize these XML standards.

This chapter examines the important XML-related classes of the .NET Framework.

Since the .NET Framework offers a wide range of classes and libraries regarding XML and its relatives, the chapter avoids exploring each class or method in detail, focusing instead on the classes and methods that provide practical solutions to common requirements.

System.Xml Namespaces

The System.Xml namespace and its derivative .Xsl, .XPath, .Schema, and .Serialization namespaces have a comprehensive set of XML classes for parsing, validating, and manipulating XML data. These actions are performed using readers, writers, and components that comply with W3C's Document Object Model (DOM). The DOM, covered in more detail below, is a treelike representation of an XML document, with different constituent parts of the document made accessible as *nodes*.

System.Xml is the overall namespace for the XML classes that provide standards-based support for processing XML. It also covers support for XML Path Language (XPath) queries and Extensible Stylesheet Language Transformations (XSLT).

The following standards are supported:

- XML 1.0 (http://www.w3.org/TR/1998/REC-xml-19980210)
- XML Namespaces (http://www.w3.org/TR/REC-xml-names/)
- XML Schemas for Structures (http://www.w3.org/TR/xmlschema-1/)
- XML Schemas for Data Types (http://www.w3.org/TR/xmlschema-2/)
- XPath Expressions (http://www.w3.org/TR/XPath)
- XSL Transformations (http://www.w3.org/TR/xslt)

- DOM Level 2 Core (http://www.w3.org/TR/DOM-Level-2/)
- SOAP 1.1 (http://msdn.microsoft.com/xml/general/soapspec.asp)

The .NET XML stack is partitioned over five important namespaces:

- **System.Xml**, which provides XML standards–based support for processing XML;
- **System.Xml.XPath**, which contains the XPath parser and evaluation engine;
- **System.Xml.Xsl**, which provides support for XSLT transforms;
- **System.Xml.Schema**, which contains the XML classes that provide XML standards–based support for schemas created with the XML Schema definition language (XSD); and
- **System.Xml.Serialization**, which contains classes that are used to serialize objects into XML format documents or streams.

These namespaces are packaged inside the System.Xml.dll assembly, which must be referenced when compiling source code that uses XML classes. For example, suppose you develop C# code that uses the Xml namespaces and call it helloxml.cs. To compile this code, you could type the following in the command prompt:

```
csc /r:System.Xml.dll helloxml.cs
```

The most common XML-related classes in the .NET Framework are as follows:

The *XmlResolver* class handles URL resolution operations to external XML resources such as entities, document type definitions (DTDs), or schemas. The class is also used to process *include* and *import* elements found in Extensible Stylesheet Language (XSL) stylesheets or XSD schemas. XmlResolver is abstract; it has a concrete subclass implementation, XmlUrlResolver, which is the default resolver for all classes in the System.Xml namespace.

- The *XmlDocument* class implements the W3C DOM. It has descendant classes such as XmlDataDocument and XPathDocument.
- The *XmlDataDocument* class is an implementation of an XmlDocument class. It can be associated with a data set.
- The *XPathDocument* class performs a cache implementation for XML document processing of XSLT.
- The *XmlNodeReader* class reads a given DOM node subtree by using XmlReader.
- The *XmlSchemaCollection* class is a library of XML-Data Reduced (XDR) and XSD schema implementations. (Schemas created with the XDR language give you a way to map elements to their respective fields in a relational database table.) These XDR and XSD schemas are cached in memory for fast accessibility.
- The *XmlTextReader* class lets you access XML data in a fast, noncached, forward-only read access direction.
- The *XmlTextWriter* class lets you generate XML data in a fast, forward-only direction.
- The *XmlSchema* class helps you reflect the W3C XSD specification. With this class, you can create an XSD schema.
- The *XmlValidatingReader* class lets you validate DTD, XDR, and XSD schemas.
- The *XPathNavigator* class lets you navigate W3C XPath data models with a cursor-style model.
- The *XslTransform* class is an implementation of W3C XSLT specification for transforming XML documents into another format such as HTML.

Document Object Model

The DOM, a cached, treelike representation of an XML document, enables the navigation and editing of the document. DOM provides a node representation of a complete XML document stored in memory, providing random access to the contents of the entire document.

The DOM implementation in the Microsoft XML Parser (MSXML) allows you to load or create a document, gather errors, and access and manipulate the information. It also allows you to manipulate structures contained within the document and resave the document as an XML file. The DOM also provides you with an interface for loading, accessing, manipulating, and serializing XML documents. The DOM allows applications to rely on the logic provided by MSXML to handle XML-based information, using its facilities rather than writing custom code to read and process XML. The DOM works better than XSLT, in which the source XML document is transformed based on the XSLT template applied. DOM allows you to create or modify a document in memory as well as to read a document from an XML source file.

In .NET, an XmlDocument class is used to represents an XML document. The XmlNode class provides methods and properties to manipulate a node in the document. Many of the other W3C classes are specializations of the XmlNode class. The XmlDocument class has a Load method that loads the document nodes from a file, a stream, or an XmlReader. The .NET framework provides the classes XmlTextReader and XmlTextWriter classes which give you quicker access to XML than the XML DOM classes do. Figure 14.1 depicts the relationship between the XmlDocument class and the XmlReader and XmlWriter classes.

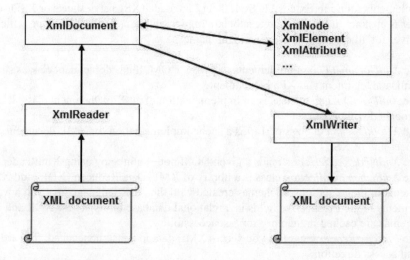

Figure 14.1: The Relationship between XmlDocument, XmlReader, and XmlWriter

DOM Document Elements

Think of an XML document as a tree with various types of *nodes* inside.

The DOM-related parts of the .NET Framework offer various classes, types, and enumerations to handle XML data representation. Some of the most common classes or nodes on the DOM tree are listed in Table 14.1.

Class or Node	Function
XmlAttribute	Refers to the Attribute content. Stores the text of the attribute.
XmlEntity	Refers to the Entity node specified within the <!ENTITY... > block.
XmlNotation	Refers to the Notation node specified within the <!NOTATION...> block.
XmlElement	Refers to the Element specified within the tag names.
XmlProcessingInstruction	Refers to the processing instructions for the XML parser. It consists of two parts: the target, such as <?xml-stylesheet, and data, such as type='text/xsl' href='library.xsl'?>.
XmlCDataSection	Refers to the CDATA node specified within the <![CDATA[...]]> block. Stores text of the CDATA section. The CDATA section is ignored by the XML parser.
XmlComment	Refers to the Comment node specified within the <!-- ... --> block. Stores the text of the comment.
XmlText	Refers to the text inside the node. Stores the text content of the relevant element or attribute node.
XmlWhitespace	Refers to the white space between markup in your document. In XML, the white spaces in your document are not truncated.
XmlSignificantWhitespace	Refers to the white space between markup in a mixed content model or white space within the xml:space="preserve" scope.

Table 14.1: Common Node Types Within the DOM Tree

These common DOM classes are derived from one of three abstract classes: XmlNode, XmlLinkedNode, and XmlCharacterData.

The XmlComment, XmlText, XmlWhitespace, XmlCDataSection, and XmlSignificantWhitespace classes derive from the abstract class XmlCharacterData, which provides text-manipulation methods for these and other classes. The others classes included in Table 14.1 are directly derived from the XmlNode or XmlLinkedNode classes.

The inheritance hierarchy (Figure 14.2) for these three base classes is as follows:

- XmlNode, which represents a single node in the document.
- XmlLinkedNode, which gets the node immediately preceding or following this node.
- XmlCharacterData, which provides text-manipulation methods used by its derivative classes.

Because these three abstract classes share many members, demonstrating one base class should give you a feel for the mechanics of all the classes. Table 14.2 lists some of the XmlNode class members.

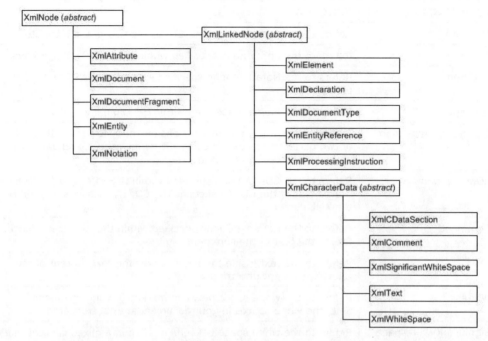

Figure 14.2: Hierarchy of Elements in the XML.NET Document Object Model

XmlNode Class Members	Description
Attributes	Returns a collection comprising attributes of the node.
BaseURI	Returns the base universal resource identifier of the node.
ChildNodes	Returns the children of the node as a node list.
FirstChild	Returns the first child node of the node.
HasChildNodes	Returns a Boolean value. Returns *true* if the node has child nodes. Otherwise returns *false*.
InnerText	The contents of the current node and its child nodes concatenated together as a single string, including only the element values—that is, the text between the start and end markup tags, excluding the markup tags and attributes of the current node and its child nodes.
InnerXml	The contents of the current node and its child nodes excluding the markup tags and attributes of the current node.
IsReadOnly	Returns a Boolean value. Returns *true* if the node is read-only. Otherwise returns *false*.
LastChild	Returns the last child node of the node.
LocalName	Gets the local name of the node.
Name	Returns the name of the node without the name prefix. The returned value depends on the type of the node.
NamespaceURI	Returns the name space universal resource identifier of the node. This attribute is defined with the *xmlns:* specifier.

XmlNode Class Members	Description
NextSibling	Returns the sibling node of the node. This is the next node that is at the same level in the node hierarchy.
NodeType	Returns the type of the node, such as Comment, Attribute, and Element.
OuterXml	The contents of the current node and its child nodes.
ParentNode	Returns the parent node of the node.
Prefix	Used to read and write the namespace prefix of the node.
Value	Used to read and write the value of the node, depending on the type of the node.
CreateNavigator()	Returns an XPathNavigator object that is positioned on the node.
RemoveAll	Removes all child nodes of the node.
RemoveChild	Removes the child node passed as a parameter.
ReplaceChild	Replaces an existing child node with a new node sent as a parameter.
SelectNodes	Returns a list of nodes that are filtered with the XPath expression.
SelectSingleNode	Returns the first node that is filtered with the XPath expression.

Table 14.2: Significant Members of the XmlNode Class

The XmlNode class contains many other members in addition to those listed in Table 14.2. For example, the CreateComment(), CreateProcessingInstruction(), and CreateElement() methods are used to create comments, processing instructions, and elements of XML documents, respectively. Another handy method, AppendChild(), is used to add a new node to the end of an XML document. This method takes an XmlNode object as its sole argument and returns an XmlNode object.

To give you an idea how to manipulate the DOM with some of the XML .NET classes we've created Listing 14.1 which shows how to create an XML document with the DOM and how to send the output generated by the XML document to the console. This listing employs the XmlTextWriter class (covered in greater detail soon) to make generated XML data persistent as text.

Listing 14.1— Example DOM Usage0

```
// Generate a document using the DOM

using System;
using System.Xml;

public class class1
{
  public static void Main( String[] args)
  {
   try
   {
    XmlDocument doc = new XmlDocument();
    // Create a comment and append
    XmlNode node = doc.CreateComment("example document");
    doc.AppendChild(node);
    node = doc.CreateProcessingInstruction("hack", "individual");
    doc.AppendChild(node);

    // Create the person element within the urn:person namespace
    node = doc.CreateElement("p", "person", "urn:person");
```

```
     doc.AppendChild(node);
     // Create the name/age elements in no namespace
     node = doc.CreateElement("name");
     node.InnerText = "bulentozkir";
     doc.DocumentElement.AppendChild(node);
     node = doc.CreateElement("age");
     node.InnerText = "27";
     doc.DocumentElement.AppendChild(node);

     // Serialize the document to the console
     XmlTextWriter tw = new XmlTextWriter(Console.Out);
     // Produce indented XML data
     tw.Formatting = Formatting.Indented;
     // Save the document, serialize it to console this time!
     doc.Save(tw);
   }
   catch(Exception e)
   {
       Console.WriteLine ("Exception: {0}", e.ToString());

   }
  }
}
```

DOM loading is built on top of XmlReader whereas DOM saving is built on XmlWriter. These classes make it possible to extend how the DOM interacts with your applications in numerous ways.

As mentioned above, the abstract XmlNode and XmlLinkedNode classes serve as base classes for any XML data type class. Another class, XmlNodeList, represents an ordered collection of nodes. XmlNodeList ultimately allows you to selectively iterate through the DOM document consisting of XmlNode and XmlLinkedNode items. After constructing the document, you can obtain an XmlNodeList object using the ChildNodes property of an XmlNode. You can also obtain selective lists of XML nodes populated in an XmlNodeList object using the SelectNodes method of the XmlNode or the GetElementsByTagName of the XmlDocument. You can iterate through the entire XmlNodeList using the Item method in conjunction with the Count property. You can use the Count property to determine how many nodes to iterate through in the XmlNodeList, and use the Item method to retrieve an XmlNode at a particular index.

Listing 14.2 shows how to pass some XML text containing first and last names as a string to YourMethod, which processes the XML data and produces the first and last names as output. The code makes use of the XmlNodeList class to cycle through all the nodes in the XML document.. As the comment in the listing's midsection points out, you can instead use the XmlDocument.Load() method to read the XML from a file.

Listing 14.2— DOM Example1

```
// XMLDocument example

using System;
using System.Xml;

public class XMLApp
{
 public void YourMethod( String strFirst, String strLast)
 {
  Console.WriteLine("{0}, {1}", strLast, strFirst);
 }

 public void ProcessXML( String xmlText)
 {
  XmlDocument _doc = new XmlDocument();
  _doc.LoadXml( xmlText);
```

```
 // Alternatively you can use _doc.Load(strFilename) to read from a file
 XmlNodeList _fnames = _doc.GetElementsByTagName("FirstName");
 XmlNodeList _lnames = _doc.GetElementsByTagName("LastName");

 // I'm assuming every FirstName has a LastName in this example
 for (int _i = 0; _i < _fnames.Count; ++_i)
 {
  YourMethod(_fnames[_i].InnerText, _lnames[_i].InnerText);
 }
}

public static void Main(String[] args)
{
 XMLApp _app = new XMLApp();
 _app.ProcessXML(@"<Authors>
  <Author>
  <FirstName>John</FirstName>
  <LastName>Doe</LastName>
  </Author>
  <Author>
  <FirstName>Jane</FirstName>
  <LastName>Eod</LastName>
  </Author>
  </Authors>");
 }
}
```

The following two-part example reads the library1.xml file and then processes through it. First, Listing 14.3 contains the XML document to be read.

Listing 14.3—Library1.xml, Sample XML Data

```
<?xml version="1.0"?>
<library>
        <book book_number="1201">
                <author>Author1</author>
                <title>Title1</title>
                <photo src="photo1.jpg"/>
        </book>
        <book book_number="1202">
                <author>Author2</author>
                <title>Title2</title>
                <photo src="photo2.jpg"/>
        </book>
</library>
```

Next, Listing 14.4 contains the code that traverses the library1.xml XML document for the author elements and writes them to the console.

Listing 14.4—DOM Example2

```
using System;
using System.IO;
using System.Xml;

public class XmlExample00
{
  public static void Main()
  {
    XmlDocument doc = new XmlDocument();
    doc.Load("library1.xml");
    XmlElement root = doc.DocumentElement;
    XmlNodeList elemList = root.GetElementsByTagName("author");
    for (int i=0; i < elemList.Count; i++)
```

```
        {
            Console.WriteLine(elemList[i].InnerXml);
             Console.WriteLine(elemList[i].OuterXml);
        }
    }
}
```

Listings 14.5 and 14.6 present another simple content-scanning application. This simple yet interesting example shows how to read XML document content selectively from a Web site. Then the read XML data is parsed and sent to the console to show just the story title and the URL.

First, you need to create an XML document like story1.xml in Listing 14.5. Then you must publish it as a Web page on a public Web site—for example, http://127.0.0.1/story1.xml, http://localhost/story1.xml, or http://www.mindcracker.com/story1.xml. The *localhost* host name resolves to the 127.0.0.1 IP address, so the first two web addresses listed above are identical. (Note: The 127.0.0.1 IP address, which is called the local loopback address, is used for local TCP/IP stack diagnostics. The IP packets targeted to the 127.0.0.1 IP address are not relayed over the network!)

Listing 14.5—Http://localhost/story1.xml, XML Document Example

```
<?xml version="1.0" ?>
<!DOCTYPE backslash [
        <!ELEMENT backslash (story*)>
        <!ELEMENT story (title, url, time, author, department, topic,
comments, section, image)>
        <!ELEMENT title (#PCDATA)>
        <!ELEMENT url (#PCDATA)>
        <!ELEMENT time (#PCDATA)>
        <!ELEMENT author (#PCDATA)>
        <!ELEMENT department (#PCDATA)>
        <!ELEMENT topic (#PCDATA)>
        <!ELEMENT comments (#PCDATA)>
        <!ELEMENT section (#PCDATA)>
        <!ELEMENT image (#PCDATA)>
]>

<backslash>
 <story>
  <title>Microsoft Instant Messenger Virus Sweeps Net</title>
  <url>http://www.mindcracker.com/url1.html</url>
   <time>2002-02-13 23:59:39</time>
   <author>michael</author>
   <department>RISKs-of-homogeneous-computing</department>
   <topic>109</topic>
   <comments>356</comments>
   <section>articles</section>
   <image>topicms.gif</image>
 </story>
 <story>
  <title>What is .NET?</title>
  <url>http://www.mindcracker.com/url2.html</url>
  <time>2002-02-13 22:20:35</time>
  <author>CmdrTaco</author>
  <department>funny-you-should-ask</department>
  <topic>109</topic>
  <comments>469</comments>
  <section>articles</section>
  <image>topicms.gif</image>
 </story>
</backslash>
```

Once you've published this document to a Web site, execute the code in Listing 14.6 to send the title and URL of the story to output to your computer screen. The listing uses the XmlDocument class to Load in the XML web page locally and the method GetElementsByTagName of the XmlNodeList class to output the XML node data.

Listing 14.6— an XML Document Searcher over the Web

```
using System;
using System.IO;
using System.Net;
using System.Text;
using System.Xml;

public class MainClass
{
 public static void Main(string[] args)
 {
    XmlDocument doc = new XmlDocument();
    WebRequest wr;
    WebResponse ws;
    StreamReader sr;
    String line;

    try
    {
        // We assume that you serve the story1.xml
        // file at LOCALHOST webserver.
       wr = WebRequest.Create(@"http://127.0.0.1/story1.xml");
       ws =  wr.GetResponse();
       sr = new StreamReader(ws.GetResponseStream(),
              Encoding.ASCII);
       line = sr.ReadToEnd();    //Read entire document
       doc.LoadXml(line);        //Load the text into the XML document

       //Get the story and url nodes
       XmlNodeList titles = doc.GetElementsByTagName("title");
       XmlNodeList urls = doc.GetElementsByTagName("url");

       for (int i=0; i < titles.Count; i++)
       {
         Console.WriteLine(titles.Item(i).InnerXml);
         Console.WriteLine(urls.Item(i).InnerXml);
       }
    }
    catch(Exception e)
    {
        Console.WriteLine ("Exception: {0}", e.ToString());
    }
 }
}
```

The SelectNodes method of the XmlNode class returns an XmlNodeList object containing the results of the selection. In Listing 14.7, we traverse the nodes list, matching our XPath expression passed into SelectNodes.

Listing 14.7—SelectNodes Example

```
void ShowStudentNames (XmlNode node)
{
  XmlNodeList nl = node.SelectNodes("Book/@Author");
  foreach(XmlNode n in nl)
       Console.WriteLine("Student:{0}", n.Value);
}
```

The SelectSingleNode method returns an XmlNode object containing only the first node in the selection result. Listing 14.8 shows you how to use the XmlNode class's SelectSingleNode method by passing it an XPath expression. Observe that we can easily jump to any word we want! Then we read the LastChild property, namely Spanish, and change it to the correct meaning.

Listing 14.8—SelectSingleNode

```
using System;
using System.IO;
using System.Xml;

public class MainClass
{
  public static void Main()
  {
    XmlDocument doc = new XmlDocument();
    doc.LoadXml(@"<Vocabulary>
        <Word type='noun' level='1'>
                <English>cat</English>
                <Spanish>gato</Spanish>
        </Word>
        <Word type='verb' level='1'>
                <English>speak</English>
                <Spanish>hablar</Spanish>
        </Word>
        <Word type='adj' level='1'>
                <English>big</English>
                <Spanish>grand</Spanish>
        </Word>
        </Vocabulary>");

    XmlNode word;

    // get the root element
    XmlNode root = doc.DocumentElement;

    // select the node where big word resides
    word = root.SelectSingleNode(@"descendant::Word[English='big']");

    // change the meaning of big in Spanish.
    word.LastChild.InnerText = "grande";

    Console.WriteLine("Display the modified XML document....");
    doc.Save(Console.Out);
  }
}
```

Another interesting example uses an XPath query to select all of the unique namespaces and URIs inside an XML document. Using the XmlDocument class and the SelectNodes method with an XPath query, you can obtain the unique namespaces in an XML document, as shown in Listing 14.9. An XPath query works like a filter to help you create a sublist of nodes from the XML document dependent on an evaluated expression.

Listing 14.9— XPath Query for Namespaces

```
// XPath namespace query sample
// Create an XPath query to return to me all of the xmlns items.
// Query all unique namespaces inside an XML document.

using System;
using System.Xml;
using System.Xml.XPath;
using System.Collections;
```

```
public class XMLApp
{
 public static void Main( String[] args)
 {

  try
  {
   // namespace_URI array
   ArrayList arr1 = new ArrayList();
   // namespace_name array
   ArrayList arr2 = new ArrayList();

   XmlDocument _doc = new XmlDocument();
   _doc.LoadXml(@"<Schema name=""BlankSpecification"" xmlns=""urn:schemas-
microsoft-com:xml-data"" xmlns:b=""urn:schemas-microsoft-com:BizTalkServer""
xmlns:d=""urn:schemas-microsoft-com:datatypes""></Schema>");
   XmlNodeList nl2 = _doc.SelectNodes(@"//namespace::node()");

   foreach (XmlNode n in nl2)
   {
    if( arr1.IndexOf(n.Value) == -1 && arr2.IndexOf(n.Name) == -1)
    {
     Console.WriteLine("<" + n.Value + ">");
     Console.WriteLine("<" + n.Name + ">");
     arr1.Add(n.Value);
     arr2.Add(n.Name);
    }
   }
   Console.WriteLine("Total Number of namespace URIs=" + arr1.Count);
   Console.WriteLine("Total Number of namespace names=" + arr2.Count);
  }
  catch(Exception e)
  {
   Console.WriteLine ("Exception: {0}", e.ToString());
  }
 }
}
```

XPath expressions are exteremely powerful for searching XML document content. Listing 14.10 searches an XML document for all authors whose first name begins with the letter J. This specific node selection is accomplished with the following XPath expression:

```
"descendant::Author[starts-with(FirstName, 'J')]"
```

Listing 14.10— XPath Query Starts-with Function

```
// XPath starts-with function sample

using System;
using System.Xml;

public class XMLApp
{
    public void ProcessXML(String xmlText)
    {
        XmlDocument _doc = new XmlDocument();
        String strXPath = @"descendant::Author[starts-with(FirstName, 'J')]";
        _doc.LoadXml(xmlText);
        XmlNodeList nl = _doc.SelectNodes(strXPath);
        foreach (XmlNode n in nl)
            Console.WriteLine("FirstName:{0}", n.InnerXml);
    }

    public static void Main( String[] args)
    {
        XMLApp _app = new XMLApp();
```

```
        try
        {
            _app.ProcessXML(@"<Authors>
                                <Author>
                                 <FirstName>John</FirstName>
                                 <LastName>TurkishDude</LastName>
                                </Author>
                                <Author>
                                 <FirstName>Bulent</FirstName>
                                 <LastName>Ozkir</LastName>
                                </Author>
                                <Author>
                                 <FirstName>Jane</FirstName>
                                 <LastName>TurkishLady</LastName>
                                </Author>
                              </Authors>");
        }
        catch(Exception e)
        {
            Console.WriteLine ("Exception: {0}", e.ToString());
        }
    }
}
```

Reading and Writing XML Documents

At the core of the .NET Framework's XML classes are two abstract classes: XmlReader and XmlWriter. *XmlReader* provides a fast, forward-only, read-only cursor for processing an XML document stream. *XmlWriter* provides an interface for producing XML document streams. Applications that want to *process* XML documents use XmlReader, whereas applications that want to *produce* XML documents employ XmlWriter. Both classes employ a streaming model that doesn't require expensive in-memory cache.

As base classes, XmlReader and XmlWriter define the functionality that all derived classes must support. Let's take a closer look at these derived classes and how they function.

XML Reader Classes

XmlReader has three concrete implementations: XmlTextReader, XmlNodeReader, and XmlValidatingReader. XmlTextReader supports reading from text-based XML streams, whereas XmlNodeReader is designed to read from in-memory XML DOM trees. XmlValidatingReader can validate data using DTD, XDR, or other schemas.

XmlNodeReader provides fast data in an XML node. Since XmlNodeReader can be constructed with any XML node within the XML document, XmlNodeReader reads only the subtree of a given node.

All of the classes deriving from XmlReader expose information, such as NodeType, Name, NamespaceURI, and Value, for only the current node position. The XmlReader class has several members, the most common of which are shown in Table 14.3.

XmlReader Class Members	Description
AttributeCount	Returns the total number of attributes inside the node.
Depth	Returns the level of nesting within the node where the root is Depth = 0.
EOF	Returns a Boolean value. Returns *true* if the reader cursor is at the end of the file. Otherwise it returns *false*.
HasAttributes	Returns a Boolean value. Returns *true* if the node has one or more attributes. Otherwise it returns *false*.
HasValue	Returns a Boolean value. Returns *true* if the node can store a value depending on its node type. Otherwise it returns *false*.
IsEmptyElement	Returns a Boolean value. Returns *true* if the element is written in short form and has no value. Otherwise returns *false*. For example, for the markup *<element1/>* with no value it returns *true*.
Name	Returns the name of the node, including namespace prefix, depending on its type.
Value	Gets the text value of the node.
XmlSpace	Returns the recent *xml:space* scope, which determines whether to preserve or remove white spaces.
Close()	Releases any of the outstanding and open resources.
GetAttribute()	Returns the value of an attribute located either with an index, with a Name, or with LocalName followed by a NamespaceURI pair.
IsStartElement()	Returns a Boolean value. Returns *true* if the node is an element start tag. Otherwise, it returns *false*.
LookupNamespace()	Returns the namespace URI of the namespace prefix specified.
MoveToAttribute()	Moves the reader cursor to the attribute. The attribute is located with either an index, a Name, or a LocalName plus NamespaceURI pair.
MoveToContent()	Checks whether the node at the current reader position is a content node of type element, attribute, entity or a CDATA block. If it is not a content node, then it moves to the next node and tests its type until it reaches the end of the file.

Table 14.3: XmlReader Class Members

The following list provides additional details about some of these readily used methods:

- The Read method supports generic document processing and reads the next hierarchical node. Application code must manage the details of each node. Attributes must be specifically read.
- The MoveToFirstAttribute and MoveToNextAttribute methods iterate through the attribute list.
- The MoveToAttribute method moves to a named attribute or attribute position.
- The ReadStartElement and ReadEndElement methods provide element optimization. The reader verifies that the node is an element. These methods support name and namespace verification.
- The ReadElementString method reads and returns the text contained inside the element containing a simple string and moves the navigation cursor to the next element. Be careful

when using this method, because if the element contains any child elements, the method throws an XmlException.

- The MoveToContent method skips over white space, comments, and processing instructions and jumps directly to the actual data content.

Listing 14.11 illustrates the use of ReadStartElement, ReadEndElement, and ReadElementString:

Listing 14.11—ReadStartElement-ReadEndElement vs. ReadElementString

```
using System;
using System.IO;
using System.Xml;

public class Sample
{
/* name.xml looks like this -
   <?xml version="1.0" encoding="utf-8" ?>
   <name attrib1='1'> Full Name
   <first attrib2='2'>Bulent</first>
   <last>Ozkir</last>
   <number num='123'> TheNumber</number>
   </name>
*/
      public static void Main()
      {
              XmlTextReader r = null;
              try
              {
               r = new XmlTextReader("name.xml");

              // start at the name element
              r.ReadStartElement("name");

              // This next commented line will throw an XmlException!
              // You cannot read the name element with
          // ReadElementString because it has child nodes.
              // r.ReadElementString("name");

              // output name element text and move cursor forward one
              // node
              Console.WriteLine("name: {0}", r.Value);
              r.Read();

              // read the "first" element
              Console.WriteLine("first: {0}",
                          r.ReadElementString("first"));

              // read the "last" element
              // Remember calling ReadElementString is equal to
          // calling:
              // ReadStartElement -> return r.Value -> Read ->
              // ReadEndElement
              r.ReadStartElement("last");
              Console.WriteLine("last: {0}", r.Value);
              r.Read();
              r.ReadEndElement();

              // read the number element
              Console.WriteLine("number: {0}",
                  r.ReadElementString("number"));

              /* The application will output:

              name: Full Name
```

```
            first: Bulent
            last: Ozkir
            number: TheNumber
            */
        }
        catch(Exception e)
        {
                Console.WriteLine(e.ToString());
        }
        finally
        {
                if (r!=null)
                        r.Close();
        }
    }
}
```

Because XmlTextReader is specific to XML text files, XmlTextReader has additional methods such as LineNumber, LinePosition, and Encoding that enable you to view file information and methods such as ReadBase64, ReadBinHex, and ReadChars that simplify the handling of large blocks of data.

XmlValidatingReader provides document validation for XML documents. The XmlValidatingReader validates errors in an XML document against an XML schema, DTD, or XDR document. Delegates are registered with a ValidationEventHandler class. If no delegate is registered, an XmlException is thrown.

Figure 14.3 shows the class hierarchy of XmlReader, XmlWriter, and their descendants, including XmlSchemaCollection (which receives more attention later in this chapter).

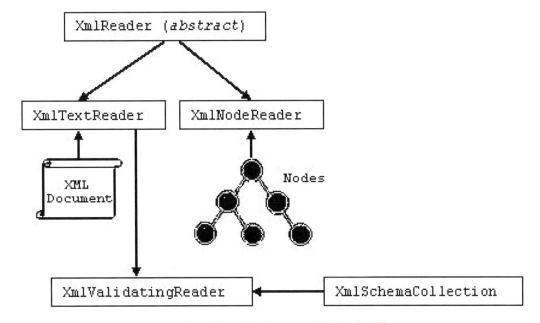

Figure 14.3:Relationship Between XmlReader Classes

XmlReader provides several methods for moving the cursor through the document stream. The most fundamental of these, the Read() method, walks through the stream in document order, one node at a time. An XmlException is thrown if there is an error in the way the XML is formed. XmlReader defines the following properties: Name, LocalName, Depth, NamespaceURI, NodeType, Value, HasAttributes, and AttributeCount. Some of these were covered in Table 14.3 and others will be illustrated in later examples.

The XmlTextReader class has different constructors to specify the location (e.g., the URL) of the XML data, as shown in Listing 14.12.

Listing 14.12—XmlTextReader

```
String URLString = @"http://www.mindcracker.com/library1.xml";

// Load the XmlTextReader from the URL
myXmlURLreader = new XmlTextReader(URLString);
```

The XmlTextReader provides fast read access to XML data, while implementing the W3C's XML 1.0 and Namespaces in XML specifications. The XmlTextReader provides constructors to read XML from a file, a stream, or a TextReader object. The Read method moves the reader sequentially through the nodes.

For element nodes, the value of an attribute can be obtained by using the index operators. Attributes are represented as a node list off the current node and can be traversed through the HasAttributes property. The Depth property reports the depth of the current node, which can be useful for formatting. Nodes at the root level are at depth 0.

When an XMLReader class is initialized, there is no current node, so the first call to Read() moves the reader to the first node in the document. When the Read method reaches the end of the document, it doesn't "walk off" and leave the reader in an indeterminate state; it simply returns false when there are no more nodes to process.

The Read method does not process attribute nodes because they are not regarded as part of the document's hierarchical structure. Attributes are typically considered metadata attached to structural elements. When the current node is an element, its attributes can be accessed through calls to GetAttribute by name or index. Listing 14.13 cycles through the attributes of an element sequentially by indexing each attribute.

Listing 14.13—XmlTextReader Reading Attributes

```
while(reader.Read())
{
    if (reader.NodeType == XmlNodeType.Element)
      // process all of the element's attributes
      for (int i=0; i<reader.AttributeCount; i++)
        Console.WriteLine(reader.GetAttribute(i));
}

/*
//you can also iterate through attributes like this:

while (reader.MoveToNextAttribute())
    Console.Write(" " + reader.Name + "='" + reader.Value + "'");
*/
```

While reading a document stream, it's possible to optimize entity node expansion. When the XML reader encounters a node of type EntityReference, it's up to the consumer to decide whether expansion is necessary by explicitly calling the ResolveEntity method. If the consumer doesn't call ResolveEntity, but rather continues with a subsequent Read call, the entity's replacement content is skipped. If ResolveEntity() is called, the replacement content is processed as everything else is, one node at a time. The XML reader also inserts an EndEntity node into the stream, making it possible for consumers to detect the end of the replacement content. Listing 14.14 shows how you can read entities and call the ResolveEntity method appropriately.

Listing 14.14—XmlTextReader Reading Elements

```
while (reader.Read())
{
  if (reader.NodeType == XmlNodeType.Element)
    Console.WriteLine(reader.Name);
  if (reader.NodeType == XmlNodeType.EntityReference)
  {
    Console.WriteLine("*** resolve entity called ***");
    // after this call, the reader
    // iterates over the entity's content.
    reader.ResolveEntity();
  }
  if (reader.NodeType == XmlNodeType.EndEntity)
    Console.WriteLine("*** end of current entity ***");
}
```

Running the code from Listing 14.14 against the XML document in Listing 14.15 will generate output to the console in listing 14.16.

Listing 14.15—XML Data for ResolveEntity

```
<!DOCTYPE person [
  <!ENTITY fl "<first>John</first><last>Rambo</last>">
]>
<person>
  <name>&fl;</name>
  <age>35</age>
</person>
```

Listing 14.16 contains the resultant output.

Listing 14.16—XML Converted Data

```
Person
name
*** resolve entity called ***
first
last
*** end of entity ***
age
```

Other than the sequential read operations, XmlReader also provides several methods for moving to specific nodes within the document stream. When positioned on an element node, the reader can move sideways through the attached attribute nodes by calling MoveToAttribute, MoveToFirstAttribute, and MoveToNextAttribute. You can also use the more convenient GetAttribute method mentioned earlier, but it returns attribute values only. Conversely, when positioned on an attribute node, you can move the reader back to the owner element node by calling MoveToElement. If you're positioned on a node that does not have content (one that has white space, comments, or processing instructions) but you want to move to the next content node (containing an element or text), you can use the handy MoveToContent method illustrated in Listing 14.17.

Listing 14.17—Read and MoveToContent Example

```
if(reader.Read())
{
  Console.WriteLine(reader.Name);
  reader.MoveToContent();
```

```
    Console.WriteLine(reader.Name);
}
```

Running the code from Listing 14.17 against the XML document in Listing 14.18 produces the following output to the console:

```
Skip
foo
```

Listing 14.18—Example XML Data for MoveToContent

```
<?skip me?>
<!--skip me too-->
<?and me too...?>

<goo>
  <bar/>
</goo>
```

Listing 14.19 illustrates how you could use the XmlTextReader class properties mentioned earlier—Depth, HasAttributes, and AttributeCount—depending on the XML node type. Here we use nodes of type Element and DocumentType. To execute this example, you need to have library1.xml, the XML document file we used in the first example in this chapter.

Listing 14.19— XmlTextReader Example

```
// XmlReader example

using System;
using System.Xml;

class TestMyApp
{
 public static XmlTextReader reader;
 public static string filename = "library1.xml";

 public static void Main()
 {
   try
    {
        reader = new XmlTextReader("library1.xml");
        while (reader.Read())
        {
        switch (reader.NodeType)
         {
           case XmlNodeType.Element: // The node is an Element
             Console.WriteLine("Element" + "<" + reader.Name + ">"
                            + reader.Value);
              Console.Write(reader.Depth + " ");
          Console.Write(reader.AttributeCount + " ");

           for (int i=0; i < reader.Depth; i++)
           {
                Console.Write('\t');
           }

          Console.Write(reader.Prefix + "Element" + "<"
                      + reader.Name + ">" + reader.Value);

           if (reader.HasAttributes)
           {
            Console.Write(" Attributes:");

            for (int j=0; j < reader.AttributeCount; j++)
```

```
      {
       Console.Write(" [{0}] " + reader[j], j);
      }
     }

   Console.WriteLine();
   break;
  case XmlNodeType.DocumentType: // The node is a DocumentType
    Console.WriteLine("DocumentType" + "<" +
        reader.Name + ">" + reader.Value);
   Console.Write(reader.Depth + " ");

  Console.Write(reader.AttributeCount + " ");

  for (int i=0; i < reader.Depth; i++)
  {
   Console.Write('\t');
  }

  Console.Write(reader.Prefix + "DocumentType" + "<" +
        reader.Name + ">" + reader.Value);

  if (reader.HasAttributes)
  {
   Console.Write(" Attributes:");

   for (int j=0; j < reader.AttributeCount; j++)
   {
    Console.Write(" [{0}] " + reader[j], j);
   }
  }

    Console.WriteLine();
    break;
   }
  }
 }
 catch(XmlException e)
 {
        Console.WriteLine("###error: " + e.Message);
 }
 finally
 {
        Console.WriteLine("\r\ndone {0} ...", filename);
        if (reader != null)
                reader.Close();
 }
    }
   }
}
```

XML Writer Classes

The XmlWriter class has various base methods and properties for writing XML content. Like XmlReader, XmlWriter is an abstract class that defines the basic functionality of its derivative classes, XmlTextWriter and XmlNodeWriter. These implementations are just like the XmlReader counterparts except that they *produce* data streams rather than read them. Figure 14.4 illustrates the relationship between the XmlWriter classes

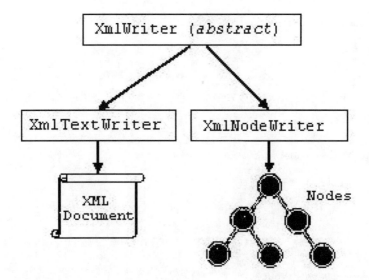

Figure 14.4: XmlWriter Classes and Their Relationship to Each Other

XmlTextWriter lets you write XML documents that conform to the W3C's XML 1.0 specification and Namespaces in XML specification. The XmlTextWriter provides constructors to write XML to a file, a stream, or a TextWriter.

The XmlNodeWriter class is designed to write to in-memory XML DOM trees. Each XML node type has corresponding XML write methods provided by this class.

XmlWriter checks that the generated content is well formed but does not validate the content. The XmlWriter class provides many methods; the most common ones are included among the class members listed in Table 14.4.

XmlWriter Members	Description
Close()	Closes the streams opened for writing.
Flush()	Immediately sends whatever is in the buffers to the streams.
WriteAttributes()	Writes out all the attributes found at the current element of the specified XmlReader.
WriteAttributeString()	Writes an attribute at the current position in the stream with the string that is passed.
WriteBinHex()	Takes an array of bytes and encodes them into binary hex, then writes the resulting string to the stream.
WriteCData()	Constructs the *<![CDATA[...]]>* section with the specified text and writes this block.
WriteChars()	Writes the specified number of characters from the buffer.
WriteComment()	Constructs a comment section *<!--...-->* with the specified text and writes this block.
WriteElementString()	Writes the element and its text.
WriteEndAttribute()	Used to close the recent WriteStartAttribute invocation.

XmlWriter Members	Description
WriteEndDocument()	Used to close the recent WriteStartDocument invocation.
WriteEndElement()	Closes the element markup tag with the namespace prefix. With no data content in the current element it writes a short end tag, />; otherwise it writes a full end tag, such as </element1>.
WriteFullEndElement()	Closes the element markup tag with the namespace prefix. Regardless of data content in the current element, it always writes a full end tag, such as </element1>.
WriteNode()	Copies the node from an XmlReader to the XmlWriter object and advances the reader to the next element.
WriteProcessingInstruction()	Writes a processing instruction with a space between the name and text.
WriteQualifiedName()	Constructs a section <?...?> with the specified text and writes this block.
WriteRaw()	Writes the markup without special characters. For example, while WriteString(">") writes >, WriteRaw(">") writes > to the writer.
WriteStartAttribute()	Starts an attribute write operation.
WriteStartDocument()	Starts an XML declaration write operation.
WriteStartElement()	Starts an element write operation.
WriteString()	Writes the text in the current write cursor context.
WriteWhitespace()	Writes a text of white spaces. Used mostly for manual document formatting.

Table 14.4: XmlWriter Class Members

The following list summarizes the functions of some prominent members of the XmlWriter class:

- XmlWriter provides write methods such as WriteStartElement, WriteEndElement, WriteString, and WriteComment for the various node types.
- WriteElementString writes a start tag, end tag, and character child in a single call.
- WriteDocType method supports writing DTD entries.
- WriteRaw method allows pass-through writing of raw XML, but the writer does not check how well formed the raw XML is.
- XmlWriter provides formatting control through properties such as Formatting, Indentation, IndentChar, and QuoteChar.
- XmlWriter has methods such as WriteBase64, WriteBinHex, and WriteChars to simplify the handling of large blocks of data.

Let's take a look at an XmlTextWriter example. Listing 14.20 shows you how to create an XML library document using the XmlTextWriter class. The paragraphs after the listing explain how the example uses some of the methods and properties described in Table 14.4.

Listing 14.20—XmlTextWriter Example

```
// XmlTextWriter example

namespace www.mindcracker.com
{
    using System;
```

```csharp
using System.IO;
using System.Xml;

public class WriteXmlFileExample
{
        private const string filename = "library2.xml";

        public static void Main()
        {
                XmlTextWriter writer = null;
                XmlTextReader reader = null;

                try
                {
                writer = new XmlTextWriter (filename,
                null);
                writer.Formatting = Formatting.Indented;
                writer.Namespaces = true;
                writer.Indentation = 4;
                writer.WriteStartDocument(false);
                writer.WriteDocType("library", null,
                        "library.dtd", null);
                writer.WriteComment("another section of a
                        library");
                writer.WriteStartElement("library");
                writer.WriteStartElement("book", null);
            writer.WriteAttributeString("book_number",
                                    "1203");
          writer.WriteAttributeString("ISBN","8888888");
                writer.WriteElementString("title", null,
                            "Title3");
                writer.WriteStartElement("author", null);
                writer.WriteElementString("first-name",
                                "fname3");
                writer.WriteElementString("last-name", "lname3");
                writer.WriteEndElement();
                writer.WriteElementString("photo", "photo3.jpg");
                writer.WriteEndElement();
                writer.WriteEndElement();
                writer.Flush();
                writer.Close();
                }
                catch (XmlException e)
                {
                Console.WriteLine ("Exception: {0}",
                            e.ToString());
                }
                finally
                {
                        Console.WriteLine("\r\ndone {0} ...",
                                    filename);
                    if (reader != null)
                    reader.Close();
                    if (writer != null)
                    writer.Close();
                }
        }

}
}
```

First, the Formatting property of the XmlTextWriter sets the output to be formatted. This causes child elements to be indented using the Indentation property in this example, although you can also use the IndentChar property. The XML declaration with the version "1.0" contained inside is written with the WriteStartDocument method.

The WriteStartDocument method starts a new document. The WriteStartElement and WriteEndElement method pairs are used signal the addition and finalization, respectively, of new elements to the document. The WriteString writes a string to the document.

The Flush method causes any remaining data in memory to be written to a file. Only the Close method is really required to flush a file; however, on occasion, the generated XML needs to be made persistent without closing the file so the writer can continue to use the XMLWriter instance from the persisted state.

The XML document file in Listing 14.21 is produced after the code in Listing 14.20 executes.

Listing 14.21—Library2.xml, XML Data

```
<?xml version="1.0" standalone="no"?>
<!DOCTYPE library SYSTEM "library.dtd">
<!--another section of a library-->
<library>
    <book book_number="1203" ISBN="8888888">
        <title>Title3</title>
        <author>
            <first-name>fname3</first-name>
            <last-name>lname3</last-name>
        </author>
        <photo>photo3.jpg</photo>
    </book>
</library>
```

Validating XML

Validation is the process of enforcing rules on the XML content either against a DocumentDTD or a schema. You can validate your XML data through a DTD or an XDR schema file using the XmlValidatingReader class. The type of validation required—Auto, None, DTD, Schema, or XDR—is set through the ValidationType property of XmlValidatingReader. The ValidationEventHandle property must be set with a ValidationEventHandler class to receive notification of validation errors.

Listing 14.22 shows how to validate XML against a DTD document using the XmlValidatingReader.

Listing 14.22—XmlValidatingReader of Type DTD

```
XmlTextReader myXmlTextReader = new XmlTextReader(document1);
XmlValidatingReader myXmlValidatingReader = new
XmlValidatingReader(myXmlTextReader);
myXmlValidatingReader.ValidationType = ValidationType.DTD;
```

The XML parser does not stop when it encounters a validation error; it stops only if it finds data that is not well formed. This way, you can find all the validation errors in one pass without having to parse the XML document repeatedly.

To illustrate validation, we have constructed an example that checks the XML in the users.xml file (in Listing 14.23) against two XDR files. (Listings 14.24 and 14.25). The validation routine in Listing 14.26 performs this validation and reports errors. First, take a quick look at the XML file.

Listing 14.23—Users.xml, XML Data

```
<?xml version="1.0"?>
<x:Users xmlns:x="x-schema:Users.xdr" xmlns:y="x-schema:UsersActive.xdr">
  <x:User Role="Bozo" y:Active="1">
```

```
    <x:first-name>Hursit</x:first-name>
    <x:last-name>Yenigun</x:last-name>
    <x:user-name>hursity</x:user-name>
  </x:User>
</x:Users>
```

Next, let's look at the individual XDR schema files, which are actually XML documents. The general structure used for XDR schemas includes the Schema start tag, which indicates the root element. The name of the schema is contained in the name attribute. The Schema start tag includes two namespaces: one for structures and the other for defining the data types used in the schema. Each ElementType element declares an element and indicates its contents. Attributes are declared with the AttributeType element. After attributes are declared for each element, they must be placed using the attribute element. The element indicates the elements that can be placed inside the element.

Listing 14.24 presents the first XDR file, called users.xdr.

Listing 14.24—Users.xdr, XDR File

```
<?xml version="1.0"?>
<Schema xmlns="urn:schemas-microsoft-com:xml-data" xmlns:dt="urn:schemas-microsoft-
com:datatypes">
  <ElementType name="first-name" content="textOnly"/>
  <ElementType name="last-name" content="textOnly"/>
  <ElementType name="user-name" content="textOnly"/>
  <AttributeType name="Role"/>
  <ElementType name="User" content="eltOnly" model="open">
    <attribute type="Role" required="yes"/>
    <group order="seq">
      <element type="first-name"/>
      <element type="last-name"/>
      <element type="user-name"/>
    </group>
  </ElementType>
  <ElementType name="Users">
    <element type="User"/>
  </ElementType>
</Schema>
```

Listing 14.25 contains the other XDR file, usersactive.xdr.

Listing 14.25—Usersactive.xdr, XDR File

```
<?xml version="1.0"?>
<Schema xmlns="urn:schemas-microsoft-com:xml-data" xmlns:dt="urn:schemas-microsoft-
com:datatypes">
  <AttributeType name="Active"/>
</Schema>
```

Listing 14.26 validates the users.xml document against the users.xdr and usersactive.xdr schemas and reports validation errors via the ValidationHandler method.

Listing 14.26— ValidationEventHandler XDR Schema

```
// validating XML document against an XDR schema
using System;
using System.IO;
using System.Xml;
using System.Xml.Schema;

namespace XMLValidation
{
```

```
class XDRExample
{
    public static void Main()
    {
      XmlTextReader tr = new XmlTextReader("Users.xml");
      XmlValidatingReader vr = new XmlValidatingReader(tr);
      vr.ValidationType = ValidationType.XDR;
      vr.ValidationEventHandler += new
              ValidationEventHandler(ValidationHandler);
      while(vr.Read());
      Console.WriteLine("Validation Finished");
      vr.Close();
    }

    static void ValidationHandler(Object sender,
            ValidationEventArgs args)
    {
      Console.WriteLine("***Validation Error***");
      Console.WriteLine("\tSeverity:\t{0}", args.Severity);
      Console.WriteLine("\tMessage:\t{0}", args.Message);
    }
  }
}
```

Any validation error that occurs in the example will call the handler method that was set by the ValidationEventHandler class before the XML document was read. If this handler method is not provided, XmlValidatingReader throws an XmlSchema exception after the first validation error. The success variable indicates the validation state.

If you want to validate your XML document against an XML schema, you may use the code shown in Listing 14.29. The most significant difference is that the ValidationType property is changed to Schema. Listing 14.27 contains the XML document to be validated in this example.

Listing 14.27—Holdings.xml, Sample XML Document

```
<?xml version="1.0"?>
<account xmlns="http://www.mindcracker.com"
xmlns:xsi="http://www.w3.org/2001/XMLSchema-instance"
xsi:schemaLocation="http://www.mindcracker.com account.xsd">
        <holding>
          <security>
            <symbol>msft</symbol>
            <industry>technology</industry>
          </security>
          <position>
            <purchaseDate>2002-04-19</purchaseDate>
            <purchasePrice>100.75</purchasePrice>
          </position>
          <position>
            <purchaseDate>2002-04-19</purchaseDate>
            <purchasePrice>100.75</purchasePrice>
          </position>
        </holding>
</account>
```

Listing 14.28 contains the XML schema to be used for validation.

Listing 14.28—Account.xsd, Sample XML Schema

```
<?xml version="1.0" ?>
<xsd:schema xmlns:xsd="http://www.w3.org/2001/XMLSchema" xmlns:dt="urn:schemas-
microsoft-com:datatypes" targetNamespace="http://www.mindcracker.com"
xmlns="http://www.mindcracker.com" elementFormDefault="qualified">
        <xsd:element name="account" type="accountType"/>
```

```xsd
<xsd:complexType name="accountType">
        <xsd:sequence>
                <xsd:element name="holding" type="holdingType"
                  minOccurs="0" maxOccurs="unbounded"/>
        </xsd:sequence>
</xsd:complexType>
<xsd:complexType name="holdingType">
        <xsd:sequence>
                <xsd:element name="security"
                        type="securityType"/>
                <xsd:element name="position" type="positionType"
                minOccurs="1" maxOccurs="unbounded"/>
        </xsd:sequence>
</xsd:complexType>
<xsd:complexType name="securityType">
        <xsd:sequence>
                <xsd:element name="symbol" type="xsd:string"
                minOccurs="1"/>
                <xsd:element name="industry" type="xsd:string"/>
        </xsd:sequence>
</xsd:complexType>
<xsd:complexType name="positionType">
        <xsd:sequence>
                <xsd:element name="purchaseDate"
                type="xsd:date"/>
                <xsd:element name="purchasePrice"
                type="xsd:decimal"/>
        </xsd:sequence>
</xsd:complexType>
</xsd:schema>
```

The code in Listing 14.29 validates the holdings.xml document against the account.xsd schema.

Listing 14.29— Validate Against an XML Document and XML Schema

```csharp
using System;
using System.IO;
using System.Xml;
using System.Xml.Schema;

namespace XMLValidation
{
    class XDRExample
    {
        public static void Main()
        {
            XmlTextReader tr = new
            XmlTextReader("holdings.xml");
            XmlValidatingReader vr = new
            XmlValidatingReader(tr);
            vr.ValidationType = ValidationType.Schema;
            vr.ValidationEventHandler += new
        ValidationEventHandler(ValidationHandler);
            while(vr.Read());
            Console.WriteLine("Validation Finished");
            vr.Close();
        }

        static void ValidationHandler(Object sender,
            ValidationEventArgs args)
        {
            Console.WriteLine("***Validation Error***");
            Console.WriteLine("\tSeverity:\t{0}",
             args.Severity);
            Console.WriteLine("\tMessage:\t{0}",
             args.Message);
```

```
        }
    }
}
```

Navigation in XML Documents

The System.Xml.XPath namespace contains the XPath parser and evaluation engine. You use three classes to navigate through XML documents with XPath expressions, XPathNavigator, XPathDocument, and XPathExpression:

- XPathNavigator reads data from any data store using a cursor model.
- XPathDocument provides a fast cache for XML document processing using XSLT.
- XPathExpression encapsulates a compiled XPath expression. An instance of an XPathExpression is returned from a call to the Compile method of XPathNavigator. The XPathExpression object is used by the Select, Evaluate, and Matches methods of XPathNavigator.

Figure 14.5 shows how you can use XPathNavigator over any kind of XML data store in the .NET Framework, giving you great flexibility. Note that the XmlDocument, XmlDataDocument, and XPathDocument classes implement the IXPathNavigable interface, and all three implement and provide the CreateNavigator method for creating an XPathNavigator. By utilizing the XPathNavigator class, you can use XPath to access XmlDocument, XPathDocument, and XmlDataDocument data stores.

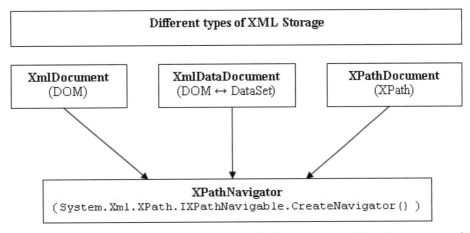

Figure 14.5: Relationship of XPathNavigator, XmlDocument, XmlDataDocument, and XPathDocument

The XPathDocument class provides a fast cache for XML document processing using XSLT and XPath. You use the XPathDocument constructor to create an instance of XPathDocument, which has various overridables. These overloads include constructors that you can pass in an XmlReader, a TextReader, or even an XML filename to create your XPathDocument. For example, the following line creates an XPathDocument from an XML file:

```
XPathDocument xmlDoc = new
            XPathDocument(@"C:\LargeXmlDocument.xml");
```

The XPathNavigator class implements the functionality to navigate through a document with convenient methods. Below we create an instance of XPathNavigator by calling XPathDocument's CreateNavigator method:

```
XPathNavigator navigator = xmlDoc.CreateNavigator();
```

The XPathDocument is geared to XPathNavigator methods, such as these:

- SelectAncestors—selects all the ancestor element nodes of the current node matching the selection criteria
- SelectDescendants—selects all the descendant nodes of the current node matching the selection criteria
- SelectChildren—selects all the child nodes of the current node matching the selection criteria
- ComparePosition—determines one node position in relation to another using fast pointer-based arithmetic internally rather than the XPathNavigator Move methods

If you use the XPathNavigator class, try to use the XPathDocument class navigator creation method for faster XML iterations rather than the XmlDocument and XmlDataDocument implementations of this method.

The XPathNavigator's navigation cursor is controlled by the MoveTo methods which allow you to traverse through an XPath document. For example MoveToRoot moves the navigation cursor to the root node of the current node, MoveToParent moves the navigation cursor to the parent of the current node, and MoveToFirstChild moves the navigation cursor to the first child of the current node. You can use MoveToFirst to move the navigation cursor to the first sibling of the current node, MoveToNext to move the navigation cursor to the next sibling of the current node, and MoveToPrevious to move the navigation cursor back to the previous sibling of the current node. Additional methods such as MoveToFirstAttribute moves the navigation cursor to the first attribute of the current node and MoveToNextAttribute moves the navigation cursor to the next attribute of the current node.

Listing 14.30 illustrates how to navigate records with XPath style access. The Select method applies the XPath query to the XML document. We can use XPath expressions to evaluate expressions like the ones in this listing. (There are overloads for Select and Evaluate methods of XPathNavigator to accept XPathExpression. We will talk about the XPathExpression class later.). The Evaluate function of the XPathNavigator class evaluates a given XPath expression and returns the result, by either selecting the relevant nodes or converting the relevant nodes, or applying a function to the relevant nodes. Evaluate is mostly useful in adhoc and aggregate query operations on XML tree nodes. Evaluate can be used to return the sum of the values in a set of nodes, the number of nodes in a node set, and the arithmetic average of the values contained in a set of nodes.

Listing 14.30—XPath Evaluation

```
// evaluate an XPath expression
// to count the total price for products.
Object obj = nav.Evaluate("count(//*[local-name()='UnitPrice'])");
// evaluate an XPath expression to calculate total sheeps.
double total = (double) nav.Evaluate("sum(//sheeps)");
```

The XPathNavigator current cursor is controlled by using MoveTo methods like MoveToRoot, MoveToParent, MoveToFirstChild, MoveToFirst, MoveToPrevious, MoveToNext, MoveToFirstAttribute, and MoveToNextAttribute.

Table 14.5 shows some XPathNavigator class members.

XPathNavigator Members	Description
HasAttributes	Returns a Boolean value: *true* if the element node has attributes; *false* otherwise.
HasChildren	Returns *true* if the element node has child nodes. Otherwise returns *false*. Applies only to Root and Element node types.
IsEmptyElement	Returns *true* if the current node is an empty element like *<element1/>* with no value. Otherwise returns *false*.
Value	Returns the content inside the node.
Compile()	Creates an XpathExpression object based on the passed XPath expression string.
Evaluate()	Evaluates an XPath expression string or XpathExpression object and returns either a Boolean, string, or node list resulting from the expression.
GetAttribute()	Returns the content of the attribute specified with LocalName and NamespaceURI parameters in the element node.
MoveTo()	Moves the navigator cursor to the same position as XPathNavigator parameter passed.
MoveToAttribute()	Moves the navigator cursor to the attribute specified with LocalName and NamespaceURI parameters in the element node.
MoveToFirst()	Moves the navigator cursor to the first node at the same level.
MoveToFirstAttribute()	Moves the navigator cursor to the first attribute in the element node.
MoveToFirstChild()	Moves the navigator cursor to the first child node of the current cursor position.
MoveToId()	Moves to the node that has an attribute matching the passed ID string. The ID attribute should be marked in the DTD to use this method.
MoveToNext()	Moves the navigator cursor to the next node at the same level.
MoveToNextAttribute()	Moves the navigator cursor to the next attribute in the element node.
MoveToNextNamespace()	Moves the XPathNavigator to the next namespace node.
MoveToParent()	Moves the navigator cursor to the parent node of the current node.
MoveToPrevious()	Moves the cursor to the previous node at the same level as the current node.
MoveToRoot()	Moves the navigator cursor to the root node.
Select()	Returns an XPathIterator with the contents filtered with the XPath expression string or XPathExpression object passed as a parameter.
SelectAncestors()	Returns an XPathIterator with contents of the ancestor nodes of the current node.
SelectChildren()	Returns an XPathIterator with contents of the child nodes of the current node.

XPathNavigator Members	Description
SelectDescendants()	Returns an XPathIterator with contents of all of the descendant nodes of the current node.

Table 14.5: XPathNavigator Members

Listing 14.31 shows you how to recursively traverse an XML tree via XPathNavigator—a sample that could be quite helpful in your .NET projects.

Listing 14.31—Walking in an XML Tree

```
// XPathNavigator tree walk example

using System;
using System.IO;
using System.Xml;
using System.Xml.Schema;
using System.Xml.XPath;

class MainClass
{

 public static void Main(string[] args)
 {
  String strXMLPath  = "library1.xml";
  XPathDocument objXMLDataDoc = new XPathDocument(strXMLPath);

  XPathNavigator nav = objXMLDataDoc.CreateNavigator();
  TreeXPathWalk(nav);
 }

// XML Tree Walk with XPathNavigator
public static void TreeXPathWalk(XPathNavigator nav)
{
  Console.WriteLine("Type: {0}\tName: {1}\tValue: {2}",
          nav.NodeType, nav.Name, nav.Value);
  if (nav.HasAttributes)
  {
    while (nav.MoveToNextAttribute())
    Console.WriteLine("\tAttr: {0}={1}",
        nav.Name, nav.Value);
  }

  if (nav.HasChildren)
  {
    nav.MoveToFirstChild();
    TreeXPathWalk(nav);
    nav.MoveToParent();
  }

  if (nav.MoveToNext())
    TreeXPathWalk(nav);
 }
}
```

Listing 14.32 shows how to use the XPathNavigator class to search for a specific element inside an XML document. This listing is also recursive and finds all occurrences of the author element.

Listing 14.32—XPathNavigator: Searching for an Element

```
// XPathNavigator searching for an element example
```

```
using System;
using System.IO;
using System.Xml;
using System.Xml.Schema;
using System.Xml.XPath;

class MainClass
{
    public static void Main()
    {
     String strXMLPath = "library1.xml";
     XPathDocument objXMLDataDoc = new XPathDocument(strXMLPath);
     XPathNavigator objXPNav = objXMLDataDoc.CreateNavigator();
     objXPNav.MoveToRoot();
     Console.WriteLine(SearchForElement(objXPNav, "author"));
    }

    public static string SearchForElement(XPathNavigator objXPNav,
 String strNodeName)
    {
     String strResults = "";
     do
     {
         if(objXPNav.Name == strNodeName)
         {
             objXPNav.MoveToFirstChild();
             strResults += objXPNav.Value + "\r\n";
             objXPNav.MoveToParent();
         }
         if(objXPNav.HasChildren)
         {
             objXPNav.MoveToFirstChild();
             strResults += SearchForElement(objXPNav, strNodeName);
             objXPNav.MoveToParent();
         }
     } while(objXPNav.MoveToNext());

     return strResults;
    }
}
```

Precompiled XPathExpression

If you have a frequently used XPath query expression, then there is a performance gain in using compiled expressions in your queries. The XPath queries can also be performed using an XPathExpression class, which provides an interface for namespace-prefixed queries in XPath. There are two main reasons for using the XPathExpression class over using the string expression in the Select method for querying your XML document. First, the expression is compiled only once and can be reused several times, thus improving performance. Second, prefixes used in the XPath expression can be bound to a namespace using an XmlNamespaceManager class. This manager class allows for prefixed XPath expressions when selecting a set of nodes.

We develop code that utilizes the XPathExpression class in the following order:

- Compile and generate an XPathExpression instance.
- Create an XmlNamespaceManager instance.
- Call AddNamespace for each namespace prefix that will be used in the XPathExpression class.
- Call SetContext on the XPathExpression instance and pass in the namespace manager.
- To execute the expression, call Select and pass in the XPathExpression instance.

Table 14.6 lists some System.Xml.XPath.XPathExpression class members:

XPathExpression Members	Description
Expression	Returns the XPathExpression as a string. Used for diagnostic purposes or for passing this string to any method that requires a String type.
ReturnType	Gets the result type of the XPathExpression.
AddSort()	Sorts the nodes filtered with the XPath expression using either the IComparer interface or by passing a set of sorting criteria parameters.
Clone()	Returns a duplicate of the XPathExpression.
SetContext()	Sets an XmlNamespaceManager to be used to resolve namespaces. The XmlNamespaceManager resolves namespaces from prefixes that are mapped to them.

Table 14.6: XPathExpression Members

The XPathNodeIterator class represents a cursor over the selected node set. It allows you to access XPath nodes that will be utilized by the XPathNavigator methods. All of the Select, SelectChildren, SelectDescendants, and SelectAncestors methods of the XPathNavigator class return an XPathNodeIterator object. We will use the XPathNodeIterator class in the next two listings with the Select method of the XPathNavigator class.

The XPathNodeIterator class provides a few members. Here are the important ones:

- The MoveNext method advances the XPath node cursor.
- The Current property returns an XPathNavigator positioned at the current node.
- The Count property returns the index of the last node in the selected set of nodes. It clones the XPathNodeIterator, so that it does not change the current position, and then walks through the node set.

Listing 14.33 implements a query utilizing XPathExpression and walks through the selected node list. In this example, we are selecting all the books whose sales rank greater than 1,000 copies.

Listing 14.33—Using an XPathNodeIterator to Walk Through a Selected Set of Nodes

```
// first compile the expression
XPathExpression expr = nav.Compile("book/@mybk:SalesRank > 1000");

// set namespaces used in the expression
XmlNamespaceManager mngr = new XmlNamespaceManager(new NameTable());
mngr.AddNamespace("mybk", "urn:examples");
expr.SetContext(mngr);

// select the nodes and iterate through them
XPathNodeIterator nodes = nav.Select(expr);

while (nodes.MoveNext())
{
    XPathNavigator classNav = nodes.Current;
    classNav.MoveToAttribute("name", "");
    Console.WriteLine("Class: {0}", classNav.Value);
}
```

Now we will develop a complete listing to further explain the XPathExpression topic. We will use the XML document shown in Listing 14.34.

Listing 14.34—XML Document with lb Namespace

```xml
<?xml version="1.0"?>
<library xmlns:lb="urn:mcbsamples">
        <book lb:book_number="1201">
                <author>Author1</author>
                <title>Title1</title>
                <photo src="photo1.jpg"/>
        </book>
        <book lb:book_number="1202">
                <author>Author2</author>
                <title>Title2</title>
                <photo src="photo2.jpg"/>
        </book>
</library>
```

Listing 14.35 selects specific XPath nodes and then outputs them to the console. The XPath expression, */library/book/@lb:book_number,* is an absolute location path and selects the node in two steps. Starting at the document root, the first step selects the *<library>* document element. The next step selects the *<book>* child elements of the *<library>* element. Within the book elements, this step selects the *book_number* attribute in the *lb* namespace.

Listing 14.35—XPathExpression Class Illustration Sample

```csharp
// XPathExpression sample
using System;
using System.IO;
using System.Xml;
using System.Xml.XPath;

public class MainClass
{
  public static void Main()
  {

      XPathDocument doc = new XPathDocument("library1919.xml");
      XPathNavigator nav = doc.CreateNavigator();
      XPathExpression expr =
        nav.Compile("/library/book/@lb:book_number");
      XmlNamespaceManager nsmgr = new
            XmlNamespaceManager(nav.NameTable);
      nsmgr.AddNamespace("lb", "urn:mcbsamples");
      expr.SetContext(nsmgr);
      XPathNodeIterator iterator = nav.Select(expr);
      while (iterator.MoveNext())
      {
        Console.WriteLine(iterator.Current.ToString());
      }
    }
}
```

XML and ADO.NET

You can construct the XmlDataDocument class from a data set to provide an XML API into the relational data. Data that is entered through DataSet relation methods can be accessed via XML methods on the XmlDataDocument class. You can save XML data over the data set using the WriteXml and WriteXmlSchema methods. The Dataset.WriteXml method saves a normalized view of the relationally mapped data to an XML document with or without a schema. The Dataset.WriteXmlSchema method creates the corresponding XML schema for the data set.

XmlDataDocument provides that same functionality in ADO.NET. The XmlDataDocument class is inherited from the XmlDocument class (the .NET version of the W3C-DOM), so it is a full-blown representation of the XML document. But unlike XmlDocument, XmlDataDocument is a special kind of DOM. XmlDataDocument can be loaded with schema mappings, and that schema is used at load time to determine how to map the document relationally. When the document is loaded, the relational subset can be obtained using the DataSet property on the XmlDataDocument class.

Figure 14.6 depicts the relationship among various XML.NET classes.

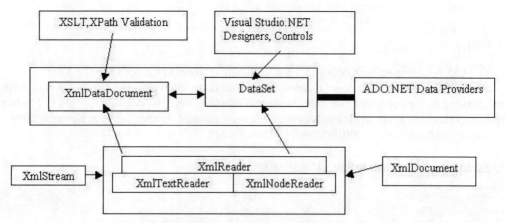

Figure 14.6: XML Classes Hierarchy

You can navigate any data set using the foreach control structure—as in the code segment in Listing 14.36. We will use this traversing technique for data sets later in the examples.

Listing 14.36—Database Objects Navigation

```
foreach(DataTable table in dataset.Tables)
{
        foreach(DataColumn column in table.Columns)
        {
        }
        foreach(DataRow row in table.Rows)
        {
                foreach(Object value in row.ItemArray)
                {
                }

        }
}
```

Reading and Writing XML Documents Using a DataSet

The DataSet class is the juncture point between XML and ADO.NET. We can create a DataSet object because we are in a relational database environment. Then we can convert it to XML easily with methods provided by the DataSet class. The WriteXml method writes the current data (schema and data) of a DataSet object to an XML file. Figure 14.7 depicts the relationships among the XmlReader, XmlWriter, DataSet, and XmlDataDocument classes.

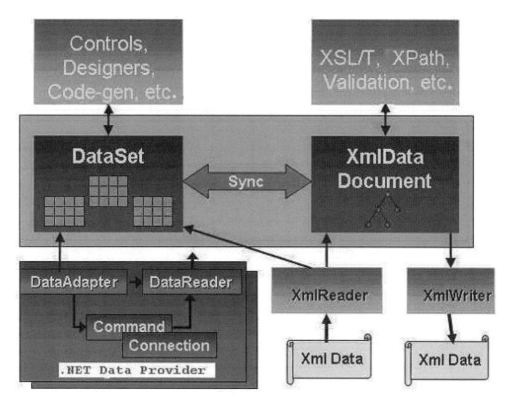

Figure 14.7: XML documents and DataSet relationships

XmlDataDocument Class

The XmlDataDocument class allows structured data to be stored, retrieved, and manipulated through a relational data set. The XmlDataDocument class provides an in-memory cache for XML data. XmlDataDocument extends the XmlDocument class, and XmlDataDocument can be used anywhere the XmlDocument class is used. The XmlDataDocument can be thought of as a DataSet-aware XmlDocument class.

Table 14.7 lists some of the XmlDataDocument class members.

XmlDataDocument Members	Description
Attributes	Returns a collection comprised of attributes of the node.
ChildNodes	Returns the children of the node as a node list.
DataSet	Returns a data set that can be used to access the XML data in a relational model.
FirstChild	Returns the first child node of the node.
HasChildNodes	Returns *true* if the node has child nodes
InnerText	Gets or sets the values of the contents of the node without the markup tags.
InnerXml	Gets or sets the XML children node text, including the markup tags and attributes representing this node.

XmlDataDocument Members	Description
IsReadOnly	Returns *true* if the node is read-only.
LastChild	Returns the last child node of the node.
NextSibling	Returns the node following this node.
OuterXml	The contents of the current node and its child nodes.
ParentNode	Gets the parent node of the node.
Prefix	Used to get and set the namespace prefix of the node.
PreviousSibling	Returns the previous node of the node at the same level.
Value	Gets or sets a string representing the value of the node. The contents returned depends upon how NodeType is set.
AppendChild	Appends the specified node to the end of the child node list.
CloneNode	Duplicates the node to the specified depth. Pass *true* to duplicate the node and all of its subnodes.
CreateAttribute	Creates a new XmlAttribute object
CreateCDataSection	Creates a new XmlCDataSection object
CreateComment	Creates a new XmlComment.
CreateDocumentFragment	Creates a new XmlDocumentFragment.
CreateDocumentType	Creates a new XmlDocumentType object.
CreateElement	Creates a new XmlElement object.
CreateEntityReference	Creates a new XmlEntityReference object.
CreateNavigator	Returns an XPathNavigator object that is positioned on the node.
CreateNode	Creates an XmlNode. You need to call AppendChild or a similar method to add the node to the document.
CreateProcessingInstruction	Creates an XmlProcessingInstruction.
CreateSignificantWhitespace	Creates an XmlSignificantWhitespace node.
CreateTextNode	Creates a new XmlText with the specified text.
CreateWhitespace	Creates a new XmlWhitespace node.
CreateXmlDeclaration	Creates a new XmlDeclaration node.
GetElementById	Gets the XmlElement with the specified ID.
GetElementFromRow	Returns an XmlElement object that is specified with a DataRow object.
GetElementsByTagName	Returns an XmlNodeList of the nodes matching the element name in the current node descendants.
GetEnumerator	Returns an object that implements the IEnumerator interface.
GetRowFromElement	Returns a DataRow object that is specified with an XmlElement object.

XmlDataDocument Members	Description
Load	Loads the current document object with data from a data source.
LoadXml	Loads the current document object with XML data passed as a string parameter.
PrependChild	Adds the XmlNode object to the beginning of the node list of children.
ReadNode	Returns a new XmlNode object from an XmlReader object.
RemoveAll	Removes all child nodes of the node.
RemoveChild	Removes the passed child node.
ReplaceChild	Replaces the old child node with a new node.
Save	Serializes the document.
SelectNodes	Returns a list of nodes that are filtered with the XPath expression
SelectSingleNode	Returns the first node that is filtered with the XPath expression.
WriteContentTo	Serializes the child nodes of the node to an XmlWriter object.
WriteTo	Serializes the document to an XmlWriter object.

Table 14.7: XmlDataDocument Members

Listing 14.37 constructs an XML data document from a data set filled from an OLE DB data provider. The data set is filled based on an SQL query to an Access table called *days* and then used to produce an XML representation of the database table in the XML data document. An XPathNavigator is then created from the XML data document so that we can navigate the XML data. Note that data that has been loaded into an XML data document can also be accessed via the relational methods in the DataSet property.

The database used in Listing 14.37 uses a Microsoft Access database called cards.mdb representing a collection of holiday cards. cards.mdb contains a table called days with the columns id, day , and description.

Listing 14.37—XmlDataDocument and Data Sets

```
// XmlDataDocument and ADO.NET integration

namespace www.mindcracker.com
{

 using System;
 using System.Xml;
 using System.Xml.XPath;
 using System.Data.OleDb;
 using System.IO;
 using System.Data;

 public class LoadDataSetXMLDataExample
  {
    private XmlDataDocument datadoc = null;
    private string ConnectionString = @"Provider=Microsoft.JET.OLEDB.4.0;
Data Source=C:\work\14\cards.mdb";
    private string XmlDataFile = @"c:\work\14\library4.xml";
```

```csharp
    private string XmlSchemaFile = @"c:\work\14\library4.xsd";

    public LoadDataSetXMLDataExample()
    {
        try
        {
            OleDbConnection mySqlConnection = new
             OleDbConnection(ConnectionString);
              mySqlConnection.Open();
              OleDbDataAdapter mySqlDataAdapter =
            new OleDbDataAdapter(@"select * from days",
                                  mySqlConnection);
            DataSet dsDays = new DataSet();
            mySqlDataAdapter.Fill(dsDays, "days");

            // Auto convert Relational data to XML data!!!
            datadoc = new XmlDataDocument(dsDays);

            datadoc.DataSet.WriteXml(XmlDataFile,
            XmlWriteMode.IgnoreSchema);
            datadoc.DataSet.WriteXmlSchema(XmlSchemaFile);

            datadoc = new XmlDataDocument();

            try
            {
                Console.WriteLine("Reading Schema file ...");
                datadoc.DataSet.ReadXmlSchema(XmlSchemaFile);
                datadoc.Load(XmlDataFile);
            }
            catch (Exception e)
            {
                Console.WriteLine ("Exception: {0}",
                                   e.ToString());
            }
            finally
            {
            }

            // navigate through the xml data via XPathNavigator
            XPathNavigator docnav = datadoc.CreateNavigator();
            WalkNavigator(docnav);
        }
        catch(Exception e)
        {
            Console.WriteLine ("Exception: {0}", e.ToString());
        }
    }

    public static void WalkNavigator(XPathNavigator nav)
    {
     switch (nav.NodeType)
     {
      case XPathNodeType.Element:
        if (nav.Prefix==String.Empty)
         {
          Console.WriteLine("<{0}>", nav.LocalName);
         }
        else
         {
          Console.Write("<{0}:{1}>", nav.Prefix, nav.LocalName);
         }
        Console.WriteLine("\t" + nav.NamespaceURI);
        break;
      case XPathNodeType.Text:
        Console.WriteLine("\t" + nav.Value);
        break;
```

```
        }

        if ( nav.MoveToFirstChild() )
        {
          do{
             WalkNavigator(nav);
          } while ( nav.MoveToNext() );

          nav.MoveToParent();
          if (nav.NodeType == XPathNodeType.Element)
            Console.WriteLine("</{0}>", nav.Name);
        }
    }

    public static void Main()
    {
        LoadDataSetXMLDataExample xmltransform = new
                LoadDataSetXMLDataExample();
    }

  }
}
```

After execution, Listing 14.37 creates the XML document in Listing 14.38.

Listing 14.38—Library4.xml, Created XML Document

```xml
<?xml version="1.0" standalone="yes"?>
<NewDataSet>
  <days>
    <id>1</id>
    <day>New Year - Christmas</day>
    <description>New Year - Christmas</description>
  </days>
  <days>
    <id>2</id>
    <day>Valentine Day</day>
    <description>Valentine Day</description>
  </days>
</NewDataSet>
```

After execution, Listing 14.37 will create the XML schema in Listing 14.39.

Listing 14.39—Library4.xsd, Created XML Schema

```xml
<?xml version="1.0" standalone="yes"?>
<xsd:schema id="NewDataSet" targetNamespace="" xmlns="" xmlns:xsd="http://www.w3
.org/1999/XMLSchema" xmlns:msdata="urn:schemas-microsoft-com:xml-msdata">
  <xsd:element name="days">
    <xsd:complexType content="elementOnly">
      <xsd:all>
        <xsd:element name="id" minOccurs="0" type="xsd:int"/>
        <xsd:element name="day" minOccurs="0" type="xsd:string"/>
        <xsd:element name="description" minOccurs="0" type="xsd:string"/>
      </xsd:all>
    </xsd:complexType>
  </xsd:element>
  <xsd:element name="NewDataSet" msdata:IsDataSet="True">
    <xsd:complexType>
      <xsd:choice maxOccurs="unbounded">
        <xsd:element ref="days"/>
      </xsd:choice>
    </xsd:complexType>
  </xsd:element>
</xsd:schema>
```

The XmlDataDocument class can be used to provide synchronization between DataSet and XML documents. You can use XmlDataDocument to read an XML document and generate a data set or read data from a data set and generate an XML file. Listing 14.40 shows how to create a data set on the fly and then generate an XML document and schema.

Listing 14.40— Dataset Creation on the Fly

```
// DataSet example

using System;
using System.Xml;
using System.IO;
using System.Data;

class TestApp
{

 public static void Main()
 {
  // Create a DataSet, namespace, and table with columns
  DataSet ds = new DataSet("daysDS");
  ds.Namespace = "daysNamespace";
  DataTable daysTable = new DataTable("daysTB");
  DataColumn col1 = new DataColumn("id");
  DataColumn col2 = new DataColumn("day");
  daysTable.Columns.Add(col1);
  daysTable.Columns.Add(col2);
  ds.Tables.Add(daysTable);

  // add some data
  DataRow newRow;
  newRow = daysTable.NewRow();
  newRow["id"]= "1";
  newRow["day"]= "Christmas";
  daysTable.Rows.Add(newRow);
  newRow = daysTable.NewRow();
  newRow["id"]= "2";
  newRow["day"]= "Valentine";
  daysTable.Rows.Add(newRow);

  ds.AcceptChanges();

  // Write out schema representation
  ds.WriteXmlSchema("library5.xsd");

  // Write out XML data from relational data
  // with schema
  ds.WriteXml("library51.xml", 0);
  // without schema
  ds.WriteXml("library52.xml", XmlWriteMode.IgnoreSchema);

  // Create an XmlDataDocument for the DataSet
  XmlDataDocument datadoc = new XmlDataDocument(ds);
  // use datadoc..
 }
}
```

After execution, Listing 14.40 creates the XML schema in Listing 14.41.

Listing 14.41—Library5.xsd, Created XML Schema

```
<?xml version="1.0" standalone="yes" ?>
<xs:schema id="daysDS" targetNamespace="daysNamespace" xmlns:mstns="daysNamespace"
xmlns="daysNamespace" xmlns:xs="http://www.w3.org/2001/XMLSchema"
```

```
xmlns:msdata="urn:schemas-microsoft-com:xml-msdata"
attributeFormDefault="qualified" elementFormDefault="qualified">
        <xs:element name="daysDS" msdata:IsDataSet="true">
                <xs:complexType>
                        <xs:choice maxOccurs="unbounded">
                                <xs:element name="daysTB">
                                        <xs:complexType>
                                                <xs:sequence>
                                                        <xs:element name="id"
                                        type="xs:string" minOccurs="0" />
                                                        <xs:element name="day"
                                        type="xs:string" minOccurs="0" />
                                                </xs:sequence>
                                        </xs:complexType>
                                </xs:element>
                        </xs:choice>
                </xs:complexType>
        </xs:element>
</xs:schema>
```

After execution, Listing 14.40 creates the XML document (with schema included) in Listing 14.42.

Listing 14.42—Library51.xml, Created XML Document (with Schema)

```
<?xml version="1.0" standalone="yes"?>
<daysDS xmlns="daysNamespace">
  <xs:schema id="daysDS" targetNamespace="daysNamespace"
xmlns:mstns="daysNamespace" xmlns="daysNamespace"
xmlns:xs="http://www.w3.org/2001/XMLSchema" xmlns:msdata="urn:schemas-microsoft-
com:xml-msdata" attributeFormDefault="qualified" elementFormDefault="qualified">
    <xs:element name="daysDS" msdata:IsDataSet="true" msdata:Locale="tr-TR">
      <xs:complexType>
        <xs:choice maxOccurs="unbounded">
          <xs:element name="daysTB">
            <xs:complexType>
              <xs:sequence>
              <xs:element name="id" type="xs:string" minOccurs="0" />
              <xs:element name="day" type="xs:string" minOccurs="0"/>
              </xs:sequence>
            </xs:complexType>
          </xs:element>
        </xs:choice>
      </xs:complexType>
    </xs:element>
  </xs:schema>
  <daysTB>
    <id>1</id>
    <day>Christmas</day>
  </daysTB>
  <daysTB>
    <id>2</id>
    <day>Valentine</day>
  </daysTB>
</daysDS>
```

Listing 14.40 also creates the XML document (without schema) in Listing 14.43 when XmlWriteMode.IgnoreSchema is passed to the WriteXml method of the DataSet class.

Listing 14.43—Library52.xml, Created XML Document (Without Schema)

```
<?xml version="1.0" standalone="yes"?>
<daysDS xmlns="daysNamespace">
  <daysTB>
    <id>1</id>
    <day>Christmas</day>
```

```
    </daysTB>
    <daysTB>
      <id>2</id>
      <day>Valentine</day>
    </daysTB>
</daysDS>
```

Transformation with XslTransform

The System.Xml.Xsl namespace provides support for Extensible Stylesheet Language
Transformations (XSLT). XslTransform supports the XSLT 1.0 syntax. The XSLT stylesheet
transformation must include the namespace declaration *xmlns:xsl=*
http://www.w3.org/1999/XSL/Transform.

XSL is an XML-based language designed to transform one XML document into another XML
document or an XML document into any other structured document. The XslTransform class
manages XSLT transformations in the new framework.

Figure 14.8 depicts the typical transformation process to other tree formats for any XML document.

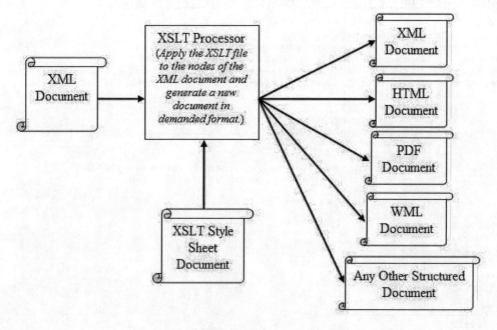

Figure 14.8: XSL Transformation Process

XML Transformation with XSL

Often, an XML document's structure does not match the structure needed to process the XML data.
To transform the existing structure into one that can be processed, you use an XSLT processor and
an XSLT style sheet (or XSLT file) that defines how to do the transformation. The XSLT file
consists of templates that specify how each node of the source XML document should appear in the
destination XML document. Thus, the XSLT processor holds three trees: one tree for the source
XML, one tree for the destination structure, and one tree for the XSLT file.

With XSL, you can maintain your data representation products either by changing the style sheet or
by adding a new style sheet and switching to it for the new view consumer. You can think of XSL as

a set of DataViews: A database table can have different views based on different user viewing requirements. The underlying data of a table remains the same, but the browsing window changes. XSLT transforms one XML document into another XML document using XPath as the query language.

You can plug any storage class implementing an IXPathNavigable interface into the XslTransform class for XSLT processing. So, you can pass the XmlDocument, XmlDataDocument, and XPathDocument storage classes, which expose XPathNavigator via IXPathNavigable, to an instance of the XslTransform class for XSLT processing. Using XSLT through an XmlDataDocument class provides transformation over relational data stored in a data set, as well as formatting capability to the XmlDocument class.

Figure 14.9 shows the XPathNavigator class and XslTransform class working together.

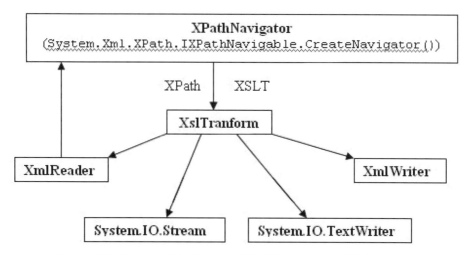

Figure 14.9: Relationship Between XPathNavigator and XslTransform

You can use the Load method of the XslTransform class to load an XSLT style sheet. The Transform method of the XslTransform class accepts an XPathDocument object, and this method can be used to either return an XmlReader for reading data transformed through the use of the style sheet or write the transformed data into a supplied XmlWriter or stream. The XSLT files can be combined to produce the required structured output format, such as XML or HTML.

Table 14.8 lists two of the System.Xml.Xsl.XslTransform class members.

XslTransform Member	Description
Load()	Loads the XSLT style sheet into the XslTransform objects by following the inclusions with xsl:include and xsl:import attributes.
Tranform()	Returns the resultant data that is generated by transforming a given XML data with the loaded XSLT style sheet applied on it.

Table 14.8: XslTransform Class Members

Listing 14.44 shows overloads of the XslTranform.Load() method for loading style sheet information used for transformation. An XmlResolver class can be optionally loaded to validate DTD and schema information.

Listing 14.44—XslTransform.Load() Overloads

```
// the XSLT style sheet contained in the IXPathNavigable.
Load(IXPathNavigable);
// the XSLT style sheet specified by a URL.
Load(string);
// the XSLT style sheet contained in the XmlReader.
Load(XmlReader);
// the XSLT style sheet contained in the XPathNavigator.
// Load(XPathNavigator);
// the XSLT style sheet contained in the IXPathNavigable.
Load(IXPathNavigable, XmlResolver);
// the XSLT style sheet specified by a URL.
Load(string, XmlResolver);
// the XSLT style sheet contained in the XmlReader.
Load(XmlReader, XmlResolver);
// the XSLT style sheet contained in the XPathNavigator.
Load(XPathNavigator, XmlResolver);
```

Listing 14.45 shows overloads for the XslTranform.Transform() method. Most of these methods take XPathNavigator as the first parameter. The last parameter indicates how the transform will output the data—whether to a file, a stream, a TextWriter class, or an XmlWriter class.

Listing 14.45—XslTransform.Transform() Overloads

```
// output to XmlReader
XmlReader Transform(IXPathNavigable, XsltArgumentList);
// output to XML file
void Transform(string, string);
// output to SmlReader
XmlReader Transform(XPathNavigator, XsltArgumentList);
// output to stream
void Transform(IXPathNavigable, XsltArgumentList, Stream);
// output to TextWriter
void Transform(IXPathNavigable, XsltArgumentList, TextWriter);
// output to XmlWriter
void Transform(IXPathNavigable, XsltArgumentList, XmlWriter);
// output to Stream
void Transform(XPathNavigator, XsltArgumentList, Stream);
// output to TextWriter
void Transform(XPathNavigator, XsltArgumentList, TextWriter);
// output to XmlWriter
void Transform(XPathNavigator, XsltArgumentList, XmlWriter);
```

The System.Xml.Xsl.XsltArgumentList class holds a variable number of arguments, which are either XSLT parameters or extension objects. During the call to the XslTransform.Tranform() method, the method invokes the parameters and extension objects from within the style sheet. XSLT parameters are appended with the AddParam method, which takes three parameters—a qualified name, namespace URI, and object value of one of the following types: System.String, System.Boolean, System.Double, System.Xml.XPath.XPathNavigator, or System.Xml.XPath.XPathNodeIterator.

For example, assume that you have an XSLT *<xsl:value-of select="$sampiyon"/>* tag where *sampiyon* is a variable/parameter of System.String type with no namespace in your XSL file. Then typically you will call the transform method to change all *$sampiyon* links with *AntepSpor*. The resultant XML document will be serialized to the TextWriter as illustrated below:

```
xslArg.AddParam("sampiyon", "", "AntepSpor");
xslt.Transform(xpdoc, xslArg, txwriter);
```

Listing 14.46 shows the typical scenario of how to transform XML documents using XSLT style sheets.

Listing 14.46—XslTransform

```
//Create a new XslTransform object.
XslTransform xslt = new XslTransform();

//Load the style sheet.
xslt.Load("http://www.mindcracker.com/schema1.xsl");

//Create a new XPathDocument and load the XML data to be transformed.
XPathDocument mydata = new
XPathDocument("http://www.mindcracker.com/data1.xml");

//Create an XmlTextWriter which outputs to the console.
XmlWriter writer = new XmlTextWriter(Console.Out);

//Transform the data and send the output to the console.
xslt.Transform(mydata, null, writer);
```

The style sheet is made up of templates that specify how each node of the source XML document should appear in the destination XML document. Thus the XSLT processor holds three trees: the source XML, the destination structure, and the style sheet. Listing 14.47 shows how to efficiently use XslTransform and XPathNavigator together to produce an XmlWriter that will apply a style sheet to an XML document.

Listing 14.47—XslTransform and XPathNavigator

```
// a simple typical XSL transformation block

    try
    {
      // load the source document (to be transformed)
      XmlDocument docSource = new XmlDocument();
      docSource.Load(strXML);
      // wrap it with an XmlNavigator
      XPathNavigator navSource = docSource.CreateNavigator();

      // create the XslTransform object
      XslTransform tr = new XslTransform();
      // load it with the stylesheet
      tr.Load(strXSLT);

      // call transform - output streamed to console
      tr.Transform(navSource, null, xw);
    }
    catch(Exception e)
    {
      Console.WriteLine("###error: " + e.Message);
    }
```

Now we will develop a real-world example that transforms an XML document into another XML document by applying an XSL file to it. Listing 14.48 displays the XML document that we are going to transform.

Listing 14.48—Library6.xml, XML Data

```
<?xml version="1.0"?>
<!-- library6.xml -->
<xml>
        <row id="1">
                <AikidoEnergyTypes/>Ki
```

```
        </row>
        <row  id="2">
                <AikidoEnergyTypes/>Chi
        </row>
        <row id="3">
                <AikidoEnergyTypes/>Chai
        </row>
</xml>
```

Listing 14.49 is the XSL file applied to the document used to convert rows to records.

Listing 14.49—Library6.xsl, XSL File

```
<?xml version="1.0"?>
<xsl:stylesheet version="1.0" xmlns:xsl="http://www.w3.org/1999/XSL/Transform">
<!-- library6.xsl -->

<xsl:output omit-xml-declaration="yes"/>

        <xsl:template match="/">
        <Dataset>
                <xsl:apply-templates/>
        </Dataset>
        </xsl:template>

        <xsl:template match="xml">
                <Aikido>
                        <xsl:apply-templates select="row"/>
                </Aikido>
        </xsl:template>

        <xsl:template match="row">
                <record>
                        <xsl:attribute name="id">
                        <xsl:value-of select="@*"/>
                        </xsl:attribute>
                        <EnergyTypes><xsl:value-of select="."/>
                        </EnergyTypes>
                </record>
        </xsl:template>
</xsl:stylesheet>
```

Listing 14.50 performs the transformation process using the XmlDocument, XPathNavigator, and XslTransform classes.

Listing 14.50—XSL Transformation Example

```
// XSLT Transformation example

using System;
using System.IO;
using System.Xml;
using System.Xml.XPath;
using System.Xml.Xsl;

public class XSLTApp
{
    public static string Stylesheet = @"library6.xsl";
    public static string Document = @"library6.xml";
    public static string TransformedDocument = @"library6t.xml";

     public static void Main()
     {
         // Read an XML document by applying a style sheet
         try
```

```
    {
        XmlDocument xmldocument = new XmlDocument();
        xmldocument.Load(Document);
        XPathNavigator navigator =
            xmldocument.CreateNavigator();

        XslTransform xsltransform = new XslTransform();
            // load XSL style sheet
        xsltransform.Load(Stylesheet);
            // transform the XML document
        XmlReader reader = xsltransform.Transform(navigator,
          null);

            // Output the transformed XML document

// Moves the reader to the root element.
        reader.MoveToContent();
            // Moves to root content node.
        reader.Read();
            // ReadOuterXml returns the markup
// for the current node and its children.
        Console.WriteLine(reader.ReadOuterXml());
    }
    catch (Exception e)
    {
        Console.WriteLine ("Exception: {0}", e.ToString());
    }

      // Write an XML document by applying a style sheet
    StreamReader stream = null;
    try
    {
        XmlDocument xmldocument = new XmlDocument();
        xmldocument.Load(Document);
        XPathNavigator navigator =
            xmldocument.CreateNavigator();
        XslTransform xsltransform = new XslTransform();
        XmlTextWriter writer = new
            XmlTextWriter(TransformedDocument, null);

            // load XSL style sheet
            xsltransform.Load(Stylesheet);
            // serialize the transformed XML document to the
            // XmlTextWriter
        xsltransform.Transform(navigator, null, writer);

          writer.Close();

        stream = new StreamReader(TransformedDocument);
        Console.Write(stream.ReadToEnd());
    }
    catch (Exception e)
    {
        Console.WriteLine ("Exception: {0}", e.ToString());
    }
    finally
    {
        if (stream != null)
            stream.Close();
    }
    }
}
```

After execution, Listing 14.50 produces the transformed XML document shown in Listing 14.51.

Listing 14.51—Library6t.xml, File Created After Execution of Code

```
<?xml version="1.0"?><Dataset><Aikido><record id="1"><EnergyTypes>Ki
     </EnergyTypes></record><record id="2"><EnergyTypes>Chi
     </EnergyTypes></record><record id="3"><EnergyTypes>Chai
     </EnergyTypes></record></Aikido></Dataset>
```

XML Serialization

In object-oriented programming, serialization of class objects is practical technique for storing information. With serialization, you can persist an object's state and then revert to its persisted state on the fly. XML-based serialization is quite handy for configuration files where objects need to be easily serializable and shared by multiple clients in a distributed application.

The System.Xml.Serialization namespace contains classes that use streams to serialize objects into XML-format documents. XML serialization is the process of converting an object's public properties and fields into an XML format for storage or transport. Deserialization re-creates the object in its original state from the XML output.

You can thus think of serialization as a way of saving the state of an object in a stream or buffer. For example, ASP.NET Web services use the XmlSerializer class to encode Web service messages. Serialization provides an easy approach for using XML in application configuration files. You can use the same approach in XML.NET applications, along with its caching capabilities, to dynamically update an application by just changing the values in the XML file.

Because serialization automatically maps elements and attributes stored in an XML file to properties of a class, you can freely update the classes in your applications without having to change the serialization code. The XML file contains application metadata that can be added to or updated as needed to enhance a class. Using this approach in class design lets the class be as dynamic as necessary. If you only want to save the states of an object, you do not need to modify the class. However, if your class reads and writes XML documents that conform to an exact XML schema, you can control the XML output to a great extent by setting certain attributes of the class's public properties and fields.

Serialization can take place in two directions: an object can be created from an XML document—known as deserializing—or an XML document can be created from an object—known as serializing. To handle these operations, the .NET Framework exposes the Serialize and Deserialize methods of the XmlSerializer class located in the System.Xml.Serialization namespace. Using the XmlSerializer class, you can easily serialize and deserialize your objects to and from disk files or to and from any .NET Framework stream class, such as BufferedStream, FileStream, MemoryStream, NetworkStream, and CryptoStream.

By using the following XmlSerializer directives in your classes, you can dictate to the classes the contents of your XML serialized/deserialized file. You can use these directives in the public fields and properties of your class to determine which ones are serialized and how they are serialized to the XML file. By editing the contents of an XML serialized file representing your class, you can change the object's state before it is deserialized from this file. In addition to files, you can serialize with streams supported in the .NET Framework and the TextReader, TextWriter, XmlReader, and XmlWriter classes.

Here are the XML serialization directives used above the public properties and fields of your class:

- [XmlElement]—serializes the public property or field into the XML structure as an element
- [XmlIgnore]—ignores the public property or field during the serialization process

- [XmlRoot]—identifies the class or struct as the root element of the XML document
- [XmlAttribute]—serializes the public property or field into the XML structure as an attribute
- [XmlArray]—serializes the public property or field into the XML structure as an element array
- [XmlArrayItem]—identifies a type that can be placed into a serialized array

The XmlSerializer attributes appear in brackets above the property definitions. Qualifiers like *ElementName= "xxx "* are primarily used when element or attribute tags do not match the property names. Once you've defined your class, instantiate an object from the XmlSerializer class, passing the data type of your class to its constructor. To map the XML structure from the configuration file to the class properties, call the Deserialize method of the XmlSerializer object with a MemoryReader or StreamReader object parameter. Listing 14.52 shows how to serialize and deserialize a custom class, MyClass, object over a MemoryStream.

Listing 14.52—XML Serialization

```
// Serialize a custom class over MemoryStream
using System;
using System.IO;
using System.Xml;
using System.Xml.Serialization;

[XmlRoot(ElementName="MyClass")]
public class MyClass
    {
        public long MyLong;
        private string MyString = "AString";

        [XmlIgnore]
         public int MyInteger;

        [XmlAttribute(AttributeName="MyAttribute")]
        public string MyAttribute
        {
                get {
                        return MyString;
                }
                set {
                        MyString = value;
                }
        }

        public MyClass()
         {
            MyLong = 1919;
             MyInteger = 19;
         }
}

public class MySerializingClass
{
 public static void Main()
  {
        Byte[] buffer = new Byte[200];
        MyClass x = new MyClass();
        x.MyInteger = 99;
        x.MyLong = 9999;
        x.MyAttribute = "Baltaci Mehmet Pasa";
        XmlSerializer xs = new XmlSerializer(x.GetType());
        MemoryStream ms = new MemoryStream();
        xs.Serialize(ms,x);
        ms.Seek(0,0);
```

```
        MyClass y;
        y = (MyClass) xs.Deserialize(ms);
        ms.Seek(0, 0);
        ms.Read(buffer, 0, 200);
        string s = System.Text.Encoding.ASCII.GetString(buffer, 0, 200);
        Console.WriteLine(s);
    }
}
```

DiffGrams

A DiffGram is an XML document formed by complying with a particular schema that represents the contents of a data set. A DiffGram includes the original and current data of a data element, as well as a unique identifier that associates the original and current versions with one another. You use DataSet's ReadXml and WriteXml functions for reading and writing DiffGram-formatted XML data streams. To write a data set to a file, stream, or XmlWriter, you use DataSet's WriteXml method. You can pass the string containing the filename for output, pass a TextWriter object, or pass an XmlWriter object to the WriteXml method.

To write your DataSet object as a DiffGram, you pass XmlWriteMode.DiffGram as the second parameter in the WriteXml method. DiffGrams are generally used for marshalling the data within a data set across a network connection so that different versions (Original, Current) and RowState values (Added, Modified, Deleted, Unchanged, Detached) of the DataRow objects can be persisted. The code snippets in Listings 14.50 and 14.51 show how to serialize and deserialize a DataSet object to a DiffGram.

Listing 14.53—Writing a DiffGram

```
DataSet myDS = new DataSet();
// place code here for filling the DataSet
System.IO.StreamWriter xmlSW = new
System.IO.StreamWriter("library007.xml");
myDS.WriteXml(xmlSW, XmlWriteMode.DiffGram);
xmlSW.Close();
```

Listing 14.54—Reading a DiffGram

```
System.IO.StreamReader xmlStream = new
System.IO.StreamReader("library007.xml");
DataSet myDS = new DataSet();
myDS.ReadXml(xmlStream, XmlReadMode.DiffGram);
xmlStream.Close();
```

After the write operation, the XML document root is *<diffgr:diffgram>* node. The resultant XML document has at most three separate data sections: the current data (whether modified or unchanged), the original data (before changes occurred), and an error section. Listing 14.55 is a pseudo XML document illustrating the entire DiffGram XML structure.

Listing 14.55—DiffGram XML Document

```
<?xml version="1.0"?>
<diffgr:diffgram
        xmlns:msdata="urn:schemas-microsoft-com:xml-msdata"
        xmlns:diffgr="urn:schemas-microsoft-com:xml-diffgram-v1"
        xmlns:xsd="http://www.w3.org/2001/XMLSchema">
        <DataSet>
                <current Rows>
                </current Rows>
        </DataSet>
<diffgr:before>
                < original of modified or inserted Rows >
                </original of modified or inserted Rows>
```

```
        </diffgr:before>
        <diffgr:errors>
              <DataSet error descriptions of faulty Rows>
        </diffgr:errors>
</diffgr:diffgram>
```

Listing 14.56 shows the entire DiffGram created after executing the .NET Framework XML write methods.

Listing 14.56—Diffgram XML Data

```
<?xml version="1.0"?>
<diffgr:diffgram xmlns:msdata="urn:schemas-microsoft-com:xml-msdata"
xmlns:diffgr="urn:schemas-microsoft-com:xml-diffgram-v1">

  <LibraryDataSet>
    <Library diffgr:id="Library1" msdata:rowOrder="0" diffgr:hasChanges="modified">
      <BookID>1919</BookID>
      <Book>Yasar Kemal</Book>
    </Library>
    <Library diffgr:id="Library2" msdata:rowOrder="1" diffgr:hasChanges="inserted">
      <BookID>1920</BookID>
      <Book>Mehmet Akif Ersoy</Book>
    </Library>
    <Library diffgr:id="Library3" msdata:rowOrder="2" diffgr:hasErrors="true">
      <BookID>1921</BookID>
      <Book>Peyami Safa</Book>
    </Library>
    <Library diffgr:id="Library4" msdata:rowOrder="3">
      <BookID>1922</BookID>
      <Book>Arif Nihat Asya</Book>
    </Library>
  </LibraryDataSet>

  <diffgr:before>
    <Library diffgr:id="Library1" msdata:rowOrder="0">
      <BookID>1919</BookID>
      <Book>Necip Fazil Kisakurek</Book>
    </Library>
  </diffgr:before>

  <diffgr:errors>
<Library diffgr:id="Library3" diffgr:Error="An error has occurred for this row."/>
  </diffgr:errors>

</diffgr:diffgram>
```

The *<LibraryDataSet>...</LibraryDataSet>* section of the DiffGram is mandatory and represents the current DataSet object. This section resembles the XML output you can get from DataSet serialization, but the DiffGram format does not include the schema information. The *<LibraryDataSet>...</LibraryDataSet>* section includes the current row values in the data set. Newly added records are also listed here since they have no previous match. The *<diffgr:before>...</diffgr:before>* section stores only the original rows that are modified or deleted. The rows in the *<LibraryDataSet>...</LibraryDataSet>* and *<diffgr:before>...</diffgr:before>* sections are tracked with a unique ID. With IDs you can pursue rows that are different between the original and the current versions of the DataSet object.

The *<diffgr:errors>* section lists messages related to pending errors on rows. The unique row ID is also used here for tracking an erroneous record, along with the error description. DiffGram nodes have many special attributes related to elements across the three different DiffGram sections mentioned above.

Here are the DiffGram attributes found in the three DiffGram sections discussed above along with some additional attributes:

- *diffgr:hasChanges* identifies a row that has been modified or inserted.
- *diffgr:hasErrors* indictates that the row has an error.
- *diffgr:id* is a unique identifier (Diffgram Identifier) for the row which is also used to match rows across sections, e.g. the elements inside the *<diffgr:before>* and *<diffgr:errors>* blocks refer to the elements. Its format is the concatenation of the TableName and RowIdentifier information.
- *msdata:rowOrder* tracks the ordinal position of the row in the data set.
- *msdata:hidden[ColumnName]=[value]* identifies a DataColumn as having a MappingType of MappingType.Hidden. The MappingType property defines how a DataColumn of a DataTable will be written in XML when calling the WriteXml method in the DataSet. (The MappingType will be of Attribute, Element, Hidden, or SimpleContent type). For example, the XML attribute takes the following form if the DataColumn in the DataSet called BookName is marked as hidden:

```
msdata:hiddenBookName="DesignPatterns"
```

Hidden means that the column is mapped to an internal structure. Hidden columns are ignored if a row column does not have data. They are only written as a DiffGram attribute if the row column contains data.

- *diffgr:parentID* identifies which element is the parent element of the current element.
- *diffgr:error* contains the error text for the row in *<diffgr:errors>*.

Let's restate the DiffGram concept: a DiffGram is in XML format and is used to identify current and original versions of data elements. The DataSet object uses the DiffGram format for serializing and deserializing its contents, without any schema information, across different computing entities over the network. This information consists of column values from the original and current row versions, of row error information, and of row order.

So, other platforms can use the DiffGram-formatted XML document data to exchange information with .NET Framework applications. For example, when exchanging a DataSet with an XML Web service, the DiffGram format is implicitly used for passing the data in the exchange. We can explicitly read and write a DiffGram document by calling the DataSet ReadXml and WriteXml methods if we explicitly state that the read or write operation mode is DiffGram.

Listing 14.57 shows how to instantiate a DataSet object and then generate a DiffGram XML document from it.

Listing 14.57— Creating a DiffGram from a Data Set

```
// DataSet example
using System;
using System.Xml;
using System.IO;
using System.Data;

class MainClass
{
  public static void Main()
  {
```

```
// Create a DataSet, namespace and Student
// table with Name and Address columns
DataSet ds = new DataSet("LibraryDataSet");
ds.Namespace = "libraryNamespace";
DataTable libraryTable = new DataTable("libraryTB");
DataColumn col1 = new DataColumn("BookID");
DataColumn col2 = new DataColumn("Book");
libraryTable.Columns.Add(col1);
libraryTable.Columns.Add(col2);
ds.Tables.Add(libraryTable);

// add some data
DataRow newRow = libraryTable.NewRow();
newRow["BookID"]= "19";
newRow["Book"]= "Necip Fazil Kisakurek";
libraryTable.Rows.Add(newRow);
newRow = libraryTable.NewRow();
newRow["BookID"]= "2";
newRow["Book"]= "Mehmet Akif Ersoy";
libraryTable.Rows.Add(newRow);

ds.AcceptChanges();

System.IO.StreamWriter xmlSW = new
            System.IO.StreamWriter("diffgram1.xml");
ds.WriteXml(xmlSW, XmlWriteMode.DiffGram);

xmlSW.Close();
Console.Read();
 }
}
```

Listing 14.57 creates the diffgram1.xml file shown in Listing 14.58.

Listing 14.58— Diffgram XML document

```
<diffgr:diffgram xmlns:msdata="urn:schemas-microsoft-com:xml-msdata"
xmlns:diffgr="urn:schemas-microsoft-com:xml-diffgram-v1">
  <LibraryDataSet xmlns="libraryNamespace">
    <libraryTB diffgr:id="libraryTB1" msdata:rowOrder="0">
      <BookID>19</BookID>
      <Book>Necip Fazil Kisakurek</Book>
    </libraryTB>
    <libraryTB diffgr:id="libraryTB2" msdata:rowOrder="1">
      <BookID>2</BookID>
      <Book>Mehmet Akif Ersoy</Book>
    </libraryTB>
  </LibraryDataSet>
</diffgr:diffgram>
```

XML Conversions

The XmlConvert class simply encodes and decodes XML names and provides methods for converting between common language runtime types and XSD types. If you already have an XML-formatted data file or stream, you can easily convert and use it in your application with the XmlConvert class.

XmlConvert has many methods for mapping XML types to ordinary .NET Framework data types. Its many public static functions free you from the need to initialize a class object. Table 14.9 lists and explains common XML conversion functions.

XmlConvert Members	Description
ToBoolean	Converts the string to a Boolean. (*1, true, 0,* and *false* are legitimate for converting to Boolean.)
ToByte	Converts the string to a byte.
ToChar	Converts the string to a char.
ToDateTime	Converts the string to a datetime.
ToDecimal	Converts the string to a decimal.
ToDouble	Converts the string to a double.
ToGuid	Converts the string to a GUID.
ToInt16	Converts the string to a 16-bit integer (negative or positive).
ToInt32	Converts the string to a 32-bit integer (negative or positive).
ToInt64	Converts the string to a 64-bit integer (negative or positive).
ToSByte	Converts the string to a signed byte.
ToSingle	Converts the string to a single.
ToString	Returns a string equivalent of any strongly typed data passed to this method.
ToTimeSpan	Converts the string to a TimeSpan.
ToUInt16	Converts the string to an unsigned 16-bit integer.
ToUInt32	Converts the string to an unsigned 32-bit integer.
ToUInt64	Converts the string to a unsigned 64-bit integer.

Table 14.9: XmlConvert Members

Listing 14.59 shows a few XML conversions using the XmlConvert class.

Listing 14.59—XmlConvert Example

```
using System;
using System.IO;
using System.Xml;

public class SomeClass
{
  public static void Main()
  {
    Int16 int1 = 19;
    String str1 = "1919";
    DateTime date1 = new DateTime(19191919);
    Double dbl1 = 19.191919;
    XmlTextWriter writer = new XmlTextWriter (Console.Out);
    writer.Formatting = Formatting.Indented;
    writer.WriteStartElement("SomeClass");
    writer.WriteAttributeString("date1", XmlConvert.ToString(date1));
    writer.WriteElementString("int1", XmlConvert.ToString(int1));
    writer.WriteElementString("dbl1", XmlConvert.ToString(dbl1));
    writer.WriteElementString("str1",
    Convert.ToString(XmlConvert.ToInt64(str1)));
    writer.WriteEndElement();
    writer.Flush();
    writer.Close();
  }
}
```

Listing 14.59 yields the output shown in Listing 14.60. The output reflects the output produced by the XmlConvert object in converting a date, an integer, a double, and a Int64 into a string.

Listing 14.60—Output of XmlConvert Example

```
<SomeClass date1="0001-01-01T00:00:01.9191919+02:00">
  <int1>19</int1>
  <dbl1>19.191919</dbl1>
  <str1>1919</str1>
</SomeClass>
```

Schema Object Model

The Schema Object Model (SOM) loads and saves valid XSD schemas, providing an easy way to create in-memory schemas using strongly typed classes. The SOM works with the XmlValidatingReader class through XmlSchemaCollection, which you can use to cache and retrieve multiple schemas. These preloaded schemas are loaded once and then reused, which results in much better parsing performance. XmlSchemaCollection supports both XDR and XSD schemas, providing a library of both, which can be used for validation purposes.

The SOM is the XSD schema equivalent of the DOM. In the XSD specification, there is a one-to-one relationship between XSD elements and classes in the SOM. This provides an editable model for XSD that allows a programmer to generate XSD schemas. Once built programmatically, the XSD schema compiles into a post-schema validation infoset. Figure 14.10 depicts the relationship of the SOM and the XmlReader and XmlWriter classes.

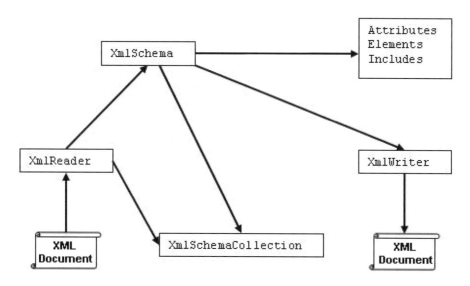

Figure 14.10: Relationship of XmlSchema, XmlReader, and XmlWriter

Listing 14.61—Reading and Writing an XML Schema Using the XmlSchema Object Model

```
private const String document = "library5.xsd";
XmlSchema mySchema = XmlSchema.Read(new XmlTextReader(document));
mySchema.Write(myXmlWriter);
Console.WriteLine(myStringWriter.ToString());
```

Now we will develop a complete XML validation example that checks XML data against two XDR files, users.xdr and usersactive.xdr (see Listings 14.24 and 14.25 earlier in this chapter), which incorporates the XmlSchemaCollection class. Listing 14.62 contains the XML data we will work with.

Listing 14.62—Users2.xml, XML Data

```
<?xml version="1.0"?>
<x:Users xmlns:x="urn:Users-Schema" xmlns:y="urn:ActiveUser-Schema">
  <x:User Role="Bozo" y:Active="1">
    <x:first-name>Ecevit</x:first-name>
    <x:last-name>Bahceli</x:last-name>
    <x:user-name>Mesut</x:user-name>
  </x:User>
</x:Users>
```

Listing 14.63 adds the two XDR schemas to its library collection. Then it uses a validating reader to prove that the XML document in Listing 14.62 is well-formed against the two reduced schemas: users.xdr and usersactive.xdr.

Listing 14.63— ValidationEventHandler XDR Schema

```
// validate an XML document against an XDR schema
using System;
using System.IO;
using System.Xml;
using System.Xml.Schema;

  class XDRExample2
  {
      public static void Main()
      {
        XmlTextReader tr = new XmlTextReader("Users2.xml");
        XmlValidatingReader vr = new XmlValidatingReader(tr);

        XmlSchemaCollection xs = new XmlSchemaCollection();
        xs.Add("urn:Users-Schema", "Users.xdr");
        xs.Add("urn:ActiveUser-Schema", "UsersActive.xdr");

        vr.Schemas.Add(xs);

        vr.ValidationEventHandler += new
         ValidationEventHandler(ValidationHandler);

        while(vr.Read());
        Console.WriteLine("Validation Finished");
        vr.Close();
      }

    static void ValidationHandler(Object sender, ValidationEventArgs args)
    {
        Console.WriteLine("***Validation Error***");
        Console.WriteLine("\tSeverity:\t{0}", args.Severity);
        Console.WriteLine("\tMessage:\t{0}", args.Message);
    }
  }
```

XML Namespace Management

The XmlNamespaceManager class allows you to map namespaces to a namespace prefix. You can pass an XmlNamespaceManager object to the SelectSingleNode method of an XmlNode class, which quite handily lets you choose all of the namespaces mapped to the prefix in the query string. The XmlNamespaceManager class constructor takes an XmlNameTable object as a parameter to save the prefix-namespace pairs. This table lets the XML parser efficiently use the same string prefix for all repeated namespaces in an XML document.

We will use the XML document, with namespace ns1, in Listing 14.64 for our application.

Listing 14.64—Xml99.xml, XML Document of Namespace ns1

```
<?xml version="1.0" ?>
<authors>
    <ns1:author xmlns:ns1="http://www.mindcracker.com/namespace">
        <name>MCB</name>
    </ns1:author>
</authors>
```

Listing 14.65 uses the XmlNamespaceManager class and the SelectSingleNode method of the XmlNode class. You could also map additional namespaces to a prefix, if necessary, by calling the AddNameSpace method multiple times. Listing 14.65 selects only the first specific XPath node, along the path *authors/ns1:author/name,* and outputs its contents to the consoleConsole. The XPath expression, */authors/ns1:author/name,* is an absolute location path, and the call to SelectSingleNode selects the node in three steps:

- Starting at the document root, the query walks down the node tree and selects the *<authors>* document element.
- Then the query selects the *<author>* element (a child element of the *<authors>* node) that is part of the ns1 namespace. The NamespaceManager maps the namespace prefix *ns1* to the URL http://www.mindcracker.com//namespace so the XPath query will check that the prefix is specifically mapped to this URL.
- The third step of the query selects the *<name>* node inside the parent node, *<author>*.

Listing 14.65—Namespace Management

```
// SelectSingle node in a specific namespace
using System;
using System.Xml;

class MainClass
{
 public static void Main()
 {
  Console.WriteLine("we will select a single node in ns1..");
  XmlDocument doc = new XmlDocument();
  doc.Load("xml99.xml");
  XmlNamespaceManager ns = new XmlNamespaceManager(doc.NameTable);
  ns.AddNamespace("ns1", "http://www.mindcracker.com/namespace");
  XmlNode node = doc.SelectSingleNode("/authors/ns1:author/name", ns);
  Console.WriteLine(node.InnerText);
 }
}
```

Summary

XML is the standard method for exchanging data between different platforms. In contrast with its descendants, it is extensible. The XML.NET classes let you exploit XML and its promising derivative technologies. As XML evolves through the demand for it, so does XML.NET. XML has different aspects that will help you ease the development maintenance cycle. Once you utilize it for data exchange and realize its benefits and ease of transferring data, you will never put it aside. XML.NET offers one the best performing infrastructures for developing XML standard applications.

You can refer to the following links for information on general XML concepts on which the .NET Framework is based:

- XML 1.0, including DTD support (http://www.w3.org/TR/1998/REC-xml-19980210)
- XML namespaces, both stream level and DOM (http://www.w3.org/TR/REC-xml-names/)
- DOM Level 1 core (http://www.w3.org/TR/REC-DOM-Level-1/)
- DOM Level 2 core (http://www.w3.org/TR/DOM-Level-2/)
- XML schemas for structures (http://www.w3.org/TR/xmlschema-1/)
- XML schemas for data types (http://www.w3.org/TR/xmlschema-2/)
- XPath expressions (http://www.w3.org/TR/XPath)
- XSLT transformations (http://www.w3.org/TR/xslt)
- SOAP 1.1 (http://msdn.microsoft.com/xml/general/soapspec.asp))

The next chapter will take you into the realm of graphics programming in .NET using the built in GDI+ library.

Chapter 15:
GDI+ Programming

Working with graphics under the Microsoft Windows Software Development Kit (SDK) has in the past been a tedious task. This chapter discusses how to work with graphics objects in the Microsoft .NET Framework using C# and GDI+. GDI+ is a new and greatly improved version of GDI, and the GDI+ application programming interface is included as part of the Microsoft XP operating system. In this chapter we cover the basics of GDI+ and the GDI+ .NET classes followed by some simple applications. We also show you some more complex examples, such as animation.

Overview of GDI+

In the Microsoft Windows platform, all graphical work is handled by Graphical Device Interface (GDI) components. The GDI layer sits between the hardware drivers and the application. Hardware-specific device drivers, such as the printer or the screen drivers, are responsible for rendering the digital data from your application to pixels. The GDI layer talks to the driver, and the driver sends the data to the output device. Device drivers take care of rendering data into human-readable format on the screen, printer, or other output device.

GDI+ is the next evolution of GDI. The GDI+ layer is based on the .NET Framework. GDI+ is a set of C++ classes and is a part of the Microsoft XP operating system. The .NET GDI+ classes provide access to the GDI+ application programming interface in an elegant, clear, object-oriented architecture. All the .NET GDI+ classes are defined in the System.Drawing namespace and the namespace's helper interfaces. We will discuss these interfaces shortly.

In GDI+ Microsoft has rectified many previously painful GDI problems. If you have programmed GDI applications using Visual Basic, C++, or Microsoft Foundation Classes (MFC), you are probably familiar with the difficulties in working with GDI objects. Simply changing the color and fonts of Windows controls using Win32 and MFC was an involved exercise. It was necessary to write at least six lines of code to change the font of a text box. Remember how many ways there were to call SelectObject and how many times you needed to call it?

Besides fixing problems in GDI, Microsoft has added more functionality to GDI+, including two-dimensional support, such as alpha blending, anti-aliasing, gradient and texture, scalable regions, cardinal splines, wide and compound lines, and floating point coordinates. In addition, Microsoft has added image support, such as native support for JPEG (Joint Photographic Experts Group), PNG (Portable Network Graphics), GIF(Graphics Interchange Format), TIFF (Tagged Image File Format), BMP (bitmap), and other image files; encoding and decoding raster image formats; support for contrast, brightness, color balance, blur, and rotation; and more. Other additions to GDI+ are new color management, including the sRGB, iCM2, and sRGB64 formats. Typographic support is also a part of GDI+ and includes texture and gradient-filled text, support for Windows 2000 scripts, and more.

GDI+ Namespaces and Classes

Before we step into GDI+ programming, let's take a brief look at the .NET GDI+ namespaces and classes. In the release candidate of .NET, all of GDI+ is defined in six namespaces. The basic GDI+ primitives are defined in the System.Drawing namespace. Table 15.1 lists the GDI+ namespaces and their descriptions.

Namespace	Description
System.Drawing	Contains the basic GDI+ classes such as Graphics, Pen, Font, Image, and Bitmap.
System.Drawing.Design	Extends the functionality of custom toolbox controls, so you can provide editors—such as font, color, image, or bitmap editors—for your custom controls.
System.Drawing.Drawing2D	Provides classes for working with advanced 2-D and vector graphics. Some of the classes defined in this namespace are Blend, GraphicsPath, Matrix, and the classes for gradient brushes.
System.Drawing.Printing	Defines classes—such as PageSize, PageSettings, PrinterSettings, and PrintDocument—that you can use to customize paging in your application.
System.Drawing.Imaging	Provides advanced imaging functionality. BitmapData, ColorMatrix, MetaFile, and ImageFormat are some of the classes defined in this namespace.
System.Drawing.Text	Provides functionality for advanced typography. In the current release, three classes are defined in this namespace—FontCollection, InstalledFontCollection, and PrivateFontCollection. FontCollections allow you to use different fonts located on your system.

Table 15.1: GDI+ Namespaces

The System.Drawing Namespace

The System.Drawing namespace is the primary namespace you need to access GDI+ objects and classes. It is in this namespace that you will find yourself doing most GDI+ programming. Table 15.2 shows the classes defined in the System.Drawing namespace and their descriptions.

GDI+ Primitive	Description
Bitmap	Encapsulates images stored in pixel data. The Bitmap class is derived from the Image class, which defines the functionality to save images; rotate and flip images; formats, pixel formats, height, width; convert images from a file, hbitmap, and streams; and so on.
Brush, Brushes, SolidBrush, SystemBrushes, TextureBrush	Different brushes used to fill GDI objects.
Color, SystemColor, ColorTranslator, ColorConverter	Used to define the color of GDI objects. ColorConverter and ColorTranslator provide a way to build new color types and convert one color type to another, such as Win32 or OLE_COLOR types.
Font, Pen, Pens, Region	Basic classes discussed previously.
FontConverter, ImageConverter,	Used to convert one data type object to another. All these converter classes are accessed through the TypeDescriptor object.

GDI+ Primitive	Description
PointConverter, RectangleConverter, SizeConverter, ImageFormatConverter	
FontFamily	Defines a family of fonts having a similar basic design and certain variations in styles.
Graphics	The surface where you draw graphical objects; the printer paper; the Windows form; a bitmap.
Icon	Represents a Windows icon, which is a small bitmap image used to represent an object.
Image	Provides functionality for the Bitmap, Icon, and Metafile classes.
ImageAnimator	Used to handle image animation.

Table 15.2: System.Drawing Graphics Classes

GDI+ has a series of structures that are useful in working with many of the graphics classes. These structures are used to work with color, size and positions. Table 15.3 describes some of these structures. Note that some structures such as points and rectangles have both an integer and floating point representation.

Structure	Description
Color	Represents an ARGB (alpha, red, green, blue) color.
Point, PointF	Represents a point, an ordered pair of x and y coordinates. The x, y are integers for Point and floats for PointF.
Rectangle, RectangleF	Stores the location and size of a rectangular region. All members of Rectangle such as height, width, x, y, top, and bottom are integer types, while RectangleFs are the floating point versions.
Size, SizeF	Represents the size of a rectangular region with integer and floating values respectively.

Table 15.3: Important GDI+ Structures

Coordinate Systems in GDI+

Some of you will remember MM_TEXT and MM_HIMETRICS from the Windows coordinate systems. GDI+ has three different coordinate systems known as *world, page,* and *device*. When a graphics drawing method is called, the coordinates of the call are translated from world to page to device and are drawn on the device. The default world coordinates map the upper-left corner of the form client to point 0,0. The default also keeps the world and page coordinate systems the same. The mapping of world coordinates to page coordinates is called the *world transformation*. If you want to change how the world coordinates of the form map to the page coordinates, you can call TranslateTransform on the Graphics object. This method will offset the mapping of the world coordinates, contained in the Transform property, to the page coordinates in the x and y direction. For example, the code in Listing 15.1 draws two rectangles with the same world coordinates but different page coordinates. The drawings are shown in Figure 15.1.

Listing 15.1—Changing the Form's Coordinate System

```
private void OffsetWorldCoordinates(Graphics g)
{
    g.DrawRectangle(Pens.Black, 0, 0, 100, 100);
    g.TranslateTransform(150, 150);
```

```
                        g.DrawRectangle(Pens.Black, 0,0, 100, 100);
    }
```

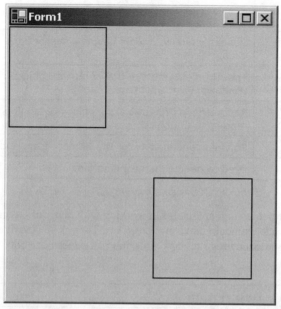

Figure 15.1: Two Rectangles Drawn in Different Page Coordinates

You can change the coordinate system so that the *y* axis points up and the origin is at the bottom-left corner of the client. Do this by changing the Transform matrix of the Graphics object to reflect the vertical direction.

Listing 15.2—Flipping the *y* Coordinate System

```
private void OffsetWorldCoordinatesNegative(Graphics g)
{
 g.Transform = new Matrix(1, 0, 0, -1, 0, 0);
 g.TranslateTransform(0, ClientRectangle.Height,
  MatrixOrder.Append);
 g.DrawLine(Pens.Black, 0,0, 100, 100);
}
```

This produces the line shown in Figure 15.2, drawn from the bottom-left corner to the new 100,100 position.

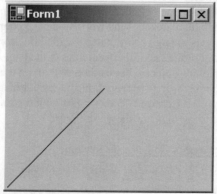

Figure 15.2: Flipped Coordinate System

You can use RotateTransform or ScaleTransform to manipulate the coordinate system. ScaleTransform is useful for zooming in and out on the form. Matrix transformations also can be applied to GraphicsPaths, Pens, and Brushes to get some interesting effects.

In addition, you can change the mapping of page coordinates to device coordinates. This is called *page transformation.* To alter this mapping, use the PageUnit property and PageScale property. The PageUnit property is an enumeration of different GraphicsUnits for mapping the page to the device, as itemized in Table 15.4.

GraphicsUnit Enumeration	Description
Display	1/75 of an inch.
Document	1/300 of an inch.
Pixel	Device pixel (often but not always 1/96 of an inch). This is the default.
Inch	1 inch.
Point	1/72 of an inch.
Millimeter	1 millimeter.
World	The world unit.

Table 15.4: GraphicsUnit Enumeration Measurements

Thus, if you want to draw a circle with a 1-inch radius (Figure 15.3), you would write the code shown in Listing 15.3. Once you change PageUnit to inches, every number applied to a graphics Draw function is measured in inches.

Listing 15.3—Changing the Page Transformation to Inches

```
private void DrawOneInchCircle(Graphics g)
{
  g.PageUnit = GraphicsUnit.Inch;
  g.DrawEllipse(new Pen(Brushes.Black, 0.10f), 0.5f, 0.5f, 2.0f,
      2.0f);
}
```

Note that the pen width needs to be specified; otherwise, the pen is drawn with a default width of 1.0, which means the thickness of the pen would be 1 inch!

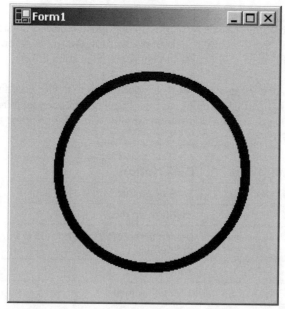

Figure 15.3: Circle Drawn with 1-Inch Radius

Now let's examine some common GDI+ classes and how to work with them. We begin with the Graphics class. After that, we discuss other common GDI+ classes and structures such as the Pen, Brush, and Rectangle, followed by examples. Later in the chapter, we see some advanced classes and how to work with them.

The Graphics Class

The Graphics class encapsulates GDI+ drawing surfaces. Before drawing an object—a circle or rectangle, for example—you have to create a surface using the Graphics class. There are a few ways to acquire a graphics drawing surface object in an application:

- Use the event argument in the Paint event of a form.
- Override the OnPaint method and extract the Graphics object from the Paint event argument.
- Create the Graphics object directly from the CreateGraphics method of a form.
- Acquire the object from a Windows handle using Graphics.FromHwnd.
- Acquire the object from an Image object using Graphics.FromImage, which draws to a bitmap.
- Acquire the object from a handle to a device context using Graphics.FromHdc.

Listings 15.4 and 15.5 demonstrate ways to get a reference to the Graphics object in the Paint event.

Listing 15.4—Form Paint Event Handler

```
private void form1_Paint(object sender, PaintEventArgs pe)
{
      Graphics g = pe.Graphics;
}
```

Listing 15.5—Override of Form Paint Event Handler

```
protected override void OnPaint(PaintEventArgs pe)
{
      Graphics g = pe.Graphics;
```

}

You can even add a Paint event by using the Properties dialog box of a form. See Figure 15.4 and Listing 15.6.

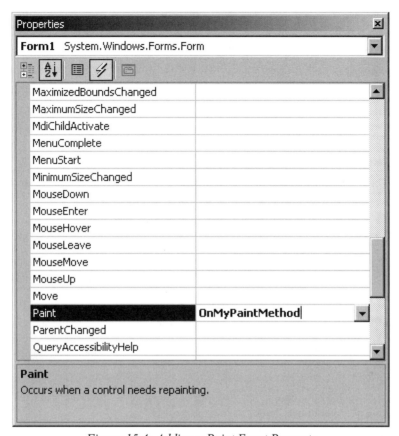

Figure 15.4: Adding a Paint Event Property

Listing 15.6—Creating Your Own Form Event Handler Name

```
private void OnMyPaintMethod(object sender,
 System.Windows.Forms.PaintEventArgs e)
{
     Graphics g = pe.Graphics;
}
```

In Listing 15.6, the PaintEventArgs.Graphics property returns the Graphics object. Once you have the Graphics object, you can call any of its class members to draw GDI objects such as lines, rectangles, polygons, or ellipses. Some of the Graphics class methods are DrawArc, DrawBezier, DrawCurve, DrawEllipse, DrawImage, DrawLine, DrawPath, DrawPie, DrawPolygon, DrawRectangle, DrawString, FillEllipse, FillPath, FillPie, FillRectangle, and FillRegion. We will see examples of these methods later in the chapter.

Graphics Objects

Several graphics objects are needed to draw lines, rectangles, text, images, graphics paths, polygons, and blends on the graphics surface. Table 15.5 lists some of the chief primitives and structures used for drawing.

Graphics Object	Function
Brush	Used to fill enclosed surfaces with patterns, colors, or bitmaps.
Pen	Used to draw lines and polygons, including rectangles, arcs, and pies.
Font	Used to describe the font to be used to render text.
Image	An abstract base class that provides the functionality for images including bitmaps, JPEGS, and metafiles.
Rectangle	Stores the location and size of a rectangular region.
Size	Represents the size of a rectangular region with an ordered pair of width and height.
Color	Describes the color used to render a particular object. In GDI+ color can be alpha blended.
Region	The interior of a shape described in terms of GraphicsPaths and rectangles.

Table 15.5: Other Important GDI+ Primitives and Structures

The Pen Class

A pen draws a line of a specified width and style. You must use a pen constructor to create a pen or use the existing system pens. The constructor initializes a new instance of the Pen class. You can initialize your pen with a color or a brush.

The constructor that follows initializes a new instance of the Pen class with the specified color. The color is the only parameter passed to the constructor:

```
public Pen(Color aColor);
```

The following constructor initializes a new instance of the Pen class with the specified brush. The Brush object is the only parameter passed as an argument:

```
public Pen(Brush aBrush);
```

To initialize a new instance of the Pen class with a specified brush and width, use this constructor:

```
public Pen(Brush aBrush, float aWidth);
```

To initialize a new instance of the Pen class with a specified color and width, pass a Color object followed by the width:

```
public Pen(Color aColor, float aWidth);
```

Here is an example of how to create a thick red pen:

```
Pen pn = new Pen(Brushes.Red, 3.0f);
```

Some of a pen's more commonly used properties are the Alignment, Brush, Color, and Width properties. Remember, you can use existing system pens if you don't want to construct new ones. System pens are contained in the Pens class. This class returns a Pen object for all its color properties and is convenient to use if you don't need a pen with an unusual thickness or style. Following is an example of using a pen from this class:

```
private void DrawingExampleWithPens(Graphics g)
{
```

```
      g.DrawLine(Pens.DarkTurquoise, 40, 50, 100, 150);
    }
```

Working with Pens

Many of the Graphics class drawing methods are passed a pen to perform the drawing task. Methods such as DrawLine, DrawRectangle, and DrawArc use pens to draw objects. A pen draws a line with a specified color, width, and style. The System.Drawing.Pen and System.Drawing.Pens classes help you create pens in GDI+. Some of the System.Drawing.Pen class properties are defined in Table 15.6.

Pen Property	Description
Brush	Attached brush with a pen
Color	Color of a pen
DashStyle	Dashed line style
DashPattern	Dash pattern
StartCap, EndCap	Starts and ends the cap style
PenStyle	Style of lines of a pen
Transform	Geometric transformation of a pen
Width	Width of the pen

Table 15.6: Properties of the Pen Class

The code in Listing 15.7 shows how to construct a pen and later set its properties.

Listing 15.7—Constructing a Green Dashed Pen

```
Pen pnGreen = new Pen( Color.Green); // construct a green pen
pnGreen.Width = 4;  // set the pen width to 4
pnGreen.DashStyle = DashStyle.DashDot; // use a DashDot style
```

The DashStyle members and their descriptions are shown in Table 15.7.

Member	Description
Custom	Custom dash style
Dash	A line consisting of dashes
DashDot	A line of a repeating pattern of dash-dot
DashDotDot	A line of a repeating pattern of dash-dot-dot
Dot	A line consisting of dots
Solid	A solid line

Table 15.7: DashStyle Enumeration for a Pen

To draw a custom dashed line, set the DashStyle to Custom and the DashPattern to an array of specified dash lengths. The code in Listing 15.8 draws a custom dashed rectangle with a pattern following the format of a dash of 5, a space of 10, a dash of 15, and a space of 20.

Listing 15.8—Drawing a Custom DashStyle

```
      private void DrawCustomDashedRectangle(Graphics g)
```

```
{
        float[] dashValues = {5, 10, 15, 20};
        Pen purplePen = new Pen(Color.Purple, 2);
        purplePen.DashStyle = DashStyle.Custom;
        purplePen.DashPattern = dashValues;
        g.DrawRectangle(purplePen, 50, 50, 150, 100);
}
```

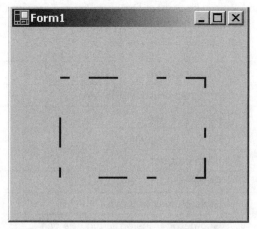

Figure 15.5: Custom Dashed Rectangle

The Brush Class

You can create different brush types in GDI+. This section illustrates how to create a few of them.

The Brush class is an abstract base class and cannot be instantiated. We always use its derived classes—such as SolidBrush, TextureBrush, RectangleGradientBrush, and LinearGradientBrush—to instantiate a Brush object.

Brushes are used to fill graphical shapes such as rectangles, ellipses, pies, polygons, and paths. The SolidBrush class defines a brush made up of a single color. The TextureBrush encapsulates a brush that uses and fills the interior of a shape with an image. The LinearGradientBrush encapsulates both two-color gradients and custom multicolor gradients. See Listings 15.9, 15.10, and 15.11 for some examples.

Listing 15.9—Constructing a Red-and-Yellow LinearGradient Brush

```
LinearGradientBrush lBrush = new LinearGradientBrush(rect, Color.Red, Color.Yellow,
 LinearGradientMode.BackwardDiagonal);
```

Listing 15.10—Constructing a Solid Red Brush

```
Brush brsh = new SolidBrush(Color.Red);
```

Listing 15.11—Filling a Rectangle with a Texture Brush

```
Image img = new Bitmap("myfile.bmp");
TextureBrush txtBrush = new TextureBrush(img);
g.FillRectangle(txtBrush, ClientRectangle);
```

The Color Structure

The Color structure represents the ARGB (alpha, red, green, blue) value of a color. You can access a color from a static set of color names, such as Aqua, Beige, Red, Black, White, Green, Blue, Yellow, and DarkRed. You also can access colors directly through their numeric ARGB value. If you know the name of the color from the enumeration of KnownColors, you can access the color through a string. Finally, you can use the KnownColors enumeration to access all the colors known by the system. Listing 15.12 demonstrates the four ways to use colors in the Color structure and paint a color strip on your form (see also Figure 15.6).

Listing 15.12—Retrieving Colors Four Different Ways

```
private void UtilizingColors(Graphics g)
{
        Rectangle aRect = new Rectangle(10, 100, 30, 30);
        Color aColor = Color.BlueViolet;
        g.FillRectangle(new SolidBrush(aColor), aRect);

        aRect.Offset(aRect.Width, 0);
        aColor = Color.FromArgb(255, 25, 25);
        g.FillRectangle(new SolidBrush(aColor), aRect);

        aRect.Offset(aRect.Width, 0);
        aColor = Color.FromKnownColor(KnownColor.Window);
        g.FillRectangle(new SolidBrush(aColor), aRect);

        aRect.Offset(aRect.Width, 0);
        aColor = Color.FromName("Yellow");
        g.FillRectangle(new SolidBrush(aColor), aRect);
}
```

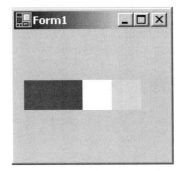

Figure 15.6: Using the Color Structure

The Font Class

The Font class defines a particular format for text, such as the font type, size, and style attributes. The following font constructor initializes a new instance of the Font class with the specified attributes:

```
public Font(string, float);
```

The following constructor initializes a new instance of the Font class from the specified existing Font and FontStyle:

```
public Font(Font, FontStyle);
```

FontStyle is an enumeration that includes the values Bold, Italic, Regular, StrikeOut, and Underline. Listing 15.13 shows one example of constructing fonts with different FontStyles and drawing them in the form.

Listing 15.13—Displays Different Font Styles

```
private void DisplayingFontStyles(Graphics g)
```

```
{
        string strFonts = "The Font Styles";
        float xcoord = 10.0f;
        float ycoord = 10.0f;
        Font afont = new Font("Times New Roman", 26);
        g.DrawString(strFonts, afont, Brushes.Black, xcoord,
                    ycoord, new StringFormat());
        ycoord += afont.Height + 5;
        afont = new Font("Times New Roman", 26, FontStyle.Bold);
                            g.DrawString(strFonts, afont, Brushes.Black,
                xcoord, ycoord,                    new StringFormat());

    ycoord += afont.Height + 5;
      afont = new Font("Times New Roman", 26, FontStyle.Underline);
      g.DrawString(strFonts, afont, Brushes.Black, xcoord, ycoord,
                    new StringFormat());

      ycoord += afont.Height + 5;
      afont = new Font("Times New Roman", 26,
                    FontStyle.Strikeout);
      g.DrawString(strFonts, afont, Brushes.Black, xcoord,
                    ycoord, new StringFormat());
      ycoord += afont.Height + 5;
      afont = new Font("Times New Roman", 26,
                        FontStyle.Bold | FontStyle.Italic);
      g.DrawString(strFonts, afont, Brushes.Black, xcoord,
                        ycoord, new StringFormat());
}
```

The corresponding output appears in Figure 15.7. Note that for the last style we were able to combine italic and bold by performing a logical *or* on the two FontStyles.

Figure 15.7: Outputting Different Font Styles

Font Properties

Fonts define several properties as shown in Table 15.8. These properties are read-only and cannot be altered after the font is constructed.

Font Property	Description
Bold	Gets a value indicating whether the font is bold
FontFamily	Gets the FontFamily of the font
Height	Gets the height of the font
Italic	Gets a value indicating whether the font is italic
Name	Gets the face name of the font
Size	Gets the size of the font
SizeInPoints	Gets the size, in points, of the font
Strikeout	Gets a value indicating whether the font is strikeout (has a line through it)
Style	Gets the style information for the font
Underline	Gets a value indicating whether the font is underlined
Unit	Gets the unit of measure for the font

Table 15.8: Properties of the Font Class

The FontFamily class represents a particular font type, such as Arial. The FontFamily is used to work with similar kinds of fonts that vary in size and style. For example, the following line constructs an object representing the Tahoma font family:

```
FontFamily fontFmly = new FontFamily("Tahoma");
```

We can then use this family to construct the font:

```
Font green28 = new Font(fontFmly, 28);
```

The FontFamily class provides members with which to get information about a family of fonts. The methods include GetName, GetLineSpacing, GetEmHeight, and IsStyleAvailable. GetName returns the family name, such as Arial. GetLineSpacing gets the space between typed lines. GetEmHeight retrieves the height of a letter. The IsStyleAvailable method tells you if the specified FontStyle exists.

The Rectangle Structure

The Rectangle structure is used to draw a rectangle on a form. Besides its constructor, the Rectangle structure's members include the properties Bottom, Height, IsEmpty, Left, Location, Right, Size, Top, Width, X, and Y. The constructors initialize a new instance of the Rectangle class. Following are two examples:

```
public Rectangle(Point, Size);
public Rectangle(int x, int y, int width, int height);
```

RectangleF is the floating point version of the Rectangle structure. Many of the Graphics class functions take either Rectangle or RectangleF as parameters. To convert a RectangleF to a Rectangle, use the static Truncate, Ceiling, or Round methods of the Rectangle class:

```
RectangleF theRectangleF = new RectangleF(5.0f, 7.0f, 100.60f, 240.3f);
Rectangle rint = Rectangle.Truncate(theRectangleF);
```

The Point Structure

The Point structure is similar to the POINT structure in C++. It represents an ordered pair of x and y coordinates that defines a point in a two-dimensional plane. The member x represents the x coordinates, and y represents the y coordinates of the plane. To instantiate a point structure, you can use the following constructors:

```
Point pt1 = new Point( 30, 30);
Point pt2 = new Point( 110, 100);
```

As with the Rectangle object, the Point structure has a floating point version—in this case called PointF. Many of the Graphics class functions take either a Point or PointF object as one of their parameters. Conversion of a PointF to a Point uses the Truncate, Ceiling, and Round functions:

```
    PointF thePointF = new PointF(73.34f, 81.93f);
Point thePoint = Point.Round(thePointF);
```

The Size Structure

The Size structure represents the size of a rectangle and is represented with an ordered pair of Width and Height properties. The Size.Empty property is used to initialize the structure. The IsEmpty method can be used to test whether the Size structure has zero Width and Height. The SizeF structure is the floating point version of the Size structure. You can convert the SizeF to a Size structure by using the static methods of the Size structure: Size.Truncate, Size.Ceiling, and Size.Round. Listing 15.14 shows an example of how to use the Size structure to draw an ellipse.

Listing 15.14—Using the Size Structure to Draw an Ellipse

```
    private void EllipseUsingSize(Graphics g)
    {
        Size sz = Size.Empty;
        sz.Height = 50;
        sz.Width = 200;
        Rectangle rect = new Rectangle(new Point(50,50), sz);
        g.DrawEllipse(new Pen(Color.Red), rect);
    }
```

Drawing Objects Using the Graphics Class

The Graphics class allows you to draw several objects.

Drawing a Rectangle

Use the Graphics class's FillRectangle or DrawRectangle method to draw a rectangle. The DrawRectangle is an overloaded method that takes the following forms:

```
public void DrawRectangle(Pen, Rectangle);
public void DrawRectangle(Pen, int, int, int, int);
public void DrawRectangle(Pen, float, float, float, float);
```

The example in Listing 15.15 draws a blue rectangle.

Listing 15.15—Drawing an Unfilled Blue Rectangle

```
protected override void OnPaint(PaintEventArgs pe)
{
Graphics g = pe.Graphics ;
Pen pn = new Pen( Color.Blue );
Rectangle rect = new Rectangle(50, 50, 200, 100);
g.DrawRectangle( pn, rect );
```

}

You can even use FillRectangle to draw a rectangle (see Listing 15.16). The LinearGradientBrush encapsulates a brush and linear gradient. The LinearGradientBrush is defined in the namespace System.Drawing.Drawing2D. Don't forget to include it.

Listing 15.16—Filling a Rectangle with a Red-Green LinearGradient

```
protected override void OnPaint(PaintEventArgs pe)
{
    Graphics g = pe.Graphics ;
    Rectangle rect = new Rectangle(50, 30, 200, 200);
    LinearGradientBrush lBrush = new LinearGradientBrush(rect,
 Color.Red, Color.Green,
    LinearGradientMode.BackwardDiagonal);
    g.FillRectangle(lBrush, rect);
}
```

Drawing an Arc

An arc is drawn from the starting angle and curves clockwise through the sweep angle, within the confines of a rectangle. To sweep counterclockwise, simply change the sign of the angle to a negative value.

```
public void DrawArc(Pen pn, Rectangle rect, float startAngle, float sweepAngle );
```

The example in Listing 15.17 draws an arc from 45 degrees above the x axis counterclockwise, sweeping through 135 degrees.

Listing 15.17—Drawing an Arc

```
private void Form1_Paint(object sender,
System.Windows.Forms.PaintEventArgs e)
        {
                Graphics g = e.Graphics;
                Pen aPen  = new Pen(Brushes.Red, 2.0f);
                Rectangle rect = new Rectangle(50, 50, 100, 50);

                // sweep 135 degree counterclockwise starting at 45 degrees
                // above the x-axis and draw an arc in the rectangle

                g.DrawArc(aPen, rect, -45, -135);
        }
```

The result of the code is displayed in the form's output in Figure 15.8.

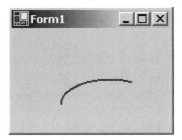

Figure 15.8: Drawing an Arc

You can draw other curves with GDI+. The DrawCurve method draws a fitted spline curve based on an array of points (see Listing 15.18). The last parameter of the DrawCurve function is a value between 0.0 and 1.0, representing the tension of the curve. A value of 0.0 would be the highest tension, producing straight lines between the point array.

Listing 15.18—Drawing a Spline Curve

```
private void Form1_Paint(object sender,
                System.Windows.Forms.PaintEventArgs e)
{
        Graphics g = e.Graphics;
        Pen aPen  = new Pen(Brushes.Red, 2.0f);


        PointF[] points = new PointF[4];
        points[0] = new PointF(30, 40);
        points[1] = new PointF(50, 100);
        points[2] = new PointF(20, 150);
        points[3] = new PointF(40, 180);
        g.DrawCurve(aPen, points, 0.5f);
}
```

The output of the DrawCurve function is shown in Figure 15.9.

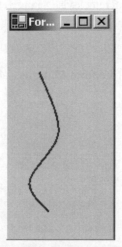

Figure 15.9: Drawing a Curve

Drawing a Line

The DrawLine function of the Graphics class draws a straight line. It has two overloaded functions: one takes a pen and a start and end point; the other takes a pen and two sets of *x, y* coordinates. You have the choice of using floating point, single, or integer types for your coordinates, as shown in the following lines of code:

```
public void DrawLine( Pen pen, Point startpt, Point endpt );

public void DrawLine( Pen pen, int xstart, int ystart, int xend, float yend);
public void DrawLine( Pen pen, float xstart, float ystart, float xend, float
        yend);

public void DrawLine( Pen pen, single xstart, single ystart, single xend,
single yend);
```

The Point class constructor takes an *x, y* argument. Listing 15.19 shows an example of drawing a blue diagonal line on the form.

Listing 15.19—Drawing a Blue Line

```
protected override void OnPaint(PaintEventArgs pe)
{
Graphics g = pe.Graphics ;
Pen pn = new Pen( Color.Blue );
Point pt1 = new Point( 30, 30);
Point pt2 = new Point( 110, 100);
g.DrawLine( pn, pt1, pt2 );
}
```

Drawing a Group of Lines

The DrawLines method allows you to draw several attached segments. This is useful if you want to connect points. The DrawLines function takes a pen and an array of points. The code in Listing 15.20 connects several points to form a sine curve using the DrawLines method. The output of the sine curve is displayed in Figure 15.10.

Listing 15.20—Drawing a Sine Curve with the DrawLines Method

```
private void DrawSineCurve(Graphics g)
{
   PointF[] points = new PointF[30];
   for (int i = 0; i < points.Length; i++)
   {
        points[i] = new PointF((float)i * 5.0f + 50,
                (float)Math.Sin(Math.PI*2.0f * (float)i/ 30.0f) * 50.0f
                + 100.0f);
   }

   g.DrawLines(Pens.Black, points);
}
```

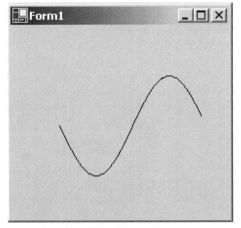

Figure 15.10: A Sine Curve Using DrawLines

Drawing an Ellipse

You can use the DrawEllipse method to draw a circle or an ellipse. This method can take either a rectangle or a set of coordinates representing a rectangle:

```
public DrawEllipse(Pen aPen, Rectangle boundingRect);
public DrawEllipse(Pen aPen, int left, int top, int right, int bottom);
```

The code in Listing 15.21 draws a hollow red circle with a pixel radius of 50 and a pixel border width of 5 in the center of the form.

Listing 15.21—Drawing a Red Circle

```
private void DrawThickRedCircle(Graphics g)
  {
   Pen pn = new Pen( Color.Red, 5 );
   Point midPoint = new Point(ClientRectangle.X + ClientRectangle.Width/2,
                    ClientRectangle.Y + ClientRectangle.Height/2);
   Rectangle circleRect = new Rectangle(midPoint.X - 50, midPoint.Y - 50,
                                 100, 100);
    g.DrawEllipse( pn,  circleRect);
  }
```

Drawing a Polygon

The DrawPolygon method draws a polygon using a set of points. This method takes two parameters: as with most drawn shapes, the first parameter is a pen; the second parameter is an array of PointF or Point objects. The code in Listing 15.22 draws a chocolate trapezoid on the screen (see Figure 15.11).

Listing 15.22—Drawing a Large Trapezoid

```
private void DrawTrapezoid(Graphics g)
{
        PointF point1 = new PointF(50.0f, 250.0f);
        PointF point2 = new PointF(250.0f, 250.0f);
        PointF point3 = new PointF(200.0f, 100.0f);
        PointF point4 = new PointF(150.0f, 100.0f);
        PointF point5 = new PointF(50.0f, 250.0f);
        PointF[] trapezoidPoints = {point1, point2, point3, point4, point5 };
        g.DrawPolygon(new Pen(Color.Chocolate, 10), trapezoidPoints);
}
```

Figure 15.11: A Trapezoid Polygon

Filling Shapes

Most shapes have a corresponding Fill function in the Graphics class if filling the shape makes sense. For example, you can fill rectangles, ellipses, regions, polygons, graphics paths, and closed curves. The Fill functions look almost identical to their corresponding Draw functions except that they take a Brush parameter instead of a Pen. See Table 15.9 for a list of the Fill functions and what each can fill.

Fill Method	Description
FillRectangle	Fills a rectangular region
FillEllipse	Fills an elliptical region
FillRegion	Fills a region
FillPolygon	Fills a polygon whose boundary is defined by a set of points
FillPath	Fills a graphics path's interior
FillClosedCurve	Fills a curved shape defined by a set of points representing spline endpoints
FillPie	Fills a pie region using the same parameters as an arc
FillRectangles	Fills the inside of an array of rectangles

Table 15.9: Fill Functions in the Graphics Class

To fill a circle with pie sections, you call FillPie, sweeping each angle of the circle. To divide a circle into three sections, you could sweep each section with 360 ÷ 3, or 120, degrees. The code for drawing a three-section color wheel is shown in Listing 15.23. Each call to FillPie sweeps another third of the pie.

Listing 15.23—Filling Pie Sections in a Circle

```
private void DrawColorWheel(Graphics g)
{
        Rectangle r  = new Rectangle(20, 20, 100, 100);
        g.FillPie(Brushes.Gray, r, 60, 120);
        g.FillPie(Brushes.DarkGray, r, 180, 120);
        g.FillPie(Brushes.White, r, 300, 120);
}
```

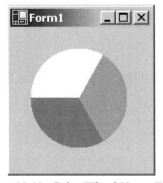

Figure 15.12: Color Wheel Using FillPie

Drawing a String

You can even use a Graphics object to draw strings. The DrawString function has several overloads and takes a font, a brush, positional information, and a StringFormat object. By manipulating the fonts, formats, and brushes, you can draw some interesting-looking messages on your form. The code in Listing 15.24 draws a big "Hello" with a cloud texture, shown in Figure 15.13.

Listing 15.24—Drawing a String with a Textured Brush

```
private void DrawCloudText(Graphics g)
  {
   g.DrawString("Hello", new Font("Comic Sans MS", 70.0f, FontStyle.Bold),
       new TextureBrush(CloudImage,
            new RectangleF(0.0f, 0.0f, 20.0f, 20.0f)),
        30, 30,
        new StringFormat());
  }
```

Figure 15.13: Output of DrawString Function

The StringFormat object is used to determine how the text is formatted. The StringFormat has two properties that help to do this: FormatFlags and Alignment. FormatFlags takes a StringFormatFlags enumeration value, which includes DirectionRightToLeft, DirectionVertical, NoClip, NoWrap, and DisplayFormatControl. NoClip specifies that the text is displayed, regardless of whether it fits in the specified display rectangle. NoWrap prevents the text from wrapping to another line, even if it is too long for the width of the display rectangle. DisplayFormatControl will show a visible representation of format characters, such as tabs or line feeds.

Listing 15.25 shows the same cloud-textured *Hello* coded for vertical text.

Listing 15.25—Using StringFormatFlags to Draw Vertical Text

```
private void DrawVerticalCloudText(Graphics g)
  {
   g.DrawString("Hello", new Font("Comic Sans MS", 70.0f, FontStyle.Bold),
       new TextureBrush(CloudImage,
            new RectangleF(0.0f, 0.0f, 20.0f, 20.0f)),
        30, 30,
  new StringFormat(StringFormatFlags.DirectionVertical));
  }
```

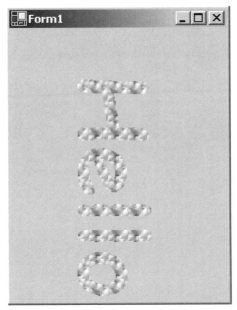

Figure 15.14: Cloud Hello Text in the Vertical Direction

The Alignment property is assigned a StringAlignment enumeration of either Center, Near, or Far. StringAlignment.Center centers the text inside the specified rectangular region. Depending on the StringFormatFlag's Direction setting, the Near property will align the beginning of the text nearest the edge of the start of the enclosing rectangular region.

StringFormat also includes a Trimming property that allows you to assign a StringTrimming enumeration of Character, EllipsisCharacter, EllipsisPath, EllipsisWord, None, or Word. This property allows you to specify how a string is trimmed inside its specified region. For example, StringTrimming.Character trims the string to the nearest character.

StringTrimming.EllipsisCharacter trims the string to the nearest character and inserts an ellipsis ("…") into the string if it doesn't fit into the display rectangle. The code in Listing 15.26 shows the *Hello* fitted into a display rectangle too short for it. We have applied the EllipseCharacter trimming to our StringFormat object and passed it into the DrawString function. The results can be seen in Figure 15.15.

Listing 15.26—Using StringFormat to Truncate a Drawn String

```
private void DrawCloudTextWithEllipse(Graphics g)
{
    const int LESS_CHARACTERS = 3;
    Font FunFont = new Font("Comic Sans MS", 70.0f, FontStyle.Bold);
    StringFormat EllipseFormat = new StringFormat();
    EllipseFormat.Trimming = StringTrimming.EllipsisCharacter ;
    g.DrawString("Hello", FunFont,
      new TextureBrush(CloudImage,
      new RectangleF(0.0f, 0.0f, 20.0f, 20.0f)),
      new RectangleF(30.0f, 30.0f,
    (float)FunFont.SizeInPoints*LESS_CHARACTERS,
    (float)FunFont.Height),
    EllipseFormat);
}
```

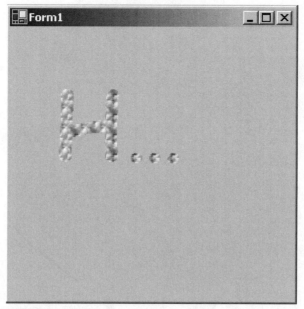

Figure 15.15: Hello Text Trimmed with the Ellipse Function

The Image Class

The Image class provides basic functionality from Bitmap, Icon, and Metafile classes. You can create a bitmap from a file, a window handle, or stream using the FromFile, FromHBitmap, and FromStream methods respectively. The GetBounds, Save, and RotateFlip methods are other useful members. We will use these members in examples in a moment.

Because the Image class is an abstract base class you cannot instantiate it directly. You can, however, retrieve an image from the From static methods mentioned in the previous paragraph. The Graphics class has two methods for drawing images. Both have many overloaded variations called DrawImage and DrawImageUnscaled. These functions can be used to draw, size, and position the image on the form. In Listing 15.27 we create an image with the FromFile method and draw it with the DrawImageUnscaled method.

Listing 15.27—Drawing an Image

```
void DrawFootballImage(Graphics g)
{
        Image theImage = Image.FromFile("football.jpg");
        for (int i = 0; i < ClientRectangle.Width - theImage.Width;
                                        i += theImage.Width)
        {
            g.DrawRectangle(Pens.Red, i, 28, theImage.Width + 2,
                                theImage.Height + 2);
            g.DrawImageUnscaled(theImage, i+2, 30, theImage.Width,
                                theImage.Height);

        }
}
```

The picture in Figure 15.16 is generated from Listing 15.27.

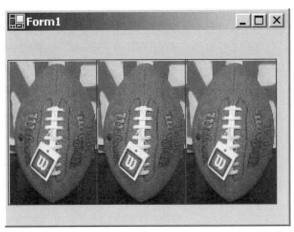

Figure 15.16: Drawing from DrawImageUnscaled

Some of the Image class properties and methods are described in Table 15.10.

Image Properties	Description
Height, Width	Represent the height and width of an image
HorizontalResolution, VerticalResolution	The horizontal and vertical resolution, in pixels per inch
PixelFormat	Gets the pixel format for the Image object
RawFormat	Gets the format of the Image object
Size	Gets the width and height of the Image object
Palette	Gets or sets the ColorPalette of the Image object

Table 15.10: Properties of the Image Class

The Image class is the base class for the Bitmap, Icon, and Metafile classes and provides the common functionality they need. These classes are described in detail in the sections that follow.

The Bitmap Class

A Bitmap object encapsulates images stored in pixel data. The Bitmap class is derived from the Image class, which defines the functionality to save images, rotate and flip images, retrieve formats, retrieve dimensions, retrieve resolutions, and convert images to files and streams. You can use the Bitmap class to construct an image from a file path, a resource in a DLL, a stream of data, an icon, or another image. You can even construct a blank bitmap with just its dimensions. This is useful when you want to draw your graphics in memory. Table 15.11 shows some of the constructors of a bitmap.

Bitmap Constructor	Description
Bitmap(Image)	Constructs an image from an existing image.
Bitmap(int width, int height)	Constructs a blank image with the specified width and height.
Bitmap(string filename)	Constructs an image from a file (JPG, GIF, BMP, etc.). The image format is automatically determined from the extension.
Bitmap(Stream, bool bUseColorCorrection)	Constructs an image from a data stream.
Bitmap(Type aResourceType, string resourceName)	Constructs a bitmap from a resource type and the name of the resource.
Bitmap (int width, int height, Graphics g)	Initializes a blank bitmap with the dimensions passed and the resolution of the Graphics object.
Bitmap(int width, int height, int rowsize, PixelFormat format, IntPtr PixelDataAddress)	Constructs a bitmap from data pointed to by a memory location.

Table 15.11: Fill Functions in the Graphics Class

The code to construct our football image as a bitmap and draw it (see Listing 15.28) is almost identical to Listing 15.27.

Listing 15.28—Using the Bitmap Class to Draw an Image

```
void DrawFootballImageBitmap(Graphics g)
{

        Bitmap theImage = new Bitmap("football.jpg");
        for (int i = 0; i < ClientRectangle.Width - theImage.Width;
            i += theImage.Width)
        {
            g.DrawRectangle(Pens.Red, i, 28, theImage.Width + 2,
                theImage.Height + 2);
            g.DrawImageUnscaled(theImage, i+2, 30, theImage.Width,
                theImage.Height);

        }
}
```

Positioning and Sizing an Image on a Form

All the overloaded functions in the Graphics.DrawImage method allow you to size and position your image anywhere you want on a drawing surface. You can draw an image with its original size and position:

```
g.DrawImage( bmp, AutoScrollPosition.X, AutoScrollPosition.Y,
bmp.Width, bmp.Height );
```

Or you can expand the image dimensions to suit your needs. By using the form's ClientRectangle, you can draw an image to fill the full client area of the form:

```
Bitmap theImage = new Bitmap("football.jpg");
g.DrawImage(theImage, ClientRectangle);
```

Figure 15.17: Football Sized to Fit Entire Form

Of course, as is apparent in Figure 15.17, this may look a bit warped because the image is stretched unequally, so you may want to size the form but scale the width and height with the same factor. See Listing 15.29 and Figure 15.18.

Listing 15.29—Drawing an Image and Maintaining the Aspect Ratio

```
void DrawFootballToFullScreenMaintainAspect(Graphics g)
{

    Bitmap theImage = new Bitmap("football.jpg");
    Rectangle r = ClientRectangle;
    float aspectx = (float)r.Width/(float)theImage.Width;
    float aspecty = (float)r.Height/(float)theImage.Height;
    if (aspectx < aspecty)
    {
      r.Width = (int)((float)theImage.Width * aspectx);
      r.Height = (int)((float)theImage.Height * aspectx);
    }
    else
    {
        r.Width = (int)((float)theImage.Width * aspecty);
        r.Height = (int)((float)theImage.Height * aspecty);
    }

    g.DrawImage(theImage, r);
}
```

Figure 15.18: Football Scaled to Fit Form

Saving an Image to a File

GDI+ supports the saving and loading of several popular file formats. The formats available are defined by the ImageFormat enumerations shown in Table 15.12.

ImageFormat Enumeration	Description
Bmp	Windows BMP (bitmap) file format
Jpeg	JPEG and JPG (Joint Photographic Experts Group) file formats
Wmf	Windows metafile
Emf	Windows enhanced metafile
Gif	Graphics Interchange Format, developed by CompuServe
Tiff	Tagged Image File Format
Png	Portable Network Graphics
Exif	Exchangeable Image File Format
Icon	Windows icon image format, to save as an icon

Table 15.12: Image Formats in .NET

To save an image, simply call the static Image.Save method. If you don't specify an image format, the save method will try to figure out the format based on the file name's extension.

Drawing to a Bitmap

To draw to a bitmap, you need a Graphics object obtained from the bitmap that you can use as a drawing surface. Listing 15.30 shows some sample code for drawing to a bitmap using the FromImage method to extract the Graphics object. The code draws a black circle on a white background to a bitmap in memory. It then saves the bitmap to a GIF file.

Listing 15.30—Drawing a Circle to a Bitmap

```
private void DrawToBitmap()
{
        Bitmap theBitmap = new Bitmap(200, 200);
        Graphics g = Graphics.FromImage(theBitmap);
        g.FillRectangle(Brushes.White, 0, 0, 200, 200);
        g.DrawEllipse(Pens.Black, 20, 20, 100, 100);
        theBitmap.Save("circle.gif", ImageFormat.Gif);
        g.Dispose();
        theBitmap.Dispose();
}
```

Working with Metafiles

The .NET Framework provides a few objects in the System.Drawing.Imaging namespace to help you work with metafiles. Metafiles are not ordinary graphics files such as GIF and BMP files that contain pixel information about each pixel's color and location. Metafiles are like recordings that play back the instructions for drawing to the form. The initial release of .NET supports three kinds of metafiles: the Windows metafile (WMF—the earliest version), the enhanced metafile (EMF), and, new for GDI+, the enhanced metafile+ (EMF+). The EMF+ files can be divided into two types: *EMF+ only* and *EMF+ dual*. EMF+ only allows you to record and play GDI+ commands but not GDI commands. EMF+ dual allows you to record and play both GDI and GDI+ commands.

In Listing 15.31 we record an EMF file and then play it back. In this example, the metafile records the drawing of a simple piece of text inside a rectangle. To create a metafile, we need to obtain the handle to the device context of the form, using the GetHdc method. Then a graphics surface is needed to draw specifically to the metafile. Once we have a Graphics object that points to the metafile, we can simply draw to this graphics surface as if it were any other Graphics object.

Listing 15.31—Recording a Metafile

```
private void CreateMetaFile()
{
Graphics g = CreateGraphics();
  IntPtr theDeviceContext = g.GetHdc();
  Metafile theMetaFile = new Metafile("FramedHello.emf",
 theDeviceContext);
  Graphics metaFileGraphics = Graphics.FromImage(theMetaFile);
  metaFileGraphics.DrawRectangle(Pens.Blue, 30, 30, 200, 100);
  metaFileGraphics.DrawString("Hi Everyone", new Font("Arial",
  20), Brushes.Red, 40, 40, new StringFormat());
  metaFileGraphics.Dispose();
  g.ReleaseHdc(theDeviceContext);
  g.Dispose();
}
```

It's important that after we have finished drawing to the graphics surface we dispose of the graphics objects and then release the device context. Otherwise, .NET starts throwing all kinds of exceptions.

To play back the metafile, construct the metafile in the same way we constructed a bitmap. We can use a metafile like any other image because it inherits from the Image class. Therefore, drawing the metafile is performed by calling DrawImage from the form's Graphics object (see Listing 15.32).

Listing 15.32—Playing a Metafile

```
private void PlayMetaFile(Graphics g)
{
        Metafile theMetaFile = new Metafile("FramedHello.emf");
        g.DrawImage(theMetaFile, 0, 0, ClientRectangle.Width,
        ClientRectangle.Height);
```

```
        }
```

Invalidation of a Form

The form's Invalidate method tells the form to repaint itself. In other words, it sends the form a Paint event and this fires the Paint event handler. If you call the Invalidate method with no parameters, it will invalidate the entire drawing and force the whole drawing to redraw. If you pass the Invalidate method a rectangle, it will invalidate only the area you want to redraw. Although the entire Paint event handler is called in any invalidation, only the specified area will actually repaint itself. Listing 15.33 shows an example of using Invalidate to tell the form to repaint itself after a button is pressed.

Listing 15.33—Invalidating a Form

```
protected void button1_Click (object sender, System.EventArgs e)
{
        AutoScroll = true;
        AutoScrollMinSize = bmp.Size;
        Invalidate();
}
```

Another useful time to invalidate a form is after the form resizes, especially if your graphics are dependent on the size of the form. You can handle a Resize event in the Resize event handler (see Listing 15.34).

Listing 15.34—Invalidating a Form During a Resize Event

```
        private void Form1_Resize(object sender, System.EventArgs e)
        {
                Invalidate();
        }
```

Invalidation is also useful for performing animation, as we see later in this chapter. Invalidating areas quickly and changing the graphics on the form gives the effect that the graphics are moving.

If you want to optimize your paint routine, you probably don't want to paint everything if you have invalidated only a small portion of the form. You can use *smart painting* by evaluating the ClipRegion in the Paint event handler and painting only those areas. This technique can speed up any animation program you are writing.

To understand the smart-painting techniques, refer to Listing 15.35. When you click inside the form, a 100-by-100-pixel area is invalidated around the point clicked. This causes a Paint message to be sent to the form and the Form1_Paint event handler to be called. The clipped region is extracted from the Paint event handler's event argument and passed along with the Graphics object to the DrawFourRectangle routine. This routine checks whether the clipping region rectangle intersects with the rectangle to be drawn before painting it using the rectangle's IntersectWith method. The output of Listing 15.35 is shown in Figure 15.19.

Listing 15.35—Smart Invalidation Using ClipRectangles

```
private void Form1_MouseDown(object sender,
                System.Windows.Forms.MouseEventArgs e)
        {
                Rectangle rectMouseArea = new Rectangle(e.X - 50,
                        e.Y - 50, 100, 100);
                Invalidate(rectMouseArea);
        }

    private void Form1_Paint(object sender,
```

```
        System.Windows.Forms.PaintEventArgs e)
        {
                Graphics g = e.Graphics;
                DrawFourRectangles(g, e.ClipRectangle);
        }


    private void DrawFourRectangles(Graphics g,
                    Rectangle clipRect)
    {
        for (int i = 0;  i < 4; i++)
        {
                int RComp = pRandom.Next(255);
                int GComp = pRandom.Next(255);
                int BComp = pRandom.Next(255);

                Color aColor = Color.FromArgb(RComp, GComp,
                BComp);
                Rectangle r = new Rectangle((i%2)*100, (i/2) *
                    100, 70, 70);

                if (clipRect.IntersectsWith(r))
                    {
                     g.FillRectangle(new SolidBrush(aColor),
                                        r);
                    }
        }

    }
```

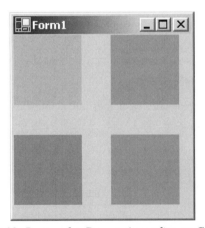

Figure 15.19: Rectangles Drawn According to Clip Region

System.Drawing.Drawing2D Namespace

The System.Drawing.Drawing2D namespace consists of classes and enumerations for advanced two-dimensional and vector graphics functionality. It contains classes for gradient brushes, matrix transformations, and graphics paths. Some of the common classes are defined in Table 15.13.

Class	Description
Blend and ColorBlend	Define the blend for gradient brushes. ColorBlend defines the array of colors and position for a multicolor gradient.
GraphicsPath	Represents a set of connected lines and curves.
HatchBrush	A brush with hatch style, foreground color, and background color.
LinearGradientBrush	Provides the brush functionality with linear gradient.
Matrix	A 3 x 3 matrix that represents geometric transformation.

Table 15.13: Classes in the Drawing2D Namespace

The System.Drawing.Drawing.2D namespace consists of several enumerations that help you work with brush and pen styles, as well as the quality of the drawing modes. See Table 15.14 for a list of some of those enumerations.

Enumeration	Description
CombineMode	Different clipping types
CompositingQuality	The quality of compositing
DashStyle	The style of dashed lines drawn with a pen
HatchStyle	Represents different patterns available for HatchBrush
QualityMode	Specifies the quality of GDI+ objects
SmoothingMode	Specifies the quality of GDI+ objects

Table 15.14: Enumerations in the Drawing2D Namespace

Working with GraphicsPath

Sometimes it is desirable to group a series of shapes into a single entity. The GraphicsPath class allows you to create a shape from a series of GDI+ lines and curves. Some GraphicsPath properties are shown in Table 15.15.

GraphicsPath Property	Description
PathData	An object containing an array of points representing the path
PathPoints	The array of points representing the path
PointCount	The number of points in the path
FillMode	Enumeration that determines how the path will be filled (alternate or winding)
PathTypes	An array of bytes describing the types of data in the PathPoints array

Table 15.15: Properties of the GraphicsPath Class

A GraphicsPath includes several methods to draw a part of the path. These methods are almost identical to the methods used by the Graphics object itself and include AddArc, AddBezier, AddBeziers, AddClosedCurve, AddCurve, AddEllipse, AddLine, AddLines, AddPath, AddPie, AddPolygon, AddRectangle, AddRectangles, and AddString. These methods take the same parameters as the corresponding Draw functions in the Graphics object. The GraphicsPath includes other useful methods as well, such as CloseFigure, which closes the points between the start point and endpoint. Also notable is the Flatten method, which converts curve segments into a sequence of connected segments. But the most useful is the Transform method, which allows you to scale, translate, rotate, or skew the GraphicsPath by applying a Matrix object.

Transforming the GraphicsPath

A GraphicsPath uses a matrix to transform drawings into two dimensions. The matrix is a 3 × 3 matrix representing a geometric transform. When you construct a matrix with no parameters, it constructs the identity matrix seen in Figure 15.20. Applying an identity matrix has no effect on the GraphicsPath.

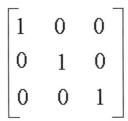

$$\begin{bmatrix} 1 & 0 & 0 \\ 0 & 1 & 0 \\ 0 & 0 & 1 \end{bmatrix}$$

Figure 15.20: Identity Matrix for Geometric Transform

This matrix can be rotated, translated, scaled, or skewed using the Matrix methods Rotate, RotateAt, Translate, Scale, and Shear. By applying these methods and then passing the matrix to the GraphicsPath Transform method, we can transfer the effects on the matrix to the GraphicsPath. Let's look at an example. Listing 15.36 creates a GraphicsPath consisting of a stick figure. The GraphicsPath is drawn on the form in the Paint event handler using the DrawPath method (see Listing 15.37). Note that we needed to backtrack along some of the lines to avoid the figure closing along the path.

Listing 15.36—Creating a GraphicsPath

```
private GraphicsPath m_StickFigure = null;

private void CreateStickFigure()
{
        // draw a stick figure graphics path

        m_StickFigure = new GraphicsPath();
        m_StickFigure.AddEllipse(50, 50, 30, 30);
        m_StickFigure.AddLine(65, 80, 65, 110);
        m_StickFigure.AddLine(65, 110, 10, 110);
        m_StickFigure.AddLine(10, 110, 120, 110);
        m_StickFigure.AddLine(120, 110, 65, 110);
        m_StickFigure.AddLine(65, 110, 65, 150);
        m_StickFigure.AddLine(65, 150, 50, 200);
        m_StickFigure.AddLine(50, 200, 20, 200);
        m_StickFigure.AddLine(20, 200, 50, 200);
        m_StickFigure.AddLine(50, 200, 65, 150);
        m_StickFigure.AddLine(65, 150, 80, 200);
        m_StickFigure.AddLine(80, 200, 110, 200);
}
```

Listing 15.37—Drawing a GraphicsPath

```
private void DrawStickFigure(Graphics g)
{
        g.DrawPath(Pens.Black, m_StickFigure);
}

private void Form1_Paint(object sender,
        System.Windows.Forms.PaintEventArgs e)
```

```
        {
                Graphics g = e.Graphics;
                DrawStickFigure(g);
}
```

The output of the graphics path is shown in Figure 15.21.

Figure 15.21: Stick Figure GraphicsPath

Now, let's shrink our man down by half in the *x* direction and half in the *y* direction. This will shrink the man to ½ *x* and ½ *y,* or one-fourth the size. Shrinking the figure is accomplished by using the Scale method of the matrix and the Transform method of the GraphicsPath. See Listing 15.38.

Listing 15.38—Using a Transform to Scale a GraphicsPath

```
        private void ShrinkStickFigure()
        {
                Matrix scalingMatrix = new Matrix();
                scalingMatrix.Scale(0.5f, 0.5f);
                m_StickFigure.Transform(scalingMatrix);
        }
```

Figure 15.22: Stick Figure Scaled Down to One-Quarter Size

To move the stick figure to the center of the form employ the Translate method, and to stand him on his head use the Rotate method. See Listing 15.39.

Listing 15.39—Using a Transform to Rotate a GraphicsPath

```
private void CenterWithHeadStand()
{
 Matrix theMatrix = new Matrix();
 theMatrix.Translate(ClientRectangle.Width/2 +
        m_StickFigure.GetBounds().Width/2,
        ClientRectangle.Height/2 +
        m_StickFigure.GetBounds().Height/2);
   theMatrix.Rotate(180);
   m_StickFigure.Transform(theMatrix);
}
```

We translated the stick figure one-half the size of the path beyond the center of the form because the Rotate method rotates around the origin, in this case, the upper-left corner of the figure. If we wanted to rotate around the center of the path, we could calculate the midpoint of the path and use the RotateAt method, which takes both an angle and the point of rotation. Figure 15.23 shows the output of our acrobatic stick figure.

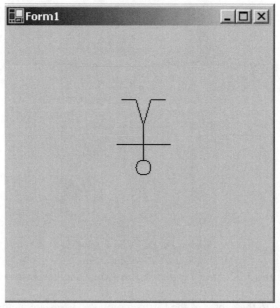

Figure 15.23: GraphicsPath Rotated and Translated

Setting Rendering Quality

QualityMode (see Table 15.16) and SmoothingMode (see Table 15.17) are two enumerations used to set the quality of image rendering. We will use these enumerations in our example (Listing 15.40)to set the rendering quality. SmoothingMode specifies the overall quality.

Enumeration Value	Description
Default	Default mode
High	High-quality, low-speed rendering
Invalid	Invalid mode
Low	Low-quality, high-speed rendering

Table 15.16: QualityMode Enumeration Values

Enumeration Value	Description
AntiAlias	Anti-aliased rendering for smoother line drawing
Default	Default mode
HighQuality	High-quality, low-speed rendering
HighSpeed	High-speed, low-quality rendering
Invalid	Invalid mode
None	No anti-aliasing

Table 15.17: SmoothingMode Enumeration Values

Listing 15.40—Using Anti-Aliasing When Drawing a Line

```
Graphics g = e.Graphics;
```

```
Pen redPn = Pens.Red;
g.SmoothingMode = SmoothingMode.AntiAlias;
g.DrawLine(redPn, 10, 10, 100, 80);
```

System.Drawing.Printing Namespace

The System.Drawing.Printing namespace defines the classes you use to implement printing functionality in your applications. Some of its major classes are defined in Table 15.18.

Printing Class	Description
PageSettings	Page settings
PaperSize	Size of paper
PreviewPageInfo	Prints preview information for a single page
PrintController	Controls document printing
PrintDocument	Sends output to a printer
PrinterResolution	Sets resolution of a printer
PrinterSettings	Printer settings

Table 15.18: Printing Classes and Structures

Printing in GDI+

.NET provides several components to make it easy for you to program printing. Those components include PrintDocument, PrintDialog, PrintPreviewControl, and PrintPreviewDialog. The components work together in different ways to enable you to construct printing in your GDI+ application with ease. Printing is handled in the PrintPage event handler. This event handler passes in a Graphics object that can be painted to exactly as you would paint in a form. If you are printing the same graphics to the printer as you are to a form, it is probably a good idea to encapsulate your custom drawing in a separate method, so that it can be called from both the PrintPage and Paint event handlers. The PrintPage event is activated by calling either the Print method from the PrintDocument or the ShowDialog from the PrintPreviewDialog. The following listings (Listing 15.41 through 15.43) is an example of printing a title page for a book to the printer. The PrintPreviewDialog, PrintDialog, and PrintDocument are created in Visual Studio .NET by dragging and dropping those components onto the form. You then need to set the PrintPreviewDialog and PrintDialog's Document property to printDocument1, the instance of the PrintDocument.

Double-clicking the PrintPage event of the printDocument1 object in the Property window creates the PrintPage event handler, where we do the drawing to the printed page. In Listing 15.41, we call the custom method DrawCenteredText inside our PrintPage handler, which handles all the drawing to the Graphics object. The DrawCenteredText method is passed the top margin and the page width (i.e., "8.5" for standard letter). See Listing 15.41.

Listing 15.41—Drawing in the PrintPage Event Handler

```
private string[] TitlePageLines = new string[] {"The Complete Visual C#
   Programmer's", "Reference Guide", "C# Corner", "Feb 15, 2001"};

private void printDocument1_PrintPage(object sender,
   System.Drawing.Printing.PrintPageEventArgs e)
      {
        DrawCenteredText(e.PageSettings.Margins.Top,
            e.PageBounds.Width, e.Graphics, TitlePageLines);
      }
```

PrintPreview is a fairly painless operation in .NET. It is carried out by calling ShowDialog on the printPreviewDialog object. See Listing 15.42.

Listing 15.42—Bringing Up the Print Preview Dialog Box

```
private void PrintPreview_Click(object sender, System.EventArgs e)
  {
   this.printPreviewDialog1.ShowDialog();
  }
```

The printing routine (to the printer driver) is performed by first opening the Printer Setup dialog box and, if OK is clicked, calling Print on the PrintDocument. See Listing 15.43.

Listing 15.43—Printing to the Printer Using the PrintDocument

```
private void Print_Click(object sender, System.EventArgs e)
   {
    if (printDialog1.ShowDialog() == DialogResult.OK)
       {
          printDocument1.Print();
       }
   }
```

The DrawCenteredText routine creates a large font and loops through the list of strings passed to the routine (see Listing 15.44). DrawCenteredText uses the MeasureString method to determine the point of the string on the page where the text will be centered. You also could use the StringFormat object to align the text.

Listing 15.44—Drawing a Title Page to the Printing Graphics Object

```
private void DrawCenteredText(int top, int pagewidth, Graphics g, string[] myText)
       {
        Font BigFont = new Font("Times new Roman", 20);
        float nextLine = (float)top;
        for (int i = 0; i < myText.Length; i++)
          {
             SizeF theFontSize = g.MeasureString(myText[i],
                                        BigFont);
             PointF midPt = new PointF(((float)pagewidth -
              theFontSize.Width)/2, nextLine);
             g.DrawString(myText[i], BigFont, Brushes.Black,
                   midPt, new  StringFormat());
             nextLine += theFontSize.Height + 5;
          }
       }
```

The results of displaying the Print Preview dialog box are shown in Figure 15.24. This dialog box gives you the option of going ahead and printing the page or zooming and displaying multiple pages in the preview screen.

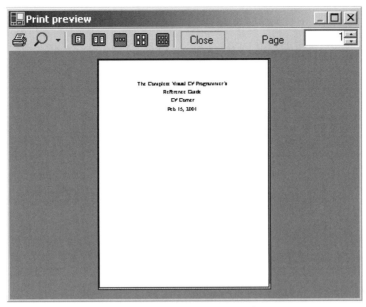

Figure 15.24: Print Preview Dialog Box

Here's a tip: If you want to change the size or orientation of the page you are printing, trap the QueryPageSettings event in the PrintDocument and make changes to the page settings there; otherwise, the changes won't occur.

System.Drawing.Text Namespace

Although most of a font's functionality is defined in the System.Drawing namespace, System.Drawing.Text provides advanced typography functionality, such as the capability to create a collection of fonts. In the current release of .NET, this namespace has only three classes: FontCollection, InstalledFontCollection, and PrivateFontCollection.

Working with Installed Fonts

One way to access the list of all the font families is to use the InstalledFontCollection class. By instantiating this class, you can loop through the collection of font families and determine which font faces are installed on your system. Listing 14.45 does just that. The method displays *C# Corner* in every font family on your system. We have added exception handling, because an exception is thrown if a font cannot be created with a regular style—for example, if the font can only be bold. The font families that cannot be displayed are outputted to the console of Visual Studio .NET.

Listing 15.45—Displaying the Installed Fonts

```
private void ShowInstalledFonts(Graphics g)
        {
                InstalledFontCollection theFonts = new
                        InstalledFontCollection();
                float xcoord = 10.0f;
                float ycoord = 10.0f;
                for (int i = 0; i < theFonts.Families.Length;
                        i++)
                  {
                    string strFonts = "C# Corner";
                    try
                    {
                        Font afont = new
```

```
                    Font(theFonts.Families[i].Name, 14);
            g.DrawString(strFonts, afont,
                Brushes.Black, xcoord,
                ycoord, new StringFormat());
            ycoord += g.MeasureString(strFonts,
                afont).Height + 3;
    }
    catch (Exception ex)
    {
        System.Console.WriteLine(
            ex.Message.ToString());
    }
    }
}
```

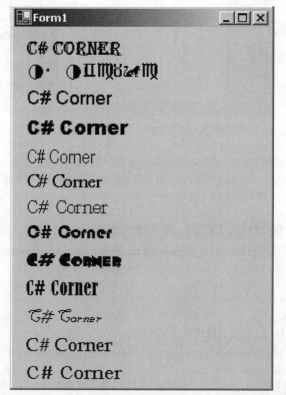

Figure 15.25: Font Families Displayed from InstalledFontCollection

Advanced Topics in GDI+

This section covers some advanced topics and techniques in GDI+. First we look at how to access your old GDI methods using GDI+ and the .NET Framework. Next we show you how to display GDI+ on a Web page in ASP.NET. Finally, we talk a little bit about animating, using double buffering, and adding sound to your application.

Using GDI with GDI+

Although GDI+ is a giant leap beyond the functionality GDI provides, some GDI functionality is not contained in GDI+. An example of something we might need to do in GDI+ is bit blasting. To bring in the calls for GDI, we need to use the attribute DllImport to bring in the gdi32.dll for the Windows operating system. (See Listing 15.46.) Note that when .NET is ported to other platforms, you probably will need to import a different native library than gdi32.dll.

Listing 15.46—Declaring and Importing a GDI Function

```
[System.Runtime.InteropServices.DllImportAttribute("gdi32.dll")]
        private static extern bool BitBlt(
            IntPtr hdcDest, // handle to destination DC
            int nXDest,   // x-coord of destination upper-left corner
            int nYDest,   // y-coord of destination upper-left corner
            int nWidth,   // width of destination rectangle
            int nHeight,  // height of destination rectangle
            IntPtr hdcSrc,  // handle to source DC
            int nXSrc,    // x-coordinate of source upper-left corner
            int nYSrc,    // y-coordinate of source upper-left corner
            System.Int32 dwRop  // raster operation code
            );
```

Now we can use the BitBlt function in our GDI+ application. To capture an image of the form, we need to blast the bits from the form to a blank bitmap of the same size. First, we acquire the Graphics object of the form. Then we create a blank target bitmap using the coordinates of the ClientRectangle. We use the FromImage method of the Graphics class to create a Graphics object for the bitmap. The graphics objects can be used to get the device contexts needed for the BitBlt GDI call using the GetHdc method. Now that we have everything we need to blast the bits, we can call the BitBlt function just as it is written in the import. After making the call, we need to release the handles to the device contexts, so that GDI+ will continue to function properly. To capture the form in a file, we can use the Save function of the Image class. See Listing 15.47.

Listing 15.47—Using a GDI Call in Your .NET Form

```
        private void button2_Click(object sender, System.EventArgs e)
        {

            Graphics g1 = this.CreateGraphics();
            Image MyImage = new Bitmap(this.ClientRectangle.Width,
                              this.ClientRectangle.Height, g1);
            Graphics g2 = Graphics.FromImage(MyImage);
            IntPtr dc1 = g1.GetHdc();
            IntPtr dc2 = g2.GetHdc();
            BitBlt(dc2, 0, 0, this.ClientRectangle.Width,
                    this.ClientRectangle.Height, dc1, 0, 0, 13369376);
            g1.ReleaseHdc(dc1);
            g2.ReleaseHdc(dc2);
            MyImage.Save(@"c:\Captured.jpg", ImageFormat.Jpeg);
            MessageBox.Show("Finished Saving Image");
        }
```

Using GDI+ in ASP.NET

There are a few ways to use GDI+ on your Web page. One is to create a bitmap and then save it as a file that points to an image already on the page. Another and faster technique is to blast the bitmap in memory out to the ASP.NET page's Response.OutputStream object.

First, you need a routine to draw to a bitmap in memory. The method in Listing 15.48 draws a C# Corner greeting in a fancy blue-and-red-filled rectangle. The greeting is drawn to a blank 500×200 bitmap that has been created in memory. A Graphics object is obtained to allow us to use the Graphics object drawing functions to draw into the bitmap.

Listing 15.48—Printing a Greeting to a Bitmap

```
        public Bitmap GenerateHelloGraphic()
        {
          Bitmap bmp = new Bitmap(500, 200);
```

```
    Graphics g = Graphics.FromImage(bmp);
    g.Clear(Color.White);
    g.DrawRectangle(new Pen(Brushes.Green, 3), 3, 3, bmp.Width - 6,
    bmp.Height - 6);
    g.FillRectangle(new LinearGradientBrush(new Point(0, 0), new
     Point(50, 50), Color.Blue, Color.Red),
        50, 50, bmp.Width - 100, bmp.Height - 100);
     g.DrawString("Hello From C# Corner", new Font("Arial", 25),
    Brushes.Yellow, 80, 75);
     return bmp;
}
```

The second step is to send the bitmap to the Response object. In order to display this in the browser, it should be done in the PageLoad event handler of the .aspx Web page. First, the Bitmap drawing routine is called to create the bitmap. Then the ContentType of the Response is set to *image,* so the browser knows what to display. Finally, the bitmap calls its Save method to send the bitmap data to the Response object's OutputStream. See Listing 15.49.

Listing 15.49—Saving the Bitmap to the Response OutputStream

```
private void Page_Load(object sender, System.EventArgs e)
{
        // Put user code to initialize the page here
        Bitmap thePageBmp = GenerateHelloGraphic();
        Response.ContentType="image/jpeg";
        thePageBmp.Save(Response.OutputStream,ImageFormat.Jpeg);


}
```

Figure 15.26 shows the resulting output in Internet Explorer.

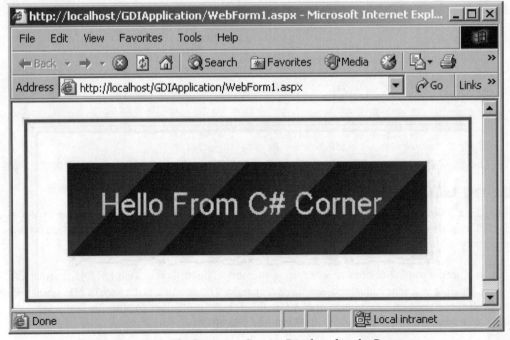

Figure 15.26: The Response Stream Displayed in the Browser

Animating in GDI+

Double Buffering in a Form

Double buffering occurs when you do all your painting behind the scenes to a bitmap in memory and then later paint the bitmap to the form. You use this technique to reduce screen flicker when graphics are animated. Double buffering is accomplished in a control simply by setting the style bits of the form. The style bits that need to be set are in the enumeration ControlStyles, and they are DoubleBuffer, AllPaintingInWmPaint, and UserPaint. The UserPaint style tells the control to draw itself rather than the operating system drawing it. The AllPaintingInWmPaint style causes the form to ignore the WM_ERASEBKGND message and causes the OnPaint and OnPaintBackground functions both to be called as a result of the WM_PAINT message. The code in Listing 15.50 tells the form to use double buffering for all of its drawing, and the code is carried out in the form's constructor.

Listing 15.50—Setting Up the Form to Perform Double Buffering

```
public Form1()
{
        InitializeComponent();


        // reduce flicker

        SetStyle(ControlStyles.UserPaint, true);
        SetStyle(ControlStyles.AllPaintingInWmPaint, true);
        SetStyle(ControlStyles.DoubleBuffer, true);

}
```

Now all drawing in the form will be subject to double buffering, and you will definitely notice a reduction of flicker for any animation that is performed.

Animating with Graphics Paths and Timers

There are a few ways to animate in .NET. One is to move bitmaps around the screen; another is to treat the GraphicPaths as sprites and move them around using transforms. The code in Listings 15.51 and 15.52 will draw our infamous stick figure and have him perform cartwheels across the form.

To add a timer to the form, drag and drop the Timer control from the Toolbox onto the form. Set the Interval property of the timer to 200, so that the stickman will draw every 200 milliseconds, or one-fifth of a second. The timer instance is set to start in the constructor using the Start method:

```
timer1.Start();
```

In Design view double-click the timer to add a Timer event handler that will be triggered every one-fifth of a second. The code in the event handler calculates the graphics path to draw and invalidates the region in which the graphics path is located. In addition, it invalidates the new region in which the graphics will be drawn when the Paint event handler is called.

Listing 15.51—Rotating and Translating the Stickman in the Timer Event Handler

```
private void timer1_Tick(object sender, System.EventArgs e)
{
        Rectangle rInvalidate =
                Rectangle.Truncate(m_gpDrawingPath.GetBounds());
```

```
                // inflate the invalidation region to account for rotation
                rInvalidate.Inflate(rInvalidate.Width/4, rInvalidate.Height/4);
                Invalidate(rInvalidate);

                // translate the stick figure 50 pixels along the line
                MoveStickFigureMatrix.Translate(10, 0);

                PointF thePoint = m_StickFigure.GetBounds().Location;

                // calculate the midpoint to rotate around
                thePoint.X += m_StickFigure.GetBounds().Width/2;
                thePoint.Y += m_StickFigure.GetBounds().Height/2;

                // rotate the matrix 20 degrees
                RotateStickFigureMatrix.RotateAt(40, thePoint);

                // rotate and translate the stick figure using the original
          // upright stick figure
                m_gpDrawingPath = (GraphicsPath)m_StickFigure.Clone();

                m_gpDrawingPath.Transform(RotateStickFigureMatrix);
                m_gpDrawingPath.Transform(MoveStickFigureMatrix);

                // inflate the invalidation region to account for rotation
                rInvalidate.Inflate(rInvalidate.Width/4, rInvalidate.Height/4);

                // force the stick figure to redraw
                Invalidate(rInvalidate);
        }
```

The stick figure drawing is done in the Paint handler. As previously stated, this event is triggered from the Invalidate call in the Timer event handler. Only the invalidated regions are erased and redrawn, and the double buffering makes the redrawing and erasing very smooth.

Listing 15.52—Painting the Moving Stickman

```
        private void Form1_Paint(object sender,
            System.Windows.Forms.PaintEventArgs e)
        {
        Graphics g = e.Graphics;

        // draw transformed figure
        g.DrawPath(Pens.Black, m_gpDrawingPath);

        // draw line below figure
        g.DrawLine(Pens.Red, 0,
                        m_StickFigure.GetBounds().Bottom + 3,
                        ClientRectangle.Right,
                        m_StickFigure.GetBounds().Bottom + 3);
}
```

When you run the code, the stick figure appears to spin head over feet across the form, as shown in Figure 15.27.

Figure 15.27: Cartwheeling Stick Figure

Adding Sound to Your Animation

To demonstrate the use of sound in our application, we will add a beep every time the cartwheel man finishes his turn. To add a sound, you need to go outside the .NET Framework and import one of the multimedia DLLs. To play a beep wave file on the Windows operating system, you can simply use the winmd.dll. Listing 15.53 shows the attribute you need to declare in your file to bring in the DLL and the corresponding PlaySound function.

Listing 15.53—Importing the PlaySound Function

```
        [DllImport("winmm.dll")]
    public static extern long PlaySound(String lpszName, long hModule,
long dwFlags);
```

Once we've imported the DLL, it is easy to use it in our .NET application. Listing 15.54 shows the code we have added to play the sound when the cartwheel man reaches zero degrees in his rotation.

Listing 15.54—Playing a Sound After Every Cartwheel

```
        int anglesum = 0;
        private void timer1_Tick(object sender, System.EventArgs e)
        {
                // code to rotate and translate stick figure

                …

                Invalidate(rInvalidate);


                anglesum += 40;

                // play the sound when the figure completes his rotation

                if (anglesum > 360)
                {
                  anglesum = 40;
                  PlaySound(Application.StartupPath + "\\beep.wav", 0, 0);
                }

        }
```

Although this does exactly what it is supposed to do, which is play a sound every 360 degrees, the graphics will stop until the sound is played. To have the sound play simultaneously along with the graphics, we need to put the playing of the sound into a thread. See Chapter 16 for more details on threading. Listing 15.55 shows the methods for playing the beep sound in a thread. The thread is created in the PlaySoundInThread method so that it is played in a thread separate from the form application.

Listing 15.55—Playing the Sound in a Thread

```
Thread oThread = null;
public void PlayASound()
{
        PlaySound(Application.StartupPath + "\\beep.wav",
                0, 0);
        oThread.Abort();
}

public void PlaySoundInThread()
{
        oThread = new Thread(new
                ThreadStart(PlayASound));
        oThread.Start();
}
```

The thread is then called in place of the PlaySound call in the Timer event handler:

```
if (anglesum > 360)
{
  anglesum = 40;
  PlaySoundInThread();
}
```

Animating with Bitmaps

There are two common techniques for using bitmaps with animation. One is to translate the bitmap image across the screen, as we did with the graphics path. The other is to overlay a bitmap on top of another, showing the image in a position different from its position in the previous bitmap. This is the same technique used in cartoons and flip books. Each image is displayed one after another, giving the illusion of motion. In the example to follow, we take advantage of two .NET components: the Timer object, used in the previous example, and the ImageList object. ImageList allows us to store a series of images to use for animation. To store images in the ImageList component, click on the ImageList component in the Design view and go to the Properties window. Click on the ellipsis in the Images property. This will bring up the window shown in Figure 15.28 in which you can add your images easily.

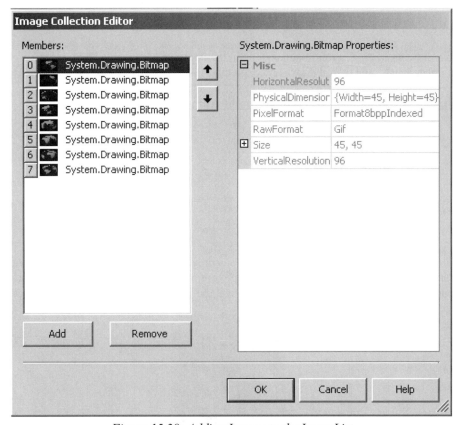

Figure 15.28: Adding Images to the ImageList

To implement our animation, we just need to pop up the images into the form, one by one, in the order we stored them in the collection. The routine in Listing 15.56 will pick the next consecutive image from our image list for drawing.

Listing 15.56—Getting the Next Image in the ImageList

```
int ImageIndex = 0;
Image CurrentImage = null;

void AnimateImages()
{
  // choose the next image in the ImageList
  CurrentImage = this.imageList1.Images[ImageIndex];
  ImageIndex++;
  if (ImageIndex >= imageList1.Images.Count)
  ImageIndex = 0;

  // force the whole form to redraw the image
  Invalidate();
}
```

The AnimateImages routine is called every 100 milliseconds, or one-tenth of a second, from our Timer event handler. See Listing 15.57.

Listing 15.57—Using the Timer to Perform the Animation

```
private void timer2_Tick(object sender, System.EventArgs e)
{
```

```
        this.AnimateImages();
}
```

The actual drawing of the CurrentImage is done in the Paint handler event. This event first checks to see if an image exists, and then it draws an image that fills the form. See Listing 15.58.

Listing 15.58—Painting the CurrentImage in the Animation

```
private void Form1_Paint(object sender,
        System.Windows.Forms.PaintEventArgs e)
{
        Graphics g = e.Graphics;
        if (CurrentImage != null)
        {
           g.DrawImage(CurrentImage, 0, 0,
               ClientRectangle.Width, ClientRectangle.Height);
        }
}
```

The resulting image is seen in Figure 15.29. You can create such animations for yourself with a digital camera and a little patience. Just snap the picture with your camera, and move the object a little. Snap the picture; move the object. Then upload the images to your computer and place them in the ImageList component as previously shown.

Figure 15.29: Spinning Globe Bitmap Animation

The ImageAnimator Class

Microsoft provides a custom class for displaying animated GIF files. Basically, this class consists of static methods that let you display the animated GIF. To get the process started, you call the Animate function, passing it the animated GIF and the event that indicates the next frame has occurred. This can be called in the constructor of the form. See Listing 15.59.

Listing 15.59—Setting Up the Animated GIF for Animating on the Form

```
Bitmap MyImage = null;

private void SetupRunningMoose()
{
        MyImage = new Bitmap("runningmoose.gif");
        ImageAnimator.Animate(MyImage, new
            EventHandler(this.OnGIFFrameChanged));
}
```

Now, you just need to handle the ImageAnimator frame change event and the Paint event. The OnGIFFrameChanged event can be used to invalidate the region of the bitmap to force the next paint. See Listing 15.60.

Listing 15.60—Handling the ImageAnimator FrameChanged Event

```
void OnGIFFrameChanged(object sender, EventArgs e)
{
 // get the area to invalidate
 GraphicsUnit PixelUnit = GraphicsUnit.Pixel;
  RectangleF myRect = MyImage.GetBounds(ref PixelUnit);

  // invalidate to force the animated gif to paint the next frame
   this.Invalidate(Rectangle.Truncate(myRect));
}
```

Painting of the GIF is done by calling the UpdateFrame method of the ImageAnimator class to get the Image reference to point to the next image and then calling the Graphics class's DrawImage method on the bitmap. See Listing 15.61.

Listing 15.61—Painting the Next GIF Image for the Animation and Triggering the Update

```
private void Form1_Paint(object sender,
        System.Windows.Forms.PaintEventArgs e)
{

    Graphics g = e.Graphics;

    if (MyImage != null)
    {
     ImageAnimator.UpdateFrames();
     g.DrawImage(MyImage, 20, 20, MyImage.Width,
                MyImage.Height);
    }
}
```

The resulting animated GIF is shown in Figure 15.30.

Figure 15.30: Animated GIF Using GDI+

Summary

The new version of GDI, GDI+, is a marked improvement over the former GDI library, giving you a host of namespaces and classes to make graphics programming quicker and easier. In this chapter you learned to use the Graphics class and paint to a graphics surface. You used brushes and pens to draw lines, curves, shapes, and fonts. You were introduced to transforms and used them to change coordinate systems on the form and rotate a graphics path. We also demonstrated how to use GDI+ on the World Wide Web and work with bitmaps. Finally, this chapter gave you some ideas for animating and for using sound in a thread. The next chapter leads you deeper into the world of threaded processes and teaches you how to write multithreaded applications in .NET.

Chapter 16:
Threading

Introduction

In a preemptive, multitasking environment, the operating system divides processor time between running processes. Threads are the basic unit of execution within a process or, in the case of .NET, an AppDomain. Each AppDomain starts with a single thread. On single-processor machines, the appeal of threads is their ability to seemingly execute multiple operations in parallel. Parallel processing becomes an actuality on multiprocessor machines, with threads executing simultaneously on each processor.

Every thread in a process is allocated a prescribed unit of processor time, called a *time slice,* in which to execute code. Once a thread's time slice, measured in milliseconds, has expired, the runtime saves the thread's context and activates another thread. This context, while processor dependent, can be summarized as containing the values of the processor's registers and stack. The duration of the time slice varies between threads, depending on their priority. A thread with the *highest* priority executes for a longer period of time, and more frequently, than one set to the *lowest* priority. Altering a thread's priority can give the impression that it or other processes and threads have stalled and should be approached with caution. Caution should also be exercised when creating threads.

Creating multiple threads within an AppDomain is both a blessing and a curse. It is a blessing with respect to the ability to order tasks in the background and ensure a timely response to user interface input. Threads allow developers to promote or demote a task's importance by changing a thread's priority. Finally, the judicious use of threads avoids hanging an application during long periods of blocking, such as file I/O and extended database queries. It is a curse when the number of threads is not kept in check. Each thread requires memory for its context, thereby reducing the amount available to application data. Managing threads devours valuable CPU cycles while the runtime schedules, runs, and switches threads and their contexts. Finally, unchecked creation and destruction of threads can cripple any application's performance.

This chapter examines .NET's System.Threading namespace and its principal classes. We start by creating a simple thread and then move on to the classes responsible for synchronizing threads. Next, we take a closer look at the Thread class and some of its members. After surveying the ThreadPool class, we investigate what goes into building a message loop application.

A Simple Thread

The project for this example is located in the ThreadSimpleExe folder. It is a simple executable (see Listing 16.1) that writes two strings to the console window (see Figure 16.1).

Listing 16.1—ThreadSimple.cs

```
using System.Threading;

static int Main(string[] args)
{
ThreadStart startMethod = null;

        startMethod = new ThreadStart( ThreadSimple.ThreadStart);

Thread thread = null;

        thread = new Thread( startMethod);
        thread.Start();
        //thread.Join();
        Console.WriteLine( "Main exiting.");
        return( 0);
}

internal static void ThreadStart()
{
        Console.WriteLine( "In ThreadStart method.");
}
```

Figure 16.1: Simple Thread Output

To the uninitiated, the resulting output may seem backward. Any confusion will be cleared up momentarily, but let's start at the beginning. The first order of business, after importing the threading classes with the *using System.Threading* statement, is to create a delegate. The ThreadStart delegate's constructor takes a reference to the method that the runtime will call when the thread begins execution. As an aside, be aware that the parameter ThreadSimple.ThreadStart, a static method, could simply have been ThreadStart. Now back to the code. An instance of the Thread class is created, with a delegate parameter, and its Start method is called. The Start method signals the runtime to schedule the newly created thread for execution. How does the runtime accomplish this?

The answer is *asynchronously*. The call to the Start method returns immediately, most likely before the thread has actually started running. As the code in Listing 16.1 is currently written, there is no way to state categorically which string will be written to the console first. In most cases, it is probable that *Main exiting* will be first. Only if the comments are removed from the Thread.Join() call can the order of the strings be guaranteed. Recompiling and running the project results in the output shown in Figure 16.2.

![Console window showing: F:\Chapter 16 Threading\ThreadSimpleExe\bin\Debug\ThreadSimpleExe.exe — In ThreadStart method. Main exiting.]

Figure 16.2: Simple Thread Output with Thread.Join() Uncommented

Thread.Join() is an overloaded method that blocks until the calling thread terminates or a timeout occurs. The parameterless method blocks indefinitely. The other methods block for a specified number of milliseconds or a System.TimeSpan before continuing to execute subsequent code. There are a number of other mechanisms to synchronize threads.

Blocking is an expression denoting that a thread's execution has been programmatically halted and will not continue until a compensating event releases the thread from its suspended state. In this case, the event that permits the main thread to resume execution is the *thread* variable's termination. The term *synchronize* stands for the ordering of operations.

In the code in Listing 16.1, the order in which the strings are written to the console is not terribly critical. However, in the case of opening and writing to a file, the operational sequence is crucial. If the main thread is to write to a file, while relying on the *thread* variable to first open that file, the lack of thread synchronization makes for a predictable result. When the main thread attempts to write to the file, an exception will be thrown at least 90 times out of 100. The next section addresses the various ways of implementing thread synchronization in an application.

Thread Synchronization

Thread.Join(), as discussed in the previous section, is a particular type of synchronization used in thread termination. Other, more general synchronization classes are explored here. They are also located in the System.Threading namespace. They are the Monitor, ResetEvent, and Mutex classes.

The project for this segment is in the ThreadSyncExe folder. To demonstrate each synchronization type, there is a file and entry point for each. Set each entry point type as in Figure 16.3.

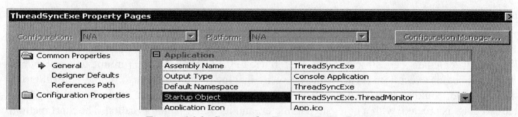

Figure 16.3: Setting the Project Entry Point

Before examining the classes in detail, a discussion of the pitfalls associated with multiple threads and synchronization is warranted. In a multithreaded application, the operating system can preempt one thread for another at any point in time. The term *preempt* can be thought of as "blocking" instigated by the operating system. Unless the developer synchronizes access to variables, bugs will invade an application. Even the most level-headed developer finds it frustrating to track down these sorts of bugs. In an ideal world, the runtime would detect such bugs and throw an exception. Unfortunately, what usually happens is that data becomes corrupted and, in the worst-case scenario, this is not noticed for months or years.

For example, suppose you have two threads inserting records into a database. Thread one is creating a first and last name record with the data *Napoleon Bonaparte,* while thread two's data is *Francis Drake.* Thread one successfully assigns *Napoleon* to a variable firstName when the operating system preempts thread one in favor of two. Now, two is able to set firstName to *Francis* before being preempted. Thread one then assigns *Bonaparte* to the lastName variable and inserts the record into the database. The end result is two records with the names *Francis Bonaparte* and *Napoleon Drake.* This mistimed chain of events is called a *race condition.* So does synchronizing access to variables solve all our threading problems? Well, not quite—there is still the issue of deadlocks, a much less subtle bug.

Monitors and the Lock Keyword

Avoiding a race condition by locking objects during access can cause a deadlock, which results in a hung application. A *deadlock* is a condition where two threads are each waiting for a resource the other has locked. The example shown in Listing 16.2 demonstrates a deadlock using the Monitor class and C#'s lock keyword. Those familiar with the Win32 application programming interface will recognize that the Monitor class and lock keyword are similar to EnterCriticalSection and LeaveCriticalSection, except that the .NET locks define sequential access to objects, whereas Win32 defines a critical section for a block of code. The first two lines of code in Listing 16.2 are located in the Main method, where two threads are created. As is evident, each thread has a different startup method.

Listing 16.2—ThreadMonitor.cs

```
        threadOne = new Thread( new ThreadStart( monitorOne.MonitorOne));
        threadTwo = new Thread( new ThreadStart( monitorOne.LockTwo));

public class ThreadMonitor
{
        private ArrayList       arrayOne = new ArrayList();
        private ArrayList       arrayTwo = new ArrayList();

        public ThreadMonitor()
        {
                arrayOne.Add( "Array one.");
                arrayTwo.Add( "Array two.");
        }


        public void MonitorOne()
        {
                for( int x = 0; x < 100; x++)
                {
                        Monitor.Enter( arrayOne);
                        Monitor.Enter( arrayTwo);
                        try
                        {
                                Console.Write( "{0}  {1}", x.ToString(),
                                                arrayOne[0]);
                                Console.WriteLine( " {0}", arrayTwo[0]);
                        }
                        finally
                        {
                                Monitor.Exit( arrayTwo);
                                Monitor.Exit( arrayOne);
                        }
                }
        }

        public void LockTwo()
        {
                for( int x = 0; x < 100; x++)
                {
                        lock( arrayTwo)
                        //lock( arrayOne)
                        {
                                lock( arrayOne)
                                //lock( arrayTwo)
                                {
                                        Console.Write( "{0}  {1}", x.ToString(),
                                                        arrayTwo[0]);
```

```
                                Console.WriteLine( " {0}", arrayOne[0]);
                          }
                    }
              }
        }
```

When the program runs, the MonitorOne thread executes until it is preempted and the LockTwo thread begins. Upon hitting the call to lock(arrayTwo), the thread blocks until Monitor.Exit(arrayTwo) is called. Then the LockTwo thread locks arrayTwo and attempts to perform the same call on arrayOne. In the interim, the MonitorOne thread has called Monitor.Enter(arrayOne) and locks arrayOne and then attempts to call Monitor.Enter(arrayTwo). The result is that the MonitorOne thread is waiting for arrayTwo to be released, and LockTwo is waiting for the same to happen to arrayOne. The application is hung. The bug can be rectified simply by switching the comments (//) in LockTwo, so that now both methods access the arrays in the same order.

There are two points to consider before we close the topic of the Monitor class. It is wise to use a try-finally block when using a Monitor, because if an exception is thrown without calling Monitor.Exit, any threads waiting on the Monitor will be blocked in perpetuity. An alternative to a lock statement or a Monitor is to use the MethodImplAttribute where a lock is desired on the entire method. The attribute is located in the System.Runtime.CompilerServices and takes the form of [MethodImplAttribute(MethodImplOptions.Synchronized)].

ResetEvent Classes

Two classes fall under the heading ResetEvent: they are AutoResetEvent and ManualResetEvent. The difference between the two classes lies in how their state is reset to *nonsignaled;* otherwise they are identical. The former is automatically reset by the runtime once a waiting thread has been released, while the latter must be done manually. Because of their similarity, ManualResetEvent is not covered with sample code. The output of the code in Listing 16.3 is the same as shown in Figure 16.2. These two classes and the Mutex class, in the next section, share a common lineage. All three classes derive from the WaitHandle class located in the Threading namespace.

Listing 16.3—ThreadReset.cs

```
class ThreadReset
{
        private AutoResetEvent waitStart = null;
        public ThreadReset()
        {
                waitStart = new AutoResetEvent( false);
        }

        public void Wait()
        {
                waitStart.WaitOne();
        }

        public void ThreadStart()
        {
                waitStart.Set();
                Console.WriteLine( "In ThreadStart method.");
        //waitStart.Set();
        }

        static int Main(string[] args)
        {
        ThreadSync reset = null;

                reset = new ThreadSync();
```

```
      Thread thread = null;

            thread = new Thread( new ThreadStart( reset.ThreadStart));
            thread.Start();
            reset.Wait();
            Console.WriteLine( "Main exiting.");
            return( 0);
      }
}
```

In the Main(), a new ThreadReset object is created, which in turn creates an AutoResetEvent
instance. AutoResetEvent's single constructor requires a Boolean value to indicate that its state is to
be set to either *signaled* or *nonsignaled*. A value of *false* specifies *nonsignaled*. A new thread is then
constructed and started. At this point, ThreadSync.Wait() is called. On the call to
WaitStart.WaitOne(), the current thread blocks and will remain blocked until
ThreadReset.ThreadStart is called by the runtime. Once ThreadStart is triggered, the state of the
reset event is set to *signaled* with waitStart.Set(), thus permitting the AppDomain's main thread to
continue execution. In real-world application development, there should be a call to
WaitHandle.Close() when it or one of its derived classes is no longer needed. Another point should
be made about this example. As the code currently stands, there is no guarantee of the order in
which the strings will be written. In all likelihood, "In ThreadStart method" will be first. The only
way to ensure the order of the output is to either switch the comment tag in ThreadStart or use
Thread.Join(). The final synchronization type is the Mutex class.

The Mutex Class

The Mutex class ensures that threads attempting to access a shared resource do so on a mutually
exclusive basis. Again, those familiar with Win32 will recognize the resemblance to the
CreateMutex and ReleaseMutex functions. Once a thread obtains ownership of a resource, it retains
that ownership until it releases the object. If a thread terminates normally, without releasing the
Mutex, its state is set to *signaled* and a waiting thread becomes the Mutex's owner. Without using
the Mutex, the code shown in Listing 16.4 produces a race condition.

Listing 16.4—ThreadMutex.cs

```
        threadOne = new Thread( new ThreadStart( mutexOne.ThreadOne));
        threadTwo = new Thread( new ThreadStart( mutexTwo.ThreadTwo));

public class ThreadMutex
{
        private         Mutex           mutex = null;
        private static ArrayList        list = null;

        static ThreadMutex()
        {
                list = new ArrayList();
                list.Add( "1st string, thread 1");
                list.Add( "1st, thread 2");
                list.Add( "2nd string, thread 1");
                list.Add( "2nd, thread 2");
        }

        public ThreadMutex( string mutexName)
        {
                mutex = new Mutex( false, mutexName);
        }

        public void ThreadOne()
        {
                for( int x = 0; x < 500; x++)
```

```
            {
                //mutex.WaitOne();
                        Console.Write("{0} {1}", x, list[0]);
                        Console.WriteLine( " - {0}", list[2]);
                //mutex.ReleaseMutex();
            }
    }

    public void ThreadTwo()
    {
            for( int x = 0; x < 500; x++)
            {
                //mutex.WaitOne();
                        Console.Write("{0} {1}", x, list[1]);
                        Console.WriteLine( " - {0}", list[3]);
                //mutex.ReleaseMutex();
            }
    }
```

```
Select F:\Chapter 16 Threading\ThreadSyncExe\bin\Debug\ThreadSyncExe.exe
458 1st, thread 2 - 2nd, thread 2
459 1st, thread 2 - 2nd, thread 2
460 1st, thread 2 - 2nd, thread 2
461 1st, thread 2 - 2nd string, thread 1
404 1st string, thread 1 - 2nd string, thread 1
405 1st string, thread 1 - 2nd string, thread 1
406 1st string, thread 1 - 2nd string, thread 1
```

Figure 16.4: Mutex Output to Create a Race Condition

The race condition can be seen in the highlighted line of output in Figure 16.4. To remedy the bug, simply remove the comments around the calls to the Mutex objects in the ThreadOne and ThreadTwo methods.

The Thread Class

As the section's title might lead one to suspect, we will review a number of methods and properties contained in the sealed Thread class. The examples are located in the ThreadClassExe folder. While it might be logical to break this segment into method and property subsections, the following examples intermix the two to clearly demonstrate the various facets of the Thread class. The Sleep method and IsBackground property are a case in point (see Listing 16.5).

Thread.Sleep() is a static, overloaded method that blocks the current thread for a specified time in milliseconds. The two overloaded methods take an int32 or a System.TimeSpan respectively. A *zero* value indicates the thread is to be suspended for the remainder of its time slice, to permit waiting threads to execute. Timeout.Infinite, in the Threading namespace, blocks until it is broken out of an infinite sleep by a call to Thread.Interrupt().

IsBackground is a Boolean type property, to identify a thread as being in the foreground or background. The only difference between the two is that a foreground thread's execution is not interrupted as a process terminates. When set to *false,* a thread prevents the process from terminating until the thread terminates. The default value for this property is *false.*

Listing 16.5—BackgroundThread.cs

```
public static void ThreadStart()
{
        Console.WriteLine( "Thread about to sleep.");
```

```
        Thread.Sleep( 10000);
}

static void Main(string[] args)
{
Thread thread = null;

        thread = new Thread( new ThreadStart( ThreadStart));
        //thread.IsBackground = true;
        thread.Start();
}
```

Running the example as it stands, the Main method exits after the call to Thread.Start(), but the process continues to execute until the sleep call in ThreadStart times out and the thread terminates. Removing the comments from the Thread.IsBackground statement causes the process to end upon exiting the Main method.

Another property that developers can set is the thread's priority. The Priority property can have one of five ThreadPriority values. The enumeration ranges from *lowest* to *highest* with the default value being *normal*. As threads can have different priorities, they can also be distinguished from one another by use of the Name property. Name is a write-once string property that has an empty string as its default value. Once set, any attempt to change the property results in a System.InvalidOperation exception being thrown.

There are also a number of read-only property members. Thread.CurrentThread is a static property that returns a reference to the currently running thread. To establish that a thread has started or is running, use the Boolean IsAlive property. A return value of *true* denotes a running thread, while *false* signals that a thread has yet to start or has terminated. A more precise enumeration of a thread's state is available through the ThreadState property.

The state diagram shown in Figure 16.5 is an overly simplified illustration of the various states and transitions a thread may go through. Starting from the left, a thread's initial state is always Unstarted and the only possible transition is to a Running state. Once a thread has been started, there are a number of possible transitions. In an AbortRequested state, the only possible transformation is to a Stopped state. The Suspended and WaitSleepJoin states may transition to a Running state prior to attaining a Stopped state.

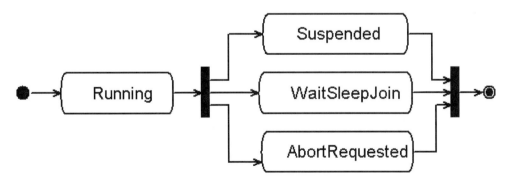

Figure 16.5: States of a Thread

The ThreadState enumeration has seven possible states. Table 16.1 lists the thread states.

State	Method
Unstarted	After thread creation and prior to calling Start().
Running	From Start() to termination or Abort() and when Interrupt() or Resume() is called.
WaitSleepJoin	A call to Sleep(), Join(), or one of the wait objects.
SuspendRequested	A call to Suspend().
AbortRequested	A call to Abort().
Suspended	The thread is in a suspended state.
Stopped	The thread has terminated or responded to an Abort().

Table 16.1: Thread States

The Thread.Sleep method applies only to the currently running thread. To selectively pause any thread, the Thread class provides Suspend() and Resume() to restart a suspended thread.

The code in Listing 16.6 and the resulting output in Figure 16.6 are fairly self-explanatory, except for the "while" loop in the Main method. If Suspend() is called prior to the thread being started, a ThreadStateException is thrown. Given that, the application remains in the while loop until the thread has started. The while loop was used for demonstration purposes only; a more elegant approach would be to use Thread.Sleep(0).

Listing 16.6—SuspendThread.cs

```
public static void ThreadStart()
{
        Console.WriteLine( "Thread running.");
        Console.WriteLine( "Sleep entered.");
        Thread.Sleep( 1000);
        Console.WriteLine( "Sleep exited.");
        Console.WriteLine( "Thread exiting.");
}

static int Main(string[] args)
{
Thread thread = null;

        thread = new Thread( new ThreadStart( ThreadStart));
        thread.Start();
        while( thread.ThreadState == ThreadState.Unstarted)
        {
                ;
        }

        thread.Suspend();
        Console.WriteLine( "Suspend called.");

        Thread.Sleep( 100);

        thread.Resume();
        Console.WriteLine( "Resume called.");
        thread.Join();
        return( 0);
}
```

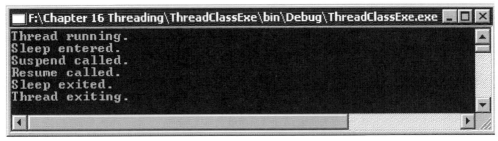

Figure 16.6: SuspendThread Output

Be aware that a call to Suspend() does not immediately block a thread. Before the runtime can halt a thread's execution, it must reach what is termed a *safe point*. A safe point is actually a point where a thread can safely be suspended, so that garbage collection can take place without corrupting any references on the thread's stack.

We'll wrap up the Thread class with a discussion about thread local storage (TLS) and the Abort() method.

TLS is a means to allocate memory for thread-specific data. This memory, called a *data slot,* may be named or unnamed and is obtained via calls to either Thread.AllocateDataSlot or Thread.AllocateNamedDataSlot. A System.LocalDataStoreSlot reference is returned by both methods. Data is set with a call to SetData() using the data slot reference and an object as parameters. Data is retrieved by calling GetData() with the data slot reference. A particular data slot cannot be shared across threads, and a developer must find another mechanism for interthread communication. An alternative to using TLS is to define a System.ThreadStaticAttribute, which is a field that has a separate instance for every executing thread.

Finally, the Abort() terminates a thread by raising a special exception, ThreadAbortException. The exception is special because although it can be caught, it will be rethrown once it leaves a catch block. Thread termination can be halted if the static method Thread.ResetAbort is called within the catch. In either case, any finally blocks are executed prior to thread termination. As with the suspend method, the runtime marks the thread as requesting termination and the thread continues executing to a safe point. Once the thread has terminated, the state is set to ThreadState.Stopped.

The ThreadPool Class

In many situations, it becomes evident that the constant creation and destruction of threads affects an application's performance. In other circumstances, threads may spend the majority of their lifetime in a sleeping state. In an effort to alleviate these problems, the Threading namespace offers a pool of worker threads administered by the runtime. The ThreadPool is a sealed class of static methods, providing up to 25 threads on a per-processor basis. Only three methods are of interest to us in this section: QueueUserWorkItem, an overloaded method; GetAvailableThreads; and GetMaxThreads. The thread pool is also capable of handling asynchronous I/O and timers, both of which are beyond the scope of this chapter. The example project is ThreadPoolingExe, and the output can be seen in Figure 16.7.

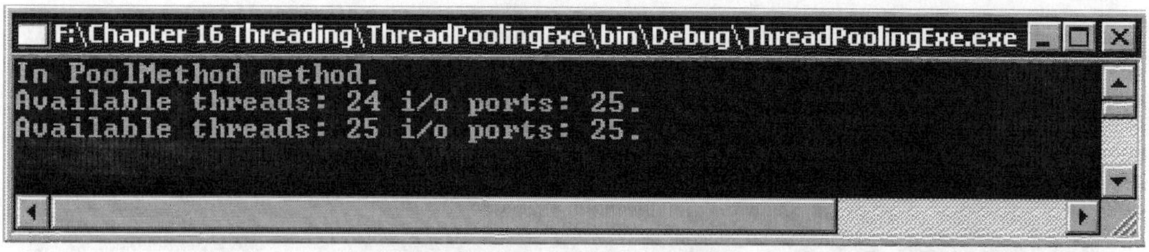

```
F:\Chapter 16 Threading\ThreadPoolingExe\bin\Debug\ThreadPoolingExe.exe
In PoolMethod method.
Available threads: 24 i/o ports: 25.
Available threads: 25 i/o ports: 25.
```

Figure 16.7: Thread Pool Output

Listing 16.7—ThreadPooling.cs

```csharp
public static void PoolMethod( object state)
{
        Console.WriteLine( "In PoolMethod method.");
        if( state != null)
        {
                ((AutoResetEvent)state).Set();
        }
}

static int Main(string[] args)
{
        AutoResetEvent wait = null;

        wait = new AutoResetEvent( false);
        ThreadPool.QueueUserWorkItem( new WaitCallback( PoolMethod), wait);
        wait.WaitOne();
        /*
        ThreadPool.QueueUserWorkItem( new WaitCallback( PoolMethod));
        Thread.Sleep( 10000);
        */

        int threads = 0;
        int ioPorts = 0;

        ThreadPool.GetAvailableThreads( out threads, out ioPorts);
        Console.WriteLine( "Available threads: {0} i/o ports: {1}.",
                                        threads, ioPorts);

        ThreadPool.GetMaxThreads( out threads, out ioPorts);
        Console.WriteLine( "Available threads: {0} i/o ports: {1}.",
                                        threads, ioPorts);
        return( 0);
}
```

In the uncommented code shown in Listing 16.7, the ThreadPool.QueueUserWorkItem is called on the main thread with a delegate and an AutoResetEvent reference as parameters. The thread pool calls PoolMethod, which writes a string to the console and sets the event to *signaled*. Once the main thread is released, it writes the thread pool's available and maximum resources to the console and exits. The commented-out ThreadPool.QueueUserWorkItem only works if the main thread stays alive for the duration of the PoolMethod execution. The reason for this has to do with the type of thread the thread pool creates, which is a background thread. As explained in the Thread Class section, a background thread ends with the termination of the last foreground thread. Hence, with the main thread sleeping 10 seconds, we are assured that the delegate will have more than enough time to complete its execution before it is destroyed. If the project being created is a Windows Application, the second QueueUserWorkItem can be used. This is because System.Windows.Forms.Application.Run creates an internal message loop and the program must be explicitly terminated. In the next section, an alternate technique to the ThreadPool is investigated.

A Message Thread

In the Windows world the utilization of message loops is prevalent only in user interfaces and Component Object Model "out-of-proc" servers, although the Win32 application programming interface does support the PostThreadMessage function. This has always seemed somewhat bizarre, considering the overhead that goes into creating a thread. As has been shown, .NET tips its hat to this overhead with the ThreadPool class, but no inherent mechanism exists to communicate with a particular thread, order tasks, or have an ever-present thread to juggle foreground and background chores in a synchronous or asynchronous fashion. In order to rectify this shortcoming, we'll create a custom message loop application in the MessageThreadExe folder. The application consists of four source files, which we will look at on a class-by-class basis. This basic project could be enhanced to handle callbacks, in the case of failure, or maintain a series of objects in multiple states. The output from this application can be seen in Figure 16.8, and it goes without saying that the output may vary each time the program is run.

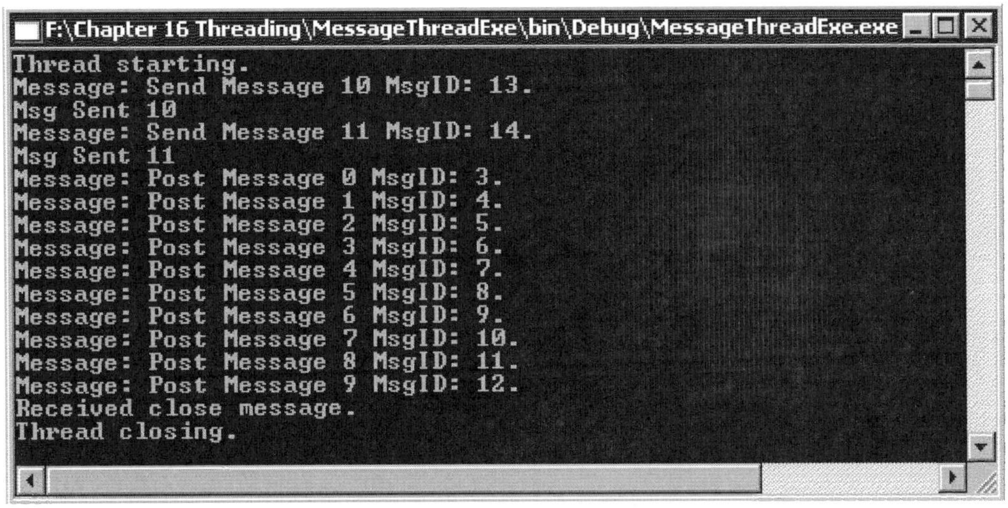

Figure 16.8: Message Thread Output

The MessageUser class, in MessageUser.cs, contains the Main method, which serves as the entry point for the console application. To use the message loop, a consumer must implement the methods defined in the IMsgInterface interface in Listing 16.8.

Listing 16.8—MsgInterface.cs

```
public interface IMsgInterface
{
        void MsgThreadStarting();
        bool Msg( int msgId, MsgPacket packet);
        void MsgThreadClosing();
}
```

The MsgThreadStarting and MsgThreadClosing methods are simply event handlers to inform the consumer when the thread starts and is about to exit. The main point of interest in the interface is the Msg method and its parameters. The method is the event handler for all messages. The first parameter is the message identifier. Unlike Win32 messages, there are only two predefined message identifier values: a ThreadClose and a UserMessage (see MsgID class in Listing 16.9). The MsgPacket class serves as the data container, much in the same manner as Win32's WPARAM and LPARAM parameters.

Listing 16.9—MsgPacket.cs

```csharp
public class MsgID
{
        public const int ThreadClose = 2;
        public const int UserMessage = 3;
}

public class MsgPacket
{
        private int    msgId = 0;
        private object msgObj = null;
        private bool   isSend = false;

        public MsgPacket( int msgId, object msgObj)
        {
                this.msgId = msgId;
                this.msgObj = msgObj;
        }

        public int MsgId
        {
                get
                {
                        return( msgId);
                }
        }

        public object MsgObj
        {
                get
                {
                        return( msgObj);
                }
        }

        internal bool IsSend
        {
                get
                {
                        return( isSend);
                }
                set
                {
                        isSend = value;
                }
        }
}
```

Together IMsgInterface (see Listing 16.8) and MsgPacket (see Listing 16.9) make up the mechanism that allows objects to communicate either synchronously or asynchronously through the MsgThread class, whose fields and public methods are defined in Listing 16.10.

Listing 16.10—MsgThread.cs

```csharp
public class MsgThread
{
        private ArrayList         msgColl = new ArrayList();
        private Thread        thread = null;
        private AutoResetEvent startEvent = null;
        private AutoResetEvent sendEvent = new AutoResetEvent( false);
        private IMsgInterface  receiver = null;

        public MsgThread( IMsgInterface receiver)
        {
                this.receiver = receiver;
```

```
            startEvent = new AutoResetEvent( false);
            thread = new Thread( new ThreadStart( this.ThreadStart));
            thread.Start();
            startEvent.WaitOne();
            startEvent.Close();
            startEvent = null;
    }

    public void SendMessage( MsgPacket packet)
    {
            if( packet.MsgId == MsgID.ThreadClose)
            {
                    PostMessage( packet);
            }
            else
            {
                    packet.IsSend = true;
                    SetMsg( packet, false);
                    sendEvent.WaitOne();
                    packet.IsSend = false;
            }
    }

    public void PostMessage( MsgPacket packet)
    {
            SetMsg( packet, true);
            if( packet.MsgId == MsgID.ThreadClose)
            {
                    thread.Join();
                    thread = null;
            }
    }
}
```

In the single constructor, the IMsgInterface parameter is used instead of an *object* reference, so that a class not implementing the interface is informed at compile time. The receiver field, which handles future callbacks, is assigned the parameter. Once that has been accomplished, the thread is instantiated and startEvent blocks until the thread actually commences running. Upon release, startEvent is no longer needed and is disposed. The SendMessage method simply calls PostMessage if a MsgID.ThreadClose message is received. This is done to ensure that the message queue is flushed prior to the thread's termination. When PostMessage receives a close message, it blocks until the thread has terminated to guarantee no more messages will be accepted. This solution is adequate in the present circumstances, with only one thread using our MsgThread object. If multiple threads were calling MsgThread, a more sophisticated solution would have to be provided.

Notice also that to conform with the Win32 definition of SendMessage, the calling thread blocks until the message has been processed. The MsgPacket's internal IsSend property also aids in realizing the SendMessage definition, but this discussion will be left for later in the chapter.

Whereas Listing 16.10 deals with the fields and public methods of MsgThread, Listings 16.11 and 16.12 delve into the class's inner workings, the private methods. The public SendMessage and PostMessage methods in Listing 16.10 call the private SetMsg() defined in Listing 16.11. The first item on the agenda in SetMsg is to ensure that the thread has not terminated and that there is a valid MsgPacket to dispatch. In a production environment, if either the thread or the message packet proves to be *null,* an exception would be raised. The dispatch container is then locked so that the ArrayList is not tampered with. The isPost parameter indicates the origin of the message. If the message is to be sent, the packet is inserted at the head of the container. If it is a posted message, the packet is added to the container's tail. The GetMsg method retrieves the first MsgPacket from the ArrayList, after locking *msgColl*, then removes the packet and returns it for processing.

Listing 16.11—MsgThread.cs

```
private void SetMsg( MsgPacket packet, bool isPost)
{
        if( thread != null)
        {
                if( packet != null)
                {
                        lock( msgColl)
                        {
                                if( isPost == false)
                                {
                                        msgColl.Insert( 0, packet);
                                }
                                else
                                {
                                        msgColl.Add( packet);
                                }
                        }
                }
        }
}

private MsgPacket GetMsg()
{
MsgPacket packet = null;

        lock( msgColl)
        {
                if( msgColl.Count != 0)
                {
                        packet = (MsgPacket)msgColl[0];
                        msgColl.Remove( packet);
                }
        }

        return( packet);
}
```

Listing 16.12—MsgThread.cs

```
private void ThreadStart()
{
        receiver.MsgThreadStarting();
        startEvent.Set();

bool stop = false;

        do
        {
MsgPacket packet = null;

                if( (packet = GetMsg()) != null)
                {

                        receiver.Msg( packet.MsgId, packet);
                        if( packet.IsSend == true)
                        {
                                sendEvent.Set();
                        }
                        else if( packet.MsgId == MsgID.ThreadClose)
                        {
                                stop = true;
                        }
                }
                else
                {
```

```
                    Thread.Sleep( 0);
            }
    }
    while( stop == false);

    receiver.MsgThreadClosing();
}
```

The heart of the MsgThread class is the ThreadStart() in Listing 16.12. Once the registered receiver has been notified that the message thread is running, via the call to MsgThreadStarting(), the creating thread is unblocked with the call to startEvent.Set(). The path of execution falls into the do-while loop and continues looping until a close message is received. With each iteration, the dispatcher is called. If a message is present, it is processed. In the event no messages are available, the thread foregoes the rest of its time slice and permits other waiting threads to continue to execute. At this juncture, a word of explanation is necessary about sendEvent.Set() and the MsgPacket.IsSend property.

The AutoResetEvent.Set method sets the event state to *signaled*. If a thread is waiting, it is released and the runtime resets the state to *nonsignaled*. If no threads are blocking, the event state remains *signaled*. Given that behavior, without the IsSend property it is possible that the event would be set by a posted message, rather than by a send message, and a nasty bug would be introduced into any application employing MsgThread. Why not use ManualResetEvent and insert a Reset call in SendMessage() just before the thread is blocked? Would this eliminate the need for the IsSend property? The short answer is you cannot. There is still the possibility, however remote, that a posted message would set the event state to *signaled* between the call to Reset() and the call to WaitOne().

In the Main method, not shown, an instance of MessageUser is created and StartMessage(), Listing 16.13, is called.

Listing 16.13—MessageUser.cs

```
public void StartMessage()
{
MsgThread       msg = null;
MsgPacket       packet = null;
int             x = 0;

    msg = new MsgThread( this);
    for( ; x < 10; x++)
    {
            packet = new MsgPacket( (MsgID.UserMessage + x),
                            "Post Message " + x.ToString());
            msg.PostMessage( packet);
    }

    packet = new MsgPacket( (MsgID.UserMessage + x),
                    "Send Message " + x.ToString());
    msg.SendMessage( packet);
    Console.WriteLine( "Msg Sent {0}", x++.ToString());

    packet = new MsgPacket( (MsgID.UserMessage + x),
                    "Send Message " + x.ToString());
    msg.SendMessage( packet);
    Console.WriteLine( "Msg Sent {0}", x++);

    packet = new MsgPacket( MsgID.ThreadClose, null);
    msg.SendMessage( packet);
}
```

The StartMessage method is where all the work on the main thread takes place. The test harness code is straightforward. A series of post messages are created in a "for" loop; then three send messages are fired off, the last being a MsgID.ThreadClose message.

Summary

We hope this chapter has demonstrated that there is an upside and a downside to threads. On the upside, threads are an easily implemented mechanism to create seemingly simultaneous operations. Multiple threads can go a long way toward maximizing an application's performance. The downside cuts a much wider swath, if time and effort are not expended considering the consequences of threads. Performance and bugs are the watchwords when implementing threads. Constant thread creation and destruction weighs heavily on an application's performance. Deadlocks or worse, race conditions, can make the most brilliantly conceived application a candidate for the junk heap. Any application worth its weight in gold, if examined closely, will be using multiple threads. Any program except for the most elementary can benefit from the use of multithreading. The keys to success are thread lightly and think before threading. The next chapter talks about how to work with Windows Services in .NET.

Chapter 17:
Windows Services

Introduction to Windows Services

An application installed as a service on the Windows Operating System (OS) is known as a Windows service—or by its old name, a Windows NT service. It was very difficult to develop and monitor Windows service programs before the .NET Framework; now this tricky task is easy because of the .NET Framework's useful wrapper classes.

Services do not provide functionality directly to users. Rather, they manage resources that other applications or users share and provide functionality that is always available, regardless of who is using the computer. You can start and stop services manually or executed them from system boot to shutdown. They almost never have a user interface, performing their work quietly in the background—like Unix daemon processes. Services often require configuration interfaces, which are invoked by administrators and communicate settings to the service. The configuration parameters are stored in the registry or in an initialization file.

While services do not require a user interface and are normally console programs, you can set a service startup option to open a graphical user interface (GUI) and use them interactively. Do this by checking *Allow service to interact with desktop* on the log-on tab of service properties. If you do not specify this option and your service application has a GUI, it will seem to hang since it does not receive any user input from the mouse or keyboard. You should be aware of this condition and act accordingly.

Behind the scenes, a Windows service application links to the advapi32.dll and calls its CreateService function to register a service in unmanaged code. We will later do this with a simple utility. When a Windows service is registered, a corresponding registry key is created under HKEY_LOCAL_MACHINE\SYSTEM\CurrentControlSet\Services\ hive. This is the place to store nonvolatile service parameters.

A Windows service application has these typical characteristics:

- Windows service names must be unique on a computer.
- You cannot run a service or step through the code directly. After installing the service with its executable image, you can attach to the service with .NET Debugger. For better debugging, you should write interim output to an ordinary text file or the event log. After the testing phase is complete, you can compile and distribute the executable with debugging disabled and verbose tracing turned off, which would slow down the execution speed.
- The main entry point of the service must invoke the Run function. The Run function loads the service into the Service Control Manager of the Windows OS.
- Windows services run in a different, distinct user session and workstation than that of the currently logged-on user. By default, they cannot show any GUI-based forms and dialog

boxes. If you show any forms and wait for a user interaction, but without setting the "Allow service to interact with desktop" flag, your service will halt until the process is killed.

- You can explicitly specify in which security context the service will run during its lifetime, but be careful to not open security holes when altering the context.

- Though it is not a must, you should develop your services to serve many network clients—like Microsoft Internet Information Server.

- If the startup option is set to automatic, a service can be started automatically as the hosting computer boots. Dependent services can also be started by the service control manager, even if their startup configuration is set to manual.

- For service applications, you must create installation components, which install and register the service on the server and create an entry for your service with the Windows Service Control Manager. You can manually develop this installer class, but the VS.NET IDE provides a wizard to create an installer link.

- ServiceBase, ServiceProcessInstaller, and ServiceInstaller are the main classes that you inherit from. To implement the body of the service's actions and implement some service events—such as pause and continue—you derive a service from the ServiceBase class. You use the ServiceProcessInstaller and ServiceInstaller classes to install and uninstall services. You can use the ServiceController class to manipulate services. You must add a reference to System.ServiceProcess.dll and System.Diagnostics.dll to use these namespaces.

- The ServiceName property for the class must match the one set in the installer's constructor. Remember that a Windows service has two implementation code blocks: one you inherit from ServiceBase and the other you inherit from the ServiceProcessInstaller and ServiceInstaller classes.

- The Windows Service Manager waits for the return from the service's OnStart method for 30 seconds by default. If the method does not return in this 30 seconds, you are shown an error indicating that the service cannot be started. When debugging a service, you must consider this timeout duration. If you put any breakpoints in the OnStart method of your service, you will observe that it will likely timeout while debugging.

- A service moves through many states during its lifecycle. Each service state has a corresponding system event that you can override and respond to—like OnStart, OnPause, OnStop, OnContinue, OnShutDown, OnCustomCommand, and OnPowerEvent. A service performs regular actions—or serves clients—only if it is in the running state. In the starting phase, the service allocates the services that it will require during its lifetime. In the stopping phase, the service will free its resources and finish incomplete tasks to prevent memory leaks and provide system stability.

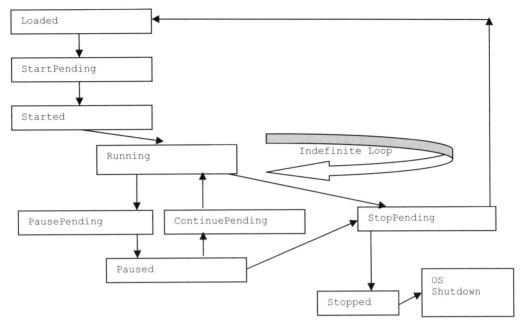

Figure 17.1: A Typical Windows Service State Flow Diagram
(Ignoring Service Dependency for the Sake of Brevity)

A Windows service has many characteristics, including service type, location of the service image file, description of the service, startup style, how the system reacts to service startup failures, and its service group membership, which specifies when the service starts in relation to other services. These characteristics are stored as values in the registry key, mentioned earlier.

Services types are the Adapter (a hardware device driver), FileSystemDriver (a kernel device driver for the file systems), InteractiveProcess (a service that can communicate with the desktop), KernelDriver (the kernel device driver for a low-level hardware device), RecognizerDriver (a file system driver used during startup to identify the file systems present on the computer), Win32OwnProcess (a Win32 service that runs in a process by itself), and Win32ShareProcess (a Win32 service that can share a process with other Win32 services). We will only delve into the latter two in managed code.

The Win32ShareProcess type is an executable that can host more than one service. Inetinfo.exe, for example, hosts IISADMIN, FTP, WWW, gopher, and other services in one executable. You can debug inetinfo and see which services are hosted by the executable. An advantage to having a process run more than one service is that it saves system resources. A potential disadvantage of this capability, however, is that if one of the hosted services causes an error that terminates the process, then all services in that process terminate.

By default, all service programs run in the LocalSystem security context, a built-in system account. This account is extremely powerful in terms of privileges. Generally, all Win2000 components run in this security context. The LocalSystem account owns virtually all predefined privileges, like taking ownership, rebooting, and the creation of security tokens. Besides, most of the folders, files, and registry keys allow access to this system account. Even if that access is not assigned, the LocalSystem account has the ability to take ownership and redefine access entry lists with rights. The LocalSystem account is not associated with a particular user; it uses the default profile of HKEY_CURRENT_USER. By default, the LocalSystem account cannot access profile information for other accounts, and it also has limited network access to resources. Services started within the

LocalSystem security context can access only file and printer shares and named pipes over null sessions. Null sessions do not require any credentials, and computers can share their resources by modifying the NullSessionPipes and NullSessionShares keys under the HKEY_LOCAL_MACHINE\SYSTEM\CurrentControlSet\Services\LanmanServer\Parameters hive. In Win2000/XP, the LocalSystem account also represents the machine's computer account. So a service running in the LocalSystem security account can be granted access by adding the computer's account to the Access Control Entry (ACE) list and assigning it an appropriate privilege. This is impossible in Windows NT, however.

By default, services cannot receive any user input or display windows. If a service were to show a GUI, it would appear to be hung up because the user would not be able to see the dialog box or send keyboard and mouse messages to that window. Some services may need to interact with users through dialog boxes or may need to access profile information for a particular user account. If you specify the ServiceType as an InteractiveProcess or set the service startup option *Allow service to interact with desktop* to enabled, then the service can display GUIs and dialog boxes.

A service can also run in the security context of a particular user rather than in that of the LocalSystem account. A service running in a user's security context has access to the relevant account's HKEY_CURRENT_USER profile information and to any network resources that the user can access.

Win2000 and XP introduced a "service failure action" capability, meaning that a service has optional FailureAction and FailureCommand values set in its registry key. When a service process terminates unexpectedly, Win2000/XP determines which services ran in the process and takes the recovery steps specified in failure-related registry values. Actions that a service can configure include restarting the service, running a program with parameters, rebooting the computer, and sending messages to network users. Additionally, a service can specify what failure actions take place the first, second, and subsequent times the service fails. A service can also specify a period of time that Win2000/XP must wait before restarting the service, if it demands a restart.

Let's look at a simple Windows service installed on Win2000—say, a computer browser. The service maintains a list of computers and other resources on the network, based on an announcement system. If you are not using Win2000's Active Directory (AD), you may have to start this service. Even if you have AD in place, you may need this service for backward compatibility with the WinNT, Win9x, and ME OSs.

You can open the service management MMC console in two ways: My Computer→Manage (Figures 17.2 and 17.3) or Control Panel→Administrative Tools→Services. Figures 17.2 below shows the service management console.

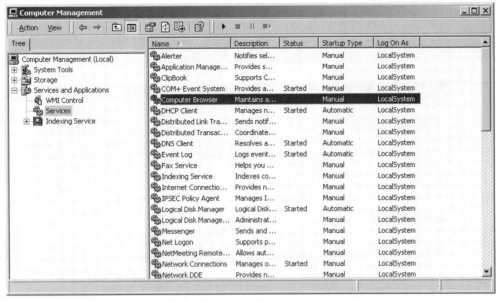

Figure 17.2: Computer Management→Services

Once you've opened the management console, you can start your service by clicking on the service start button in the toolbar of the console shown as the black triangle pointing to the right in figure 17.3.

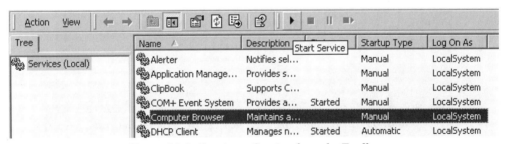

Figure 17.3: Starting a Service from the Toolbar

Stopping the service manually can be accomplished by selecting the running service and pressing the active black square in the toolbar of the console shown in figure 17.4.

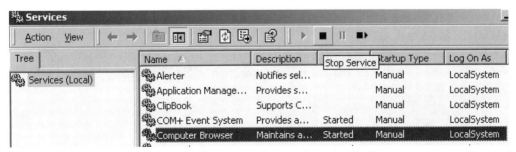

Figure 17.4: Stopping a Service from the Toolbar

Double clicking on a service in the service management console brings up a properties windows for the service. Shown in figure 17.5. In this window, you can change different aspects of the service such as how the service should recover if it fails or how the service will logon to the system. It also shows you what other windows services the service is dependent upon.

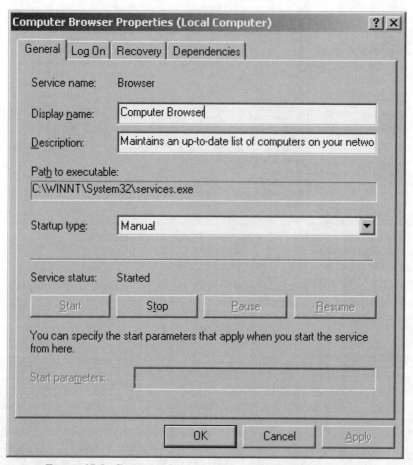

Figure 17.5: Computer Browser Service Properties—General

System.ServiceProcess Namespace Classes

The .NET Framework provides the System.ServiceProcess namespace, which contains all the classes you need to write and install service applications. Every Windows service application class has to be derived from the ServiceProcess.ServiceBase.

ServiceBase Class

You must inherit the ServiceBase class and override some of its methods to develop Windows Service applications. Table 17.1 shows important properties of the ServiceBase class, and Table 17.2 show important methods of the ServiceBase class.

Property	Description
AutoLog	If set to true, you can report Start, Stop, Pause, and Continue commands in the event log. If set to false, you can implement custom logging.
CanHandlePowerEvent	If set to true, you can handle notifications of computer power status changes.
EventLog	Returns an event log reference you can use to write notifications.
CanStop	If set to true, you can stop the service later.
CanShutdown	If set to true, the service will be notified that the system is shutting down in the OnShutdown event handler
CanPauseAndContinue	If set to true, you can pause the service first and then continue it later.
ServiceName	Sets the service's name, which must be the same as the ServiceInstaller.ServiceName.

Table 17.1: ServiceBase Class İmportant Properties

Method	Description
GetService	Returns an object that refers to the current service.
OnStart	Code that is executed when the service is started.
OnStop	Code that is executed when the service is stopped.
OnPause	Code that is executed when the service is paused.
OnShutdown	Code that is executed when the computer is shut down.
OnPowerEvent	Code that is executed when the computer's power status has changed.
OnContinue	executes when a continue command is sent from the SCM to the service
Run	The main entry code block for the service application.

Table 17.2: ServiceBase Class İmportant Methods

ServiceController Class

The ServiceController class is used to control service states by retrieving an array of all installed device services and non-device services in an array letting you connect to and control the behavior of these services. You can also enumerate through each array element to get details about each service. With the ServiceController, you can obtain the device driver services or non-device driver service list for any local or authorized remote computer.. To obtain the device services from the local machine or from a specific computer, you would use the lines below:

```
ServiceController [] devices = ServiceController.GetDevices();
ServiceController [] devices = ServiceController.GetDevices("Computer");
```

To obtain the non-device services from the local machine or from a specific computer and place them in array, you would use the following code:

```
ServiceController [] services = ServiceController.GetServices();
ServiceController [] services = ServiceController.GetServices("Computer");
```

Table 17.3 shows important properties of the ServiceController class. These properties allow you retrieve information about the Windows service as well as alter certain properties such as the DisplayName or the Service Name.

Property	Description
Status	Status of a service—e.g., running, stopped, etc.
DisplayName	Gets or Sets the Descriptive name shown for this service in the service applet.
ServiceType	Type of the service.
ServiceName	Gets or sets the Short name of the service.
CanStop	Indicates if the service can be stopped later.
CanShutDown	Indicates if the service can be shut down later.
CanPauseAndContinue	Indicates if the service can be paused first and then can be continued later.
DependentServices	List of services that depend on this service.
ServicesDependOn	List of services that this service depends on.

Table 17.3: ServiceController Class Important Properties

Table 17.4 provides methods of the ServiceController class that allow you to call methods that affect the state of the Windows service. Using these methods you can start, stop, pause, or close the service.

Method	Description
Close	Closes connection of the ServiceController object and releases all the allocated resources for that connection.
Start	Starts the relevant service.
Stop	Stops the relevant service.
Pause	Pauses the relevant service.
Refresh	Refreshes the relevant service properties with new updated values.
WaitForStatus	Waits for the service to enter a specified state, when an event can be triggered to perform some specific actions.

Table 17.4: ServiceController Class Important Methods

ServiceInstaller Class

With the ServiceInstaller class you can set some service attributes during installation. Table 17.5 shows the class's import properties.

Property	Description
DisplayName	Sets the friendly name that identifies the service to the user.
ServiceName	Sets the name that the system uses to identify the service. This name must be the same as ServiceBase.ServiceName.
ServicesDependedOn	Specify the services that must be running for this service to run.
StartType	Sets how and when the service will be started. The possible values for this property are automatic (service starts automatically when system starts), manual (the user manually starts the service from SCM), or disabled (the service starts in disabled mode).

Table 17.5: ServiceInstaller Class Important Properties

ServiceProcessInstaller Class

As shown in Table 17.6, the ServiceProcessInstaller class has some very important properties concerning security issues of your service application.

Properties	Description
Account	An enumeration of type ServiceAccount that gets or sets the type of security account the user will be running under. An account can be assigned values of User, LocalService, LocalSystem, or NetworkService. If Account is of type User, then you need to set the Username and Password properties (otherwise the system will prompt for them when the service is installed)
Username	Sets the user name under which the service will run. It is required only if the the Account is a User Account.
Password	Sets the password associated with the user account under which the service will run. Like the Username property, this is required only if the Account is of type User.
HelpText	Sets the help text displayed for service installation options.

Table 17.6: ServiceProcessInstaller Class Important Properties

ServiceType

A service type is an enumeration that tells you in what capacity the service will be used by the computer system. For example, an Adapter Service type is a device service that needs to have a driver supplied with it. The services that you can create using Visual Studio.NET are both non-device services either of type Win32OwnProcess or Win32ShareProcess. You can retrieve service types by querying the ServiceController.ServiceType property. The service types should match those in the ServiceController.ServiceType enumeration.

Enumeration	Description
Adapter	Hardware device driver that requires its own driver.
FileSystemDriver	Kernel device driver for file systems.
InteractiveProcess	Service can communicate with the desktop
KernelDriver	Kernel device driver for low-level hardware device.
RecognizerDriver	The file system driver used during startup. This is used to identify the file systems present on the system.
Win32OwnProcess	A Win32 service that runs in a process by itself.
Win32ShareProcess	A Win32 service that can share its process with other Win32 services.

Table 17.7: ServiceType Enumeration

Installing and Uninstalling Windows Services

In the folder where the executable for your service application resides, run the installutil.exe utility provided by the .NET Framework to install or uninstall the application.

This is the syntax for installing a Windows service:

```
installutil myService.exe
```

This is the syntax for uninstalling a Windows service:

```
installutil /u myService.exe
```

If you type instalutil at the command prompt, it will list all the other options available to you with this utility shown in Figure 17.6. Some options include printing a log of the installation to a file and printing the call stack of the installation to the log.

In order for your Windows Service to have the ability to work with the Install Utility, you need to add an Install class to your assembly. Follow these simple steps to add a minimum installer for your Windows service application:

1. Add a class derived from System.Configuration.Install.Installer class.
2. Set the RunInstallerAttribute attribue for this class to true.
3. In the constructor, create a new instance of ServiceProcessInstaller per service application and a new instance of ServiceInstaller class for each service in the application.
4. Add these installer objects to the InstallerCollection of your Installer class.

The methods associated with these two classes are called by the install utility during the install and uninstall process. You don't have to specifically call any of these methods in your Installer class.

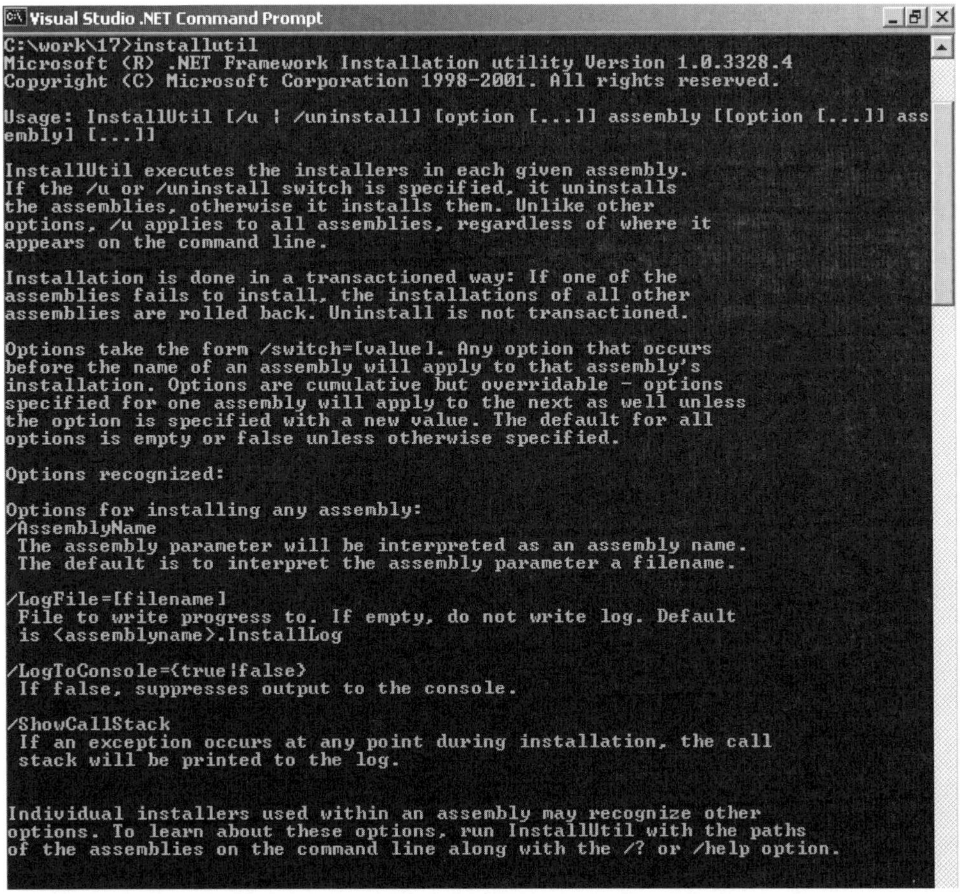

Figure 17.6: Installutil of .NET Framework SDK

Please note that the VS.NET IDE environment wizard provides you with an Add Installer wizard (explained later in this chapter), which saves time by generating the service installer files, but as a professional developer, you should become familiar with the internals of the service installation process anyway. Listing 17.1 shows you how to write the custom ServiceInstaller class.

Listing 17.1—Service and Process Installer Constructor Method

```
[RunInstallerAttribute(true)]
public class MCB_ServiceInstall : Installer
{
// pseudo code
public MCB_ServiceInstall()
 {
       this.m_ServiceInstaller = new ServiceInstaller ();
       this.m_ServiceInstaller.StartType = ServiceStart.Manual;
       this.m_ServiceInstaller.ServiceName = "My Service Short Name";
       this.m_ServiceInstaller.DisplayName = "My Service Long Name";
       Installers.Add (this.m_ServiceInstaller);

       this.m_ProcessInstaller = new ServiceProcessInstaller ();
       this.m_ProcessInstaller.RunUnderSystemAccount = true;
       Installers.Add (this.m_ProcessInstaller);
 }
}
```

Samples in the Windows Service World

Here are five samples of various kinds to take you through the steps and thus help you improve your theoretical knowledge of Windows services.

Sample 1 – Creating a Windows Service with a text editor

The following sample is the simplest skeleton of a Windows service containing an installer. It just adds simple entries to the EventLog upon starting and stopping the service. It also logs messages in the EventLog for Pause and Continue.

Listing 17.2—Service1.cs, Simple Windows Service

```csharp
using System;
using System.ServiceProcess;
using System.Diagnostics;

public class SimpleService: ServiceBase
{

    public static void Main()
    {
        ServiceBase.Run(new SimpleService());
    }

    public SimpleService()
    {
        CanPauseAndContinue = true;
        ServiceName = "MCB Service";
    }

    protected override void OnStart(string[] args)
    {
        EventLog.WriteEntry("MCB Service started");
    }

    protected override void OnStop()
    {
        EventLog.WriteEntry("MCB Service stopped");
    }

    protected override void OnPause()
    {
        EventLog.WriteEntry("MCB Service paused");
    }

    protected override void OnContinue()
    {
        EventLog.WriteEntry("MCB Service continued");
    }
}
```

Listing 17.3 shows the bare bones Installer class for this service.

Listing 17.3—Installer1.cs, Simple Windows Service Installer

```csharp
using System;
using System.Collections;
using System.Configuration.Install;
using System.ServiceProcess;
using System.ComponentModel;

[RunInstallerAttribute(true)]
```

```
public class MyInstaller: Installer
{

    private ServiceInstaller myserviceInstaller;
    private ServiceProcessInstaller myprocessInstaller;

    public MyInstaller(){

        myprocessInstaller = new ServiceProcessInstaller();
        myserviceInstaller = new ServiceInstaller();

        // Service will run under system account
        myprocessInstaller.Account = ServiceAccount.LocalSystem;

        // Service will have Start Type of Manual
        myserviceInstaller.StartType = ServiceStartMode.Manual;

        myserviceInstaller.ServiceName = "MCB Service";

        Installers.Add(myserviceInstaller);
        Installers.Add(myprocessInstaller);
    }
}
```

The service can be compiled on the command line using the csharp compiler. The command line passes the two class files making up the simple service as arguments(service1.cs and installer1.cs) and specifies the output for the IL executable as mcbservice.exe.

Figure 17.7: Compiling mcbservice.exe

Afterwords, we can run the install utility to install our service onto the local system by typing the command below:

```
installutil.exe mcbservice.exe
```

This will produce the following output on the console shown in Figure 17.8:

```
C:\work\17>installutil mcbservice.exe
Microsoft (R) .NET Framework Installation utility Version 1.0.3328.4
Copyright (C) Microsoft Corporation 1998-2001. All rights reserved.


Running a transacted installation.

Beginning the Install phase of the installation.
See the contents of the log file for the c:\work\17\mcbservice.exe assembly's pr
ogress.
The file is located at c:\work\17\mcbservice.InstallLog.
Installing assembly 'c:\work\17\mcbservice.exe'.
Affected parameters are:
    assemblypath = c:\work\17\mcbservice.exe
    logfile = c:\work\17\mcbservice.InstallLog
Installing service MCB Service...
Service MCB Service has been successfully installed.
Creating EventLog source MCB Service in log Application...

The Install phase completed successfully, and the Commit phase is beginning.
See the contents of the log file for the c:\work\17\mcbservice.exe assembly's pr
ogress.
The file is located at c:\work\17\mcbservice.InstallLog.
Committing assembly 'c:\work\17\mcbservice.exe'.
Affected parameters are:
    assemblypath = c:\work\17\mcbservice.exe
    logfile = c:\work\17\mcbservice.InstallLog

The Commit phase completed successfully.

The transacted install has completed.
```

Figure 17.8: Installing mcbservice.exe

To start your service, go to the Service Manager under the Administrative Tools in the Control
Panel, click on the MCB service, and press the black triangle start button on the toolbar. The Service
should be shown as Started as in Figure 17.9:

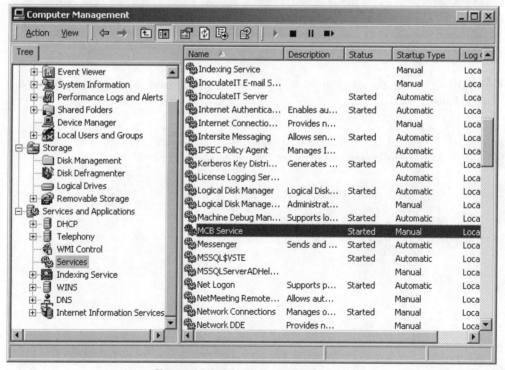

Figure 17.9: Managing MCB Service

If we now go to the Event Viewer node in the Computer Management Adminstration Tool, we can
see if the message in the OnStart event handler was logged correctly. To check the event log, click

on the Application node in the Event Viewer. Then check the Messages logged by MCBService by double-clicking in the right hand pane on the line with MCBService as the Source of the Event Log message as shown in Figure 17.10.

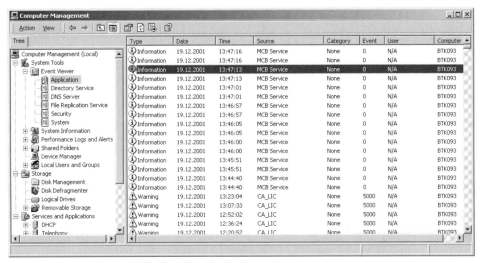

Figure 17.10: MCB Service Stopped Entry in EventLog

The Log Entry should display the Message generated in the service by the OnStart event handler indicating that the service as started as shown in Figure 17.11.

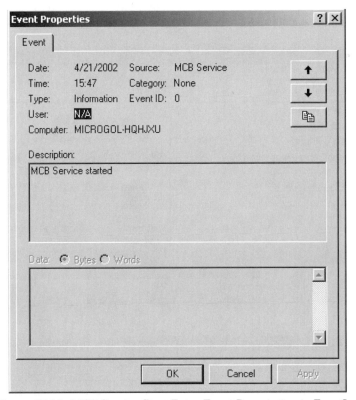

Figure 17.11: MCB Service Start Entry Event Description in EventLog

Sample 2 – Creating a Windows Service with Visual Studio.NET

The VS.NET Windows Service Wizard provides a minimum skeleton for service applications, along with an option to add the Windows service installer classes. In its initial skeleton, the wizard provides the OnStart and OnStop methods, which are essential events in the life of a Windows service application. The OnStart method is called when the service starts, and the OnStop method is called when the service stops.

Your service application can implement other methods on demand, but their use depends on the architecture and options you want for the application. For example, you can implement the OnPause, OnContinue, and OnShutdown methods, but if your service application does not support pause and continue, there is no need to implement them.

You can set the characteristics of your application by setting the values for the properties supported by the ServiceBase class. (It is strongly recommended that you review these properties in Table 17.1.) Since debugging a Windows service application is no small job, it is important to set the EventLog properties. EventLog should be used extensively in your project's initial phase so that you can log trace messages.

Note: We do not need to deal with installer classes (ServiceProcessInstaller and ServiceInstaller) when using the VS.NET Windows Service Wizard because it creates an implementation of these classes on demand.

Now let's step into the creation process for a simple Windows service application. As shown in Figure 17.12, to create a new service, select the Windows service option from your Visual C# Projects, give it a name, and click OK.

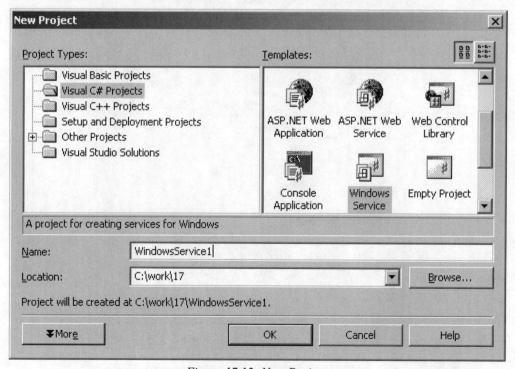

Figure 17.12: New Project

The resulting window will look like Figure 17.13. The wizard adds the WebService1.cs class to the project.

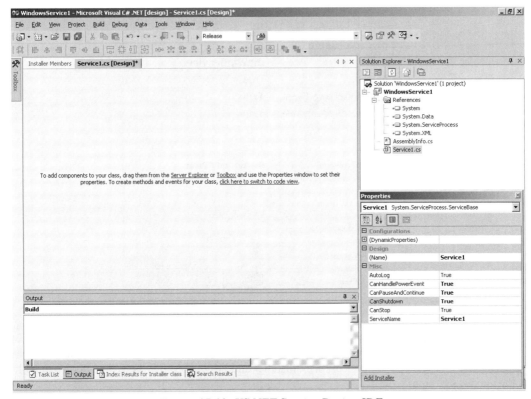

Figure 17.13: VS.NET Service Design IDE

You can set the ServiceName property to an easily identifiable name so that it will be easier to recognize your service during testing. The service name can be set either using the service's Property window or programmatically using the following syntax:

```
this.ServiceName = "mcWinService";
```

This creates the name of the Windows service that you will be manipulating later. Figure 17.14 below shows the property window for setting the ServiceName.

Figure 17.14: Windows Service Property window to set the ServiceName

The properties Window also contains a helpful hyperlink, Add Installer, for generating install functionality for the service automatically. Clicking the Add Installer link generate a custom derived Installer class that sets up the ServiceProcessInstaller and ServiceInstaller as we had done manually in the previous section.

Note:If you find you are having trouble recognizing the installer assemblies, System.Configuration.Install and System.Service.Process when you compile your Windows service, you can add the assemblies to your project by right-clicking on Add Reference and bringing up the Add Reference dialog. Choose the System.Service.Process.dll and the System.Configuration.Install.dll assemblies here. The Add Reference dialog for the chosen assemblies is shown below in Figure 17.15.

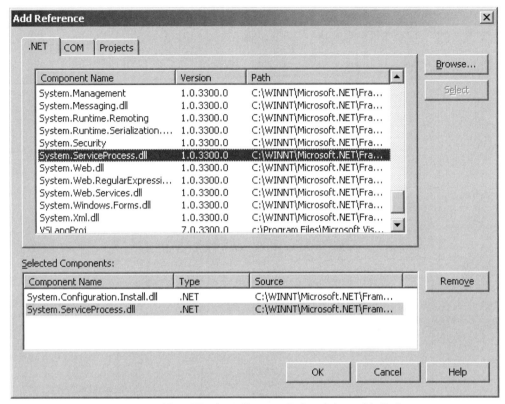

Figure 17.15: Adding Windows Service–Related Assembly References

The wizard does much of the work writing your actual service for you. You can also use the service Property Window to the service's properties and service name. The code generated by the framework is shown in Listing 17.4. Notice the generated code looks similar to the Windows Forms generated code with a call to Initialize component to construct the Windows service.

Listing 17.4—Service1.cs, Created by the Wizard and Some Custom Code

```
using System;
using System.Collections;
using System.ComponentModel;
using System.Data;
using System.IO;
using System.Diagnostics;
using System.ServiceProcess;

namespace mcWinService
{
        public class mcWinService : System.ServiceProcess.ServiceBase
        {
                private System.ComponentModel.Container components = null;

                public mcWinService()
                {
                        InitializeComponent();
                }

                // The main entry point for the process
                static void Main()
                {
```

```
            System.ServiceProcess.ServiceBase[] ServicesToRun;

      // More than one user Service may run within the same process.
      // To add another service to this process, change
      // the following line to
      // create a second service object. For example,
      //
      //   ServicesToRun = new
      // System.ServiceProcess.ServiceBase[] {new Service1(), new
      // MySecondUserService()};

            ServicesToRun = new System.ServiceProcess.ServiceBase[] {
                  new mcWinService() };

            System.ServiceProcess.ServiceBase.Run(ServicesToRun);
      }

   /// <summary>
   /// Required method for Designer support - do not modify
   /// the contents of this method with the code editor.
   /// </summary>
   private void InitializeComponent()
   {
         //
         // mcWinService
         //
         this.CanHandlePowerEvent = true;
         this.CanPauseAndContinue = true;
         this.CanShutdown = true;
         this.ServiceName = "mcWinService";

   }

   /// <summary>
   /// Clean up any resources being used.
   /// </summary>
   protected override void Dispose( bool disposing )
   {
         if( disposing )
         {
               if (components != null)
               {
                     components.Dispose();
               }
         }
         base.Dispose( disposing );
   }

   /// <summary>
   /// Set things in motion so your service can do its work.
   /// </summary>
   protected override void OnStart(string[] args)
   {
   }

   /// <summary>
   /// Stop this service.
   /// </summary>
   protected override void OnStop()
   {
   }
   }
}
```

As you saw in probably noticed in Listing 17.4 two methods—the OnStart and OnStop methods—are overridden by default. However, you can override other available service actions, like the

OnPause method. The OnStart function executes when you start your service, and the OnStop function executes when you stop your service. In Listing 17.5, we use the OnStart and OnStop event handler methods in conjunction with the StreamWriter to log service start and stop events to a file called mcWindowsService.txt.

Listing 17.5—Overriding OnStart and OnStop Methods

```
/// <summary>
/// Set things in motion so your service can do its work.
/// </summary>
protected override void OnStart(string[] args)
{
 FileStream fs = new FileStream(@"c:\temp\mcWindowsService.txt",
FileMode.OpenOrCreate, FileAccess.Write);
 StreamWriter m_streamWriter = new StreamWriter(fs);
 m_streamWriter.BaseStream.Seek(0, SeekOrigin.End);
 m_streamWriter.WriteLine(" mcWindowsService: Service Started \n");
 m_streamWriter.Flush();
 m_streamWriter.Close();
 fs.Close();
}

/// <summary>
/// Stop this service.
/// </summary>
protected override void OnStop()
{
 FileStream fs = new FileStream(@"c:\temp\mcWindowsService.txt",
FileMode.OpenOrCreate, FileAccess.Write);
 StreamWriter m_streamWriter = new StreamWriter(fs);
 m_streamWriter.BaseStream.Seek(0, SeekOrigin.End);
 m_streamWriter.WriteLine(" mcWindowsService: Service Stopped \n");
 m_streamWriter.Flush();
 m_streamWriter.Close();
 fs.Close();
}
```

Listing 17.6: ProjectInstaller.cs File Created by VS.NET IDE Add Installer Wizard

```
using System;

using System.Collections;

using System.ComponentModel;

using System.Configuration.Install;

namespace WindowsService1

{

 /// <summary>

 /// Summary description for ProjectInstaller.

 /// </summary>

 [RunInstaller(true)]

 public class ProjectInstaller : System.Configuration.Install.Installer

 {

  private System.ServiceProcess.ServiceProcessInstaller serviceProcessInstaller1;
```

```csharp
    private System.ServiceProcess.ServiceInstaller serviceInstaller1;

    /// <summary>
    /// Required designer variable.
    /// </summary>
    private System.ComponentModel.Container components = null;

    public ProjectInstaller()
    {
      // This call is required by the Designer.
      InitializeComponent();
      // TODO: Add any initialization after the InitComponent call
    }

    #region Component Designer generated code

    /// <summary>
    /// Required method for Designer support - do not modify
    /// the contents of this method with the code editor.
    /// </summary>
    private void InitializeComponent()
    {
      this.serviceProcessInstaller1 = new
System.ServiceProcess.ServiceProcessInstaller();
      this.serviceInstaller1 = new System.ServiceProcess.ServiceInstaller();
      //
      // serviceProcessInstaller1
      //
      this.serviceProcessInstaller1.Password = null;
      this.serviceProcessInstaller1.Username = null;
      //
      // serviceInstaller1
      //
      this.serviceInstaller1.ServiceName = "mcWinService";
      //
      // ProjectInstaller
      //
      this.Installers.AddRange(new System.Configuration.Install.Installer[] {
```

```
                    this.serviceProcessInstaller1,

                    this.serviceInstaller1});

   }

   #endregion

 }

}
```

Building this application generates a single executable, Service1.exe. From the command line, you need to call the installutil utility to register this service:

```
installutil C:\mcWebService\bin\Debug\Service1.exe
```

Next you need to go to the Computer Management window to start and stop the service. You can use the Manage menu item by right-clicking on My Computer. Under Services and Applications, you will see the service myWinService. The Start and Stop menu items start and stop the service.

When installing your service and defining the security context it will run in, if you do not provide a user name and password (or do not specify the LocalSystem security context), you will be prompted to provide them, as illustrated in Figure 17.16. Note that you can later change these credentials from Windows Service Manager.

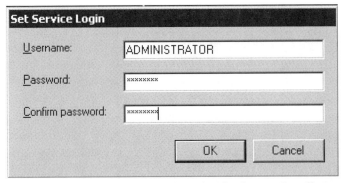

Figure 17.16: Set Service Log-in Dialog for Service Installation

Logging Events

One of the ways to monitor what your Windows service is doing, is to log events to the Event Viewer. This way, as your Windows service is out their running, if something goes wrong, you can check the EventLog and see what happened. You can also use event logging for capturing debug information as you would in an event trace. Listing 17.7 illustrates a few options in which to log events from your service. If you set AutoLog to true, it will log your events to the Application event log on your system. You can also set AutoLog to false, so that you can log events to your own custom event log.

Listing 17.7: Different ways to log events to the EventLog

```
// pseudo code
// logging a windows service service

// enable default logging for your service
MyService1.AutoLog = true;
```

```
// or
// you can do your custom logging
// first disable default logging for your service
MyService1.AutoLog = false;
// create an event source specifying log name
EventLog eventlog1 = new System.Diagnostics.EventLog();

if(!System.Diagnostics.Eventlog.SourceExists("mcbSource"))
{
 System.Diagnostics.EventLog.CreateEventSource("mcbSource", "mcbLog");
}
//configure event log to use this source name
eventLog1.Source = "mcbSource";


// later in any of the action trigger events, write an event log entry
eventLog1.WriteEntry("My Service is Running Smoothly! ");
```

Sample 3 – Service Manager

The following program manages services running on your computer. It allows you to start and stop services by clicking on a Windows service node in a tree and choosing the service action from the Form menu. The code uses the GetServices method of the ServiceController class to retrieve a list of services on a particular computer. As mentioned earlier in the chapter, the GetServices method returns an array of all of a computer's available services, except for those associated with device drivers.

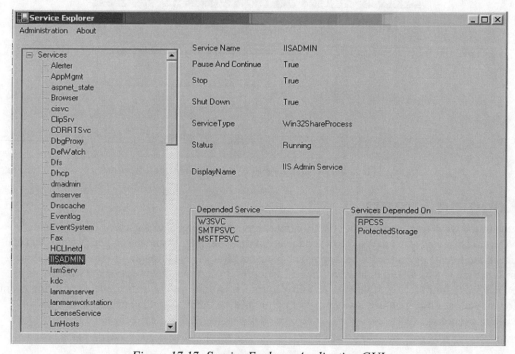

Figure 17.17: Service Explorer Application GUI

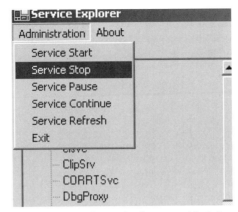

Figure 17.18: Service Explorer Application Administration Menu

Listing 17.8—Managing States of Windows Services Installed on a System

```csharp
using System;
using System.Drawing;
using System.Collections;
using System.ComponentModel;
using System.Windows.Forms;
using System.Data;
using System.ServiceProcess;

namespace ServiceExplorer
{
        /// <summary>
        /// Summary description for Form1.
        /// </summary>
        public class Form1 : System.Windows.Forms.Form
        {
                private System.Windows.Forms.TreeView treeService;
                //Create an array of type ServiceController to contain
                //the results
                private ServiceController[] services;
                private ServiceController SelectedService;

        …   // more control declarations


                /// <summary>
                /// Required designer variable.
                /// </summary>
                private System.ComponentModel.Container components = null;

                public Form1()
                {
                        //
                        // Required for Windows Form Designer support
                        //
                        InitializeComponent();

                        services = ServiceController.GetServices();

                        PopulateTreeView();
                        //
                        // TODO: Add any constructor code after InitializeComponent
                        // call
                        //
                }

                /// <summary>
```

```
        /// Clean up any resources being used.
        /// </summary>
        protected override void Dispose( bool disposing )
        {
                if( disposing )
                {
                        if (components != null)
                        {
                                components.Dispose();
                        }
                }
                base.Dispose( disposing );
        }


        protected void PopulateTreeView()
        {
                TreeNode RootNode = new TreeNode("Services",0,0);
                treeService.Nodes.Add(RootNode);

                //Call GetServices on the ServiceController class.
                //GetServices returns an array of ServiceController
                //objects.

                foreach(ServiceController service in services)
                {

                        TreeNode ServiceNode = new
                                TreeNode(service.ServiceName);
                        RootNode.Nodes.Add(ServiceNode);
                }

                treeService.ExpandAll();
        }

        /// <summary>
        /// The main entry point for the application.
        /// </summary>

        [STAThread]
        static void Main()
        {
                Application.Run(new Form1());
        }

        private void treeService_AfterSelect(object sender,
                        System.Windows.Forms.TreeViewEventArgs e)
        {
                lstDependedService.Items.Clear();
                lstServicesDependedOn.Items.Clear();

                foreach(ServiceController service in services)
                {
                        if(service.ServiceName==e.Node.Text)
                        {
                                SelectedService=service;
                                FillForm(service);
                                break;
                        }
                }

                //MessageBox.Show(((TreeView)sender).SelectedNode.Text);
        }

        private void FillForm(ServiceController service)
        {
                lblServiceName.Text=service.ServiceName;
```

```csharp
        lblCanPauseAndContinue.Text=service.CanPauseAndContinue.ToString();
        lblCanShutdown.Text=service.CanShutdown.ToString();
        lblDisplayName.Text=service.DisplayName;
        lblServiceType.Text=service.ServiceType.ToString();
        lblStatus.Text=service.Status.ToString();
        lblStop.Text=service.CanStop.ToString();

        foreach(ServiceController dependent in
                    service.DependentServices)
        {
            lstDependedService.Items.Add(dependent.ServiceName);
        }

        foreach(ServiceController dependsOn in
                    service.ServicesDependedOn)
        {
            lstServicesDependedOn.Items.Add(
                dependsOn.ServiceName);
        }

    }

private void menuStart_Click(object sender, System.EventArgs e)
{

        if(SelectedService.Status.ToString()=="Stopped")
        {
            SelectedService.Start();
            SelectedService.Refresh();
            PrepareForm(SelectedService);
        }
        else
        {
         MessageBox.Show("You cannot use Start menu because " +
                        SelectedService.ServiceName+" is "
                        +SelectedService.Status.ToString());
        }
}


private void menuStop_Click(object sender, System.EventArgs e)
{
        if(SelectedService.CanStop==true)
        {
                if(SelectedService.Status.ToString()!="Stopped")
                {
                    SelectedService.Stop();
                    SelectedService.Refresh();
                    PrepareForm(SelectedService);
                }
                else
                {
                MessageBox.Show("You cannot use Stop menu because " +
                    SelectedService.ServiceName +" is     "
                    +SelectedService.Status.ToString());
                }
        }
        else
        {
                MessageBox.Show("You cannot use Stop menu because " +
                SelectedService.ServiceName+" does not support
                                        Stop");
        }

 }

private void menuPause_Click(object sender, System.EventArgs e)
```

```
        {
                if(SelectedService.CanPauseAndContinue==true)
                {
                        if(SelectedService.Status.ToString()=="Running")
                        {
                                SelectedService.Pause();
                                SelectedService.Refresh();
                                PrepareForm(SelectedService);
                        }
                        else
                        {
                                MessageBox.Show(
                                "You cannot use Pause menu because "
                                + SelectedService.ServiceName+" is "
                                + SelectedService.Status.ToString());
                        }
                }
                else
                {
                        MessageBox.Show("You cannot use Pause menu because "
                        + SelectedService.ServiceName +
                        " does not support PauseAndContinue");
                }
        }

        private void menuContinue_Click(object sender, System.EventArgs e)
        {
                if(SelectedService.CanPauseAndContinue==true)
                {
                        if(SelectedService.Status.ToString()=="Paused")
                        {
                                SelectedService.Continue();
                                SelectedService.Refresh();
                                PrepareForm(SelectedService);
                        }
                        else
                        {
                                MessageBox.Show(
                                "You cannot use Continue menu because " +
                                 SelectedService.ServiceName+" is "
                                + SelectedService.Status.ToString());
                        }
                }
                else
                {
                MessageBox.Show("You cannot use Continue menu because " +
                        SelectedService.ServiceName+" does not support
                        PauseAndContinue");
                }
        }

        private void menuRefresh_Click(object sender, System.EventArgs e)
        {
                SelectedService.Refresh();
                PrepareForm(SelectedService);
        }


        private void PrepareForm(ServiceController service)
        {
                lstDependedService.Items.Clear();
                lstServicesDependedOn.Items.Clear();
                FillForm(service);
        }

private void menuExit_Click(object sender, System.EventArgs e)
        {
```

```
                Application.Exit();
        }

        private void menuAbout_Click(object sender, System.EventArgs e)
        {
                new About().ShowDialog();
        }

    }
}
```

Sample 4 – Using the ServiceController to List Device Drivers

The following code lists the attributes of the device drivers installed on your computer. Initially we get the collection of all of the device drivers installed on the computer by calling the static ServiceController method GetDevices. Then we loop through the list of device drivers and displays the service name, display name, and service type to the console.

Listing 17.9—Devices.cs, Browsing Device Drivers Installed on a Workstation

```csharp
using System;
using System.ServiceProcess;

public class DeviceDriverDisplayer
{
 public static void Main()
 {
  ServiceController [] controllers = ServiceController.GetDevices();
  int nNum = controllers.Length;
  String strType = "";

  for (int i = 0; i < nNum; i++)
  {
    // Get the short name of service.
    Console.WriteLine(controllers[i].ServiceName);
    // Get the display name of the service.
    Console.WriteLine(controllers[i].DisplayName);
    // Get the service type.
    ServiceType type = controllers[i].ServiceType;

    switch (type)
    {
      case ServiceType.Adapter:
      strType = "Adapter";
      break;

      case ServiceType.FileSystemDriver:
      strType = "File System Driver";
      break;

      case ServiceType.InteractiveProcess:
      strType = "Interactive Process";
      break;

      case ServiceType.KernelDriver:
      strType = "Kernel Mode Driver";
      break;

      case ServiceType.RecognizerDriver:
      strType = "Recognizer Driver";
      break;

      case ServiceType.Win32OwnProcess:
      strType = "Win32 Process";
```

```
            break;

            case ServiceType.Win32ShareProcess:
            strType = "Win32 Share Process";
            break;

            default:
            strType = "Unknown";
            break;
        }
        Console.WriteLine(strType);

        // Check if the service can be stopped or not.
        Console.WriteLine((controllers[i].CanStop == true) ? "Can be stopped" : "Cannot
be stopped");
        // You cen perform a Stop action on this service if this is true!
    Console.WriteLine("===========================================================");
    }
  }
}
```

Summary

In this chapter you learned how to create a Windows Service using the .NET framework and its classes. You learned about three important classes: the ServiceBase, ServiceController, and ServiceInstaller classes and how these classes are important in creating your Windows Service. You learned how to create a Windows service with a text editor as well as how to create one in the Visual Studio environment. You learned how to do event logging with the framework and how to use event handlers such as OnStart and OnStop. In the next chapter we will examine how the .NET Framework can be used to create applications that interact with COM.

Chapter 18:
COM Interoperability

Introduction

If you are wondering how to use your existing software investment in Component Object Model (COM) components in the .NET world, this chapter gives you that information. In the Active Server Pages (ASP) world, COM is the glue that connects all the components. In ASP, for example, COM acts as the glue to access ActiveX Data Objects (ADO), whereas ADO.NET is not dependent on COM in .NET. However, .NET can leverage the COM infrastructure, and we'll look at the details in this chapter.

What Is COM, and Why Do We Need It?

The Component Object Model (or COM) is Microsoft's answer to component-based distributed computing called Microsoft Windows Distributed interNet Applications Architecture (Windows DNA). COM addresses the problem of code reusability that many programmers face. One of the advantages of COM is that it can be written in any COM-enabled language, such as Visual Basic (VB), Visual C++, and so on. Another advantage is that COM components can be consumed from any COM-enabled tool such as ASP, Microsoft Word Visual Basic for Applications macros, Windows scripting components, and so on.

What Is Wrong with COM?

Of course, COM has a few problems. One of those is called "DLL Hell." Upgrading an existing COM component is difficult. When you upgrade an existing COM component with a newer version, it could break the applications that use the older version, and vice versa. Plus, moving an application from one directory to another could be a major problem. You must first unregister the COM component from the old directory and then reregister it in the new directory.

Another problem is that of upgrading the COM component when it is in use. This is difficult because you have to reboot the server to remove the COM component reference from the memory, upgrade the COM component, and reboot the server if necessary. This process is impossible if the server is used around the clock.

Differences Between COM and .NET Components

.NET components rely on the .NET Framework, whereas COM components rely on the COM infrastructure. When a COM object is created with a client such as VB or ASP, the client maintains the lifetime of the COM object, including creating the object, calling the properties and methods, and destroying the object. The .NET Framework maintains the .NET objects, and it provides all the necessary information, including garbage collection.

COM objects depend on the Windows registry to expose information about the components, and all the components' definitions are either in the .tlb file or embedded in the .dll, .exe, or .ocx files.

.NET components store the metadata information inside the component in an area called the *manifest.*

Accessing COM Components from .NET

The .NET Framework provides options for accessing COM components from a .NET application. The first and easiest is the Type Library Importer (Tlbimp.exe) utility. The Type Library Importer takes the COM type library file (*.tlb) or the .dll or .exe file and generates the .NET-aware metadata dynamic-link library (DLL) out of it. This .NET-aware metadata DLL can be used in .NET applications to call the COM components.

How Does It Work?

COM components run based on the interfaces and location information found in the Windows registry. As for .NET components, they reside in either the application directory or the global assembly cache. In addition, all of the .NET components include information about themselves. This is crucial for .NET components to work properly.

When we use the Type Library Importer, it generates a proxy DLL called the runtime callable wrapper (RCW). The RCW DLL will have all the metadata required for the .NET applications to instantiate the COM objects. The RCW will marshal the calls between .NET applications and COM components, and vice versa. Figure 18.1 illustrates the architecture of the RCW.

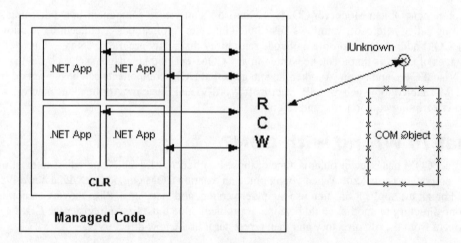

Figure 18.1: Runtime Callable Wrapper Architecture

The RCW will appear as a native .NET component to the .NET client, but in fact the RCW just marshals the calls between the .NET client and COM component. Every COM component instantiated outside the .NET Framework will share the single RCW, regardless of the number of instances of the component.

Note that certain COM component interfaces—such as IUnknown, IDispatch, IDispatchEx—will not be accessible from the .NET client. These interfaces will be consumed by the RCW.

Let's look at a simple example of how the RCW marshals calls between .NET and the COM component. Consider the following Visual Basic 6.0 (VB6) method signature:

```
Function GetData(Category As String, CutOffDate As Date) As Integer
```

When the method shown is compiled into a COM component, the VB6 method signature will be converted into the following Interface Definition Language (IDL) format:

```
HRESULT GetData(BSTR Category, DATE CutOffDate, [out, retval] int *retval);
```

When we create an RCW for the COM component, the COM method signature will be converted to the following C# syntax:

```
int GetData(String Category, DateTime CutOffDate);
```

In the conversion process, the VB6 string variable is converted into a BSTR-type IDL definition, and it is converted back into the System.String type in .NET. The Date Data type is converted into the System.DateTime type in .NET. Moreover, we're getting a pointer back from the COM method to get the integer result.

A Simple COM Component

To understand this process, let's build a simple COM component with VB. Start VB6 and select the ActiveX DLL project (as shown in Figure 18.2).

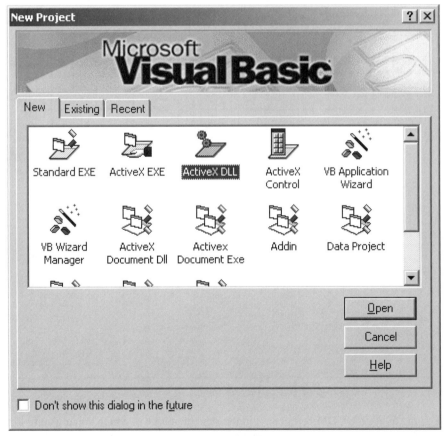

Figure 18.2: ActiveX Project

Change the project name to VB6Comp and the class name to COMComp (as shown in Figure 18.2).

Figure 18.3: Project Attributes

Create a method called SayHelloFromVB6COMComp as shown in Figure 18.4.

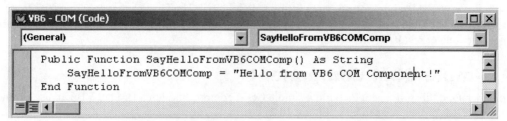

Figure 18.4: SayHelloFromVB6COMComp Method

Compile the COM component as VB6Comp.dll (as shown in Figure 18.5).

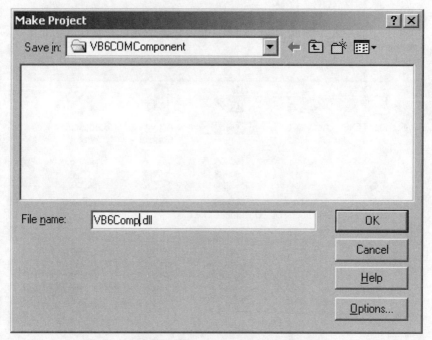

Figure 18.5: Compile the COM Component

If you are going to use the COM component in the same machine in which you are compiling it, you don't have to register the component in the registry. If not, you must register the COM component in the registry with the Regsvr32 tool (as shown in Figure 18.6).

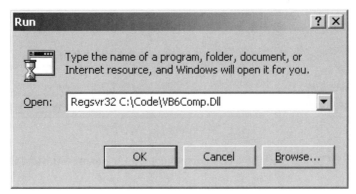

Figure 18.6: Compile the COM Component

Our COM component is ready now. Let's test it from an ASP page (see Listing 18.1).

Listing 18.1—Accessing a COM Component

```
<Html>
<Head>
<Title>Accessing a COM component</Title>
</Head>
<Body>
<%
      Dim ObjCOMClient
      Set ObjCOMClient = CreateObject("VB6Comp.COMComp")

      Response.Write ObjCOMClient.SayHelloFromVB6COMComp

      Set ObjCOMClient = Nothing
%>
</Body>
</Html>
```

Let's save the ASP code as default.asp and access it from Internet Explorer (as shown in Figure 18.7).

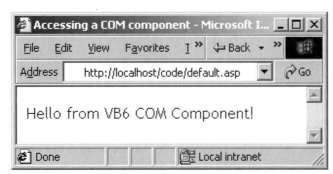

Figure 18.7: Accessing the COM Component from ASP

Building a Runtime Callable Wrapper

Everything works fine so far. Let's build an RCW proxy DLL for the COM component. For that, we're going to use the Type Library Importer. Go to the command prompt and change the current directory to wherever you've placed the COM component. Then type the command line to build the RCW for the COM component (as shown in Figure 18.8).

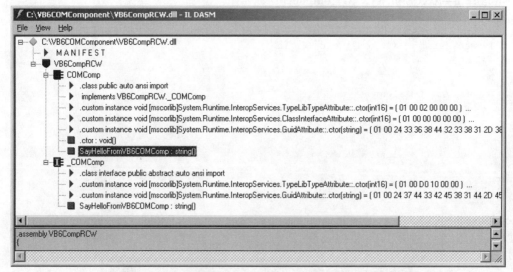

Figure 18.8: Building the RCW

We've just built an RCW for the VB6 COM component with the name VB6CompRCW.dll.

Inspecting the Metadata

Microsoft ships a utility called the MSIL Disassembler (Ildasm.exe) with .NET Framework, which you can view the content of an assembly. It is kind of an object viewer utility in VB. Let's use the MSIL Disassembler to view the content of the RCW (see Figure 18.9).

Figure 18.9: Metadata Information Stored in the RCW

As you can see, the RCW contains the metadata about the COM component including the method name SayHelloFromVB6COMComp. If we double-click that method name, we'll see the details about the method (as shown Figure 18.10).

Figure 18.10: SayHelloFromVB6COMComp Method Signature

The method signature includes the return type as *string,* and the string will be marshaled between .NET and COM using the BSTR data type.

An ASP.NET Client

Create a Bin folder in the Internet Information Server virtual directory, and put the RCW .dll file in that Bin folder. When we're accessing the COM component from a .NET client such as ASP.NET, we can access it by using either *early binding* or *late binding.* The early-binding method is strongly typed, and at the compilation time the .NET client will be aware of all the properties, methods, and events exposed by the COM component using the RCW.

Early Binding

Now that our runtime callable wrapper is ready, lets build an ASP.NET client to access it (see Listing 18.2).

Listing 18.2—RCW Example

```
<%@Import Namespace="VB6CompRCW" %>
<html>
<head>
<Title>Accessing a COM component -- From ASP.NET</Title>
</head>
<body>
<script language="C#" runat="server">
protected void Page_Load(object sender, EventArgs e){
        COMComp objCOMRCW = new COMComp();
        Label1.Text = objCOMRCW.SayHelloFromVB6COMComp();
}
</script>
<form runat="server">
<b>Result:</b> <asp:Label id="Label1" runat="server" />
</form>
</body>
</html>
```

First of all, we import the namespace VB6CompRCW. You will remember that the RCW DLL that we generated holds the same name. In the Page_Load event we're instantiating an object of the type COMComp as we do with all other .NET objects. Notice that the VB6 project name becomes the name of the namespace, and the VB6 class name is the same as the class name for the RCW. Then we call the method SayHelloFromVB6COMComp and assign the result in an ASP.NET label server control. Figure 18.11 shows the result of the ASP.NET page.

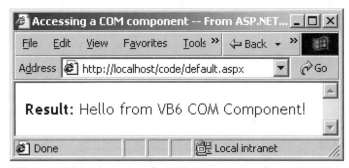

Figure 18.11: Accessing the COM Component from ASP.NET

Behind the scene, the runtime creates an RCW and maps the metadata proxy's class methods and properties to methods and properties exposed by the COM component. The .NET runtime manages the lifetime of the RCW with Garbage Collector. The RCW takes care of maintaining reference counts of the COM object and helps the .NET runtime manage the reference counts of the COM objects.

Accessing COM Components from Visual Studio .NET

Accessing COM components from Visual Studio .NET (VS.NET) is easy. VS.NET hides all the complexities of generating an RCW. Let's look at the steps in accessing the COM component from VS.NET.

Fire up VS.NET and select a C# Windows Forms application (as shown in Figure 18.12).

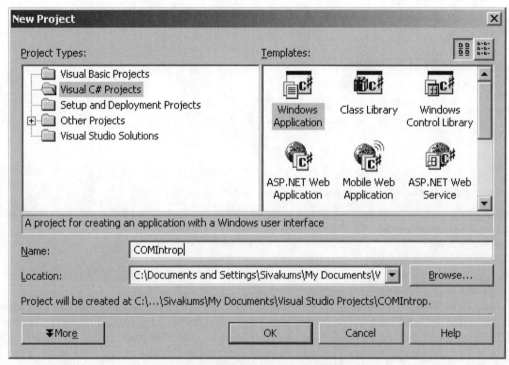

Figure 18.12: C# Windows Forms Application

Go to the Solutions Explorer and right-click the References item. You'll see a shortcut menu as shown in Figure 18.13.

Figure 18.13: References Shortcut Menu

Select Add Reference . . . from the shortcut menu. You'll see a new dialog box, Add Reference. Select the COM tab at the top as shown in Figure 18.14.

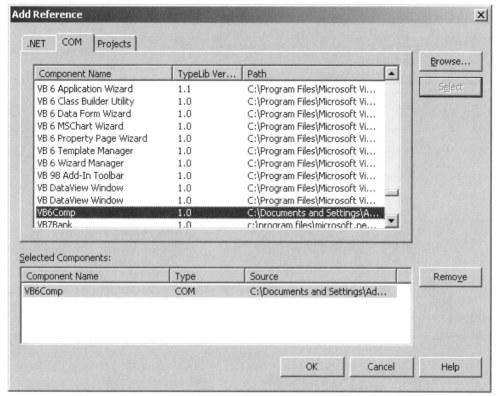

Figure 18.14: COM Tab on Add Reference Dialog Box

Now scroll down and select the VB6Comp COM component and click the Select button. The selected COM component will be added to the selected components list. Click the OK button now. You'll see one more message box as shown in Figure 18.15.

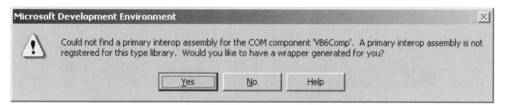

Figure 18.15: Message Box

The message box asks you if you want to generate an RCW for the COM component since it could find the RCW for the COM component. Click Yes. When you do that, VS.NET will use the Type Library Importer to generate the RCW for the COM component, and it'll add the RCW to the Windows Forms project (as shown in Figure 18.16).

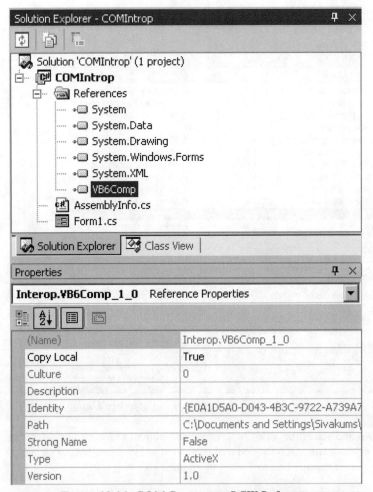

Figure 18.16: COM Component RCW Reference

Let's add a label and a command button control to the Windows form (as shown in Figure 18.17).

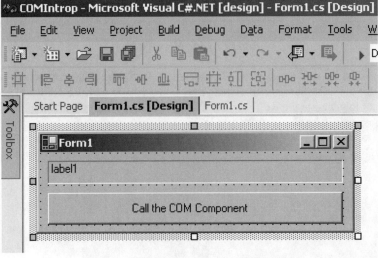

Figure 18.17: Windows Form Design

Double-click the command button and add the code in Listing 18.3 to the button's Click event.

Listing 18.3—VB6 COM Component

```
//Create an object type of the VB6 COM component
VB6Comp.COMComp objCOM = new VB6Comp.COMComp();

//Call the SayHelloFromVB6COMComp Method
label1.Text = objCOM.SayHelloFromVB6COMComp();
```

In the button's Click event we've created an object type of the COM component. We've then accessed the SayHelloFromVB6COMComp method and assigned the result to a label control.

Press F5 to build and run the Windows Forms application (as shown in Figure 18.18).

Figure 18.18: Windows Forms Runtime

Now click the button. You'll see the result in the label control as shown in Figure 18.19.

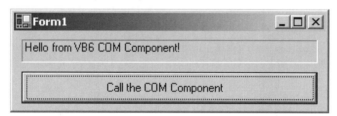

Figure 18.19: Result from COM Component

Late Binding

We can access COM components through late binding by using *reflection.* Reflection is a technology that allows us to examine metadata that describes types and members or an assembly. In .NET every type is either a reference type or a value type, and it is derived from the base type System.Object. The object has a method called GetType that returns an instance of the type System.Type. This type provides numerous application programming interfaces to retrieve information about types, constructors, methods, properties, fields, interfaces, events, and so on. Reflection provides runtime access to method signatures, superclass information, and interfaces supported by a type, among other things.

Let's use reflection to access the COM component in the late-bound mode. Fire up your favorite editor and save the code shown in Listing 18.4 as LateBinding.aspx.

Listing 18.4—Late-Binding Example

```
<%@Import Namespace="System" %>
<%@Import Namespace="System.Runtime.InteropServices" %>
<%@Import Namespace="System.Reflection" %>
<%@Import Namespace="VB6CompRCW" %>
```

```
<html>
<head>
<Title>Accessing a COM component -- From ASP.NET (Late Bound)</Title>
</head>
<body>
<script language="C#" runat="server">
protected void Page_Load(object sender, EventArgs e){

        try{
                //A String variable to get the return
                //value form the COM component
                String RtnValue;

                //Declare an object type to hold
                //the latebound COM component
                object objLateBound;

                //Declare a Type variable to get the
                //type of the COM component using the
                //Reflection classes
                Type objType;

                //Get the type information from the
                //ProgID "VB6Comp.COMComp"
                objType = Type.GetTypeFromProgID("VB6Comp.COMComp");

                //Create an instance of the object using the
                //type information that we've retrieved
                objLateBound = Activator.CreateInstance(objType);

                // Invoke the SayHelloFromVB6COMComp method
                RtnValue = (String)objType.InvokeMember
                  ("SayHelloFromVB6COMComp", BindingFlags.Default |
                 BindingFlags.InvokeMethod, null, objLateBound, null);

                //Show the return value in the Label control.
                Label1.Text = RtnValue;

        }
        catch (Exception Ex1) {
                //Show the exception in the Label control
                Label1.Text = Ex1.ToString();
        }
}
</script>
<form runat="server">
<b>Result:</b> <asp:Label id="Label1" runat="server" />
</form>
</body>
</html>
```

First, we import a few namespaces such as System, System.Reflection, VB6CompRCW, and System.Runtime.InteropServices. The System.Reflection namespace holds all the class references for reflection operations, and the System.Runtime.InteropServices namespace holds the classes to access the COM components from the managed code. VB6CompRCW is our RCW for the COM component.

In the Page_Load event, we have three variables of the types *string, object,* and *type.* The string variable (RtnValue) is used to retrieve the return value from the COM component; the object variable (objLateBound) is used to get a reference to the COM object; and the type variable (objType) is used to get the reference of the COM component (See listing 18.5).

Listing 18.5—Getting Return Values

```
//A String variable to get the return
//value from the COM component
String RtnValue;

//Declare an object type to hold
//the latebound COM component
object objLateBound;

//Declare a Type variable to get the
//type of the COM component using the
//Reflection classes
Type objType;
```

We use the GetTypeFromProgID method of the Type class (in the System namespace) to get the reference of the type VB6Comp.COMComp.

```
//Get the type information from the ProgID "VB6Comp.COMComp"
objType = Type.GetTypeFromProgID("VB6Comp.COMComp");
```

Then we use the CreateInstance method of the Activator class to create an instance of the type VB6Comp.COMComp that we've stored in the variable objType.

```
//Create an instance of the object using the
//type information that we've retrieved
objLateBound = Activator.CreateInstance(objType);
```

Then we use the InvokeMember method of the Type class, invoke the method SayHelloFromVB6COMComp in the COM component, and store the result back in the string variable. Then we assign the result of the COM component to a label control. (See Listing 18.6.)

Listing 18.6—InvokeMember Example

```
// Invoke the SayHelloFromVB6COMComp method
RtnValue = (String)objType.InvokeMember("SayHelloFromVB6COMComp",
                BindingFlags.Default | BindingFlags.InvokeMethod,
                null, objLateBound, null);

//Show the return value in the Label control.
Label1.Text = RtnValue;
```

Figure 18.20 shows the output of the late-bound COM component.

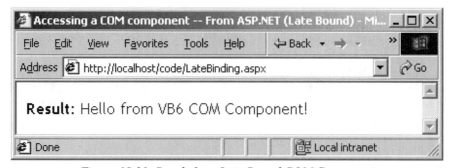

Figure 18.20: Result from Late-Bound COM Component

Handling COM Events

COM handles events in an entirely different way than .NET. The COM event-handling mechanism is based on *connection points,* whereas .NET event handling is based on *delegates.* The RCW handles the event source difference clearly. When an event is raised in the COM object, the RCW receives the event connection point and generates the necessary delegates for the .NET client to understand the event (as shown in Figure 18.21).

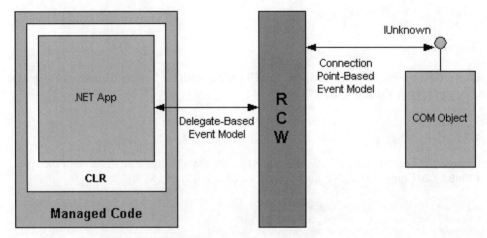

Figure 18.21: Event Conversion

When a .NET client sees the RCW, it'll see only the event delegate. During this process, the event delegate will act as translator between the managed and unmanaged code based the COM connection point event handler.

ActiveX Controls and .NET

ActiveX controls have found a whole new market in the desktop world; you can find ActiveX controls ranging from spreadsheets to MP3 players. ActiveX controls are COM-based components, and they are not directly supported by Windows Forms. However, we can build a wrapper class to make the ActiveX controls usable in the .NET world.

All the Windows Forms controls are derived from the System.Windows.Forms.Control class. If we need to use an ActiveX control in Windows Forms, we have to build a wrapper class that inherits from the System.Windows.Forms.AxHost class. The .NET Framework ships with a utility called the ActiveX Control Importer (Aximp.exe). When we use the ActiveX Control Importer against an ActiveX control, it generates one or more assemblies to be consumed by the .NET Framework.

Let's look at an example. We'll take the Microsoft Tabbed Dialog Control 6.0 ActiveX control that comes with VB6 and build a wrapper for it. The Microsoft Tabbed Dialog Control 6.0 ActiveX control is stored as an .ocx file in C:\Winnt\System32\tabctl32.ocx. Go to the command prompt and type the following command to convert the ActiveX control:

```
AxImp "C:\Winnt\System32\tabctl32.ocx"
```

When you press ENTER, the wrapper classes will be generated (as shown in Figure 18.22).

Figure 18.22: Wrapper Class Generation

As you can see, the ActiveX Control Importer generates two assembles, TabDlg.dll and AxTabDlg.dll, from the tab ActiveX control. The TabDlg.dll file is the common language runtime proxy for the ActiveX control, and AxTabDlg.dll is the Windows Forms proxy file. Now the ActiveX control is ready to be placed in a Windows Forms application.

We can examine the wrapper assemblies generated by the ActiveX Control Importer by using the MSIL Disassembler utility. Figure 18.23 shows the content of the assembly TabDlg.dll.

You can see this assembly including all the information about the ActiveX control right from constants to the event information.

Figure 18.23: Content of the Assembly TabDlg.dll

Figure 18.24 shows the content of the assembly AxTabDlg.dll. As you can see, this assembly stores only information about the events in it. This is the assembly consumed by Windows Forms.

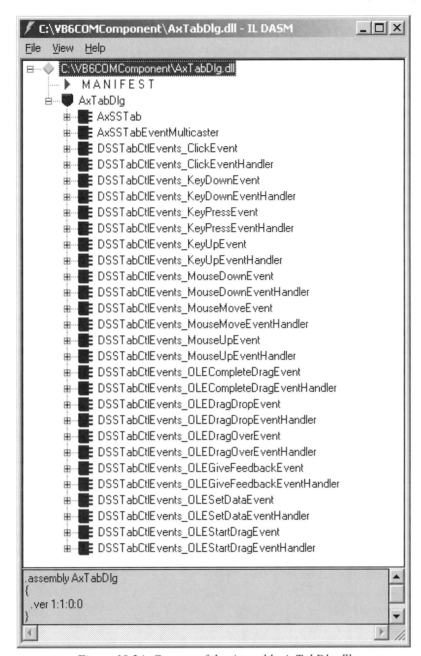

Figure 18.24: Content of the Assembly AxTabDlg.dll

VS.NET makes this process seamless, and we'll never know about the AxImp.exe file if we use the Visual Studio .NET integrated development environment.

We'll use the tab control that comes with VB6 in the Windows Forms application. Fire up VS.NET and create a C# Windows Forms application. Then right-click the toolbar and select the option Customize Toolbox ... from the shortcut menu (as shown in Figure 18.25).

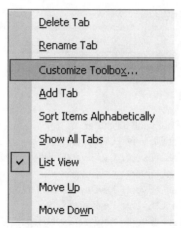

Figure 18.25: Shortcut Menu

You'll see a new dialog box with COM Components and .NET Components tabs. In the COM Components tab, select Microsoft Tabbed Dialog Control 6.0 (SP4) from the list and click OK (as shown in Figure 18.26).

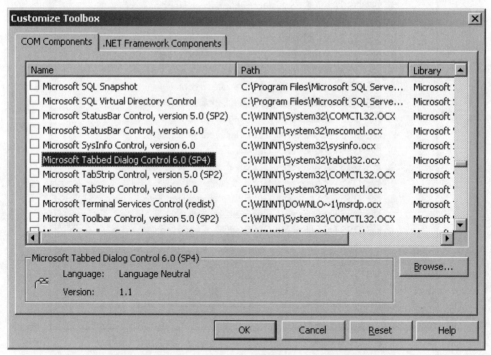

Figure 18.26: Component Selection Dialog

Once you've selected the COM component, you can see the two assemblies VS.NET generates using the AxImp.exe utility behind the scene and adds to the Solution Explorer (as shown in Figure 18.27).

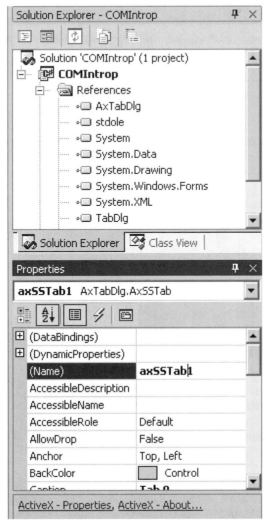

Figure 18.27: Component Selection Dialog

Let's drag and drop the tab control into the Windows form as shown in Figure 18.28.

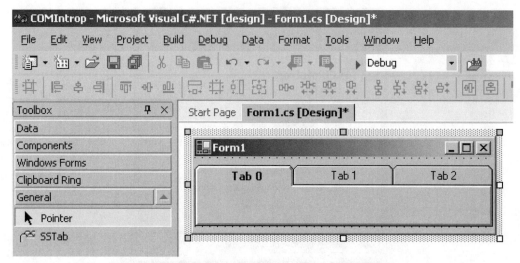

Figure 18.28: Tab ActiveX Control on a Windows Form

If you press F5, the code will run without errors because both of the assemblies are generated by the AxImp.exe utility.

Exception Handling

.NET and COM each handle exceptions differently. In .NET each exception is based on an Exception definition, and in COM error handling is done through the HRESULT parameter in the IDL definition. The HRESULT parameter tells whether the method call went through. When a COM method call fails, a system- or user-defined exception needs to be raised in the .NET client. When we create the RCW for a COM component, the RCW takes care of the exception transition from HRESULT to an exception.

Each exception class in .NET maps to an HRESULT. For example, if the COM component encounters a *Divide by zero* error, it reports the HRESULT parameter with COR_E_DIVIDEBYZERO, and this will be transformed into the DivideByZeroException in .NET.

Threading Affinity

The COM components support three different threading models: single-threaded apartments (STAs), multithreaded apartments (MTAs), and unknown. However, all of the .NET components are by default MTA (free threaded). When a COM component is called from .NET, the common language runtime creates and initializes an apartment. That apartment can be either an STA or an MTA, and if an MTA accesses an STA COM component (e.g., a VB6 COM component), there will be performance implications. Each STA has one thread, and the MTAs have more than one thread. When incompatible apartments are created, the COM marshals the calls between STAs and MTAs using a proxy. To overcome the problem, we can set the kind of apartment that needs to be created when using the COM components.

For example, if we're accessing an STA COM component from .NET, we ask .NET to create an STA to access this component. The code in Listing 18.7 creates an STA before calling the COM component.

Listing 18.7—STA COM Component

```
//Include the Threading namespace
```

```
using System.Threading;

//Include the RCW of the COM component
using VB6CompRCW;

//Set the current apartment to use STA threading
//Since we're calling an VB6 component
Thread.CurrentThread.ApartmentState = ApartmentState.STA;

//Create a COM component
COMComp objCOMRCW = new COMComp();

//Call its method
Console.Write(objCOMRCW.SayHelloFromVB6COMComp());
```

Note that when accessing COM components from .NET, it is always a good idea to situate the threading information as the first line of code, since the threading information code will not take effect after the common language runtime creates the apartment to access the COM component.

Calling Native DLL Functions

The .NET Framework provides the *platform invoke* service, which allows calling native functions in DLLs such as Win32 DLLs. Platform invoke marshals the calls between the .NET application and the DLL (as illustrated in Figure 18.29).

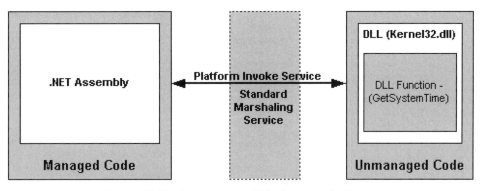

Figure 18.29: Architecture of Platform Invoke Service

When we want to consume a DLL function, we must first declare the DLL function as a static function with the attribute DllImport with the DLL file name inside a class (see Listing 18.8).

Listing 18.8—DllImport Example

```
public class DLLclass
{
    [DllImport("MyDLL.dll")]
    public static extern void MyDLLFunction(Parameters...);
}
```

Let's look at a simple example. We're going to consume the GetSystemTime function, which is in Kernel32.dll. The GetSystemTime function accepts a *struct* variable by reference and returns the system data and time information. Let's access the GetSystemTime function from an ASP.NET page. The code is shown in Listing 18.9.

Listing 18.9—GetSystemTime Function

```
<%@ Import Namespace="System" %>
<%@ Import Namespace="System.Runtime.InteropServices" %>
```

```
<html>
<head>
<Title>Accessing a Win32 API -- From ASP.NET</Title>
</head>
<body>
<script language="C#" runat="server">

//Declare a SystemDateTime Structure
public struct SystemTime
{
    public ushort wYear;
    public ushort wMonth;
    public ushort wDayOfWeek;
    public ushort wDay;
    public ushort wHour;
    public ushort wMinute;
    public ushort wSecond;
    public ushort wMiliseconds;
}


//Declare a class
public class Win32API
{
        //Import the Win32API into the class and make it
        //a static method
        [DllImport("Kernel32.dll")]
        public static extern void GetSystemTime(ref
        SystemTime sysTime);
}

protected void Page_Load(object sender, EventArgs e){
        try{
                //Declare a variable type of
                //the SystemTime struct
                SystemTime sysTime = new SystemTime();

                //Call the GetSystemTime API with the
                //struct variable as reference.
                Win32API.GetSystemTime(ref sysTime);

                //Show the result.
                Label1.Text = sysTime.wMonth + "/" + sysTime.wDay + "/" +
                sysTime.wYear + " " + sysTime.wHour + ":" +
                sysTime.wMinute + ":" + sysTime.wSecond;
        }
        catch (Exception Ex1) {
                Label1.Text = Ex1.ToString();
        }
}
</script>
<form runat="server">
<b>System Date-Time is:</b> <asp:Label id="Label1" runat="server" />
</form>
</body>
</html>
```

First, we import System and System.Runtime.InteropServices. Classes inside the System.Runtime.InteropServices namespace is used for interoperating between managed and unmanaged code. Then we define the struct type supported by the GetSystemTime function. (See Listing 18.10.)

Listing 18.10—Part1 Explanation

```
//Declare a SystemDateTime Structure
public struct SystemTime
{
```

```
    public ushort wYear;
    public ushort wMonth;
    public ushort wDayOfWeek;
    public ushort wDay;
    public ushort wHour;
    public ushort wMinute;
    public ushort wSecond;
    public ushort wMiliseconds;
}
```

Then we define a public class with the name Win32API, and we define the GetSystemTime function as an extern function. We specify the location of the function using the attribute DllImport with the DLL file name. (See Listing 18.11.)

Listing 18.11—Part2 Explanation

```
//Declare a class
public class Win32API
{
      //Import the Win32API into the class and make it
      //a static method
    [DllImport("Kernel32.dll")]
    public static extern void GetSystemTime(ref
    SystemTime sysTime);
}
```

In the Page_Load event, we create a variable of the type struct. We then call the function GetSystemTime and pass the struct variable as reference. Then we concatenate a string variable with date. (See Listing 18.12.)

Listing 18.12—Part3 Explanation

```
protected void Page_Load(object sender, EventArgs e){
      try
      {
              //Declare a variable type of
              //the SystemTime struct
              SystemTime sysTime = new SystemTime();

              //Call the GetSystemTime API with the
              //struct variable as reference.
              Win32API.GetSystemTime(ref sysTime);

          //Show the result.
          Label1.Text = sysTime.wMonth + "/" + sysTime.wDay +
          "/" + sysTime.wYear + " " + sysTime.wHour + ":" +
sysTime.wMinute + ":" + sysTime.wSecond;
      }
      catch (Exception Ex1) {
              Label1.Text = Ex1.ToString();
      }
}
```

Figure 18.30 shows the output of the code.

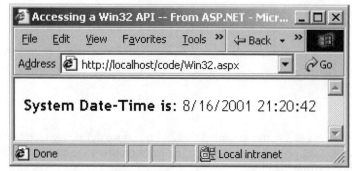

Figure 18.30: Output of the DLL Function

What Do We Lose?

Accessing COM components from .NET can have performance implications. Because COM components are not native to .NET, the calls to the COM components go through a proxy such as an RCW. Thus, if possible, it is advisable to convert the COM component into a .NET component. The .NET components solve the DLL Hell problem; when we use COM components from .NET, our application is still a target for DLL Hell.

The common language runtime exposes a few performance counters to be used with the Performance Monitor utility that comes with Windows. The performance counters are available under the category .NET CLR Interop (as shown in Figure 18.31).

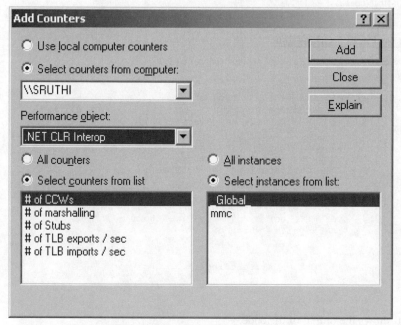

Figure 18.31: .NET Interop Performance Counters

The performance counters can tell us, for instance, how much time the marshaling and stub take per second (as shown in Figure 18.32).

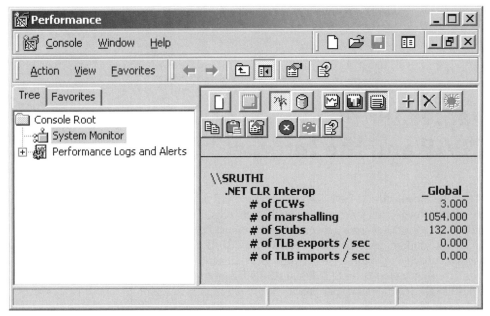

Figure 18.32: .NET Interop Performance Counters Summary

Summary

In this chapter, we looked at how to use unmanaged code inside managed code, including using COM components, ActiveX controls, and a function from a native DLL. The .NET interop services bridge the gap between the managed and unmanaged code. When using .NET interop services, the .NET application pays a performance penalty because the class to the COM component goes through the process of marshaling. Therefore, you should be careful when planning such implementation. Moreover, watch the performance counters using the Windows Performance Monitor tool when stress-testing the .NET interop application.

Chapter 19:
TCP/IP and the Internet

The TCP/IP protocol suite is the bricks and mortar of all networked applications and the most widely used protocol among private and public networks. The .NET Framework provides robust and versatile classes for developing networked applications. For example, classes for SOAP and ASP.NET programming use the .NET Framework TCP/IP classes as base/parent classes or as member components to accomplish network operations—by inheritance, aggregation, or composition—since classes for SOAP and ASP.NET programming are network-centric. The TCP/IP classes inside the .NET Framework provide the required infrastructure for any software that is network enabled.

TCP/IP Programming

A Department of Defense (DOD) research project developed TCP (transmission control protocol) and IP (Internet protocol) to connect a number of different networks designed by different vendors into a network of networks—the Internet. TCP/IP-based Internet was immediately successful because it delivered a few basic services that everyone needed (file transfer, electronic mail, and remote log-on) across a very large number of client and server systems.

On the battlefield, a communications network must be able to sustain damage, so the DOD designed TCP/IP to be robust and automatically recover from any node or phone-line failure. This design allows the construction of very large networks with less central management. (However, because of the automatic recovery, network problems can go undiagnosed and uncorrected for long periods of time.)

TCP/IP is the underlying communication protocol for local LANs/WANs and for the Internet. It has been a widely adopted standard since the days of legacy operating systems. The TCP/IP protocol stack is made up of four layers: application, transport, network, and link. IP resides in the network layer, and TCP is a part of the transport layer.

The *link layer* is normally a device driver that handles the hardware interface. The *application layer* provides particular services to the user, such as FTP (file transfer protocol) and SMTP (simple mail transfer protocol).

The *network layer* describes how a series of exchanges over various data links can deliver data between any two nodes in a network. This layer, then, defines the Internet's addressing and routing structure. IP is the mailroom of the TCP/IP stack where packet sorting and delivery take place. At this layer, each incoming or outgoing packet is referred to as a *datagram*. Each IP datagram bears the source IP address of the sender and the destination IP address of the intended recipient. Unlike media access control addresses, IP addresses in a datagram remain the same throughout a packet's journey across an internetwork.

IP is responsible for moving a packet of data from node to node based on a four-byte destination address (the IP number). The Internet authorities assign to organizations ranges of numbers. The organizations then assign to their departments groups of their numbers. IP, then, operates on gateway machines that move data from department to organization to region and then around the world.

The *transport layer* describes the quality and nature of data delivery. This layer defines if and how retransmissions will be used to ensure data delivery. TCP provides a connection-based, reliable byte-stream service to applications.

TCP is responsible for verifying the correct delivery of data from client to server. Data can be lost in the intermediate network, so TCP adds support to detect errors or lost data, triggering retransmission until the data is correctly and completely received. It does so by utilizing sockets. A *socket* refers to the package of high-level subroutines that provide access to TCP/IP on most systems.

Microsoft networking relies upon TCP transport for log-on, file and print sharing, replication of information between domain controllers, transfer of browse lists, and other common functions. But TCP can be used for only one-to-one communications. On the other hand, UDP (User Datagram Protocol) is connectionless and used for multicast operations generally.

However, higher-level interfaces are available to user-mode applications, the most common being Windows sockets, RPC, and NetBIOS. (If you are interested in TCP/IP protocol suite internals, refer to a solid book like *TCP/IP Illustrated,* volumes 1, 2, and 3.)

Figure 19.1 depicts the fundamental architecture of a network frame that carries a TCP/IP packet. Each source layer in the stack adds header information to the frame, critical to its corresponding destination layer.

Preamble	Destination Address	Source Addresss	Type or Length	Ethernet Data	CRC
8 Bytes	6 Bytes	6 Bytes	2 Bytes	0-1500 Bytes	4 Bytes

IP Headers	IP Data
20 Bytes	0-1480 Bytes

TCP Headers	TCP Data
20 Bytes	0-1460

Application Header	User Data
Defined by Application	Defined by Application

```
Ethernet Data = IP Headers + IP Data
IP Data = TCP Headers + TCP Data
TCP Data = Application Header + User Data
```

Figure 19.1: TCP/IP Network Package Over Ethernet Frame

Listing 19.1 shows a network data capture from the Microsoft Network Monitor program.

Listing 19.1—Captured Header Information

```
ETHERNET: ETYPE = 0x0800 : Protocol = IP: DOD Internet Protocol
ETHERNET: Destination address : 02608C8D95F8
ETHERNET: Source address : 02608C8D5B7B
ETHERNET: Frame Length : 60 (0x003C)
ETHERNET: Ethernet Type : 0x0800 (IP: DOD Internet Protocol)
IP: Total Length = 44 (0x2C)
IP: Fragment Offset = 0 (0x0) bytes
   IP: Time to Live = 32 (0x20)
   IP: Protocol = TCP - Transmission Control
   IP: CheckSum = 0x3B4F
   IP: Source Address = 131.107.2.211
   IP: Destination Address = 131.107.2.212
   IP: Data: Number of data bytes remaining = 24 (0x0018)
 TCP: ....S., len:  4, seq:   17357, ack:     0, win: 8192, src: 1025 dst: 139 (NBT
Session)
   TCP: Source Port = 0x0401
   TCP: Destination Port = NETBIOS Session Service
   TCP: Sequence Number = 17357 (0x43CD)
   TCP: Acknowledgement Number = 0 (0x0)
TCP: Flags = 0x02 : ....S.
TCP: Window = 8192 (0x2000)
   TCP: CheckSum = 0x2350
TCP: Option Value = 1460 (0x5B4)
```

The TCP destination port—for example, HTTP 80—defines which application you are requesting from the remote server. The TCP source port defines the client computer's port for this communication. When the connection occurs, the parties (server and client) will use these ports by designating source and destination ports for themselves on each packet when exchanging data. For the server, the source port is 80 and the destination port—for example, 2334—is one of the ephemeral ports. For the client in this example, the source port is 2334 and the destination port is HTTP 80. In general, port numbers are divided into three ranges:

- Well-known ports like HTTP, FTP, HTTPS (0 through 1023)
- Registered ports (1024 through 49151)
- Dynamic and/or private ports (49152 through 65535)

For a list of the well-known and registered ports, check out the IANA port assignments list at http://www.iana.org/assignments/port-numbers.

Requests for Comments

The Internet community uses requests for comments (RFCs) to publish all standards for TCP/IP. They are a constantly evolving series of reports, proposals, and protocol standards. You can obtain RFCs in a number of ways using HTTP, FTP, or e-mail. See the RFC Editor Web page at http://www.rfc-editor.org, which provides a table of well-known RFC numbers. For a complete list sorted latest to earliest, refer to http://www.rfc-editor.org/rfc-index2.html, and for a list sorted earliest to latest, refer to http://www.rfc-editor.org/rfc-index.html.

Socket Programming

The Socket class creates a managed version of an Internet transport service. Once the socket is created, it is bound to a specific endpoint with the Bind method, and the connection to the endpoint is established with the Connect method. Then data is sent to the socket using the Send method and SendTo method, and the data is read from the socket using the Receive method and ReceiveFrom method. After completion, the Shutdown method disables the socket, and the Close method closes the socket.

The Socket class is used by the .NET Framework to provide Internet connections to the TCPClient, UDPClient, WebRequest, and descendent classes. Below is the general protocol data flow during a simple socket application where the connected server drops the connection after sending the last byte (such as with HTTP and WHOIS protocols):

- Create/initiate socket.
- Create IPAddress, resolve host DNS to IP.
- Create IPEndpoint, IPAddress, and TCP application port.
- Connect to remote server using this endpoint.
- Send some application-specific data to connected server.
- Receive data until the buffer is empty.
- Process completed data.
- Return back to step 5 if looping for any reason.
- Socket connection is terminated by the remote server or by us explicitly.

TCPClient is used to create a client connection to a remote host. Data sent to and from the network goes through a NetworkStream instance. The TCPClient class builds upon the Socket class to provide TCP services at a higher level of abstraction. Application level protocols such as FTP and HTTP build on the TCPClient class.

Listing 19.2 creates a TCP connection to the server, time.mindcracker.com, on port 13 and gets the response stream. (Note that port 13 is the destination port for the client and the source port for the server. You generally do not need to specify the client source port for connections when it is also the destination port for the server, since both ports are automatically managed by the TCP/IP stack after initiating the connection.)

Listing 19.2—TCPClient, Example 1 Connection with Constructor

```
TcpClient myClient = new TcpClient("time.mindcracker.com",13);
Stream myStream = myClient.GetStream();
```

Listing 19.3—TCPClient, Example 2 Explicit Connection

```
TcpClient myClient = new TcpClient()
MyClient.Connect("time. mindcracker.com",13);
NetworkStream myStream = myClient.GetStream();
```

System.Net.Sockets Namespace and Its SubClasses

The Socket classes act as the transition point between managed and native code within the .NET classes. In most cases, Socket calls simply marshal data into their native Win32 counterparts and handle any necessary security checks. The System.Net.Sockets namespace provides a managed implementation of the Windows Sockets interface for developers who need to tightly control access to the network. Developers familiar with the Winsock API should have no problem developing applications using the Socket class. Table 19.1 shows the important Socket classes and their functions.

Socket Class	Function
LingerOption	Determines the amount of time the socket will stay open after closing if data remains to be sent.
MulticastOption	Multicast is a means of sending the same data to numerous recipients simultaneously. The MulticastOption class is used when joining or leaving multicast groups. Refer to the "UDP Multicasting" section for more clarification.
NetworkStream	Provides streams to send and receive network data through network sockets. Supports both synchronous and asynchronous access.
Socket	The basic class for sending or receiving raw network data. It is an implementation of Berkeley sockets. Used by TCPClient, UDPClient, and WebRequest (and descendent classes).
TCPClient	Used for connecting to a remote host with TCP services. Also used by application-level protocols such as FTP and HTTP.
TCPListener	Used for listening connections from a remote host with TCP services. Also used by application-level protocols such as FTP and HTTP.
UDPClient	Used for both listening and connecting to remote hosts with UDP services. But it is unlike separate TCPClient and TCPListener classes because of the characteristics of the UDP protocol.

Table 19.1: Important Socket Classes

The Socket class allows raw data exchange. You can implement any TCP/IP suite protocol with it. But TCP and UDP classes are higher descendants, making your life easier and letting you develop TCP and UDP protocol client/server applications easily.

LingerOption Class

If LingerOption is not enabled, calling the Close method of the Socket class (and its descendants) will immediately close the connection to the network. If it is enabled, the data stream will continue to relay until LingerTime (in seconds) is timed out. If the time-out is reached or the data is sent with acknowledgment, the connection is closed. However, if there is no data to send, or in other words the TCP/IP send queue length is 0, the connection is closed immediately. Listing 19.4 shows an example of using the LingerOption class.

Listing 19.4—LingerOption Example

```
// set linger to 1 second
LingerOption myOpts = new LingerOption(true, 1);
mySoc.SetSocketOption(SocketOptionLevel.IP,SocketOptionName.Linger,
myOpts);
```

MulticastOption Class

The MulticastOption class is used when joining or leaving multicast groups. Listing 19.5 shows how this class might be used. Notice that the protocol is UDP and socket type is datagram.

Listing 19.5—MulticastOption Example

```
// create a multicast address
IPAddress myaddr = IPAddress.Parse("224.0.0.1");

// create a UDP Datagram socket
Socket sock = new Socket(AddressFamily.InterNetwork, SocketType.Dgram,
ProtocolType.Udp );
```

```
// set socket options for multicast
sock.SetSocketOption(SocketOptionLevel.IP,
   SocketOptionName.AddMembership,
   new MulticastOption( myaddr ) );
```

NetworkStream Class

The NetworkStream class provides streams to send and receive network data through network sockets. It supports both synchronous and asynchronous access.

TCPClient Class

The TCPClient class provides a simplified way of connecting to an endpoint by using the TCP protocol. It also exposes data being read or written over the connection through a NetworkStream object.

TCPListener Class

The TCPListener class facilitates the work of listening on a particular socket for a TCP connection from a client.

Socket Class

The basic Socket class is for sending or receiving raw network data. It is an implementation of Berkeley sockets and is used by TCPClient, UDPClient, and WebRequest (and descendent classes) using inheritance, aggregation, or composition. After the socket is created, the socket object is bound (Bind method) to an IPEndPoint and connected (Connect method). Packets are sent using the Send or SendTo methods and read using the Receive or ReceiveFrom methods. The socket can be disabled with the ShutDown method and can be closed with the Close method.

UDPClient Class

Unlike TCP protocol classes, the UDP protocol class has only a client class to both receive and send UDP datagrams. UDPClient—like TCPClient and TCPListener—is an implementation of the Socket class. UDPClient can both listen for incoming requests and send data to listening servers.

The .NET examples below are based on the Socket class or its descendants. Notice that all TCP/IP packets that you send and receive are nothing but bytes. So, before sending data to a network stream, you should convert it to bytes, and after you receive data from a network, you should convert it from bytes to the data type you need.

The function in Listing 19.6 shows how the Socket class can be used to send data to an HTTP server and receive the response.

Listing 19.6—Socket1.cs, Socket Example to Request Synchronous HTTP

```
using System;
using System.Runtime.InteropServices;
using System.Net;
using System.Net.Sockets;
using System.IO;
using System.Text;

class MyApp
{

 public static void Main()
 {
  MyApp theapp = new MyApp();
```

```
  theapp.DoSocketGet();
}

public void DoSocketGet()
{
  //Set up variables and String to write to the strServer
  Encoding ASCII = Encoding.ASCII;
  string Get = "";
  Byte[] ByteGet;
  Byte[] RecvBytes = new Byte[256];
  StringBuilder strRetPage = new StringBuilder("");
  Socket s = null;

 Console.WriteLine("Please specify an HTTP server name...
 (type q or quit to exit)");

 for( string strServer = Console.ReadLine();
      strServer != "q" && strServer !="quit";
      strServer = Console.ReadLine() )
 {
  try
  {
   strRetPage.Remove(0, strRetPage.Length);
   //Create the Socket for sending data over TCP
   s = new Socket(AddressFamily.InterNetwork, SocketType.Stream,
ProtocolType.Tcp);

   // IPAddress and IPEndPoint represent the endpoint that will
   //  receive the request

   IPHostEntry iphe = Dns.Resolve(strServer);
   IPAddress[] iparr = iphe.AddressList;
   IPAddress hostip = iparr[0];
   IPEndPoint EPhost = new IPEndPoint(hostip, 80);
   Console.WriteLine("Resolved host: " + strServer +
" to IP: " + hostip);

   // define HTTP GET ...
   Get = "GET / HTTP/1.1\r\nHost: " + strServer +
   "\r\nConnection: Close\r\n\r\n";
   ByteGet = ASCII.GetBytes(Get);

   // Connect to host using IPEndPoint
   s.Connect(EPhost);

    Console.WriteLine("Winsock connect error: " + Convert.ToString(
    Marshal.GetLastWin32Error()));

   // Sent the GET text to the host
   s.Send(ByteGet, ByteGet.Length, 0);

   // Receive the page, loop until all bytes are received
   Int32 bytes = s.Receive(RecvBytes, RecvBytes.Length, 0);
   strRetPage.Append("Default HTML page on " + strServer + ":\r\n");
   strRetPage.Append(ASCII.GetString(RecvBytes, 0, bytes));

   while (bytes > 0)
   {
     bytes = s.Receive(RecvBytes, RecvBytes.Length, 0);
     strRetPage.Append(ASCII.GetString(RecvBytes, 0, bytes));
   }
  }
  catch(Exception e)
  {
    Console.WriteLine("Exception:" + e.ToString());
  }
  finally
```

```
      {
         s.Shutdown(SocketShutdown.Both);
         s.Close();
         s = null;
      if(strRetPage.Length > 0)
         {
          Console.WriteLine(strRetPage);
          Console.WriteLine("\r\nNumber of #Bytes received: " + strRetPage.Length);
         }
      Console.WriteLine("\r\nPlease specify an HTTP server name...(type q or quit to
exit)");
   }
  }
 }
}
```

Coding a Simple TCP Client Application: WHOIS

In Listing 19.7 we develop a simple WHOIS client to query the owners of Internet domain names. A stream is read until it returns 0, when the underlying connection is finalized. For TCP clients, you can create a connection, write data to the stream, and receive data from the stream until it is closed. The TCPClient, while easy to code, has limited functionality compared to its base—the Socket class.

Listing 19.7—Whois.cs, Example of the WHOIS Client

```csharp
using System;
using System.Net;
using System.Net.Sockets;
using System.IO;
using System.Text;

class MyApp
{

 public static void Main()
  {
   // read buffer size
   const int BUFFER_SIZE = 128;
   // TCP network stream
   NetworkStream stream = null;
   // TCP client
   TcpClient tcpc = null;

   string strWHOIS = "whois.networksolutions.com";
   Console.WriteLine("Please specify a domain name for WHOIS query...(type q or quit
to exit)");

   for( string strDomain = Console.ReadLine();
        strDomain != "q" && strDomain !="quit";
        strDomain = Console.ReadLine() )
   {

    tcpc = new TcpClient();
    // Gets or sets the receive time-out value of the connection in seconds.
    tcpc.ReceiveTimeout = 5000; // 5 seconds
   // Gets or sets the send time-out value of the connection in seconds.
    tcpc.SendTimeout = 5000; // 5 seconds

    if (strDomain == "")
        {
        Console.WriteLine("ERROR: You must specify a domain name.");
        continue;
        }
```

```
    // Verify that your DNS server can resolve that this host name exists
      if (Dns.GetHostByName(strWHOIS) == null)
          {
          Console.WriteLine("ERROR: DNS cannot resolve whois server: " + strWHOIS);
          continue;
          }
      else
          {
          Console.WriteLine("SUCCESS: DNS resolved whois server: " + strWHOIS);
          }

      // Connects the client to the specified port on the specified host.
      tcpc.Connect(strWHOIS, 43);

      // get the stream
      stream = tcpc.GetStream();
      if(stream == null && !stream.CanWrite)
        {
          Console.WriteLine("null Stream returned from TCP or stream not writeable.");
           continue;
        }

      // send the request
      strDomain += "\r\n";
      // Encodes a range of an array of characters into a array of bytes.
      Byte[] bDomArr = Encoding.ASCII.GetBytes(strDomain.ToCharArray());
      stream.Write(bDomArr, 0, bDomArr.Length);

      // buffer to read stream data in
      Byte[] Buffer = new Byte[BUFFER_SIZE];
      // string will be modified too often, so we prefer StringBuilder to String
      StringBuilder strWhoisResponse = new StringBuilder("");

      Console.Write("\r\n");

      // read until the response buffer is empty
      int BytesRead = stream.Read(Buffer, 0, BUFFER_SIZE);
      while (BytesRead != 0 )
      {
        // get ASCII encoded string from bytes
        strWhoisResponse.Append(Encoding.ASCII.GetString(Buffer,0,BytesRead));
        // Stream.Read returns the number of bytes read from the stream,
        // or 0 if the underlying socket is closed
        BytesRead = stream.Read(Buffer, 0, BUFFER_SIZE);
      }

    // closes the network stream and the underlying socket
    stream.Close();

    Console.WriteLine(strWhoisResponse);
    Console.WriteLine("\r\nTotal #Bytes received: " + strWhoisResponse.Length);
    Console.WriteLine("\r\nPlease specify a domain name for WHOIS query...(type q or
quit to exit)");
   }
 }
}
```

SMTP client

The objective of SMTP (Simple Mail Transfer Protocol) is to transfer mail reliably and efficiently. SMTP is independent of the particular transmission subsystem and requires only a reliable ordered data stream channel. (Refer to RFC 2821 for more up-to-date details.) Figure 19.2 diagrams SMTP protocol flow.

Figure 19.2: SMTP Protocol

SMTP does not have a log-on session before relaying messages. Some new SMTP implementations, however, do require user names and passwords to prevent unsolicited relaying from external users. Others have options like IP address range restrictions to limit use to predetermined clients.

Listing 19.8 makes a simple e-mail transfer via an SMTP gateway using the SMTP protocol. The program receives a response from the SMTP server each time it sends a stream of bytes. This mutual request and response is necessary for e-mail delivery traffic. In Socket-based applications, you can loop communicating until the connection is closed. Figure 19.3 shows the program's response.

Listing 19.8—SMTP.cs, Example Program to Send E-mail with SMTP

```
//simple SMTP mailer

using System;
using System.Net;
using System.Net.Sockets;
using System.IO;
using System.Text;

class MyApp
{
 public static void Main()
 {
    string SMTPServer = "mail.mindcracker.com"; // smtp gateway

    TcpClient sender = new TcpClient(SMTPServer, 25);
    Byte[] outbytes;
    string input;

    string strFrom = "bulentozkir@hotmail.com";
    string strTo = "mcb@mindcracker.com";
    string strSubject = "Hello!";
    string strBody = "This is a test...";

    try{
            NetworkStream ns = sender.GetStream();
             StreamReader sr = new StreamReader(sender.GetStream() );
            Console.WriteLine(sr.ReadLine());

            input = "HELO " + SMTPServer + "\r\n";
            outbytes = System.Text.Encoding.ASCII.GetBytes(input.ToCharArray());
            ns.Write(outbytes,0,outbytes.Length) ;
            Console.WriteLine(sr.ReadLine());

            input = "MAIL FROM: " +"<" + strFrom + ">" + "\r\n";
            outbytes = System.Text.Encoding.ASCII.GetBytes(input.ToCharArray());
            ns.Write(outbytes,0,outbytes.Length) ;
            Console.WriteLine(sr.ReadLine());

            input = "RCPT TO: " + "<" + strTo + ">" + "\r\n";
            outbytes = System.Text.Encoding.ASCII.GetBytes(input.ToCharArray());
            ns.Write(outbytes,0,outbytes.Length) ;
            Console.WriteLine(sr.ReadLine());
```

```
            input = "DATA" + "\r\n";
            outbytes = System.Text.Encoding.ASCII.GetBytes(input.ToCharArray());
            ns.Write(outbytes,0,outbytes.Length) ;
            Console.WriteLine(sr.ReadLine());

            input ="Subject: " + strSubject + "\r\n" + strBody + "\r\n" + "." +
"\r\n";
            outbytes = System.Text.Encoding.ASCII.GetBytes(input.ToCharArray());
            ns.Write(outbytes,0,outbytes.Length) ;
            Console.WriteLine(sr.ReadLine());

            input ="QUIT" + "\r\n";
            outbytes = System.Text.Encoding.ASCII.GetBytes(input.ToCharArray());
            ns.Write(outbytes,0,outbytes.Length) ;
            Console.WriteLine(sr.ReadLine());

            sr.Close();
            ns.Close();
        }
    catch(Exception e)
        {
            Console.WriteLine("Exception:" + e.ToString());
        }
    }
}
```

```
C:\work\19>19.3.exe
220 X1 NT-ESMTP Server mail2.fiberspeed.net (IMail 7.00 16404-1)
250 hello mail2.fiberspeed.net
250 ok
250 ok its for <mcb@mindcracker.com>
354 ok, send it; end with <CRLF>.<CRLF>
250 Message queued
221 Goodbye
```

Figure 19.3: Response from Program in Listing 19.8

POP3 Protocol

SMTP's companion is POP3. You can send e-mail with SMTP and receive it with POP3. POP3 is an old protocol but still commonly used for retrieving e-mail. (Its successors include IMAP4 and HTTP.) The POP3 client connects to a server on port 110, and then sends the user name and password to connect to the server. After connecting, the POP3 client sends the Stat command to the server to obtain statistics about the mailbox stored for that user.

Listing 19.9 shows a simple POP3 client and Figure 19.4 shows a snapshot taken from a sample execution.

Listing 19.9—POP3.cs, A POP3 Client to Retrieve a Number of New Unread Items

```
// simple POP3 client to retrieve number of new unread items

using System.Net.Sockets;
using System.IO;
using System.Net;
using System;
using System.Threading;
using System.Globalization;

class POP3
{

public static void Main()
```

```
{
 try
 {
  Console.Write("POP3Server: ");
  string POP3Server = Console.ReadLine();
  Console.Write("Username: ");
  string user = Console.ReadLine();
  Console.Write("Password: ");
  string pwd = Console.ReadLine();

  Byte[] outbytes;
  string input = "", resp = "";

  // Connect to POP3 port on 110...
  TcpClient sender = new TcpClient();
  sender.ReceiveTimeout = 5000;
  sender.SendTimeout = 5000;
  sender.Connect(POP3Server, 110);

  NetworkStream ns = sender.GetStream();
  StreamReader sr = new StreamReader(ns);
  StreamWriter wr = new StreamWriter(ns);
  wr.AutoFlush = true;
  resp = sr.ReadLine();
  while(resp == null || resp.Length == 0)
  {
   resp = sr.ReadLine();
  }
  Console.WriteLine(resp);

  input = "user " + user + "\r\n";
  outbytes = System.Text.Encoding.ASCII.GetBytes(input.ToCharArray());
  wr.Write(input.ToCharArray(), 0, input.Length) ;
  Console.Write(input);
  resp = sr.ReadLine();
  while(resp == null || resp.Length == 0)
  {
   resp = sr.ReadLine();
  }
  Console.WriteLine(resp);

  input = "pass " + pwd  + "\r\n";
  outbytes = System.Text.Encoding.ASCII.GetBytes(input.ToCharArray());
  wr.Write(input.ToCharArray(), 0, input.Length) ;
  Console.Write(input);
  resp = sr.ReadLine();
  while(resp == null || resp.Length == 0)
  {
   resp = sr.ReadLine();
  }
  Console.WriteLine(resp);

  input = "stat \r\n";
  outbytes = System.Text.Encoding.ASCII.GetBytes(input.ToCharArray());
  wr.Write(input.ToCharArray(), 0, input.Length) ;
  Console.Write(input);
  resp = sr.ReadLine();
  while(resp == null || resp.Length == 0)
  {
   resp = sr.ReadLine();
  }
  Console.WriteLine(resp);

  string[] tokens = resp.Split(new Char[] {' '});

  input = "quit \r\n";
  outbytes = System.Text.Encoding.ASCII.GetBytes(input.ToCharArray());
```

```
    wr.WriteLine(input.ToCharArray(), 0, input.Length) ;
    Console.Write(input);
    resp = sr.ReadLine();
    while(resp == null || resp.Length == 0)
    {
     resp = sr.ReadLine();
    }
    Console.WriteLine(resp);
    sr.Close();
    wr.Close();
    ns.Close();
    Console.WriteLine("Number New Messages# {0}", Int32.Parse(tokens[1],
                NumberStyles.AllowTrailingWhite) );
   }
  catch(Exception e)
  {
   Console.WriteLine("Exception:" + e.ToString());
  }
 }
}
```

```
[OX] Visual Studio.NET Command Prompt                        _ |□| x|
C:\work\19>19.4.exe
POP3Server: mail.kkk.tsk.mil.tr
Username: mcb
Password: password
+OK Microsoft Exchange POP3 sunucusu srm 5.5.2652.42 hazr
user mcb
+OK
pass password
```

Figure 19.4: Screen Response for Listing 19.9

Sample TCP application: GUID Server and Client

Listing 19.10 shows the code for a TCPListener server application that listens on port 5555 and responds with new GUID (globally unique identifier) strings to the client. The TCPClient application, Listing 19.11, simply connects to this server and gets a response from it, namely the GUID generated by the server, shown in Figures 19.5 and 19.6.

Listing 19.10—TcpGuidSrv.cs, TCP GUID Server

```
// TCP guid server

using System;
using System.Net;
using System.Net.Sockets;
using System.Text;

class TCPGUIDServer
{
 public static void Main()
 {
  string strGUID;
  Encoding ASCII = Encoding.ASCII;

  TcpListener tcpl = new TcpListener(5555); // listen on port 5555

  tcpl.Start();

  Console.WriteLine("<Waiting for clients to connect to the guid server>");
  Console.WriteLine("press Ctrl+C or Ctrl+Break to quit...");

  // loop infinitely...
  while (true)
  {
    // Accept will block until someone connects
```

```
    Socket s = tcpl.AcceptSocket();

    // GUID is a 128-bit integer that identifies an interface to an
    // object across all computers and networks
    // ToString converts this value to eg 382c74c3-721d-4f34-80e5-57657b6cbc27
    Guid myguid = Guid.NewGuid();
    strGUID = myguid.ToString();

    // Convert the string to a Byte Array and send it
    Byte[] byteGUID = ASCII.GetBytes(strGUID.ToCharArray());
    s.Send(byteGUID, byteGUID.Length, 0);
    Console.WriteLine("Sent " + strGUID);
   }
  }
 }
```

Figure 19.5: Screen Response for Listing 19.10

Listing 19.11—TcpGuidClnt.cs, TCP GUID Client

```
// TCP GUID client

using System;
using System.Net;
using System.Net.Sockets;
using System.IO;
using System.Text;

class TCPGUIDClient {
 public static void Main() {

   TcpClient tcpc = new TcpClient();
   Byte[] read = new Byte[64];

   // loopback address
   String server = "localhost";

    // Verify that the server exists
   if (Dns.GetHostByName(server) == null)
   {
    Console.WriteLine("Cannot find server: " + server);
    return;
   }

   // Try to connect to the server
   tcpc.Connect(server, 5555);

   // Get the stream
   Stream s = tcpc.GetStream();

   // Read the stream and convert it to ASII
   int bytes = s.Read(read, 0, read.Length);
   String strGUID = Encoding.ASCII.GetString(read);

   // Display the data
   Console.WriteLine("Received " + bytes + " bytes");
   Console.WriteLine("My GUID: " + strGUID);

   s.Close();
```

```
    }
}
```

Figure 19.6: Screen Response for Listing 19.11

Sample TCP Application for File Uploading

Listing 19.12 shows coding for a file receiver and creator server, and Listing 19.13 shows coding for a TCP file upload client that connects to the server and sends a local file. This client/server application is based on TCPClient and TCPListener and uses 127.0.0.1, the localhost loopback address, so both server and client are localhost.

Before executing this example, create the temporary file C:\temp\delete_me.txt, the client file. After the server receives the file, it will save it as C:\temp\delete_you.txt. Make sure that C:\temp\delete_me.txt is not zero bytes in length or you will receive an exception. If you have time, please modify the example to implement various file-related operations like deleting and renaming remote files in a real networked environment.

Figure 19.7 shows the screen response of the server when executing, and Figure 19.8 shows the screen response of the client when executing.

Listing 19.12—TcpFileSrv.cs, TCP File Receiver and Creator Server

```csharp
// file receiver and creator server - TCPListener

using System;
using System.Net;
using System.Net.Sockets;
using System.IO;
using System.Text;

class Receive
{
 public static void Main()
 {
    try
    {
        Encoding ASCII = Encoding.ASCII;
        TcpListener tcpl = new TcpListener(8081);
        int read = 0;
        byte[] bytes = new byte[1024];
        tcpl.Start();

        Console.WriteLine("<Waiting for clients to connect and upload a file on
port 8081>");
        Console.WriteLine("press Ctrl+C or Ctrl+Break to quit...");

        while (true)
        {
            // Accept will block until someone connects
            Socket s = tcpl.AcceptSocket();
            Stream DataStream = new NetworkStream(s);
            String filename;
            Byte[] Buffer = new Byte[32];
            Byte[] Buffer2 = new Byte[3];
            DataStream.Read(Buffer, 0, 32);
```

```
            filename = Encoding.ASCII.GetString(Buffer);
            StringBuilder dummy = new StringBuilder(filename);
            dummy.Replace("me", "you");
            Console.WriteLine("Original filename1:<" + dummy + ">");
            Console.WriteLine("Original filename2:<" + filename + ">");
            String str1 =  dummy.ToString();
            int i = str1.IndexOf(@"^^^", 0);
            str1 = str1.Substring(0, i);

            Console.WriteLine("Received filename:<" + str1 + ">");

            while(filename != @"%%%")
            {
             DataStream.Read(Buffer2, 0, 3);
              filename = Encoding.ASCII.GetString(Buffer2);
              Console.WriteLine("dummy data: " + filename);
            }

            FileStream fs = new FileStream(str1, FileMode.OpenOrCreate);
            BinaryWriter w = new BinaryWriter(fs);

            // Read the stream
            while( (read = DataStream.Read(bytes, 0, bytes.Length)) != 0)
            {
                w.Write(bytes, 0, read);
                 Console.WriteLine("#bytes: " + read);
            }

            DataStream.Flush();
            DataStream.Close();
            fs.Close();
            w.Close();
            Console.WriteLine("Received file...\r\n");
            Console.WriteLine("<Waiting for clients to connect and upload a file on
port 8081>");
            Console.WriteLine("press Ctrl+C or Ctrl+Break to quit...");
        }
    }
    catch(Exception ex)
    {
        //MessageBox.Show(ex.ToString());
        Console.WriteLine("Exception: " + ex.ToString());
    }
  }
}
```

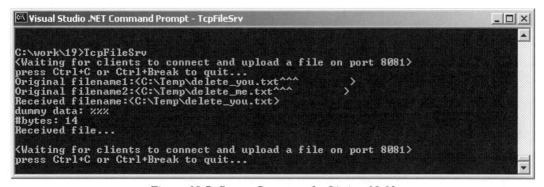

Figure 19.7: Screen Response for Listing 19.12

Listing 19.13—TcpFileClnt.cs, TCP File Upload Client

```csharp
// file upload client...

using System;
using System.Net;
using System.Net.Sockets;
using System.Threading;
using System.IO;
using System.Text;

class UploadFile
{
 public static void Main()
  {
    try
    {
        // we will use %%% as filename delimiter
        String remotefilename = @"C:\Temp\delete_me.txt^^^";
        String localfilename = @"C:\Temp\delete_me.txt";
        String server = "127.0.0.1";

        TcpClient tcpc = new TcpClient();
        int read = 0;
        byte[] bytes = new byte[1024];

        // Try to connect to the server
        tcpc.Connect(server, 8081);

        // Get the stream
            NetworkStream DataStream = tcpc.GetStream();

            Byte[] b = Encoding.ASCII.GetBytes(remotefilename.ToCharArray());
            DataStream.Write( b, 0,  b.Length );
            Console.WriteLine("Sent remotefilename: " + remotefilename);
//          Thread.Sleep(5000);
            b = Encoding.ASCII.GetBytes("%%%".ToCharArray());
            DataStream.Write( b, 0,  b.Length );
            Thread.Sleep(5000);

            FileStream fs = new FileStream(localfilename, FileMode.Open,
FileAccess.Read);

            BinaryReader reader = new BinaryReader(fs);

            while((read = reader.Read(bytes, 0, bytes.Length)) != 0)
            {
                // Read from the file and write the data to the network
                DataStream.Write(bytes, 0, read);
                Console.WriteLine("#bytes: " + read);
            }

            reader.Close();
            DataStream.Flush();
            DataStream.Close();
            Console.WriteLine("Sent file.");
    }
    catch(Exception ex)
    {
        //MessageBox.Show(ex.ToString());
        Console.WriteLine("Exception: " + ex.ToString());
    }
  }
}
```

Figure 19.8: Screen Response of Listing 19.13

UDP Client/Server Application

Listing 19.14 is code for a UDP server, and Listing 19.15 is code for the client. After compiling, run the server, then run the client. The server listens for any client activity on port 2000 until it receives a termination signal in the form of a *q* or *quit* stream. As with the TCP example above, both server and client use the loopback address. The IP stacks do not forward the stream to the network, but rather back into the TCP/IP stack.

Listing 19.14—UdpSrv.cs, Example UDP Server

```
// example UDP Server

using System;
using System.Net;
using System.Net.Sockets;
using System.IO;
using System.Text;


class MyServer{
 public static void Main(String[] args)
 {
  Socket Listener = new
  Socket(AddressFamily.InterNetwork,SocketType.Dgram,ProtocolType.Udp);
  IPEndPoint ipEnd = new IPEndPoint(IPAddress.Any, 2000);
  EndPoint end = (EndPoint)ipEnd;
  Listener.Bind(ipEnd );

  byte[] msg=new byte[256];
  int cnt;
  String str = "";
  Console.WriteLine("sleeping...");

  while(str != "q" && str != "quit")
  {
   cnt=Listener.ReceiveFrom(msg,256,0,ref end );
   char[] message=new char[cnt];

   for(int i=0;i<cnt;i++)
         message[i] = Convert.ToChar(msg[i]);

   str=new String(message);

   Console.WriteLine(str);
  }
 }
}
```

Figure 19.9: Screen Response for Listing 19.14

Listing 19.15—UdpClnt.cs, Example UDP Client

```
// example UDP Client

using System;
using System.Net;
using System.Net.Sockets;
using System.IO;
using System.Text;

class MyClient
{

private static Socket Listener = null;

public static void sendUDP(char[] message)
{
        byte[] msg=new byte[message.Length];
        for(int i=0;i<message.Length;i++)
            msg[i] = Convert.ToByte(message[i]);
        Listener.SendTo(msg, msg.Length, 0, new
IPEndPoint((IPAddress.Parse("127.0.0.1")), 2000));

}

public static void Main(String[] args)
{
        Listener = new
Socket(AddressFamily.InterNetwork,SocketType.Dgram,ProtocolType.Udp);
        Console.WriteLine("sending requests...");
        char[] message1 = "is this a test?".ToCharArray();
        sendUDP(message1);
        char[] message2 = { 'n','o',' ','i','t',' ','a','i','n','t','!' };
        sendUDP(message2);
        sendUDP("q".ToCharArray());
    }
}
```

Figure 19.10: Screen Response for Listing 19.15

UDP Multicasting

Multicasting is extremely powerful when sending the same data to multiple clients at the same time. In routers, multicasting is generally disabled to preserve performance and utilization of the Internet. But there are alternative, private multicast networks for the Internet, and for intranets it is up to you to enable/disable multicasting on your routers.

The UdpClient class makes it easier to send network datagram packets and IP multicast with group management methods such as UdpClient.JoinMulticastGroup and UdpClient.DropMulticastGroup.

You can create both UDP listener and client to join a multicast address, listen on that address and specified port, and send the messages you write to the multicast clients.

The UdpClient object is initialized with a constructor call, which sets the port that the object will listen on. The object then joins a Multicast group. Once initialized, the UdpClient can listen for incoming messages with the Receive function, which can be found in the Listener function. The Receive function returns an array of bytes, containing the data received. This data can be easily converted into a string.

Sending data is just as easy. The UdpClient has a function called Send which sends out a byte array to every class that is listening on the Multicast group. You can safely implement the above logic in your real-world applications. Listing 19.16 shows how to join a multicast group.

Listing 19.16—Joining a Multicast Group

```
try
{
UdpClient Client = new UdpClient(9999);
IPAddress GroupAddress = IPAddress.Parse("224.0.0.1");
Client.JoinMulticastGroup(GroupAddress);
IPEndPoint RemoteEP = new IPEndPoint(GroupAddress,RemotePort);
}
catch(Exception e)
{
Console.WriteLine("Exception!" + e.ToString());
}
```

Listing 19.17 shows how to leave a multicast group.

Listing 19.17—To leave a multicast group

```
try
{
Client.DropMulticastGroup(GroupAddress);
}
catch(Exception e)
{
Console.WriteLine("Exception:" + e.ToString());
}
```

Ping and ICMP Echo

Internet Control Message Protocol (ICMP), documented in RFC 792, is a required protocol tightly integrated with IP. ICMP messages, delivered in IP packets, are used for out-of-band messages related to network operation or faulty operation. Since ICMP uses IP, ICMP packet delivery is unreliable. Therefore, hosts can't count on receiving ICMP packets for any network problem.

For troubleshooting, ICMP supports an Echo function that just sends a packet on a round trip between two hosts. Ping, a common network management tool, is based on this feature. Ping transmits a series of packets, measuring average round-trip times and computing loss percentages. Two of the most frequently seen ICMP messages are Echo and Echo Reply, which are used for simple request response testing. A host sends an Echo (type = 8) to a destination host and then awaits an Echo Reply (type = 0). Incoming replies are associated with specific requests through use of an identifier, and when a number of Echo requests are sent in succession, each request message contains an incremented sequence number.

The data in the Echo message must be returned verbatim in the Echo Reply message, which usually includes a time stamp followed by some data pattern. Because ICMP messages traverse the network encapsulated in IP datagrams, successful receipt of an Echo Reply would indicate that a large portion of the datagram delivery mechanism is functioning. Indeed, the most commonly used diagnostic utility—ping—makes use of the Echo/Echo Reply transaction.

Note that RFC 1122 (section 3.2.2.6) states that ICMP Echo messages sent to IP broadcast or multicast addresses may be silently discarded. One reason for this is to prevent denial-of-service attacks, such as Smurf.

Listing 19.18 is a basic program for pinging a host. You can enhance it and encapsulate it as a library class to use in your custom applications.

Listing 19.18—Ping.cs, Example Ping/ICMP Echo

```
// Ping example

using System;
 using System.Net;
 using System.Net.Sockets;

  class Ping
  {
    const int SOCKET_ERROR = -1;
    const int ICMP_ECHO = 8;

    public static void Main(string[] argv)
    {
      Console.WriteLine(@"Press CTRL+C to exit...");
      while(true)
      {
       Console.WriteLine(@"Enter hostname or localhost will be pinged as
               default...");
       string host = Console.ReadLine();
       if(host == @"")
         host = @"127.0.0.1";
       PingHost(host);
      }
    }

    //takes the "hostname" of the server
    //and then it pings it and shows the response time
    public static void PingHost(string host)
    {
        IPHostEntry serverHE, fromHE;
        int nBytes = 0;
        int dwStart = 0, dwStop = 0;

        Socket socket = new Socket(AddressFamily.InterNetwork, SocketType.Raw,
                ProtocolType.Icmp);


        try
        {
          serverHE = Dns.GetHostByName(host);
        }
        catch(Exception)
        {
          Console.WriteLine("Host not found"); // fail
          return ;
        }

        IPEndPoint ipepServer = new IPEndPoint(serverHE.AddressList[0], 0);
        EndPoint epServer = (ipepServer);

        fromHE = Dns.GetHostByName(Dns.GetHostName());
```

```
IPEndPoint ipEndPointFrom = new IPEndPoint(fromHE.AddressList[0], 0);
EndPoint EndPointFrom = (ipEndPointFrom);

int PacketSize = 0;
IcmpPacket packet = new IcmpPacket();

packet.Type = ICMP_ECHO;
packet.SubCode = 0;
packet.CheckSum = UInt16.Parse("0");
packet.Identifier  = UInt16.Parse("45");
packet.SequenceNumber = UInt16.Parse("0");
int PingData = 32;
packet.Data = new Byte[PingData];

for (int i = 0; i < PingData; i++)
{
  packet.Data[i] = (byte)'#';
}

PacketSize = PingData + 8;
Byte [] icmp_pkt_buffer = new Byte[ PacketSize ];
Int32 Index = 0;

Index = Serialize(packet, icmp_pkt_buffer, PacketSize, PingData);

if( Index == -1 )
{
  Console.WriteLine("Error in Making Packet");
  return ;
}

Double double_length = Convert.ToDouble(Index);
Double dtemp = Math.Ceiling( double_length / 2);
int cksum_buffer_length = Convert.ToInt32(dtemp);
UInt16 [] cksum_buffer = new UInt16[cksum_buffer_length];

int icmp_header_buffer_index = 0;
for( int i = 0; i < cksum_buffer_length; i++ ) {
  cksum_buffer[i] =
      BitConverter.ToUInt16(icmp_pkt_buffer,icmp_header_buffer_index);
  icmp_header_buffer_index += 2;
}

UInt16 u_cksum = checksum(cksum_buffer, cksum_buffer_length);

packet.CheckSum  = u_cksum;

Byte [] sendbuf = new Byte[ PacketSize ];

Index = Serialize(packet, sendbuf, PacketSize, PingData);

if( Index == -1 )
{
  Console.WriteLine("Error in Making Packet");
  return ;
}


dwStart = System.Environment.TickCount; // Start timing

if ((nBytes = socket.SendTo(sendbuf, PacketSize, 0, epServer)) ==
        SOCKET_ERROR)
{
  Console.WriteLine("Socket Error cannot Send Packet");
}

Byte [] ReceiveBuffer = new Byte[256];
```

```csharp
    nBytes = 0;

    bool recd =false ;
    int timeout=0 ;

    while(!recd)
    {
      nBytes = socket.ReceiveFrom(ReceiveBuffer, 256, 0, ref EndPointFrom);
      if (nBytes == SOCKET_ERROR)
      {
        Console.WriteLine("Host not Responding") ;
        recd=true ;
        break;
      }
      else if(nBytes>0)
      {
        dwStop = System.Environment.TickCount - dwStart; // stop timing
        Console.WriteLine("Reply from "+epServer.ToString()+" in "
            +dwStop+" miliseconds, Bytes Received "+nBytes);
        recd=true;
        break;
      }

      timeout = System.Environment.TickCount - dwStart;
      if(timeout>1000)
      {
        Console.WriteLine("Timed Out") ;
        recd=true;
      }
  }

    socket.Close();
}

//get the packet and calculates the total size
//of the packet by converting it to byte array
public static Int32 Serialize(IcmpPacket packet, Byte[] Buffer,
                Int32 PacketSize, Int32 PingData )
{
    Int32 cbReturn = 0;

    int Index=0;

    Byte [] b_type = new Byte[1];
    b_type[0] = (packet.Type);

    Byte [] b_code = new Byte[1];
    b_code[0] = (packet.SubCode);

    Byte [] b_cksum = BitConverter.GetBytes(packet.CheckSum);
    Byte [] b_id = BitConverter.GetBytes(packet.Identifier);
    Byte [] b_seq = BitConverter.GetBytes(packet.SequenceNumber);

    Array.Copy( b_type, 0, Buffer, Index, b_type.Length );
    Index += b_type.Length;

    Array.Copy( b_code, 0, Buffer, Index, b_code.Length );
    Index += b_code.Length;

    Array.Copy( b_cksum, 0, Buffer, Index, b_cksum.Length );
    Index += b_cksum.Length;

    Array.Copy( b_id, 0, Buffer, Index, b_id.Length );
    Index += b_id.Length;

    Array.Copy( b_seq, 0, Buffer, Index, b_seq.Length );
    Index += b_seq.Length;
```

```
    Array.Copy( packet.Data, 0, Buffer, Index, PingData );
    Index += PingData;
    if( Index != PacketSize/* sizeof(IcmpPacket)  */) {
      cbReturn = -1;
      return cbReturn;
    }

    cbReturn = Index;
    return cbReturn;
}

//has the algorithm to make a checksum
public static UInt16 checksum( UInt16[] buffer, int size )
{
    Int32 cksum = 0;
    int counter;
    counter = 0;

    while ( size > 0 ) {
    UInt16 val = buffer[counter];

      cksum += Convert.ToInt32( buffer[counter] );
      counter += 1;
      size -= 1;
    }

    cksum = (cksum >> 16) + (cksum & 0xffff);
    cksum += (cksum >> 16);
    return (UInt16)(~cksum);
}
}

//Class that holds the Pack information
public class IcmpPacket
{
 public Byte   Type;      // type of message
 public Byte   SubCode;     // type of sub code
 public UInt16 CheckSum;    // ones complement checksum of struct
 public UInt16 Identifier;    // identifier
 public UInt16 SequenceNumber;    // sequence number
 public Byte [] Data;

  }
```

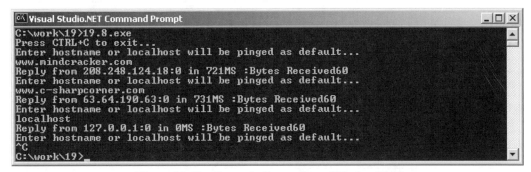

Figure 19.11: Example Screenshot of Listing 19.18

Internet Programming

It has become common programming practice to provide Internet browser features in applications.
Programs download data from a Web page and upload data to a Web page through HTTP.

The Microsoft .NET Framework makes these functionalities possible with classes defined under the System.NET namespace. Table 19.2 lists and describes these classes, but we'll explore some in more detail later.

Class	Description
AuthenticationManager	Handles authentication modules. If a protected resource is accessed, the credentials are passed by using basic, digest, negotiate, NTLM, and Kerberos authentication types.
Authorization	Handles authentication messages. AuthenticationManager class returns an Authorization object indicating the client is permitted to access the Internet server when using the WebRequest class (or one of its descendants).
Cookie	Class used to manage cookies. It has the following properties: Comment, CommentUri, Discard, Domain, Expired, Expires, Name, Path, Port, Secure, TimeStamp, Value, and Version. Cookies, first introduced by Netscape, keep some user data temporarily on the client side. They are used widely in Web applications for such things as personalization and membership.
DNS	Provides DNS functionality—namely domain name resolution. DNS servers resolve host names to IP addresses, or by the reverse DNS mechanism, IP addresses to host names.
FileWebRequest, FileWebResponse	File system implementation of WebRequest and WebResponse classes, respectively. These classes use `file://` instead of `http://`.

HttpVersion	Used by the HttpWebRequest and HttpWebResponse classes to control version-specific features of HTTP, such as chunking and pipelining. Refer to the relevant RFCs for differences between HTTP protocol implementations.
HttpWebRequest, HttpWebResponse	Classes derived from WebRequest and WebResponse to work with HTTP protocol.
IPAddress	Contains the IP address.
IPHostEntry	Provides host address information.
IPEndPoint	A consolidated class for combining an IP address with a port number.
WebClient	Provides client functionality to send and receive data.
WebHeaderCollection	Contains the collection of protocol headers, which are accessed through the WebRequest or WebResponse Headers property.
WebProxy	When using WebRequest (or descendant) class objects, it is used to override proxy settings set by GlobalProxySelection class.
WebRequest	A base class for all WebRequest classes, it implements methods and properties to receive data from the Web. FileWebRequest and HttpWebRequest are its derived classes.
WebResponse	A base class for WebResponse classes—HttpWebResponse and FileWebResponse—it implements methods and properties to provide a response from a URL.

Table 19.2: Important System.NET Classes

WebClient Class

The System.Net.WebClient class provides functionality for uploading data to or downloading data from the Internet, an intranet, or a local file system. Table 19.3 briefly describes WebClient class methods and properties.

Member	Description
BaseAddress	Current base URL address.
Headers	Headers in the form of name and value pair associated with the request.
QueryString	Queries in the form of name and value pair associated with the request.
ResponseHeaders	Headers in the form of name and value pair associated with the response.
DownloadData()	Downloads data from a URI and returns data as a byte array.
DownloadFile()	Downloads data from a URI and saves it as a local file.
OpenRead()	Opens and reads a URI in stream form.
OpenWrite()	Opens a stream to write data to a URI.
UploadData()	Uploads data buffer to a URI.
UploadFile()	Uploads a local file to the given URI.
UploadValues()	Uploads name and value collection.

Table 19.3: Important Methods and Properties for the WebClient Class

Downloading Data

WebClient provides three different methods for downloading data from the Internet, an intranet, or a local file system. The WebClient constructor doesn't take any argument. In the following code, the URL is the file name you want to download, such as http://www.c-sharpcorner.com/index.asp. Using these methods, you can download any type of file, such as image and HTML files.

```
string URL = textBox1.Text;
WebClient client = new WebClient();
```

The DownloadData method takes the URI as a parameter, downloads data from a resource URI, and returns a byte array.

```
byte [] bytedata = client.DownloadData(URL);
```

The DownloadFile method downloads data from a resource and saves it in the local file system. Hence it takes parameters, first the URI name and second the local file name:

```
client.DownloadFile(URL, "C:\\temp.asp");
```

The OpenRead method downloads data from a resource and return data as a stream:

```
Stream data = client.OpenRead(URL);
```

Listing 19.19 illustrates WebClient downloading.

Listing 19.19—WebClient Downloading

```
// Downloading web pages using WebClient Class

// Address of URL
string URL = textBox1.Text;
try
{
        // Get HTML data
        WebClient client = new WebClient();
        Stream data = client.OpenRead(URL);
        StreamReader reader = new StreamReader(data);
        string str = "";
        str = reader.ReadLine();

        while( str != null)
        {
                Console.WriteLine(str);
                str = reader.ReadLine();
        }
        data.Close();
}
catch(WebException exp)
{
        MessageBox.Show(exp.Message, "Exception");
}
```

Uploading Data

The WebClient class provides four ways to upload data. The *OpenWrite method* sends a data stream to the resource—the reverse of the OpenRead method. With OpenWrite, the first parameter is a URI string:

```
OpenWrite(string);
```

The *UploadData method* sends a byte array to the resource and returns a byte array containing any response—the reverse of the DownloadData method. It takes two arguments, a URI string and array of bytes:

```
UploadData(string, byte[]);
client.UploadData("http://www.mindcracker.com/testfile.bmp", data);
```

The *UploadFile method* sends a local file to the resource and returns a byte array containing any response—the reverse of the DownloadFile method. UploadFile also takes two parameters, a URI name and the uploaded file name.

```
UploadFile(string, string);
client.UploadFile("http://www.mindcracker.com/tst.gif", @"c:\mcb.gif");
```

Or:

```
client.UploadFile("http://www.mindcracker.com/test.htm", @"c:\test.htm");
```

The *UploadValues method* sends a NameValueCollection to the resource and returns a byte array containing any response:

```
UploadValues(string, NameValueCollection);
```

WebRequest and WebResponse Classes

Although you can use the WebClient class to upload and download data, it does not handle all things involved in uploading and downloading data. For example, what if you don't have permission to upload to the server? You'd get the error in Figure 19.12.

Figure 19.12: Authorization Error Received with WebClient Class

The WebRequest and WebResponse classes can deal with this and other issues.

The WebRequest Class

WebRequest is an abstract base class: You don't directly use it. You use it through its derived classes—HttpWebRequest and FileWebRequest. Table 19.4 describes some WebRequest class members.

Members	Description
ConnectionGroupName	Name of the connection group for the request.
ContentLength	Content length of the request data.
ContentType	Content type of the request data being sent.
Headers	The collection of header name-value pairs associated with a request.
Method	The protocol method to use in a request.
Proxy	The network proxy used to access an Internet resource.
RequestUri	The URI of the Internet resource associated with the request.
Timeout	The length of time before the request times out.
Create()	Used to create an instance of WebRequest derived classes.
CreateDefault()	Used to create an instance of WebRequest derived class for the specified URI.
BeginGetResponse()	Starts an asynchronous request.
EndGetRequestStream()	Returns a stream for writing data to the source.
EndGetResponse()	Returns a WebResponse object.
GetRequestStream()	Returns a stream for writing data to the source.
GetResponse()	Returns a response to a request.

Members	Description
Abort()	Cancels an asynchronous request.

Table 19.4: Important WebRequest Properties and Methods

WebResponse Class

WebResponse is an abstract base class from which protocol-specific classes are derived. Applications, then, can use the WebResponse class to handle responses without dealing with the protocol. The WebResponse class can be used to access any resource on the network that is addressable with a URI. You can enter a URL with *https://* instead of *http://*, and WebRequest will work exactly the same. Client applications should never directly create WebResponse objects, which should be created by calling the GetResponse method on a WebRequest instance. Table 19.5 shows important WebResponse members.

Members	Description
ContentLength	Gets or sets the content length of data being received.
ContentType	Gets or sets the content type of data being received.
Headers	Gets a collection of header name-value pairs associated with this request.
ResponseUri	Gets the URI of the Internet resource that actually responded to the request.
GetResponseStream()	Returns the data stream from the Internet resource.

Table 19.5: Import WebResponse Properties and Methods

Listing 19.20 shows the standard way to use the WebRequest and WebResponse classes.

Listing 19.20—WebRequest and WebResponse Usage Example

```
// Classical recommended way to use WebRequest/WebResponse classes

WebRequest req = WebRequest.Create("http://www.mindcracker.com/");
WebResponse result = req.GetResponse();
Stream ReceiveStream = result.GetResponseStream();
Encoding encode = System.Text.Encoding.GetEncoding("utf-8");
StreamReader sr = new StreamReader( ReceiveStream, encode );

Char[] read = new Char[256];
int count = sr.Read( read, 0, 256 );
String str = new String(read, 0, count);
Console.Write(str);

while (count > 0)
{
 str = new String(read, 0, count);
 Console.Write(str);
 count = sr.Read(read, 0, 256);
}
```

You can use the WebRequest.Create method to create an instance of WebRequest. The GetResponseStream method returns the data stream. The following example, Listing 19.21, downloads a data stream from a Web page. The example shows how to use Get and Post to send data to a Web page. WebRequest and WebResponse classes default to Get protocol. Notice that the reserved characters are encoded in the way we want before sending to the IIS server.

Although missing from the example, you should wrap your code with the WebException and UriFormatException exceptions when using the WebRequest and WebResponse classes.

With the WebRequest and WebResponse classes, you can submit form data as in HTML using the Post and Get actions. Get is used to pass data in the URL:

http://www.server1.com/blah.asp?var1=sometext&var2=moretext

But data length is limited to 1,024 bytes. On the other hand, Post sends data in the HTTP headers and has no limits on data length.

Listing 19.21—Sending Parameters with HTTP Get/Post

```
// Sending parameters with HTTP GET/POST methods
// using WebRequest and WebResponse classes

String url = " http://www.mindcracker.com/cgi-bin/cgisrch.exe";
 String payload = "StartAt=0&Count=20&Search=alloca";

WebRequest req = WebRequest.Create(url);
req.Method = "POST";
req.ContentType = "application/x-www-form-urlencoded";
StringBuilder UrlEncoded = new StringBuilder();
Char[] reserved = {'?', '=', '&'};
byte[] SomeBytes = null;

if (payload != null)
{
 int i=0, j;
 while(i<payload.Length)
 {
  j=payload.IndexOfAny(reserved, i);
  if (j==-1)
  {
   UrlEncoded.Append(HttpUtility.UrlEncode(payload.Substring(i, payload.Length-
i)));
   break;
  }
  UrlEncoded.Append(HttpUtility.UrlEncode(payload.Substring(i, j-i)));
  UrlEncoded.Append(payload.Substring(j,1));
  i = j+1;
 }
SomeBytes = Encoding.UTF8.GetBytes(UrlEncoded.ToString());
req.ContentLength = SomeBytes.Length;
Stream newStream = req.GetRequestStream();
newStream.Write(SomeBytes, 0, SomeBytes.Length);
newStream.Close();

}
else
{
 req.ContentLength = 0;
}

WebResponse result = req.GetResponse();
Stream ReceiveStream = result.GetResponseStream();
Encoding encode = System.Text.Encoding.GetEncoding("utf-8");
StreamReader sr = new StreamReader( ReceiveStream, encode );

Char[] read = new Char[256];
int count = sr.Read( read, 0, 256 );
String str = new String(read, 0, count);
Console.Write(str);
```

```
while (count > 0)
{
 str = new String(read, 0, count);
 Console.Write(str);
 count = sr.Read(read, 0, 256);
}
```

Listing 19.22—WebReqResp.cs, WebRequest and WebResponse Usage

```
using System;
using System.Net;
using System.IO;


namespace WebRequestSamp
{
        /// <summary>
        /// Summary description for Class1.
        /// </summary>
        class Class1
        {
                static void Main(string[] args)
                {
                        WebRequest request =
                         WebRequest.Create("http://www.mindcracker.com/");
                        WebResponse response = request.GetResponse();

                        StreamReader reader = new
                          StreamReader(response.GetResponseStream());

                        string str = reader.ReadLine();
                        while(str != null)
                        {
                                Console.WriteLine(str);
                                str = reader.ReadLine();
                        }


                }
        }
}
```

WebProxy Class

You can also use a Web proxy when requesting content using HTTP, FTP, and other TCP/IP suite application-level protocols. Proxies submit requests on your behalf externally and send back to you the retrieved data. They are useful for caching content and thus saving network overhead for such things as duplicate file requests from various clients. Proxies also provide secure access to internal/external resources. For example, the Microsoft ISA server is a well-known proxy server and firewall.

As Listing 19.23 shows, using the WebProxy class, you can make requests and receive responses via a proxy server, an intermediate provider. (Note that HttpWebRequest also has a Proxy property which can override your global proxy settings for specific requests.)

Listing 19.23—WebProxy Example

```
string proxy = "proxy.mindcracker.com";

WebProxy proxyObject = new WebProxy(proxy, 80);

// Disable Proxy use when the host is local i.e. without periods.
proxyObject.BypassProxyOnLocal = true;
```

```
// Now actually take over the global with our new settings,
// all new requests use this proxy info
GlobalProxySelection.Select = proxyObject;

// now use webrequest,webresponse,
// httpwebrequest, httpwebresponse classes in your application…
```

HttpWebRequest and HttpWebResponse Classes

The HTTP protocol accounts for a large share of Internet traffic, and the .NET Framework provides robust support for HTTP with the HttpWebRequest and HttpWebResponse classes. There are the derived WebRequest and WebResponse classes returned when a URI beginning with *http* or *https* is presented to the Create method. In most cases WebRequest and WebResponse will provide all functionality that is necessary to make the request. However, when access to HTTP-specific features is required, the request or response can be typecast to HttpWebRequest or HttpWebResponse.

The HttpWebRequest and HttpWebResponse classes encapsulate a standard HTTP request and response transaction and provide access to common HTTP headers through properties. These classes also support most HTTP 1.1 protocol features, including pipelining, chunking, authentication, preauthentication, encryption, proxy support, server certificate validation, connection management, and HTTP extensions. Custom headers and headers not provided through properties can be accessed by storing them in the Headers property.

Listing 19.24 shows use of HttpWebRequest.

Listing 19.24—HttpWebRequest Example

```
HttpWebRequest request = (HttpWebRequest)WebRequest.Create
("http://www.microsoft.com ");
HttpWebResponse response = (HttpWebResponse)request.GetResponse();
String ver = response.ProtocolVersion.ToString();

StreamReader reader = new StreamReader(response.GetResponseStream());

string str = reader.ReadLine();
while(str != null)
{
        Console.WriteLine(str);
        str = reader.ReadLine();
}
```

You can also use the following streams, in Listing 19.25, for asynchronous reads from and writes to the network stream:

- The HttpWebRequest.BeginGetRequestStream method begins an asynchronous request for a stream that the application can use to write data.
- The HttpWebRequest.EndGetRequestStream method ends an asynchronous request for a stream that the application can use to write data.

Though the MyClass object is the second parameter for BeginGetResponseStream, you can pass any object. So, you could encapsulate the wreq, a HttpWebRequest object, along with other aggregated or composed objects in a separate class and send it to the asynchronous functions. Listing 19.25 demonstrates using HttpWebRequest and HttpWebResponse asynchronously. We register a callback function to receive responses. (Remember that callbacks are delegates in C#.) The function begins getting a response asynchronously from a request to an Internet resource.

Listing 19.25—HttpAsync.cs, Asynchronous Usage of HttpWebRequest and HttpWebResponse

```
using System;
using System.Net;
using System.Threading;
using System.Text;
using System.IO;

public class MyClass
{
  public HttpWebRequest wreq;
  public Int32 iAnyInteger;
  public Byte[] BufferRead = new byte[1024];
  public Stream ResponseStream;
}

public class dummy
{
 public static void Main()
 {
  string suri = null;
  Console.WriteLine(@"Enter site url : (The default is
http://www.mindcracker.com)");
  suri = Console.ReadLine();
  if(suri == "") suri = @"http://www.mindcracker.com";
  Console.WriteLine("Fetching " + suri + " asynchronously...");
  Uri HttpSite = new Uri(suri);
  HttpWebRequest wreq = (HttpWebRequest) WebRequest.Create(HttpSite);
  MyClass obj1 = new MyClass();
  obj1.wreq = wreq;
  obj1.iAnyInteger = 19;
  IAsyncResult r = (IAsyncResult) wreq.BeginGetResponse(new
AsyncCallback(RespCallback), obj1);
  Thread.Sleep(45000); // wait 45 seconds at most
  Console.WriteLine("\r\nExiting...");
 }

 // callback or delegate function
 private static void RespCallback(IAsyncResult ar)
 {
  const int BUFFER_SIZE = 1024;
  MyClass obj2 = (MyClass) ar.AsyncState;
  HttpWebRequest req = (HttpWebRequest) obj2.wreq;
  HttpWebResponse resp = (HttpWebResponse) req.EndGetResponse(ar);
  Stream responseStream = resp.GetResponseStream();
  obj2.ResponseStream = responseStream;
  Console.WriteLine("verifying object iAnyInteger ##" + obj2.iAnyInteger);
   IAsyncResult iarRead = responseStream.BeginRead(obj2.BufferRead, 0, BUFFER_SIZE,
new AsyncCallback(ReadCallBack), obj2);
 }

 private static void ReadCallBack(IAsyncResult ar)
 {
  const int BUFFER_SIZE = 1024;
  int BytesRead;
  char[] Buffer = new char[BUFFER_SIZE];
  MyClass obj3 = (MyClass) ar.AsyncState;
  Stream responseStream = obj3.ResponseStream;
  BytesRead = responseStream.EndRead(ar);
  Char[] charBuffer = new Char[BUFFER_SIZE];
  Decoder StreamDecode =  Encoding.UTF8.GetDecoder();
  int len = StreamDecode.GetChars( obj3.BufferRead, 0, BytesRead, charBuffer, 0 );
  String str = new String( charBuffer, 0, len);
  Console.WriteLine(str);
  Console.WriteLine("xx" + len);
  if(len <= 0) return;
```

```
 IAsyncResult iarRead = responseStream.BeginRead(obj3.BufferRead, 0, BUFFER_SIZE,
new AsyncCallback(ReadCallBack), obj3);
 }
}
```

The HttpWebRequest class has some important properties, described in Table 19.6. These are specific to HTTP 1.0 and 1.1 protocols. Refer to the Microsoft Developer Network (MSDN) for more details.

Members	Description
KeepAlive	Allows a client using HTTP to conserve network resources and behave in a more efficient manner by keeping an existing TCP connection to the server alive and reusing that connection, rather than closing it and creating a new one for each request.
SendChunked	Used when an application needs to send data whose exact size is not known at the time the upload begins.
Pipelined	An HTTP 1.1 feature that allows Net classes to send multiple HTTP requests to a backend server over a persistent connection without waiting for a response from the server. This can have a dramatic effect on performance, as applications requesting multiple resources from a server don't get blocked waiting for one particular resource.
Proxy	Identifies the WebProxy instance to use when processing requests sent to Internet resources. To specify that no proxy should be used, set the Proxy property to the proxy instance returned by the GlobalProxySelection.GetEmptyWebProxy method.
ConnectionGroupName	Enables you to associate a request with a connection group. This is useful when your application makes requests to one server for different users, such as a Web site that retrieves customer information from a database server.

Table 19.6: Important HttpWebRequest Properties

Using Credentials

Many .Net classes support a variety of client authentication mechanisms, including digest, basic, Kerberos, NTLM (Windows NT, LAN Manager), and custom mechanisms. Authentication is achieved by setting the WebRequest.Credentials object before making a request. Digest and basic require a user name and password. NTLM and Kerberos use Windows security, and the Credential object can be set either to a user name, password, and domain combination or to the system defaults.

For the conceptual details of credentials, authentication methods, and supported security infrastructures, refer to Microsoft operating system manuals and documentation. Microsoft also has a Web site for security concepts and issues: http://www.microsoft.com/security/.

Kerberos is an industry-standard authentication protocol providing high security while scaling well. Developed under MIT's Project Athena, it is based on symmetric key cryptography. At the heart of the protocol is a trusted server called a Key Distribution Center (KDC). When the user logs on to the network, the KDC verifies the user's identity and provides credentials called "tickets"—one for each network service that the user wants to use. Each ticket introduces the user to the appropriate service and optionally carries information indicating the user's privileges for the service. For more information about Microsoft security products and technologies go to http://www.microsoft.com/technet/security/prodtech/prodtech.asp.

The NetworkCredential class is a base class that supplies credentials in password-based authentication schemes, such as basic, digest, NTLM, and Kerberos. The DefaultCredentials property applies only to NTLM, negotiate, and Kerberos, and represents the system credentials for the current security context in which the application is running. For client-side applications, these are usually the Windows credentials (user name, password, and domain) of the user running the application. For ASP.NET applications, the default credentials are the user credentials of the logged-in user or the user being impersonated. Listing 19.26 demonstrates use of NetworkCredential.

Listing 19.26—NetworkCredential Example

```
NetworkCredential myCred = new NetworkCredential("mcb","csharp","corner");

CredentialCache myCache = new CredentialCache();
myCache.Add(new Uri("www.c-sharpcorner.com"), "Basic", myCred);
myCache.Add(new Uri("www.mindcracker.com"), "Digest", myCred);

WebRequest wr = WebRequest.Create("www.mindcracker.com");
wr.Credentials = myCache;

// or
WebRequest wr2 = WebRequest.Create("www.c-sharpcorner.com");
Wr2.Credentials = CredentialCache.DefaultCredentials;
```

IP Address and DNS Programming

DNS (Domain Name System) servers are essential for Internet applications like FTP and HTTP. Users would find it difficult to remember hundreds of IP addresses—like 208.248.124.18—but friendly FQDNs (fully qualified domain names)—like www.mindcracker.com—are easier to remember and use.

IPAddress Class

The IPAddress class contains the address of a computer on an IP network. The address is a made up of four 8-bit numbers separated by dots: 10.0.23.251. It must be unique to a computer on a network, thus allowing one-to-one communication. There are also shared IP addresses used when broadcasting to a specific group of computers, allowing one-to-many communication. Then there is the loopback address—127.0.0.1—which does not send packets to the network interface card but instead returns them to the TCP/IP stack as if they came from the network. The loopback address is extremely useful for testing. Listing 19.27 demonstrates use of the IPAddress class, and Figure 19.13 shows its screenshot.

Listing 19.27—IPAddress.cs, Example IPAddress Class Usage

```
using System;
using System.Net;

namespace Application1
{
        /// <summary>
        /// Summary description for Class1.
        /// </summary>
        class Class1
        {
                static void Main(string[] args)
                {
                        IPAddress myIP = IPAddress.Parse("10.0.23.251");
                        Console.WriteLine("10.0.23.251: " + myIP.ToString());
                        IPAddress mynewIP = new IPAddress(myIP.Address);
                        Console.WriteLine("new IP: " + mynewIP.ToString());
                        myIP = IPAddress.Any;
```

```
                        Console.WriteLine("Any: " + myIP.ToString());
                        myIP = IPAddress.Loopback;
                        Console.WriteLine("Loopback: " + myIP.ToString());
                        myIP = IPAddress.Broadcast;
                        Console.WriteLine("Broadcast: " + myIP.ToString());
                        myIP = IPAddress.None;
                        Console.WriteLine("None: " + myIP.ToString());
                        Console.ReadLine();
                }
        }
}
```

Figure 19.13: Example Screenshot of Listing 19.27

IPHostEntry Class

The DNS class is a static class that provides a means of obtaining information about a Internet DNS host. The DNS class returns an IPHostEntry object containing the hostname and an array of IP addresses and aliases. Note that a host may specify more than one entry in the DNS database. A typical host has a primary hostname associated with a unique IP in a DNS server configuration file. Along with the DNS record about this host, can be many other A and CNAME records. (Refer to the DNS RFC for details.) Multiple aliases and addresses provide flexibility for hosts that work with many distinct applications. Listing 19.28 demonstrates use of IPHostEntry, and Figure 19.14 shows its example screenshot.

Listing 19.28—IPHostEntry.cs, Example IPHostEntry Class Usage

```
using System;
using System.Net;

namespace Application1
{
        /// <summary>
        /// Summary description for Class1.
        /// </summary>
        class Class1
        {
                static void Main(string[] args)
                {
                        IPAddress myIP = IPAddress.Loopback;
                        Console.WriteLine("Loopback: " + myIP.ToString());
                        IPHostEntry hostInfo = Dns.GetHostByAddress(myIP);
                        //IPHostEntry hostInfo = Dns.GetHostByName("heaven");
                        Console.WriteLine("Aliases:");
                        for(int i=0; i <= hostInfo.Aliases.GetUpperBound(0); ++i)
                                Console.WriteLine(hostInfo.Aliases[i]);
                        Console.WriteLine("AddressList:");
                        for(int i=0; i <=
hostInfo.AddressList.GetUpperBound(0); ++i)
                                Console.WriteLine(hostInfo.AddressList[i]);

                }
        }
}
```

Figure 19.14: Example Screenshot of Listing 19.28

IPEndPoint Class

The IPEndPoint class combines the IP address and service port number, forming a connection point to a service on a server. Listing 19.29 shows how IPEndPoint is used.

Listing 19.29—IPEndPoint Example

```
IPEndPoint RemoteEP = new IPEndPoint( "10.0.0.1", 99 );

//Initializes a new instance of the TcpClient class with the specified endpoint.
TcpClient tcpc = new TcpClient(RemoteEP);

//or
//Initializes a new instance of the TcpListener class with the specified local
endpoint.
TcpListener tcpc = new TcpListener(RemoteEP);

//or
// Initializes a new instance of the UdpClient class that communicates on a
specified local endpoint.
UdpClient udpc = new UdpClient(RemoteEP);
```

DNS Class

The DNS class provides a simple domain name resolution functionality. With it, clients connecting to system-defined DNS addresses make normal (hostname to IP address) or reverse (IP address to hostname) queries. In other words, they can get the hostname of a machine or get the IP address if the hostname is already known.

The DNS class is a static class that provides access to information from the Internet DNS. The information returned includes multiple IP addresses and aliases if the host specified has more than one entry in the DNS database. The list is returned as a IPHostEntry object.

IPHostEntry can contain multiple IP addresses and aliases if the specified host has more than one entry in the DNS database. The Dns.GetHostByName and Dns.GetHostByAddress have been illustrated, which creates an IPHostEntry instance from a specified IPAddress instance or a string.

The DNS has a few more static member functions: GetHostName gets a string containing the DNS hostname of the local machine. GetHostByAddress, GetHostByName, GetHostName, and Resolve are synchronous static DNS functions, and BeginGetHostByName, BeginResolve, EndGetHostByName, and EndResolve are asynchronous static DNS functions. Refer to MSDN for more details.

Listing 19.30 demonstrates usage of the DNS class, and Figure 19.15 shows its example screenshot.

Listing 19.30—DnsClnt.cs, Example DNS Class Usage

```
using System;
using System.Net;
```

```
namespace Application1
{
        /// <summary>
        /// Summary description for Class1.
        /// </summary>
        class Class1
        {
                static void Main(string[] args)
                {
                        IPAddress myIP = IPAddress.Loopback;
                        Console.WriteLine("Loopback: " + myIP.ToString());
                        Console.WriteLine("Dns.HostName: " + Dns.GetHostName());
                        Console.WriteLine("IPAddress.Address: " + myIP.Address);
                }
        }
}
```

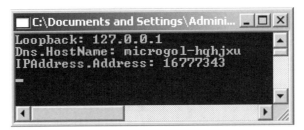

Figure 19.15: Example Screenshot of Listing 19.30

DNS, IPAddress, and IPHostEntry Example

Listing 19.31 demonstrates use of DNS, IPAddress, and IPHostEntry.

Listing 19.31—DnsIpHost.cs, Example DNS, IPAddress, and IPHostEntry

```
using System;
using System.Net;
using System.Net.Sockets;

class MyApp
{

 public static void Main()
 {
  MyApp theapp = new MyApp();
  theapp.DNSexample();
 }

 public static void dumpIPHE(IPHostEntry iphe, string str1)
 {
  Console.WriteLine("dumping IPHostEntry: " + str1);
  Console.WriteLine("AddressList:");
  for(int i=0; i <= iphe.AddressList.GetUpperBound(0); ++i)
   {
        Console.WriteLine(iphe.AddressList[i]);
//Provides an array of IPAddress objects
   }
  Console.WriteLine("Aliases:");
  for(int i=0; i <= iphe.Aliases.GetUpperBound(0); ++i)
   {
        Console.WriteLine(iphe.Aliases[i]);
//Provides an array of strings containing other
//DNS names that resolve to the IP addresses in AddressList
   }
  Console.WriteLine("Hostname:");
```

```
   Console.WriteLine(iphe.HostName);
//Contains the DNS name of the host
  }

public void DNSexample()
{
 try
 {
  // Gets the host name of the local machine.
  Console.WriteLine("\r\nHostname:" + Dns.GetHostName());
  try
  {
   // DNS query - Resolves a DNS hostname to an IPAddress instance
   IPHostEntry iphe = Dns.GetHostByName("www.microsoft.com");
   IPAddress[] m_arrIPs = iphe.AddressList;
   dumpIPHE(iphe, "iphe");
   Console.WriteLine("\r\nIP Addresses:");
   for(int i=0; i <= m_arrIPs.GetUpperBound(0); ++i)
       Console.WriteLine(m_arrIPs[i]);
  }
  catch(Exception e)
  {
   Console.WriteLine("Exception:" + e.ToString());
  }

  // reverse DNS - Retrieves the IPHostEntry information corresponding to
  // the DNS name provided in the host parameter
  IPHostEntry iphe2 = Dns.GetHostByAddress("208.248.124.18");
  string[] m_arrAlias = iphe2.Aliases ;
  dumpIPHE(iphe2, "iphe2");
  Console.WriteLine("\r\nDomain Names:");
  for(int i=0; i <= m_arrAlias.GetUpperBound(0); ++i)
      Console.WriteLine(m_arrAlias[i]);

  // Creates a string containing the DNS name of the host specified in address
  // 10.20.30.40 => 00001010.00010100.00011110.00101000 => 673059850
  // how=> the bytes are reversed 00101000000111100001010000001010 = 673059850
  int intIP = 673059850;
  string strIP = (new IPAddress(intIP)).ToString();
  Console.WriteLine("converted IP:" + strIP);
  IPAddress myIP = new IPAddress(intIP);
  Console.WriteLine("\r\nIPAddress:" + myIP.ToString());
 }
 catch(Exception e)
 {
  Console.WriteLine("Exception:" + e.ToString());
 }
 }

}
```

Sending E-mail with the System.Web.Mail Class

You can use the SmtpMail class to send e-mail from your C# application. By default, the system queues mail, ensuring that the calling program does not block network traffic. The SmtpMail class is defined in the namespace System.Web.Mail, so before using it, you need to make this call:

```
using System.Web.Mail;
```

This class has only one member function: Send. The Send method is overloaded. You can pass either four arguments to the Send message (the direct method) or a MailMessage class.

Before sending the message, you must specify your SMTP relay server, with or without calling System.Web.Mail:

```
System.Web.Mail.SmtpMail.SmtpServer = "mail.mindcracker.com";
```

Or:

```
SmtpMail.SmtpServer = "mail.mindcracker.com";
```

You can call the Send method with or without calling System.Web.Mail:

```
System.Web.Mail.SmtpMail.Send(txtFrom.Text, txtTo.Text, txtSubject.Text,
txtMessage.Text);
```

Or:

```
SmtpMail.Send(txtFrom.Text, txtTo.Text, txtSubject.Text, txtMessage.Text);
```

You can call the Send method in two ways, first using the direct method:

```
public static void Send(string from, string to, string subject, string
messageText);
```

Example:

```
SmtpMail.Send("mcb@mindcracker.com", "mcb@mindcracker.com", "Subject", "Message
body");
```

Table 19.7 lists the direct method's parameters. Listing 19.32 shows use of the direct method.

Members	Description
From	E-mail address of sender.
To	E-mail address of recipient.
Subject	E-mail subject line.
MessageText	Body of e-mail message.

Table 19.7: Smtp.Mail Send Method Direct Usage Parameters

Listing 19.32—MailMessage Properties

```
MailMessage mailMsg = new MailMessage();
mailMsg .From = "from@fromServer.com";
mailMsg .To = "to@toServer.com";
mailMsg .Cc = "cc@ccServer.com"";
mailMsg .Bcc = "bcc@bccServer.com";
mailMsg .Subject = "SubjectOfTheMailString";
mailMsg .Body = "BodyOfTheMailString";
SmtpMail.Send(mailMsg );
```

Or you can pass MailMessage as a parameter:

```
public static void Send(MailMessage);
```

MailMessage Class

You can use the MailMessage class to send mail with copies (cc), blind copies (bcc), and attachments. The MailMessage constructor initializes a new instance of the MailMessage class. It doesn't take any parameters:

```
MailMessage mail = new MailMessage();
```

Table 19.8 lists important MailMessage properties.

Members	Description
Bcc	A semicolon-separated list of e-mail addresses that will receive a private copy of the e-mail message.
Body	The body content of the e-mail message.
BodyEncoding	The encoding type of the e-mail message.
BodyFormat	The type of the e-mail message body (text or HTML).
Cc	A semicolon-separated list of e-mail addresses that will receive a copy of the e-mail message.
From	The e-mail address of sender.
Priority	The priority of the e-mail message.
Subject	The subject line of the e-mail.
To	The e-mail address of the recipient.
UrlContentBase	The base of all relative URLs used within an HTML-encoded message.
Attachments	List of MailAttachments to be transmitted with the message. This property is read-only.
Headers	The dictionary of custom headers to be transmitted with the message. This property is read-only.

Table 19.8: MailMessage Class Important Properties

Each class member is easy to understand. For example, if you want to send an attachment, you simply use the Attachment member. This coding attaches mcb.jpg to the e-mail:

```
mail.Attachments.Add(new MailAttachment(@"C:\mcb.jpg"));
```

Summary

TCP/IP, the bricks and mortar of all networked applications, is the most widely used protocol in private and public networks. The .NET Framework provides robust and versatile classes for developing networked applications. Most other classes of interest—like SOAP and ASP.NET—use .NET TCP/IP classes as a base or component by inheritance, aggregation, or composition. The .NET TCP/IP classes are network-centric that give SOAP and ASP.NET the necessary infrastructure to build upon.

In this chapter we have learned how to program with TCP, UDP and other Internet-related .NET Framework classes. You can deepen your experience in this topic by developing networked applications like an FTP client and server or a simple Internet Relay Chat client. When in doubt, you can refer to the RFC documents. The next chapter will explore the manipulation of strings and arrays in .NET.

Chapter 20:
Strings and Arrays

Arrays

An array in C# is simply a set of sequential memory locations that can be accessed using either indices or references. A mechanism in C# prevents a program from writing outside the bounds of an array and destroying the contents of memory in the process: The declaration of an array simply sets aside the requisite block of memory and treats the name of the array as a synonym for the address of the block's beginning.

On our behalf, .NET Framework handles memory allocation behind the scenes. Arrays can be multidimensional, but their elements must be of the same base type. Arrays can store integers, strings, and any other type of object, including references and other arrays.

Arrays and Array Initializations

In C#, before using an array, you must declare it, providing two important pieces of information:

- The name of the array
- The type of data to be stored in it

Arrays may be declared in C# using the format below:

```
int[] myArray;
```

As with other objects in C#, the declaration does not allocate memory for the array data but rather allocates memory for a reference to the array. Memory to contain the array data must be allocated from dynamic memory using statements such as the one below:

```
int[] myArray = new int[15];
```

C# saves space until you explicitly assign a value to a reference type. For value types, however, the space is allocated immediately (see the example in the "System.Array Class" section).

The two statements above simultaneously declare the name of the array and cause memory to be allocated to contain it. The references are allocated but do not refer to anything until the array is actually assigned data.

It is not necessary, however, to combine these two processes. You can execute one statement to declare the array and another statement to allocate the memory:

```
int[] myArray;
//. . .
myArray = new int[25];
```

Causing memory to be set aside to contain the array data is commonly referred to as *instantiating the array object*—or creating an instance of the array object. If you prefer to declare and instantiate the array at different points in your program, you can use the syntax above. This pattern is very similar to the declaration and instantiation of all objects in C#.

This is the general syntax for declaring and instantiating an array:

```
typeOfElements[] nameOfArray = new typeOfElements[sizeOfArray];
```

Having instantiated an array in C#, you can access the elements of the array using index syntax similar to C++ and many other languages:

```
myArray[5] = 6;
myVar = myArray[5];
```

As in C++, array indices in C# always begin with 0.

The following code fragment illustrates another interesting aspect of arrays in C#:

```
for(int cnt = 0; cnt < myArray.Length; cnt++)
  myArray[j] = j;
```

All array objects in C# have a Length property that can be accessed to determine the number of elements stored in the array.

Single–Dimensional Arrays

A single-dimensional array of size *N* has elements ranging from 0 to *N*–1 subscripts:

```
int[] myIntArray = new int[5] { 5, 4, 3, 2, 1 };
// or
Array myArr = Array.CreateInstance( typeof(int), 5 );
```

Listing 20.1 illustrates the use of single-dimensional arrays.

Listing 20.1—Outputting an array of strings to the Console

```
// array example - single dimensional

using System;

public class ArrayMembers
{
    public static void Main()
    {
        Console.WriteLine("Enter a sentence");
        String str1 = Console.ReadLine();
        Console.WriteLine("");

        //Iterate through the items of array args using  foreach
        foreach(char s in str1)
        {
          Console.WriteLine(s);
        }

        Console.WriteLine("");
        //Declare array strNames
        string[] strNames = {"Ahmet","Mustafa","Mehmet","Mahmut"};
```

```
            //Iterate through the items of array strNames
            for(int i = 0;i < strNames.Length;i++)
            {
               Console.WriteLine("strNames[{0}] = {1}",i,strNames[i]);
            }
      }
}
```

Multidimensional Arrays

A multidimensional array of dimension *n* is a collection of items accessed via *n* subscript
expressions. It can be declared with a different notation but in the same way as single-dimensional
arrays, as shown in Listing 20.2.

Listing 20.2—Creating and Assigning values to Multidimensional Arrays

```
// simply like below
// 3*2 member two-dimensional arrays
int[,] intCount = new int[,] {{1, 2, 3}, {4, 5, 6}};
// 1*3 member three-dimesional arrays
int[,,] intDec = new int[10, 20, 30];

//or...

// Create and initialize a new three-dimensional array instance of type int
 Array myArr = Array.CreateInstance( typeof(int), 2, 3, 4 );
 for ( int i = myArr.GetLowerBound(0); i <= myArr.GetUpperBound(0); i++ )
    for ( int j = myArr.GetLowerBound(1); j <= myArr.GetUpperBound(1); j++ )
       for (int k = myArr.GetLowerBound(2); k <= myArr.GetUpperBound(2); k++ )
          {
             myArr.SetValue( (i*i)+(j*j)+k, i, j, k );
          }
```

Listing 20.3 provides another example of multidimensional arrays that incorporates an enumerator
class.

Listing 20.3—Multidimensional Arrays using an Enumerator

```
// array example - multidimensional

using System;

public class ArrayMembers
{
     public static void Main()
     {
        int[,] myIntArray = new int[,] {{1, 2, 3}, {4, 5, 6}};
       int i = 0;
       Console.WriteLine("myIntArray.GetUpperBound(0):" +
myIntArray.GetUpperBound(0));
        Console.WriteLine("myIntArray.GetUpperBound(1):" +
myIntArray.GetUpperBound(1));

      System.Collections.IEnumerator myEnumerator = myIntArray.GetEnumerator();
      int cols = myIntArray.GetLength( myIntArray.Rank - 1 );
      while ( myEnumerator.MoveNext() )
      {
        if ( i < cols )
        {
          i++;
        }
        else
        {
          Console.WriteLine();
```

```
                i = 1;
            }
        Console.Write( "\t{0}", myEnumerator.Current );
        }
    Console.WriteLine();
    }
}
```

Rectangular Arrays

Rectangular arrays may be single-dimensional or multidimensional but always have a rectangular shape. Rectangular means that the length of each subarray in the same dimension are the same length.

Single-dimensional rectangular arrays are declared this way:

```
short[] shtEmpNo;
int[] intSalary;
```

Multidimensional rectangular arrays are declared this way:

```
// two-dimensional arrays of short
short[,] shtEmpNo;
// three-dimensional arrays of int
int[,,] intSalary;
```

This is the syntax for a rectangular array:

```
Element-type (int, short, long) Rank-specifiers ([], [,,]) Name (Arrays Name)
```

Array types are reference types, so the declaration of an array variable merely sets aside space for the reference to the array. Array instances are actually created via array initializers and array creation expressions, as shown in Listing 20.4.

Listing 20.4—Rectangular Array Creation

```
// 5 member single-dimensional arrays intialized
short[] shtEmpNo = new short[5];
// 3 member single-dimensional arrays
int[] intSlNo = new int[] {1, 2, 3};
// 3*2 member two-dimensional arrays
int[,] intCount = new int[,] {{1, 2, 3}, {4, 5, 6}};
// 1*3 member three-dimesional arrays
int[,,] intDec = new int[10, 20, 30];
```

In fact, in all languages developed for the .NET Framework, rectangular arrays are zero-based arrays, as shown in Listings 20.5 and 20.6 which start assigning array values to elements indexed at zero.

Listing 20.5—Rectangular Arrays Are Zero-Subscript-Based

```
shtEmpNo[0] = 0;
shtEmpNo[1] = 0;
shtEmpNo[2] = 0;
shtEmpNo[3] = 0;
shtEmpNo[4] = 0;
intSlNo[0] = 1 , intSlNo[1] = 2 and intSlNo[2] = 3;
intCount[0,0] = 1, intCount[1,0] = 2, intCount[0,1] = 4 ,
    intCount[2,2] = 6;
intDec[0,0,0] = 10 , intDec[0,0,2] = 30;
```

Listing 20.6—Rectangular Array Example

```
using System;

class MyClass
{
        static void Main() {
                int[] intDec = new int[5];
                for (int i = 0; i < intDec.Length; i++)
                        intDec[i] = i * 10;
                for (int i = 0; i < intDec.Length; i++)
                    Console.WriteLine("intDec[{0}] = {1}", i, intDec[i]);
        }
}
```

Jagged Arrays

Jagged arrrays are arrays of arrays . The syntax for a jagged array uses the square brackets after the type declaration for each dimension of the array:

```
// "jagged" array: array of (array of int)
int[][] j2;
// array of (array of (array of int))
int[][][] j3;
```

Listing 20.7 compares rectangular and jagged arrays.

Listing 20.7—Rectangular and Jagged Arrays

```
//single-dimensional rectangular arrays
int[] r1 = new int[] {1, 2, 3};
//two-dimensional rectangular arrays
int[,] r2 = new int[,] {{1, 2, 3}, {4, 5, 6}};
//three-dimesional rectangular arrays
int[,,] r3 = new int[10, 20, 30];
//"jagged" array: array of (array of int)
int[][] j2 = new int[3][];
j2[0] = new int[] {1, 2, 3};
j2[1] = new int[] {1, 2, 3, 4, 5, 6};
j2[2] = new int[] {1, 2, 3, 4, 5, 6, 7, 8, 9};
```

The code in Listing 20.7 includes various expressions for creating both rectangular and jagged arrays. The variables *r1*, *r2*, and *r3* are rectangular arrays, and the variable *j2* is a jagged array.

Rectangular arrays always have a rectangular shape. For example, the length of *r3's* three dimensions are 10, 20, and 30, and it is easy to see that this array contains 10 x 20 x 30 elements.

The variable *j2* is a jagged array—an array of an array of integers, or a single-dimensional array of type int[]. Each of these int[] variables can be initialized individually, and this allows the array to take on a jagged shape. Listing 20.7 gives each of the int[] arrays a different length. Specifically, the length of j2[0] is 3, the length of j2[1] is 6, and the length of j2[2] is 9. Listing 20.8 illustrates how to create and loop through a jagged array.

Listing 20.8—Creating and Outputting Jagged Arrays

```
// Jagged Array example

using System;

public class MyArrayc2
{
 public static void Main()
```

```
{
 int [][] JaggedArray = new int[4][];
 JaggedArray[0]=new int[3];
 JaggedArray[1]=new int[2];
 JaggedArray[2]=new int[5];
 JaggedArray[3]=new int[4];

 Console.WriteLine("Enter the numbers for Jagged Array");

 for(int i=0 ; i < JaggedArray.Length ; i++)
 {
  for(int x=0 ; x < JaggedArray[i].Length ; x++)
  {
   String st= Console.ReadLine();
   int num=Int32.Parse(st);
   JaggedArray[i][x]=num;
  }
 }

 Console.WriteLine("");
 Console.WriteLine("Printing the Elements");

 for(int x=0 ; x < JaggedArray.Length ; x++)
 {
  for(int y=0 ; y < JaggedArray[x].Length ; y++)
  {
   Console.Write(JaggedArray[x][y]);
   Console.Write("\0");
  }
  Console.WriteLine("");
 }
}
}
```

Array Conversions

The Type property of Array objects provides information about array type declarations. Array objects with the same array type share the same Type object, so the array is said to be homogenous. But you can store wrapper classes as objects with aggregation or composition, which can store or link references to other objects. Listing 20.9 shows conversion of an Int32 array to a double array by copying and then modifying elements with changed values.

Listing 20.9— Array Copy and Conversion

```
// copying and converting array elements

using System;

class Test
{
    public static void TestForEach (ref int[] myArray)
    {
        foreach (int x in myArray)
        {
            Console.WriteLine(x);
        }
    }

    public static void TestForEach (ref double[] myArray)
    {
        foreach (double x in myArray)
        {
            Console.WriteLine(x);
        }
    }
```

```
public static void Main()
{
    // an int array and an Object array
    int[] myIntArray = new int[5] { 5, 4, 3, 2, 1 };
    TestForEach(ref myIntArray);
    Console.WriteLine("myIntArray: Type is {0}", myIntArray.GetType());
    double[] myDblArray = new double[5];
    Array.Copy(myIntArray, myDblArray, myIntArray.Length);
    for(int i=0;i<myDblArray.Length;i++)
      myDblArray[i] += myDblArray[i] / 19;
    TestForEach(ref myDblArray);
}
}
```

System.Array Class

Arrays are one of the fundamental data structures in programming languages, providing a storage area for sequential data values. System.Array is the base class for all arrays in the common language runtime. It has methods for creating, manipulating, searching, and sorting the arrays we have talked about so far.   System.Array implements several interfaces, like ICloneable, IList, ICollection, and IEnumerable. It also has many properties and methods to aid you in determining information about your array.

The Length property of the array returns the total number of elements in all of the array's dimensions.

The Rank property returns the rank—the number of dimensions—of the array, which is useful in multidimensional arrays.

You can use the Clear function to reset a range of array elements to zero or to a null reference.

The GetLowerBound function returns the lower bound of the specified dimension in an array. GetLowerBound(0) returns the lower bound for the indexes of the first dimension of an array, and GetLowerBound(Rank–1) returns the lower bound for the indexes of the last dimension of an array.

The GetUpperBound function returns the upper bound of the specified dimension in an array. GetUpperBound(0) returns the upper bound for the indexes of the first dimension of an array, and GetUpperBound(Rank–1) returns the upper bound for the indexes of the last dimension of an array.

Using the Copy function, you can copy a range of elements from one array, starting at the specified source index, and paste them into another array, starting at the specified destination index:

```
// Copy the first 2 elements from mySourceArray to myDestinationArray
Array.Copy( mySourceArray, mySourceArray.GetLowerBound(0),
       myDestinationArray, myDestinationArray.GetLowerBound(0), 2);
```

There are three ways to enumerate array elements:

- Using the foreach loop structure
- Looping with a for loop along the length of the array
- Using the GetEnumerator function and implementing IEnumerator

Listing 20.10 illustrates these three enumeration methods.

Listing 20.10—Looping Through Array Class Objects

```csharp
//enumerating array elements
using System;

class Test
{
    public static void TestForEach (ref int[] myArray)
    {
        foreach (int x in myArray)
        {
            Console.WriteLine(x);
        }
    }

    public static void TestForWithLength (ref Object[] myArray)
    {
        for (int x=0; x < myArray.Length; x++)
        {
            Console.WriteLine(myArray[x]);
        }
    }

    public static void TestForEnum(ref System.Array myArray)
    {
        System.Collections.IEnumerator myEnumerator = myArray.GetEnumerator();
        int i = 0;
        int cols = myArray.GetLength( myArray.Rank - 1 );
        while ( myEnumerator.MoveNext() )  {
            if ( i < cols )
            {
                i++;
            }
            else
            {
                Console.WriteLine();
                i = 1;
            }
            Console.WriteLine(myEnumerator.Current );
        }
    }

    public static void Main()
    {
        // an int array and an Object array
        int[] myIntArray = new int[5] { 5, 4, 3, 2, 1 };
        TestForEach(ref myIntArray);
        // an Object array
        Object[] myObjArray = new Object[5] { 99, 98, 97, 96, 95 };
        TestForWithLength(ref myObjArray);
        // another object array
        Array myObjArray2 = Array.CreateInstance( Type.GetType("System.Object"), 5);
        for ( int i = myObjArray2.GetLowerBound(0); i <=
myObjArray2.GetUpperBound(0); i++ )
            myObjArray2.SetValue(i*i, i );
        TestForEnum(ref myObjArray2);
    }
}
```

The .NET Framework provides IEnumerable and IEnumerator interfaces to implement and provide a collectionlike behavior to user-defined classes. These interfaces are implemented through inner classes. An inner or nested-type class is enclosed inside another class. Listing 20.11 is the pseudocode for the implementation of the enumerator.

Listing 20.11—Creating a custom Enumerator

```
class ItemCollection : IEnumerable      // COLLECTION
{
}

class ItemIterator : IEnumerator     // ITERATOR
{
  class ItemCollection ;
// class ItemCollection  is an Inner Class or Nested Type in class ItemIterator
}

//IEnumerator and IEnumerable interfaces are defined in System.Collections
//namespace as:
public interface IEnumerable
{
  IEnumerator GetEnumerator(); //returns an enumerator
}

public interface IEnumerator
{
  bool MoveNext();
//After an enumerator is created or after a Reset,
//an enumerator is positioned before the first element
//of the collection, and the first call to MoveNext
//moves the enumerator over the first element of the
//collection.
// And next calls move the cursor one further till the end.

  object Current { get ; }
// Returns the current object from the collection.
// You should throw an InvalidOperationException exception
// if index pointing to wrong position.

  void Reset();
// Resets enumerator to just before the first element of the collection.
// Resets pointer to -1.
}
```

In C# all array elements are initialized to their default values. For reference-type variables, the default value is null. You need to instantiate the reference element before you can access any member property; otherwise you receive an error. As shown in Listing 20.12, you can also use the Array.Initialize member function to initialize every element of a value-type array by calling the default constructor of the value type.

Listing 20.12— Array Initialization Example

```
// array initialization

using System;

public class DisplayPreferences
{
 string m_PropertyID;
 public DisplayPreferences()
 {
  m_PropertyID = null;
 }
 public string PropertyID
 {
  get { return m_PropertyID; }
  set { m_PropertyID = value; }
 }
}
```

```
public class MySampleClass
{
 public static void Main()
 {
  DisplayPreferences[] oPrefs = new DisplayPreferences[10];
  // you have to initiliaze array items before use... otherwise
  /*
The following error message is displayed if the array initialization below is not
included.
  An unhandled exception of type 'System.NullReferenceException' occurred in
displaypreferences.exe
Additional information: Value null was found where an instance of an object was
required.
   at MySampleClass.Main()
  */

  for(int i = 0; i < oPrefs.Length; i++)
    oPrefs[i] = new DisplayPreferences();
  oPrefs[0].PropertyID = "ID007";
  // or if the array is of value-type, not necessary but...
  int[] intarr = new int[10];
  intarr.Initialize();
  intarr[0] = 7;
 }
}
```

Sorting, Reversing, and Searching in Arrays

You can search for the occurence of a value in an array with the IndexOf and LastIndexOf member functions. IndexOf starts the search from a lower subscript and moves forward, and LastIndexOf starts the search from an upper subscript and moves backwards. Both functions achieve a linear search, visiting each element sequentially until they find the match—forward or backward. Listing 20.13 illustrates a linear search through an array using the IndexOf and LastIndexOf methods.

Listing 20.13— Array Linear Search

```
// Linear Search
using System;

public class LinearSearcher
{
 public static void Main()
 {
  String[] myArray = new String[7] {"kama", "dama", "lama", "yama", "pama", "rama",
"lama"};
  String myString = "lama";
  Int32 myIndex;

  // Search for the first occurrence of the duplicated value in a section of the
Array.
  myIndex = Array.IndexOf( myArray, myString, 0, 7 );
  Console.WriteLine( "The first occurrence of \"{0}\" between index 0 and index 6
is at index {1}.", myString, myIndex );


  // Search for the last occurrence of the duplicated value in a section of the
Array.   myIndex = Array.LastIndexOf( myArray, myString, 6, 7 );
  Console.WriteLine( "The last occurrence of \"{0}\" between index 0 and index 6 is
at index {1}.", myString, myIndex );
 }
}
```

The program in Listing 20.13, has this output:

```
The first occurrence of "lama" between index 0 and index 6 is at index 2.
The last occurrence of "lama" between index 0 and index 6 is at index 6.
```

The String class provides methods for sorting, searching, and reversing that are easy to use. Note that Sort, BinarySearch, and Reverse are all static functions and are used for single-dimensional arrays.

Listing 20.14 illustrates usage of the Sort, BinarySearch, and Reverse functions.

Listing 20.14—Array Sort, Binarysearch, and Reverse Examples

```csharp
// Binary Search
// Note an EXCEPTION occurs if the search element is not in the list
// We leave adding this functionality as homework!

using System;

class linSearch

{
  public static void Main()
  {
    int[] a= new int[3];
    Console.WriteLine("Enter number of elements you want to hold in the array (max
3)?");
    string s=Console.ReadLine();
    int x=Int32.Parse(s);
    Console.WriteLine("---------------------------------------------------");
    Console.WriteLine("\n Enter array elements \n");
    Console.WriteLine("---------------------------------------------------");
    for(int i=0;i<x;i++)
    {
      string s1=Console.ReadLine();
      a[i]=Int32.Parse(s1);
    }

    Console.WriteLine("Enter Search element\n");
    Console.WriteLine("---------------------------------------------------");
    string s3 = Console.ReadLine();
    int x2 = Int32.Parse(s3);

    // Sort the values of the Array.
    Array.Sort(a);
    for(int i=0;i<x;i++)
    {
        Console.WriteLine("-------------Sorted----------------------");
        Console.WriteLine("Element{0} is {1}", i+1, a[i]);
    }

    // BinarySearch the values of the Array.
    int x3 = Array.BinarySearch(a, (Object) x2);
    Console.WriteLine("---------------------------------------------------");
    Console.WriteLine("BinarySearch: " + x3);
    Console.WriteLine("Element{0} is {1}", x3, a[x3]);
    Console.WriteLine("---------------------------------------------------");

    // Reverse the values of the Array.
    Array.Reverse(a);
    Console.WriteLine("----------Reversed---------------------------");
    for(int i=0;i<x;i++)
    {
        Console.WriteLine("---------------------------------------------");
        Console.WriteLine("Element{0} is {1}", i+1, a[i]);
    }
  }
}
```

```
}
```

Listing 20.15 is a more sophisticated example of using the IComparer interface and Sort function together. The IComparer interface allows you to define a Compare method in order to do a comparison between two elements of your array. This Compare method is called repeatedly by the Sort function in order to sort the array. Listing 20.15 defines a Compare method that does a comparison between two strings.

Listing 20.15—Array Sorting

```csharp
// sort an array according to the Nth element
using System;
using System.Collections;

public class CompareX : IComparer
{

  int compareFrom = 0;

  public CompareX(int i)
  {
   compareFrom = i;
  }

  public int Compare(object a, object b)
  {
   return String.Compare(a.ToString().Substring(compareFrom),
b.ToString().Substring(compareFrom));
  }
}

public class ArrListEx
{

 ArrayList arr = new ArrayList();
 public ArrListEx()
  {
  arr.Add("aaaa9999");
  arr.Add("bbbb8888");
  arr.Add("cccc7777");
  arr.Add("dddd6666");

  arr.Sort(new CompareX(4));

  IEnumerator arrList = arr.GetEnumerator();

  while(arrList.MoveNext())
  {
   Console.WriteLine("Item: {0}", arrList.Current);
  }
 }

 public static void Main(string [] args)
 {
  new ArrListEx();
 }
}
```

System.ArrayList Class

The ArrayList class implements a collection of objects using an array whose size is dynamically increased as required. The ArrayList class is very useful if you are working with arrays and need to add, remove, index, or search for data in a collection.

Although ArrayList is very versatile and grows dynamically when you add values, it is slower than the Array class, which allows you to access its members with subscripts but does not let the array grow during runtime. When choosing between Array and ArrayList, decide which feature is important to your application. To get a better idea of how an Array compares to an ArrayList, think of an ArrayList as nothing more than a linked-list implementation of an Array. Adding data to an ArrayList is pretty easy; just call the class's Add member, as shown in Listing 20.17.

Listing 20.17—Adding an element to an ArrayList

```
ArrayList dataArray = new ArrayList();
for ( int i = 0; i<20; i++ )
{
    dataArray.Add( i );
}

// or you can add any object type like below.

dataArray.Add( "Object type" );
```

The Add member takes an argument of Object type. You can add any value to the ArrayList because all values inherit from the Object base class.

You can also insert an element into the ArrayList at a specified index. Note that if you specify the index item as the last item + 1, the Insert method works the same way as the Add method:

```
myList.Insert( 1, "real first" );
```

The Remove and RemoveAt members delete data from an ArrayList. The RemoveAt method removes the element at the specified index of the ArrayList, while the Remove method removes the first occurrence of a specific object from the ArrayList:

```
// Remove the element containing "3".
myList.Remove( "3" );
```

The BinarySearch member of ArrayList is very useful and fast for searching for elements. This member returns the zero-based index of a specific element in the sorted ArrayList or a portion of it using a binary search algorithm:

```
int myIndex = myList.BinarySearch( 3 );
```

With the ToArray function, you can copy the elements of the ArrayList to a new array of the specified type:

```
int[] myIntArr = myList.ToArray(Int32);
```

You can always set the capacity to the actual number of elements in the ArrayList with the TrimToSize function:

```
myList.TrimToSize();
```

Strings

A string in C# is simply a set of 16-bit bytes arranged in sequential memory locations. In other words, a string is simply an array of Unicode characters. C# includes a variety of standard functions to recognize this data organization as a string and emulate the actions provided by operators on true string types in other languages. C# prevents functions from writing outside the bounds of the string's memory area. Listing 20.18 is a Console application that shows some basic manipulation of strings. The program prompts the user for a string , a character to be found, and a character to replace the found characters. The program illustrates simple string initialization, assignment, concatenation and indexing.

Listing 20.18—Replacing characters in a string

```
// a string is an array of characters
class TheReplacer
{
 static string s1, s2;
 static char c2,c3;

  public static void Main()
  {
    try
    {
        System.Console.Write("Please enter a string:");
        s1=System.Console.ReadLine();
        System.Console.Write("Please enter a character to be found:");
        string temp = System.Console.ReadLine();
        c2 = temp[0];
        System.Console.Write("Please enter a character to replace the found
chars:");
        temp = System.Console.ReadLine();
        c3 = temp[0];
    }
    finally
    {
    }

    try
    {
        for (int i=0; i < s1.Length; i++)
        {
            if (c2 == s1[i])
            {
            s2 += c3;
            }
            else
            {
            s2 += s1[i];
            }
        }
    }
    finally
    {
        System.Console.WriteLine("\nNew string:" + s2);
    }

  }
}
```

The program in Listing 20.18, has this output:

```
Please enter a string:kazoo
Please enter a character to be found:o
Please enter a character to replace the found chars:u

New string:kazuu
```

String Initialization and System.String Class

C# strings stem from the String class of the System namespace: System.String. A similar class, the StringBuilder class, can be found in the System.Text namespace. We'll talk more about the StringBuilder class later in this chapter.

The String class is used to work with strings in the .NET Framework. String objects are immutable: Once they are created, their values cannot be changed. However, you can reassign the string reference to another string, freeing up the first string for garbage collection if no other reference to it exists.

String class methods that appear to manipulate a string do not change the current string but instead create a new string and return it. This process of repeatedly creating and throwing away strings can be slow. However, with immutable objects, ownership, aliasing, and threading issues are all much simpler.

Strings consist of characters in the ascii set. These characters include simple alphanumerics such as 'a' or '_'. These characters also include special characters that include <return> or <tab> characters. Return, tab and other special characters are represented in a string using escape sequences. Table 20.1 shows the escape sequences some of the common special characters.

Escape Sequence	Function
\t	Tab (Unicode 0x0009)
\r	Carriage return (0x000d)
\n	Newline (line feed) (0x000a)
\v	Vertical tab (0x000b)
\a	Alert (0x0007)
\b	Backspace (0x0008)
\f	Form feed (0x000c)
\0	Null (0x0000)
\\	Backslash (0x005c)
\'	Single quotation mark (0x0027)
\"	Double quotation mark (0x0022)
\uABCD	Unicode character 0xABCD (where A, B, C, and D are valid hexadecimal digits 0-9, a-f, A-F)
\x0058	Hexadecimal character

Table 20.1: Escape Sequences

Verbatim string literals begin with @" and end with the matching quotation mark. They do not require escape sequences. The only exception to the no-escape-sequence rule for verbatim string literals is that you can put a double quotation mark inside a verbatim string by doubling it:

```
@"A ""quote"" from Conan the Cimmerian..."
```

Verbatim string literals can also extend over a line break. If they do, they include any white space between the quotes:

```
@"First \t line
    tabbed second line"
```

Like all classes, the String class is a reference type with built-in .NET Framework support methods and operators to simplify development. Such support includes string indexing to read (but not write) individual characters (as in $s[i]$), string concatenating with the $+$ operator (as in $s + t$), and equality and inequality operators (as in $s == t$ and $s \mathrel{!=} t$). Listing 20.19 demonstrates their use.

Listing 20.19—String Assignments Comparisons

```
string strValue1 = @"verbatim C# text";
string strValue2 = @"verbatim C# text " + @" concatenated…";
string strValue3 = "regular C# text \r\n"; // beware escape sequences \r\n
char chrFirst = strValue1 [3]; // stores 't'
if (strValue1 == strValue2) {  } // value equality comparison
if (strValue1 != strValue2) {  } // value inequality comparison

if ((object) strValue1 == (object) strValue2) { } //reference equality comparison
if ((object) strValue1 != (object)  strValue2) { } //reference inequality
comparison
```

You can also concatenate any object with a string. This concatenates the return value from the object's ToString method with the string. For instance, all of the following are valid:

```
String str1 = " everyone using C# is hefty ";
String str2 = 4 + str1;    // "4 everyone using C# is hefty"
String str3 =  str2 + 19.19 ;    // "4 everyone using C# is hefty 19.19"
```

In addition, because strings are immutable, the compiler and runtime will merge duplicate string literals so that there's only one copy.

The two most common methods of initializing a string are to assign the string with a string literal or to assign a string with the value from another string:

```
String str1 = "Hello, World!";
String str2 = str1;
```

As Listing 20.20 shows, you can use the static method Copy if you want a second copy of the string.

Listing 20.20—String Assignments Comparisons

```
String str1 = "Hello, World again…";

//no copy; str1 and str2 refer to same String
String str2 = (String)str1.Clone();

// makes copy; str1 and str3 refer to different objects
String str3 = String.Copy(str1);

Console.WriteLine("str1 same as str2: {0}, str1 same as str3: {1}",
   (Object)str1 == (Object)str2, (Object)str1 == (Object)str3);
```

You can also create an array of strings, as Listing 20.21 shows.

Listing 20.21—String Arrays

```
String[] a = new String[3];
a[0] = "1";
a[1] = "2";
a[2] = "3";
//or
```

```
String[][] a = new String[3][3];
a[0][0] = "1";
a[1][0] = "2";
a[2][0] = "3";
```

Listing 20.22 shows additional ways to assign values to strings.

Listing 20.22— String Creation Styles

```
// String creation
// Note that this class is of library type and does not have a Main!


using System;

class myString
{

        public String str;

//Create the string through character Array
        public myString (char[] strValue)
        {
                str = new String(strValue);
                Console.WriteLine("The string '" + str + "' has been
                        initialized by passing an array of characters");
        }

//Create the string through a single character which is repeated a number of
// times
        public myString (char strValue,int intCount)
        {
         str = new String(strValue,intCount);
         Console.WriteLine("The string '" + str + "' has been initialized
          by a character '" + strValue + "' which is repeated '" + intCount
                            + "' times");

        }

//Create the string through character array specifying the starting and ending
places
        public myString (char[] strValue,int intStart,int intEnd)
        {
                str = new String(strValue,intStart,intEnd);
                Console.WriteLine("The string "+ str + " has been initialized
                        by array of characters starting from '"+intStart+"'
                        and ending at '"+intEnd+"'");

        }
}
```

String Class: Important Member Functions

Here are some System.String class member functions:

The ToUpper function converts a string to uppercase.: String.ToUpper().

The ToLower function converts a string to lowercase: String.ToLower().

The Concat function concatenates strings together:

- String.Concat(String[]) concatenates the string array
- String.Concat(String, String) concatenates the two strings
- String.Concat(String, String, String) concatenates the three strings

- String.Concat(String, String, String, String) concatenates the four strings

Listing 20.23 below shows an example of the String.Concat overloaded methods.

Listing 20.23—Writing concatenated strings to the console

```
Console.Write("Enter the string array length : ");
string strArr = Console.ReadLine();
int intArr = int.Parse(strArr);
for (int i = 0;i < intArr; i++)
{
        Console.Write("Enter string " + i + " : ");
        strTempArr[i] = Console.ReadLine();
}

Console.WriteLine("The Concatenated string : " + String.Concat(strTempArr));
Console.WriteLine("the concatenation of the first two string : " +
String.Concat(strTempArr[0],strTempArr[1]));

Console.WriteLine("the concatenation of the first three string : " +
String.Concat(strTempArr[0],strTempArr[1],strTempArr[2]));

Console.WriteLine("the concatenation of the first four string : " +
String.Concat(strTempArr[0], strTempArr[1], strTempArr[2], strTempArr[3]));
```

In Listing 20.24 the Copy function returns a new string with the same value as the string entered by the user.

Listing 20.24—String.Copy

```
Console.WriteLine("original string : " + objString);
Console.Write("enter the string to replace the above one : ");
string strCopy = Console.ReadLine();
objString = String.Copy(strCopy);
Console.WriteLine("the string after copying : " + objString);
```

In Listing 20.25 the CopyTo function copies a part of one string to another string.

Listing 20.25—String.CopyTo

```
Console.Write("Enter the source string : ");
string strTmp = Console.ReadLine();
Console.Write("Enter the starting index for source string : ");
string strSrcSt=Console.ReadLine();
int intSrcSt = int.Parse(strSrcSt);
Console.Write("Enter the starting index in the destination string:");
string strDstSt = Console.ReadLine();
int intDstSt = int.Parse(strDstSt);
Console.Write("Enter the number of characters to be copied from the source string :
");
string strSrcLn = Console.ReadLine();
int intSrcLn = int.Parse(strSrcLn);
chArray = objStringToCharArray();
strTmp.CopyTo(intSrcSt,chArray, intDstSt, intSrcLn);
objString = new String(chArray);
Console.WriteLine("The changed string is : " + objString);
```

In Listing 20.26 the EndsWith function returns a Boolean value, checking whether the parent string ends with the value entered by the user.

Listing 20.26—String.EndsWith

```
Console.WriteLine("The string to be checked :" + objString);
Console.Write("Enter the 'ends with' string :");
String strTmp = Console.ReadLine();
```

```
if (objString.EndsWith(strTmp))
 Console.WriteLine("'"+ objString + "' ends with '" + strTmp + "'.");
else
  Console.WriteLine("'" + objString + "' does not end with '" + strTmp + "'.");
```

The Format static function helps in formating strings containing numbers, dates, strings, and much more. Using the Format method you can pass in objects of different types and have them neatly inserted into your string. You can also handle column alignment and column width in the string. Below are some of the rules of using the overloaded static Format method.

- Format(String *str*, Object *obj*) formats the string with one object.
- Format(String *str*, Object *obj1*, Object *obj2*) formats the string with two objects.
- The string should follow the formating specification: {*N*,[*M*]:[*formatstring*]}. *N* indicates the argument to be replaced and starts from zero(0). *M* indicates the length of formatting area, padded with spaces if the value filled in is smaller. *Formatstring* represents the value of the formating code.

Refer to C#.NET help for a full list of format strings. In Listing 20.27, the *C* format parameter is used for currency. If the value before the colon is negative, it is left justified to fit the number of characters of the value; if the value is positive, it is right justified.

Listing 20.27—String.Format

```
String strTmp = "{0} is working in {1,10} to earn {2,5:C} per month.\n{0} then
works again in {1,-10} to earn the {2,-5:C} in cash";
Console.WriteLine("The source string is : " + strTmp);
Console.Write("Enter the first replacement string (a name) : ");
String strTmp1 = Console.ReadLine();
Console.Write("Enter the second replacement string (a place) : ");
String strTmp2 = Console.ReadLine();
Console.Write("Enter a numeral : ");
String strTmp3 = Console.ReadLine();
int intTmp = int.Parse(strTmp3);
Console.WriteLine("the modified string :" + String.Format(strTmp,
strTmp1, strTmp2, intTmp));
```

Figure 20.1: Output of Formatted String

The GetHashCode function returns the hash code(a 32-bit signed integer value) for the string:

```
Console.WriteLine("Hash of '"+ objString + "' is : " + objString.GetHashCode());
```

If you want to insert a string into the middle of another string, you can use the Insert method. The Insert method is illustrated in Listing 20.28 by having the user enter a string to be inserted into an existing string at a chosen position.

Listing 20.28—String.Insert

```
Console.WriteLine("the original string : " + objString);
```

```
Console.Write("Enter the string to be inserted : ");
string strTmp = Console.ReadLine();
Console.Write("Enter the position where it has to be inserted :");
int intTmp = int.Parse(Console.ReadLine());
objString = objString.Insert(intTmp, strTmp);
Console.WriteLine("the modified string : " + objString);
```

The Join function joins two strings and string arrays into one body:

- String.Join(string *str*, string[] strarr) joins the string arrays using *str*.
- String.Join(string *str*, string[] strarr, int *i*, int *j*) joins the string arrays using *str*, starting from the *i*th array element and continuing *j* number of elements after it.

The StartsWith method is similar to the EndsWith method, except it verifies that a substring exists at the beginning of the parent string. As shown in Listing 20.29, the StartsWith function returns a Boolean value indicating whether the string starts with a string entered by the user.

Listing 20.29—String.StartsWith

```
Console.WriteLine("The original string : " + objString);
Console.Write("Enter the string to search for :");
string strTmp = Console.ReadLine();
if (objString.StartsWith(strTmp))
  Console.WriteLine("The string '" + objString + "' starts with '" + strTmp +
"'.");
else
  Console.WriteLine("The string '"+objString+"' does not start with '" + strTmp +
"'.");
```

The SubString function retrieves a part of the string from the original string:

- String.Substring(int *i*) retrieves the string starting from *i* (zero based).
- String.Substring(int *i*,int *j*) retrieves the string starting from *i* and having a length *j*.

The Split function splits a string delimited with some specified characters. It identifies the substrings that are delimited by one or more characters specified in an array, then returns these substrings in a string array. Delimiter characters are not included in the substrings. The Split function has forms like this:

- string[] Split(params char[])
- string[] Split(params char[] separator)

The Split function returns one of these:

- An array consisting of a single element containing the entire string if the string contains none of the characters in the separator list.
- An array of substrings if the string is delimited by one or more of the characters specified in the separator list passed in the Split method.
- An array of substrings in a string delimited by white space characters if those characters occur and the separator array passed is a null reference or contains no delimiter characters.
- String.Empty (a static read-only field that represents the empty string) where two separator are adjacent or a separator is found at the beginning or end of the string.

For example, if we want to split string *38, \n29, 57* with a character array separator list containing comma and space characters, we will get "38", "", "29", "", "57" as string array elements returned.

Or, if we want to split string "38..29..57" with the character array delimiter list containing a period '.', we will get "38", "", "29", "", "57" as string array elements.

The Trim function removes white space characters or specified characters from the beginning and end of the string:

- String.Trim() removes white space characters from the beginning and end of the string.
- String.Trim(char[] *c*) removes all occurances of a set of characters in the array from the beginning and end of the string.

As demonstrated in Listing 20.30, the TrimEnd function removes all occurrences of the set of characters in the array from the end of the string.

Listing 20.30—String.TrimEnd

```
Console.WriteLine("The original string is : " + objString);
Console.Write("Enter the character array : ");
char[] c = Console.ReadLine().ToCharArray();
Console.WriteLine("The modified string is : " +
  objString.TrimEnd(c));
```

As demonstrated in Listing 20.31, the TrimStart function removes all occurrences of the set of characters in the array from the beginning of the string.

Listing 20.31—String.TrimStart

```
Console.WriteLine("The original string is : " + objString);
Console.Write("Enter the character array : ");
char[] c = Console.ReadLine().ToCharArray();
Console.WriteLine("The modified string is : " +
  objString.TrimStart(c));
```

The IndexOf function returns the index of the first occurence of a charcter or string in a given string. The search for the string stops when the required value is found or when the end of the string is reached. The function returns the index if the value is found or -1 if it is not found. The IndexOf function has these forms:

- IndexOf(char *c*) returns the occurence *c* in the string.
- IndexOf(string *str*) returns the occurence of *str* in the string.
- IndexOf(char *c*, int *i*) returns the occurence of *c* in the string, with the search starting from *i*.
- IndexOf(string *str*, int *i*) returns the occurence of *str* in the string, with the search starting from *i*.
- IndexOf(char *c*, int *i*, int *j*) returns the occurence of *c* in the string, with the search starting from *i* and examining *j* character positions.
- IndexOf(string *str*, int *i*, int *j*) returns the occurence of *str* in the string, with the search starting from *i* and examining *j* character positions.

The IndexOfAny function returns the index of the first occurence of any charcter of the character array in the given string. The search of the string stops when the required value is found or until the end of the string is reached. It returns the index if the value is found or -1 if it is not found. The IndexOfAny function has these forms:

- IndexOfAny(char[] *c*) returns the occurence of any character of the array in the string.
- IndexOfAny(char[] *c*, int *i*) returns the occurence of any character of the array in the string, with the search starting from *i*.

- IndexOfAny(char[] *c*, int *i*, int *j*) returns the occurence of any character of the array in the string, with the search starting from *i* and examining *j* character positions.

Custom String Methods

Below are some custom string methods for C# that are found in VB.NET and various scripting languages: PCase, Replace, ToSingleSpace, CharCount, Reverse, Left, Right, and IsPalindrome. These methods are useful in common string operations. Since the .NET Framework does not natively include these methods, you can use the methods in Listing 20.32 to build your own "super string" class. Let's start with the code, then explain it in detail.

Listing 20.32—Strings. cs, Auxiliary Custom String Methods

```
// Auxiliary custom String methods

using System;

class MyString
{
  public static void Main()
  {
    String strData="WeLcOmE tO c#.eNjoy FoLkS";
    Console.WriteLine("String Value: {0}",strData);
    Console.WriteLine("PCase Equivalent: {0}",PCase(strData));
    Console.WriteLine("Reverse Equivalent: {0}",Reverse(strData));
    Console.WriteLine("Is 'rotator'  PalinDrome: {0}",IsPalindrome("rotator"));
    Console.WriteLine("Is 'visualc#' PalinDrome: {0}",IsPalindrome("visualc#"));
    Console.WriteLine("Left(string,5): {0}",Left(strData,5));
    Console.WriteLine("Right(String,6): {0}",Right(strData,6));
    Console.WriteLine("CharCount(CharCount,c):
        {0}",CharCount("Charcount","C"));
    Console.WriteLine("CharCount(CharCount,c,true):
        {0}",CharCount("Charcount","C",true));
    Console.WriteLine("CharCount(CharCount,d,true):
        {0}",CharCount("Charcount","d",true));
    Console.WriteLine("ToSingleSpace('welcome   to     C      Sharp
        '): {0}",ToSingleSpace("welcome   to      C      Sharp      "));
    Console.WriteLine("Replace(aaaaaa,aa,a):
              {0}",Replace("aaaaaa","aa","a"));
  }

  // Convert String to ProperCase
  public static String PCase(String strParam)
  {
    String strProper = strParam.Substring(0,1).ToUpper();
    strParam = strParam.Substring(1).ToLower();
    String strPrev = "";

    for(int iIndex=0; iIndex < strParam.Length; iIndex++)
    {
      if(iIndex > 1)
      {
        strPrev = strParam.Substring(iIndex-1, 1);
      }
      if( strPrev.Equals(" ") ||
          strPrev.Equals("\t") ||
          strPrev.Equals("\n") ||
          strPrev.Equals("."))
      {
        strProper += strParam.Substring(iIndex,1).ToUpper();
      }
      else
      {
        strProper += strParam.Substring(iIndex, 1);
      }
```

```
    }
    return strProper;
  }

  // Replace string with a found string in the source string
  public static String Replace(String strText, String strFind, String
strReplace)
  {
    int iPos = strText.IndexOf(strFind);
    String strReturn = "";
    while(iPos != -1)
    {
      strReturn += strText.Substring(0,iPos) + strReplace;
      strText = strText.Substring(iPos + strFind.Length);
      iPos = strText.IndexOf(strFind);
    }
    if(strText.Length > 0)
      strReturn += strText;
    return strReturn;
  }

  // Trim the string to contain only a single whitepace between words
  public static String ToSingleSpace(String strParam)
  {
    int iPosition=strParam.IndexOf("  ");
    if(iPosition == -1)
    {
      return strParam;
    }
    else
    {
      return ToSingleSpace(strParam.Substring(0, iPosition) +
strParam.Substring(iPosition + 1));
    }
  }

  // Count the number of occurrences of a substring in a source string
  // case sensitive
  public static int CharCount(String strSource, String strToCount)
  {
    int iCount = 0;
    int iPos = strSource.IndexOf(strToCount);
    while(iPos != -1)
    {
      iCount++;
      strSource = strSource.Substring(iPos + 1);
      iPos = strSource.IndexOf(strToCount);
    }
    return iCount;
  }

  // Count the number of occurrences of a substring in a source string
  // case insensitive
  public static int CharCount(String strSource, String strToCount, bool
IgnoreCase)
  {
    if(IgnoreCase)
    {
      return CharCount(strSource.ToLower(), strToCount.ToLower());
    }
    else
    {
      return CharCount(strSource, strToCount);
    }
  }

  // Reverse the String passed
```

```
public static String Reverse(String strParam)
{
  if(strParam.Length == 1)
  {
    return strParam;
  }
  else
  {
    return Reverse(strParam.Substring(1)) + strParam.Substring(0, 1);
  }
}

// Get a number of characters of a string from the beginning
public static String Left(String strParam, int iLen)
{
  if(iLen > 0)
    return strParam.Substring(0, iLen);
  else
    return strParam;
}

// Get a number of characters of a string from then end
public static String Right(String strParam, int iLen)
{
  if(iLen > 0)
    return strParam.Substring(strParam.Length - iLen, iLen);
  else
    return strParam;
}

// Test if the string is Palindrome
public static bool IsPalindrome(String strParam)
{
  int iLength, iHalfLen;
  iLength = strParam.Length - 1;
  iHalfLen = iLength / 2;
  for(int iIndex = 0; iIndex <= iHalfLen; iIndex++)
  {
    if(strParam.Substring(iIndex, 1) != strParam.Substring(iLength -
iIndex, 1))
    {
      return false;
    }
  }
  return true;
}
}
```

The PCase method converts a string to proper case, capitalizing each word's first character. It distinguishes words using whitespace characters such as space, tab, line feed, and carriage return characters (' ', '\t', '\n', '\r'). Its usage is PCase(*String*).

The Replace method replaces strings with string phrases and characters. This function finds characters passed in the second argument within the source string in the first argument and replaces them with characters in the third argument. Its usage is Replace(*Source*, *Find*, *Replacement*). For example, Replace("abc","b","d") will return "adc".

The ToSingleSpace function converts multiple whitespace characters to single whitespace characters. Its usage is ToSingleSpace(*SourceString*). For example, ToSingleSpace("Welcome to   C#") will return "Welcome to C#".

The CharCount method returns the number of occurrences of a substring in the main string. CharCount has two overloads: one for case-sensitive operations and the other for case-insensitive operations. For case-insensitive operations, CharCount simply converts both string and substring parameters to full lowercase, then calls the case-sensitive CharCount method. The CharCount method can be useful for string-parsing operations. CharCount usages are CharCount(*Source*, *Find*) or CharCount(*Source*, *Find*, true). For example, CharCount("aaaaac", "a") and CharCount("aaaaac","A", true) will return 5, but CharCount("aaaaac", "A") and CharCount("aaaaac", "A", false) will return 0.

The Reverse method reverses and returns the characters in a string argument. Its usage is Reverse(*Source*). For example, Reverse("abc") will return *cba*.

The Left method returns a certain number of characters from the beginning, or left side, of the string. Its usage is Left(*Source*, *CharCount*). For example, Left("Welcome", 3) will return *Wel*.

The Right method returns a certain number of characters from the end, or right side, of the string. Its usage is Right(*Source*, *CharCount*). For example, Right("Welcome", 2) will return *me*.

The IsPalindrome function returns whether the passed string is a palindrome—reading the same backward as forward. Its usage is IsPalindrome(*Source*). For example, IsPalindrome("abc") will return false, whereas IsPalindrome("121") will return true.

String Encoding/Decoding and Conversions

All strings in a .NET Framework program are stored as 16-bit Unicode characters. At times you might need to convert from Unicode to some other character encoding, or from some other character encoding to Unicode. The .NET Framework provides several classes for encoding (converting Unicode characters to a block of bytes in another encoding) and decoding (converting a block of bytes in another encoding to Unicode characters).

The System.Text namespace has a number of Encoding implementations:

- The ASCIIEncoding class encodes Unicode characters as single 7-bit ASCII characters. This class supports only character values between U+0000 and U+007F.
- The UnicodeEncoding class encodes each Unicode character as two consecutive bytes. This supports both little-endian (code page 1200) and big-endian (code page 1201) byte orders.
- The UTF7Encoding class encodes Unicode characters using UTF-7 encoding (UTF-7 stands for UCS Transformation Format, 8-bit form). This supports all Unicode character values and can also be accessed as code page 65000.
- The UTF8Encoding class encodes Unicode characters using UTF-8 encoding (UTF-8 stands for UCS Transformation Format, 8-bit form). This supports all Unicode character values and can also be accessed as code page 65001.

Each of these classes has methods for both encoding (such as GetBytes) and decoding (such as GetChars) a single array all at once. In addition, each supports GetEncoder and GetDecoder, which return encoders and decoders capable of maintaining shift state so they can be used with streams and blocks.

Listing 20.33 shows various forms of the Encoding class.

Listing 20.33—Encoding and Decoding

```
// writing
FileStream fs = new FileStream("text.txt", FileMode.OpenOrCreate);
StreamWriter t = new StreamWriter (fs, Encoding.UTF8);
```

```
t.Write("This is in UTF8");

//or

// reading
FileStream fs = new FileStream("text.txt", FileMode.Open);
StreamReader t = new StreamReader(fs, Encoding.UTF8);
String s = t.ReadLine();
```

Listing 20.34 makes a Web page request and then encodes the bytes returned/read as ASCII characters.

Listing 20.34—String Encoding

```
// encoding example

using System;
using System.Net;
using System.IO;
using System.Text;

class MyApp
{
  static void Main()
  {
   try
   {
    WebRequest theRequest =
     WebRequest.Create(@"http://www.mindcracker.com");
    WebResponse theResponse = theRequest.GetResponse();

    int BytesRead = 0;
    Byte[] Buffer = new Byte[256];// Buffer Size

    Stream ResponseStream = theResponse.GetResponseStream();
    BytesRead = ResponseStream.Read(Buffer, 0, 256);

    StringBuilder strResponse = new StringBuilder(@"");
    while (BytesRead != 0 )
    {
     // Returns an encoding for the ASCII (7 bit) character set
     // ASCII characters are limited to the lowest 128 Unicode
    // characters
     // , from U+0000 to U+007f.
       strResponse.Append(Encoding.ASCII.GetString(Buffer,
                          0,BytesRead));
     BytesRead = ResponseStream.Read(Buffer, 0, 256);
    }

    Console.Write(strResponse.ToString());
   }
   catch(Exception e)
   {
    Console.Write("Exception Occured!{0}", e.ToString());
   }
  }
}
```

Conversion Classes

You can convert one data type to another type using the Convert class. The Convert class has a number of static methods, beginning with *To* and ending with the target data type—for example, ToInt32 or ToByte. If successful, the returned instance is an object of the target data type. Not all conversions will be possible when using the Convert method, so use a try-catch block if you think you may get uncertain results.

Listing 20.35—Convert Class

```
Int32 intExample = 19;

// the methods inside convert...
Console.WriteLine("Convert.ToString, result = {0}", Convert.ToString(intExample));
Console.WriteLine("Convert.ToBoolean, result = {0}",
Convert.ToBoolean(intExample)); //displays True
Console.WriteLine("Convert.ToByte, result = {0}", Convert.ToByte(intExample));
Console.WriteLine("Convert.ToChar, result = {0}", Convert.ToChar(intExample));
Console.WriteLine("Convert.ToDouble, result = {0}", Convert.ToDouble(intExample));
```

If you want to convert strings into dates, you can use the Parse method for the DateTime data type or you can use the ToDateTime method. Both achieve the same objective. Because users sometimes incorrectly enter dates, don't forget to include appropriate exception handling to make sure that any conversion errors are caught. If you want to provide more control over parsing a date, use the ParseExact method.

CultureInfo Class

As shown in Listing 20.36, the CultureInfo class contains cultural information like DisplayName, Calendar, and various official abbreviations.

Listing 20.36—CultureInfo Class

```
CultureInfo c = new CultureInfo("tr");
Console.WriteLine ("The CultureInfo is set to: {0}", c.DisplayName);
Console.WriteLine ("The parent culture is: {0}", c.Parent.DisplayName);
Console.WriteLine ("The three leter ISO language name is: {0}",
c.ThreeLetterISOLanguageName);
Console.WriteLine ("The default calendar for this culture is: {0}\n\n",
c.Calendar.ToString());
```

As demonstrated in Listing 20.37, the RegionInfo class contains regional information, including DisplayName, currency information, and official abbreviations. RegionInfo also contains a static property to retrieve the CurrentRegion.

Listing 20.37—RegionInfo Class

```
RegionInfo r = new RegionInfo("tr");
Console.WriteLine ("The name of this region is: {0}", r.Name);
Console.WriteLine ("The currency symbol for the region is: {0}", r.CurrencySymbol);
Console.WriteLine ("Is this region metric : {0} \n\n", r.IsMetric);
```

StringBuilder Class

A StringBuilder object is not a string but rather an auxiliary object used for manipulating characters. It contains a buffer, typically initialized with a string but usually larger than that string. This buffer can be manipulated in place without creating a new string: You can insert, append, remove, and replace characters. When you're done manipulating the characters, use StringBuilder's ToString method to extract the finished string from it.

Both String and StringBuilder contain Unicode characters of type Char and support an indexer that returns Char. Because the String class is immutable, its indexer is read-only, but the StringBuilder indexer is readable/writeable. Listing 20.38 illustrates how to manipulate characters with the StringBuilder class and then place the characters into a String object.

Listing 20.38—StringBuilder Class Manipulation

```
StringBuilder MyOtherName = new StringBuilder("Hello");
MyOtherName.Remove(2, 3); // produces "He"
MyOtherName.Insert(2, "lp");  // produces "Help"
MyOtherName.Replace('l', 'a'); // produces "Heap"
MyName = MyOtherName.ToString();
```

You can use either String or StringBuilder for string operations. Deciding which to use depends on the frequency of the string modification. If you modify the string frequently—in operations like reassigning, appending, removing, and replacing some characters—you should choose the StringBuilder class. However, if your methods do not change the string value much, registering the String class to the .NET Framework's internal string table will save space in memory for duplicate strings. The framework also provides you faster access to string literal values stored in variables. The .NET Framework automatically handles these operations behind the scenes for you.

For example, whenever you modify a string in the String class, the methods of the String class returns a new string as the result. Creating many String objects might degrade the performance of your program. You can avoid creating a new instance of a string by using the StringBuilder class.

Let's say you want to concatenate two strings. Here is the traditional way using the System.String class:

```
string str1 = "I like ";
string str2 = "Soccer";
string strConcat = string.Concat(str1, str2);
```

The value of strConcat is *I like Soccer*. You can use the StringBuilder class and its Append method to do the same thing:

```
StringBuilder MyStrBuilder = new StringBuilder ("I like ");
String newStr = "Soccer";
MyStrBuilder.Append(newStr);
```

The value of MyStrBuilder is *I like Soccer*.

You can use the String and StringBuilder classes whenever required and also write auxilliary functions for both classes by providing static helper functions. For example, by default StringBuilder does not provide the IndexOf member function, which does a linear search for a character in a string. But Listing 20.39 shows how you can create your own custom IndexOf function.

Listing 20.39—StringBuilder IndexOf

```
// Example IndexOf function for StringBuilder class
using System;
using System.Text;
public class App
{
        public static int sbIndexOf(StringBuilder sb, char ch)
        {
                Int32 intVal1 = -1;
                while( ++intVal1 < sb.Length )
                {
                        if(sb[intVal1] == ch)
                        {
```

```
                            return intVal1;
                        }
                }
                return -1;
        }

        // string is an alias for System.String in the .NET Framework.
public static void Main(string[] args)
{
        StringBuilder sb1 = new StringBuilder(@"Hello There");
        Console.Write("{0}", App. sbIndexOf(sb1, 'o'));
}

}
```

Let's look at the subtle difference between String and StringBuilder when passed to a Win32 API function that takes a string. GetWindowText, defined in Windows.h . LpString, points to a buffer of size nMaxCount. That means, before calling GetWindowText, we are expected to allocate a buffer for the pointer of nMaxCount characters:

```
int GetWindowText(
  HWND hWnd,          // handle to window or control
  LPTStr lpString,    // text buffer
  int nMaxCount       // maximum number of characters to copy
);
```

A fixed-length changeable character buffer must be passed to unmanaged code since LPTStr is a pointer to a character (it is either char* or wchar*, depending on the code compilation choice, ANSI or Unicode). Simply passing a string does not work in this case because GetWindowText cannot modify the contents of the passed buffer. Even if the string is passed by reference, GetWindowText cannot initialize the buffer to a given size.

The solution in this case is to pass a StringBuilder as the argument in place of a String since a StringBuilder instance can be modified by GetWindowText. Keep in mind that the StringBuilder instance should not exceed the capacity of the StringBuilder. The StringBuilder will be initialized to a fixed length before calling GetWindowText. If you initialize a StringBuilder with a capacity of N, the unmanaged code marshaler uses a buffer of size $(N + 1)$ characters. StringBuilder does not have a null terminator, while the unmanaged string pointer does.

Listing 20.40 is the code for passing a StringBuilder instance to the GetWindowText API.

Listing 20.40—GetWindowText in .NET DLL Import

```
public class Win32API
{
[DllImport("User32.Dll")]
public static extern void GetWindowText(IntPtr handle, StringBuilder s,
int nMaxCount);

public String GetText(IntPtr handle)
        {
                StringBuilder sb = new StringBuilder(256);
                GetWindowText(handle, sb, sb.Capacity);
                return sb.ToString();
        }

private void TestGetText()
  {
        MessageBox.Show(GetText(Handle));
  }
```

}

Listing 20.41 illustrates StringBuilder usage when building SQL queries. The code segment connects to a Microsoft SQL Server Pubs database, which is installed by default as an example database with predefined options. You'll need to change the SqlClient constructor for use of the example on your computer.

Listing 20.41—StringBuilder Class

```
//stringbuilder

using System;
using System.Data;// for ADO.Net
using System.Data.SqlClient; // for SQL
using System.IO;            // for FileStream class
using System.Text;          // for StringBuilder class

public class WriteXML
{ public static void Main()
  {
      // Build a connection
      SqlConnection myConn =
            new SqlConnection("server=vesnet27;uid=sa;pwd=;database=Pubs");
      // Build the SQL string
      StringBuilder mySql = new StringBuilder("SELECT emp_id, fname, lname,
        hire_date ");
      mySql.Append("FROM employee ");
      mySql.Append("WHERE lname LIKE 'A%' ");
      mySql.Append("ORDER BY lname");
      Console.WriteLine(mySql);

      // Build the DataSet Command object
      SqlCommand myCmd = new SqlCommand(mySql.ToString(), myConn);

       // Build the DataSet
      DataSet myDs = new DataSet();

      SqlDataAdapter adapter = new SqlDataAdapter();
      adapter.SelectCommand = myCmd;
      // Fill the DataSet with a dataset table named "Products"
      adapter.Fill(myDs);

      // Get a FileStream object
      FileStream myFs =
          new FileStream("myXmlData.xml",FileMode.OpenOrCreate,FileAccess.Write);

      // Use the WriteXml method of DataSet object to write an XML file from
        // the DataSet
      myDs.WriteXml(myFs);
      myFs.Close();
      Console.WriteLine("File Written");
  }
}
```

The program in Listing 20.41, has this output:

```
SELECT emp_id, fname, lname, hire_date FROM employee WHERE lname LIKE 'A%' ORDER BY
lname File Written
```

Regular Expressions

A regular expression is a string of characters that contains a pattern to find the string or strings you are looking for. In its simplest form, a regular expression is just a word or phrase to search for in the source string. Regular expressions include metacharacters which are special characters that add a great deal of flexibility and convenience to the search.

Regular expressions have their origins in automata theory and formal language theory, which study models of computation automata and ways to describe and classify formal languages. In theoretical computer science, a formal language is nothing but a set of strings.

In the 1940s, two mathematicians, Warren McCulloch and Walter Pitts, described the nervous system by modeling neurons. Later, mathematician Stephen Kleene described these models using his mathematical notation called *regular sets* and developed regular expressions as a notation for describing them.

Afterward, Ken Thompson, one of the key creators of the Unix Operating System, built regular expressions into Unix-based text tools like qed, (predecessor of the Unix ed) and grep. Since then, regular expressions have been widely used in Windows and Unix.

Patterns

Let's examine two regular expression patterns:

```
Pattern#1 Regex objNotNaturalPattern=new Regex("[^0-9]");
Pattern#2 Regex objNaturalPattern=new Regex("0*[1-9][0-9]*");
```

Pattern #1 will match for strings other than those containing numbers from 0 to 9 (^ = not). (Use brackets to give range values, such as 0–9, a–z, or A–Z.) For example the string *abc* will return true when you apply the regular expression for pattern #1, but the string *123* will return false for this same pattern.

Pattern #2 will match for strings that contain only natural numbers (numbers that are always greater than 0). The pattern *0** indicates that a natural number can be prefixed with any number of zeroes or no zeroes at all. The next pattern, *[1-9]*, means that it should contain at least one integer between 1 and 9 (including 1 and 9). The next pattern, *[0-9]**, indicates that it should end with any number of integers between 0 and 9. For example, *0007* returns true, whereas *00* returns false.

Here are basic pattern metacharacters used by RegEx:

- * = zero or more
- ? = zero or one
- ^ = not
- [] = range

Metacharacters

The period is a widely used wildcard metacharacter. It matches exactly one character and does not care what the character is. For example, the regular expression *5,.-AnyString* will match *5,8-AnyString* and *5,9-AnyString.* The period will not match a string of characters or the null string. Thus, *5,800-AnyString* and *5,-AnyString* will not be matched by the regular expression above.

What if you want to search for a string containing a period? For example, we may wish to search for references to the mathematical constant *pi*. Bear in mind that the regular expression *3.14* would match *3.14*, *3914*, *3g14*, and even *3*14*.

We can get around this with a second metacharacter, the backslash, which indicates that the character following it must be taken as a literal character. If we want to search for the string *3.14*, we would use *3\.14*. In regular expression terminology, this operation is called *quoting*, and the period in the regular expression is said to be *quoted*.

Be careful when using the backslash to quote since it has another function when used in escape sequences: such as \n, \r, \t, \f, \b, \B, \0, \1, \2, \3, \4, \5, \6, \7, \8, and \9. Note that these are forbidden search strings in regular expressions. You should quote a metacharacter that turns the search character(e.g. \..) into a normal character, but be careful when you quote a normal character(e.g. \9) that may turn the search string into a metacharacter.

The question mark indicates that the character immediately preceding it either appears zero or one time. For example, *A?nyString* would match either *nyString* and *AnyString; Another?String* would match either *AnotheString* and *AnotherString*.

The star, or asterisk, indicates that the character to its left can be repeated zero or any number of times. For example, *XY*Z* would match *XZ, XYZ, XYYZ, XYYYZ*, or *XYYYYYYYYZ*. In other words, any string is satisfactory if it starts with an *X*, is followed by a sequence of any number of *Y* characters, and ends with a *Z*.

The plus metacharacter is just like the star metacharacter except that it doesn't match the null string. For example, *XY+Z* would not match *XZ* but would match *XYZ, XYYZ, XYYYZ*, or *XYYYYYYYYZ*.

Many metacharacters can be combined. A practical combination is the period followed by the star, which matches a string of any length, even the null string. For example, *AnyString.*ade* would match *AnyStringFecade, AnyStringFacade, AnyString of steel made*, and even *AnyStringade*. It matches any string starting with *AnyString*, followed by any string or the null string, and ending with *ade*.

If you want to search for *AnyStringDecade* and *AnyStringFacade* but do not want to match *AnyString of steel made*, you could string together three periods: *AnyString...ade*. Only strings 15 characters long which start with *AnyString* and end with *ade* will be matched.

Now, with *x\.*z* you will match any string that starts with *x*, is followed by a series of periods or no period, and ends with *z*—for example, *xz, x.z, x..z*, or *x...z*.

The expression *x.*z* will match any string that starts with *x*, is followed by one arbitrary character, and ends with **z*: *xf*z, x9*z, x@*z*. The expression *x\++z* will match any string that starts with *x*, is followed by one or a series of plus signs, and is terminated by *z*. Thus, *xz* is not matched, but *x+z, x++z*, and *x+++z* are.

The expression *b.?t* will match *but, bat, bot*, and any other three-character string that begins with *b* and ends with *t*, and will also match *bt*. The expression *b\.?t* will match only *bt* and *b.t*. The expression *b.\?t* will match any four-character string that starts with *b* and ends with *?t*: *bu?t, b9?t, b@?t*. The expression *b\.\?t* will match only *b.?t*.

We mentioned that the backslash can turn ordinary characters into metacharacters and vice versa. One example is the digit metacharacter, \d, which will match exactly one digit. For example, *5,\d-AnyString* will match *5,5-AnyString* and *5,9-AnyString*. Also, *5\.\d\d\d\d* will match any five-digit floating-point number from 5.0000 to 5.9999.

We can combine the the digit metacharacter with other metacharacters. For example, *x\d+z* will match any string that starts with *x*, is followed by a string of numbers, and ends with *z*. Note that since the plus sign is used, the expression will not match *az*.

In the digit metacharacter, the letter *d* must be lowercase because the nondigit metacharacter, \D, uses the uppercase *D*. The nondigit metacharacter will match any character except a digit. For example, *x\Dz* will match *xyz*, *xYz*, or *x@z*, *but not x0z*, *x1z*, or *a9z*. Most metacharacters using a backslash take the inverse meaning with an uppercase letter.

The word metacharacter, \w, matches exactly one letter, one number, or the underscore character. Its inverse, \W, matches any one character except a letter, a number, or the underscore. For example, *x\wz* will match *xyz*, *xYz*, *x9z*, *x_z*, or any other three-character string that starts with *x*, has a second character that is either a letter, a number, or the underscore, and ends with *z*.

The white-space metacharacter, \s, matches exactly one character of white space—spaces, tabs, new lines, or any other character that cannot be seen when printed. Its opposite, \S, matches any character that is not white space. For example, *x\sz* will match any three-character string that starts with *x*, has a second character that is a space, tab, or new line, and ends with *z*. The expression *x\Sz* will match any three-character string that starts with *x*, has a second character that is not a space, tab, or new line, and ends with *z*.

The word-boundary metacharacter, \b, matches whole words bounded by spaces or punctuation that have the same beginning. Its opposite, \B, matches whole words that have a different beginning. For example, *\bcommut* will match *commuter* or *commuting*, but will not match *telecommuter* since there is no space or punctuation between *tele* and *commuter*. The expression *\Bcommut* will not match a word like *commuter* or *commuting* unless it is part of a larger word such as *telecommuter* or *telecommuting*. The underscore is considered a "word" character. For example, *tele\bcommuter* will not match *tele_commuter*, but would match *tele commuter* and *tele-commuter*.

The octal metacharacter, \nnn, where *n* is a number from zero to seven, is generally used to specify control characters that have no typed equivalent. For example, *\007* will match an embedded ASCII bell character, the ASCII value of 7.

The braces metacharacter follows a normal character and contains two numbers separated by a comma and surrounded by braces. It acts like the star metacharacter, but the length of the string it matches must be within the minimum and maximum length specified by the two numbers in braces. For example, *xy{3,5}y* will match only *xyyyz*, *xyyyyz*, and *xyyyyyz*. The expression *.{2,4}ade* will match *cascade*, *facade*, *arcade*, or *decade*, but not *fade* since *f* is only one character long.

The vertical bar metacharacter indicates an either/or choice. For example, *mystery|myth|arcane* will match strings with either *mystery* or *myth* or *arcane* or any combination of all three.

The brackets metacharacter matches one occurence of any character inside the brackets. For example, *\s[bgh]ut\s* will match *but*, *gut*, and *hut*, but not *tut*, *xut*, or *zut*. The expression *5,[89]-AnyString* will match *5,8-AnyString* and *5,9-AnyString*, but not *5,88-AnyString*, *5,89-AnyString*, or *5,-AnyString*.

A range of characters within the brackets can be indicated with a hyphen, or dash. For example, *x[j-m]z* will match only *xjz*, *xkz*, *xlz*, and *xmz*. The expression *AnyFile0[7-9]* will match only *AnyFile07*, *AnyFile08*, and *AnyFile09*.

If you want to include a dash within brackets as one of the characters to match, simply put it before the right bracket. For example, *x[1234-]z* and *x[1-4-]z* will match the same strings: *x1z*, *x2z*, *x3z*, *x4z*, and *x-z*, but nothing else.

The bracket metacharacter can also be reversed by placing a caret metacharacter after the left bracket, letting you specify a range or list to exclude. For example, *AnyFile0[^02468]* will match any nine-character string that starts with *AnyFile0* and ends with anything except an even number. You can combine inversion and ranges as well. For example, *\W[^f-h]ood\W* will match any four-letter wording ending in *ood* except for *food*, *good*, or *hood*.

Within brackets, ordinary quoting rules do not apply and other metacharacters are not available. The only characters that can be quoted are the left and right brackets and the backslash. For example, *[\[\\\]]xyz* will match any four-character string that ends with *xyz* and starts with *[*, *]*, or **.

Perhaps the most powerful element of regular expression syntax is the backreference, where results of a subpattern are loaded into a buffer for reuse later in the expression. Parentheses identify backreference patterns, and the buffers are numbered as each begin parenthesis is encountered from left to right in the expression. Buffer numbers begin at 1 and continue up to a maximum of *n* subexpressions allowed by the .NET Framework:

- If you search *[abc]([def])* in *be*, the first backreference match will be *e*.
- If you search *([abc])([def])* in *be*, the first backreference match will be *b* and the second backreference match will be *e*.
- If you search *(ab(cd))ef* in *abcdef*, the first backreference match will be *abcd* and the second backreference match will be *cd*.
- If you search *(a)+b** in *aaaabbb*, the first backreference match will be *a*.
- If you search *(a+)b** in *aaaabbb*, the first backreference match will be *aaaa*.
- If you search *([abc])+* in *aaabbbc*, the first backreference match will be *c*.

You can access each buffer by using the form *\n*, where *n* is one- or two-decimal digits identifying a specific buffer: *\1* identifies the first buffer. For example, the regular expression *(\d)\1* could match *44*, *55*, or *99*, but wouldn't match *24* or *83*.

One of the simplest, most useful applications of backreferences is to locate the occurrence of two identical words together—for example, in *Were you drunk or sober last night night night?* The expression *\b([a-z]+) \1\b* will match *night night*.

To be complete, a backreference expression must be enclosed in parentheses. The expression *(\w(\1))* contains an invalid backreference since the first set of parentheses is not complete where the backreference appears.

Here is a more advanced example where we validate a URI (universal resource identifier), such as *http://www.mindcracker.com:8080/myfolder/index.html#content1*. The regular expression *(\w+)://([^/:]+)(:\d*)?([^#]*)* does the following:

- *(\w+)://* matches any word that precedes a colon and two forward slashes.
- *([^/:]+)* captures the domain address part: any sequence of characters that does not include the caret, forward slash, or colon.
- *(:\d*)* captures a Web site port number, if it is specified: zero or more digits following a colon.
- *([^#]*)* captures the subdirectory and the page address specified by the Web URI: one or more characters other than # or the space character.

The first backreference will be *http*, the second backreference will be *www.mindcracker.com*, the third backreference will be *:8080*, and the fourth backreference will be */myfolder/index.html*.

Backreferences allow for strings of data that change slightly from instance to instance—such as page numbering schemes. We may have a document that numbers each page with the notation *<page n="[some number]" id n="[some chapter name]">*; the number and the chapter name change from page to page, but the rest of the string stays the same. We can write a simple regular expression that matches these subpatterns:

```
<page n="\([0-9]+\)" id="\([A-Za-z]+\)">/Page \1, Chapter \2
```

Buffer number one (\1) holds the first matched sequence, ([0-9]+); buffer number two (\2) holds the second, ([A-Za-z]+).

Listing 20.42 shows the code for validating strings entered against various regular expression patterns.

Listing 20.42—Regular Expressions

```
//regular expressions

using System.Text.RegularExpressions;
using System;

class Validation
{

  public static void Main()
  {
    String strToTest;
    Validation objValidate=new Validation();

    Console.Write("Enter a String to Test for Natural Numbers:");
    strToTest = Console.ReadLine();
    if(objValidate.IsNaturalNumber(strToTest))
    {
      Console.WriteLine("{0} is a Valid Natural Number",
                          strToTest);
    }
    else
    {
      Console.WriteLine("{0} is not a Valid Natural Number",
                          strToTest);
    }

    Console.Write("Enter a String to Test for Whole Numbers:");
    strToTest = Console.ReadLine();
    if(objValidate.IsWholeNumber(strToTest))
    {
      Console.WriteLine("{0} is a Valid Whole Number", strToTest);
    }
    else
    {
      Console.WriteLine("{0} is not a Valid Whole Number",
                          strToTest);
    }

    Console.Write("Enter a String to Test for Integers:");
    strToTest = Console.ReadLine();
    if(objValidate.IsInteger(strToTest))
    {
      Console.WriteLine("{0} is a Valid Integer", strToTest);
    }
    else
    {
      Console.WriteLine("{0} is not a Valid Integer", strToTest);
    }

    Console.Write("Enter a String to Test for Positive Numbers:");
    strToTest = Console.ReadLine();
    if(objValidate.IsPositiveNumber(strToTest))
```

```csharp
    {
      Console.WriteLine("{0} is a Valid Positive Number",
                            strToTest);
    }
    else
    {
      Console.WriteLine("{0} is not a Valid Positive Number",
                            strToTest);
    }

    Console.Write("Enter a String to Test for Numbers:");
    strToTest = Console.ReadLine();
    if(objValidate.IsNumber(strToTest))
    {
      Console.WriteLine("{0} is a Valid Number", strToTest);
    }
    else
    {
      Console.WriteLine("{0} is not a Valid Number", strToTest);
    }

    Console.Write("Enter a String to Test for Alpha Numerics:");
    strToTest = Console.ReadLine();
    if(objValidate.IsAlphaNumeric(strToTest))
    {
      Console.WriteLine("{0} is a Valid Alpha Numeric", strToTest);
    }
    else
    {
      Console.WriteLine("{0} is not a Valid Alpha Numeric",
                            strToTest);
    }

    Console.Write("Enter a String to Test for Alphabets:");
    strToTest = Console.ReadLine();
    if(objValidate.IsAlpha(strToTest))
    {
      Console.WriteLine("{0} is a Valid Alpha String", strToTest);
    }
    else
    {
      Console.WriteLine("{0} is not a Valid Alpha String",
                            strToTest);
    }

}

// Function to test for Positive Integers
public bool IsNaturalNumber(String strNumber)
{
  Regex objNotNaturalPattern=new Regex("[^0-9]");
  Regex objNaturalPattern=new Regex("0*[1-9][0-9]*");
  return  !objNotNaturalPattern.IsMatch(strNumber) &&
          objNaturalPattern.IsMatch(strNumber);
}

// Function to test for Positive Integers with zero inclusive
  public bool IsWholeNumber(String strNumber)
  {
    Regex objNotWholePattern=new Regex("[^0-9]");
    return !objNotWholePattern.IsMatch(strNumber);
  }

  // Function to Test for Integers both Positive & Negative
  public bool IsInteger(String strNumber)
  {
    Regex objNotIntPattern=new Regex("[^0-9-]");
```

```
        Regex objIntPattern=new Regex("^-[0-9]+$|^[0-9]+$");
        return  !objNotIntPattern.IsMatch(strNumber) &&
                        objIntPattern.IsMatch(strNumber);
    }

  // Function to Test for Positive Number both Integer & Real
  public bool IsPositiveNumber(String strNumber)
  {
    Regex objNotPositivePattern=new Regex("[^0-9.]");
    Regex objPositivePattern=new Regex(
                        "^[.][0-9]+$|[0-9]*[.]*[0-9]+$");
    Regex objTwoDotPattern=new Regex("[0-9]*[.][0-9]*[.][0-9]*");
    return !objNotPositivePattern.IsMatch(strNumber) &&
          objPositivePattern.IsMatch(strNumber)   &&
          !objTwoDotPattern.IsMatch(strNumber);
  }

  // Function to test whether the string is valid number or not
  public bool IsNumber(String strNumber)
  {
    Regex objNotNumberPattern=new Regex("[^0-9.-]");
    Regex objTwoDotPattern=new Regex("[0-9]*[.][0-9]*[.][0-9]*");
    Regex objTwoMinusPattern=new Regex("[0-9]*[-][0-9]*[-][0-9]*");
    String strValidRealPattern=
                        "^([-]|[.]|[-.]|[0-9])[0-9]*[.]*[0-9]+$";
    String strValidIntegerPattern="^([-]|[0-9])[0-9]*$";
    Regex objNumberPattern =new Regex("(" + strValidRealPattern
        +")|(" + strValidIntegerPattern + ")");
    return !objNotNumberPattern.IsMatch(strNumber) &&
          !objTwoDotPattern.IsMatch(strNumber) &&
          !objTwoMinusPattern.IsMatch(strNumber) &&
          objNumberPattern.IsMatch(strNumber);
  }

  // Function To test for Alphabets.
  public bool IsAlpha(String strToCheck)
  {
    Regex objAlphaPattern=new Regex("[^a-zA-Z]");
    return !objAlphaPattern.IsMatch(strToCheck);
  }

  // Function to Check for AlphaNumeric.
  public bool IsAlphaNumeric(String strToCheck)
  {
    Regex objAlphaNumericPattern=new Regex("[^a-zA-Z0-9]");
    return !objAlphaNumericPattern.IsMatch(strToCheck);
  }

}
```

Split and Match Methods

There are a few significant RegEx methods:

The RegEx.Split method splits an input string into an array of substrings at the positions defined by a regular expression match.

The RegEx.Replace method replaces all occurrences of a character pattern defined by a regular expression with a specified replacement character string.

The RegEx.Matches method searches an input string for all occurrences of a regular expression and returns all the successful matches as if Match were called numerous times.

There is also a MatchCollection class that represents the set of successful matches found by iteratively applying a regular expression pattern to the input string.

Listing 20.43 illustrates the Split and Matches methods and the MatchCollection class.

Listing 20.43—Split and Match Examples

```
using System;
using System.Text.RegularExpressions;

public class RegExpSplit
{

    public static void Main(string[] args)
    {
        Console.WriteLine(@"Enter a split delimeter ( default is
                [0-9 a-z A-Z]* ) : ");
        metaExp = Console.ReadLine();
        Console.WriteLine(@"Enter a meta string: ");
        string [] rets = ParseExtnSplit(Console.ReadLine());
        if(rets == null)
        {
            Console.WriteLine("Sorry no match");
        }
        else
        {
            Console.WriteLine(rets.Length);
            foreach(string x in rets)
              Console.WriteLine(x);

        }

        Console.WriteLine(
         @"Enter a match pattern ( default is [0-9 a-z A-Z]* ) : ");
        metaExp = Console.ReadLine();
        Console.WriteLine(@"Enter a meta string: ");
        rets = ParseExtnMatch(Console.ReadLine());
        if(rets == null)
        {
            Console.WriteLine("Sorry no match");
        }
        else
        {
            Console.WriteLine(rets.Length);
            foreach(string x in rets)
              Console.WriteLine(x);

        }

    }

    public static string[] ParseExtnSplit(String ext)
    {
        Regex rx = new Regex(metaExp);

        return rx.Split(ext);
    }

    public static string[] ParseExtnMatch(String ext)
    {
        // case insensitive match
        Regex rx = new Regex(metaExp, RegexOptions.IgnoreCase);
        MatchCollection rez = rx.Matches(ext);
        string[] ret = null;
        if(rez.Count > 0)
        {
```

```
        ret = new string[rez.Count];
        for(int i=0;  i < rez.Count;i++)
        {
            ret[i] = rez[i].ToString();
        }
    }

    return ret;
}

private static string metaExp = "[0-9 a-z A-Z]*" ;
}
```

Summary

In this chapter we examined Array, ArrayList, String, StringBuilder, and regular expressions. An array in C# is simply a set of sequential memory locations that can be accessed using either indices or references. C# has a mechanism that prevents a program from writing outside the bounds of an array and destroying the contents of memory. The declaration of an array in C# simply sets aside the requisite block of memory and treats the name of the array as a synonym for the address of the beginning of the memory block.

Arrays can be single- or multidimensional. Rectangular arrays—what most of us are familiar with—may be single-dimensional or multidimensional. Jagged arrrays are nothing but arrays of arrays. The ArrayList class implements a collection of objects using an array whose size is dynamically increased as required. The ArrayList class is very useful if you are working with arrays and need to add, remove, or search data in a collection.

The String class is the string type in the .NET Framework. String objects are immutable, meaning once they're created their values cannot be changed. You can reassign the string reference to another string, freeing up the first string for garbage collection if no other reference to it exists.

A StringBuilder object is not a string but rather an auxiliary object used for manipulating characters. It contains a buffer, typically initialized with a string but usually larger than that string.

A regular expression is a string of characters used in searching for a matching string pattern. The RegEx class helps you split, match, and replace patterns found in strings. In the next chapter we will talk about the SOAP protocol and its role in .NET.

Chapter 21: Miscellaneous Topics

In this chapter we address some miscellaneous topics that were not treated in other chapters. We discuss the usage and advantages of System.Diagnostics classes, the Environment class, the Buffer class, the Math class, Reflection.Emit classes, the Random class, Windows registry classes, the Timer class, directory services, and Windows Management Instrumentation.

Diagnostics

The System.Diagnostics namespace provides classes that enable you to debug and trace code; start, stop, and kill processes; monitor system performance; and read and write event logs. Table 21.1 describes some System.Diagnostics namespace classes.

System.Diagnostic Class	Description
Debug	Provides methods used to help debug code.
Trace	Provides methods for tracing through code.
EventLog	Helps log messages to the Windows EventLog.
Process	Used to spawn processes on the system and start and stop system processes.

Table 21.1: System.Diagnostics Classes

The Process Class

The Process class retrieves various information pertaining to a process running on the system and caches the information in memory. This means that if your application requires up-to-date process information, you should frequently refresh the process cache by calling the Process.Refresh() method. In addition to simply retrieving the name of the current process, this class can provide more information, such as the following:

- Memory statistics
- Process times
- Thread statistics
- Handle statistics

Table 21.2 describes the members of this class.

Process Member	Description
BasePriority	Read-only property to obtain base priority.
EnableRaisingEvents	Boolean value that lets the Exited event be called when set to *true*.
ExitCode	An integer value that represents the status of the process when it terminates.
ExitTime	Represents a DateTime value—date and time of day—when the process terminates.
Handle	Represents the handle assigned to the process by the underlying operating system or virtual machine.
HandleCount	Represents the total number of open handles.
Id	Represents the unique identifier assigned to the process by the underlying operating system or virtual machine.
MachineName	Represents the computer name on which the process executes.
MaxWorkingSet	Used to manage maximum amount of memory pages in the program's virtual address space that have recently been referenced in terms of private and shared data.
MinWorkingSet	Used to manage minimum amount of memory pages in the program's virtual address space that have recently been referenced in terms of private and shared data.
Modules	Represents a collection of DLL and EXE files that have been loaded into the process.
PagedMemorySize	Represents the memory allocated that can be written to the paging file.
PrivilegedProcessorTime	Represents a TimeSpan value that has been spent at the operating system level.
ProcessName	Represents the process name used by the underlying operating system.
Responding	Represent a Boolean value that indicates whether the user interface associated with the process is alive.
StartTime	Represents a DateTime value that shows when the process was started.
TotalProcessorTime	Represents a TimeSpan value that is the sum of UserProcessorTime and PrivilegedProcessorTime that the CPU has spent for running the process.
UserProcessorTime	Represents a TimeSpan value that has been spent at the application level.
VirtualMemorySize	Represents the virtual memory associated with the process.
WorkingSet	Represents the total physical memory used by the process.
Close()	Terminates the process and releases all the opened resources.
GetCurrentProcess()	Returns a process object for the current process.
GetProcessById()	Returns a process object that is the unique process identifier running on the local computer or on a computer on the network.
GetProcesses()	Returns an array of process objects that are running on the local computer or on a computer on the network.
GetProcessesByName()	Returns an array of process objects that are the processes associated with the same executable file running on the local

Process Member	Description
	computer or on a computer on the network.
Kill()	Terminates the process immediately and abnormally.
Refresh()	Refreshes the properties of the process object that has been cached.
Start()	Launches and begins the process with the StartInfo parameters.
WaitForExit()	Specifies if the process will wait indefinitely or for a specified number of milliseconds to exit. This operation blocks the current thread execution.

Table 21.2: Process Class Members

Listing 21.1 illustrates how to get the current process from the Process class. In this case, the process would be the application name you gave to the following code(Listing 21-1) after the code is compiled into an assembly.

Listing 21.1—Getting a Current Process

```
using System;
using System.Diagnostics;

public class Test
{
 public static void Main ( String[] args )
  {
    Process CurrentProcess = Process.GetCurrentProcess() ;
    Console.WriteLine("ProcessName: {0}", CurrentProcess.ProcessName);
   }
}
```

Although you plan to enumerate processes currently running on the system, you may not be authorized to access process-specific information. If any of the Process class methods fail (usually with ACCESS_DENIED), that may throw an exception corresponding to the failure. For example:

System.ComponentModel.Win32Exception: Access is denied

It has a method named GetProcesses() that returns all running processes on the machine. The GetProcesses has two overloads: one for the local machine and another for the remote machine. To see processes on the local machine, use GetProcesses(); otherwise use GetProcesses(string machinename). Listing 21.2 shows how to list the first 20 running processes on your computer. You may opt to loop or enumerate through all the processes from the returned array, but here we just list 20.

Listing 21.2—Using GetProcess

```
using System;
using System.Diagnostics;

public class Test
{

 public static void Main ( String[] args )
  {

    Process[] procList =  Process.GetProcesses();

    // or you can specify a computer name
    // Process[] procList =  Process.GetProcesses(@"MCBcomputer");

    // output the first 20 processes in the array
```

```
    for ( int i=0; i<20; i++)
    {
        Console.WriteLine ("ProcessID: {0}", procList[i].Id);
        Console.WriteLine ("ProcessName: {0}", procList[i].ProcessName);
    }

  }
}
```

The Process class offers properties from which you can learn things about a process. You can also start a process, close it, and kill it if you have the right authorization. Listing 21.3 depicts some of the important process methods with inline comments.

Listing 21.3—Various Process Methods

```
// you can start process with Start method
process.Start();

// wait until the application is in an idle message loop state indefinitely
process.WaitForInputIdle();

// wait until the application is in an idle message loop state 500miliseconds
// process.WaitForInputIdle(500);

// try to close the application main window GUI.
// you cannot close processes on remote computers!
// use Close() for console and GUI-based applications!
// but always prefer using CloseMainWindow() for GUI apps!

if(!process.CloseMainWindow())
{
// you can Kill process with Kill method if you cannot close it
process.Kill();
}

// wait for the application to exit indefinitely or 500miliseconds
// process.WaitForExit();
// process.WaitForExit(500);
```

The EnterDebugMode method of the Process class puts the process in the debug state, and the LeaveDebugMode method forces the process to exit the debug state and return to the normal state.

Process Threads

A process consists of at least one thread, the primary execution thread, which can spawn more needed threads. You should limit the total number of threads because synchronization and context-switching operations can drain the performance of the thread actions. The number of threads you allow depends on your resources and code. Thus, at the outset, we recommend you limit the maximum concurrent threads to a modest number, but do leave the maximum number of threads option of your process as configurable via the registry or other means such as the application *.ini file. The application consumer can monitor the default application performance and then reduce or augment the maximum number of threads if fine-tuning is necessary.

All process threads share the address space of the primary execution thread. A thread is made up of code, data, and other resources such as open files, semaphores, and dynamically allocated memory. Process threads share process resources. Each thread has a private thread local storage (TLS) area for its memory operations. Threads run in various intervals inside a process according to priorities assigned by the code and operating system. An atomic system scheduler gives execution control to threads in a round-robin fashion. The threads are run in clockwise order, each thread running in a time slice inside a virtual ring. The system scheduler determines which threads should run and when, so you do not need to worry about this aspect of thread execution. However, threads with lower priority use less CPU cycles to execute their code than higher-priority threads. To balance the CPU load on systems with multiple CPUs, the system scheduler may opt to move some threads to other CPUs. Listing 21.4 shows how you can list the running processes and their spawned threads on your system.

Listing 21.4—Listing Threads

```
using System;
using System.Diagnostics;

public class Test
{

    public static void Main ( String[] args )
    {

        Process CurrentProcess = Process.GetCurrentProcess() ;
        ProcessThreadCollection threadList =  CurrentProcess.Threads;

        Console.WriteLine("ProcessName: {0}", CurrentProcess.ProcessName);

        foreach(ProcessThread thr in threadList)
        {
          Console.WriteLine ( "Thread ID: {0}", thr.Id);
         Console.WriteLine ( "Thread Priority Level: {0}", thr.PriorityLevel);
          Console.WriteLine ( "Thread Total Processor Time: {0}",
thr.TotalProcessorTime);
        }
    }
}
```

Debugging and Tracing

Among the many diagnostic classes the .NET Framework provides are the Debug and Trace classes. The Debug class helps us debug code, and the Trace class helps us trace the execution of code. The Debug class is intended for debug builds, and the Trace class is used for release builds.

Table 21.3 describe the members of the Debug and Trace classes.

Debug/Trace Class Members	Description
AutoFlush	Represents a Boolean value that when set to *true* is identical to calling the Flush method automatically after each write operation to the Listeners.
IndentLevel	An integer value to adjust the output indent level.
IndentSize	An integer value to adjust the number of indent white spaces.
Listeners	Specifies a collection of Listener objects that Debug/Trace will send output to.
Assert()	Checks whether a given Boolean condition is *false*.
Close()	Closes the Listener objects after flushing the outstanding buffer contents that have not been written yet.
Fail()	Outputs the error message and behaves as if you are calling Assert(*false*, error_message, detailed_error_message).
Flush()	Immediately serializes the outstanding buffer content to the Listeners.
Indent()	Adds one to the current indent level. It is identical to executing IndentLevel += 1.

Debug/Trace Class Members	Description
Unindent()	Substracts one from the current indent level. It is identical to executing IndentLevel -= 1.
Write()	Performs write operation to the Listeners.
WriteIf()	Performs write operation to the Listeners if the given boolean condition is *true*.
WriteLine()	Performs a write operation to the Listeners, adding a line terminator to the content.
WriteLineIf()	Performs a write operation to the Listeners, adding a line terminator to the content if the given Boolean condition is *true*

Table 21.3: Debug/Trace Class Members

You must define the DEBUG and TRACE compiler directives to activate debugging and tracing respectively. If you neglect to define either of these directives, Trace or Debug calls will be ignored during compilation. You can define these in Visual Studio .NET by choosing Properties from the Project menu.

It is generally recommended that you define TRACE in your code, since at a minimum, end users and administrators may turn on lightweight diagnostic tracing out in the field when they encounter a problem related to the application. Microsoft tends to deliver both versions of its applications, release and checked (or the debug) build. The checked build versions of commercial applications are larger in size and slower in performance than the release build versions, because they perform verbose and extensive logging to the computer disk to help you find the culprits or bugs in support issues. Both the Debug and Trace classes contain the exact same methods. But unlike Debug, Trace is meant for monitoring the application's well-being in the field. Even if you debugged things in your testing phase, you may find it difficult to find some of the fuzzy problems, particularly in distributed n-tier environments. For example, some types of problems arise only when the application is under an intense load, or the problems may occur randomly or intermittently. Tracing may prove more useful in finding these problems.

Although Debug and Trace have identical members, you should use Debug during development and Trace for diagnosing an application after deployment. The output methods of the Trace and Debug classes are Write(), WriteIf(), WriteLine(), and WriteLineIf(). WriteLine puts a carriage return and line feed (CRLF) on the end of the output, but Write does not. WriteIf and WriteLineIf are similar to Write and WriteLine respectively, but they provide conditional tracing capabilities since they trace only if the first parameter evaluates to *true*. The Indent() and UnIndent() methods of the Debug and Trace classes increase and decrease the current IndentLevel, which determines how much the output will be indented by one, respectively. The Fail() method of the Trace and Debug classes produces an error message so you can handle exceptions and errors during debugging more easily. The Flush() method of the Trace and Debug classes forces buffered data to pour to the Listeners collection immediately. We will talk about listeners later. The Close() method of the Trace and Debug classes performs a Flush() implicitly and then closes the Listeners. The Assert() method of the Trace and Debug classes evaluates the passed condition, then if the condition is *false,* it pours out its diagnostics messages into the Listeners collection. The Assert method has three overloads, as shown in Listing 21.5.

Listing 21.5—Assert Overloads

```
// Assert without description
Debug.Assert ( a > b );
```

```
// Assert with description
Debug.Assert ( a > b , "a is not greater than b" );

// Assert with description and more detail
Debug.Assert ( x > y , " x is not greater than y", "Assertion... y is less than
x");
```

Although there are many debug and trace methods, when in the past you used Microsoft Foundation Classes in Visual Studio 6, Microsoft made extensive use of methods similar to the Debug.Assert() and Trace.WriteLine() methods. You should consider that an implicit, but strong, recommendation for your code. You can enable debugging or tracing by adding a #define DEBUG or #define TRACE line to the top of your code or using the /d:DEBUG or /d:TRACE compiler switch when you compile. See the example in Listing 21.7.

The C# .NET compiler provides the following techniques to define compilation variables:

- *Compiler command-line switches.* For example, /define:DEBUG or /d:DEBUG;
  /define:TRACE or /d:TRACE.
- *Environment variables in the operating system shell.* For example, SET DEBUG=1, SET
  TRACE=1.
- *Pragmas in the source code.* For example, #define DEBUG to define the compilation
  variable or #undef DEBUG to undefine it; #define TRACE to define the compilation
  variable or #undef TRACE to undefine it.

Autoflush is used to automatically flush the output buffer after each write to the listeners if set to *true*. In the code you can enable it with a Debug.AutoFlush = true; statement.

IndentSize is the number of spaces in an indent, with the default being 4. The IndentLevel property and Indent() methods indent the content IndentSize times any and 1 respectively.
In the code you can enable it with a Debug.IndentSize = 6; statement.

Other than programmatic options, you can change your <Application>.EXE.CONFIG application configuration file such as in Listing 21.6 to set the AutoFlush and IndentSize properties.

Listing 21.6—Configuration file EXE.CONFIG

```
<configuration>
    <system.diagnostics>
        <debug autoflush="true" indentsize="6"/>
            <listeners>

            </listeners>
        </debug>
        <trace autoflush="true" indentsize="6"/>
            <listeners>

            </listeners>
        </trace>
    </system.diagnostics>
 </configuration>
```

The sample code in Listing 21.7 uses the configuration file shown in Listing 21.6 and outputs with Debug and Trace statements to the console.

Please note the following. Open the Debug Monitor utility (DbMon.exe) of the Platform SDK for Windows NT, 2000, and XP in a separate command prompt console before running the listing. DbMon.exe will show any debug and trace messages coming from any application running on your system that are sent to DefaultTraceListener (OutputDebugString application programming interface

[API] method of the Windows operating system). We will talk about TraceListener classes later. For now just know that Debug Monitor runs in its own console window and displays messages sent by your application using the OutputDebugString function. If you do not have or do not want to use DbMon.exe, uncomment the two following code lines to send debug and trace output to the console:

```
Debug.Listeners.Add(new TextWriterTraceListener(Console.Out));
Trace.Listeners.Add(new TextWriterTraceListener(Console.Out));
```

Listing 21.7—Using Debug and Trace

```
#define DEBUG // for debugging
//or
#define TRACE // for tracing

using System;
using System.IO;
using System.Diagnostics;

public class TraceListenerExample
{
 public static void Main()
  {

  // If you do not have DBMON.EXE, then to watch debug and trace messages,
  // make sure that the system will output debug and trace to the console.
  // Otherwise you cannot monitor Debug and Trace messages.
  // The DefaultTraceListener will output
  // to OutputDebugString of Windows operating systems.
  // We will talk about TraceListener classes later.

  // Debug.Listeners.Add(new TextWriterTraceListener(Console.Out));
  // Trace.Listeners.Add(new TextWriterTraceListener(Console.Out));


  // Indent by one IndentSize times 1. Indent this time 6 x 1 = 6!
  Debug.Indent();
  Trace.Indent();

  Debug.WriteLine("Debugged 1!");
  Trace.WriteLine("Traced 1!");

  bool bDebugTrace = false;
  // test for a boolean flag to output debug or trace.
  Debug.WriteLineIf(bDebugTrace, "Not Debugged 1!");
  Trace.WriteLineIf(bDebugTrace, "Not Traced 1!");

  bDebugTrace = true;
  // test for a boolean flag to output debug or trace.
  Debug.WriteLineIf(bDebugTrace, "Debugged 2!");
  Trace.WriteLineIf(bDebugTrace, "Traced 2!");

  // this is faster than WriteLineIf! So prefer the block below.
  if (bDebugTrace == true)
  {
   Debug.WriteLine("Debugged 3!");
   Trace.WriteLine("Traced 3!");
  }
  Console.Read();
 }
}
```

Conditional Debug Attributes

You can use a conditional attribute in front of the method declaration so your method is callable when the condition is *true*. Conditional attributes, like other C# attributes, do not put any burden on the code calling them. For example, in Listing 21.8, if you put *#define IwantDEBUG* at the top of your code or compile your code with the /D:IwantDEBUG option, then myMethod can be called. Otherwise, the Microsoft intermediate language code for the myMethod code will be omitted (not generated) in your final assembly.

Listing 21.8—Conditional Attribute Example 1 (debug1.cs)

```csharp
using System ;
using System.Diagnostics;

class Test
{

    [Conditional("IwantDEBUG")]
    public static void myMethod()
    {
        Console.WriteLine("only for conditional DEBUG..." );
    }

    public static void Main()
    {
        myMethod();
    }
}
```

Listing 21.9 is a more sophisticated example of using conditional attributes.

Listing 21.9—Conditional Attribute Example 2 (debug2.cs)

```csharp
using System;
using System.Diagnostics;

public class Debugging
{
        private int r = 0;

        public Debugging (int r)
        {
                this.r = r;
        }

        public int R
        {
                get { return r; }
                set { r = value;}
        }

        public static void Main()
        {
                methodA();
                methodB();
                methodC();
                methodD();
                methodE();
                methodF();
        }

        public static void methodA()
        {
                Console.WriteLine("Method A");
        }

        [Conditional("saygin")]
        public static void methodB()
        {
```

```
        Console.WriteLine("Method B - has [conditional(saygin)]");
    }

    public static void methodC()
    {
        Console.WriteLine("Method C");
    }

    public static void methodD()
    {
        Console.WriteLine("Method D");
    }

    [Conditional("alex")]
    public static void methodE()
    {
        Console.WriteLine("Method E - has [conditional(alex)]");
    }

    [Conditional("saygin"), Conditional("alex")]
    public static void methodF()
    {
        Console.WriteLine("Method F - has
        [conditional(saygin),conditional(alex)]");
    }
}
```

The Switch Class

A trace switch is a way to control tracing and debugging output at runtime using various settings. The Switch class is the parent of the BooleanSwitch and TraceSwitch classes. Despite our being able to derive and create custom switches, the BooleanSwitch and TraceSwitch classes will be satisfactory for our debugging and tracing needs. Table 21.4 describes two members of the Switch class.

Switch Member	Description
Description	Returns a detailed introduction text of the switch.
DisplayName	Returns the name of the switch. Mainly it is used for finding initial switch settings.

Table 21.4: Switch Class Members

The TraceSwitch class provides per assembly, per module, or per class tracing. This is more powerful and easier than the single-trace options because it lets you specify various output options at once. Therefore, the extreme debugging or tracing outputs do not overwhelm us with the various options that we have specified when we don't want them. Table 21.5 describes members of the TraceSwitch class. The TraceSwitch constructor takes two parameters: the descriptive display name ("descriptive trace switch name") and the switch name.

TraceSwitch Member	Description
Level	Specifies the Level value (Off, Error, Warning, Info, or Verbose) that will affect the detail of the messages to output for tracing and debugging.
TraceError	Returns *true* if Level is set to Error, Warning, Info, or Verbose.
TraceInfo	Returns *true* if Level is set to Info or Verbose.
TraceVerbose	Returns *true* if Level is set to Verbose.
TraceWarning	Returns *true* if Level is set to Warning, Info, or Verbose.

Table 21.5: TraceSwitch Class Members

We generally define the switches for the executable in the EXE.CONFIG configuration file (see Listing 21.10). The application configuration file name is <program>. Inside switch elements of the XML file, the "name" attribute refers to the switch name and the "value" attribute is the numerical value the corresponding trace level is set to. Note that we can also define the autoflush and the indent size parameters in the configuration file.

Listing 21.10—Switches defined in the EXE.CONFIG file

```
<?xml version="1.0" encoding="UTF-8" ?>
<configuration>
    <system.diagnostics>
        <switches>
            <add name="Switch1" value="3" />
            <add name="Switch2" value="2" />
        </switches>
        <!--additional diagnostics -->
        <trace autoflush="true" indentsize="3" />
    </system.diagnostics>
</configuration>
```

Each assembly should have its own trace switch.

Possible TraceSwitch tracing levels are as follows:

- 0—None
- 1—Errors only; TraceError
- 2—Warning (warnings and errors); TraceWarning
- 3—Info (warnings, errors, and information); TraceInfo
- 4—Verbose (all kinds of traces); TraceVerbose

An example is shown in Listing 21.11.

Listing 21.11—Using TraceSwitch

```
TraceSwitch MySwitch = new MySwitch ("Switch1",
                            "my switch1 at Info mode");

// do you see which one will run?
Trace.WriteLineIf ( MySwitch.TraceError ,
                    "Error tracing is on!" ) ;
Trace.WriteLineIf ( MySwitch.TraceWarning ,
                    "Warning tracing is on!" ) ;
Trace.WriteLineIf ( MySwitch.TraceInfo ,
                    "Info tracing is on!" ) ;
Trace.WriteLineIf ( MySwitch.TraceVerbose ,
```

```
"VerboseSwitching is on!" ) ;
```

Boolean switches can be used as a switch in your code to either turn on or turn off the printing of a debug statement. Possible BooleanSwitch tracing levels are as follows:

- 0—False; Disabled
- 1—True; Enabled

In Listing 21.12 we enable the Boolean switch in the XML-formatted application configuration file.

Listing 21.12—Enabling a Boolean switch in the EXE.CONFIG

```
<?xml version="1.0" encoding="UTF-8" ?>
<configuration>
    <system.diagnostics>
        <switches>
            <add name="Switch3" value="1" />
        </switches>
        <!—additional diagnostic settings -->
        <trace autoflush="true" indentsize="5" />
    </system.diagnostics>
</configuration>
```

The BooleanSwitch example in Listing 21.13 is set to the Verbose mode.

Listing 21.13—Using BoolSwitch

```
BooleanSwitch boolSwitch= new BooleanSwitch("Switch3", "my boolean switch");

Debug.WriteLine("DEBUG");
Trace.WriteLine("TRACE");

Trace.WriteLineIf(boolSwitch.Enabled, "boolSwitch");
```

We can also derive custom switch classes from the Switch class but generally do not need to do so.

TraceListener Classes

The Listener property of the Trace and Debug classes retrieves the active Listeners collection. The TraceListener-derived classes control the tracing output. The members of this class are shown in Table 21.6.

TraceListener Member	Description
IndentLevel	An integer value to adjust the output indent level.
IndentSize	An integer value to adjust the number of indent white spaces.
Name	Manages the name of the Listener.
Close()	Closes the streams after flushing the outstanding buffer contents that have not been written yet.
Fail()	Outputs the error message to the listener and by default behaves as if calling Assert(*false*, error_message, detailed_error_message).
Flush()	Serializes the outstanding buffer content to the stream immediately.
Write()	Performs write operation to the Listener with a message, category name, or object.ToString method.
WriteLine()	Performs write operation to the Listener with a message, category name, or object.ToString method prepending a line terminator to the content.

Table 21.6: TraceListener Class Members

The TextWriterTraceListener sends output to a text file, while the EventLogTraceListener sends output to the event log. In other words, we can say that the listeners monitor trace and debug output and generate formatted output of the trace. By default, the output of all methods is directed to the DefaultTraceListener. Therefore, the environment that executes your code sets where the DefaultTraceListener output is directed. The TraceListener class (the thread-safe parent class for other listeners) has the following subclasses:

- *DefaultTraceListener*. Sends your debugging or tracing write output through the OutputDebugString API function of the operating system. If you have no active debugger, OutputDebugString will not do anything. If you are inside the Visual Studio .NET integrated development environment, it will output the trace output to the debug window. If you are in console mode, you should use the Debug Monitor utility (DbMon.exe) of the Platform SDK. The Debug Monitor has its own console window and displays debugging and tracing messages sent by your application using the OutputDebugString—the DefaultListener—function.
- *EventLogTraceListener*. Sends tracing or debugging output to the event log.
- *TextWriterTraceListener*. Sends tracing or debugging output to Console.Out, FileStream, or other Stream and TextWriter classes.

Listing 21.14 shows a typical application configuration file (named <Application>.EXE.CONFIG) with various diagnostic settings.

Listing 21.14—Configuration File with Various Settings

```
<configuration>
<system.diagnostics>
    <trace autoflush="true" indentsize="1">
        <listeners>
            <add name="myTextFileListener"
type="System.Diagnostics.TextWriterTraceListener,System"
initializeData="c:\mylog.txt" />
            <remove type="System.Diagnostics.DefaultTraceListener,System"/>
        </listeners>
    </trace>
</system.diagnostics>
</configuration>
```

If you want to remove a listener that you created, use the Remove method in the Listeners collection. For example, to remove the DefaultListener use the following code:

```
Debug.Listeners.Remove("Default");
```

The example in Listing 21.15 shows how you can use TraceListeners. The application outputs trace code to the system console, to a file, and to the event log (a new event source named *Demo*) separately to illustrate all of the possible TraceListener styles. Note that you can replace the Debug class with the Trace class if you wish in the example.

Listing 21.15—Using TraceListeners (listener1.cs)

```
using System;
using System.IO;
using System.Diagnostics;

public class Test
{

 public static void Main()
 {
        TextWriterTraceListener myWriter = new
            TextWriterTraceListener(System.Console.Out);
        Debug.Listeners.Add(myWriter);

        Debug.WriteLine("Test output 1 ");

        Stream myFile = File.Create("output.txt");

        TextWriterTraceListener myTextListener = new
            TextWriterTraceListener(myFile);
        Debug.Listeners.Add(myTextListener);

        Debug.WriteLine("Test output 2 ");

        if(!EventLog.SourceExists("Demo"))
        {
         EventLog.CreateEventSource("Demo","Demo");
        }

        Debug.Listeners.Add(new EventLogTraceListener("Demo"));
        Debug.WriteLine("Test output 3 ");

        myWriter.Flush();
        myWriter.Close();

        myFile.Flush();
        myFile.Close();
 }

}
```

The EventLog Class

The EventLog class allows you to access or customize Windows NT, 2000, and XP event logs, which record information about important software or hardware events. Using the EventLog class, you can read from existing logs, write entries to logs, create or delete event sources, delete logs, and respond to log entries. You can also create new logs when creating an event source. Table 21.7 describes the members of the EventLog class.

EventLog Member	Description
EnableRaisingEvents	Represents a Boolean value. If set to *true*, the EntryWritten event will be notified when any entry is written to the event log.
Entries	Returns a collection that represents all of the event log entries.
Log	Specifies the name of the log, like Application, System and Security.
LogDisplayName	Returns the long friendly name of the event log that you can also see in the event viewer.
MachineName	Specifies the computer to read or write event logs.
Source	Specicifes the source name of the event log entry creator.
Clear()	Removes the contents of the log.
Close()	Releases the log handle along with its other open handles and closes the log.
CreateEventSource()	Registers a source to an existing log on a computer or creates a new log and then registers the source with this log.
Delete()	Deletes an event log from the specified computer.
DeleteEventSource()	Used for removing the registration of your application as a valid source of events on a computer.
Exists()	Returns a Boolean value that indicates whether a log exists on a specified computer.
GetEventLogs()	Returns an array of the log objects on a specified computer.
LogNameFromSourceName()	Returns the log for which the source (application or a subcomponent of the application) is registered on the specified computer.
SourceExists()	Returns a Boolean value that indicates whether a source is registered on a specified computer.
WriteEntry()	Used to write detailed information when creating a new event log entry.
EnableRaisingEvents	Represents a Boolean value. If it is set to true, the EntryWritten event will be notified when any entry is written to the event log.
Entries	Returns a collection that represents all of the event log entries.

Table 21.7: EventLog Class Members

Event logging provides a standard, centralized way for you to have your applications record important software and hardware events. Windows supplies a standard user interface for viewing the event logs (you can open Event Viewer MMC from Control Panel→Administrative Tools→Computer Management→Event Viewer). Using the Microsoft .NET Framework's EventLog component, you can easily connect to existing event logs on both local and remote computers and read entries from those logs programmatically.

The types of event logs are defined under the HKEY_LOCAL_MACHINE\SYSTEM\ControlSet\ Services\Eventlog registry hive. Windows 2000 includes Application, Security, System, Active Directory, and Domain Name System (DNS) logs by default. In an earlier example, we also added a "Demo" event log source hive in our listener program. Listing 21.16 illustrates how you can create an event source, check the existence of the Application and Demo event sources (which will be created by us) as an event log or in Event Viewer, enumerate and read event log entries, write entries to a log, and monitor the event log source for any new entries written to the log.

Listing 21.16—Using EventLog

```csharp
using System;
using System.IO;
using System.Diagnostics;

public class Test
{

 public static void Main()
 {

        // check for the event log source on specified machine
       // the Application event log source on MCBcomputer
       if(!EventLog.Exists("Application", "MCBcomputer"))
       {
           Console.WriteLine("The log does not exist!");
           return;
       }

       EventLog myLog = new EventLog();
       myLog.Log = "Application";
       myLog.MachineName = "MCBcomputer";

       Console.WriteLine("There are " + myLog.Entries.Count + " entr[y|ies] in the
                          Application log:");
       foreach (EventLogEntry entry in myLog.Entries)
       {
           Console.WriteLine("\tEntry: " + entry.Message);
       }

      // check for Demo event log source existence
      // create it if it not exist
      if ( !EventLog.SourceExists("Demo") ) {
           EventLog.CreateEventSource("Demo","Demo");
       }

      EventLog.WriteEntry("AnySource", "writing error to demo log.",
                          EventLogEntryType.Error);

    Console.WriteLine("Monitoring of Application event log began...");

    Console.WriteLine(@"Press 'q' and 'Enter' to quit");
    while(Console.Read()!='q')
    {

// Now we will monitor the new entries that will be written.
// When you create an EntryWrittenEventHandler delegate
// you identify the method that will handle the event.

       myLog.EntryWritten += new EntryWrittenEventHandler(OnEntryWritten);

// EnableRaisingEvents gets or sets a value indicating whether the
// EventLog instance receives EntryWritten event notifications.

       myLog.EnableRaisingEvents = true;
     }

 }

 public static void OnEntryWritten(Object source, EntryWrittenEventArgs e)
 {
     Console.WriteLine("written entry: " + e.Entry.Message);
 }

}
```

The PerformanceCounter Class

We always measure the performance of our code (applications, services, drivers, etc.) in the field in real time or in a testing environment. Then we can diagnose problems and fix them in the future. Performance counters enable us to publish, capture, and analyze the performance data of running code. A performance graph is a two-dimensional plot with one axis indicating time elapsed and the other reporting relevant relative or actual performance statistics.

The common language runtime (CLR) provides a PerformanceCounter class, with which we can read and write performance data on computers running Windows NT, 2000, or XP. We need to call counters in which the performance data is placed. The names of the counters are stored in the Windows registry along with the counters' various settings. Every performance counter has a unique name and location. Another attribute of a counter is its category (the performance object for which the counter measures data). For example, the Processor performance category has the % Processor Time performance counter object (and others), which has the _Total performance counter instance (and others). Please use Performance Monitor MMC if you have Windows NT, 2000, or XP installed (it's found on the Administrative Tools menu) to discover other PerformanceCounter categories, objects, and instances. PerformanceCounter class members are defined in Table 21.8.

PerformanceCounter Member	Description
CategoryName	Gets or sets the category name that stands for physical components and system objects, like Cache, Memory, Objects, PhysicalDisk, Process, Processor, Server, System, and Thread categories.
CounterHelp	Returns the detailed text that describes what the counter monitors.
CounterName	Gets or sets the short name of the counter that is being monitored.
CounterType	Gets an enumeration that defines the way that the counter behaves and its nature. It can be of NumberOfItems32, NumberOfItems64, RateOfCountsPerSecond32, RateOfCountsPerSecond64, or AverageTimer32 values.
InstanceName	Gets the name of the instance of this counter. Categories are subdivided into instances. Instances have performance counters associated with them.
MachineName	Specifies the computer on which the performance counters are processed or created.
RawValue	Gets or sets the raw values of the counters.
ReadOnly	Gets or sets a value indicating whether this PerformanceCounter instance is in read-only mode.
BeginInit()	Begins the initialization of a PerformanceCounter instance used on a form or by another component.
Close()	It closes the performance counter and frees all the resources allocated by the performance counter instance
CloseSharedResources()	It frees the performance counter library shared state allocated by the counters
Decrement()	Decreases the performance counter by one for custom counters.
Increment()	Increases the performance counter by one for custom counters.
IncrementBy()	Increases or decreases the performance counter by a specified amount (e.g., 1, 2, -1).
NextSample()	Returns a raw value for the next recent counter measure.

PerformanceCounter Member	Description
NextValue()	Returns a calculated value for the next recent counter measure.
RemoveInstance()	Removes the custom created category instance that is specified by the InstanceName property.

Table 21.8: PerformanceCounter Class Members

Listing 21.17 illustrates how we might use performance counters. In this example we measure the total processing time with the Processor performance counter.

Listing 21.17—Using PerformanceCounter (perf1.cs)

```
using System;
using System.Threading;
using System.Diagnostics;

public class TestPerfCounter
{
 static PerformanceCounter myCounter;
 public static void Main()
 {
      if ( !PerformanceCounterCategory.Exists("Processor"))
      {
          Console.WriteLine("Object Processor does not exist!");
          return;
      }

      if ( !PerformanceCounterCategory.CounterExists(@"% Processor Time",
                                                "Processor") )
      {
          Console.WriteLine(@"Counter % Processor Time does not exist!");
          return;
      }

      myCounter = new PerformanceCounter("Processor", @"% Processor Time" ,
                               @"_Total");

// The raw value of a counter can be set in your applications as shown below
// if the object is not read-only
      try
      {
          myCounter.RawValue = 19;
      }
      catch
      {
          Console.WriteLine(@"Processor, % Processor Time, _Total
                               instance is READONLY!");
      }

       Console.WriteLine(@"Press 'CTRL+C' to quit...");
      while ( true )
      {
         Console.WriteLine("@");
       try
       {
         Console.WriteLine(@"Current value of Processor, %Processor Time,
             _Total= " + myCounter.NextValue().ToString());
       }
       catch
       {
         Console.WriteLine(@"_Total instance does not exist!");
          return;
       }
```

```
            Thread.Sleep(1000);
            Console.WriteLine(@"Press 'CTRL+C' to quit...");
        }

    }

}
```

The Windows Registry

The Windows registry acts as a central repository of information for the operating system and the applications on a computer. This database is organized in a hierarchical format, based on a logical ordering of the elements stored within it. When storing information in the registry, select the appropriate location based on the type of information being stored. Be sure to avoid destroying information created by other applications because this can cause those applications to exhibit unexpected behavior and can adversely affect your own application.

Windows NT, 2000, and XP provide two versions of a Registry Editor: Regedt32.exe and Regedit.exe. Regedt32.exe is automatically installed in the %systemroot%\System32 folder. Regedit.exe is automatically installed in the %systemroot% folder. You can modify the registry using either of these Registry Editor utilities. However, if possible, you should use other utilities and tools provided with Windows 2000 to modify your system settings, such as those in the Control Panel. When you modify the registry with Registry Editor, the editor does not check for syntax or other errors. In addition, one modification to the registry may cause a cascade of changes throughout it. The results of an incorrect edit made with Registry Editor are unpredictable and may impair or disable the Windows 2000 operating system. However, by using other tools and utilities, you can ensure that modifications made to the registry are logical and valid, and you can manage any subsequent cascade of changes an edit may cause.

You can use Regedt32.exe in read-only mode (on the Options menu, click Read Only Mode) to safely view the registry and not inadvertently make changes. Switch off read-only mode when you are certain of the changes you wish to make.

Registry keys are the base unit of organization in the registry; they can be compared to folders in Windows Explorer. A particular key can have subkeys (just as a folder can have subfolders). Each key can also have multiple values associated with it, which are used to store information about your application. Each value holds one particular piece of information, which can be retrieved and updated when required. For instance, you can create a registry key for your company under the key HKEY_LOCAL_MACHINE\Software and then a subkey for each application that your company creates. Each subkey holds information specific to that application such as color settings, screen location, and product-specific file extensions.

The information stored in the registry is available to other applications and users, and therefore you should not use the registry to store security or critical application information. The main base Registry categories for the Microsoft operating systems are as follows:

- *CurrentUser*. Stores information about user preferences.
- *LocalMachine*. Stores configuration information for the local machine.
- *ClassesRoot*. Stores information about types (and classes) and their properties.
- *Users*. Stores information about the default user configuration.
- *PerformanceData*. Stores performance information for software components.
- *CurrentConfig*. Stores non-user-specific hardware information.
- *DynData*. Stores dynamic data.

The Registry class has a static field corresponding to each of these key types. The Registry class members are described as follows:

- *ClassesRoot.* Returns a RegistryKey type that provides access to the HKEY_CLASSES_ROOT key.
- *CurrentConfig.* Returns a RegistryKey type that provides access to the HKEY_CURRENT_CONFIG key.
- *CurrentUser.* Returns a RegistryKey type that provides access to the HKEY_CURRENT_USER key.
- *DynData.* Returns a RegistryKey type that provides access to the HKEY_DYN_DATA key.
- *LocalMachine.* Returns a RegistryKey type that provides access to the HKEY_LOCAL_MACHINE key.
- *PerformanceData.* Returns a RegistryKey type that provides access to the HKEY_PERFORMANCE_DATA key.
- *Users.* Returns a RegistryKey type that provides access to the HKEY_USERS key.

For example, if you want to access the HKEY_LOCAL_MACHINE key, you need to call the Registry.LocalMachine member that returns a RegistryKey instance pointing to the local machine key.

```
RegistryKey pRegKey = Registry.LocalMachine;
```

The RegistryKey class enables you to manipulate data in a registry key; it contains members to add, remove, replace, and read registry data. Some of its common methods and properties are defined in Table 21.9.

RegistryKey Member	Description
Name	The name of the key.
SubKeyCount	The number of keys under the current key.
ValueCount	The number of values under the current key.
Close()	Closes the key.
CreateSubKey()	Creates a new subkey if one does not exist; otherwise opens an existing subkey.
DeleteSubKey()	Deletes the subkey passed by this method.
DeleteSubKeyTree()	Deletes the subkey passed and any children of the subkey.
DeleteValue()	Deletes the value specified from the current key.
GetSubKeyNames()	Returns an array of names of all the subkeys.
GetValue()	Gets the value specified by the value name passed; returns null if the value does not exist.
GetValueNames()	Retrieves an array of names of all of the values.
OpenSubKey()	Opens a subkey specified by the string passed.
SetValue()	Sets a value in the registry with the value passed into the second parameter of this method. The first parameter is the name of the value.

Table 21.9: Registry Class Members

Let's see how to use these methods to add, remove, and update keys and their values. First we will add a subkey called HKEY_LOCAL_MACHINE/Software/MCBInc and place a value entry and a value inside (see Listing 21.18).

Let's perform some actions against the registry. We can use CreateSubKey to add a new key to the Registry and call the SetValue method to write a value and key. The code in Listing 21.18 does this for us. The second parameter of the OpenSubKey method is a Boolean that identifies whether our access is for reading or writing. Use *false* in the second parameter for reading a value, and use *true* for writing a value. That way you can prevent unplanned, unwanted write operations. The public void SetValue (string name, object value) function sets the specified value to the registry key. The key must be opened for write access, and the key name is not case sensitive. Values allowed in the registry must be of the type DWORD, binary, or string. You pass these object types as the second parameter to the SetValue method, which accepts Object as the parameter type. You should format your string values appropriately before setting their values. String values can be represented in the following categories in the registry:

- *SZ*. Data is represented as a null-terminated Unicode string value.
- *MULTI_SZ*. Data is represented as an array of null-terminated Unicode strings.
- *EXPANDED_SZ*. Data is represented as a null-terminated Unicode string with expanded references to environment variables.

Since many values can be stored in each key in the registry, the name parameter specifies the particular value you wish to manipulate. To set the default value for a particular registry key, the name can be set to either a null reference or an empty string (""). Notice in Listing 21.18 that the second parameter to OpenSubKey is set to *true* to enable the registry writing operation on that key.

Listing 21.18—Using CreateSubKey and SetValue

```
// Create a new key under HKEY_LOCAL_MACHINE\Software as MCBInc
RegistryKey key = Registry.LocalMachine.OpenSubKey("Software", true);
// Add one more sub key
RegistryKey newkey = key.CreateSubKey("MCBInc");
// Set value of sub key
newkey.SetValue("MCBInc", "NET Developer");
```

The GetValue method returns the value of a subkey in the form of an object. In the example in Listing 21.19, we read the value of the CenteralProcessor\0 subkey and write it to the console. To get the default value for a particular registry key, set the name of the value in GetValue to either a null reference or an empty string ("").

Listing 21.19—Using GetValue

```
// Retrieve data from other part of the registry
// find out your processor
RegistryKey pRegKey = Registry.LocalMachine;
pRegKey = pRegKey.OpenSubKey(@"HARDWARE\DESCRIPTION\System\CentralProcessor\0");
Object val = pRegKey.GetValue("VendorIdentifier");
Console.WriteLine("The central processor of this machine is:" + val);
```

You can also loop through all the subkeys inside a registry key by getting a collection of the subkeys as shown in Listing 21.20.

Listing 21.20—Using GetSubkeyNames

```
RegistryKey regkey =
    Registry.LocalMachine.OpenSubKey(@"Software\Mindcracker", false);
foreach (String s in regkey.GetSubKeyNames())
```

```
Console.WriteLine(s);
```

Furthermore, you can loop through all the values of the registry key by getting a collection of all the values in the key, as Listing 21.21 demonstrates.

Listing 21.21—Using GetValueNames

```
//retrieve the array of values for that key
String [] sarray = regkey.GetValueNames();

//write the values to the screen
foreach (String s in sarray)
    Console.WriteLine(s);
```

If you want to delete a key, use the DeleteSubKey or the DeleteSubKeyTree methods. The RegistryKey.DeleteSubKey method deletes the specified subkey. The RegistryKey.DeleteSubKeyTree method deletes a subkey, its data, and all of its child subkeys recursively in one shot. If you want to delete a value, use the DeleteValue method of the RegistryKey class. The RegistryKey.DeleteValue method deletes the specified value from the key. These methods are illustrated in Listing 21.22.

Listing 21.22—Using DeleteValue and DeleteSubKey

```
// Deleting registry keys and values
// Delete the key value
RegistryKey delKey = Registry.LocalMachine.OpenSubKey("Software\\");
delKey.DeleteValue("MCBInc");

// Delete the key value
RegistryKey delKey = Registry.LocalMachine.OpenSubKey("Software", true);
delKey.DeleteSubKey("MCBInc");

The sample source code in Listing 21.23 illustrates all the registry operations
we've discussed.

Listing 21.23—Various Registry Options (reg1.cs)
using System;
using Microsoft.Win32;

class Class1
{
 static void Main(string[] args)
 {
  // Create a new key under HKEY_LOCAL_MACHINE\Software as MCBInc
  RegistryKey key = Registry.LocalMachine.OpenSubKey("Software", true);
  // Add one more sub key
  RegistryKey newkey = key.CreateSubKey("MCBInc");
  // Set value of sub key
  newkey.SetValue("MCBInc", "NET Developer");
  // Retrieve data from other part of the registry
  // find out your processor
  RegistryKey pRegKey = Registry.LocalMachine;
  pRegKey =
    pRegKey.OpenSubKey("HARDWARE\\DESCRIPTION\\System\\CentralProcessor\\0");
  Object val = pRegKey.GetValue("VendorIdentifier");
  Console.WriteLine("The central processor of this machine is:"+ val);
  // Delete the key value
  RegistryKey delKey = Registry.LocalMachine.OpenSubKey("Software", true);
  delKey.DeleteSubKey("MCBInc");
 }
}
```

There is another useful way to retrieve top-level registry handles (an alternative to the direct OpenSubKey method) for both local and remote computers. We can use the OpenRemoteBaseKey method:

```
RegistryKey rgkey =
    RegistryKey.OpenRemoteBaseKey(RegistryHive.LocalMachine, "MCBcomputer");
```

RegistryHive values are used by the OpenRemoteBaseKey method to represent the top-level node of a requested key on a foreign (remote) machine. The only nodes that can be opened with the OpenRemoteBaseKey method must be among the following top-level RegistryKeys. Further access to the subkeys of the identified node is available using methods in the RegistryKey class as long as the user has appropriate permission.

ClassesRoot: Represents the HKEY_CLASSES_ROOT base key on a foreign machine. This value can be passed to the OpenRemoteBaseKey method, to open this node remotely.

CurrentConfig: Represents the HKEY_CURRENT_CONFIG base key on a foreign machine. This value can be passed to the OpenRemoteBaseKey method, to open this node remotely.

CurrentUser: Represents the HKEY_CURRENT_USER base key on a foreign machine. This value can be passed to the OpenRemoteBaseKey method, to open this node remotely.

DynData: Represents the HKEY_DYN_DATA base key on a foreign machine. This value can be passed to the OpenRemoteBaseKey method, to open this node remotely.

LocalMachine: Represents the HKEY_LOCAL_MACHINE base key on a foreign machine. This value can be passed to the OpenRemoteBaseKey method, to open this node remotely.

PerformanceData: Represents the HKEY_PERFORMANCE_DATA base key on a foreign machine. This value can be passed to the OpenRemoteBaseKey method, to open this node remotely.

Users: Represents the HKEY_USERS base key on a foreign machine. This value can be passed to the OpenRemoteBaseKey method, to open this node remotely.

Listing 21.24 shows an example of reading some registry values on a foreign machine. Note that OpenRemoteBaseKey is opening the HKEY_LOCAL_MACHINE registry key on the machine named "ComputerNAME". Also note that OpenSubKey may not need a second Boolean parameter to indicate whether we are reading or writing to the registry because the single parameter call to OpenSubKey is read-only.

Listing 21.24—OpenRemoteBaseKey Illustrated (reg2.cs)

```
// Processor and Bios Information

using System;
using Microsoft.Win32;

public class MyRegistry {
  static void Main() {
  RegistryKey hklm = Registry.LocalMachine;

//or for a remote machine
//    RegistryKey hklm = RegistryKey.OpenRemoteBaseKey(RegistryHive.LocalMachine,
"ComputerNAME");

  hklm=hklm.OpenSubKey(@"HARDWARE\DESCRIPTION\System\CentralProcessor\0");
  Object obp = hklm.GetValue("Identifier");
```

```
  Console.WriteLine("Processor Identifier :{0}", obp);

  hklm = Registry.LocalMachine;
  hklm = hklm.OpenSubKey(@"HARDWARE\DESCRIPTION\System\CentralProcessor\0");
  obp = hklm.GetValue("VendorIdentifier");
  Console.WriteLine("Vendor Identifier    :{0}", obp);

  hklm = Registry.LocalMachine;
  hklm = hklm.OpenSubKey(@"HARDWARE\DESCRIPTION\System\MultiFunctionAdapter\4");
  obp = hklm.GetValue("Identifier");
  Console.WriteLine("Bios Status          :{0}", obp);

  hklm = Registry.LocalMachine;
  hklm = hklm.OpenSubKey(@"HARDWARE\DESCRIPTION\System\");
  obp = hklm.GetValue("SystemBiosDate");
  Console.WriteLine("Bios Date            :{0}", obp);

  hklm = Registry.LocalMachine;
  hklm = hklm.OpenSubKey(@"HARDWARE\DESCRIPTION\System\");
  obp = hklm.GetValue("Identifier");
  Console.WriteLine("System Identifer     :{0}", obp);
  }
}
```

Understanding Timers

The Timer class (server-based timer) lets you specify a recurring interval at which the elapsed event is raised. This way we can do regular processing inside the event code block when the timer event occurs. Timers are used to generate recurring events in an application. Some members of the Timer class are described in Table 21.10.

Timer Member	Description
AutoReset	Represents a Boolean value. If set to *true*, it indicates the timer will raise the elapsed event each time the specified interval elapses. Otherwise it will raise the elapsed event only once after the first time is elapsed. If set to *false*, either Enabled must be set to *true* or the Start method must be called to begin the timer again.
Enabled	Represents a Boolean value that indicates whether the timer will raise the elapsed event or not. If set to *true*, it is identical to calling the Start method. If set to *false*, it is identical to calling the Stop method.
Interval	Represents the interval in milliseconds at which to trigger the elapsed event. It has a default value of 100 milliseconds.
BeginInit()	Called to make sure that the timer is initialized before it is used.
Close()	Closes resources opened by the timer.
EndInit()	Ends the initialization of a timer during runtime.
Start()	Starts the timer and triggers the associated elapsed event by setting Enabled to *true*.
Stop()	Halts event triggering by the elapsed event by setting Enabled to *false*.

Table 21.10: Timer Class Members

We use the Timer class to work with worker threads in a multithreaded environment; it is based on server-based timers rather than Windows timers. Server-based timers are more reliable than Windows timers. With server-based timers, we can move among threads to handle the raised elapsed event. Windows timers, on the other hand, were not really intended for switching between threads. The Windows timer is optimized for use in Windows Forms applications and is assumed to be thread-safe. The server-based timer is an updated Windows timer that has been optimized to run in a multithreaded server environment. The Windows timer lives in the System.Windows.Forms namespace, and the server-based timer resides in the System.Timers namespace. Intervals are specified in milliseconds for timers, to trigger events after that time has gone. When the AutoReset field of the Timer class is set to *false,* the elapsed event is triggered only once by the timer after the first interval has elapsed. If you want to raise the elapsed event each time the time interval occurs in perpetuity, set AutoReset to *true.* Since both timer usages are almost identical, we choose to demonstrate the server-based timer because of its multithreaded nature. The sample code in Listing 21.25 shows how to use a Timer object that is triggered on 1,000-millisecond intervals.

Listing 21.25—Using Timers (timer1.cs)

```
using System;
using System.Timers;
using System.Threading;

public class Test
{

 public static void Main()
 {

        System.Timers.Timer myTimer = new System.Timers.Timer();
        myTimer.Elapsed += new ElapsedEventHandler(OnTimer);

        myTimer.Interval = 1000;
        myTimer.Enabled = true;
        myTimer.AutoReset = false;

        Console.WriteLine(@"Press 'q' and 'Enter' to quit...");
        while ( Console.Read()!='q' )
        {
           Thread.Sleep(1000);
        }

 }

 public static void OnTimer(Object source, ElapsedEventArgs e)
 {

        Console.WriteLine("DateTime: " + DateTime.Now);
        System.Timers.Timer theTimer = (System.Timers.Timer)source;
        theTimer.Interval += 1000;
        theTimer.Enabled = true;
 }
}
```

Figure 21.1: Timer Output from One-Second Timer

Notice the time difference between each time trigger. This shows that the server-based timers are not pulsing as we expected, because although we enabled our timer to trigger every one second, the event handler was delayed in order to handle other activity of the CPU. Server-based timers are dependent on the operating system's multithreading character on which our code runs, and the program must obey the CPU priority rules when using these timers.

Working with Directory Services

Microsoft has provided the Active Directory Service Interface (ADSI), an API for directory services, for many years. ADSI allows us to access the directory services of various network providers in a distributed computing environment, and it presents a single set of directory service interfaces for managing network resources. We can list and manage the resources in a directory service via the ADSI service, but we do not need to know where the actual resource is located. We can use ADSI to perform common administrative tasks such as searching resources like computers, users, printers, shares, and groups on an enterprise computer network.

When you install a Windows 2000 domain controller and are creating a new forest and domain, you install the Active Directory (and optionally an Active Directory-integrated DNS if one does not exist), in which all resource information is stored. The Windows 2000 Active Directory allows you to store information about all kinds of resources such as computers, groups, printers, shares, users, and so on. If you want to surf through an Active Directory, you would use the basic program named LDP.EXE from theWindows2000 support tools, in the Windows 2000 CD's support directory. Active Directory is a database that has a storage structure similar to that of the Registry—namely, hierarchical rather than relational. This statement is also valid for other LDAP (Lightweight Directory Access Protocol) servers and stores. You can also think of it as an XML Document Object Model tree. Every object inside Active Directory is created based on a schema object type, has an LDAP path relative to the root, and has particular attributes such as name and global unique identifier (GUID). The created objects of valid schema types reside as nodes in the Active Directory tree.

Figure 21.2 shows a simple model of an Active Directory tree and node. (Note that the same logic applies to all LDAP servers such as Microsoft Internet Information Server.)

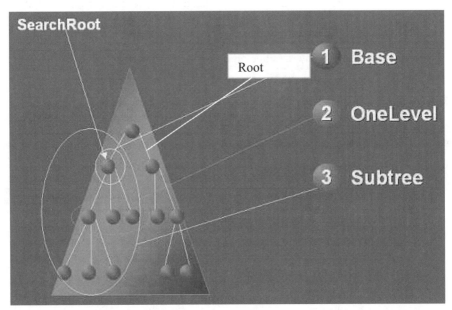

Figure 21.2: Active Directory Data and Search Model

The DirectoryEntry class presents a node or object in the Active Directory hierarchy. The Add method creates a request to create a new entry in the container. The Find method returns the child with the specified name. The Remove method deletes a child DirectoryEntry from this collection. Table 21.11 describes the members of the DirectoryEntry class.

DirectoryEntry Member	Description
AuthenticationType	Specifies the type of authentication against the LDAP provider for binding (e.g., Anonymous, Delegation, Secure, Encryption, None, Sealing, Signing, FastBind).
Children	Returns a collection of DirectoryEntries that consists of the child entries of the current node.
Guid	Gets the GUID of the directory entry.
Name	Returns the name of the object inside the schema.
NativeGuid	Gets the GUID of the directory entry.
NativeObject	Gets the native ADSI object to be used when calling methods of COM interfaces with this property.
Parent	Returns the parent node of the current entry node.
Password	Gets or sets the password used with the credentials when authenticating the client.
Path	Gets or sets the path of the directory entry.
Properties	Gets a PropertyCollection of properties.
SchemaEntry	Returns the directory entry that stores the schema information.
SchemaClassName	Same as the SchemaEntry.Name property.
UsePropertyCache	Represents a Boolean value that indicates whether the cache should be committed or not after each operation performed on the entry.
Username	Gets or sets the user name used for authenticating access to the directory entry along with the password.
Close()	Closes the directory entry.
CommitChanges()	Writes any outstanding changes to the entry.
CopyTo()	Duplicates the directory entry with a new name.
DeleteTree()	Deletes the node, including the entire subtree.
Exists()	Searches the existence of a directory entry at the specified path.
Invoke()	Invokes a method with the object parameter of the native LDAP server.
MoveTo()	Moves the entry to another container either by preserving the same name or by using the new name supplied.
RefreshCache()	Loads the properties cache with values from the current directory entry.
Rename()	Renames the directory entry.

Table 21.11: DirectoryEntry Class Members

The DirectorySearcher class performs queries against the Active Directory. But of the system-supplied ADSI providers like LDAP, Internet Information Services (IIS), and Novell NetWare Directory Service (NDS), only LDAP supports searching. The Filter property of the

DirectorySearcher class gets or sets the LDAP filter string format. The FindAll method in the DirectorySearcher class executes the search and returns a collection of entries found. Table 21.12 describes the members of the DirectorySearcher class.

DirectorySearcher Member	Description
CacheResults	Represents a Boolean value. When set to *true*, the result will be cached on the computer.
ClientTimeout	Represents the maximum amount of time in seconds for the return of the search result.
Filter	Manages the filter string in LDAP format, such as "(&(objectClass=user)(|(manager=mcb)(homepage=mindcracker)))", which filters all user objects that have either *mcb* as manager or *mindcracker* as homepage.
PageSize	Gets or sets the page size in a paged search.
PropertiesToLoad	Gets or sets a StringCollection of the properties returned from the search results.
PropertyNamesOnly	Represents a Boolean value. If set to *true*, the search operation returns only the names of attributes, not the values. If set to *false*, the search operation returns both the names of attributes and their values.
ReferralChasing	Gets or sets how referrals are chased.
SearchRoot	Gets or sets the root in which the search begins.
SearchScope	Gets or sets the scope of the search performed. Scope includes Base, OneLevel, and Subtree.
ServerPageTimeLimit	Gets or sets the time limit the server should observe to search an individual page of results.
ServerTimeLimit	Gets or sets the maximum amount of time the server spends searching.
SizeLimit	Gets or sets the maximum number of objects the server returns in a search.
Sort	Returns the property that the search result is sorted on.
FindAll()	Returns all of the entries found in a collection after the search.
FindOne()	Returns only the first entry found after the search.

Table 21.12: DirectorySearcher Class Members

You can use Active Directory Users and Computers MMC to manage your Active Directory resources. It resides on the Administrative Tools menu on Windows 2000 servers.

The code in Listing 21.26 searches the MCBCorp.Com Windows 2000 Active Directory domain. It outputs all of the Active Directory objects and their properties, and then all the data inside, recursively.

Listing 21.26—Using DirectoryEntry (ldapdir1.cs)

```
using System;
using System.DirectoryServices;

class Test
  {
    static void Main (string[] args)
    {
```

```
    // the name of the domain
    DirectoryEntry entry = new DirectoryEntry(@"LDAP://MCBcorp, DC=com");

    Console.WriteLine("Name            = " + entry.Name);
    Console.WriteLine("Path            = " + entry.Path);
    Console.WriteLine("SchemaClassName = " + entry.SchemaClassName);
    Console.WriteLine("Properties:");
    Console.WriteLine("======================================");
    foreach(string key in entry.Properties.PropertyNames)
    {
       try
       {
        Console.WriteLine("\t" + key + " = ");
        foreach(Object objCollection in entry.Properties[key])
            Console.WriteLine("\t\t" + objCollection);
        Console.WriteLine("======================================");
       }
       catch
       {
       }
    }


      System.DirectoryServices.DirectorySearcher mySearcher = new
            System.DirectoryServices.DirectorySearcher(entry);
      mySearcher.Filter = ("(objectClass=*)");
      Console.WriteLine("Active Directory Information");
      Console.WriteLine("======================================");
     foreach(System.DirectoryServices.SearchResult resEnt
            in mySearcher.FindAll())
      {
       try
       {
        Console.WriteLine(
          resEnt.GetDirectoryEntry().Name.ToString() );
        Console.WriteLine(
          resEnt.GetDirectoryEntry().Path.ToString() );
        Console.WriteLine(
          resEnt.GetDirectoryEntry().NativeGuid.ToString() );
        Console.WriteLine("======================================");
       }
       catch
       {
       }
      }


    }
  }
```

You can create entries and properties in the Active Directory. You simply create a new directory or use an existing one with the DirectoryEntry class and then assign the values you want to the specific properties. When you have finished assigning the values, call the CommitChanges() method to cause the changes to occur in the Active Directory. The sample code in Listing 21.27 achieves this update operation.

Listing 21.27 also shows you how to pick individual properties of Active Directory objects! The *properties* term of Active Directory is not related to the C# class properties used with get and set. Active Directory properties are an array of adjustable object property members with specific names determined by the Active Directory schema. For example, you can set the following properties for objects: sn, givenName, title, or mycustomproperty. The properties change depending on their class definition in the Active Directory schema. Refer to the Active Directory Schema MMC to discover possible object types and definitions.

Listing 21.27—Updating Active Directory

```
// get the handle to MCBuser from Active Directory database
DirectoryEntry entry = new DirectoryEntry("LDAP://DC=MyDC, O=MyOrg, OU=MyOU,
cn=MCBuser");
Entry.Password = "mcb"; // password
(entry.Properties["myprop") [0] = "myvalue"; // properties
entry.CommitChanges();
```

Reflection and Reflection.Emit

The Reflection.Emit namespace classes can be used to emit Microsoft intermediate language (MSIL) code on the fly so that the generated code can be executed directly. Reflection is also used to obtain information about a class and its members. In other words, reflection is a technology that allows you to examine metadata that describes types and their members. You may have programmatically accessed Component Object Model type libraries before; reflection in .NET is very similar, but it is a lot more powerful and a lot easier to use. When you compile a source file with a .NET compiler, the compiler emits the MSIL of the statements within the source file, along with the metadata that describes the types defined within the file. It is this metadata that the reflection APIs in .NET enable you to examine. The MSIL and metadata are contained in assembly files (typically .dll and .exe files).

The reflection API in .NET uses the System.Reflection namespace. In this namespace are classes used to help you access structures inherent in a program such as classes, types, fields, structs, enums, members, and methods. For example, you use the Type class to identify the type of the class being reflected, and the FieldInfo class represents the fields of a struct or enum. The MemberInfo class represents the members of the reflected class, and you use the MethodInfo class to represent methods of the reflected class. The ParameterInfo class represents the parameters of a method in the reflected class.

You can create code at runtime with the System.Reflection.Emit namespace classes, but we must warn you that you must have some knowledge of the MSIL operation codes and the MSIL language to take advantage of the emitting commands. In fact, what you are actually emitting is the MSIL itself behind the scenes. You can use reflection to define an assembly in memory, create a class/module for that assembly, and then create other module members plus new types for that module. You can construct the assembly using emitting. Reflection.Emit is a powerful namespace in which we can dynamically emit transient and persisting assemblies at runtime. Reflection.Emit produces a low-level, language-neutral MSIL. Normally, we create an assembly by saving its source code to disk and then compiling that source code. Then we call the methods of classes that we need to use from that assembly, which was compiled on disk. But as you can imagine, this involves extra disk write and read effort! With reflection emit, we can omit this overhead and immediately emit the operation codes directly into memory. Reflection emitting is nothing but writing any assembly code directly within your code and then invoking the resulting code on the fly.

You should use Reflection.Emit members for the following reasons:

- You have your own macro languages, compilers, or script compilers in your applications.
- You want to improve performance of your algorithms by creating assemblies, classes, modules, and new types during runtime.
- You want to improve performance of late-bound objects. You can emit the code necessary to call bound types directly, and then call through your emitted method. Although you cannot perform calls as speedily as with early binding, you will perform better than late binding.

The System.Reflection.Emit namespace provides the classes necessary for a user to create an .exe file on the fly. Its classes allow a compiler or tool to emit metadata and MSIL. So you can create .exe files on your disk on the fly as if you were running the code, saving it, and calling the compiler to compile the code. Mostly you will need this feature and this namespace for your custom script engines and compilers.

The Reflection.Emit namespace has many members you can use for emitting. Here are the two most important ones:

- The AssemblyBuilder class is the starting point for any application that emits code at runtime and has methods for creating dynamic modules.
- The ModuleBuilder class is used as the starting point for adding types such as classes and structures to a dynamic assembly at runtime.

The ILGenerator.OpCodes class, which generates MSIL instructions, includes all the MSIL operation codes in its fields that you will need (operation codes are a portion of a set of operation descriptions that specifies the operation to be performed or the set of operations in a computer). MSIL is the typeless operation code of the base assembly language for the CLR or intermediate language. When you code any C# code and compile it, it is transformed into MSIL first. Then when you invoke an assembly in MSIL, it is converted and executed in the corresponding machine language. The easiest way to learn MSIL is to disassemble simple codes that you have compiled. You can disassemble any compiled .NET code by using ILDasm.exe (the IL Disassembler), one of the .NET SDK utilities. After you have compiled the code in Listing 21.28 and run it on the console, a new file is generated in your current folder called TestAsm.exe. This .exe file prints the message "Hello World" on the console.

Listing 21.28—Creating an .exe File on the Fly (ReflectionEmit.cs)

```
using System;
using System.Runtime;
using System.Reflection;
using System.Reflection.Emit;

public class class1
{

        public static void Main()
        {
                AppDomain ad = AppDomain.CurrentDomain;
                AssemblyName am = new AssemblyName();
                am.Name = "TestAsm";

                AssemblyBuilder ab =
                        ad.DefineDynamicAssembly(am,AssemblyBuilderAccess.Save);
                ModuleBuilder mb = ab.DefineDynamicModule("testmod","TestAsm.exe");
                TypeBuilder tb = mb.DefineType("mytype",TypeAttributes.Public);
                MethodBuilder metb = tb.DefineMethod("hi",MethodAttributes.Public |
                        MethodAttributes.Static,null,null);

                ab.SetEntryPoint( metb);
                //
                ILGenerator il = metb.GetILGenerator();
                il.EmitWriteLine("Hello World");
                il.Emit(OpCodes.Ret);
                tb.CreateType();
                ab.Save("TestAsm.exe");
        }
}
```

Try executing TestAsm.exe, and see whether it works as you expect. Indeed, we can accomplish anything by emitting operation codes that we can do with normal C# code, since they both produce corresponding MSIL in the end. Listing 21.29 is a more sophisticated example that shows how to emit an assembly that contains a method to calculate a factorial on the fly.

Listing 21.29—Calculating Factorial by Emitting Operation Codes (emitfactorial.cs)

```
using System;
using System.Reflection;
using System.Reflection.Emit;
using System.IO;
using System.Threading;
using System.Diagnostics;

// declare the interface
public interface IFactorial
{
  int myfactorial();
}

public class SampleFactorialFromEmission
{
   // emit the assembly using op codes
   private Assembly EmitAssembly(int theValue)
   {
     // create assembly name
     AssemblyName assemblyName = new AssemblyName();
     assemblyName.Name = "FactorialAssembly";

     // create assembly with one module
     AssemblyBuilder newAssembly =
      Thread.GetDomain( ).DefineDynamicAssembly(
      assemblyName, AssemblyBuilderAccess.Run);
     ModuleBuilder newModule =
       newAssembly.DefineDynamicModule("MFactorial");

     // define a public class named "CFactorial" in the assembly
     TypeBuilder myType = newModule.DefineType("CFactorial",
                         TypeAttributes.Public);

     // Mark the class as implementing IFactorial.
     myType.AddInterfaceImplementation(typeof(IFactorial));

     // define myfactorial method by passing an array that defines
     // the types of the parameters, the type of the return type,
     // the name of the method, and the method attributes.
     Type[] paramTypes = new Type[0];
     Type returnType = typeof(Int32);
     MethodBuilder simpleMethod = myType.DefineMethod(
                   "myfactorial",
                             MethodAttributes.Public |
                             MethodAttributes.Virtual,
                             returnType,
                             paramTypes);

     // obtain an ILGenerator to emit the IL
     ILGenerator generator = simpleMethod.GetILGenerator();

     // Ldc_I4 pushes a supplied value of type int32
     // onto the evaluation stack as an int32.

     // push 1 onto the evaluation stack.
     // foreach i less than theValue,
     // push i onto the stack as a constant
     // multiply the two values at the top of the stack.
     // The result multiplication is pushed onto the evaluation
```

```
      // stack.
      generator.Emit(OpCodes.Ldc_I4, 1);
      for (Int32 i = 1; i <= theValue; ++i)
      {
       generator.Emit(OpCodes.Ldc_I4, i);
       generator.Emit(OpCodes.Mul);
      }

      // emit the return value on the top of the evaluation stack.
      // Ret returns from method, possibly returning a value.
      generator.Emit(OpCodes.Ret);

      // encapsulate information about the method and
      // provide access to the method metadata
      MethodInfo factorialInfo =
          typeof(IFactorial).GetMethod("myfactorial");

      // specify the method implementation.
      // pass in the MethodBuilder that was returned
      // by calling DefineMethod and the methodInfo just created
      myType.DefineMethodOverride(simpleMethod, factorialInfo);

      // create the type and return new on-the-fly assembly
      myType.CreateType();
      return newAssembly;
   }

   // check if the interface is null, generate assembly
   // otherwise it is already there, where it is to be...
   public double DoFactorial(int theValue)
   {
      if (thesample == null)
      {
       GenerateCode(theValue);
      }

      // call the method through the interface
      return (thesample.myfactorial());
   }

   // emit the assembly, create an instance and
   // get the interface IFactorial
   public void GenerateCode(int theValue)
   {
      Assembly theAssembly = EmitAssembly(theValue);
      thesample = (IFactorial) theAssembly.CreateInstance("CFactorial");
   }

   // private member data
   IFactorial thesample = null;

}

class Class1
    {
            [STAThread]
            static void Main(string[] args)
            {
             Int32 aValue = 5;
             SampleFactorialFromEmission t = new SampleFactorialFromEmission ();
             double result = t.DoFactorial(aValue);
             Console.WriteLine("Factorial of " + aValue + " is " +
                        result);
            }

    }
```

The Environment Class

The Environment class of the System namespace is handy for getting and setting various operating system–related information. You can use this class to retrieve information such as command-line arguments, exit codes, environment variable settings, contents of the call stack, time since last system boot in milliseconds (tick count), and version of the CLR. Members of the Environment class are described in Table 21.13.

Environment Member	Description
CommandLine	Returns a string that includes the command line arguments.
CurrentDirectory	Gets or sets the full path of the current directory in which this process starts with the format of drivename + backslash character + subdirectory (e.g., C:\ or C:\dir1).
ExitCode	Returns a success or failure status from a process.
HasShutdownStarted	Represents a Boolean value that reads *true* if the CLR is shutting down.
MachineName	Returns the NetBIOS name of the computer. There are two types of naming standards for a computer: NETBIOS and FQDN.
NewLine	Returns the defined NewLine string. This is mostly \r\n on Windows-related operating systems but on other operating systems this value may differ.
OSVersion	Returns an operating system object with the current version information.
StackTrace	Returns a string that shows the call stack.
SystemDirectory	Returns the fully qualified path where the underlying operating system is installed.
TickCount	Returns the number of milliseconds passed since the operating system was last started.
UserDomainName	Returns the domain name of the current user.
UserInteractive	Returns a Boolean that indicates whether the process is running in user-interactive mode or not. For service and Web applications, this value will return *false*.
UserName	Returns the name of the user who started the current thread of this process.
Version	Returns a version object from which we can learn the major, minor, build, and revision numbers of the CLR.
WorkingSet	Returns a 64-bit number representing the amount of physical memory used by the process.
Exit()	Quits this process with a specified exit code to pass to the operating system.
ExpandEnvironmentVariables()	Sets the environment variables by parsing the specified string containing environment variables quoted with the percent sign. Returns the new environment variable settings in a string.
GetCommandLineArgs()	Returns an array of strings where each element contains a command line argument passed to the process.
GetEnvironmentVariable()	Gets the value of the passed environment variable.
GetEnvironmentVariables()	Gets all environment variables and their values and returns an IDictionary interface for accessing them

Environment Member	Description
GetFolderPath()	Returns the fully qualified path to the system special folder (set by the system and on demand explicitly by the user) of the passed-in-type SpecialFolder enumeration. This enumeration has values such as Favorites, History, Cookies, Startup, Startup, and InternetCache, all indicating a special folder of the operating system.
GetLogicalDrives()	Gets the names of the logical drives that exist on the computer as an array of strings.

Table 21.13: Environment Class Members

The System.Environment.SystemDirectory property returns a string containing the operating system's directory (e.g., c:\winnt\system32). You can use the Environment.UserInteractive property to get a Boolean value indicating whether the current process is running in user-interactive mode. (User-interactive mode means the user can send inputs to the process and see outputs with his or her eyes!) UserInteractive will be *true* if the current process is running in user-interactive mode.

To list the environment variables, open the command prompt console, type "SET," and press ENTER. You can obtain the values of any of these environment variables by using the Environment.GetEnvironmentVariable method. Simply pass it the name of the environment variable for which you want to obtain a value, and it will return the value as a string. For example, if you want the name of the user who is currently logged in, you can use the following:

```
Environment.GetEnvironmentVariable("USERNAME");
```

You can use the Environment.NewLine property to get the newline string defined for this environment. (In our case it's a string containing \r\n.)

You can quit our application program anytime and return an Int32 exit code to the operating system, using the Environment.Exit(<exit_code>) method.

You can use the Environment.GetCommandLineArgs() method to return an array of strings where each element contains a command-line argument.

```
String str1[] = Environment.GetCommandLineArgs();

str1[0] ; // the executable file name.

str1[1]; // zero or more command line arguments.
str1[2]; // zero or more command line arguments.
. .
```

Listing 21.30 uses various Environment class methods, fields, and properties to illustrate the power of this class.

Listing 21.30—Using the Environment Class (environment1.cs)

```
using System;
using System.Diagnostics;

namespace EnvironmentTestConsole
{
        /// <summary>
        /// Summary description for Class1.
        /// </summary>
        class Class1
        {
```

```csharp
        /// <summary>
        /// The main entry point for the application.
        /// </summary>
        [STAThread]
        public static void Main(string[] args)
        {
                // reading the entire command line
                // including the path to the application:
                String s = Environment.CommandLine;
                Console.WriteLine(s);

                // reading each argument individually:
                foreach (String s1 in
                    Environment.GetCommandLineArgs())
                    Console.WriteLine(s1  + "\n");

                // reading a specific argument:
                if (Environment.GetCommandLineArgs().Length > 0)
                {
                 s =
            Environment.GetCommandLineArgs().
            GetValue(0).ToString();
                 Console.WriteLine(s + "\n");
                }

                // manipulating the current working directory:
                Environment.CurrentDirectory = @"C:\Temp";
            Console.WriteLine("Current directory is: " +
                        Environment.CurrentDirectory);

                // getting the computer and user names:
                Console.WriteLine("Machine= " +
                        Environment.MachineName);
                Console.WriteLine("User= " +
                        Environment.UserDomainName +
                    "\\" + Environment.UserName);
                Console.WriteLine("Is Interactive= " +
                    Environment.UserInteractive.ToString());

    // reading all environment variables
    foreach(String s2 in
            Environment.GetEnvironmentVariables().Keys)
        Console.WriteLine(s2 + "=" +

    Environment.GetEnvironmentVariable(s2).ToString());

    // reading a specific variable
    s = Environment.GetEnvironmentVariable("PATH").ToString();

    // translating or expanding strings containing
// variable references
    Console.WriteLine(Environment.ExpandEnvironmentVariables(
        @"User%userdomain%\%username% on %computername%\n"));

    // identifying logical drive letters
    foreach(String s3 in Environment.GetLogicalDrives())
                Console.WriteLine("Drive: " + s3 + "\n");

    // locating the system folder
    Console.WriteLine("System Dir= " +
                Environment.SystemDirectory  +
                "\n");

                // locating all system and other special folders
                String sFolderName = "";
                String sFolderPath = "";
    foreach(Environment.SpecialFolder eFolderID in
```

```
Enum.GetValues(typeof(System.Environment.SpecialFolder)))
    {
    sFolderName =
    Enum.GetName(typeof(System.Environment.SpecialFolder),
    eFolderID);
    sFolderPath = Environment.GetFolderPath(eFolderID);
    Console.WriteLine(sFolderName + "=" + sFolderPath + "\n");
    }

    // locating a specific special folder
    sFolderPath =
    Environment.GetFolderPath(Environment.SpecialFolder.
                             ApplicationData);

    // identifying OS parameters:
    s = Environment.NewLine;  // New Line sequence for the
                             // current OS
    switch(Environment.OSVersion.Platform)
  {
   case PlatformID.Win32NT:
    Console.WriteLine("Running under Windows NT or Windows
                     2000\n");
    break;
   case PlatformID.Win32S:
     Console.WriteLine("Running under Win32s\n");
     break;
   case PlatformID.Win32Windows:
     Console.WriteLine("Running under win9x\n");
     break;
  }

    Console.WriteLine("OS Version= " +
    Environment.OSVersion.Version.ToString() + "\n");
    Console.WriteLine("Stack size= " + Environment.StackTrace +
                     "\n");
    Console.WriteLine("Tick Count= " +
                     Environment.TickCount.ToString()+
                     "\n");
    Debug.WriteLine("CLR Version= " +
                 Environment.Version.ToString() + "\n");
    Debug.WriteLine("WorkingSet size= " +
                 Environment.WorkingSet.ToString() + "\n");

    // setting an exit code for the current process
    Environment.ExitCode = 19;
    Console.WriteLine("Exit code=" +
                     Environment.ExitCode.ToString() + "\n");

    Console.WriteLine("\nHit any key to continue\n");
    Console.ReadLine();

    //Setting an exit code and terminating immediately:
    Environment.Exit(1919);

    // the exit codes are ignored in debugging and are only valid
    // for releases.
  }
 }
}
```

The Win32 SDK includes an API called GetVersionEx that returns the information in the OSVERSIONINFO structure. Once we have populated this structure, we can look at the values of its various members to see what version of the operating system we are running. To accomplish the same task using the Environment class, simply examine the Environment.OSVersion property that returns an OperatingSystem object. This object can be used to get the value of the operating system version.

The OperatingSystem class has three properties that contain all the information you need to return attributes about the operating system. Following is a list of these properties:

- *Platform property*. Returns a PlatformID value. This enumeration has three possible values: Win32NT—the operating system is Windows NT/2000/XP; Win32Windows—the operating system is Windows 95/98/ME; Win32S—the operating system is a Win32 subsystem running on a 16-bit version of Windows 3.0/3.1/3.11WFW. We leave the honor of running of the code on the MAC and Linux operating systems to you, so you can see how the .NET Framework is implemented there. Just run Listing 21.31.
- *CSD property*. Indicates the Corrected Service Diskette number of the operating system. In other words, this is a string representing the recent service pack installed for the operating system.
- *Version property*. Returns a Version class. This class is nothing but the standard version class used for indicating any assembly's version. .NET defines a version value in the format major.minor.build.revision. The Version class has four properties that completely define the version of an operating system or an assembly:
  - Major—major version number
  - Minor—minor version number
  - Build—build number
  - Revision—revision number

You can use the values returned by the preceding three properties to get the exact version of the operating system (Windows) running on your computer.

Note that the build and revision numbers are optional!

Listing 21.31 shows how to use the Environment class in the System namespace to get an OperatingSystem object.

Listing 21.31—Getting Operating System Details

```
using System;

public class EnvironmentVersionSample
{
 public static void Main(string[] args)
 {
  // Get the operating system from Environment Class
  OperatingSystem os = Environment.OSVersion;

  // Get the version information
  Version vs = os.Version;

  Console.WriteLine("Major" + vs.Major);
  Console.WriteLine("Minor" + vs.Minor);
  Console.WriteLine("Revision" + vs.Revision);
  Console.WriteLine("BuildNumber" + vs.Build);
 }
}
```

The Buffer Class

The word *buffer* implies something that works directly on memory. In the C# language, buffering is basically a manipulation of unmanaged memory that is represented as arrays of bytes. Table 21.14

describes some members of the Buffer class. Let's look at an example of a program where we copy one array of data into another using the Array class, and then we will compare that with a Buffer class example doing the same thing.

Buffer Member	Description
BlockCopy()	Copies some bytes from a source array object beginning at the specified offset to the destination array object beginning at the specified offset.
ByteLength()	Gets the total number of bytes in the array.
GetByte()	Gets the byte at a specific index location in an array object.
SetByte()	Sets the byte at a specific index location in an array object.

Table 21.14: Buffer Class Members

In the System.Array class the Copy() member allows us to copy from one array to another. Let's take an array of five elements, Myarr1[5], initialized with the data 1, 2, 3, 4, 5 and another array of 10 elements, Myarr2[10], with the data 0, 0, 0, 0, 0, 6, 7, 8, 9, 10. In arrays, *length* refers to the number of elements in the array. In our example, Myarr1 has five elements, so the array length is 5, and Myarr2 has 10 elements, so the array length is 10. The Array class includes the Copy() method, which copies the contents of one array into another. It copies a range of elements from an array starting at the specified source index and pastes it to another array starting at the specified destination index. The Copy() method takes five parameters: source array, source index, destination array, destination index, and number of elements to copy.

The method Array.Copy(Array sourceArray, int sourceIndex, Array destinationArray, int destinationIndex, int length) takes five parameters: first, the array that contains the data to copy; second, the index in the sourceArray at which copying begins; third, the array that receives the data; fourth, DestinationIndex, the index in the destinationArray at which storing begins; and, fifth, the number of elements to copy.

Listing 21.32 demonstrates the use of the Array.Copy() method. In the listing we perform Array.Copy(myarr1, 0, myarr2, 0, 5) for the following arrays:

int[] myarr1 = new int[5] {1, 2, 3, 4, 5};
int[] myarr2 = new int[10] {0, 0, 0, 0, 0, 6, 7, 8, 9, 10};

Listing 21.32—Using Array.Copy (array1buffer.cs)

```
using System;

public class Array1
{
 public static void Main(string[] args)
 {
  int[] myarr1 = new int[5] {1, 2, 3, 4, 5};
  int[] myarr2 = new int[10] {0, 0, 0, 0, 0, 6, 7, 8, 9, 10};
  Console.Write("Before Array copy operation\n");
  Console.Write("Myarr1 and Byte Length{0}\n", myarr1.Length);
  foreach(int i in myarr1)
   Console.Write("{0} \t", i);
  Console.WriteLine("\nMyarr2 and Byte Length:{0} \n", myarr2.Length);
  foreach(int i in myarr2)
   Console.Write("{0} \t", i);
  Array.Copy(myarr1, 0, myarr2, 0, 5);
  Console.Write("After Array copy operation\n");
  Console.Write("Myarr1 :\n");
  foreach(int i in myarr1)
   Console.Write("{0} \t", i);
```

```
  Console.WriteLine("\nMyarr2: \n");
  foreach(int i in myarr2)
   Console.Write("{0} \t", i);
  Console.ReadLine();
 }
}
```

Listing 21.32 outputs the following:

```
Before Array.Copy operation

Myarr1 and Byte Length :5

1       2       3       4       5

Myarr2 and Byte Length:10

0       0       0       0       0       6       7       8       9       10

After Array.Copy operation

Myarr1 :

1       2       3       4       5

Myarr2:

1       2       3       4       5       6       7       8       9       10
```

Now let's see how the same thing is done using the BlockCopy() method of the System.Buffer class. The major difference between the two types of copying, Array.Copy and BlockCopy, is that the copy made in the Buffer class is not an index-to-index copy. It is from offset to offset in memory. The Buffer class copies a specified number of bytes from a source array starting at a particular offset to a destination array starting at a particular offset in memory. In our example, we are using arrays of integers, and we know that each integer occupies four bytes. Therefore, the offset values will be the addition of four bytes from the starting offset value.

Let's look at an example of copying using BlockCopy with an array of five elements, Myarr1[5], initialized with the data 1, 2, 3, 4, 5 and another array of 10 elements, Myarr2[10], with the data 0, 0, 0, 0, 0, 6, 7, 8, 9, 10.

In the Buffer class the *length* refers to the number of bytes in the array. In our example, Myarr1 has five elements, so the byte length is 5 (elements) × 4 (number of bytes in an integer) = 20 bytes. Myarr2 has 10 elements, so the byte length is 10 (elements) × 4 = 40 bytes. Note that you can get the byte length of the entire array by using Buffer.ByteLength(Myarr1).

The BlockCopy method in the Buffer class copies a range of elements from an array starting at the specified source offset value to another array starting at the specified destination offset value. The BlockCopy() method takes five parameters: source array, source offset value, destination array, destination offset value, and the number of bytes to copy. In our example, we need to copy five elements, so 5 × 4 = 20 bytes is the number of bytes to copy.

The BlockCopy(Array src, int srcOffset, Array dst, int dstOffset, int count) method takes five parameters. The first is the source buffer, the second is the byte offset into src, the third is the destination buffer, the fourth is the byte offset into dst, and the fifth is the number of bytes to copy. Listing 21.33 demonstrates the use of the Buffer.BlockCopy() method.

Listing 21.33—Using Buffer.BlockCopy (buffer1.cs)

```
using System;

public class buffer1
{
 public static void Main(string[] args)
 {
  int[] myarr1 = new int[5] {1, 2, 3, 4, 5};
  int[] myarr2=new int[10] {0, 0 ,0 ,0 ,0 ,6 , 7, 8, 9, 10};
  Console.Write("Before Block copy operation\n");
  Console.Write("Myarr1 and Byte Length :{0}\n", Buffer.ByteLength(myarr1));

  foreach(int i in myarr1)
       Console.Write("{0} \t", i);
  Console.WriteLine("\nMyarr2 and Byte Length:{0} \n",Buffer.ByteLength(myarr2));
  foreach(int i in myarr2)
       Console.Write("{0} \t", i);
  Buffer.BlockCopy(myarr1, 0, myarr2, 0, 20);
  Console.Write("After Block copy operation\n");
  Console.Write("Myarr1 :\n");
  foreach(int i in myarr1)
       Console.Write("{0} \t", i);
  Console.WriteLine("\nMyarr2: \n");
  foreach(int i in myarr2)
       Console.Write("{0} \t", i);
  Console.ReadLine();
 }
}
```

Listing 21.33 ouputs the following:

```
Before BlockCopy operation

Myarr1 and Byte Length :20

1       2       3       4       5

Myarr2 and Byte Length:40

0       0       0       0       0       6       7       8       9       10

After BlockCopy operation

Myarr1 :

1       2       3       4       5

Myarr2:

1       2       3       4       5       6       7       8       9       10
```

Math Class

The System.Math class offers many constant fields and static methods that you can use to do trigonometric, logarithmic, and other mathematical calculations. For example, the Pow method of the System.Math class can be used to raise a number to a power of x. Let's use the Pow method and the Math.PI field (returns the value of π, the ratio of a circle's circumference to its diameter) to calculate the area of a circle (dblRadius is the radius of a circle, and $\pi \approx 3.14159265358979323846$):

```
// Area of a Circle = πr²
```

double answer = Math.PI * Math.Pow(dblRadius, 2);

Another constant, other than pi, is the natural logarithmic base or Euler constant, specified by the constant Math.E (e ≈ 2.7182818284590452354). The double Log method calculates the logarithm of a specified number in a specified base. The Log(double a, double newBase) method takes two parameters. The first is the number whose logarithm is to be found, and the second is the base of the logarithm. Let's prove that log10e = 0.43429448190325182765, which we already know from high school math lessons.

```
// log10e = 0.43429448190325182765 ??? yes!
answer = Math.Log(Math.E, 10);
```

The Math.Max and Math.Min return the larger and the smaller of two numbers passed in, respectively. They support almost all number types as parameters. Their overloads are shown in Listing 21.34.

Listing 21.34—Math.Max and Math.Min Overloads

```
byte Max(byte, byte);
decimal Max(decimal, decimal);
double Max(double, double);
short Max(short, short);
int Max(int, int);
long Max(long, long);
sbyte Max(sbyte, sbyte);
float Max(float, float);
ushort Max(ushort, ushort);
uint Max(uint, uint);
ulong Max(ulong, ulong);

byte Min(byte, byte);
decimal Min(decimal, decimal);
double Min(double, double);
short Min(short, short);
int Min(int, int);
long Min(long, long);
sbyte Min(sbyte, sbyte);
float Min(float, float);
ushort Min(ushort, ushort);
uint Min(uint, uint);
ulong Min(ulong, ulong);
```

You can use the Sqrt method to return the square root of a number. For example, the following code calculates the square root of 49, or 7.

```
answer = Math.Sqrt(49);
```

The Abs method returns the absolute value of a number (the positive value of a number regardless of its sign). For example, the following code returns the absolute value of –3, which is 3.

```
answer = Math.Abs(-3);
```

The Math.Abs method has many overloads matching common value types such as Int16, Int32, In32, Single, SByte, Decimal, and Double.

The Sign method returns the sign of a number. The function returns one of three mathematical results. If the number is negative, Sign returns –1; if it's positive, Sign returns 1; if the number is equal to 0, Sign returns 0.

The Round method rounds a number to the nearest whole number. Math.Round (banker's rounding or rounding to nearest) applies IEEE Standard 754, section 4. For example, the following code is used to round the number 5.499999.

```
answer = Math.Round(5.499999);
```

The answer would be 5. If you use Round to round a number that is exactly halfway between two numbers, such as 5.5, Round always returns the even number closest to the number. Thus, Math.Round(5.5) would return 6, but Math.Round(8.5) would return 8.

Math.Round has another overload with which you can specify the number of digits beyond the decimal point in the returned value. In other words, it returns the number's nearest value with precision equal to the second parameter passed. If the value to round is exactly halfway between an even and an odd number (e.g., .45 with precision of 1), then the even number is returned. If the number of digits behind the decimal in the first parameter is less than the precision number in the second parameter, then the Round method returns the passed value untouched. Some examples are shown in Listing 21.35.

Listing 21.35—Rounding with Precision

```
Math.Round(5.44, 1); // returns 5.4
Math.Round(5.45, 1); // returns 5.4
Math.Round(5.46, 1); // returns 5.5
Math.Round(5.54, 1); // returns 5.5
Math.Round(5.55, 1); // returns 5.6
Math.Round(5.56, 1); // returns 5.6
```

You can use the Floor method to truncate a real number. Floor returns the largest whole number smaller than the original number. For example, use the following to return the floor of 4.8.

```
answer = Math.Floor(4.8);
```

The answer would be 4. Note that the Floor method may behave differently than you might expect for negative values. For example, Math.Floor(–4.8) returns –5.

The Ceiling method does the opposite, returning the smallest whole number greater than the original.

```
answer = Math.Ceiling(4.8);  // returns 5
```

The Math class contains a number of additional methods for making trigonometric and logarithmic calculations such as Sin, Asin, Sinh, Cos, Acos, Acosh, Tan, Atan, Tanh, Log, and Log10.

In Listing 21.36 we use the Math.Sin function to output a sine wave cycle to the console.

Listing 21.36—Outputting Sine Wave Values to Console

```
using System;
class SineWaveToConsole
{
        private static string spaces(double val)
        {
                string SpaceString = new String(' ', ((int)(val *
                                                               10.0)) +
10);
                return SpaceString;
        }
```

```
[STAThread]
static void Main(string[] args)
{
        for (float i = 0; i < Math.PI * 2.0F; i += 0.3F)
        {
                        Console.WriteLine("The sine of {0,10:F} = {1,-10:F6}"
                          + spaces(Math.Sin(i)) + "*", i, Math.Sin(i));
        }

        Console.ReadLine();
    }
}
```

The listing will output a numeric representation of a sine wave along with a text character graph (see Figure 21.3). Note the use of composite formatting to ensure that the sine value is trimmed to six digits beyond the decimal.

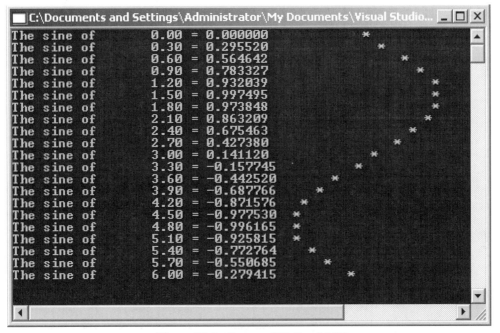

Figure 21.3: Output of Listing 21.36

Generating Random Numbers Using the System.Random Class

Before we dive into the details of the System.Random class, we should talk about randomness in discrete mathematics. The two most common scenarios for generating random numbers are generating integers uniformly between 1 and n and generating real numbers uniformly between 0 and 1. Most random-number-generation algorithms are not influenced by the outside universe; they are inherently pseudorandom: predictable and following a pattern (ideally not an obvious one). You should keep in mind the following two statements on pseudorandomness made by respected computer science masters:

- "Anyone who considers arithmetical methods of producing random digits is, of course, in a state of sin."—John Von Neumann (1951)
- "Random number generators should not be chosen at random."—Donald Knuth (1986)

Let's go back to our main focus now. We use the System.Random class to produce a random number. System.Random can return both decimal and integer random numbers. In addition, System.Random by design can seed its random number generator with a random value derived from the computer system clock.

```
System.Random rnd = new System.Random();
```

You can initialize the seed with any Int32 value on demand at times when the system clock is not fast enough to refresh or when you need to synchronize your random number generators across a network. This is also the common use of a seed to synchronize two random number generators.

```
System.Random rnd = new System.Random((int)DateTime.Now.Ticks);
```

The Random class includes a series of methods allowing you to retrieve the next number produced by the random number generator. The NextDouble method returns a double random number between 0.0 and 1.0. The Next method returns an integer random number between two integer values. The NextBytes method fills the elements of a specified array of bytes with random numbers. The NextDouble, Next, and NextBytes methods are instance methods; therefore, you must instantiate a System.Random object before using them.

The Next() method has three overloads:

```
// a positive random number
public virtual int Next();
// a positive random number less than the specified maximum
public virtual int Next(int);
// a random number within a specified range
public virtual int Next(int, int);
```

You can use the Next method overloads as shown in Listing 21.37.

Listing 21.37—Using the Next Property

```
// any valid integer random number
Int32 dbl1 = rnd.Next();

// an integer between 0< and UpperBound where UpperBound + 1 >= 0
Int32 dbl1 = rnd.Next(UpperBound + 1);

// an integer between LowerBound< and UpperBound where UpperBound + 1 >= 0
// and LowerBound <= UpperBound + 1
Int32 dbl1 = rnd.Next(LowerBound, UpperBound + 1);

Using the NextDouble method of the Random class produces the next pseudorandom
double value that is greater than 0.0 and less than 1.0.

Double dbl1 = rnd.NextDouble();

The NextBytes method of the Random class produces an array of random bytes with
values ranging from 0 to MaxValue (MaxValue = 255).

Byte[] mybytes = new Byte[5];
// mybytes is filled with 5 bytes of random data
rnd.NextBytes(mybytes);
```

The program in Listing 21.38 generates unique integer random numbers in the ranges that you send to the application and then displays them on the console.

Listing 21.38—Generating Unique Random Numbers with Next(Int32, Int32)

```
using System;
class testrandom
{
 public static void Main(string[] args)
 {
  int intno;
  if (args.Length == 0)
  {
   Console.WriteLine ("Please enter a parameter eg. unique 5");
   return;
  }
  else
  {
  intno = Int32.Parse (args[0]);
   if (intno < 1)
   {
    // Check to see if user has entered value >= 1
    // because my LowerBound is  hardcoded to 1
    Console.WriteLine ("Enter value greater than or equal to 1" );
    return;
   }
  }

  unique_random generateit = new unique_random();
  generateit.create_random(intno);
 }
}

class unique_random
{
 public void create_random (int passed_intno)
 {

  int LowerBound = 1;
  int UpperBound = passed_intno;
  bool firsttime = true;
  int starti = 0;
  int[] vararray;
  vararray = new int[UpperBound];

  // Random Class used here
  Random randomGenerator = new Random (DateTime.Now.Millisecond);

  do
  {
  int nogenerated = randomGenerator.Next(LowerBound, UpperBound+1);

  // Note: randomGenerator.Next generates no. to UpperBound - 1 hence +1
  // .... i got stuck at this pt & had to use the debugger.

  if (firsttime) // if (firsttime == true)
  {
   vararray[starti] = nogenerated;
   // we simply store the nogenerated in  vararray
   firsttime = false;
   starti++;
  }
  else // if (firsttime == false)
  {
   bool duplicate_flag = CheckDuplicate(nogenerated, starti, vararray);
   // call to check in array
    if (!duplicate_flag) // duplicate_flag == false
    {
      vararray[starti] = nogenerated;
      starti++;
```

```
      }
    }
  } while (starti < UpperBound);

  PrintArray (vararray); // Print the array
}

public bool CheckDuplicate (int newrandomNum, int loopcount, int [] function_array)
{
  bool temp_duplicate = false;

  for (int j = 0; j < loopcount; j++)
  {
   if (function_array[j] == newrandomNum)
   {
    temp_duplicate = true;
    break;
   }
  }
 return temp_duplicate;
}

// Print Array

public static void PrintArray(Array arr)
{
  Console.Write ("{");
  int count = 0;
  int li = arr.Length;
  foreach (object o in arr)
  {
   Console.Write("{0}", o);
   count++;
   //Condition to check whether ',' should be added in printing arrray
   if (count < li)
   Console.Write(", ");
  }
  Console.WriteLine ("}");
 }
}
```

Windows Management Instrumentation

Windows Management Instrumentation (WMI) helps to ease administrative enterprise system management tasks such as starting and stopping remote services and rebooting a remote machine. With WMI you can create management applications to control and modify operating system elements contained in systems, applications, networks, and devices such as CPUs, disks, memory, services, and network status. But you are required to have authorization to perform the relevant tasks. All of the .NET WMI classes live in the System.Management namespace.

Although WMI is a great feature, it may prove to be a security risk because intruders may use WMI objects accidentally or maliciously to their advantage without your control. If you have no intention of using the features of WMI on your network, you may want to disable it on certain computers. Note that all of the WMI operations are controlled by the Windows Management Instrumentation Windows service on computers on which Windows NT, 2000, or XP is installed.

WMI is an interface designed to interact with parts of the Windows operating system. Without it we would have to address administrative tasks individually rather than remotely and automatically. WMI works with the Common Information Model Object Manager (CIMOM). CIMOM is a database of objects representing different operating system elements such as applications and services . CIMOM provides a common interface to these operating system elements.

WMI is the Microsoft implementation of Web-Based Enterprise Management (WBEM). WBEM is an industry initiative to develop a standardized technology for accessing management information such as details about the state of system memory, inventories of currently installed client applications, and other information about client status in an enterprise environment. WMI enables the Common Information Model (CIM) designed by the Distributed Management Task Force (DMTF) to represent systems, applications, networks, and other managed components. CIM can model every component in the managed environment, regardless of the data source location. As well as data modeling, WMI provides a powerful set of basic services that include query-based information retrieval and event notification.

CIM is a model for describing overall management information in a network or enterprise environment. It comprises both a specification and a schema. The specification defines the details for integration with other management models, while the schema provides the actual model descriptions.

More details about WBEM, CIM, and other DMTF standards are available at http://www.dmtf.org/standards/.

WMI can help you accomplish a horde of tasks:

- Control remote workstations and severs in bulk from your own workstation
- Audit or configure Windows 2000 systems automatically and remotely
- Centrally archive Windows NT event logs
- Block server render down with WMI event notification
- Integrate WMI with Active Directory
- Manipulate remote processes and files
- Identify, list, and adjust all the services on a server
- Identify, list, and adjust all the NT file system partitions on a server that have less than 10 percent free space
- Execute a backup on a Microsoft Exchange Server machine and then dump the transaction log
- Use any existing WMI method to launch a program on a server remotely
- Set up an event consumer that subscribes to a system that watches for a specific event in the system log and sends an SMS (System Management Service) or e-mail message when that event occurs
- Reconfigure an event consumer to request a system event whenever a server's CPU use exceeds 85 percent

WMI has a query language named WQL (Windows Management Instrumentation Query Language). WQL is a subset of the American National Standards Institute Structured Query Language (ANSI SQL) with small semantic changes to support WMI. For example, you can perform a WQL query such as "SELECT * FROM Win32_Processor" on the root\CIMV2 namespace path.

The code samples in Listings 21.39 through 21.46 demonstrate various ways to employ WMI in the .NET Framework.

Listing 21.39—Retrieving Local WMI Objects

```
ManagementObject mo = new ManagementObject("Win32_Share.Name=\"X$\"");
mo.Get();
Console.WriteLine("Win32_Share.Name=\"X$\" path is {0}", mo["Path"]);
```

Listing 21.40—Retrieving Remote WMI Objects

```
ManagementPath path = new ManagementPath();
```

```
path.Path = "Win32_Share.Name=\"X$\"";
path.Server = "MCBcomputer";
path.NamespacePath = @"root\CIMV2";

ManagementObject mo = new ManagementObject(path);

Console.WriteLine("Win32_Share.Name=\"X$\" path is {0}", mo["Path"]);
```

Listing 21.41—Enumerating WMI Objects

```
ManagementClass mc = new ManagementClass("Win32_Share");
ManagementObjectCollection mcCollection = mc.GetInstances();

foreach( ManagementObject mo in mcCollection )
{
        Console.WriteLine( "'{0}' path is '{1}'",
                mo["__RELPATH"], mo["Path"]);
}
```

Listing 21.42—Performing Queries on WMI Objects

```
ManagementObjectSearcher query =
        new ManagementObjectSearcher(
                "SELECT * FROM Win32_Service WHERE Started=true");

ManagementObjectCollection queryCollection = query.Get();

foreach( ManagementObject mo in queryCollection )
{
        Console.WriteLine( "Service: '{0}'", mo["DisplayName"]);
}
```

Listing 21.43—Calling a WMI Object Method to Create TEMP Share to C:\TEMP

```
ManagementClass mc = new ManagementClass("Win32_Share");

// Get the methods in parameters
ManagementBaseObject inParams =
        mc.GetMethodParameters("Create");

// Setup method parameters
inParams["Name"] = "TEMP";
inParams["Path"] = @"C:\TEMP";
inParams["Type"] = 0;

ManagementBaseObject outParams =
        mc.InvokeMethod("Create", inParams, null);

// inspect out parameters for return value
uint retVal = (uint)outParams["ReturnValue"];
```

Listing 21.44—Managing Remote WMI Connections

```
ConnectionOptions options = new ConnectionOptions();
options.Authentication  = AuthenticationLevel.Call;
options.Impersonation   = ImpersonationLevel.Impersonate;
options.EnablePrivileges = true;
options.Locale = "MS_409";
options.Username = @"MCBDOMAIN\mcb";
options.Password = "password";

ManagementScope ms =
        new ManagementScope(@"\\MCBcomputer\root\CIMV2", options);

// Explicit connection to WMI namespace
ms.Connect();
```

```
ManagementObject mo =
        new ManagementObject("Win32_Share.Name=\"X$\"");

// Reuse existing connection for this
// ManagementObject retrieval
mo.Scope = ms;

// Connection scope used when object is retrieved here!
mo.Get();

Console.WriteLine("Win32_Share.Name=\"X$\" path is {0}", mo["Path"]);


Listing 21.45—Rebooting a Remote Computer with WMI (reboot1.cs)
using System;
using System.Management;

class RemoteWMI
{
   static void Main(string[] args)
   {
     //Connect to the remote computer
     ConnectionOptions co = new ConnectionOptions();
     co.Username = "mcb";
     co.Password = "password";
     ManagementScope ms = new ManagementScope(@"\\MCBcomputer\root\cimv2", co);

     //Query remote computer across the connection
     ObjectQuery oq = new ObjectQuery("SELECT * FROM Win32_OperatingSystem");

     ManagementObjectSearcher query1 = new ManagementObjectSearcher(ms,oq);
     ManagementObjectCollection queryCollection1 = query1.Get();

     foreach( ManagementObject mo in queryCollection1 )
     {
       string[] ss={""};
       mo.InvokeMethod("Reboot",ss);
       Console.WriteLine(mo.ToString());
     }
   }
}
```

Listing 21.46—Clearing the Application Logs using WMI

```
using System;
using System.Management;
namespace ClearEventLog
{
    class ClearEventLog
    {
        [STAThread]
        static void Main(string[] args)
        {
          try
          {
                // create conncetion options
                ConnectionOptions options = new
ConnectionOptions();
      options.Authentication  = AuthenticationLevel.Call;
      options.Impersonation  = ImpersonationLevel.Impersonate;
      options.EnablePrivileges  = true;
      options.Locale = @"MS_409"; // LocaleID
      options.Username = @"mcb"; // username for connection
      options.Password = @"mindcracker"; // password for the
```

```
// create management scope for CIM/WMI
 ManagementScope ms =  new
ManagementScope(@"\\MCBComputer\root\CIMV2",
                 options);

 // query Application event log
ManagementObjectSearcher query1 =
new ManagementObjectSearcher(@"select * from
Win32_NTEventLogFile where LogfileName='Application'");

 // get the query collection
 ManagementObjectCollection queryCollection1 =
                 query1.Get();

// clear the Application event log
foreach(ManagementObject mo in queryCollection1)
    {
        mo.Get();
        ManagementBaseObject inParams =
           mo.GetMethodParameters("ClearEventLog");
        ManagementBaseObject outParams =
         mo.InvokeMethod("ClearEventLog", inParams, null);
        mo.Dispose();
        Console.WriteLine();
        if (0 ==    (int)(uint)
           (outParams.
           Properties["ReturnValue"].Value)
         )
           Console.WriteLine("cleared...");
       else
           Console.WriteLine("not cleared!!!");
    }
   }
   catch(Exception e)
   {
     Console.WriteLine("Error: {0}", e.ToString());
   }
  }
 }
}
```

Summary

In this chapter we discussed the following:

- Using the Debug, Process, ProcessThread, Switch, TraceListener, EventLog, and PerformanceCounter classes to diagnose operating systems, code, and computers
- The Registry class and how to read and write to the Windows registry
- The Timer class, which helps us trigger a code routine continually at specified time intervals
- Accessing LDAP servers such as Microsoft Windows 2000 Active Directory and the Internet Information Server metabase
- The Reflection namespace and how to effectively find all the types in an assembly and dynamically invoke methods in an assembly
- The Reflection.Emit namespace and how to use emitting to generate MSIL codes and .exe files on the fly
- Using the Environment class to manage system environment variables
- The differences between the Array.Copy() and Buffer.Copy() methods
- Using the Math class methods and fields within the .NET Framework to perform mathematical operations
- Generating pseudorandom numbers of various types (e.g., Int32, Double, and Bytes)
- Managing computer enterprise resources with WMI

The .NET Framework offers a myriad of classes for use in development projects. The features covered in this chapter constitute just the tip of the iceberg. Much more exists under the surface for you to explore.

Chapter 22:
Security in .NET

Introduction

This chapter addresses the security aspects of assemblies, which are the building blocks of .NET Framework applications. They form the fundamental unit of deployment, version control, reuse, activation scope, and security authorization. This last aspect, security authorization, is the focal point of this chapter; more general information about assembly deployment can be found in Chapter 26.

Microsoft took a big stride toward improved configuration and maintenance of software systems by allowing administrators rather than developers to determine the permissions a segment of code should have at runtime. Now such decisions fall under the domain of professionals who really know the runtime environment.

During installation of a new application in the Windows Operating System (OS), the setup package may overwrite existing shared dynamic-link libraries (DLLs) to update the module. (Of course, well-designed installation programs prompt you about duplicate file names.) The overwriting occurs because you cannot have multiple versions of DLLs in a shared environment. This often causes existing applications to function incorrectly because they may depend on a specific version of the shared DLL—which may have been overwritten! The most recently installed version of the shared DLL can overwrite a previously installed yet *more current* version. The version most recently installed prevails for all of the installed applications referencing that DLL module, potentially causing enormous problems for administrators.

The C# compiler processes your source code and produces Microsoft intermediate language (MSIL) assembly files. Additionally, it embeds *metadata* in your assemblies. The .NET metadata is merely a cluster of information—specifically, the declared types, methods, fields, properties, and events implemented in the files of the assembly—made persistent in binary data. The metadata is always embedded in the same executable file and DLL as the MSIL code. For example, the metadata contains reference data to find the actual code for every implemented method that the common language runtime (CLR) uses.

Not surprisingly, in the .NET Framework, assemblies are also versioned like DLLs that are based on the Component Object Model (COM). However, multiple versions of an assembly can coexist on the same computer without causing trouble. This allows applications to run with the assemblies they were built with. Assemblies contain all the metadata related to them, so no separate files are necessary to describe the contents of an assembly.

As with COM+, the .NET Framework code that accesses computing resources must be assigned permission to use those resources. The system administrator can configure security policies to grant access to resources based on the caller's identity and the origin of the code. For example, suppose you develop code that accesses any registry key. At execution time, the framework requests permission to access the registry. This way the system can make sure that the assembly in which the executed program exists has permission to access the registry key.

Formerly, all applications installed on a computer had to be registered before they could be used. Most installation programs not only copy files to the computer but also add various information to the registry and create various hard settings needed to uninstall that application later.

It is safe to say that we have reached the end of the COM+ era and the beginning of the .NET era. With the advent of .NET Framework, we no longer need to develop COM+ components unless they are truly necessary in order to interact with legacy applications. Of course, we will still use legacy COM+ components with our current Web services and other .NET applications during the migration to .NET applications.

Figure 22.1 depicts the typical way of exposing a COM+ component interface via the .NET framework. You can use any .NET client application, such as a Web service in which the .NET client application itself is a server application, to expose the component interface. In other words, the .NET client application (Web service) is an intermediary application to the actual COM+ component or server.

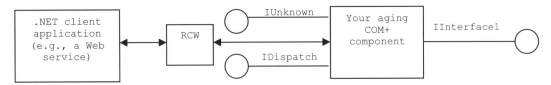

Figure 22.1: Client Access Through Runtime Callable Wrapper

The runtime callable wrapper (RCW) of .NET wraps the COM+ components' exposed interfaces. The RCW mediates between the COM+ component and the CLR. RCW exposes the COM+ components to .NET clients as if they were native .NET components. RCW exposes the .NET clients to COM+ components as if they were standard COM clients.

As a .NET client developer, you can generate the RCW using either Visual Studio .NET (VS.NET) or the command-line–based type library import utility of the .NET software development kit (SDK). With the VS.NET approach, you add a COM+ reference to your active project; with the .NET SDK approach, you use a command-line tool called tlbimp.exe.

To install an application within the .NET Framework, you just copy the application's files into a directory on the client computer. There are two assembly types in .NET: private and public. You usually copy the private assemblies to the application installation directory. Any subfolder within the installation directory is also an appropriate place for private assemblies. You can uninstall private assemblies by deleting them from the local directory. You install shared public assemblies either to the global assembly cache (GAC) or to another global location on the computer disk. When any client application wants to reference and use those classes in a public (shared) or private assembly, it consults its configuration files to locate and then load the shared or private assembly. If the desired assembly cannot be found in the client application's configuration files, the application has the option of searching the system's configuration files.

The manifest information cluster is the most significant part of an assembly. The manifest of an assembly contains the following metadata information:

- Assembly name—a textual string name of the assembly.

- Version information—a major and minor version number, a revision number, and a build number. Version information is used by the CLR to enforce version policy. It defines which version of the assembly is loaded and run when an assembly is referenced from an application.
- Strong-name information—a cryptographic identifier, which the author of the assembly provides, and the public key of the publisher, which is used to create the strong-name signature for the assembly.
- Culture information—the culture information that the assembly supports.
- List of all files in the assembly—a hash of each file that was present when the manifest was built and the relative path to the files. The list also contains the simple name, public key, and versioning information of each dependent assembly.
- Type reference list—a list that identifies supported types.

Figure 22.2 depicts the differences between single-file and multifile assemblies. In some instances, the manifest actually resides inside an assembly.

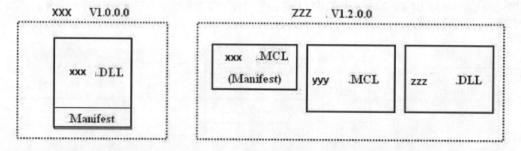

Figure 22.2: Single-file (XXX) and Multifile (ZZZ) Assemblies and Their Manifests

Signing an Assembly

You can ensure an assembly's identity by signing it. This signing operation employs public-key infrastructure algorithms. Assembly manifests are hashed and signed with a private key. When any assembly is deployed, the hashed value is calculated and compared with the hashed value stored in the assembly. If the runtime hash value matches the hard-coded hash, the installation is allowed to continue.

Note that the digital signature is found elsewhere in the metadata, in a section that is not included in the manifest. The digital signature of an assembly is just a secure hash of the manifest, which ensures that no one can modify the assembly contents after shipment. The CLR also provides support for embedding digital certificates, Authenticode, into assemblies.

You must use a private key to sign the assembly to create a strong-named assembly. (The *strong name* is a cryptographically strong identifier provided by the author or publisher of the assembly). The public key is by design incorporated into the assembly when it is signed, so your clients can verify the strong name. A .NET Framework SDK utility, the Strong Name tool (Sn.exe), is used to build strong-name key files. Various uses of the Sn.exe tool are explained in detail later in this chapter.

Strong-name (SN) signatures and Authenticode signatures do not override each other; they coexist. You must be sure that the strong-name signing operation takes place before the Authenticode signing.

You can identify managed code by using Authenticode signatures with strong-name signing. You can consider using both if you already have a security trust structure that depends on Authenticode signatures. The Authenticode signature is stored in a special section of the assembly if an assembly is also signed by using Authenticode. Only the file containing the manifest should be signed when you use Authenticode for multifile assemblies.

Together, SN and Authenticode signatures are nearly impenetrable by hackers. Authenticode signatures warrant that a particular publisher signed an assembly. Authenticode signatures also guarantee that the publisher has not yet revoked the certificate that signed the assembly. However, strong names do not warrant that a signature has not been revoked. Strong names allow you to ensure that the contents of a given assembly have not been tampered with. Therefore, you can make sure that the assembly loaded at runtime is from the same publisher who coded and compiled your program.

For several reasons, the cost of verifying assemblies signed by Authenticode is significantly greater than the cost of verifying a strong-named assembly. Strong-name signing does not involve certificates, but Authenticode does. Similarly, strong-name signing does not depend on a certification hierarchy, but Authenticode does. Remember, an Authenticode signature will make your assembly invalid if you assign a strong-name signature *after* an Authenticode signature, but the converse is not true.

To summarize, digital signatures and public-key encryption are used for code signing and strong names. After the publisher or author assigns a strong name to an assembly, the strong-name information, which includes a unique public key to the assembly, is stored in the manifest. Each strong-named assembly is digitally signed with a private key corresponding to its public key. This digital signature can be verified by using the public key that is stored in the manifest. You can also further sign an assembly with Authenticode on demand.

So much for theory—now let's examine a few realistic scenarios for signing assemblies.

- You want to build a strong-named assembly and sign it. Each file in the assembly is hashed, and the hash values are stored in the manifest. Your public key is stored in the manifest. The manifest file is digitally signed with your private key, and this signature is stored in a nonhashed segment of the assembly.
- You develop some code that references some other class of another strong-named assembly. The strong-named assembly's public key is read from the manifest and hashed to create a unique public-key token. This public-key token is a unique hash of the public key. This public-key token is stored, along with the version, simple name, and culture of the target assembly in the assembly references section (one entry for each external assembly referenced by the current module). The .NET Framework uses the assembly references section information at runtime to identify and locate the target assemblies.
- You want to load or install a strong-named assembly. The framework verifies the strong-name signature when you install the assembly in the GAC. If your assembly is not strong-named, then the framework verifies the signature whenever the assembly is loaded. If the system cannot verify the signature, the assembly cannot be installed in the GAC or you cannot load it. At runtime, whenever the system loads a module of an assembly, first its contents are hashed, and then the system compares that resultant value with the hash value stored in the manifest. If both hashes do not match, the system will not load the module of the assembly.

When an application calls a method that is found in another assembly, the runtime tries to locate the assembly by examining binding policy information. The binding policy information is created at compile time and is stored in the application's metadata. Binding is the operation of mapping assembly references to physical assemblies (typically dll's). The policy rules are used to determine how binding is done. An application will be bound to an assembly it was built and tested with, even if a newer version of the assembly is available. Default binding policy is always used unless it is explicitly overridden. Through the use of policy configuration files, binding policy can be altered without having to rebuild the assembly or the application. There are three policy resolution stages that the runtime may goes through before choosing which assembly to load. These stages, in order, are:

Application Policy:
- Modifies binding rules for a single application.
- Modified by Administrator.
- Can be provided with the application.
- Captured in XML configuration file in application directory in the format of *assembly_file_name.file_extension.config*.

Publisher Policy:
- Compiled into an assembly.
- Modifies binding rules for all applications using a specific assembly.
- Provided by publisher as a statement about compatibility.
- Captured in XML file wrapped as assembly that is signed by the publisher.
- Deployable with msi (Microsoft Installation) packages.
- Policy can be versioned.
- Stored in the global assembly cache.
- Found by naming convention.
- Forces applications to use the latest version of an assembly.
- Overrides application policy unless individual app refuses publisher policy.

Administrator Policy:
- Modifies binding rules for all applications on the machine.
- Modified by administrator.
- Overrides all other policy on machine.
- Mostly used security fixes to existing assemblies.
- Captured in *machine.config* file in CONFIG subdirectory of the runtime install path, *C:\Windows\Microsoft.net\Frameworks\<Version>\config*.

Because the CLR cache is a vital part of the framework, we should delve a bit into the topic. The CLR cache consists of two parts:

- *Download cache* can be managed with al.exe (an assembly generation tool), Windows Installer, and Windows Explorer. Downloaded code is placed in a special download cache and is not globally available on the machine. Downloaded code does not affect existing assemblies because of the versioning mechanism.
- *Global assembly cache* can be managed with gacutil.exe (a global assembly cache management utility) and mscorcfg.msc (the .NET Framework Configuration tool). It is a local cache of the shared assemblies maintained by the .NET Framework for the locally installed applications.

From the command prompt in the same directory where MyComponent.dll resides, run gacutil.exe of .NET Framework SDK as shown below.

```
gacutil /i MyComponent.dll
```

With this command you have placed the assembly in the GAC; and that assembly is said to be a public, shared assembly. It can now be used from other assemblies on the server, regardless of their location on the computer.

The .NET Framework requires developers to specifically identify as partially trusted any strong-named assembly and components that will be called by mobile code downloaded from the Internet or intranet and any code to which their security policy grants less than full trust.

Without the [assembly:AllowPartiallyTrustedCallers] attribute declaration (a custom attribute of the System.Security.AllowPartiallyTrustedCallersAttribute class) in the assembly configuration file, only fully trusted callers will be able to use the assembly. This attribute makes the assembly callable from any other partially or fully trusted assembly.

The AllowPartiallyTrustedCallers attribute removes the implicit LinkDemand (the permission check conducted on the caller) for the FullTrust permission set that is otherwise automatically placed on each assembly. Following are just some of the .NET Framework assemblies that have the AllowPartiallyTrustedCallers attribute declared:

- System.dll
- mscorlib.dll
- System.XML.dll
- System.Web.Services.dll
- System.Data.dll
- System.Windows.Forms.dll
- System.Drawing.dll

Refer to the Microsoft .NET Web site for updates to the .NET security framework.

Also note that even with the AllowPartiallyTrustedCallers attribute enabled, assemblies cannot be called by partially trusted code if one of the following security attributes is declared in the code:

- [PermissionSet(SecurityAction.LinkDemand, Name="FullTrust")]
- [SecurityPermission(SecurityAction.LinkDemand, UnmanagedCode=true)]
- [PermissionSet(SecurityAction.InheritanceDemand, Name="FullTrust")]
- [FileIOPermissionAttribute(SecurityAction.RequestMinimum, Unrestricted=true)]

Security and Microsoft .NET

The .NET Framework security system is built to provide protection as software undergoes the metamorphosis to multiple mobile components. The .NET security system provides a fine-grained, extensible policy and permission system so that people can run more powerful software code without compromising the system to security-related risks. The .NET security system enables administrators to create robust security policies at all levels because administrators are not forced to determine the trust of users at runtime.

As you will see later, .NET security policies are completely customizable. Developers can focus mainly on the application logic rather than delving into security details. Thus they do not need to deal with security at the core level. Security is handled capably by the CLR in the .NET Framework. Developers can use and extend .NET security at any time.

Security, an essential part of the .NET Framework, starts immediately after a class is loaded in the .NET runtime memory area; the framework performs many initial verification checks to ensure that the code is accessing memory in a controlled way. Then the framework controls code access to the resources via code access security.

In the .NET Framework, all code is essentially type safe because it references only memory blocks that have been reserved for its use and it accesses objects only through valid, exposed interfaces. From a security point of view, referencing only designated memory allows multiple objects to safely share a single address space and allows the accessing of objects only through their exposed interfaces, thus ensuring that security checks connected with these specific interfaces are not omitted.

The .NET Framework's security model checks code security not only during load time but also during runtime. It also allows security checks based on the identity of the code and of the user. Security policies established and maintained by administrators or developers govern the access to resources granted to a given assembly.

The .NET Framework's security model has six major areas:

- type safety and verification, which ensures that code accesses memory in a controlled way;
- code signing, which ensures that code has not been tampered with after release by establishing an identity for the code;
- cryptographic services and data signing, which protect application data;
- code access security, which, based on the caller's identity and origin, provides permission to access resources;
- role-based security, which controls code access based on the user's identity; and
- isolated storage, which persists data in a safe way on a client computer.

Figure 22.3 depicts some significant features of the code access security mechanism.

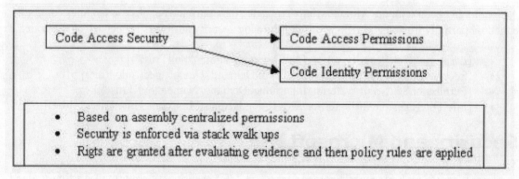

Figure 22.3: Code Access Security in Action

Figure 22.4 outlines some significant features of the role-based security mechanism.

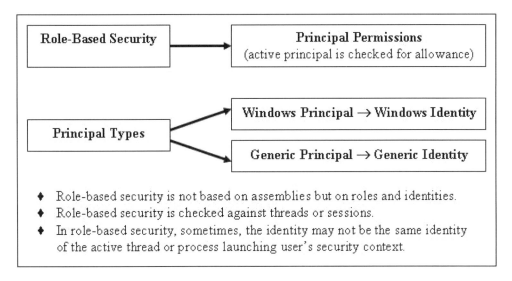

Figure 22.4: Role-Based Security in Action

The CLR associates strong typing in the metadata, like members, parameters of methods, array elements, return values of methods, and static values, with strong typing in the MSIL code, like local variables and stack slots. This two-way strong-typing enforcement ensures type safety. Thus, regardless of the language used to develop the program, the resultant executable files or or DLLs are sure to be type safe, because they are all ultimately MSIL code. The CLR verifies all of the loaded code before it is run. On demand, you can skip this verification process by explicitly trusting an assembly through the use of policies.

The .NET Framework security solution is based on the notion of managed code, with security rules imposed by the CLR. Most managed code is verified to ensure type safety and the predictable behavior of other security properties. In a verified code block, a method declared to accept an Int16 value, for example, will disallow a call attempt with a 16-byte parameter as unsafe. Verification also ensures that execution flows only to recognized locations (e.g., method entry points), a process that prevents execution from jumping to an arbitrary location.

The verification mechanism prevents nontype-safe code from executing and catches many common programming errors before they cause damage. Well-known system vulnerabilities, such as access to memory that has not been initialized and the arbitrary transfer of execution control, are completely disallowed. This mechanism benefits users because the code they run is checked prior to each execution. It also benefits developers, who will find that many common, security-related bugs that have traditionally caused trouble during development are now identified during the verification process and thus prevented from damaging system resources.

Besides preventing unauthorized users from accessing the system, the framework further protects application code and data by enforcing security restrictions on managed code. These restrictions arise from the six-pronged approach to security found in the .NET Framework. Let's delve into the details of these six .NET security areas mentioned earlier.

- **Type-safe code** can read from or write to allowed memory locations only. During Just-In-Time (JIT) compilation, the MSIL code and metadata are examined to verify that the MSIL code is genuinely type safe and well formed. You can skip this verification if you set your policies that way.

- **Code signing** sets an assembly's uniqueness so that other external processes cannot change the assembly. With strong-named assemblies, each file in the assembly loaded at runtime is hashed and that hash value is compared to the hash value stored in the manifest for that file. If the hash values do not match, the system refuses to load the file and throws an exception. As an alternative or as an added precaution, you may want to sign strong-named assemblies by using Microsoft Authenticode. This is useful in environments where a trust hierarchy is already in place and certificates are required. For example, Microsoft ActiveX controls are expected to have certificates that are downloaded and run inside Microsoft Internet Explorer.
- **Cryptographic services and data signing** (encryption of data) classes of .NET help you to offer a secure environment for your data by providing nearly all of the common cryptography algorithms. Thus, you can encrypt and decrypt your data with various cryptography algorithms.
- **Code access security** permits code to access protected resources as long as code really has the requested permission (the right to access protected resources). Your code has a permission set that is constructed according to the active security policy. When your code accesses system resources, the system checks the code for the required permission.
- **Role-based security** allows the system to make decisions about a user's authority to access resources based on the user's identity and role membership information, which is determined by the code.
- **Isolated storage,** a virtual file system for data storage, is isolated per assembly and user. For example, Web-based applications downloaded from intranet or Internet sites may not have access to the ordinary file system. Such applications can have their data, files, and directories stored in this isolated virtual file system. You can limit the size of isolated storage.

Security Choices for Developers and Administrators

Code access security and role-based security are the two main types of security available to developers. Code access security deals with assigning permissions to code, which allows code to access protected resources (such as disk files or the registry) or carry out certain operations (such as accessing unmanaged code). Code access security is built around the notion of permission objects, which control who can access protected resources and what level of access is granted. These permissions are usually based on a permission policy specified by administrators on a given machine or domain.

Role-based security deals with identifying the user who is attempting to execute the code, allowing or disallowing certain operations based on the privileges that the user possesses. User identity is the underlying notion, but role-based security also deals with permissions. Identities are closely tied to principals, which contain information as to which roles a user has. The .NET Framework provides an extensible architecture that allows developers to build their own principals and identities for use with .NET role-based security.

The .NET Framework also introduces another security model, *evidence-based security. Evidence* simply refers to input to the security policy about code. Code that targets the CLR is deployed in single- or multiple-file units called *assemblies*, which are the building blocks of .NET Framework applications. At load time, the CLR examines each assembly for evidence identifying the assembly—for example, the digital signature of the code's author and the location where the code originates. Based on this evidence, the CLR security manager maps the assembly to a code group. Code groups are defined to test for specific forms of evidence and have permission sets associated with them. Assemblies that belong to a code group receive the permissions defined by the associated permission sets.

For illustrative purposes, suppose some assemblies belonging to an application are downloaded to the client computer from a Web site. Based on evidence about the assemblies such as the URL, zone, strong name, and Web site from which the assemblies are downloaded, the security system can determine the proper set of permissions to be granted to the assemblies. Evidence information can be obtained from multiple sources—the CLR, Microsoft Internet Explorer, Microsoft ASP.NET, and the operating system shell, depending on the source of the code.

When an assembly is loaded, the CLR policy system gathers the assembly evidence and evaluates it in the context of the security policy. The CLR policy system then determines which set of permissions it should grant to the assembly based on the evaluated evidence and any specific permission requests that the assembly makes.

Permission requests may be used to stipulate certain permissions or limit the permissions granted to an assembly. Assembly publishers know that some assemblies will operate properly only when granted a certain minimum set of permissions and that other assemblies will never need certain permissions. Depending on the form of permission request, the policy system may grant permissions to an assembly or remove unnecessary permissions. The system may even refuse to load the assembly, if the minimum set of permissions needed to run the assembly is not granted by system policy. An assembly can never be assigned more permission than the policy system would grant in the absence of permission requests.

Security policy consists of a collection of code groups, each with associated permissions to be granted based on the evidence obtained. Policy has two aspects: permissions granted to code rather than to users and permissions granted on a per-assembly basis. Code groups describe the permissions available to assemblies acquired from a specific security zone, or those that are signed by a specific publisher, and so forth. While the CLR ships with a default set of code groups and associated permissions, system administrators can modify these CLR security definitions to fit their needs. Almost any characteristic can be submitted as evidence, provided that the security policy has a use for it. The administrator merely needs to define a code group related to that evidence.

The procedure for granting permission involves evaluating the evidence to determine which code groups are applicable at each of four levels (detailed later): enterprise, machine, user, and application domain. The policy evaluates these four levels in order and then creates a permission set that represents the intersection of all four. System administrators may designate any policy level as final, thus preventing the evaluation of policies at subordinate levels. For example, an administrator can finalize policy for an assembly at the machine level and prevent the application of user-level policies to that assembly. Once the policy processing is complete, an initial set of permissions is created. Assemblies may adjust these grants by making specific requests in three areas:

- The first step is to specify a minimal set of permissions that the assembly must have to operate. If these permissions are not present, the assembly fails to load and an exception is thrown.
- Next, an optional set of permissions may be specified. While the assembly would like any of these permissions, it still loads if they are not available.
- Finally, particularly obedient assemblies may actually reject hazardous permissions that they don't need.

These three enhancement options are accomplished as load-time declarative statements. At runtime, permissions are evaluated based on the execution of code. Actions such as reading or writing files, displaying dialog boxes, and reading or writing environment variables are accomplished using .NET Framework methods that are included within the framework security infrastructure. Thus the .NET Framework allows or disallows actions based on the security policy without imposing additional work on the developer. While programmers of managed classes that expose protected resources must make appropriate security demands in their libraries, programmers who use the .NET Framework class libraries to access a protected resource benefit from the code access security system for free; they do not need to make any explicit security calls.

Administrators may adjust the security policy by determining which permissions are granted and then rely on the .NET Framework to handle all security operations. Code access security prevents most attacks, and the verification of code eliminates buffer overruns and other unexpected behaviors that can lead to security susceptibility. Thus, applications and components are inherently protected against the vast majority of security problems that have plagued native code implementations.

Sometimes it is appropriate for authorization decisions to be based on an authenticated identity or on the code's function. For example, financial or business software may enforce security policy through business logic that evaluates role information. The amount of a financial transaction may be limited based on the role of the user making the request. Tellers may be allowed to process transactions up to a certain dollar amount, whereas a supervisor may need to process transactions involving higher amounts. The .NET Framework provides services that enable applications to incorporate such logic easily, building it around the concept of identities and principals. An *identity* may map to the user logged into the operating system or may be defined by the application. The corresponding *principal* encapsulates the identity, along with any related role information—for example, the user's "group" as defined by the operating system.

Authentication

Authentication is the process of accepting credentials from a user and validating those credentials against authority. If the credentials are valid, the identity is said to be authenticated. *Authorization* is the process of determining whether that authenticated identity has access to a requested resource. Authentication can be accomplished by either system or business logic, and is available through a single application programming interface (API). The authentication API is fully extensible, so developers can use their own business logic as needed. Developers may code their authentication needs to this single API and may revise the underlying authentication methods without making major changes in their code. In addition to Microsoft Windows' identity authentication, other available authentication methods include basic Hypertext Transfer Protocol (HTTP), Digest, and Kerberos, as well as Microsoft Passport and ASP.NET forms-based authentication. These methods of authentication are also fully integrated into ASP.NET.

For example, in ASP.NET forms authentication, the user provides credentials and submits the forms using HTTP GET, POST, or PUT. If the application authenticates the requester, the system issues a cookie that contains the credentials in some form or a key for reacquiring the identity. Subsequent requests are issued with the cookie in the request headers, and they are authenticated and authorized by an ASP.NET handler using whatever validation method the application desires.

If a request is not authenticated, HTTP client-side redirection is used to send that request to an authentication form, where the user can supply authentication credentials. Forms authentication is sometimes used for personalization, the customization of content for a known user. In some of these cases, identification rather than authentication is the issue, so a user's personalized information can be obtained simply by accessing the user name.

ASP.NET offers two types of authorization services: file authorization and URL authorization. File authorization determines which access control lists are consulted based on both the HTTP method being used and the identity making the request. URL authorization is a logical mapping between pieces of the Uniform Resource Identifier namespace and various users or roles.

Isolated Storage

Applications frequently need to store state information or user data while they execute and perform some tasks during their run. Conventionally, this information is stored in a temporary place such as the Windows TEMP directory on your root disk. Usually, the path of this folder is a hard-coded value in the application resource files or is automatically set by the environment variables of the environment shell. This path can also be provided to the application from the registry or from a configuration file. Sometimes malicious code can misuse this information to adversely affect your computer systems.

The .NET Framework eliminates this risk by providing a special capability, *isolated storage*, for storing data even when no file access is allowed. For example, when a managed control is downloaded from the Internet and run, it is given a limited set of permissions but not the right to perform risky actions such as reading or writing to files. Isolated storage provides a virtual file system that is assigned to an assembly based on the evidence that the assembly presents.

Isolated storage is a set of types and methods provided by the .NET Framework for local data storage operations. Essentially, each assembly is given access to a distinct storage area on the computer disk. No access to other data is allowed, and isolated storage is available only to the specific assembly for which it is created. For example, isolated storage may be used by an application to keep its activity logs, save settings, or save user or system state data to disk for later use (e.g., for personalization). Because the location of isolated storage is predetermined, isolated storage provides a suitable way to specify unique space for storage without the need to determine file paths as is done for the Windows TEMP directory. Eventually on demand, administrators can remove all user data from isolated storage and perform other tasks using the isolated storage tool named Storeadm.exe.

On Windows NT/2000/XP operating systems, the isolated storage files are physically stored under different directories, depending upon whether roaming profiles are enabled or not. Roaming profiles allow users to log on to any computer without losing personal settings. If your user profile has roaming enabled, the profile is stored at the server hard disk, as designated by the enterprise administrators. You may consider roaming profiles only if you are part of an administered Windows domain.

If roaming profiles are enabled, the isolated storage files are stored in this path:

```
<%SYSTEMDRIVE%>\Documents and Settings\user\Application Data
```

For nonroaming stores, the path for isolated storage files is this:

```
<%SYSTEMDRIVE%>\Documents and Settings\user\Local Settings\Application Data
```

While restricted code from the local intranet can access and use isolated storage, restricted code from the Restricted Sites zone and from sites that are not trusted has no access to isolated storage.

Security Policy Levels

Security policy is nothing but a configurable set of rules established for *code groups*— groups to which assemblies are assigned depending on evidence gathered about them. As mentioned earlier, the .NET Framework provides four levels of security policy:

- Enterprise policy—defined by enterprise administrators who set policy for enterprise domains.
- Machine policy—defined by machine administrators who set policy for one computer.

- User policy—defined by users who set policy for a system log-on account.
- Application domain policy—defined by the runtime host (essentially any application that hosts the CLR for the purpose of setting load-time policy).

The CLR determines the permission set for an assembly from the intersection of the defined permission sets granted by each of the four policy levels. Policy-level checking is performed in a certain order, with enterprise level coming first, as shown in Figure 22.5. EMUAD is a useful acronym for remembering the order.

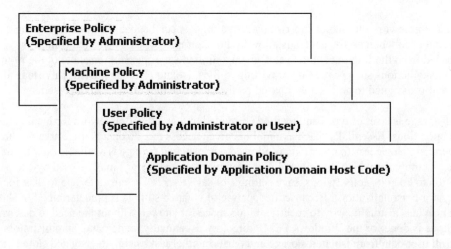

Figure 22.5: Security Policy Levels in Hierarchical Order

You cannot administer application domain policy as you do enterprise, machine, and user policies. It cannot be governed; instead, it is an optional policy level provided by the host. For example, a browser host like Microsoft Internet Explorer, which runs code within the context of a Web site, may require a more restrictive policy option for its application domain than a shell host which spawns applications from the shell.

The rules for the various levels of security policy are all stored in relevant security configuration files, which are merely Extensible Markup Language (XML) files that you can edit with your favorite XML editor or with the Code Access Security Policy (CASPOL) tool. Microsoft recommends the use of CASPOL (covered later in this chapter). Table 22.1 lists the areas in which the configuration files are stored on systems running Windows NT, 2000, or XP.

Policy Level	Location of Configuration File
Enterprise	%CLR installDir%\config\enterprise.config
Machine	%CLR installDir%\config\security.config
User	%USERPROFILE%\application data\Microsoft\CLR security config\vxx.xx\security.config

Table 22.1: Location of Security Policy Configuration Files

Suppose a .NET security administrator decides to change the default user policy of user Caroline. The administrator follows these steps:

- From the command line, he or she runs *caspol –user –reset* to generate a default user security.cfg file at the administrator's user policy–level directory.
- Next, he or she copies the security.cfg file to the user's policy configuration directory of Caroline.
- Finally, the adminstrator uses an XML editor or CASPOL tool to modify security.cfg.

The permission set that the CLR gives to an assembly actually consists of the common, overlapping permissions granted by each level of security policy. Bear in mind that, by default, machine and enterprise policies are more restrictive than user and application domain policies. (Remember the EMUAD hierarchy!)

Let's see what machine-level policy includes, by default:

- local system zone (unrestricted)
- intranet zone (read environment variables, user interface, isolated storage, assertion, network access to same site, file read to same directory)
- Internet zone (safe user interface, isolated storage, network access to same site)
- restricted zone (no authorization; code cannot run)
- Microsoft strong name (.NET Framework classes are unrestricted!)

When the CLR tries to grant permissions to assemblies requested automatically during assembly load, CLR considers the requirements of the enterprise, machine, user, and application domain policies together with the assembly's requested permissions. For application domains, the CLR initially steps through enterprise, machine, and user policies.

Security policy can be easily deployed using a Windows Installer (.msi) file, a self-contained installation package that you can deploy, install, and uninstall in various ways. Your Windows operating system manual lists a number of setup preparation programs you can use to create .msi files, but you already have one such program, compliments of .NET. The .NET Framework Configuration tool, Mscorcfg.msc, provides the Create Deployment Package Wizard for creating Windows Installer files. The wizard can create an Installer file that corresponds to any one—but only one—of the three configurable policy levels. Thus, if you intend to configure several policy levels, you must create a different Windows Installer file for each policy level and deploy those files individually. The wizard creates the Installer file using the current policy settings of the computer from which the wizard executes. For example, in order to create a user policy for deployment to a group of users, you configure the user policy on your current computer to the policy settings you wish to deploy to the target computer, create the Installer file with the wizard, and then return the user policy of the current computer to its original state.

Code Groups

A *code group* is a logical grouping of code that fulfills a specific condition for membership. Any code that meets a code group's membership condition is said to be in that code group. All security-level administrators configure security policy by managing code groups. Code groups that build a policy tree are composed of two parts: a membership condition and a named permission set.

Table 22.2 lists the membership conditions for code groups and includes descriptions excerpted from the .NET Framework Configuration tool's MMC console.

Code Group	Condition Base	Description
Application directory	For checking if an assembly is part of a code group in terms of the directory in which the application resides.	Condition is true for all assemblies in the same directory or in a child directory of the running application.
Cryptographic hash	For checking if an assembly is part of a code group in terms of its MD5 or SHA-1 cryptographic hash.	Condition is true for all assemblies with a hash that matches the cryptographic algorithm.
Software publisher	For checking if an assembly is part of a code group in terms of its software publisher's Authenticode X.509v3 certificate	Condition is true if an assembly is digitally signed with a certificate that matches the one of the Publisher Certificate (Name, Issuer Name, Hash, etc).
Strong name	For checking if an assembly is part of a code group in terms of its cryptographically strong signature.	Condition is true for all assemblies with a strong name that matches the strong name (Public Key, Name, Version, etc).
URL	For checking if an assembly is part of a code group in terms of its URL where the code originates, including the final wildcard (http://mcb/book/*)	Condition is true for all assemblies that originate from the URL specified, such as http://www.mindcracker.com/search/. The URLs must include the protocol such as *ftp://* or *http://*. An asterisk (*) can be used as a wildcard character at the end of the URL.
Web site	For checking if an assembly is part of a code group in terms of the Web site where the code originates (e.g., www.ms.com or *.ms.com)	Condition is true for all assemblies that come from the site name specified.
Zone	For checking if an assembly is part of a code group in terms of the zone where the code originates.	Condition is true for all assemblies that originate from the zone specified, like Internet, Local Intranet, My Computer, Trusted Sites, and Untrusted Sites. The Internet Zone, for example, contains all applications that come from the Internet.
Custom	An application-defined or system-defined condition; this must be imported from an XML file.	Implements a custom code group specific to your app using an XML file that contains a definition of the new code group in the form: *<CodeGroup [Attributes]=[Attribute Values]> </CodeGroup>* where *[Attributes]* and *[Attribute Values]* represent atributes of that custom code group and their values respectively.

Table 22.2: Code Groups and Conditions

Named Permission Sets

A named permission set is a set of permissions that security administrators associate with code groups—in other words, a group of permissions given a unique name. A named permission set consists of one or more permissions and a name and description for the permission set. Administrators can establish or modify the security policy for code groups by using named permission sets. Of course, more than one code group can be associated with the same named permission set.

The .NET Security Framework has built-in named permission sets that the system administrator cannot modify. The administrator can create custom named permission sets and modify security policy to use these customized sets in lieu of the built-in ones. When naming the custom permission sets, you must ensure that the names do not conflict with those of the built-ins.

The CLR provides the following permission set flags:

- Nothing—gives no permissions or prevents code from running.
- Execution—gives permission to run or execute but does not give permission to use protected resources.
- Internet—the default policy permission set for content from unknown origin.
- LocalIntranet—the default policy permission set within an enterprise.
- Everything—gives all standard built-in permissions but does not include permission to skip verification.
- FullTrust—gives full access to all resources protected by permissions. It can be unrestricted.

You can modify only the Internet, LocalInternet, and Everything permission sets.

Listing 22.1 contains code extracted from a typical policy configuration file that sets Internet permissions, the default rights given to Internet applications.

Listing 22.1—Internet Permission Set

```
<PermissionSet class="NamedPermissionSet"
 version="1"
 Name="Internet"
 Description="Default rights given to internet applications">
 <IPermission class="FileDialogPermission"
    version="1"
    Access="Open"/>
 <IPermission class="IsolatedStorageFilePermission"
    version="1"
    Allowed="DomainIsolationByUser"
    UserQuota="10240"/>
 <IPermission class="SecurityPermission"
    version="1"
    Flags="Execution"/>
 <IPermission class="UIPermission"
    version="1"
    Window="SafeTopLevelWindows"
    Clipboard="OwnClipboard"/>
  <IPermission class="PrintingPermission"
    version="1"
    Level="SafePrinting"/>
</PermissionSet>
```

Listing 22.2 generates output that lists all known policy levels and named permission sets at all policy levels.

Listing 22.2—Output Named Permission Sets

```
using System;
using System.Collections;
using System.Security;
using System.Security.Policy;

class testsecurity
{
```

```
public static void Main(string[] args)
{
        IEnumerator ienum1 = SecurityManager.PolicyHierarchy();
        while(ienum1.MoveNext())
        {
                PolicyLevel pol = (PolicyLevel) ienum1.Current;
                Console.WriteLine(pol.Label);
                IEnumerator ienum2 =
pol.NamedPermissionSets.GetEnumerator();
                while (ienum2.MoveNext())
                {
                        NamedPermissionSet permset =
(NamedPermissionSet) ienum2.Current;
                        Console.WriteLine(permset.Name
+ ", " + permset.Description);
                }
        }

    }
}
```

Evidence

Although you briefly encountered the concept of evidence in the earlier discussion of code groups, let's expand the concept here. *Evidence* is information that the CLR uses to make decisions regarding security policy. The CLR decides that the code has particular membership to a code group depending on evidence gathered about the code. Evidence can include digital signatures and the location where code originates.

Although the following list of all evidence types looks much like the list of coding groups, the two serve totally different purposes.

- Application directory—the application's installation directory.
- Hash—the cryptographic hash, such as SHA-1.
- Publisher—the software publisher signature; that is, the Authenticode signer of the code.
- Site—the site of origin, such as http://www.mindcracker.com.
- Strong name—the cryptographically strong name of the assembly.
- URL—the URL of origin.
- Zone—the zone of origin, such as Internet Zone.
- Custom—an application- or system-defined custom condition. Administrators and developers can define these new types of evidence and extend security policy to recognize and use them.

Other than the different types of evidence shown above (Application directory, Hash, Publisher, Site, Strong name, URL, Zone), application-defined or system-defined evidence can also be provided to the runtime by trusted application domain hosts. CLR uses this system-defined evidence to evaluate enterprise, machine, user policy and an application domain policy for assemblies and return the set of permissions to grant to the assembly or application domain. Objects of any type that are recognized by security policy represent evidence.

Let us look at an example of examining the evidence contained in an assembly. Listing 22.3 displays the evidence that is passed to the security system for the mscorlib.dll assembly. The .NET Framework generates a permission set for the assembly based on security policy using the evidence according to policy files adjusted by administrators.

Listing 22-3 Outputting Evidence from an Assembly

```
using System;
using System.Reflection;
using System.Security.Policy;
using System.Collections;

public class XMLApp
{
 public static void Main( String[] args)
 {

  try
  {
   // temporary Int64 object
   Int64 bigint1 = new Int64();
   // get the target class type
   Type mytype = bigint1.GetType();
   // get the assembly which hosts the Integer type.
   Assembly myassembly = Assembly.GetAssembly(mytype);
   Evidence myevidence = myassembly.Evidence;
   Console.WriteLine("How many evidences? " + myevidence.Count +
"\r\n");
   IEnumerator ienum = myevidence.GetEnumerator();
   while(ienum.MoveNext())
   {
    Console.WriteLine(ienum.Current);
   }
   /* The listing will output:
    How many evidences? 4

    <System.Security.Policy.Zone version="1">
        <Zone>MyComputer</Zone>
    </System.Security.Policy.Zone>

    <System.Security.Policy.Url version="1">
    <Url>file://C:/windows/microsoft.net/framework/v1.0.3705/
mscorlib.dll</Url>
    </System.Security.Policy.Url>

    <StrongName version="1"
            Key="00000000000000000400000000000000"
            Name="mscorlib"
            Version="1.0.3300.0"/>
    <System.Security.Policy.Hash version="1">
        <RawData>
        ...
        ...
        ...
        </RawData>
    </System.Security.Policy.Hash>
   */
  }
  catch(Exception e)
  {
   Console.WriteLine ("Exception: {0}", e.ToString());
  }
 }
}
```

Application Domains

In .NET, each application runs in an application domain under the control of a host. The host creates the application domain and loads assemblies into it. The host has access to information about the code via evidence. This information can include the zone in which the code originates or the digital signatures of the assemblies in the application domain. The System.AppDomain class provides the application domain functionality and is used by hosts. A host can be trusted if it provides the CLR with all the evidence the security policy requires.

There are several types of application hosts:

- *Browser host*—includes applications hosted by Microsoft Internet Explorer; runs code within the context of a Web site.
- *Server host*—regarding ASP.NET, refers to the host that runs the code that handles requests submitted to a server.
- *Shell host*—refers to a host that launches applications, namely .exe files, from the operating system shell.
- *Custom-designed host*—a host that creates domains or loads assemblies into domains (e.g., dynamic assemblies).

Listing 22.4 executes the managed application MyApp.exe, with specific evidence inside the Internet security zone, in which code has minimal access to local resources.

Listing 22.4—Running an Application with a Specific Evidence and Zone

```
String myApplication = @"C:\MyApp.exe";
String[] argsToApp = null;
String myURL = @"http://www.mindcracker.com";
SecurityZone myZone = SecurityZone.Internet;

Evidence myEvidence = new Evidence();
myEvidence.AddHost(new Zone(myZone));
myEvidence.AddHost(new Url(myURL));
AppDomain app = AppDomain.CreateDomain(myApplication, myEvidence);
app.ExecuteAssembly(myApplication, myEvidence, argsToApp);
```

LevelFinal and Exclusive Attributes

Some higher-level policies can choose to exclude lower policy levels so that they are not evaluated. Simply applying the LevelFinal or Exclusive attribute to a code group creates this exclusion.

The LevelFinal attribute prevents any policy level below the current level from being evaluated. Remember that the policy levels are the following from highest to lowest: enterprise policy, machine policy, user policy, application domain policy. If, for example, you apply the LevelFinal attribute to the zone code group at the enterprise level, the policy of any code group at the machine level will not be evaluated even if a machine-level administrator has made changes. Applying the LevelFinal attribute at a particular policy level, guarantees that an assembly associated with a code group marked with the LevelFinal attribute will never have its permissions revoked because of decisions made by a lower policy level's administrator.

The Exclusive attribute prevents other code groups in the same policy level from being considered when the runtime environment computes permissions for assemblies in the exclusive code group. Policy levels above and below the current level are still evaluated. This attribute allows one specific code group to make the sole decision for the current policy level regarding which permissions to grant to assemblies that match that group. This is useful when you want to grant a specific set of permissions to specific assemblies, without allowing permissions from other code group matches on the same policy level. Note that an assembly is not allowed to execute if it belongs to more than one code group marked as exclusive; otherwise, the system throws a PolicyException error.

Listing 22.5 walks through creation of an example code group named xxx and the setting of a few properties with the mscorcfg.msc MMC tool.

Listing 22.5—Example Application Directory Code Group

```
<CodeGroup class="UnionCodeGroup"
           version="1"
           PermissionSetName="FullTrust"
           Attributes="Exclusive, LevelFinal"
           Name="xxx"
           Description="xxx description">
<IMembershipCondition class="ApplicationDirectoryMembershipCondition"
                      version="1"/>
</CodeGroup>
```

Permissions

Permissions—basically the rights to do something—are used in the .NET Framework to implement security mechanisms in managed code. As the smallest unit of the security system, permissions are the key concept upon which the whole security system is based.

Developers can and should always request the permissions that the code will need, even if they do not really *need* to make the request. This protects against unexpected situations and makes the maintenance of an application easier for both developers and administrators. Administrators too can assign permissions to an application through code access security. Regardless of your position—developer or administrator—you should never request or grant more permission than necessary. This protects the system from code segments accessing unknown resources and helps developers find bugs earlier. You can think of this as a type of defensive development.

Permissions are divided into three major groups: code access permissions, identity permissions, and role-based permissions. Code access permissions contain the set of permissions used to request the right to execute or access protected operations or devices. As they are of central interest to software developers and administrators, let's examine them first.

Code Access Permissions

Code access permissions are used to protect resources, devices, or operations from unauthorized users. They represent the right to access or execute something. Because code access permissions form a major part of the .NET security system, developers and administrators must understand how these permissions work.

Programmers who opt to use layering to simplify code may compromise security. One layer can misuse the authorization or access it obtains, which can lead to the compromise of another layer. In general, partially trusted code presents a security risk. It can be disguised and manipulated to perform actions on behalf of malicious code, even though the malicious code lacks permission to access the demanded resource. Consequently, malicious code can achieve greater security access than it should be allowed.

In .NET, code access security uses a stack-walking mechanism to defend the system against such attacks. The CLR protects managed code by running a stack walk on all calls. The stack walk checks that all code in the call stack of functions has permission to access the implicitly or explicitly demanded protected resource. Since any suspicious code, like all other code, resides somewhere in the call stack, it cannot exceed its own cumulative or intersected security permissions.

The stack walk mainly prevents an assembly with low authorization from calling a highly trusted component to perform an action on its behalf that it would not otherwise have permission to perform. Code access security uses a hidden code manager to examine the stack for special security markers indicating permissions granted to executing procedures. These markers may be allocated on the stack by the JIT compiler and are accessible only through the hidden code manager.

Figure 22.6 illustrates the stack walk that results when a method in Assembly 3 demands that its callers (Assembly 2 and Assembly 1) have Permission X.

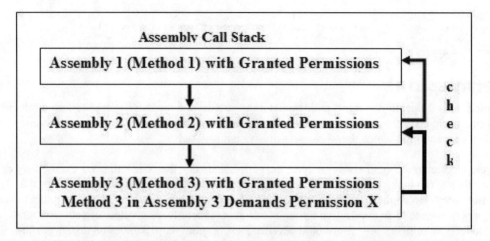

Method 1 calls Method 2; afterwards Method 2 calls Method 3. Since
Method 3 demands Permission X, Assembly 2 and Assembly 1 must have
been granted Permission X. Otherwise an exception is thrown during the
assembly stack walk-up.

Figure 22.6: Permission Stack Walk

The runtime's security system patrols the call stack to determine whether code is authorized to access a resource or perform an operation. It compares the granted permissions of each caller to the permission being demanded. If any caller in the call stack does not have the permission being demanded, a security exception is thrown and access is refused. Demanding permissions of all callers at runtime affects performance; however, it is essential to protect from attacks by partially trusted code.

What is the sense in examining the whole call stack to determine if the executing method should be granted the requested permission? Suppose you have a component that accesses your corporate employee database. This works well for your purposes, but what happens when another component connects to your database component and misuses it? You certainly do not want to explain to your supervisor how someone got confidential information through your component. Because the security system makes sure that every callee in the chain has the necessary permissions, this scenario, which presents a significant problem in other common security systems, should not happen within the .NET architecture.

With the handling of permission requests, the security system checks not only the actual context but also the whole environment in which a piece of code executes. This major step toward secure execution of code protects the operating system, your code, and the code that you access.

In general, it is desirable to have the CLR perform a stack walk whenever permissions are requested; yet, in certain situations you may want to bypass this stack walk. This gives other assemblies the opportunity to execute an operation they are not authorized to perform. Stopping stack walk-ups for an extra security check is possible by calling the Assert method of the

CodeAccessPermission object. As you will see later, use of the Assert method also requires permissions.

Understanding the process by which the CLR grants or denies requests for code access permissions starts with the administrator's actions. The administrator creates code groups, which function as connectors between identities and code access permissions. After creating a group, the administrator assigns some code access permissions to that group. Whenever the CLR loads an assembly, it examines evidence in the assembly to determine its identity and assigns the assembly to a code group. A request is thus granted or denied by examining the code access permissions of the code group to which the assembly belongs.

You can increase permissions for an assembly by following these steps:

- Use the Permission View tool (Permview.exe) to view the minimum permissions requested by the assembly. These are minimal permissions that the application needs in order to run.
- Identify the assembly characteristics. This helps you determine default evidence and host security features.
- Create a new code group with a unique code group name. (A unique name is required within a policy level.) Use the .NET Framework Configuration tool (Mscorcfg.msc) or the Code Access Security Policy tool (Caspol.exe) to create the code group.
- Create a new permission set that includes all the permissions the assembly needs in order to run by using the .NET Framework Configuration tool or CASPOL. This should be a minimal set of permissions, specifying no more permissions than necessary.
- Associate the new permission set with the new code group by using the .NET Framework Configuration tool or CASPOL.

The application can now run from any location and receive sufficient permissions to function. But this does not mean that less-trusted applications from the same location would receive extra permissions. Your system is still protected from malicious code.

Custom Code Access Permissions

You can provide custom permissions within an application or library. Any custom permission you create must be added to the security policy on the computers where the application using the permission runs.

To create custom code access permissions, just create an XML representation of the configuration you want the custom permission to have and then import the XML into your security policy. The .NET Framework security system uses XML to serialize permissions. The XML representations of the permissions that make up your security policy are stored in the policy configuration files.

To add a custom permission to a security policy, perform the following steps:

1. Load the assembly into GAC.
2. Trust the assembly.
3. Use the CASPOL tool, Notepad, or your favorite editor to generate an XML file that represents the type of permission. This can be a difficult task so, from the start, you should learn the relevant specific XML tags by copying them from existing files. Follow Microsoft's recommendation and use either the CASPOL or mscorcfg.msc tool instead of editing these files manually.
4. Apply the XML file to the security policy.

You can see whether all of your callers have been granted a specific permission by demanding the permissions for them. Demands can be made either imperatively through code or declaratively through attributes.

The Assert Method

For code access permissions, the CLR walks through the call stack, checking each caller in the stack one by one for the proper permissions to the requested resources. Yet, demanding permissions from each caller every time a call is made can create considerable overhead in big programs. Depending on how many callers are in the stack, you may encounter an unexpectedly high number of permission checks that can degrade performance. For example, if your code accesses a secure method five times, and five callers are currently above it in the call stack, 25 permission evaluations will be performed. The examples later in this chapter show how to implement code access security in situations like this, and they also walk you through a remedy to the tedious stack walk-ups: the Assert method. Using this method in your code to assert the specific permission can reduce the number of evaluations to be performed up the call stack. However, you can use the Assert method only if your code is to have the permission both to perform the request being made and to make assertions.

The Assert method is evaluated at runtime. All of the code access permission classes and permission sets may implement the Assert method. Figure 22.7 demonstrates file permissions and how the Assert method affects the call stack. Assume that assembly 2 is your DLL module and has permission to read all files on the drive. Assembly 3 can only read files with an XML extension, and assembly 1 has not been granted file I/O permissions. Assembly 1 makes a call to the library module (assembly 2), which in turn calls assembly 3.

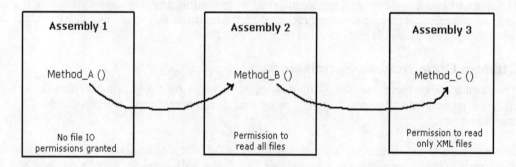

Figure 22.7: Assert Method Illustration

Under normal circumstances, when assembly 3 tries to read an XML file, the runtime security mechanism checks the permissions of its callers (assembly 2 and assembly 1). The call fails and throws a security exception because assembly 1, which originated the call, does not have the proper permissions. Using the Assert method, you can have assembly 2 assert its permissions to read files. Then when assembly 3 tries to read an XML file, the security mechanism's stack walk stops at assembly 2 because that assembly uses assertion on the same permission type (FileIOPermissions).

In this way, you can reduce the number of permission evaluations performed, but your performance gain will vary depending on the number of callers and accesses. In the scenario above, a performance gain can be realized; but a closer look reveals that assembly number 1, which would not otherwise have file I/O permissions, gains such permission when the security check stops at assembly 2. When assembly 2 asserts its file permissions, it passes those permissions along to the callers above it in the stack. The security checks for this asserted permission do not proceed beyond the assembly making the assertion.

Using the Assert method allows your code to retain permissions that it normally has but eventually allows other callers upstream in the call stack to have access that they would not normally have.

You should use Assert very carefully so as to avoid opening up backdoor security risks. It is tempting to use assertions to attain performance gains, but you should provide additional security measures when Assert is used. You should explicitly trace and evaluate the security holes that could be opened up through the use of assertion.

Imperative Demand

With *imperative demand*, developers can write the security code into the logic of the applications. You place an imperative demand in your method code body to protect the rest of the code in a method from which the Demand method is called. If the caller does not satisfy the Demand, an exception will be thrown. Demand method of CodeAccessPermission class (or any of its derived classes) will throw a SecurityException during the program execution if the function invoking assemblies in the assembly stack have not been granted the permission requested by the class object.

The order of processes required to make an imperative demand is as follows:

- Create a new instance of a permission object and then set the properties you want on the permission object. This can typically be done in a single call to the constructor for most of the security objects.
- Call the object's Demand method. In most instances, the Demand method is called in a try block so that if the demand fails, the resulting exception is caught.

If the demand fails for any reason (possibly your permission is revoked), a security exception is thrown. If the demand works as planned, execution continues after the call.

Declarative Demand

The chapter on C# syntax (Chapter 5) covered the concept of attributes. Declarative security is implemented by using attributes on assemblies, classes, or methods. These security attributes, which are stored as metadata in assemblies and modules, can be either built in or custom defined. Declarative security allows developers to specify most of the same kinds of security requirements that imperative security allows. However, as you will see in the examples, the syntaxes are quite different. You can apply Assert, Demand, and Deny methods or permit only certain permissions by placing security attributes in your classes or methods.

As you will see, all built-in permissions have a corresponding attribute. A declarative security attribute follows the syntax shown:

```
[<Permission>Attribute(<SecurityAction>,
    <PublicProp1> = <Value1>)]
```

In this pseudocode, <Permission> obviously represents the name of the permission you want to use, and <SecurityAction> is a member of the SecurityAction enumeration, such as SecurityAction.Assert. This action describes the type of security operation to be performed, with the possible actions including LinkDemand, InheritanceDemand, Demand, Assert, Deny, PermitOnly, RequestMinimum, RequestOptional, and RequestRefuse.

Permission requests are specified by using attributes for an assembly, stored in the metadata of an assembly. You have already learned that an assembly's permission requests are examined when the assembly is loaded, and the CLR continues based on the kind of permission request the assembly makes.

When you fail to make any permission requests, you are requesting the maximum amount of permissions the local security policy will allow for your code. On the other hand, when you request limited permissions to be granted to your code, you will be testing your code against the known security limitations. Where security of your code is of concern, you must be careful about requesting full set of permissions because it can affect the ability of your code to run. For example, you should consider the case, where the security policy allows your code to do something (such as read and write a file), and the requested permissions do not. You can use the RequestMinimum optional assembly attribute when you want to ask for those permissions that your assembly will probably need as a minimum to load. You can use the RequestOptional optional assembly attribute when your assembly provides features that require additional permissions. You can use the RequestRefuse optional assembly attribute when you want to deny particular permissions that will not be needed by your code within your assembly even though your assembly is granted to them by the local policy.

The three kinds of optional attribute permission requests are as follows:

- Minimum permissions (RequestMinimum)—In your programs, you should request only necessary permissions. You can use RequestMinimum to discover minimum-security requirements and output the requirements of a target assembly. So you can fine-tune policy to meet the requirements. An assembly must be granted permission to at least its minimum requirements to be loaded. Once the assembly is loaded, you are certain that it satisfied at least the minimum permissions requested.
- Optional permissions (RequestOptional)—These optional requests for additional permissions are not required for running.
- Refused permissions (RequestRefuse)—This allows you to refuse unnecessary permissions that invite abuse; thus you can effectively defend your programs and classes.

The following example makes a minimum permission request for permission to call unmanaged code. The assembly will not load if it is not granted the permission to execute unmanaged code.

```
[assembly:SecurityPermissionAttribute(
    SecurityAction.RequestMinimum, UnmanagedCode = true)]
```

Permission requests affect the final permission that an assembly receives. Microsoft offers the following official formula to calculate granted permissions, where $\cap$ equals intersection, $\cup$ equals union, and the minus sign equals exclusion:

```
Granted Permissions = (maximum allowed permission ∩ (minimum permission request ∪
optional permission request)) - refused permission request
```

It is assumed that the minimum permission request for an assembly is available all the time when calculating granted permissions.

Choosing Imperative or Declarative Security

Declarative security is simpler to implement than imperative security. Declarative security attributes can be viewed with Permview.exe or mscorcfg.msc, allowing the callers of code to see what permissions the code requires. Imperative security is not evident to the callers of code. Because the permissions requirements are embedded inside the code, you cannot see what is happening unless coding a demand.

In some cases the choice between declarative and imperative security is obvious because some security actions can be performed in only one of the two ways. For example, minimum, optional, and refused permission requests are only available declaratively.

But how do you choose which approach to use when both approaches provide equivalent support for the functions you need? If a security action can be performed both declaratively and imperatively, the decision depends on the developer's preference. The performance difference between the two is insignificant, for the most part, however, you can would have to choose imperative syntax over declarative syntax when you are going to construct the initial permission state of security in your code with information that is only available at run time.

A declarative demand is a way of invoking a security check without adding any statements to your code. You make a declarative demand by placing information at the class or member level, indicating the permissions you want callers to have. You can also implement Deny actions declaratively. If you place a declarative security check at the class level, it applies to each class member, including methods, properties, and fields. If you place a declarative security check at the member level, it applies to only that member and overrides any permission specified at the class level. Declarative demands degrade performance only at JIT compilation. In fact, the use of declarative demands can actually increase the performance of an application in which a demand is made many times.

The imperative demand that you place in your code protects all of the remaining code in the method from which the Demand method is called. The security check is performed when the Demand method executes; if the security check fails, a security exception is thrown and the rest of the code in that method or member is not executed unless the exception is caught and handled. Consider using an imperative (rather than declarative) demand when information that you need to specify permission becomes known only at runtime.

Identity Permissions

When an assembly is requested, the CLR searches for evidence of the assembly's origin. In simple terms, the CLR asks the following questions:

- From which site does the assembly come?
- From which URL does the assembly come?
- From which zone does the assembly come?
- Who has signed the assembly?
- What is the strong (public/private key–signed assembly) name of the assembly?

Based on the evidence it collects, the CLR learns the identity of the assembly and assigns the appropriate identity permissions. These identity permissions "earn" an assembly its membership to a code group. Developers and administrators do not have influence over the identity permissions of an assembly. The CLR just takes a requested assembly, examines its evidence, and assigns the identity permissions based on that evidence. To associate a set of identity permissions with a code group, the administrator must set up security policies, as described earlier in this chapter.

Some of the identity permission classes in the framework are

- SiteIdentityPermission, which represents the Web site from which the assembly originated;
- URLIdentityPermission, which represents the URL from which the assembly originated;

- ZoneIdentityPermission, which represents the security zone from which the assembly originated. The zone identity is one of the values of the System.Security.SecurityZone enumeration.
- PublisherIdentityPermission, which represents the Authenticode publisher of the assembly; and
- StrongNameIdentityPermission, which represents the strong name of the assembly.

Even if identity permissions can be demanded, they are granted only if an assembly can show evidence of the proper identity. This also holds true for code access permissions. Identity and code access permissions are very closely related in that they share the same underlying concept and derive from the same base class, CodeAccessSecurity.

Link Demands

Link demands, the permissions a caller must have when calling code, can be used to limit which classes can be linked to your classes. You must set link demands declaratively because they can be evaluated at JIT compilation time by the system and performed against the caller of the code. If the caller does not possess enough permission to satisfy the link demand, the system throws an exception. The CLR does not perform a stack walk for link demands, so you can avoid the potential impact on performance.

Link demands can be associated with identity permissions to control who or what can call your code. For example, you can develop assemblies that can be called only by other assemblies from a specific publisher. For syntax, see the examples provided in the class descriptions section later in this chapter.

Listing 22.6 illustrates how you can implement LinkDemand declarative security.

Listing 22.6—LinkDemand Illustration

```
// code to restrict callers
[ZoneIdentityPermission(SecurityAction.LinkDemand,
Zone=SecurityZone.MyComputer)]
public class test
{
//.........
}
```

Inheritance Demands

Inheritance demands are similar to link demands except that they are used to restrict how entities inherit characteristics at the class level. For example, you can place inheritance demands declaratively at the class level to ensure that only code with the specified permission can inherit from your class. You can place inheritance demands on methods to ensure that any code that overloads the method has the specified permission to do so.

Listing 22.7 illustrates how you can implement class-level InheritanceDemand declarative security.

Listing 22.7—InheritanceDemand Illustration

```
// code to restrict subclassing
[StrongNameIdentityPermission(SecurityAction.InheritanceDemand,
        PublicKey={...})]
public class test2
{
// ...
}
```

Role-Based Permissions

You know now how the CLR controls the permissions of your code. Now it's time to explore how you can control the rights of a user.

Every role you have—whether parent or child, shopper or billpayer, developer or administrator—has certain behaviors and responsibilities associated with it. Security designers have recognized how useful this concept of role-associated behaviors can be in IT and have designed a security check that grants permissions based on roles.

When you write a software system, the design phase usually reveals certain roles that users play based upon actual workflow. Role-based security allows the developer to check whether a user is functioning within a certain role when requesting access to resources.

Unlike identity permissions and code access permissions, role-based permissions have nothing to do with the rights a piece of code possesses but rather with the workflow-based permission of a user. The term *workflow-based permission* implies a sequence of steps or hierarchical permissions that colleagues require to see a task through to completion. For example, a bellhop with no permissions takes a guest's bags to a hotel room designated by a desk clerk with specific permissions. A housekeeper with very few permissions freshens the room; and at checkout, the desk manager's more extensive permissions are required to remove unauthorized charges from the guest's bill and to discount the room rate.

Role-based permissions are not derived from the CodeAccessPermission class, as identity permissions and code access permissions are. Instead they share the same base class with the common principal-based (also known as Windows identity) permissions; both are derived from the PrincipalPermission class. To understand role-based permissions, we must look at two other classes: Identity and Principal.

The Identity class represents users in a software or operating system. In contrast, the Principal class represents the security context (Windows user group) of a user (Windows identity). Basically, Principal represents all the roles to which a user is assigned. A PrincipalPermission is the object used to demand a role from a user. If the user belongs to the necessary Principal class (i.e., if the user has been assigned the requisite roles), the request succeeds. PrincipalPermission is therefore an easy way to check role assignments.

We have seen the different security concepts related to a specified software system. Yet, that software system is embedded in the operating system and the .NET runtime host, so there must be other permissions that manage your rights to control the runtime.

Security Permissions

All permissions related to the runtime environment and the controlling of it are represented through the SecurityPermission class found in the System.Security.Permissions namespace. With this class, you can request runtime environment permissions.

The class takes a SecurityPermissionFlag enumeration in its constructor. This enumeration contains an item called *Assertion*, which is responsible for trying to execute the assertion for permission. If an assembly does not possess Assertion rights, it is not possible to call the Assert method to assert specific permissions and therefore you cannot disable the stack walk of the code access permissions.

Treat with extreme caution any permissions represented by SecurityPermission objects. If you assign rights through this enumeration, be sure you know *what* the code does and whether it really needs these rights. If you obtain code over the Internet or from other uncontrollable sources, never assign it permissions if you don't know what the code contains. .

Exceptions

In .NET, any security violation throws one of three exception types—security, policy, or verification—which can be caught and handled appropriately by exception-handling routines. An object is created to represent exceptions as they occur. All three security-related exceptions that follow inherit from Object.Exception.SystemException.

- SecurityException is thrown when a security violation is detected, typically at runtime.
- PolicyException is thrown when policy forbids code to run. This exception, which usually occurs as the code is loading, is thrown when the code requests more permission than the policy will grant or the policy is configured to prohibit running the code.
- VerificationException can occur either when code that is verifiable does not pass verification rules or when code that is not verifiable is run without SkipVerify permissions enabled for that particular zone, such as the intranet zone. Verification includes memory allocations, proper casting of variables, and type safety. Code can be verified during JIT compilation because it contains nothing but MSIL statements. However, code in which SkipVerify permission is set is omitted.

.NET Framework Security Tools

The .NET Framework takes advantage of a host of security tools, enabling you to approach security in a number of ways. Table 22.3 lists many of the security tools available in the framework.

Tool Name	Description
Code Access Security Policy Tool (Caspol.exe)	Used to to view and configure security policy.
Software Publisher Certificate Test Tool (Cert2spc.exe)	Used to create a software publisher's certificate from one or more X.509 certificates.
Certificate Creation Tool (Makecert.exe)	Used to generate X.509 certificates solely for the purpose of testing.
Certificate Manager Tool (Certmgr.exe)	Used to manage certificates, certificate trust lists, and certificate revocation lists.
Certificate Verification Tool (Chktrust.exe)	Used to check the validity of a file signed with an Authenticode, X.509, certificate.
Permissions View Tool (Permview.exe)	Used to examine all the declarative permissions of an assembly.
PEVerify Tool (Peverify.exe)	Used to confirm that the JIT compilation process can verify the type safety of the assembly.
Set Registry Tool (Setreg.exe)	Used to change the registry settings that pertain to certificates and digital signatures.
Strong Name Tool (Sn.exe)	Used to create an assembly with a strong name or verify that an assembly has a strong name.
Digital Signature Wizard (Signcode.exe)	Used to attach an Authenticode signature to an assembly.

Table 22.3: .NET Framework Security Tools

Let's take a closer look at the three tools that are most often used in managing security within the .NET environment: .NET Framework Configuration tool, CASPOL (Code Access Security Policy Tool), and SN(Strong Name Tool).

.NET Framework Configuration Tool

Microsoft recommends that you configure security policy using the .NET Framework Configuration tool (Mscorcfg.msc). You can launch Mscorcfg.msc by executing the following instruction:

```
mmc <drive>:\\Winnt\Microsoft.NET\Framework\<version number>\mscorcfg.msc
```

This tool provides various wizards to help you safely set and adjust enterprise-, machine-, and user-level security policies. Therefore, you should start to spend time with this configuration tool as soon as you learn the basic concepts of .NET security.

Some of the most useful wizards allow you to

- trust an application (i.e., identify an application by publisher or strong name information and increase the application's level of trust);
- adjust security settings (i.e., increase or decrease permissions to assemblies originating from one of the following zones: My Computer, Local Intranet, Internet, Trusted Sites, and Untrusted Sites);
- reset security policy level to the default settings;
- evaluate an assembly (i.e., determine the permissions that will be granted to an assembly or the code groups that give permissions to an assembly);
- create and modify existing policies at the enterprise, machine, and user levels; and
- create a deployment package (i.e., create a Windows Installer package to deploy security policy across an enterprise).

For more information on using the wizards, see the .NET Framework Configuration tool.

If the wizards do not provide the functionality you require to administer security policy, you can edit the permission sets and code groups directly by using either the .NET Framework Configuration tool or CASPOL. For information on performing specific tasks using these tools, see Security Policy Configuration in the SDK documentation.

CASPOL Tool

Suppose a developer creates an assembly that requires access to a resource or action that is typically available to users or clients requesting that assembly. Sometimes, for maintenance or other purposes, the administrator may need to restrict the action or resource required by the developer's assembly. This restriction could cause the assembly to function improperly or fail altogether when security exceptions are thrown. Viewing the requirements of the assembly could help you identify the problem and determine whether security issues are involved.

CASPOL (Caspol.exe), a command-line tool included with the .NET runtime SDK, is used to administer policy changes as well as to view existing permissions and the code group hierarchy. Let's look at a few examples of viewing code groups and permissions with CASPOL.

Your default view in CASPOL is determined by your current access permissions (enterprise, machine, or user). If you do not currently have administrative permissions, your default view is the Users view. The examples below explicitly specify either the machine or the user policy level. When code groups from both levels should be displayed together, as in the first example, the *-all* option is used.

Running the following command from the command line shows the code groups to which a specific assembly file belongs.

```
CASPol   -all   -resolvegroup   hello.dll
```

Although this example uses a library called hello.dll, the library could be replaced with any assembly—even caspol.exe itself. Assuming that the hello.dll assembly has no custom or added restrictions, the command output from the example is as shown in Listing 22.8.

Listing 22.8—Output from CASPOL Command to View Code Groups

```
Microsoft (R) .NET Framework CasPol 1.0.2204.21
Copyright (c) Microsoft Corp 1999-2000. All rights reserved.

Level = Machine
Code Groups:

1. All code: Nothing
    1.1. Zone - MyComputer: FullTrust

Level = User
Code Groups:

1. All code: FullTrust

Success
```

While brief and simple, this output is sufficient to demonstrate what you can expect to see when viewing code groups. The first item is one of the policy levels, the machine policy, followed by a list of the code groups that the code belongs to. At the machine level, the code belongs to the All Code group, which uses the built-in permission set called Nothing. (Other nonmodifiable built-in permission sets include Execution and FullTrust). The Nothing permission set prohibits all resources, including the right to execute code. However, the All Code group has a subgroup called Zone. The Zone subgroup requires that any code within that subgroup meet the MyComputer membership condition. For any code that meets that condition, the FullTrust permission set is used to allow full access to all resources. At the next policy level listed, the user level, we have FullTrust permissions to run all code. In the final line of output, the program displays that it has run successfully.

If you plan to view an assembly's permission sets for diagnostic reasons, you may want to use the -all option so that you can be sure you're seeing all the relevant information. After all, when the assembly is run, it's being spawned by a user account, in which case the machine, user policies, and the application domain's policy(if it exists) are combined to produce the total permissions granted to that assembly. Using the -all option lets you see both the user and machine permission sets at the same time. Note that the -all option can also be abbreviated to just -*a* in the command.

The following command shows the permission sets to which a specific assembly file belongs.

```
CASPol   -all   -resolveperm   hello.dll
```

Again, the hello.dll library could be replaced with any assembly. An example of the command's output appears in Listing 22.9.

Listing 22.9—Output from CASPOL Command to View Permission Sets

```
Microsoft (R) .NET Framework CasPol 1.0.2204.21
Copyright (c) Microsoft Corp 1999-2000. All rights reserved.
```

```
Resolving permissions for level = Machine
Resolving permissions for level = User

Grant =
<PermissionSet class="System.Security.PermissionSet" version="1">
  <Unrestricted/>
    <Permission
  class="System.Security.Permissions.StrongNameIdentityPermission,
  mscorlib, Ver=1.0.2204.21, Loc='', SN=03689116d3a4ae33" version="1">
      <PublicKeyBlob>
       <Key>0024000004800000940000000602000002400005…</Key>
      </PublicKeyBlob>
      <Name>hello</Name>
      <Version>1.0.444.35256</Version>
    </Permission>
  <Permission class="System.Security.Permissions.URLIdentityPermission,
    mscorlib,
    Ver=1.0.2204.21, Loc='', SN=03689116d3a4ae33" version="1">
    <Url>file:///D:/Projects/hello.dll</Url>
  </Permission>
  <Permission class="System.Security.Permissions.ZoneIdentityPermission,
    mscorlib,
    Ver=1.0.2204.21, Loc='', SN=03689116d3a4ae33" version="1">
    <Zone>MyComputer</Zone>
  </Permission>
</PermissionSet>
Success
```

The first item in the example output is the policy levels. The output combines both the machine and user policies to display what permissions have been granted to the code.

The PermissionSet itself is set to unrestricted, allowing all permissions to be available. Next, three specific sets of permissions are being demanded:

- *StrongNameIdentityPermission*—indicates that the hello.dll library contains a strong name (a shared assembly using public-key cryptography). This permission contains the public key that must be matched for other code to make valid calls to this assembly. The cryptographic number has been shortened in this example for display.
- *URLIdentityPermission*—lists the URL where the code originated. If you are viewing one of your own assemblies, you will most likely see the path that you compiled to.
- *ZoneIdentityPermission*—determines if the calling code is from a specific *zone* (a specific caller region, such as Intranet_Zone or Internet_Zone). Only exact zone matches can be defined for this permission, and a URL can only belong to a single zone.

Another option that can be used with the CASPOL utility is the *-list* option. The -list option shows the list of code groups followed by a list of named permission sets available in the most recently displayed policy. The following command enlists the -list option to provide you with an overall look at your permissions:

```
CASPol   -list
```

The output from this command is for your entire current configuration, not just for a single assembly. If the output is too long for your shell window, then try using the following command, which saves the output to text file called output.txt:

```
CASPol   -list   > output.txt
```

To shorten the output further, you could use the following command to list just the code groups for your current configuration:

```
CASPol   -listgroups
```

This command produces output similar to that in Listing 22.10.

Listing 22.10—Output from CASPOL Command to List Code Groups Only

```
Security is ON
Execution checking is OFF
Policy change prompt is ON

Level = Machine
Code Groups:
1. All code: Nothing
   1.1. Zone - MyComputer: FullTrust
      1.1.1. Honor SkipVerification requests: SkipVerification
   1.2. Zone - Intranet: LocalIntranet
      1.2.1. All code: Same site Socket and Web.
   1.3. Zone - Internet: Internet
   1.4. Zone - Untrusted: Nothing
   1.5. Zone - Trusted: Internet
   1.6. StrongName - 00240000048000000940000000…: Everything
```

As you might expect, the following command functions in much the same way, except that it displays only the permission sets for your current configuration.

```
CASPol   -listpset
```

Although this hello.dll example had very few restricted permissions, you can see how using the CASPOL utility to view restrictions for a specific assembly allows you to discover which permissions your assembly needs to run. Similarly, using the CASPol -list command reveals the permissions available to you as a user or administrator.

SN Tool

Assemblies can be digitally signed with a strong name, which consists of a public key, simple text assembly name, version number, and culture. The public key provides an assembly with a unique name, and strong-name signing assures users that the assembly has not been altered since being signed. Strong names use public-key encryption and digital signature techniques to guarantee secure code distribution. Code signing prevents attacks from hackers who tamper with code or impersonate the identity of a publisher.

Code signing uses Public-Key Infrastructure (PKI) methods to give your code a unique identity. These PKI methods are complex mathematical functions used to prevent others from assuming the publisher's identity. Code signing ensures that your code has not been tampered with after you signed it.

You can use the Strong Name command-line tool (Sn.exe) for many purposes when working with shared components that reside in shared assemblies. You can generate a new public-private key pair and write that pair to a file by adding the -k option to the following command:

```
sn -k <outputfile>
```

You can verify an assembly has a strong-name signature with the -v[f] option, as follows:

```
sn -v[f] <assembly>
```

You can verify that a particular assembly is signed using a particular key file.

You can extract a public key from a key pair in a file and export it to a separate file with the -p option, as specified in this command:

```
sn -p <inputfile> <outputfile>
```

You can verify that the same key pair signed both components if the –t and –T options on the following commands produce the same key token:

```
sn -t <outputfile>
```

```
sn -T any.dll
```

One last example illustrates the two steps needed when you want to attach a strong-name signature to your code:

1. Create the strong-name key and compile your assembly with key you generated. You create a key pair and view the public key portion. Then you need to make an identity demand for code signed with the corresponding private key.

```
sn -k mykeypair.dat
sn -p mykeypair.dat mypublickey.dat
sn -tp mypublickey.dat
```

2. Now add a declaration to the code in your assembly to indicate the location of the file generated in step one, as shown in Listing 22.11.

Listing 22.11—AssemblyKeyFile

```
[assembly:AssemblyKeyFile("mykeypair.dat")]

public class MyClass
{
    //class
}
```

The SN tool offers yet another feature: the delayed signing of an assembly. In simple terms, this feature reserves a place for the signature in the assembly manifest, but you do not initially sign the assembly with a private key. In delayed signing, the SN signature is applied after the assembly has been built and tested. Bear in mind that assembly developing and publishing tasks can be separated and assigned to different people. Delayed signing is helpful when the assembly's developer does not have access to the private key that will be used to generate the signature—a common occurrence during the development and testing phase of applications. (In fact, it is a good security practice to limit the number of people who have access to the private key.)

When the assembly is built with AssemblyDelaySign set to true, as shown here, the CLR books space for the strong-name signature and stores the public key in the assembly.

```
[assembly:AssemblyDelaySign (true)]
```

Please note that the /delaysign+ and /keyfile options can also be used with the Assembly Generation tool (Al.exe) to create delay-signed assemblies.

Cryptography in Brief

Cryptography, an area of discrete mathematics, gives you additional means of protecting your data from security threats. Cryptographic techniques provide the following security measures:

- Confidentiality—information remains hidden from anyone for whom it is not intended. To prevent "eavesdropping," data is encrypted before it is transmitted over an insecure channel.
- Integrity—data has not been altered during transmission.
- Nonrepudiation—the sender of a message cannot deny sending the message.
- Antireplay prevention—a message is not a replay of some part of a previous communication session.
- Authentication—an entity proves its identity to other entities. Authentication prevents an entity from successfully disguising itself.

Cryptography implements these security measures through the use of mathematical techniques that encrypt and decrypt data. The process consists of two parts: the creation of codes to secure communications and data, and the deciphering of those codes.

Cryptographic algorithms associate your original data, called *plaintext* or *cleartext*, with a key to generate encrypted data, called *ciphertext*. The algorithms also associate ciphertext with a decryption key to convert the data to its original form again. The encryption and decryption keys can be the same key or two different keys, depending on the cryptography algorithms.

Let's start with a simple example to illustrate the concept. The following algorithm encrypts data with key k1 to create CipheredDATA.

```
CipheredDATA = Encrypt_{k1}(DATA)
```

To get the original DATA, you decrypt the CipheredDATA with key k1.

```
DATA = Decrypt_{k1}(CipheredDATA)
```

It is difficult but not impossible for hackers to understand the original DATA without key k1. The hackers must find what k1 is to start the decryption. This simple example illustrates *symmetric* (secret-key) cryptography, in which a single key is used to encrypt and decrypt data. In *asymmetric* (or public-key) cryptography, a public key encrypts the data, and the recipient uses his or her private key to decrypt the data.

Real cryptography algorithms are much more complex than the one in the example because the mathematicians who develop algorithms have considered almost all of the known approaches to deducing those algorithms. If you want an even greater degree of sophistication, you can use *steganography* to hide one set of data within another in a way that allows it to be extracted later. Steganography is best used with cryptography, although cryptography need not be used with steganography unless you want to conceal the fact that you are hiding data through encryption.

The .NET Framework provides a set of cryptographic classes that offer encryption, digital signatures, hashing, and random-number generation, which implement well-known algorithms such as RSA, DSA, Rijndael/AES, Triple DES, DES, and RC2, as well as the MD5, SHA-1, SHA-256, SHA-384 and SHA-512 hash algorithms. Let's briefly look at some of these cryptography algorithms:

- RSA (Rivest-Shamir-Adleman), a public-key cryptosystem for encryption and authentication, was invented in 1977 by the founders of RSA Data Security, Inc. RSA accepts a variable key length.
- Digital Signature Algorithm (DSA) is used to generate and verify signatures.
- Data Encryption Standard (DES) is an encryption block cipher defined and endorsed by the National Institute of Standards and Technology (NIST) in 1977 as a U.S. government

standard. It has become the best-known and most widely used symmetric cryptosystem in the world. DES uses a 64-bit block size and a 56-bit key.

- Triple DES (3DES) consists of running DES three times using three distinct keys.
- RC2 and the more recent RC4 and RC5 are developed by RSA Data Security for use in place of DES.
- MD2 and the more recent MD4 and MD5, developed by one of the founders of RSA Data Security, are useful for digital signature applications in which a large message must be compressed in a secure manner before being signed with a private key.
- The secure hash algorithms SHA and SHA-1 were developed by NIST and published as federal information-processing standards.

The .NET Framework also supports the XML Digital Signature specification, under development by the Internet Engineering Task Force and the World Wide Web Consortium. The framework-provided cryptographic classes support .NET's internal services, too. The classes are available as managed code to developers who require cryptographic support.

For more information about implementing cryptography algorithms, we recommend Bruce Schneier's *Applied Cryptography: Protocols, Algorithms, and Source Code in C*, 2nd edition (John Wiley & Sons, 1996). Though the examples are coded in ANSI C, this is one of the best cryptography books available.

Security Classes in .NET

System.Security

The System.Security namespace provides the underlying structure of the .NET Framework security system. It includes interfaces, attributes, exceptions, and base classes for permissions, as well as the CodeAccessPermission class, which defines the underlying structure of all code access permissions.

IPermission Interface

Many Permission classes implement the IPermission interface, which takes the form shown in Listing 22.12.

Listing 22.12—IPermission Interface

```
interface IPermission
{
        bool IsSubsetOf(IPermission target);
        void Demand();
        void DemandImmediate();
        IPermission Copy();
        IPermission Intersect(IPermission target);
        IPermission Union(IPermission target);
}
```

ISecurityEncodable Interface

The ISecurityEncodable interface is implemented to serialize permissions to and from XML format. Listing 22.13 shows the typical structure of the interface.

Listing 22.13—ISecurityEncodable Interface

```
interface ISecurityEncodable
{
        void FromXml(SecurityElement e);
        SecurityElement ToXml();
}
```

Listing 22.14 provides an example of XML security serialization.

Listing 22.14—XML Security Serialization

```
// code to show XML serialization
PermissionSet ps = new PermissionSet(PermissionState.None);
SecurityElement myDOM = ps.ToXml();
Console.WriteLine(myDom.ToString());
```

Permission Classes

All of the classes listed in Table 22.4 are derived from the CodeAccessPermission class.

Class	Function
DirectoryServicesPermission	Protects directory services.
DnsPermission	Protects DNS services.
EnvironmentPermission	Protects environment variables.
EventLogPermission	Protects event logs.
FileDialogPermission	Protects file dialog boxes in the user interface.
FileIOPermission	Protects files and folders on the file system.
IsolatedStorgeFilePermission	Protects isolated storage.
MessageQueuePermission	Protects MSMQ queues.
OleDbPermission	Protects databases accessed by the OLE DB data access provider.
PerformanceCounterPermission	Protects performance counters.
PrintingPermission	Protects printers.
ReflectionPermission	Protects type information at runtime.
RegistryPermission	Protects registry.
SecurityPermission	Cannot be inherited; protects elements of the security infrastructure (execution, assertion, unmanaged code, skip verification, serialization formatter, control domain policy, control principal, control thread).
ServiceControllerPermission	Protects running or stopping services.
SocketPermission	Protects connections to other computers via sockets.
SqlClientPermission	Protects databases accessed by the SQL Server data access provider.
UIPermission	Protects windows and other user interface elements.
WebPermission	Protects connections to other computers via HTTP.

Table 22.4: Permission Classes in the System.Security Namespace

Table 22.5 lists the most common methods used with the permission classes. Three of these methods—Assert, Deny, and PermitOnly—are called *overrides* because they override the default behavior of the security system. When different overrides are present in the same stack frame, the runtime processes these overrides in the following order: PermitOnly, Deny, and Assert.

Method	Function
Demand	Causes the CLR to perform a security check to see if all callers have demanded permission.
Assert	Allows your code to perform actions that it has permission to perform but that its callers may not have permission to perform (so use caution!).
Deny	Prevents execution of code that is called to get a specific permission. When the Deny method is called for a specific permission, all demands for that permission by callers fail even if they have been granted the permission. Yet if a caller calls Assert for the permission, calling Deny from your code has no effect.
PermitOnly	Limits callers to only the specific permission on which you call PermitOnly; can be overridden by a call to Assert.
RevertAssert RevertDeny RevertPermitOnly	Deactivate an active call to the Assert, Deny, or PermitOnly method, respectively. The deactivation occurs in the current module call chain.
RevertAll	Deactivates any active call to the Assert, Deny, and PermitOnly methods in the current stack frame.
IsSubsetOf	Compares two permissions of the same class and determines if one permission is a subset of the other.
Union	Combines two permission objects of the same class.
Intersect	Creates the intersection of two permission objects of the same class.

Table 22.5: Commonly Used Methods of Permissions Classes

If, during the stack walk, the runtime discovers more than one override of the same type (e.g., two calls to Assert in one stack frame), the second override causes an exception. To replace an override, first call the appropriate revert method (e.g., RevertAssert) and then apply the new override. Also, be aware that each stack frame can have, at most, one permission set used for denial. The most recent Deny function replaces all other denials for other permission sets in the current stack frame.

In Listing 22.15, a demand for a read operation to c:\dir1\ is called. If the system refuses that demand, an exception is thrown.

Listing 22.15—Executing the Demand method of a Permissions object

```
// Demand

try
{
   FileIOPermission p = new FileIOPermission(FileIOPermissionAccess.Read,
"C:\\dir1\\");
p.Demand();
}
catch(SecurityException ex)
{
// catch SecurityException here...
}
```

The code in Listing 22.16 compares two file permissions to determine whether one is a subset of the other. If so, the subset may derive granted permissions from the "parent." For example, if file I/O permission to c:\dir1\ is granted, then file I/O permission to c:\dir1\dir2\ is also granted. Thus, you can conclude that perm2 is a subset of perm1 in this example.

Listing 22.16—IsSubsetOf Example

```
Listing 22.16—IsSubsetOf Example
// IsSubsetOf tests
using System;
using System.Security;
using System.Security.Permissions;

class TestClass
{
    public static void Main()
    {
        try
        {
            // create two registry permissions
            RegistryPermission perm1 = new RegistryPermission(
                RegistryPermissionAccess.AllAccess,
                @"HKEY_LOCAL_MACHINE");
            RegistryPermission perm2 = new RegistryPermission(
                RegistryPermissionAccess.AllAccess,
                    @"HKEY_LOCAL_MACHINE\HARDWARE\DESCRIPTION\
                    System\FloatingPointProcessor\0");

            // and test which is subset of which?
            Console.WriteLine(perm1.IsSubsetOf(perm2)?"perm1 is
                subset of perm2.":"test1 not successful!");
            Console.WriteLine(perm2.IsSubsetOf(perm1)?"perm2 is
                subset of perm1.":"test2 not successful!");

            /* The program will output:
                test1 not successful!
                perm2 is subset of perm1.
            */
        }
        catch(Exception e)
        {
            Console.WriteLine("SecurityException occurred! " +
                                e.ToString());
        }
    }
}
```

Listing 22.17 illustrates a typical use of the Assert method. First, file I/O permission is demanded. Then the Assert method is called to affirm permission to unmanaged code. As a result, no more stack walk-ups are performed until processing of the unmanaged code is complete.

Listing 22.17—Assert Example

```
// assert unmanaged code

    try
    {
        FileIOPermission p1 = new FileIOPermission(
            FileIOPermissionAccess.Read, @"C:\dir1\");

        filePerm.Demand();

        SecurityPermission unmanagedPerm =
            new SecurityPermission(
            SecurityPermissionFlags.UnmanagedCode);
        unmanagedPerm.Assert();
        // call unmanaged code
    }
    catch
    {
        // demand for file I/O permission failed.
```

```
    }
```

Listing 22.18 uses the Demand and Assert methods together for performance tuning. First, you demand an environment variable for read permission. Then you assert that need and execute non-risky code in terms of that environment permission.

Listing 22.18—Demand and Assert Example

```
// demand and assert together

try
{
EnvironmentPermission envPerm = new EnvironmentPermission(
                 EnvironmentPermissionAccess.Read, "TEMP");
// Demand it once to see if it has been granted.
envPerm.Demand();
// Assert the permission to stop the stack walk here.
envPerm.Assert();
for (int i = 0; i < 100; i++)
{
        // code that reads TEMP environment variable
}
}
catch
{
    // The demand failed.
}
```

SecurityAction Enumeration

SecurityAction is an enumeration that encompasses the following elements:

- LinkDemand
- InheritanceDemand
- Demand
- Assert
- Deny
- PermitOnly
- RequestMinimum
- RequestOptional
- RequestRefuse

SecurityPermissionFlag Enumeration

The SecurityPermissionFlag enumeration helps to specify access flags for the security permission object. The SecurityPermission class uses this enumeration. Many of these flags are powerful and should be granted only to highly trusted code.

The enumeration contains the following elements:

- AllFlags
- Assertion
- ControlAppDomain
- ControlDomainPolicy
- ControlEvidence
- ControlPolicy
- ControlPrincipal
- ControlThread
- Execution
- Infrastructure

- NoFlags
- RemotingConfiguration
- SerializationFormatter
- SkipVerification
- UnmanagedCode

Listing 22.19 shows how to use the SecurityPermissionFlag enumeration to request minimum security in the class attributes. This causes security verification to be skipped during JIT compilation.

Listing 22.19—SecurityPermissionFlag Example

```
// SecurityPermissionFlag

[SecurityPermissionAttribute(SecurityAction.RequestMinimum,
        Flags =SecurityPermissionFlag.SkipVerification)]
public class  MySecureClass
{
        public MySecureClass ()
        {
                // code here
        }
}
```

PermissionSet Class

The PermissionSet class represents a collection of different permissions and supports the methods that use and modify those permissions. You can add, remove, assert, deny, and copy permissions.

The example in Listing 22.20 uses the PermissionSet class to obtain the permissions necessary to gain full access to a file and to read a TEMP environment variable. Before changing the permissions of a file, the file will have a default permission set.

The Deny method of the PermissionSet prevents callers from accessing the protected resource even if they have been granted permission to access it. The PermitOnly method of the PermissionSet ensures that only the resources specified by this permission object can be accessed, even if the code has been granted permission to other resources. FileIOPermissionAccess specifies the actions that can be performed on the file or folder. The EnvironmentPermission class instance, added to the PermissionSet in Listing 22.20, manages access to user and system environment variables by granting permissions on how a user queries and modifies user and system environment variables.

Listing 22.20—PermissionSet Sample1

```
using System;
using System.IO;
using System.Security.Permissions;
using System.Security;

public class TestClass
{
        public static void Main()
        {
                // Try to access resources using the permissions
            // currently available.
                AttemptAccess("Default permissions");

                // Create a permission set that allows read access to
            // the TEMP
                // environment variable and read, write, and append
            // access to C:\myfile.txt
                PermissionSet ps = new PermissionSet(PermissionState.None);
```

```
ps.AddPermission(new EnvironmentPermission(
        EnvironmentPermissionAccess.Read, "TEMP"));
ps.AddPermission(
        new FileIOPermission( FileIOPermissionAccess.Read |
                              FileIOPermissionAccess.Write |
                              FileIOPermissionAccess.Append,
                              @"c:\myfile.txt"));

// test if we can access the resource contained in ps
ps.Assert();

// Try to access resources using the permissions we've
// just asserted.
AttemptAccess("Assert permissions.");

// Remove this stack frame's Assert
CodeAccessPermission.RevertAssert();

// Deny access to the resources we specify
ps.Deny();

// Try to access resources using the permissions we've
// just denied.
AttemptAccess("Deny permissions.");

// Remove this stack frame's Deny so we're back to
// default permissions.
CodeAccessPermission.RevertDeny();

// Make the permissions indicate the only things that
// we're allowed to do.
ps.PermitOnly();

// Try to access resources using only the permissions
// we've just permitted.
AttemptAccess("PermitOnly permissions.");

// Remove this stack frame's PermitOnly so we're back
// to default permissions.
CodeAccessPermission.RevertPermitOnly();

// Remove the FileIOPermissions from the permission set
ps.RemovePermission(typeof(FileIOPermission));

// Try to access resources using only the Environment
// permissions.
ps.PermitOnly();
AttemptAccess("PermitOnly without FileIOPermission
                permissions.");

// Remove this stack frame's PermitOnly so we're back
// to default permissions.
CodeAccessPermission.RevertPermitOnly();

// Remove the EnvironmentPermission from the permission
// set
ps.RemovePermission(typeof(EnvironmentPermission));

// Try to access resources using no permissions.
ps.PermitOnly();
AttemptAccess("PermitOnly without any permissions");

// Remove this stack frame's PermitOnly so we're back
// to default permissions.
CodeAccessPermission.RevertPermitOnly();

Console.ReadLine();
```

```
        }

        public static void AttemptAccess(String strMsg)
        {
                Console.WriteLine(strMsg);
                FileStream fs = null;
                String env = null;

                // Try to access a file
                try
                {
                        fs = new FileStream("SomeFile", FileMode.OpenOrCreate);
                }
                catch (Exception)
                {
                        // ignore catch
                }

                // Try to read an environment variable
                try
                {
                        env = Environment.GetEnvironmentVariable("TEMP");
                }
                catch (Exception)
                {
                        // ignore catch
                }

                // Display what we sucessfully did and what we failed.
                Console.WriteLine("test results: " + ((fs != null) ?
                                                "File opened." :
                                                "File cannot be opened!") + " " +
                                        ((env != null) ? "Environment read." :
                                        "Environment cannot be read!"));

                // close file stream
                if (fs != null)
                {
                        fs.Close();
                }
        }
}
```

Figure 22.8 contains the output created by the various access attempts in Listing 22.20.

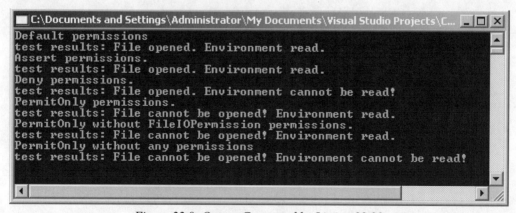

Figure 22.8: Output Generated by Listing 22.20

Listing 22.21 first denies permissions to the permission set it has created. Then it uses the RevertDeny method to allow access again.

Listing 22.21—PermissionSet Sample2, RevertDeny

```
// RevertDeny

public interface anyinterface
{
        void anyfunction(char ch1);
}

public class myclass:anyinterface
{
        PermissionSet ps = new PermissionSet(PermissionState.None);
         ps.AddPermission(new FileIOPermission(FileIOPermissionAccess.AllAccess,
                                        @"c:\dir1"));
        ps.AddPermission(new FileIOPermission(FileIOPermissionAccess.AllAccess,
                                        @"c:\dir2"));
        ps.AddPermission(new EnvironmentPermission(PermissionState.Unrestricted));
        // deny the permissions we just created
        ps.Deny();
        anyfunction('a');
        // revoke denial of the permissions just created
        CodeAccessPermission.RevertDeny();
}
```

PermissionAttribute Class

You can place security attributes in your classes or methods to assert, demand, deny, or permit only certain permissions.

There can be zero or more public properties set in the attribute, each separated by a comma. For example, the FileIOPermissionAttribute has properties for controlling how a user can append, read, and write to a file. Setting these properties in this attribute defines which files or directories you wish to check for access permissions.

In Listing 22.22, FileIOPermissionAttribute demands permission to read C:\dir1\ whenever a method in MyClass is called. The EnvironmentPermissionAttribute demands permission for reading the TEMP environment variable before a call to MyMethod can succeed. If either of the demands fails, the system throws a security exception for calls to MyMethod.

Listing 22.22—PermissionAttribute Example

```
// PermissionAttribute for class and method

[FileIOPermissionAttribute(SecurityAction.Demand,
        Read = @"c:\dir1\")]
public class MyClass
{
        [EnvironmentPermissionAttribute(SecurityAction.Demand,
                Read = "TEMP")]
        public void MyMethod()
        {
        }
}
```

In Listing 22.23, AnyClass defines two assembly permission set attributes, which will cause it to request to read, at a minimum, the minimum_permission.xml file and, optionally, the optional_permission.xml file.

Listing 22.23—PermissionSetAttribute Example

```
// PermissionSetAttribute

[assembly: PermissionSetAttribute(SecurityAction.Request.Minimum,
File="minimum_permission.xml")]
[assembly: PermissionSetAttribute(SecurityAction.RequestOptional,
File="optional_permission.xml")]

public class AnyClass
{
        public static void Main()
        {
                Console.WriteLine("Permissions");
        }
}
```

Listing 22.24 illustrates the declarative use of Deny to override security checks.
RegistryPermissionAttribute includes a SecurityAction enumeration for Deny and the registry key to
which write access will be denied.

Listing 22.24—RegistryPermissionAttribute Example

```
// Declarative demand1

[RegistryPermissionAttribute(SecurityAction.Deny, Write ="HKEY_LOCAL_MACHINE")]
public class MyClass
{

        public MyClass()
        {
        }

// no writes but read to HKLM is allowed!

        public void ReadRegistry()
        {
                //Access the registry.
        }
}
```

Listing 22.25 shows how to use Assert declaratively to override security checks. Using Assert in
FileIOPermission causes demands for access to C:\temp\trace1.txt to succeed, since the Assert
method is called during JIT compilation.

Listing 22.25—FileIOPermission Example

```
// Declarative demand2

[FileIOPermission(SecurityAction.Assert, All = @"C:\temp\trace1.txt")]
public void SaveTrace()
{
        StreamWriter TextStream = new StreamWriter(@"C:\temp\trace1.txt");
        TextStream.WriteLine("created on:" + DateTime.Now);
        TextStream.Close();
}
```

Listing 22.26 shows how a link demand can be used to check only the immediate caller of your code
during a security check performed as part of a JIT compilation. The immediate caller of the
CoolApp class must have the strong name used in the StrongNameIdentityPermissionAttribute
defined in the listing, since we used the LinkDemand security action. CoolApp class can be linked
only by the assembly that has the strong name specified in the LinkDemand attribute.

Listing 22.26—LinkDemand Example

```
// link demand

[StrongNameIdentityPermissionAttribute(SecurityAction.LinkDemand,
PublicKey="00240000048000009400000006020000002400005253413100040000010001000bf01b056
b9778a08f3b7b7a573b1a6e6e1bf18af004f8f017997a28b4378ea7b389932c9f537df90190b994c1e0
849a4222a6d87761bc96d2a16d8a36865c6d7d031fa3109ed9711d064d20e7059aa945dfe10cdd64d32
49c10b76e2759556d3554f7708ade90c9453b1118f97a492b81ba33d193ee8df19b29af7dabae691d5"
,
        Name = "CoolApp", Version = "1.0.0.2"]

public class CoolApp
{
        // Additional code here
}
```

System.Security.Principal

The System.Security.Principal namespace defines a principal object that represents the security context under which code is running.

IIdentity Interface

- AuthenticationType—this property returns a string that describes the type of authentication in place, such as basic authentication, NTLM, Kerberos, or Passport. The value for this property will be defined by each application.
- IsAuthenticated—this property returns a value that indicates whether the current user has been authenticated.
- Name—this property returns the user name of the user represented by this identity.

IPrincipal Interface

- Identity—this property returns the identity object that is associated with this principal.
- IsInRole—this method returns a value that indicates whether the user represented by this principal belongs to a specific role.

WindowsIdentity Class

The WindowsIndentity class implements the IIdentity interface. It represents the identity of the user based on a method of authentication supported by the Windows operating system. A Windows identity provides the ability to impersonate another user so resources can be accessed on that user's behalf.

WindowsPrincipal Class

The WindowsPrincipal class implements the IPrincipal interface. It represents Windows users and their *roles*, which are simply the Windows groups to which the users belong.

GenericIdentity Class

The GenericIdentity class implements the IIdentity interface. It represents the identity of the user based on a custom authentication method defined by the application.

GenericPrincipal Class

The GenericPrincipal class implements the IPrincipal interface. It represents users and roles that exist independent of Windows users and their roles. Essentially, the generic principal is a simple solution for application authentication and authorization.

PrincipalPermission Class

PrincipalPermission objects allow code to perform actions (Demand, Union, Intersect, etc.) against the current user identity in a manner consistent with the way those actions are performed for code access permissions and identity permissions. PrincipalPermission can be issued as an imperative demand, as shown at the top of Listing 22.27, or as a declarative demand, as the bottom of the listing shows.

Listing 22.27—IsInRole Example

```
PrincipalPermission p = new PrincipalPermission(null,
"BUILTIN\Administrator");
p.Demand();

// or it can be issued as a declarative demand as shown in the line below
[PrincipalPermission(SecurityAction.Demand, Role=@"BUILTIN\Administrators")]
```

CurrentPrincipal Property

The CurrentPrincipal property of the Thread class is a static proprety that allows you to get or set the current security context of the user. You can use the CurrentPrincipal property of the System.Threading.Thread class in order to get the current WindowsPrincipal object as in the line of code below:

```
WindowsPrincipal myWindowsPrincipal = (WindowsPrincipal)
Thread.CurrentPrincipal;
```

IsInRole Method

You can check role membership by calling the IsInRole method on the principal object. You can use IsInRole with WindowsPrincipal and CurrentPrincipal. Listing 22.28 shows a simple use of the IsInRole method.

Listing 22.28—IsInRole Example

```
// IsInRole

WindowsPrincipal winpr = (WindowsPrincipal) Thread.CurrentPrincipal;

// WindowsBuiltInRole is an enumeration!

// Is winpr object in role of Administrator?
winpr.IsInRole(WindowsBuiltInRole.Administrator);

// Is the current thread principal in role of Administrator?
System.Threading.Thread.CurrentPrincipal.IsInRole(@"BUILTIN\Administrator");
```

Impersonate and ImpersonateContext

If your application must impersonate a Windows account that has not been attached to the current thread, you must retrieve that account's token and use it to activate the account:

- Retrieve an account token for a particular user by making a call to the unmanaged LogonUser method, passing it the user name, password, and domain of the account you want. This method is not in the .NET Framework base class library but is located in the unmanaged advapi32.dll library. For the LogonUser call to work, a special privilege known as SE_TCB_NAME is needed. You can check this by selecting Control Panel→Administrative Tools→Local Security Policy Settings.
- Create a new instance of the WindowsIdentity class, passing the account token retrieved in the preceding step.

- Begin impersonation by creating a new instance of the WindowsImpersonationContext class and initializing it with the Impersonate method of the WindowsIdentity object created in the preceding step.
- When you no longer need to impersonate the Windows user, call the WindowsImpersonationContext.Undo method to revert the impersonation with MyImpersonation.Undo();.

Listing 22.29 illustrates how you can accomplish impersonation.

Listing 22.29—Impersonation Example

```
// impersonation

public class ImpersonationExample
{
        [DllImport("ADVAPI32")]
        private unsafe static extern int LogonUser (
                String lpszUsername,
                String lpszDomain,
                String lpszPasswords,
                int dwLogonType,
                int dwLogonProvider,
                out InPtr phToken
                );

        public void anyfunction()
        {
                InPtr lToken;
                int lRetVal = 0;
                lRetval = LogonUser (strUserName, strDomain,
                        strPassword, LOGON32_LOGON_NETWORK ,
                        LOGON32_PROVIDER_DEFAULT, out lToken);

                if(lRetval == 0)
                {
                        Console.WriteLine("Login error occurred!");
                        return;
                }

                WindowsIdentity ImpId = new WindowsIdentity(lToken);
                WindowsImpersonationContext ImpContext =
                        ImpId.Impersonate();

                // you are impersonating another user now in this
                // thread!
                // execute some managed and unmanaged code now

                ImpContext.Undo();
        }
}
```

Listing 22.30 creates two PrincipalPermission objects representing two different users. The union demand succeeds only if user mcb is in the role of director or user mindcracker is in the role of officer.

Listing 22.30—PrincipalPermission Union Example

```
// Union Demand

String id1 = "mcb";
String role1 = "Director";
PrincipalPermission PrincipalPerm1 = new PrincipalPermission(id1, role1 );
String id2 = "mindcracker";
String role2 = "Officer";
```

```
PrincipalPermission PrincipalPerm2 = new PrincipalPermission(id2, role2 );
(PrincipalPerm1.Union(PrincipalPerm2 ) ).Demand();
```

In Listing 22.31, the current WindowsIdentity class is transformed into a WindowsPrincipal class. Then all of the identity and principal properties are written to the system console.

Listing 22.31—WindowsIdentity to WindowsPrincipal Example

```
// WindowsIdentity illustrated

WindowsIdentity MyIdentity =
                    WindowsIdentity.GetCurrent();
WindowsPrincipal MyPrincipal = new
                    WindowsPrincipal(MyIdentity);

//Principal values.
Console.WriteLine(MyPrincipal.Identity.Name);
Console.WriteLine(MyPrincipal.Identity.AuthenticationType);
Console.WriteLine(MyPrincipal.Identity.IsAuthenticated.ToString());

//Identity values.
Console.WriteLine(MyIdentity.Name);
Console.WriteLine(MyIdentity.AuthenticationType);
Console.WriteLine(MyIdentity.IsAuthenticated.ToString());
Console.WriteLine(MyIdentity.IsAnonymous.ToString());
Console.WriteLine(MyIdentity.IsGuest.ToString());
Console.WriteLine(MyIdentity.IsSystem.ToString());
Console.WriteLine(MyIdentity.Token.ToString());
```

Listing 22.32 illustrates GenericIdentity class usage.

Listing 22.32—GenericIdentity Example

```
AppDomain.CurrentDomain.SetPrincipalPolicy(PrincipalPolicy.WindowsPrincipal);

WindowsPrincipal myUser =
WindowsPrincipal)System.Threading.Thread.CurrentPrincipal;

GenericIdentity MyIdentity = new
GenericIdentity(myUser.Identity.Name.ToString());

String[] MyStringArray = {"Role1", "Teller"};

GenericPrincipal MyPrincipal = new GenericPrincipal(MyIdentity,
MyStringArray);

System.Threading.Thread.CurrentPrincipal = MyPrincipal;

//Return user values

String Name =  MyPrincipal.Identity.Name;

bool Auth =  MyPrincipal.Identity.IsAuthenticated;

bool IsInRole =  MyPrincipal.IsInRole("Role2");

if(IsInRole)
{
 Console.WriteLine("The test was successful as a user in the user-defined role of
Role1");
}
else
{
 Console.WriteLine("The test was not successful!");
}
```

In Listing 22.33, declarative demands for PrincipalPermission and PrincipalPermissionAttribute are illustrated. The attribute adjustment says that only a principal in the role of Role1 may execute these functions.

Listing 22.33—Declarative Identity Example

```
[PrincipalPermission(SecurityAction.Demand, Role=@"Role1")]
private string MyFunction()
{

return "Declarative control for the role of Role1 is truly successfully. This
function can be executed by you!";

}

[PrincipalPermissionAttribute(SecurityAction.Demand, Name = "MyUser", Role =
"Role1")]
public static void PrivateInfo()

{
    //Output of private data
    Console.WriteLine("You have access to the private data!");
}
```

IsolatedStorageFile Class

The .NET Framework provides the IsolatedStorageFile class to represent a store for an assembly.

Listing 22.34 shows various aspects of IsolatedStorage namespace classes and methods.

Listing 22.34—IsolatedStorage Example

```
// isolated storage
// in System.IO.IsolatedStorage namespace

// Obtain a store
IsolatedStorageFile store1 =
        IsolatedStorageFile.GetUserStoreForDomain();

// you can also use static GetStore methods like below
/*

IsolatedStorageFile storefile1 = IsolatedStorageFile.GetStore(
    IsolatedStorageScope.User |
        IsolatedStorageScope.Assembly,
    null,
    null);

IsolatedStorageFile storefile1 = IsolatedStorageFile.GetStore(
    IsolatedStorageScope.User |
        IsolatedStorageScope.Assembly |
        IsolatedStorageScope.Domain,
    null,
    null);

IsolatedStorageFile storefile1 = IsolatedStorageFile.GetStore(
    IsolatedStorageScope.User |
        IsolatedStorageScope.Assembly |
        IsolatedStorageScope.Roaming,
    null,
    null);

IsolatedStorageFile storefile1 = IsolatedStorageFile.GetStore(
    IsolatedStorageScope.User |
```

```
            IsolatedStorageScope.Assembly |
            IsolatedStorageScope.Domain |
            IsolatedStorageScope.Roaming,
    null,
    null);

*/

IsolatedStorageFileStream stream1 =
        new IsolatedStorageFileStream("file1.txt",
        FileMode.Create, store1);

StreamWriter writer = new StreamWriter(stream1);
writer.WriteLine("Hello Isolated Storage");

writer.Close();
stream1.Close();
store1.Close();

// Read from a file in isolated storage
IsolatedStorageFileStream stream1 =
        new IsolatedStorageFileStream("file2.txt",
        FileMode.Open, store1);

StreamReader reader = new StreamReader(stream1);
String sb = reader.ReadToEnd();

reader.Close();
stream1.Close();
store1.Close();

// Obtain a store
// Create a directory
store1.CreateDirectory("dir1");

// Create two directories, one inside the other
store1.CreateDirectory("dir2/dir3");

// Create a directory
store1.CreateDirectory("dir4");

// Delete the directory
store1.DeleteDirectory("dir4");

// Obtain a store
IsolatedStorageFile store1 =
        IsolatedStorageFile.GetUserStoreForDomain();

// Create an empty file
IsolatedStorageFileStream stream1 =
        new IsolatedStorageFileStream("file3.txt",
        FileMode.Create, store1);
stream1.Close();

// Delete the file
store1.DeleteFile("file3.txt");

// Find a storage space available

// Obtain a store
IsolatedStorageFile store1 =
        IsolatedStorageFile.GetUserStoreForDomain();

// Compute the storage available in the store
ulong spaceLeft =
        store1.MaximumSize - store1.CurrentSize;
```

```
// Enumerate files and directories
// Obtain a store
IsolatedStorageFile store1 =
        IsolatedStorageFile.GetUserStoreForDomain();

// Get all of the directories in the root of the store
string [] directories = store1.GetDirectoryNames("*");

// Get all of the files in the root of the store
string [] files = store1.GetFileNames("*");
```

System.Security.Cryptography Namespace

The System.Security.Cryptography namespace contains support for the most common symmetric (DES, 3DES, RC2, Rijndael), asymmetric (RSA, DSA), and hash (MD5, SHA-1, SHA-256, SHA-384, SHA-512) cryptography algorithms. It also includes a helpful class to encrypt and decrypt streams. You can use this class, called CryptoStream, in combination with other stream classes or you can use several CryptoStream class objects together. With a little effort, you can feed the output of one CryptoStream object into another CryptoStream object.

Table 22.6 lists the classes and interfaces that are part of the System.Security.Cryptography namespace of the .NET Framework base class library. These classes and interfaces define the abstract object model for encryption algorithms within the .NET Framework. New algorithms may be added to the .NET Framework by subclassing and/or implementing a portion of these classes and interfaces.

Class or Interface	Description
SymmetricAlgorithm	The top-level abstraction for all symmetric cryptography algorithms.
AsymmetricAlgorithm	The top-level abstraction for all asymmetric cryptography algorithms.
RC2	The RC2 abstraction; a subclass of SymmetricAlgorithm.
DES	The DES algorithm abstraction; a subclass of SymmetricAlgorithm (DES.cs).
TripleDES	The Triple DES algorithm abstraction, derived from SymmetricAlgorithm.
Rijndael	The Rijndeal abstraction, derived from SymmetricAlgorithm.
RSA	The RSA public key cipher abstraction, derived from AsymmetricAlgorithm.
DSA	The DSA public key cipher abstraction, derived from AsymmetricAlgorithm.
ICryptoTransform	The interface definition for encryption and decryption transforms; objects of this type are generated by methods on SymmetricAlgorithm.

Table 22.6: Classes and Interfaces in the System.Security.Cryptography Namespace

Listing 22.35 illustrates the use of DES and CryptoStream classes to encipher and decipher a file.

Listing 22.35—Cryptostream1.cs, CryptoStream with DES

```
// NOTE: Before you execute the program, first
// create a file named c:\myfile.txt with text "myname is bozo..." in it.

// After you execute the code, two files will be created on the c: drive.
// The c:\ciphered.txt file will include weird ciphered characters like
// "¼ş□Eó□ğNª□4û  Õ?8Ò¤¤□"5"
```

```
// The c:\enciphered.txt file will be identical to c:\myfile.txt.

using System;
using System.IO;
using System.Security;
using System.Security.Cryptography;
using System.Text;

class CryptoDESSample
{
    public static void Main(string[] args)
    {
      FileStream fsInput = new FileStream(@"c:\myfile.txt",
                                      FileMode.Open,
                                      FileAccess.Read);

      FileStream fsCiphered = new FileStream(@"c:\ciphered.txt",
                                        FileMode.Create,
                                        FileAccess.Write);
      DESCryptoServiceProvider ourDESProvider = new DESCryptoServiceProvider();
      // our 8 byte DES secret key is 12345678
      ourDESProvider.Key = ASCIIEncoding.ASCII.GetBytes("12345678");
      ourDESProvider.IV = ASCIIEncoding.ASCII.GetBytes("12345678");
      ICryptoTransform des1 = ourDESProvider.CreateEncryptor();
      ICryptoTransform des2 = ourDESProvider.CreateDecryptor();
      CryptoStream cryptostream1 = new CryptoStream(fsCiphered,
                                            des1,
                                            CryptoStreamMode.Write);

      byte[] bytearrayinput = new byte[fsInput.Length];
      fsInput.Read(bytearrayinput, 0, bytearrayinput.Length);
      cryptostream1.Write(bytearrayinput, 0, bytearrayinput.Length);
      cryptostream1.Close();
      fsInput.Close();
      fsCiphered.Close();

      FileStream fsread = new FileStream(@"c:\ciphered.txt",
                                    FileMode.Open,
                                    FileAccess.Read);
      CryptoStream cryptostream2 = new CryptoStream(fsread,
                                            des2,
                                            CryptoStreamMode.Read);
      StreamWriter fsEnciphered = new StreamWriter(@"c:\enciphered.txt");
      fsEnciphered.Write(new StreamReader(cryptostream2).ReadToEnd());
      fsEnciphered.Flush();
      fsEnciphered.Close();
    }
}
```

The code in Listing 22.36 uses the SHA1 algorithm to compute the hash value of a given string.

Listing 22.36—Hash1.cs, Hashing a String Using SHA-1 Algorithm

```
using System;
using System.IO;
using System.Security;
using System.Security.Cryptography;

public class Class1
{
 public static void Main(string[] args)
 {
    String str1 = "MCBinc";
    Char[] char1a = str1.ToCharArray();
    Byte[] byte1a = new Byte[char1a.Length];
    for(int i = 0; i < byte1a.Length; i++)
```

```
byte1a[i] = (Byte)char1a[i];

  // create hash value from str1 using SHA1 instance
  // returned by CryptoConfig
  byte[] hash1 = ((HashAlgorithm)
CryptoConfig.CreateFromName("SHA1")).ComputeHash(byte1a);

  // or you can use directly created instance of the SHA1 class
  // byte[] hash1 = (new SHA1CryptoServiceProvider()).ComputeHash(byte1a );

  Console.WriteLine(str1 + @" hashed Value is <" +
BitConverter.ToString(hash1) + @">");
 }
}
```

The code in the listing writes the output in Figure 22.9 to the console.

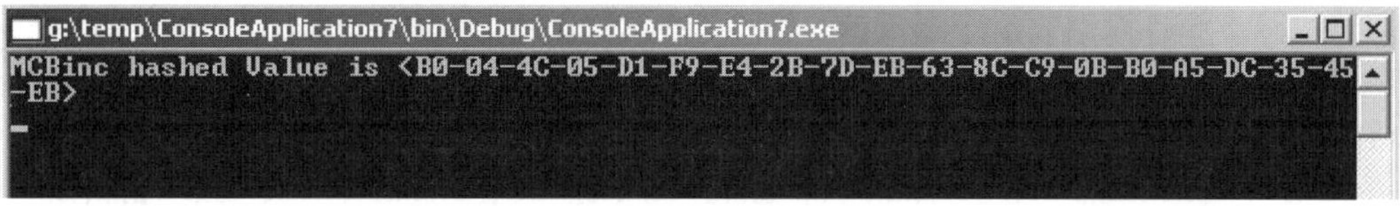

Figure 22.9: Output Generated from Listing 22.36

System.Security.Cryptography.Xml Namespace

The System.Security.Cryptography.Xml namespace contains a full implementation of the World Wide Web Consortium standard for digitally signing XML data and files. In other words, the namespace helps you to sign any XML object with a digital signature. Refer to the XML-Signature Syntax and Processing page at http://www.w3.org/TR/xmldsig-core/ for details on this progressing standard.

The sample code in Listing 22.37 shows how to sign XML data and produce an envelope for it via the RSA algorithm.

Listing 22.37—SignXML1.cs, Compute Signature for XML Data

```
using System;
using System.Xml;
using System.Security.Cryptography;
using System.Security.Cryptography.Xml;

public class DigitalSignSample {
 public static void Main()
 {
  // generate XML data
  XmlDocument document = new XmlDocument();
  XmlNode node = document.CreateNode(XmlNodeType.Element, "", @"Visual Studio
.NET", "sign xml samples");
  node.InnerText = @"C# wimps the lama's bass...";
  document.AppendChild(node);
  Console.WriteLine("OriginalXML data:\r\n" + document.OuterXml + "\r\n");

  // create signedxml variable
  RSA rsa = System.Security.Cryptography.RSA.Create();
  SignedXml signedXml = new SignedXml();
  signedXml.SigningKey = rsa;

  // create dataobject
  DataObject dataObject = new System.Security.Cryptography.Xml.DataObject();
  dataObject.Data = document.ChildNodes;
  dataObject.Id = "goo";

  // add dataobject and reference
```

```
signedXml.AddObject(dataObject);
signedXml.AddReference(new Reference("#goo"));

// add keyinfo
KeyInfo keyInfo = new KeyInfo();
keyInfo.AddClause(new RSAKeyValue(rsa));
signedXml.KeyInfo = keyInfo;

// compute signature and get an envelope for the XML data
signedXml.ComputeSignature();
XmlElement xmlDigitalSignature = signedXml.GetXml();

// output the envelope
Console.WriteLine("======================================================");
XmlTextWriter w = new XmlTextWriter(Console.Out);
w.Formatting = Formatting.Indented;
xmlDigitalSignature.WriteTo(w);
 }
}
```

Summary

Computer security deals with preventing unauthorized users from eyeing secret data or tampering with private information. Computer security decreases the frequency of unauthorized use and prevents unauthorized users from destroying valuable computer resources. Any secure computer system must guarantee the integrity, confidentiality, and availability of the resources, users, and information.Conventional security models shelter resources by preventing unauthorized users from accessing and misusing these resources. When a user runs a program, the application code starts performing and that application can access any resources on the computer whose access permission is granted to the application. Poor permissioning can create a hole for violating security.The .NET Framework provides a very neat infrastructure for developing and deploying secure applications. In the .NET Framework, role-based and code access security work very well together. Microsoft separated the logical security behavior covered by role-based security from the permissions a segment of code has during execution. This separation adds simplification to the complex topic of security. Even if code access security entails a steeper learning curve and places more responsibility on administrators, it is an effective approach.

In code access security, your code groups are traversed according to your evidence in four policy levels (Remember EMUAD!), and then your resultant permission sets are determined as an intersection of these policies. Role-based security and code-based security can be implemented through imperative or declarative means. Imperative security is implemented with policy files and modules, and declarative security is implemented via attributes. Cryptography classes supplied as part of the .NET Framework support most common symmetric, asymmetric, and hash algorithms. Role-based and code access security work very well together. Microsoft separated the logical security behavior covered by role-based security from the permissions a segment of code has during execution. This separation adds a new, simplified structure to the complex topic of security. Role-based security and code-based security can be implemented through imperative or declarative means. Imperative security is implemented with policy files and modules, and declarative security is implemented via attributes. In the next chapter we will talk about SOAP and how it is implemented in .NET.

Chapter 23:
SOAP and .NET Remoting

Simple Object Access Protocol (SOAP) is an industry-standard protocol designed to improve cross-platform interoperability by using the World Wide Web and Extensible Markup Language (XML). With the advent of XML as a standard document-tagging syntax, derivatives began appearing in the arena. XML evolved into SOAP, and SOAP has since evolved into BizTalk. Thus, SOAP and BizTalk are indeed nothing but specialized XML documents. Prior to the appearance of SOAP, Microsoft implemented COM+ (an extension of Component Object Model), Java proponents supported Enterprise JavaBeans (EJB), and other companies supported Common Object Request Broker Architecture (CORBA). In fact, all these models tried to make remote component usage easy and secure. However, they only handle components of the same style—that is, none of them is able to communicate with the others. SOAP has now made this possible. It solves the problem of platform incompatibility in accessing data. It is a syntax that allows you to build applications for remotely invoking methods on objects. SOAP removes the requirement that two systems must run on the same platform or be written in the same programming language. Instead of invoking methods through a proprietary binary protocol, a SOAP package uses an open standard syntax for making method calls. That syntax is XML.

SOAP is simply equal to XML plus Hypertext Transfer Protocol (HTTP). SOAP sends an XML request to a SOAP server over HTTP and receives the response back in XML. Because HTTP is the de facto mode of communication on the Internet, with all Web servers recognizing and responding to an HTTP request, it is an ideal protocol for enabling the integration of various systems. XML is emerging as a de facto standard to exchange information among disparate systems. SOAP's use of XML to send and receive messages ensures that any system on any platform can read and process the message, unlike with a proprietary format.

Existing technologies such as Distributed Component Object Model (DCOM) or CORBA enable components to be distributed; however, DCOM and CORBA use remote procedure call (RPC) for communication, which doesn't work well across the Internet. Further, both the client and server must have the same or similar systems and operating systems for DCOM or CORBA to work. Setup time may also be needed to make these solutions work. For these reasons, we do not regard the DCOM and CORBA solutions as supporting true distributed components. With true distributed components, the client and server can be disparate. The client and server can have different operating systems and run on different kinds of machines and networks. Because SOAP uses XML over HTTP to communicate, it offers true distributed component support.

SOAP is not a replacement for COM or CORBA; however, COM and CORBA can use SOAP to enable them to work across the Internet. SOAP uses the common standards XML and HTTP to promote interoperability between heterogeneous systems anywhere on the Internet. Web services are fast emerging as a new solution paradigm, and it won't be too long before you start using SOAP to build Web services. Web services expose data through the Web without formatting it. Think of Web services as applications that make it possible for you to program using data available on the Web, just as you can program now using data available internally. Applications on different platforms have only a limited ability to share data. In recognition of those limitations, developers have pushed overwhelmingly for the establishment of standards for data formats and for data exchange. This push stems from a vision that is rapidly evolving into a new computing paradigm: the seamless, Web-enabled integration of services across traditional hardware and software barriers.

Introduction to SOAP

A SOAP document is an electronic envelope into which you place your payload. The payload consists of the tags that describe the method you want to invoke and the data that method invocation needs to do its job. A SOAP envelope document has two subelements—the SOAP:Header and SOAP:Body. The SOAP:Header element contains information about the transaction. The Body contains the content data. (Note that in our examples we will refer to HTTP protocol when we mean SOAP communication protocol, but other protocols will be supported by new SOAP versions.)

As you can see in Figure 23.1, a SOAP client submits a request (XML-formatted) over any SOAP-supported protocol (e.g., HTTP) to a "listener" SOAP server at another site. This listening server captures the message, interprets the request, and invokes a method on an object in its domain. That object returns something useful (XML-formatted response) to our application by responding through the SOAP server to our waiting client application.

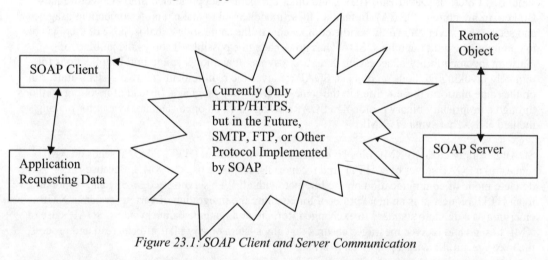

Figure 23.1: SOAP Client and Server Communication

Please note that the object being invoked does not need any kind of modification. The SOAP server will interpret the SOAP XML document that comes over the HTTP, Transmission Control Protocol (TCP), or Simple Mail Transfer Protocol (SMTP) connection. Then the SOAP server turns the XML document into something meaningful that the object understands. The SOAP server speaks both the SOAP language and the language of the object being called, translating conversation between them. We can say that the SOAP server acts as an interpreter. Consequently, the object can be developed in any programming language on any operating system or platform.

A SOAP package (Figure 23.2) simply contains information used to call a method. But the SOAP specification does not define how that method is to be called. It just contains what to call with what, not how to call. This makes the client and server communication loosely coupled and more free. On the other hand, some things SOAP does not do as well. It does not provide any means for bidirectional communication, type safety, distributed garbage collection, or messages that contain more than one business document (a SOAP message can contain only one business document!). However, SOAP allows us to pass parameters and commands between HTTP, TCP, and SMTP clients and servers, and this is done independent of any platforms, operating systems, or applications. Of course, the commands and parameters passed back and forth are all encoded in

XML syntax. XML provides us a formatting syntax with which to express almost any kind of data. Refer to the XML chapter if you need a refresher on XML.

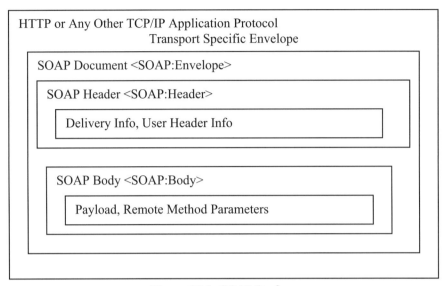

Figure 23.2: SOAP Package

The SOAP specification defines the SOAP elements that can be used with a SOAP request: they are the envelope, head, and body. The envelope is a container for the head and body. The head contains information about the SOAP message, and the body contains the actual message. Namespaces are used to distinguish the SOAP elements from the other elements of the payload. For example, SOAP-ENV:Envelope, SOAP-ENV:Head, and SOAP-ENV:Body are used in a SOAP document. Listing 23.1 shows a SOAP schema for the envelope of SOAP 1.1.

Listing 23.1—SOAP Schema for the Envelope of SOAP 1.1

```
<?xml version="1.0" ?>
<!-- XML Schema for SOAP v 1.1 Envelope -->
<!-- Copyright 2000 DevelopMentor, International Business
Machines Corporation, Lotus Development Corporation,
Microsoft, UserLand Software -->
<schema xmlns="http://www.w3.org/1999/XMLSchema"
    xmlns:tns="http://schemas.xmlsoap.org/soap/envelope/"
    targetNamespace="http://schemas.xmlsoap.org/soap/envelope/">
    <!-- SOAP envelope, header, and body -->
    <element name="Envelope" type="tns:Envelope"/>
    <complexType name="Envelope">
        <element ref="tns:Header" minOccurs="0"/>
        <element ref="tns:Body" minOccurs="1"/>
        <any minOccurs="0" maxOccurs="*"/>
        <anyAttribute/>
    </complexType>
    <element name="Header" type="tns:Header"/>
    <complexType name="Header">
        <any minOccurs="0" maxOccurs="*"/>
        <anyAttribute/>
    </complexType>
    <element name="Body" type="tns:Body"/>
    <complexType name="Body">
        <any minOccurs="0" maxOccurs="*"/>
        <anyAttribute/>
    </complexType>
    <!-- Global Attributes.  The following attributes are
```

```
            intended to be usable via qualified attribute names on
            any complex type referencing them.
    -->
    <attribute name="mustUnderstand" default="0">
        <simpleType base="boolean">
            <pattern value="0|1"/>
        </simpleType>
    </attribute>
    <attribute name="actor" type="uri-reference"/>
    <!-- 'encodingStyle' indicates any canonicalization
     conventions followed in the contents of the containing
     element.  For example, the value
     'http://schemas.xmlsoap.org/soap/encoding/' indicates
     the pattern described in SOAP specification.
    -->
<simpleType name="encodingStyle" base="uri-reference"
    derivedBy="list"/>
    <attributeGroup name="encodingStyle">
        <attribute name="encodingStyle"
            type="tns:encodingStyle"/>
    </attributeGroup>
    <!-- SOAP fault reporting structure -->
    <complexType name="Fault" final="extension">
        <element name="faultcode" type="qname"/>
        <element name="faultstring" type="string"/>
        <element name="faultactor" type="uri-reference"
            minOccurs="0"/>
        <element name="detail" type="tns:detail" minOccurs="0"/>
    </complexType>
    <complexType name="detail">
        <any minOccurs="0" maxOccurs="*"/>
        <anyAttribute/>
    </complexType>
</schema>
```

When we use HTTP, we use the POST request method because with this method, as opposed to the GET method, the size of the HTTP headers is unlimited. We will see two types of headers in HTTP—request headers and response headers. Please refer to the document RFC2616 (*Hypertext Transfer Protocol—HTTP 1.1* by R. Fielding et al.) for more details about HTTP implementation details. Listing 23.2 shows an example of an HTTP POST request header. You can add any headers you like to HTTP—for example, in Listing 23.2 SOAPAction is a SOAP-added HTTP header referring to the remote method, UpdateData, to be invoked and its Uniform Resource Locator (URL).

Listing 23.2—HTTP POST Request Header

```
POST /Order HTTP/1.1
Host: www.mindcracker.com
Content-Type: text/xml
Content-Length: nnnn
SOAPAction: "http://www.mindcracker.com#UpdateData"

Information being sent would be located here.
```

Listing 23.3 shows a good response-type HTTP header.

Listing 23.3—Good HTTP Response Header

```
200 OK
Content-Type: text/plain
Content-Length: nnnn

Content goes here.
```

Listing 23.4 shows a bad HTTP response header.

Listing 23.4—Bad HTTP Response Header

```
400 Bad Request
Content-Type: text/plain
Content-Length: 0
```

A SOAP request document without HTTP headers is shown in Listing 23.5.

Listing 23.5—SOAP Request Document Without HTTP Headers

```
<SOAP-ENV:Envelope
   xmlns:xsi="http://www.w3.org/1999/XMLSchema/instance"
   xmlns:SOAP-ENV="http://schemas.xmlsoap.org/soap/envelope"
   xsi:schemaLocation=
      "http://www.mindcracker.com/schemas/Schema.xsd">
<SOAP-ENV:Header xsi:type="MindcrackerHeader">
      <COM:GUID xmlns:COM="http://comobject.northwindtraders.com">
         10000000-0000-abcd-0000-000000000001
      </COM:GUID>
   </SOAP-ENV:Header>

   <SOAP-ENV:Body xsi:type="MindcrackerBody">
      <OrderUpdate>
         <orderID>0</orderID>
         <item>89</item>
      </OrderUpdate>
   </SOAP-ENV:Body>
</SOAP-ENV:Envelope>
```

Listing 23.6 shows a SOAP body schema—the contents of the file
http://www.mindcracker.com/schemas/Schema.xsd.

Listing 23.6—Schema.xsd File Contents

```
<xsd:schema xmlns:xsd="http://www.w3.org/1999/XMLSchema"
   targetNamespace="http://schemas.xmlsoap.org/soap/envelope"
   xmlns:SOAP="http://schemas.xmlsoap.org/soap/envelope">
   <xsd:complexType name="MindcrackerHeader">
      <xsd:element name="GUID" type="string"/>
   </xsd:complexType>

   <xsd:complexType name="MindcrackerBody">
      <xsd:element name="OrderUpdate">
         <xsd:complexType>
            <element name="orderID" type="integer"/>
            <element name="item" type="double"/>
         </xsd:complexType>
      </xsd:element>
   </xsd:complexType>
</xsd:schema>
```

A successful SOAP response document is shown in Listing 23.7.

Listing 23.7—Successful SOAP Response Document

```
<SOAP-ENV:Envelope
   xmlns:xsi="http://www.w3.org/1999/XMLSchema/instance"
   xmlns:SOAP-ENV="http://schemas.xmlsoap.org/soap/envelope"
   xsi:schemaLocation=
      "http://www.mindcracker.com/schemas/Schema.xsd">
   <SOAP-ENV:Body xsi:type="MindcrackerBody">
      <OrderUpdate>
```

```
        <orderID>09999</orderID>
        <return>0</return>
    </OrderUpdate>
  </SOAP-ENV:Body>
</SOAP-ENV:Envelope>
```

Listing 23.8 shows a faulty SOAP response document. The transaction has failed for the reason noted in the error message.

Listing 23.8—Faulty SOAP Response Document

```
<SOAP-ENV:Envelope
   xmlns:xsi="http://www.w3.org/1999/XMLSchema/instance"
   xmlns:SOAP-ENV="http://schemas.xmlsoap.org/soap/envelope"
   xsi:schemaLocation=
      "http://www.mindcracker.com/schemas/Schema.xsd">
      <SOAP-ENV:Fault>
         <SOAP-ENV:faultcode>200</SOAP-ENV:faultcode>
         <SOAP-ENV:faultstring>Must Understand Error
         </SOAP-ENV:faultstring>
         <SOAP-ENV:detail xsi:type="Fault">
            <errorMessage>
               The object cannot be found or is not installed.
            </errorMessage>
         </SOAP-ENV:detail>
      </SOAP-ENV:Fault >
   </SOAP-ENV:Body>
</SOAP-ENV:Envelope>
```

Following is an example of a C# SOAP server/client with the UpdateData method declaration:

```
public int OrderUpdateMethod(ref int OrderID, double Item);
```

More information about SOAP encoding is available at http://www.w3.org/tr/soap. SOAP is used extensively by developers working with .NET Remoting, Web services (ASP.NET), and Active Template Library (ATL) Server's C++ native, unmanaged Web services code.

.NET Remoting and SOAP

.NET Remoting is a framework built into the common language runtime (CLR) that can be used to build sophisticated distributed applications and network services. The CLR remoting infrastructure provides a rich set of classes that allows developers to ignore most of the complexities of deploying and managing remote objects. Although we are dealing with applications running against different runtime environments, calling methods on remote objects is nearly identical to calling local methods. This is a new procedure when compared with COM+ and CORBA; it is more platform independent because it is XML based.

When a client creates an instance of a remote object, it receives a proxy representing the class instance on the server. All methods called on the proxy are forwarded automatically to the remote class, and any result is returned to the client. From the client's perspective, this process is no different than making a local call. Any exception thrown by the remote object is returned automatically to the client. This enables the client to use normal try-and-catch blocks around sections of the code to trap and deal with exceptions.

When a client calls a method on a remote object, the remoting framework automatically serializes any data associated with the request and uses a channel to transport the data to the remote object. Some of the more popular channels supported are HTTP, TCP, and SMTP. In the case of HTTP, the framework uses the SOAP protocol to transport data in XML format from the client to the server and back. The default serialization formatter for HTTP is a SOAP formatter. Because programmers can create custom formatters to use with any channel, the remoting framework can be configured to work with any external .NET Framework on other platforms. The TCP channel uses plain sockets and binary serialization by default and can be used to communicate with any object on a remote server. Remote objects can be hosted easily in Internet Information Server (IIS). This allows any client to connect to the object by using normal HTTP on port 80. It is also possible to create Web pages that allow a user to connect to a remote object by using Internet Explorer.

A SOAP Client/Server Application in .NET

Listing 23.9 shows a simple SOAP server application.

```
Listing23.9.cs  , DateTimeServer and DateTimeServer remote object
```

Execute the following commands to generate two files from the source code—object1.dll and Listing23.9.exe:

```
csc /t:library /out:object1.dll Listing23.9.cs
csc /r:object1.dll Listing23.9.cs
```

Listing 23.9—SOAP Server1 (Listing23.9.cs)

```
// compile with:
// csc /out:object1.dll Listing23.9.cs
// csc /r:object1.dll Listing23.9.cs

/* sample output:

press <enter> to exit....
DateTime server activated
DateTime server activated
Hi Bozo the clown. Here is the current DateTime: 8/19/2002 9:22:23 AM
DateTime server activated

DateTime server Object Destroyed...

*/

using System;
using System.Runtime.Remoting;
using System.Runtime.Remoting.Channels;
using System.Runtime.Remoting.Channels.Http;

namespace ExampleRemoting
{

    public class DateTimeServer : MarshalByRefObject, IDisposable
    {

        public DateTimeServer()
        {
            Console.WriteLine("DateTime server activated");
        }
        ~DateTimeServer()
        {
            Console.WriteLine("DateTime server Object Destroyed...");
        }

        public void Dispose()
        {
            GC.SuppressFinalize(this);
        }
```

```
        public String MyMethod(String name)
        {
                String strMessage= "Hi " + name + ". Here is the current
                                DateTime: " + DateTime.Now;
                Console.WriteLine(strMessage);
                return strMessage;
        }
}

public class Server
{
        public static void Main()
        {
                HttpChannel channel = new HttpChannel(9999);
                ChannelServices.RegisterChannel(channel);
                RemotingConfiguration.RegisterWellKnownServiceType(
                        Type.GetType("ExampleRemoting.DateTimeServer,
                                Listing23.9"),
                        "SayDateTime",
                        WellKnownObjectMode.SingleCall);
                System.Console.WriteLine("press <enter> to exit....");
                System.Console.ReadLine();
        }

        public String MyMethod(String name)
        {
                String strMessage = "Hi " + name + ". Here is the current
                                DateTime: " + DateTime.Now;
                Console.WriteLine(strMessage);
                return strMessage;
        }


    }
}
```

When a client calls MyMethod on the DateTimeServer class, the server object appends the string passed from the client to the current DateTime and returns the resulting string to the client. The DateTimeServer class is derived from MarshalByRefObject to make it remotable. When the server is started, we create and register a HTTP channel that will listen for clients to connect on port 9999. We also register the remote object with the remoting framework by calling RemotingConfiguration.RegisterWellKnownServiceType.

When you start the server, the object will be instantiated as part of the registration process so the framework can extract the relevant metadata from the object. After registration, this object is destroyed, and the framework starts listening for clients to connect on the registered channels.

Clients can reach and reference remote objects in the following ways:

- When we compile the client, the server object can be compiled and specified as an EXE (executable) or a DLL (dynamic-link library) reference to the compiler.
- The server and client can both implement the same interfaces. The interfaces can be compiled to a DLL and shipped to the client site as necessary.
- The utility SOAPSUDS.EXE can be used to generate proxies for the remote component. The Soapsuds tool can extract the required metadata from a running server object. It can be pointed to a remote Uniform Resource Identifier (URI) and generate the required metadata as source code or a DLL. Notice that Soapsuds creates only metadata, as if we were using or implementing an interface. It will not generate the source code for the remote object.

Generally the preferred way is to use interfaces common to both the client and server. This is like using a type library (TLB) file of a COM+ component. When you are distributing a COM+ component, it is enough to deliver only type library, which includes only global unique identifiers (GUIDs) and function signatures. We will see an example later in the chapter in the section "Using Common Interfaces." Creating a client proxy requires us to use the Soapsuds tool provided by Microsoft. That utility reads the XML description and generates a proxy assembly (class signatures) used to access the SOAP server. For example:

```
soapsuds -url:http://<hostname>:1095/ServiceClass?WSDL -oa:Server1
```

This creates a proxy called Server1.dll that will be used for access by referencing the remote object from the client.

Microsoft .NET Remoting provides a rich and extensible framework for objects living in different application domains, in different processes, and in different machines to communicate with each other seamlessly. .NET Remoting offers a powerful yet simple programming model and runtime support for making such interactions transparent. Two types of objects can be configured to serve as .NET remote objects. The type you choose depends on the requirements of your application. SingleCall objects service one and only one request coming in. They are useful in scenarios where objects are required to do a finite amount of work and cannot store state information. SingleCall objects can be configured in a load-balanced fashion. They cannot hold state information between method calls. Singleton objects service multiple clients and should not store instance data. They are useful in cases where data needs to be explicitly shared between clients and also where the overhead of creating and maintaining objects is substantial.

Client-activated objects are server-side objects that are activated on request from the client. This way of activating server objects is very similar to the classic COM co-class activation. When the client requests a server object by using the *new* operator, an activation request message is sent to the remote application. The server then creates an instance of the requested class and returns an ObjRef back to the client application that invoked it. A proxy is then created on the client side by using the ObjRef. The client's method calls will be executed on the proxy. A client-activated object can maintain state information between method calls. Each invocation of *new* returns a proxy to an independent instance of the server type.

Execute the following command to compile the client source code in Listing 23.10 to generate proxy object object11.dll and client executable Listing23.10.exe:

soapsuds -url:http://127.0.0.1:9999/SayDateTime?WSDL -oa:object11.dll

csc /r:object11.dll Listing23.10.cs

Listing 23.10—SOAP Client1 (Listing23.10.cs)

```
/* after executing the Listing23.9.exe, use the SOAPSUDS tool to create
object11.dll proxy:

soapsuds -url:http://127.0.0.1:9999/SayDateTime?WSDL -oa:object11.dll

*/

// compile with:
// csc /r:object11.dll Listing23.10.cs

using System;
using System.Runtime.Remoting;
using System.Runtime.Remoting.Channels;
```

```csharp
using System.Runtime.Remoting.Channels.Http;

namespace ExampleRemoting
{
    public class Client
    {
        public static void Main()
        {
            ChannelServices.RegisterChannel(new HttpChannel());
            DateTimeServer obj1 = (DateTimeServer)Activator.GetObject(
                typeof(ExampleRemoting.DateTimeServer),
                "http://127.0.0.1:9999/SayDateTime");
            if (obj1 == null)
            {
                System.Console.WriteLine("Could not locate server");
            }
            else
            {
                Console.WriteLine(obj1.MyMethod("Bozo the clown"));
                obj1.Dispose();
            }
        }
    }
}
```

Listing 23.10 shows an example of a client calling the single-call server in Listing 23.9. When the client starts up, it registers an HTTP channel and proceeds to activate the object by calling the GetObject method on the Activator class. The type of class we need to activate is ExampleRemoting.DateTimeServer. Next we specify the URI of the object we need to activate. For this client the URI is simply http://127.0.0.1:9999/SayDateTime. (Remember that 127.0.0.1 refers to the local host or loopback address of the local computer.) It is important to note that the URI includes the protocol, machine name, and port number as well as the endpoint. If the server is deployed on a host named "mindcracker," clients can connect to the server by specifying http://mindcracker:9999/SayDateTime.

The .NET Remoting framework provides developers with a modern distributed object model that allows remote method invocation between different common language runtimes across a network or between different application domains in the same common language runtime. Any interaction with a remote object occurs through a proxy mechanism; a client cannot access a remote object directly because the object is meaningful only inside its own application domain.

Once a message arrives at the server, the framework reassembles the original call, activates the target object if it is not already activated, and forwards the call to the object in question. Returning a result back to the client follows exactly the opposite path—the result is packaged in a message that is transported back to the client. If the server object type is SingleCall, the object is automatically recycled after the result returns to the client. When the client code is executed, the client locates and connects to the server, retrieves a proxy for the remote object, and calls MyMethod on the remote object, passing the string "Clown Bozo" as a parameter. The server returns "Bozo the clown. Here is the current DateTime: 2001-06-11T01:52:50."

It is worth noting that all TCP channels use binary serialization when transporting local objects to and from a remote object.

Singleton Objects

Singleton objects ensure that a class has only one instance and provide a global point of access to it. Some classes must have exactly one and only one instance in a system. A global variable makes an object accessible, but it does not keep you from instantiating multiple new objects. A better solution is to make the class itself responsible for keeping track of its sole instance. The class can ensure that no other instance is created by intercepting requests to create new objects, and it can provide a way to access the instance. The Singleton patterns are adequate when there must be exactly one instance of a class and it must be accessible from a well-known access point. They are adequate as well when the sole instance should be extensible by subclassing and clients should be able to use an extended instance without modifying their code.

There are two well-known object modes in SOAP .NET Remoting:

- *SingleCall.* Every message is dispatched to a new object instance.
- *Singleton.* Every message is dispatched to the same object instance.

The term singleton is a concept where a global object services all requests. The Singleton concept is a taken from Design Patterns. It is similar to CWinApp in Microsoft Foundation Classes—the one and only application object. Although there can be many printers in a system, there should be only one printer spooler. There should be only one file system and one window manager. The Singleton object server is activated only once, and its destructor is never called unless we kill the server object explicitly. Notice that the variable returned by the server is not reset between different invocations of the client. This behavior demonstrates that the server does indeed preserve its state during its lifetime. Let's develop a sample Singleton application. Listing 23.11 shows the remote, singleton object to be created

Listing 23.11—Object Code2 (Listing23.11.cs)

```
// compile with:
// csc /t:library /out:object2.dll Listing23.11.cs

using System;

namespace ExampleRemoting
{
        public class DateTimeServer : MarshalByRefObject
        {

                private static int iSayac = 0;

                public DateTimeServer()
                {
                        Console.WriteLine("DateTime server activated");
                }

                ~DateTimeServer()
                {
                        Console.WriteLine("DateTime server Object Destroyed...");
                }

                public String MyMethod(String name)
                {
                        String strMessage = "Hi " + name + ". Here is the current
                                            DateTime: " + DateTime.Now;
                        Console.WriteLine(strMessage);
                        return strMessage;
                }

                public int BeniSay()
                {
                        // lock this object to prevent concurrent updates
                        // to single instance lock(this)...
                        {
                                Console.WriteLine("Counter: " + ++iSayac);
```

```
                                     return iSayac;
                           }
                   }
           }
}
```

Listing 23.12 displays the sample server code.

Listing 23.12—SOAP Server2 (Listing23.12.cs)

```
// compile with:
// csc /r:object2.dll Listing23.12.cs

/* sample output:

press <enter> to exit...
DateTime server activated
Counter: 1
Hi Clown Bozo. Here is the current DateTime: 8/19/2002 4:02:28 AM
Counter: 2
Hi Clown Bozo. Here is the current DateTime: 8/19/2002 4:02:28 AM
Counter: 3
Hi Clown Bozo. Here is the current DateTime: 8/19/2002 4:02:28 AM
Counter: 4
Hi Clown Bozo. Here is the current DateTime: 8/19/2002 4:02:28 AM
Counter: 5
Hi Clown Bozo. Here is the current DateTime: 8/19/2002 4:02:28 AM
Counter: 6
Hi Clown Bozo. Here is the current DateTime: 8/19/2002 4:02:28 AM
Counter: 7
Hi Clown Bozo. Here is the current DateTime: 8/19/2002 4:02:28 AM
Counter: 8
Hi Clown Bozo. Here is the current DateTime: 8/19/2002 4:02:28 AM
Counter: 9
Hi Clown Bozo. Here is the current DateTime: 8/19/2002 4:02:28 AM
Counter: 10
Hi Clown Bozo. Here is the current DateTime: 8/19/2002 4:02:28 AM

DateTime server Object Destroyed...

*/

using System;
using System.Runtime.Remoting;
using System.Runtime.Remoting.Channels;
using System.Runtime.Remoting.Channels.Http;

namespace ExampleRemoting
{
       public class Example
       {

               public static void Main()
               {
                       ChannelServices.RegisterChannel(new HttpChannel(999));
                       RemotingConfiguration.RegisterWellKnownServiceType(
                              Type.GetType("ExampleRemoting.DateTimeServer,
                              object2"),
                              "server/SayDateTime.SOAP",
                              WellKnownObjectMode.Singleton);
                       System.Console.WriteLine("press <enter> to exit...");
                       System.Console.ReadLine();
               }
       }
}
```

Listing 23.13 shows the sample client code. Note that we will use HTTP channels to connect to the remote object twice in a row.

Listing 23.13—SOAP Client2 (Listing23.13.cs)

```
/* after executing the Listing23.12.exe use the SOAPSUDS tool to create object2.dll
proxy:

soapsuds -url:http://127.0.0.1:999/server/SayDateTime.SOAP?WSDL -oa:object22.dll

*/

// compile with:
// csc /r:object22.dll Listing23.13.cs

/* sample output:

HttpChannel...
1 - HttpChannel
Hi Clown Bozo. Here is the current DateTime: 8/19/2002 4:02:28 AM
2 - HttpChannel
Hi Clown Bozo. Here is the current DateTime: 8/19/2002 4:02:28 AM
3 - HttpChannel
Hi Clown Bozo. Here is the current DateTime: 8/19/2002 4:02:28 AM
4 - HttpChannel
Hi Clown Bozo. Here is the current DateTime: 8/19/2002 4:02:28 AM
5 - HttpChannel
Hi Clown Bozo. Here is the current DateTime: 8/19/2002 4:02:28 AM
HttpChannel...
6 - HttpChannel
Hi Clown Bozo. Here is the current DateTime: 8/19/2002 4:02:28 AM
7 - HttpChannel
Hi Clown Bozo. Here is the current DateTime: 8/19/2002 4:02:28 AM
8 - HttpChannel
Hi Clown Bozo. Here is the current DateTime: 8/19/2002 4:02:28 AM
9 - HttpChannel
Hi Clown Bozo. Here is the current DateTime: 8/19/2002 4:02:28 AM
10 - HttpChannel
Hi Clown Bozo. Here is the current DateTime: 8/19/2002 4:02:28 AM

*/

using System;
using System.Runtime.Remoting;
using System.Runtime.Remoting.Channels;
using System.Runtime.Remoting.Channels.Http;

namespace ExampleRemoting
{
        public class Client
        {
                public static void Main()
                {
                        HttpChannel channel = new HttpChannel();
                        ChannelServices.RegisterChannel(channel);
                        Run(); // run 1st, singleton counter counts
                        Run(); // run 2nd, singleton counter counts
                }

                public static void Run()
                {
                        Console.WriteLine("HttpChannel...");
                        DateTimeServer obj = (DateTimeServer) Activator.GetObject(
                            typeof(DateTimeServer),
                            "http://127.0.0.1:999/server/SayDateTime.SOAP");
                        for (int i = 0; i <5; i++)
```

```
                                    {
                                        Console.WriteLine(obj.BeniSay() + " - HttpChannel");
                                        Console.WriteLine(obj.MyMethod("Clown Bozo"));
                                    }
                            }
                    }
}
```

Passing Objects by Value and by Reference

Passing arguments to a remote object can be done by *reference* or by *value*. Let's look at how to do each. If you pass by reference, derive your object class from MarshalByRefObject, on the client side, and create your channel to allow bidirectional communication (see Listing 23.14).

Listing 23.14—Passing by Reference

```
public class MyClass : MarshalByRefObject
{
    public void MyFunction (String text)
    {
        Console.WriteLine(text);
    }
}
```

The client code for passing this class object by reference is shown in Listing 23.15.

Listing 23.15—Client for Referenced Object

```
// another port for bidirectional communication : 9998 receiving , 9999 sending
ChannelServices.RegisterChannel(new TcpChannel(9998));
MyClass me1 = new MyClass();
DateTimeServer obj = (DateTimeServer)
Activator.GetObject(typeof(ExampleRemoting.DateTimeServer),
"tcp://127.0.0.1:9999/SayDateTime");
Console.WriteLine(obj.HelloMethod("clown bozo", me1));
```

To pass objects by value (Listing 23.16), just add a [serializable] attribute to your object class definition and do not derive it from MarshalByRefObject. When you pass the class, you will see that the object is not changed after the change operation at the remote object function. The rest of the code will be the same as in the previous examples.

Listing 23.16—Passing by Value

```
[serializable]
  public class MyClass {

    private int iSayac = 1;

    public void MyIncrement()
    {
        iSayac++;
    }

    public int getValueOfSayac()
    {
        return iSayac;
    }
  }
```

Using Common Interfaces

Let's see another aspect of .NET Remoting. This will put you in mind of the COM+ style of remote object usage. We will develop an example using a shared interface. The interfaces also afford us a good means for using black-box objects. We have used this feature with type library (TLB) files with COM+ objects. To develop against a type library is sufficient to use services on a COM server. The client calls GetObject on an endpoint without knowing what the exact object type is; all it knows is that the object implements an interface. This illustrates how we can build a client that does not reference a server object at compile-time. The sample code for this example consists of four parts: a shared interface, the remote object that implements this interface, a server, and a client that will use this interface method via an unknown object. Listing 23.17 displays the code for the shared interface.

Listing 23.17—SOAP Shared Interface3 (Listing23.17.cs)

```
// compile with
// csc /t:library /out:share3.dll Listing23.17.cs

using System;

namespace ExampleRemoting
{
        public interface IDateTime
        {
                string DateTimeMethod(String name);
        }
}
```

Listing 23.18 contains the code for the object that implements the shared interface.

Listing 23.18—SOAP Object That Implements Share 3 (Listing23.18.cs)

```
// compile with:
// csc /t:library /r:share3.dll /out:object3.dll Listing23.18.cs

using System;

namespace ExampleRemoting
{
        public class DateTimeServer : MarshalByRefObject , IDateTime
        {

                public DateTimeServer()
                {
                        Console.WriteLine("DateTime server activated");
                }

                ~DateTimeServer()
                {
                        Console.WriteLine("DateTime server Object Destroyed...");
                }

                public String DateTimeMethod(String name)
                {
                        String strMessage = "Hi " + name + ". Here is the current
                                            DateTime: " + DateTime.Now;
                        Console.WriteLine(strMessage);
                        return strMessage;
                }
        }
}
```

The code for the server that delivers the remote methods appears in Listing 23.19.

Listing 23.19—SOAP Server3 (Listing23.19.cs)

```
// compile with:
// csc /r:share3.dll /r:object3.dll Listing23.19.cs

/* sample output:

press <enter> to exit...
DateTime server activated
DateTime server activated
Hi Bozo the clown. Here is the current DateTime: 8/19/2002 4:32:12 AM

DateTime server Object Destroyed...
DateTime server Object Destroyed...

*/

using System;
using System.Runtime.Remoting;
using System.Runtime.Remoting.Channels;
using System.Runtime.Remoting.Channels.Http;

namespace ExampleRemoting
{
        public class Example
        {
                public static void Main()
                {
                        HttpChannel channel = new HttpChannel(8888);
                        ChannelServices.RegisterChannel(channel);
                        RemotingConfiguration.RegisterWellKnownServiceType(
                                Type.GetType("ExampleRemoting.DateTimeServer,
                                Object3"),
                                "SayDateTime",
                                WellKnownObjectMode.SingleCall);
                        System.Console.WriteLine("press <enter> to exit...");
                        System.Console.ReadLine();
                }
        }
}
```

Listing 23.20 shows the code for the client that connects to the server and uses the methods exposed.

Listing 23.20—SOAP Client3 (Listing23.20.cs)

```
/* after executing the Listing23.19.exe, use the SOAPSUDS tool to create
object3.dll proxy:

soapsuds -url:http://127.0.0.1:8888/SayDateTime?WSDL -oa:object33.dll

*/

// compile with:
// csc /r:object33.dll Listing23.20.cs

/* sample output:

Hi Bozo the clown. Here is the current DateTime: 8/19/2002 4:32:12 AM

*/

// client3

using System;
using System.Runtime.Remoting;
using System.Runtime.Remoting.Channels;
using System.Runtime.Remoting.Channels.Http;
```

```
namespace ExampleRemoting
{
      public class Client
      {
            public static void Main()
            {
                  HttpChannel channel = new HttpChannel();
                  ChannelServices.RegisterChannel(channel);
                  // create an object of type interface
                  IDateTime obj = (IDateTime)
                   Activator.GetObject(typeof(ExampleRemoting.IDateTime),
                          "http://127.0.0.1:8888/SayDateTime");
                  if (obj == null)
                        Console.WriteLine("could not locate server!");
                  else
                        Console.WriteLine(obj.DateTimeMethod("Bozo the
                                              clown"));
            }
      }
}
```

Asynchronous Calls

Synchronous means occurring at the same time, at the same rate, or with a regular or predictable time relationship or sequence. *Asynchronous* means not synchronized by a shared signal such as a clock or semaphore, proceeding independently. Refer to a basic computer science text if you are not familiar with these concepts. You must consider the trade-offs when deciding between the two types. Synchronous calls run faster but must activate and run immediately. If you have relatively few calls, that type may be preferable. Asynchronous calls run slower but activate and run whenever the response is received. If you have many calls, that type may be preferable. Multithreaded applications, in particular, should be coded in an asynchronous style because you cannot make estimations about the receive time of the relevant stream or data for any of the threads. The synchronous call strategy might not always be desirable because the remote object might have to perform a number of time-consuming tasks, and it is not advisable to block the client while a call is in progress. In our next example, we will see a variation of the SoapClientProtocol implementation.

In Listing 23.21 the callback declares an object of the type IAsyncResult as the parameter of the callback function. Once the call completes, the framework ensures that the result of the call is placed inside the result object, and the callback is then invoked back to the client, forwarding the result object to it. To retrieve the result of the call, we simply extract the delegate from the AsyncResult and call EndInvoke. We create a delegate for the callback method and one for the remote method; we call the method by calling BeginInvoke on the delegate, and simply wait for the result to return from the server. The compiler automatically generates the class MyDelegate when it encounters the declaration and adds a BeginInvoke and EndInvoke method to the delegate that maps to native calls somewhere in the CLR.

After making an asynchronous call, the next thing to do is to create the callback function that receives the result from the call. We could code the asynchronous interface client for our previous SOAP remote object server as in Listing 23.21.

Listing 23.21—Asynchronous Call SOAP with Null Parameter

```
// ...
      AsyncCallback mycallback = new AsyncCallback(Client.MyCallBack);
      MyDelegate mydelegate = new MyDelegate(obj.DateTimeMethod);
      IAsyncResult ar = mydelegate.BeginInvoke("Clown Bozo",
                        mycallback, null);
// ...
```

```
public static void MyCallBack(IAsyncResult ar)
{
  MyDelegate d  = (MyDelegate)ar.AsyncObject;
  Console.WriteLine(d.EndInvoke(ar));
}
```

Introduction to Web Services and ASP.NET

This chapter is intended only to introduce the ASP.NET and SOAP concepts together—for more details on ASP.NET please refer to the relevant chapter. A Web service is an application running as a service delivered over the Web. Web services use HTTP and SOAP-encoded XML messages to communicate with clients, which range from Web pages to applications to devices—with the only criteria being that the client can communicate over HTTP in SOAP-encoded XML messages.

The Web Services Description Language (WSDL) is the description of a Web service generated for all Web services. If you are using the .NET platform to create a client, use WSDL.EXE to create a proxy class from the WSDL of the Web service (more about WSDL.EXE in a moment). If you are consuming the Web service over .aspx pages, you need to import the proxy file <%@ Import namespace="AnyService" %>, which should reside in the folder C:\inetpub\wwwroot\Services\bin\.

Once you have the Proxy class code, compile it into a library and use the Proxy class library in your clients to call methods on a Web service. A proxy is a component that acts on behalf of the remote Web service; it allows access to the remote Web service via SOAP and takes care of all the plumbing beneath. The Web service client can use the proxy as a real object and access its properties and methods. When we access a Web service via a proxy, the proxy will convert our Web service call into a SOAP message and send the SOAP request to the Web service. When it receives the raw SOAP-based XML response back from the Web service, it converts the XML response to an object accessible by the client and returns the object to the client.

For the client to use the Web service it should have knowledge of how the Web service is implemented and how to call it. But you can talk to a Web service without knowing how it is implemented. The client cannot know automatically about the Web service. Hence all Web services automatically generate an XML document with WSDL grammar to describe themselves. If you have installed the Web service under a virtual directory called "myservice," you can get the WSDL of the service by calling the following URL in your browser: http://localhost/myservice/service.asmx?WSDL. This will generate an XML file and display it in your browser. The displayed file is the WSDL of the Web service.

The .NET SDK comes with a tool called WSDL.EXE. This tool takes the WSDL of a Web service as an input and uses reflection to generate a Proxy class that is similar to the Web service. You have to reference the System.dll, System.Web.Services.dll, and System.Xml.Serialization.dll assemblies to create your proxy library.

A number of platforms currently exist for creating applications. Each platform has traditionally used its own protocols, usually binary in nature, for machine-to-machine integration. As a result, applications across platforms have only a limited ability to share data. In recognition of these limitations, there has been an overwhelming push toward establishing standards for data formats and for data exchange. This push stems from a vision that is rapidly evolving into a new computing paradigm: the seamless, Web-enabled integration of services across traditional hardware and software barriers. At the heart of this vision is the concept of interoperability, that is, the capacity of disparate systems to communicate and to share data seamlessly. A Web service is a programmable application logic accessible using standard Internet protocols—or to put it another way, the implementation of Web-supported standards for transparent machine-to-machine and application-to-application communication.

A number of Web services technologies—such as SOAP, WSDL, and HTTP—are now used to pass messages between machines. ASP.NET provides support for Web services with the .asmx file. An .asmx file is a text file similar to an .aspx file. The .asmx files can be part of an ASP.NET application that includes .aspx files. They are then URI addressable, just as .aspx files are. Listing 23.22 shows the file for a "Hello" ASP.NET Web service.

Listing 23.22—"Hello" Web Service

```
<%@ WebService Language="C#" Class="Hello" %>

using System;
using System.Web.Services;

public class Hello : WebService
{
    [WebMethod]
    public String SayHello()
    {
        return "Hello...";
    }
}
```

This file starts with an ASP.NET directive, WebService, and sets the language to C#. Next, the class Hello is declared. This class is derived from the base class WebService. Finally, any methods that will be accessible as part of the service have the custom attribute [WebMethod] in front of their signatures. To make this service available, we might name the file HelloWorld.asmx and place it on a server called XXX.com in a virtual directory called YYY. With virtually any HTML 3.2 or later browser, you could then enter the URL http://XXX.com/YYY/Hello.asmx, and the resulting page would show the public methods for this Web service (those marked with the WebMethod attribute), as well as which protocols (such as SOAP or HTTP GET) you can use to invoke these methods. Entering http://XXX.com/YYY/Hello.asmx?WSDL into the Internet Explorer address bar produces the same information as an XML file, based on the WSDL grammar. This WSDL file is used by clients that access the service and is very important. The WSDL.EXE tool in the .NET SDK (or in the Visual Studio .NET integrated development environment, "Add Web Reference" on the Project menu) can be used to download the WSDL description of a Web service and create a proxy class that addresses the service.

```
WSDL /language:CS /n:Hello /out:Hello.cs
http://localhost/hello/HelloWorld.asmx?WSDL
```

A proxy class called Hello.cs is then created. It contains a method called SayHello that returns a string. Compiling this proxy class into an application and then calling its method results in the proxy class's packaging a SOAP request across HTTP and receiving the SOAP-encoded response, which is then marshaled as a string. We could code a client as shown in Listing 23.23.

Listing 23.23—"Hello" Web Service Client

```
using Hello;

Hello myHello = new Hello();
Console.WriteLine(myHello.SayHello());
```

A Web service allows a site to expose programmatic functionality via the Internet. Web services can accept messages and have the option to return replies to those messages. Today's sites already expose functionality that allows you to do such things as query a database, book an airline reservation, check the status of an order, and so on, but no consistent model exists for allowing you to program against these sites. Web services can be invoked via HTTP POST, HTTP GET, and

SOAP. SOAP is a remote procedure call protocol and specification developed by a group of companies including Microsoft and DevelopMentor. It is based on broadly adopted Internet standards such as XML and typically runs over HTTP.

Visual Studio .NET is the formal shipping vehicle for creating rich Web services on the .NET platform. With the release of Visual Studio .NET (http://msdn.microsoft.com/vstudio/nextgen/default.asp) we are able to create Web services by using ASP+.NET and any language that targets the common language runtime or ATL Server and unmanaged C++. ATL Server is a collection of Active Template Library classes that aid the C++ developer in writing native, unmanaged Internet Server Application Program Interface (ISAPI) extensions and filters. Instead of the .aspx file extension of an ASP Web page, Web services are saved in files with the extension .asmx.

Whenever the ASP runtime receives a request for a file with an .asmx extension, the runtime dispatches the call to the Web service handler. This mapping is established in the <httphandlers> section of the config.web files for the machine and individual applications. Config.web files are human-readable XML files used to configure almost every aspect of your Web applications. Handlers are instances of classes that implement the System.Web.IHTTPHandler interface. The IHTTPHandler interface defines two methods, IsReusable and ProcessRequest. The IsReusable property allows an instance of IHTTPHandler to indicate whether it can be recycled and used for another request. The ProcessRequest method takes an HttpContext object as a parameter and is where the developer of an HTTP handler begins to do his work. A particular handler ultimately services inbound requests that are received by the ASP+ runtime. After a handler is developed, it is configured in the config.web file of the application. A typical config.web file for a machine will have code similar to that shown in Listing 23.24.

Listing 23.24—Sample Config.web File Contents

```
<httphandlers>

< add verb="*" path="*.asmx"
type="System.Web.Services.Protocols.WebServiceHandlerFactory, System.Web.Services"
validate="false" />

</httphandlers>
```

In Listing 23.24 the <httphandlers> section states that for all requests (HTTP verbs such as GET, POST, or PUT), if the file being requested has an .asmx extension, create an instance of the WebServiceHandlerFactory, which lives in the System.Web.Services.dll assembly. If the administrator wanted this handler to accept only the GET verb, he or she would change the verb property to verb="Get". Handlers accept requests and produce a response. When the HTTP runtime sees a request for a file with the .aspx extension, the handler that is registered to handle .aspx files is called. In the case of the default ASP installation, this handler will be System.Web.UI.PageHandlerFactory. This is equivalent to how .asmx files are handled. For the default ASP+ installation, Web services are handled by System.Web.Services.Protocols.WebServiceHandlerFactory.

The custom handler enables ASP to use reflection and dynamically create an HTML page describing the service's capabilities and methods. The generated HTML page also provides the user a way to test the Web methods in the service. Another advantage of ASP is seen in publishing Web Service Definition Language contracts. As noted previously, WSDL is an XML-based grammar for describing the capabilities of Web services. WSDL allows a Web service to be queried by potential consumers of your service—you can think of it as an XML-based type library made available via the Web. For output to be generated, one must only make an HTTP request to the Web service file passing in Service Description Language (SDL) in the query string (e.g., http://localhost/services/myservice.asmx?WSDL). Another nice aspect of the Web service handler is that it creates a simple test Web page for your services. This test page allows you to confirm that everything in your Web service is working without having to write your own test client.

In the next example, we create a Web service that returns the date and time from the server. We could just return the date and time within a string type and force the caller to parse the string, but that would not be ideal. Instead, we are going to create a LocalTime struct that will be returned to the caller. For those of you unfamiliar with structs, they are synonymous with Visual Basic's user-defined types (UDTs). A walkthrough of the code shows us defining a LocalTime struct that contains all the date and time information to be returned to the client. Our LocalTime struct holds eight values: Day, Month, Year, Hour, Minute, Seconds, Milliseconds, and Timezone. The struct's definition is shown in Listing 23.25.

Listing 23.25—TimeService ASP.NET Web Service

```
<%@ WebService Language="C#" class="TimeService" %>
using System;
using System.Web.Services;

public struct LocalTime
{
        public int Day;
        public int Month;
        public int Year;
        public int Hour;
        public int Minute;
        public int Seconds;
        public int Milliseconds;
        public string Timezone;
}

public class TimeService
{
        [WebMethod]
        public LocalTime GetTime()
        {
                LocalTime lt = new LocalTime();
                DateTime dt = DateTime.Now;
                lt.Day = dt.Day;
                lt.Month = dt.Month;
                lt.Year = dt.Year;
                lt.Hour = dt.Hour;
                lt.Minute = dt.Minute;
                lt.Seconds = dt.Second;
                lt.Milliseconds = dt.Millisecond;
                lt.Timezone = TimeZone.CurrentTimeZone.StandardName;
                return lt;
        }
}
```

.NET includes a console application that takes care of requesting the WSDL contract of a remote Web service and generating a proxy to use the service. For you to use a remote Web service a few things need to happen. You need to know where the Web service resides (e.g., http://www.servername.com/wstest.asmx). Then you need to create a local proxy for the remote service. The proxy allows the developer to work with the remote service as though it were local to the machine. When instantiated, the proxy accepts method calls from your code as though it were the remote service object. Calls are packaged into SOAP methods and shipped via HTTP to the remote Web service. If the remote object is created via the specified channel, the remote service receives the request, unwraps the envelope, does the work that you asked, then returns the result in a result envelope. Once the proxy receives this returned envelope, it is unwrapped and delivered to your code as a native method call.

The WSDL.EXE utility takes care of requesting a WSDL contract from a remote Web service via HTTP and generating a proxy class for you. Although the Web services utility uses C# as its default proxy-generation language, any language (including VB and JScript) that implements the ICodeGenerator interface will work (e.g., just change the language parameter to CS for C#.NET, VB for VB.NET, or JS for JS.NET).

```
WSDL /language:CS /n:TimeService http://localhost/services/TimeService.asmx?WSDL
/out:TimeServiceProxy.cs
```

Running this command generates the TimeServiceProxy.cs file. An instance of this object is what takes care of accepting method calls, packaging up calls for SOAP, invoking via HTTP, and returning the results, if any, to the caller. Now that you have a proxy, you need to compile it using the appropriate compiler (which depends on the language you have chosen). The following command assumes that the C# compiler (csc.exe) is in the system's path and that you are working in the directory where your Web service's .asmx file resides.

```
csc /out:TimeServiceProxy.dll /t:library /r:system.web.services.dll
/r:system.xml.serialization.dll TimeServiceProxy.cs
```

This command creates a DLL named TimeServiceProxy.dll. Now we will use a Web time service via a .NET application, a simple console application in C# that prints out the time from the remote service. This application is compiled into an executable (.exe) file as opposed to a library (.dll). The TimeTestApp.exe first creates a new instance of our TimeService class that lives in the bin/TimeServiceProxy.dll assembly. Then a call is made to the GetTime method of the TimeService class (*ts*). The returned value is stored in a local variable named *lt*. The lt variable is of the type LocalTime. In case it isn't obvious, we should point out that the LocalTime object that we are now using is originally defined in our remote .asmx file. The WSDL utility is able to create a local definition of the LocalTime struct based on the SDL contract that is generated and returned from the Web service handler. Next in our code, we call GetTime and then begin simply to construct a couple of local strings that contain our formatted time and date. Then we output the results using Console.WriteLine. See Listing 23.26.

Listing 23.26—TimeService Web Service Client1

```
using System;
using TimeService;

class MyClass
{
        static void Main()
        {
                TimeService ts = new TimeService();
                LocalTime lt = ts.GetTime();
                string stime = lt.Hour + ":" + lt.Minute + ":" + lt.Seconds + "." +
                lt.Milliseconds + " " + lt.Timezone;
                string sdate = lt.Month + "/" + lt.Day + "/" + lt.Year;
                Console.WriteLine("The remote date is: " + sdate);
                Console.WriteLine("The remote time is: " + stime);
        }
}
```

To compile the TimeTest application, use the following command.

```
csc /r:system.web.services.dll /r:TimeServiceProxy.dll TimeTestApp.cs
```

This command creates an executable file named TimeTestApp.exe in the local directory. We could have explicitly told the C# compiler that we wanted an executable, but the compiler creates executables (/target:exe) by default. We assume you have copied TimeServiceProxy.dll to the C:\inetpub\wwwroot\Services\bin\ directory (the Web services directory under the default IIS installation directory). Thus, a simple draft .aspx Web page file that uses our service can be developed as in Listing 23.27 (note that the code shown is simple; please enhance it depending on your implementations).

Listing 23.27—TimeService Web Service Client2

```
<%@ Import namespace="System" %>
<%@ Import namespace="TimeService" %>
<%@ Page Language="C#" %>
<html>
<head>
</head>
<body>
<script language="C#" runat="server">
 public void getDateTime()
 {
  //Create a Instance of the Proxy Class
  TimeService tm = new TimeService() ;
  LocalTime LT = ts.GetTime();

  // now "LT" contains the time web service returned DateTime value
 }
</script>
</body>
</html>
```

XML-Based Protocols

This section reviews XML-based protocols. The information we present here is bundled from official documents. It is important to understand which component fits where. Please refer to the World Wide Web Consortium (W3C) XML Protocol Comparisons Web page (http://www.w3.org/2000/03/29-XML-protocol-matrix/) to compare and contrast a variety of XML protocols. Also note that the XML Schema Definition Tool (Xsd.exe) will help you if you want to use the produced XML files extensively, because it can output XML schema or CLR classes from XDR (XML-Data-Reduced), XML, and XSD (XML Schema Definition) files or from classes in a runtime assembly. Only XML-based protocols in which Microsoft participated are discussed here.

DISCO

Developers will need a way to discover Web services. Discovery of Web Services (DISCO) provides a way to discover and retrieve WSDL descriptions of services on remote machines. Using the discovery document format (which is also an XML grammar), one can send a discovery document to a remote server and, if any SOAP-enabled services (i.e., Web services) exist, receive back a WSDL description of the services provided. In many cases, developers will not know the URLs of the services. Universal Description, Discovery, and Integration (UDDI) specifies a mechanism whereby Web service providers advertise the existence of their Web services and Web service consumers locate Web services of interest. UDDI is a specification for distributed Web-based information registries of Web services. UDDI is also a publicly accessible set of implementations of the specification that allows businesses to register information about the Web services they offer so that other businesses can find them. UDDI registries are used to promote and discover distributed Web services. The Web Services Discovery Tool (Disco.exe) helps you discover the URLs of Web services located on a Web server. You can also save documents related to each Web service locally. Listing 23.28 shows a sample DISCO document from W3C.

Listing 23.28—A DISCO Document

```
<disco:discovery>
  <disco:discoveryRef ref='folder/discovery'/>

  <-- elements from other namespaces -->
</disco:discovery>

<disco:discovery>
  <scl:contractRef ref='my1.sdl'>
  <scl:contractRef ref='my2.sdl' docRef='my.htm'>
</disco:discovery>

<disco:discovery>
  <schema:schemaRef ref='my1.xsd' targetNamespace='http://my.org/my1.xsd'/>
  <schema:schemaRef ref='my2.xsd'/>
</disco:discovery>
```

UDDI

UDDI is a building block that enables businesses to quickly, easily, and dynamically find and transact business with one another using their preferred applications. UDDI is designed to provide a searchable directory of businesses and their Web services. A sample UDDI document from W3C appears in Listing 23.29.

Listing 23.29—An UDDI Document

```
<element name="businessEntity">
  <type content="elementOnly">
    <group order="seq">
      <element ref="discoveryURLs" minOccurs="0" maxOccurs="1"/>
      <element ref="name"/>
      <element ref="description" minOccurs="0" maxOccurs="*"/>
      <element ref="contacts" minOccurs="0" maxOccurs="1"/>
      <element ref="businessServices" minOccurs="0" maxOccurs="1"/>
      <element ref="identifierBag" minOccurs="0" maxOccurs="1"/>
      <element ref="categoryBag" minOccurs="0" maxOccurs="1"/>
    </group>
    <attribute name="businessKey" minOccurs="1" type="string"/>
    <attribute name="operator" type="string"/>
    <attribute name="authorizedName" type="string"/>
  </type>
</element>
```

WSDL

Given a Web service, it would be nice to have a standard way to document what messages the Web service accepts and generates—that is, to document the Web service contract. A standard language makes it easy for developers and developer tools to create and interpret contracts. The Web Services Description Language (WSDL) is an XML-based contract language jointly developed by Microsoft and IBM. The Web services contract written using WSDL is an XML document that defines the inputs and outputs of a Web service, including the XML schemas that should be used to create the input and output documents. Each WSDL document contains both an abstract definition of the service and how the service binds to a particular network implementation and data format bindings.

Over the years Microsoft and IBM have proposed several contract languages: Service Description Language (SDL), Service Contract Language (SCL), and Network Accessible Services Specification Language (NASSL). All these are superceded by WSDL. WDSL is a new specification to describe networked XML-based services. It provides a simple way for service providers to describe the basic format of requests to their systems regardless of the underlying protocol (such as SOAP or XML) or encoding (such as Multipurpose Internet Messaging Extensions). WSDL is a key part of the effort of the UDDI initiative to provide directories and descriptions of such online services for electronic business. You can use the Web Services Description Language Tool (Wsdl.exe) to generate WSDL files for ASP.NET Web services—in other words, usable codes from WSDL contract files, XSD schemas, and .discomap discovery documents. Listing 23.30 shows an example of a WSDL document from W3C.

Listing 23.30—A WSDL Document

```xml
<?xml version="1.0"?>
<definitions name="StockQuote"

targetNamespace="http://example.com/stockquote.wsdl"
        xmlns:tns="http://example.com/stockquote.wsdl"
        xmlns:xsd1="http://example.com/stockquote.xsd"
        xmlns:soap="http://schemas.xmlsoap.org/wsdl/soap/"
        xmlns="http://schemas.xmlsoap.org/wsdl/">

    <types>
        <schema targetNamespace="http://example.com/stockquote.xsd"
              xmlns="http://www.w3.org/1999/XMLSchema">
          <element name="TradePriceRequest">
              <complexType>
                  <all>
                      <element name="tickerSymbol" type="string"/>
                  </all>
              </complexType>
          </element>
          <element name="TradePrice">
              <complexType>
                  <all>
                      <element name="price" type="float"/>
                  </all>
              </complexType>
          </element>
        </schema>
    </types>

    <message name="GetLastTradePriceInput">
        <part name="body" element="xsd1:TradePrice"/>
     </message>

    <message name="GetLastTradePriceOutput">
        <part name="body" element="xsd1:TradePriceResult"/>
     </message>

    <portType name="StockQuotePortType">
        <operation name="GetLastTradePrice">
            <input message="tns:GetLastTradePriceInput"/>
            <output message="tns:GetLastTradePriceOutput"/>
        </operation>
    </portType>

    <binding name="StockQuoteSoapBinding" type="tns:StockQuotePortType">
        <soap:binding style="document"
transport="http://schemas.xmlsoap.org/soap/http"/>
        <operation name="GetLastTradePrice">
            <soap:operation soapAction="http://example.com/GetLastTradePrice"/>
            <input>
                <soap:body use="literal"
namespace="http://example.com/stockquote.xsd"

encodingStyle="http://schemas.xmlsoap.org/soap/encoding/"/>
            </input>
            <output>
                <soap:body use="literal"
namespace="http://example.com/stockquote.xsd"
```

```
encodingStyle="http://schemas.xmlsoap.org/soap/encoding/"/>
            </output>
        </operation>
    </binding>

    <service name="StockQuoteService">
        <documentation>My first service</documentation>
        <port name="StockQuotePort" binding="tns:StockQuoteBinding">
            <soap:address location="http://example.com/stockquote"/>
        </port>
    </service>

</definitions>
```

SOAP

Simple Object Access Protocol (SOAP) is a lightweight, XML-based protocol for exchange of information in a decentralized, distributed environment. It consists of three parts: an envelope that defines a framework for describing what is in a message and how to process it, a set of encoding rules for expressing instances of application-defined data types, and a convention for representing remote procedure calls and responses. SOAP can potentially be used in combination with a variety of other protocols; however, the only bindings defined in the SOAP specification describe how to use SOAP in combination with HTTP and HTTP Extension Framework. The Soapsuds tool (Soapsuds.exe) creates XML schemas describing services exposed so you can compile client applications that communicate with Web services using a technique called remoting. A sample SOAP document from W3C appears in Listing 23.31.

Listing 23.31—A SOAP Document

```
<SOAP-ENV:Envelope
  xmlns:SOAP-ENV="http://schemas.xmlsoap.org/soap/envelope/"
  SOAP-ENV:encodingStyle="http://schemas.xmlsoap.org/soap/encoding/"/>
  <SOAP-ENV:Body>
    <e:Book>
        <title>My Life and Work</title>
        <firstauthor href="#Person-1"/>
        <secondauthor href="#Person-2"/>
    </e:Book>
    <e:Person id="Person-1">
        <name>Henry Ford</name>
        <address xsi:type="m:Electronic-address">
            <email>mailto:henryford@hotmail.com</email>
            <web>http://www.henryford.com</web>
        </address>
    </e:Person>
    <e:Person id="Person-2">
        <name>Samuel Crowther</name>
        <address xsi:type="n:Street-address">
            <street>Martin Luther King Rd</street>
            <city>Raleigh</city>
            <state>North Carolina</state>
        </address>
    </e:Person>
  </SOAP-ENV:Body>
</SOAP-ENV:Envelope>
```

BizTalk

Official information about the BizTalk protocol is available at http://www.biztalk.org/. Microsoft has also put a back-office product called BizTalk server on the market to make it easier to develop and deploy BizTalk-based business-to-business, business-to-customer, customer-to-business, and customer-to-customer applications between internal and external commodity merchandisers.

The Microsoft BizTalk Framework is an XML framework for application integration and electronic commerce. It includes a design framework for implementing an XML schema and a set of XML tags used in messages sent between applications. Microsoft, other software companies, and industry standards groups can use the BizTalk Framework to create XML schemas in a consistent manner. The BizTalk Framework itself is not a standard: XML is the standard. The goal of the BizTalk Framework is to accelerate the rapid adoption of XML. BizTalk Framework schemas, which are business documents and messages expressed in XML, can be registered and stored on the BizTalk.org Web site.

Any individual or organization can download the framework and use it to create and submit an XML schema to the Web site. As long as the schema passes a verification test, it is considered a valid BizTalk Framework schema. Individuals and organizations can freely use XML schemas from the BizTalk.org Web site in their applications for as long as the schema is published for public use. The BizTalk Framework schema design has been submitted to W3C for adoption as an XML schema standard. A sample BizTalk document from W3C appears in Listing 23.32.

Listing 23.32—A BizTalk Document

```
<SOAP-ENV:Envelope
            xmlns:SOAP-ENV="http://schemas.xmlsoap.org/soap/envelope/"
            xmlns:xsi="http://www.w3.org/1999/XMLSchema-instance">
    <SOAP-ENV:Header>
        <dlv:delivery SOAP-ENV:mustUnderstand="1"
                xmlns:dlv="http://schemas.biztalk.org/btf-2-0/delivery"
                xmlns:agr="http://www.trading-agreements.org/types/">
            <dlv:to>
                <dlv:address xsi:type="agr:department">Book Order
Department</dlv:address>
            </dlv:to>
            <dlv:from>
                <dlv:address xsi:type="agr:organization">Booklovers
Anonymous</dlv:address>
            </dlv:from>
        </dlv:delivery>
        <prop:properties SOAP-ENV:mustUnderstand="1"

xmlns:prop="http://schemas.biztalk.org/btf-2-0/properties">

<prop:identity>uuid:74b9f5d0-33fb-4a81-b02b-5b760641c1d6</prop:identity>
            <prop:sentAt>2000-05-14T03:00:00+08:00</prop:sentAt>
            <prop:expiresAt>2000-05-15T04:00:00+08:00</prop:expiresAt>

<prop:topic>http://electrocommerce.org/purchase_order/</prop:topic>
        </prop:properties>
    </SOAP-ENV:Header>
    <SOAP-ENV:Body>
        <po:PurchaseOrder
xmlns:po="http://electrocommerce.org/purchase_order/">
            <po:Title>Essential BizTalk</po:Title>
        </po:PurchaseOrder>
    </SOAP-ENV:Body>
</SOAP-ENV:Envelope>
```

Summary

This chapter introduced you to SOAP, .NET Remoting, and ASP.NET Web services and provided some working examples. SOAP is an XML-based protocol specification for invoking methods on remote servers, services, components, and objects. The SOAP specification supports an XML vocabulary used for representing method parameters, return values, and exceptions. SOAP relies on HTTP 1.0 or greater for communication between the client and the remote server. Firewalls can easily recognize SOAP packets based on their content type (text/xml-SOAP), and they can filter based on the interface and method name exposed via HTTP headers.

One of most significant differences between TcpChannel and HttpChannel is that TcpChannel uses BinaryFormatter and HttpChannel uses SoapFormatter for serialization by default. However, you can change the formatter of each channels by specifying different formatter types during construction of the HttpChannel and TcpChannel objects.

.NET Remoting is a superior way to use remote components. It may eventually replace COM+ and CORBA or at least will be used to complement existing components. Web services are distributed business components that can be invoked remotely across wires. There is a significant difference between Web services and .NET Remoting over the HTTP channel. Although they seem to achieve the same ends, behind the scenes their serialization mechanisms are completely different. While Web services use XML serialization, found in the System.Xml.Serialization namespace, a .NET Remoting-over-HTTP client/server uses CLR serialization, found in the System.Runtime.Serialization namespace. Thus, Web services exchange XML data types and a .NET Remoting client/server exchanges CLR data type

Chapter 24:
Mobile Programming

Introduction

In today's technological world, mobile devices often are a basic requirement for running a successful business, and thus mobile programming has grown in importance. Until now, developing mobile applications has been a tedious task. As a developer, you had to address many issues, such as device capabilities, various markup languages, and physical capabilities of handheld device. Now, however, developing mobile applications using Microsoft .NET and its supported languages is no longer a monumental undertaking. Microsoft .NET has introduced a mobile SDK along with its .NET SDK. The mobile SDK is also known as the Mobile Internet Toolkit.

In this chapter, you will gain an understanding of the basics of the Mobile Internet Toolkit, the requirements for mobile programming with .NET, and the setup for different wireless clients. You will also learn how to work with mobile forms, user interface and mobile controls, validation controls, and utility controls. Finally, you will build a simple mobile application.

Requirements

Following are the basic requirements for developing mobile applications with .NET:

- Microsoft Windows 2000 Server; Microsoft Windows 2000 Advanced Server; or Microsoft Windows 2000 Professional (including Internet Information Services), Service Pack 1
- Microsoft Internet Explorer 5.5
- .NET Framework (including Premium ASP.NET)
- Microsoft Mobile Internet Toolkit Version 1.0.

The WAP Client

Briefly, the Wireless Application Protocol (WAP) is an open standard for developing wireless applications. All major players in the wireless market collaborated to come up with a standard for extending the Web to mobile devices. Applications for WAP-enabled devices usually are written in Wireless Markup Language (WML), but Microsoft .NET provides a framework to deal with WML and a higher level of abstraction to access the low-level tasks. The current version of the Mobile Internet Toolkit takes care of generating output that complies with the WML 1.1 specification.

A logical perspective of the WAP environment is illustrated in Figure 24.1.

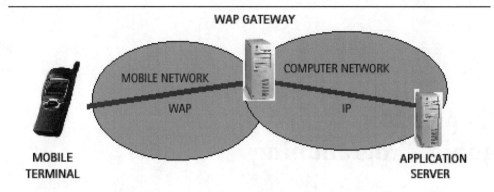

Figure 24.1: Diagram of WAP Communication

A *WAP gateway,* also called a *WAP server,* acts as a bridge between a mobile phone and the application server. The application server here is either Internet Information Server (IIS) or Personal Web Server (PWS). Here is how a wireless device's request actually works.

The user sends a request from her mobile phone to a WAP gateway for a specific URL. This request goes to the WAP gateway using the wireless protocol. The WAP gateway generates a conventional HTTP request and sends it on to the Web server. The Web server generates an HTML response and sends it back to the WAP server. Here the Web server's response is translated into a WML deck, with the added HTTP headers.

Before getting any deeper into this, let's discuss the basics of a *deck* and its *cards.* The basic unit of WML is the card, which specifies a single interaction between the user-agent and the user. Cards are grouped together into decks. A deck is the smallest unit of WML that a Web server can send to the user-agent. In many ways, a deck can be thought of as a Hypertext Markup Language (HTML) page. When a user-agent receives a deck, it typically activates the first card in the deck, although it can be directed to any particular card in the deck. The <wml> tag defines a deck and encloses all the information and cards in a deck. The <card> tag indicates the general layout and user schemes in the user-agent.

Let's look at a sample WML document (see Listing 24.1) to make things clearer.

Listing 24.1—Sample WML Code

```
<?xml version="1.0"?>
<!DOCTYPE wml PUBLIC "-//WAPFORUM//DTD WML
1.2//EN""http://www.wapforum.org/DTD/wml12.dtd ">
<wml>
<card id="Card1" title="Welcome">
<p>
Welcome to Mobile Programming
</p>
</card>
</wml>
```

A valid WML deck is a valid Extensible Markup Language (XML) document and therefore must contain an XML declaration and a document type declaration, in this case WAP 1.1, as shown in the first two lines of the listing. While the deck is the unit between the <wml> tag and the card is defined in the <card> tag, you can have any number of cards in a deck unit.

The WAP gateway verifies the HTTP header and the WML content, then encodes them into a binary format. The gateway builds the WAP response, consisting of WML, and sends it back to the mobile phone. The mobile phone receives the WAP response, parses the WML, and displays the contents.

As you see from this model, you need a Web server and a WAP-enabled mobile device to write and test mobile applications. You can test your applications on your desktop using a WAP toolkit, as major wireless companies provide a toolkit for testing applications on the desktop. In our examples, we will be using the Nokia WAP toolkit. The toolkit and documentation are available at http://forum.nokia.com.

The I-MODE Client

Nippon Telephone and Telegraph Docomo (NTT Docomo), a Japanese company, developed i-mode, a wireless technology that enables users to access Internet services via their cellular phones. In i-mode, the "i" stands for information based on packet data transmission technology. This means that even if an i-mode client is always online, the user is charged only for the information that is received. i-mode can be used to exchange e-mail with computers, personal digital assistants (PDAs), and other i-mode cellular phones. An important difference between an i-mode and a WAP client is the markup language employed. A WAP-enabled device uses WML, while i-mode draws on Compact HTML (CHTML).

There is one major distinction between the two protocols: WAP is an open standard, whereas i-mode is a proprietary service owned by NTT Docomo. There are two types of sites running with i-mode protocol. First are the official sites hosted by NTT Docomo, which have a link from the official i-mode site menu. Then there are the unofficial sites, which must be accessed by typing the URL in the device.

Many other wireless devices with different specifications are available on the market. Some of them support Handheld Markup Language (HML) or Mobile Markup Language (MML), but you can take a generic approach when you develop applications with the Mobile Internet Toolkit. The generated output conforms to a device's protocol specifications.

The Mobile Internet Toolkit supports WML 1.1, HTML 3.2, and CHTML 1.0, and it has been tested extensively for the following devices:

- Mitsubishi T250
- Nokia 7110
- Pocket PC with Microsoft Pocket Internet Explorer version 4.5
- Siemens C-35i

Limited testing has been done with many other simulators and devices. While that does not cover all devices, it can said that the toolkit is the most generic approach for developing mobile applications.

Basics of the Mobile Internet Toolkit

The Mobile Internet Toolkit is actually an extension of ASP.NET controls. When you install the toolkit, the installation program places the mobile DLL in the .NET Framework's directory and updates any necessary system files, and this provides you access to mobile controls with the .NET Framework. The Mobile Internet Toolkit consists of only one assembly, System.Web.Mobile.dll. The assembly contains two namespaces—System.Web.Mobile and System.Web.UI.MobileControls—for application development as well as a designer namespace.

When a mobile project is created with Visual Studio .NET, the setup program creates a virtual directory in IIS and stores the DLLs in the bin directory, so you can build mobile pages and run them through the server.

Mobile Web Forms Classes

Web forms in a wireless environment are called *mobile Web forms*. These forms are similar to Web forms but are designed to work with mobile devices. The mobile classes are similar to Web classes in ASP.NET. The Web Forms controls are described briefly in Table 24.1. We'll discuss these classes in more detail in the following sections.

Mobile Internet Designer Control	Brief Description
Form	Acts as a container for any number of controls. It also acts as an outer grouping within the mobile page object.
Panel	Is used to nest a control within a form. There can be any number of panels in a form. The form acts as a container for a panel control.
AdRotator	Is similar to the Web version of the AdRotator control, which allows the display of random advertisements.
Calendar	Displays a calendar with a rich functionality such as date picking.
Call	Permits the user to automatically call an associated phone number.
Command	Performs actions such as submitting information or invoking a function.
Image	Displays a specified image on a mobile device.
Label	Displays static text on a mobile device.
Link	Creates a hyperlink to a URL from the form.
List	Displays a list of items on a mobile device.
Textbox	Displays a single-line text box.
Textview	Is used to display an arbitrary amount of text.
ObjectList	Provides the ability to display multiple fields in one control and other functionality like DataBound.
SelectionList	Provides a user with a selection option from a list.
CompareValidator	Is used to compare two controls for validation purposes.
CustomValidator	Allows us to customize validation of a control.
RangeValidator	Allows us to validate a value within a specific range.
RegularExpressionValidator	Validates a value against a specified expression.

Mobile Internet Designer Control	Brief Description
RequiredFieldValidator	Makes it compulsory that the value of the control is different from its initial value.
ValidationSummary	Displays the summary of the form's validation.
DeviceSpecific	Allows a user to program according to the end device output.

Table 24.1: Mobile Web Controls

The MobilePage Control

The first class we will discuss is the System.Web.UI.MobileControls.MobilePage class. This class is inherited from the ASP.NET Page class. Below given example, is the starting point for using mobile controls in your page. Here we inherit our page from the MobilePage class.

Here is a simple scenario, where we inherit directly from the MobilePage class:

```
<%@ Page Inherits="System.Web.UI.MobileControls.MobilePage" Language="cs" %>
<%@ Register TagPrefix="mobile" Namespace="System.Web.UI.MobileControls"
Assembly="System.Web.Mobile" %>
```

The language attribute must be set with the programming language you intend to use, such as C# or Visual Basic.

The Form Control

The Form control is another very basic control. As with any other type of Web application, a mobile form acts as a container for all other controls in the page. Any other control, whether it is a user interface, validation, or utility control, is contained within the <form> tag. So there must be at least one form in a mobile page.

Listing 24.2 is a simple example of using a form as a container. We discuss other user interface controls in detail in subsequent sections. In this example we display the text "Welcome to Mobile World" on the screen.

Listing 24.2—Welcome to Mobile World

```
<%@ Register TagPrefix="Mobile" Namespace="System.Web.UI.MobileControls"
Assembly="System.Web.Mobile"%>
<%@ Page Inherits="System.Web.UI.MobileControls.MobilePage" Language="CS" %>

  <mobile:Form id=Form1 runat="server">
      <mobile:Label id=Label1 runat="server">
         WELCOME TO MOBILE WORLD
      </mobile:Label>
  </mobile:Form>
```

The code in Listing 24.2 simply displays a string on the mobile screen, as shown in Figure 24.2.

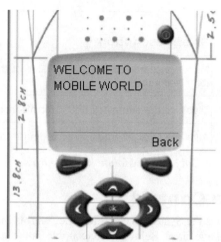

Figure 24.2: Displaying "Welcome to Mobile World"

Here we have used a Label control with the value WELCOME TO MOBILE WORLD.
Before we deal with individual controls, let's discuss some of the basic properties that apply to most controls. They are as follows:

- ID: Here you can specify an ID for almost all the controls and then reference the control using the ID attribute.
- BackColor: Here you can specify the background color of a control. It is similar to the HTML BackColor attribute and can be set by the hexadecimal values specified for different colors.
- FontSize: The size of the Font attribute can be set to Large, Small, Normal, or NotSet.
- Visible: If the specified control is visible on the page, then the return value will be *true*. You can set the Visibility property for controls to *true* or *false*.

There is also a StyleSheet property, which allows you to define your own specific style. A custom style can be given a name and then referenced in your form, using the StyleReference property for that particular control. This will become clearer in the examples that follow.

Basic User Interface Controls

Here we discuss the basic user interface (UI) controls of Label, TextBox, and Command—the three most commonly used controls.

Label

In the very first example (Listing 24.2), we saw that the Label class is used for displaying static text on the screen. You can set the text you want to display through this control's Text property. The control's syntax looks like the following:

```
<mobile:Label  id="label1" runat="server"  Text="Good Morning">
</mobile:Label>
```

TextBox

The TextBox control is used to take a single-line input from the user. This control also has a Text property, in which the input is stored. When you want to retrieve the input, you use the ID to reference that TextBox and its Text property. You can restrict input to numeric and masked values by setting the Numeric or Password properties to true.

```
<mobile:TextBox runat="server" id="TextBox1" />
```

You can set a TextBox to take only numeric input.

```
<mobile:TextBox runat="server" id="TextBox1" Numeric="true"/>
```

Or for password input, set the corresponding property to *true*.

```
<mobile:TextBox runat="server" id="TextBox1" password="true"/>
```

Command

With the Command control you can invoke an event from the user interface. This will make user input post back to the server and makes use of the Click event.

```
<mobile:Command runat="server" id="Command1" OnClick="Command1_OnClick">
    GET IN
</mobile:Command>
```

For a complete picture of what is happening, let's look at an example that uses these three basic controls (see Listing 24.3).

Listing 24.3—Example Using Basic UI Controls

```
<%@ Page Inherits=
    "System.Web.UI.MobileControls.MobilePage" Language="C#" %>
<%@ Register TagPrefix="mobile"
    Namespace="System.Web.UI.MobileControls"
    Assembly="System.Web.Mobile" %>

<script language="c#" runat="server">

public void Command1_OnClick(Object sender, EventArgs e)
{
    Label2.Text = "Good Morning " + TextBox1.Text;
    this.ActiveForm = Form2;
}
</script>

<mobile:Form id="Form1" runat="server">
    <mobile:Label id="Label1" runat="server">
        Enter Your Name
    </mobile:Label>
    <mobile:TextBox runat="server" id="TextBox1"/>
    <mobile:Command runat="server" id="Command1" OnClick="Command1_OnClick">
        GET IN
    </mobile:Command>
</mobile:Form>

<mobile:Form runat="server" id="Form2">
    <mobile:Label runat="server" id="Label2"/>
</mobile:Form>
```

Notice that in the Command_OnClick method the ActiveForm property of the MobilePage class is set to *Form2*. This is one way to traverse to a specified form programmatically. When the page is loaded, the first form is automatically made active, and the Label control asks the user to enter his name. The entered name is stored in the Text property of TextBox1, and when the user submits the form clicking on Command Button, the Command function concatenates the static text and

TextBox1 value. The ActiveForm property will make Form2 active, and you will see another screen displaying the concatenated text.

The output for the two screens is shown in Figures 24.3 and 24.4.

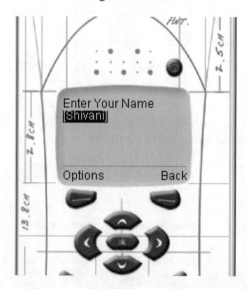

Figure 24.3: Screen Taking Input from User

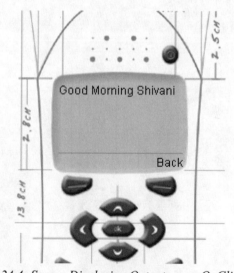

Figure 24.4: Screen Displaying Output on an OnClick Event

Advanced Controls

To this point we have used very common controls. Now we will look at somewhat more complex controls.

TextView

At some point you may find the need to display an arbitrary amount of text and even some markup tags. The TextView control takes care of this for you. To handle large amounts of text, a form's

Pagination property may come in handy. What is Pagination? There are many times when the size of a client's screen is unknown. Using the Pagination property allows a developer to partition the display of data across a number of pages. The TextView control supports both custom and internal pagination. You turn on pagination by setting the form's Pagination property to *true*.

```
<mobile:TextView runat="server"
        id="TextView1"  Alignment="Center"
        forecolor="Blue"
        Font-Bold="true">
      This is the basic entry gateway
        for Mobile Programming!!!! Have Fun
</mobile:TextView>
```

Link

The Link control creates a hyperlink in a mobile form. When the user invokes the Link control, a browser traverses to the URL provided in the NavigateURL property.

```
<mobile:Link runat="server" id="Link1" Text="Goto Link"
    NavigateURL="#Form1">
</mobile:Link>
```

If the NavigateURL property's value begins with a number sign (#), the browser searches the current mobile page for a form tag with the corresponding ID. Otherwise it is assumed to be a valid URL.

Image

Graphics can be an important part of any application, and that includes wireless devices. The Image control displays images, which the developer specifies by setting the ImageURL property. It also has a NavigateURL property, which adds a clickable area to the image, allowing a client to navigate to another destination.

```
<mobile:Image runat="server" id="image1" AlternateText=
    "Image is unvisible" ImageURL="image1.gif">
</mobile:Image>
```

List

The List control provides you with the power to show a list of items in a static as well as an interactive manner. This is an important control if you want to provide the user with choices or if you want to bind data to a control.

```
<mobile:List runat="server" id="List1" OnItemCommand="List1_Click" >
    <item Text="Shivani" Value="Shivani"/>
    <item Text="Shilpa"  Value="Shilpa"/>
</mobile:List>
```

An example of advanced user controls is shown in Listing 24.4.

Listing 24.4—Example of Advanced UI Controls

```
<%@ Page Inherits="System.Web.UI.MobileControls.MobilePage" Language="C#"%>
<%@ Register TagPrefix="mobile"  Namespace="System.Web.UI.MobileControls"
Assembly="System.Web.Mobile" %>
<script language="c#" runat="server">
public void List1_Click(Object source, ListCommandEventArgs e)
{
```

```
    Label1.Text = "Hi  "  +  e.ListItem.Text ;
    ActiveForm = Form2;
}
</script>
<mobile:Form id="Form1" runat="server" BackColor="Blue">
    <mobile:TextView runat="server" id="TextView1">
          Here you are going to select one Name!!
    </mobile:TextView>
    <mobile:List runat="server" id="List1" OnItemCommand="List1_Click">
        <item Text="Shivani" Value="Shivani" />
        <item Text="Shilpa"  Value="Shilpa" />
    </mobile:List>
</mobile:Form>
<mobile:Form id="Form2" runat = "server">
    <mobile:Label id="Label1" runat="server"/>
    <mobile:Image runat="server" id="Image1" ImageURL="Congrats.wbmp"
        AlternateText="Hey no Image for you">
    </mobile:Image>
</mobile:Form>
```

The output of the code in Listing 24.4 is shown in Figures 24.5 and 24.6.

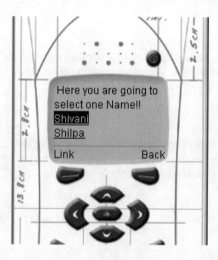

Figure 24.5: Screen Displaying a List of Names with a Link

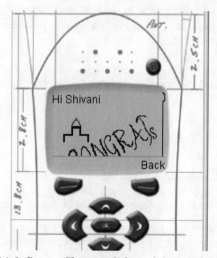

Figure 24.6: Screen Showing Selected Output from the List

Here is an important point to note. In the example, the ImageURL is in the .wbmp format. The image format supported on WAP devices is wbmp format. These images tend to be small and relatively simple, given the constraint of the devices' size. Thus, those devices that do not support the .wbmp format would display the AlternateText value rather than the image. For this problem we have the DeviceSpecific class, which gives you the power to provide the specific content. The following example shows how to use device-specific content:

```
<DeviceSpecific>
  <Choice Filter="IsHtml" ImageURL="Congrats.gif"/>
  <Choice Filter="IsWbmp" ImageURL="Congrats.wbmp"/>
  <Choice ImageURL="Congrats.bmp"/>
</DeviceSpecific>
```

The DeviceSpecific class affords a means to specify device-dependent content. If a device supports a .gif image, then the Congrats.gif will be displayed, while devices supporting an image/vnd.wap.wbmp will output Congrats.wbmp. The default behavior will display the Congrats.bmp.

Validation

Up to this point we have discussed the user interface in terms of visible controls, but any data an application collects from the user will require some form of validation. Validation is an essential part of any program, and .Net provides a number of validation controls.

Let's look at the basic properties of a validation control:

- The ControlToValidate property allows the developer to associate a graphical control with a validation control. It gets or sets the ID of a control that needs to be validated.
- The ErrorMessage property allows the developer to specify the error message text she wants displayed.
- The Display property is used to set whether the ErrorMessage property is to be shown statically or dynamically.

The preceding basic properties apply to all of the validation controls. There are a total of five validation controls, which all inherit from the BaseValidator class. Let's discuss them one by one.

RequiredFieldValidator

Required field validation takes a control where a value must be provided. The field to be validated cannot be empty.

Syntactically the RequiredFieldValidator looks like the following:

```
<mobile:RequiredFieldValidator   ControlToValidate="validator1"
runat="server">
    Required Field
</mobile:RequiredFieldValidator>
```

RangeValidator

The RangeValidator control ensures that the value of the control to be validated falls within a specified range by providing the Minimum and Maximum properties.

```
<mobile:RangeValidator ControlToValidate="validator2"
    Type="Integer"
```

```
            MaximumValue="75"
            MinimumValue="50"
            runat="server">
            Does not fall in the specified Range
        </mobile:RangeValidator>
```

Listing 25.5 contains an example of these validators.

Listing 25.5—Example of Validation Controls

```
<%@ Page Inherits="System.Web.UI.MobileControls.MobilePage" Language="C#"%>
<%@ Register TagPrefix="mobile" Namespace="System.Web.UI.MobileControls"
Assembly="System.Web.Mobile" %>

<script language="c#" runat="server">
protected void Submit_OnClick(Object sender, EventArgs e){
    if (Page.IsValid){
        ActiveForm = Form2;
    }
}
</script>

<mobile:Form id="Form1" runat="server">
  <mobile:Label runat="server">
      Enter your Name
  </mobile:Label>
  <mobile:TextBox id="validator1" runat="server"/>
  <mobile:RequiredFieldValidator ControlToValidate="validator1"
      runat="server">
       Required Field
  </mobile:RequiredFieldValidator>
  <mobile:Label runat="server">
     Enter Age
  </mobile:Label>
  <mobile:TextBox id="validator2" runat="server"/>
  <mobile:RangeValidator ControlToValidate="validator2"
      Type="Integer"
      MaximumValue="75"
      MinimumValue="50"
      runat="server">
    Your Age does not Fall in the specified Range
  </mobile:RangeValidator>
  <mobile:RequiredFieldValidator ControlToValidate="validator2"
      runat="server">
    Required Field
  </mobile:RequiredFieldValidator>
  <mobile:Command runat="server" OnClick="Submit_OnClick">
      Submit
  </mobile:Command>
</mobile:Form>

<mobile:Form id="Form2" runat="server">
    <mobile:Label runat="server">
        Your Entry is Submited
    </mobile:Label>
</mobile:Form>
```

The output, when you submit this page, will look something like that shown in Figures 24.7 and 24.8.

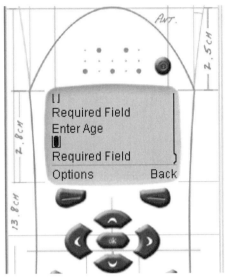

Figure 24.7: Error Message Displayed If Form Is Submitted Without Input

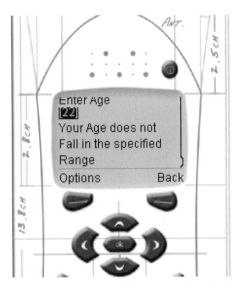

Figure 24.8: Error Message Displayed If Input Is Outside the Specified Range

If the IsValid property is missing, the page will be submitted in spite of providing the control with validation. Therefore, whenever you use a validation control make sure the Page.IsValid property is present to ensure that validation has taken place.

RegularExpressionValidator

The RegularExpressionValidator is used to validate a control using a "regular expression."

To check and make sure the "@" is present in an e-mail address, you would use the RegularExpressionValidator in the following manner:

```
<mobile:RegularExpressionValidator ControlToValidate="EmailField"
    ValidationExpression=".*@.*"
    runat="server">
```

```
        Invalid Email ID
</mobile:RegularExpressionValidator>
```

CompareValidator

The CompareValidator control is used when you want to compare a specified control with another control or value using the Operator property. The Operator property supports enumerations such as GreaterThan, LessThan, or EqualTo.

There are two properties to perform this: ControlToCompare and ValueToCompare. In the first case, you can specify any control you want to validate, as in the case of a password field. When you submit a Confirm Password field, you can validate it against another field called Choose Password for equality. Here's an example of this type of validation:

```
<mobile:CompareValidator ControlToValidate="ConfirmPassword"
    Type="String"
        Operator="Equal"
    ControlToCompare="ChoosePassword"
            runat="server">
    The Password doesn`t Match
</mobile:CompareValidator>
```

In the second case, you can specify the value with which you want a control to be compared:

```
<mobile:CompareValidator ControlToValidate="validator4"
        Type="Integer"
    Operator="GreaterThan"
        ValueToCompare="20"
        runat="server">
    The value is not in the Range
</mobile:CompareValidator>
```

CustomValidator

When you want a control to be validated using your own rules, or you want the value to be checked in a specific way, you can customize the way the control is validated.

```
<mobile:CustomValidator ControlToValidate="validator5"
        OnServerValidate="Custom_Validator"
    runat="server">
    Invalid Response
</mobile:CustomValidator>
```

This particular validation takes place on the server by means of the Custom_Validator method. In that function, you can write the required validation code.

ValidationSummary

We have seen all the major validators, but let's say you do not want an error message to be displayed for every validation that fails. There is a way to accommodate that.

The ValidationSummary control will list all the errors that occur in the form. This control has the ability to filter error messages by only displaying the text of the ErrorMessage property.

```
<mobile:ValidationSummary FormToValidate="Form1"
        HeaderText="Errors Are:"   runat="server">
</mobile:ValidationSummary>
```

Listing 24.8 gives you a fair picture of a validation summary.

Listing 24.8—Example of Validation Controls 2

```
<%@ Page Inherits="System.Web.UI.MobileControls.MobilePage" Language="C#" %>
<%@ Register TagPrefix="mobile"  Namespace="System.Web.UI.MobileControls"
Assembly="System.Web.Mobile" %>

<script language="c#" runat="server">

protected void Submit_OnClick(Object sender, EventArgs e){
     ActiveForm = Form2;
}

void Custom_Validate (object source, ServerValidateEventArgs args){
     int number = Int32.Parse(SecurityCode.Text);
     if (number % 5 == 0)
          args.IsValid = true;
     else
          args.IsValid = false;
}

</script>

<mobile:Form id="Form1" runat="server">
  <mobile:Label runat="server">
          Enter EmailId
  </mobile:Label>
  <mobile:TextBox id="EmailId" runat="server"/>
  <mobile:RegularExpressionValidator ControlToValidate="EmailId"
       ValidationExpression=".*@.*"
          runat="server" ErrorMessage="Invalid Email ID">
  </mobile:RegularExpressionValidator>
  <mobile:Label runat="server">
     Enter Password
   </mobile:Label>
  <mobile:TextBox id="EnterPass" runat="server"/>
  <mobile:Label runat="server">
     Confirm Password
  </mobile:Label>
  <mobile:TextBox id="ConfirmPass" runat="server"/>
  <mobile:CompareValidator ControlToValidate="ConfirmPass"
        Type="String"
        Operator="Equal"
        ControlToCompare="EnterPass"
   runat="server" ErrorMessage="The Password doesn`t Match">
  </mobile:CompareValidator>
  <mobile:Label runat="server">
    Enter Security Code
  </mobile:Label>
  <mobile:TextBox id="SecurityCode" runat="server"/>
  <mobile:CustomValidator ControlToValidate="SecurityCode"
          OnServerValidate="Custom_Validate"
          runat="server" ErrorMessage=" Code Not Permitted">
  </mobile:CustomValidator>
  <mobile:Command runat="server" OnClick="Submit_OnClick">
     Submit
  </mobile:Command>
</mobile:Form>

<mobile:Form id="Form2" runat="server">
  <mobile:Label runat="server">
     Valid if its empty below
  </mobile:Label>
  <mobile:ValidationSummary FormToValidate="Form1"
          HeaderText="Error listed below:"
```

```
        runat="server"/>
</mobile:Form>
```

The code in Listing 24.8 will produce the display shown in Figures 24.9 and 24.10 when the text fields are incorrectly filled out.

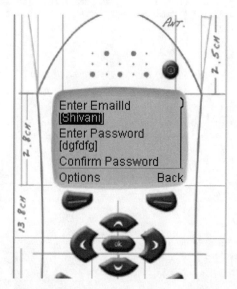

Figure 24.9: Screen for the User's Input

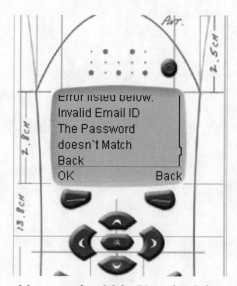

Figure 24.10: Error Messages that Make Use of ValidationSummary Control

Utility Controls

We have covered the basics of user interface controls and validation controls. Now we move on to something even more interesting to a programmer. The basic utility controls provided by the Mobile Internet Toolkit reduce some of the pain of writing code and make the most out of what you write. There are three utility controls: Calendar, Call, and AdRotator.

Calendar

The Calendar control is the most powerful of the three utility controls. This class is similar to the Web.UI.Calendar class but provides a display of the day/week/month that is dependent on the physical screen capability of the device. This control provides the date selection functionality and displays the selected date.

Listing 24.8 shows an example in which the user is asked to select the date.

Listing 24.8—Example of Calendar Control

```
<%@ Page Inherits="System.Web.UI.MobileControls.MobilePage" Language="C#" %>
<%@ Register TagPrefix="mobile"              Namespace="System.Web.UI.MobileControls"
Assembly="System.Web.Mobile" %>

<script language="c#" runat="server">

protected void Calendar_Selection(Object sender, EventArgs e){
    Label1.Text = "The selected date is " + Calendar1.SelectedDate;
    ActiveForm = Form2;
}

</script>

<mobile:Form id="Form1" runat="server">
    <mobile:Calendar id="Calendar1"
        OnSelectionChanged="Calendar_Selection"
        SelectionMode="DayWeek"
         runat=server/>
</mobile:Form>

<mobile:Form id="Form2" runat="server">
    <mobile:Label id="Label1" runat="server"/>
</mobile:Form>
```

The code in Listing 24.8 generates the output shown in Figures 24.11 through 24.15 and gives you the opportunity to select the date, as the figures show.

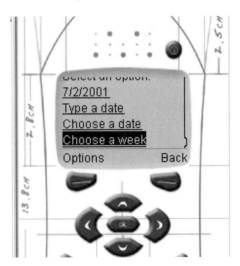

Figure 24.11: Screen Prompting User to Select a Date

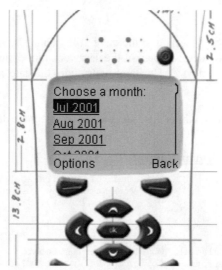

Figure 24.12: Screen Prompting User to Select a Month

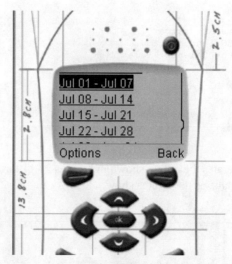

Figure 24.13: Screen Prompting User to Select a Week

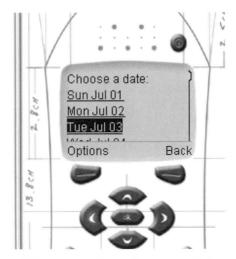

Figure 24.14: Screen Prompting User to Select a Day

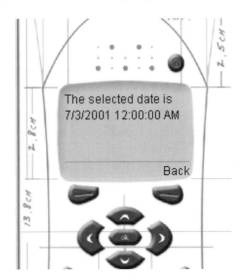

Figure 24.15: Final Output Shown After Submit, Showing Date Selected by User

Call

The second utility we are going to look at is calling functionality. You must be thinking: What is so special about calling from a mobile phone? Yes, it is from this control that you can automatically call a displayed number. Let's suppose you want to call the company number that is embedded in your company address in the display. It would be nice if the number were activated when a user clicks on the link for the phone number. There is no need to remember the number anymore. The following code shows how this is done:

```
<mobile:Call runat="server"
AlternateURL="http://c-sharpcorner.com"
            phoneNumber="9109845248004">
        Shivani`s Creation
</mobile:Call>
```

AdRotator

The final control we'll discuss is the AdRotator. This particular utility control is the same as Web.UI.WebControls.AdRotator. It picks an advertisement from the file specified in the AdvertisementFile property.

Here is what this control looks like:

```
<mobile:AdRotator runat="server" AdvertisementFile="myAd.xml">
</mobile:AdRotator>
```

If you are using images or want to provide personalization in the form of a message, you can use the DeviceSpecific control.

In this chapter we have covered the bits and bytes of the Mobile Internet Toolkit. These are the basics you need to know to start programming mobile devices in .NET. Now let's look at a couple of case studies.

Case Study 1

We want to develop an application for a bank that will provide its users with their account balance on a mobile device. Users will be authenticated against their preassigned credentials and, if that is successful, logged on. Then they will be asked for their account number, which returns their balance.

For this example, XML is used as a data source. We will interact with the XML file, which has been extracted from a database and opened with the specific field to be read only.

Let's have a look at the XML file (shown in Listing 24.8).

Listing 24.8—XML Bank Data File

```xml
<BankData>
 <customer>
     <Name>Shivani</Name>
     <Password>hishivani</Password>
     <AccountNo>117971</AccountNo>
     <Balance>5000</Balance>
 </customer>
 <customer>
     <Name>Shilpa</Name>
     <Password>hishilpa</Password>
     <AccountNo>117972</AccountNo>
     <Balance>7000</Balance>
 </customer>
 <customer>
     <Name>Neha</Name>
     <Password>hineha</Password>
     <AccountNo>117973</AccountNo>
     <Balance>9000</Balance>
 </customer>
 <customer>
     <Name>Shubham</Name>
     <Password>hishubham</Password>
     <AccountNo>117974</AccountNo>
     <Balance>11000</Balance>
 </customer>
</BankData>
```

Our requirement, once again, is to allow the customer to view her account balance, once she has been authenticated. The code in Listing 24.9 accomplishes this goal.

Listing 24.9—Mobile Banking Application

```csharp
<%@ Page Inherits="System.Web.UI.MobileControls.MobilePage" Language="C#" %>
<%@ Register TagPrefix="mobile" Namespace="System.Web.UI.MobileControls"
Assembly="System.Web.Mobile"%>
<%@ Import Namespace="System"%>
<%@ Import Namespace="System.Xml" %>

<script runat="server" language="c#">

   int flag1,flag2;
   string Balance1;

   public void SubmitBtn_Click(Object sender, EventArgs e){
        XmlDocument _doc = new XmlDocument( );
       _doc.Load("E:/ASPXSITE/Examples/casestudyxml.xml");
        XmlNodeList _snames    = _doc.GetElementsByTagName("Name");
        XmlNodeList _spasswords = _doc.GetElementsByTagName("Password");
        for ( int _i = 0; _i < _snames.Count; ++_i ){
          if(_snames[ _i].InnerText==Name.Text &&
                     _spasswords[_i].InnerText==Password.Text){
                  flag1 = 1;
                  break;
              }
          else
                  flag1 = 0;
      }

    if(flag1 == 1)
          ActiveForm = Form2;
    else
          ActiveForm = Form3;
  }


   public void SecondForm_OnActivate(Object sender, EventArgs e){
          Welcome.Text   = "u r successfully logged on";
   }

   public void AccNo_Submit(Object sender, EventArgs e){
       XmlDocument _doc = new XmlDocument( );
        _doc.Load("E:/ASPXSITE/Examples/casestudyxml.xml");
        XmlNodeList _snames    = _doc.GetElementsByTagName("Name");
       XmlNodeList _spasswords =
                          _doc.GetElementsByTagName("Password");
        XmlNodeList _sbalance   = _doc.GetElementsByTagName("Balance");
        XmlNodeList _saccno     =
                          _doc.GetElementsByTagName("AccountNo");
       for ( int _i = 0; _i < _snames.Count; ++_i ){

        if(_saccno[ _i].InnerText==AccountNo.Text &&
             _snames[ _i].InnerText==Name.Text &&
             _spasswords[ _i].InnerText==Password.Text){

           flag2 = 1;
            Balance1 = _sbalance[ _i].InnerText;
            break;
        }
          else
              flag2 = 0;
      }

  if(flag2 == 1){
```

```
        Balance.Text= "u r balance is $ "  + Balance1;
        Conclusion.Text="Thank You" ;
        ActiveForm = Form4;
    }
    else{

        Balance.Text ="Invalid Account No";
        Conclusion.Text="You need to Relogin";
        ActiveForm = Form4;
    }
}

</script>


<mobile:Form runat="server" id="Form1" BackColor="#336699" ForeColor="#ffffff">

    <mobile:Label runat="server" Font-Name="Arial">Name</mobile:Label>
    <mobile:TextBox runat="server" id="Name" ForeColor="#000000" />
    <mobile:Label runat="server" Font-Name="Arial">
        Password
    </mobile:Label>
    <mobile:TextBox runat="server" id="Password" ForeColor="#000000" />
    <mobile:Command runat="server"
        OnClick="SubmitBtn_Click" Text="Go!"/>
    </mobile:Form>
    <mobile:Form runat="server" id="Form2"
            OnActivate="SecondForm_OnActivate" Font-Name="Arial">
    <mobile:Label runat="server" id="Welcome" />
    <mobile:Label runat="server" id="Label2" Text="Enter Account No."/>
    <mobile:TextBox runat="server" id="AccountNo"
            ForeColor="#000000" />
    <mobile:Command runat="server" OnClick="AccNo_Submit" Text="Go!" />
    <mobile:Link runat="server"
            Font-Size="Small" NavigateURL="#Form1"
            Text="Return to Start"/>

</mobile:Form>
<mobile:Form runat="server" id="Form3"
        OnActivate="SecondForm_OnActivate" Font-Name="Arial">
    <mobile:Label runat="server" id="Label3" Text="Login Failed" />
    <mobile:Link runat="server" Font-Size="Small"
            NavigateURL="#Form1" Text="Return to Start"/>
</mobile:Form>
<mobile:Form runat="server" id="Form4" Font-Name="Arial">
    <mobile:Label runat="server" id="Balance"/>
    <mobile:Label runat="server" id="Conclusion"/>
    <mobile:Link runat="server"
                Font-Size="Small"
                NavigateURL="#Form1" Text="Return to Start"/>
</mobile:Form>
```

The code is self-explanatory, but it requires a basic knowledge of using XML with .NET.

The output is shown in Figures 24.16 through 24.18. This is the output as long as the input is correct. This way we can develop basic mobile applications for different domain clients.

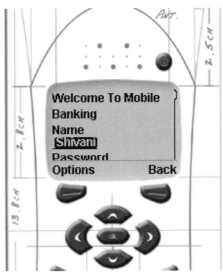

Figure 24.16: Authentication Screen Prompting for Name and Password

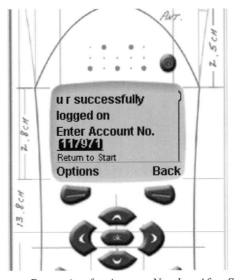

Figure 24.17: Screen Prompting for Account Number After Successful Log-on

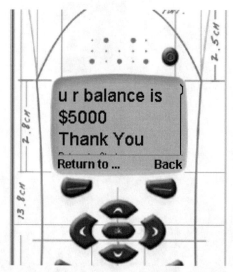

Figure 24.18: Final Screen, Showing the Balance

Let's see one more example, which will give you a fair idea of how rich the functionality of ASP.NET classes can be when deployed for mobile controls.

Case Study 2

This program will allow the user to send mail from his mobile device. Here we use a mail server and make use of the classes provided in the System.Web.Mail namespace. We also make elaborate use of validation controls.

Listing 24.10—Mail-Sending Application

```
<%@ Page Inherits="System.Web.UI.MobileControls.MobilePage" Language="C#" %>
<%@ Register TagPrefix="mobile" Namespace="System.Web.UI.MobileControls"
Assembly="System.Web.Mobile" %>
<%@ Import Namespace="System.Web.Mail" %>

<script language="c#" runat="server">

protected void Submit_OnClick(Object sender, EventArgs e){
  if(Page.IsValid){
 /// Make an object of MailMessage Class
      MailMessage message = new MailMessage();
 ///Set the Fields
      message.To = to.Text;
      message.From = from.Text;
      message.Subject = subject.Text;
 ///Set u r Mail Server here
      SmtpMail.SmtpServer = "c-sharpcorner.com" ;
/// This will send the Message
      SmtpMail.Send(message);
/// Give the Confirmation as the Message has been sent
      confirm.Text = "Mail has been sent to " + to.Text;
//Activate Second Form
      this.ActiveForm = Form2;
   }

}

</script>
```

Listing 24.10 is the final action in the example. When the user submits the form, the Submit_OnClick method is called, and once the message is e-mailed, Form2 is activated. But first we have to get input from the user for both the To and From fields. We will limit the data we collect, as it is difficult to type on a phone (see Listing 24.11).

Listing 24.11—Mail Sending: User Interface

```
<mobile:Form id="Form1" runat="server">
    <mobile:Label runat="server">
            FROM :
    </mobile:Label>
    <mobile:TextBox id="from" runat="server"/>
    <mobile:RequiredFieldValidator
            id="FromValidator1"
            ControlToValidate="from" runat="server">
                Enter from address
    </mobile:ReuiredFieldValidator>
    <mobile:RegularExpressionValidator
            id="FromValidator2"
            ControlToValidate="from"
            ValidationExpression="\w+([-+.]\w+)*@\w+([-.]\w+)
                          *\.\w+([-.]\w+)*"
            runat="server">
    Enter a valid Email Id
    </mobile:RegularExpressionValidator>
    <mobile:Label runat="server">
        TO:
    </mobile:Label>
    <mobile:TextBox id="to" runat="server"/>
    <mobile:RequiredFieldValidator
            id="toValidator1"
             ControlToValidate="to" runat="server">
            Enter to address
    </mobile:RequiredFieldValidator>
    <mobile:RegularExpressionValidator
            ControlToValidate="to"
            ValidationExpression="\w+([-+.]\w+)*@\w+
                    ([-.]\w+)*\.\w+([-.]\w+)*"
             runat="server">
             Enter a valid Email Id
    </mobile:RegularExpressionValidator>
    <mobile:Label runat="server">
        MESSAGE:
    </mobile:Label>
    <mobile:TextBox id="subject" runat="server"/>
    <mobile:Command runat="server" OnClick="Submit_OnClick">
            Submit
    </mobile:Command>
</mobile:Form>

<mobile:Form id="Form2" runat="server">
    <mobile:Label id ="confirm" runat="server">
    </mobile:Label>
</mobile:Form>
```

The validators will allow the Submit function to be called only after the page has been validated. Do not forget the IsValid property, as was mentioned earlier.

The output shown in Figure 24.19 should appear on the phone screen.

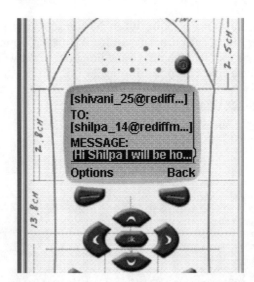

Figure 24.19: Input Screen for From and To E-Mail Address and Message

If all the fields are valid and you are pointing to a valid SMTP server, then your output should appear as shown in Figure 24.20.

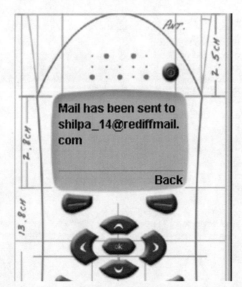

Figure 24.20: Confirmation Screen When User Clicks on Send Button

This is how easy it is to use the functionality of ASP.NET classes in your mobile controls.

Summary

In this chapter, we touched on the basics of mobile programming within the .NET Framework and how to take advantage of the Mobile Internet Toolkit. We also looked briefly at the basic controls the Mobile Internet Toolkit provides. Those controls include such things as the MobilePage control, interface controls, validation controls, and utility controls. Finally, we demonstrated how to use these controls and tools with some coding examples. After reading this chapter, you should possess the foundation you need to start programming for the mobile Internet. The next chapter will discuss the .NET Remoting Framework for client/server communication.

Chapter 25:
.NET Remoting

Introduction

Remote procedure call (RPC), the Component Object Model (COM), the Distributed Component Object Model (DCOM), Common Object Request Broker Architecture (CORBA), and remote method invocation (RMI) are technologies that provide a means to transfer data across boundaries, in what has come to be called distributed applications. A boundary can be another process, a different machine, a remote network, or, in the case of .NET, an application domain. Generally, distributed applications can be simply illustrated as shown in Figure 25.1.

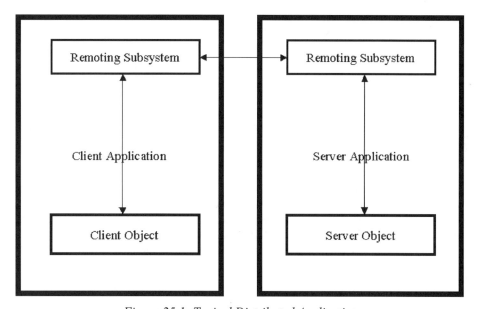

Figure 25.1: Typical Distributed Application

The .NET Remoting Framework provides an extensive array of classes enabling developers to create distributed applications with minimal effort and complexity. The framework is also highly extensible, presenting developers with a wide range of customization options that extend to Internet solutions.

The *.NET Framework Developer Specifications,* published by Microsoft, describe .NET Remoting as enabling Web Services Anywhere and CLR (Common Language Runtime) Object Remoting. Web Services Anywhere means that remoting functionality and services can be used by any application over any transport and can employ any encoding scheme. CLR Object Remoting rides on top of Web Services Anywhere. It provides all the language semantics normally associated with a local object, such as constructors, delegates, the *new* operator, and overloaded methods.

Activation, lease-based lifetime, distributed identity, and call context are also dealt with in CLR Object Remoting.

The remoting framework comprises a large segment of the System.Runtime namespace. Remoting encompasses 11 namespaces containing in excess of 50 classes and interfaces. The wealth of material in the remoting framework deserves an entire book. Unfortunately, the time and space allotted to this chapter permit only a survey of a few of those namespaces, classes, and interfaces.

This chapter explores .NET Remoting and relies heavily on examples to demonstrate various topics. Among the subjects highlighted are these:

- Remoting components
- A simple client/server sample
- Lifetime management
- Passing objects and collections as method parameters and return types
- Remoting events and delegates
- Call contexts
- Configuration files in remoting
- Remoting over the Web
- Creating a custom sink

.NET Remoting Components

At its core the .Net Remoting Framework communicates between server and client objects via object references. To qualify as a remote object, the class *must* derive from System.MarshalByRefObject. Much in the manner of COM, the remoting system uses proxies in the client's application domain. A proxy is an abstract representation of the actual remote object on the server. In the case of .NET, two proxies are created—a transparent proxy and a real proxy. The *transparent proxy* is the remote object reference returned to the client. The *real proxy* handles the forwarding of messages to the channel. Sound confusing? The diagram in Figure 25.2 will, hopefully, make the sequencing clearer.

The transparent proxy is returned when the client activates a remote object using the *new* operator or a System.Activator method. All method calls on the proxy are intercepted by the runtime to ensure the call is a valid method or property on the remote object. When a remote object's method is called, the transparent proxy calls System.Runtime.Remoting.Proxies.RealProxy.Invoke() with a System.Runtime.Remoting.Messaging.IMessage interface, which contains the called method's parameter types and their values. The actual implementation is the private Message class in mscorlib.dll.

A real proxy is created along with the transparent proxy. To create a customized proxy, a developer derives the class from the RealProxy class and overrides Invoke().The real proxy's primary responsibility is to forward messages to the channel. It does this by first creating a message sink on the channel with the call System.Runtime.Remoting.Channels.IChannelSender.CreateMessageSink and then storing the returned IMessageSink object. Then in the Invoke method, it calls either the message sink's SyncProcessMessage() or AsyncProcessMessage().

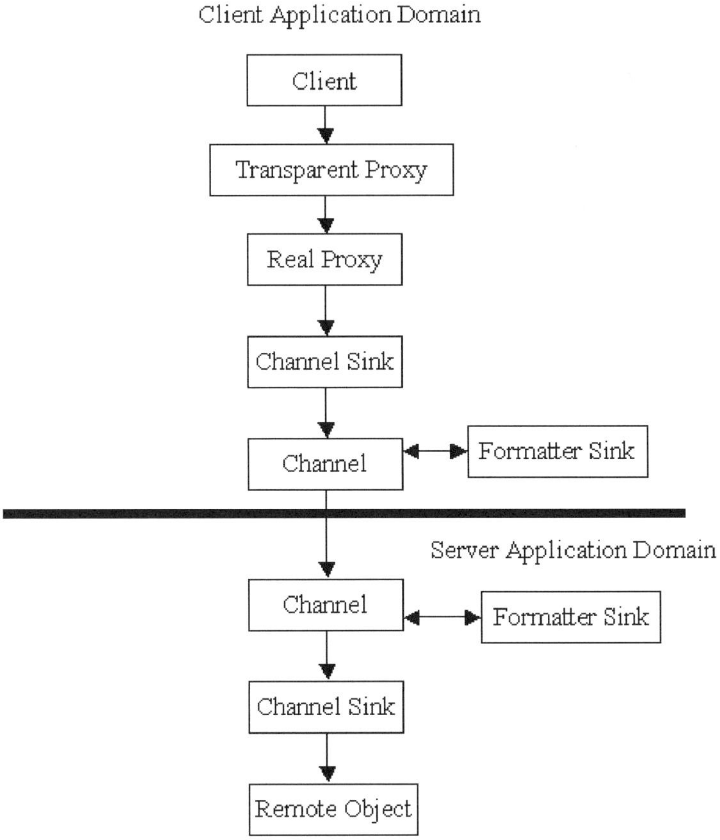

Client Application Domain

Figure 25.2: Remoting Sequence

The Channel Sink and Formatter Sink boxes in the diagram are somewhat misleading in two ways. First, neither is an independent entity but rather a member of the channel. Second, sinks are linked together in a chain. Each member in the chain retains a reference to the next sink in the chain. In the client's application domain, the first sink is a formatter and the last sink is the transport sink. In the server's domain the order is reversed. Between the formatter and transport sinks, customized user sinks may be dropped into the chain. Each sink in the chain implements the ProcessMessage() and AsyncProcessMessage() methods and is responsible for calling the respective method on the next sink in the chain.

The function of formatter sinks is to serialize and deserialize IMessage to and from a stream. The client must implement IClientChannelSink, while the server implements IServerChannelSink.

The transport sink is responsible for transporting the serialized message.

A channel can receive messages, send messages, or both. Every channel derives from IChannel. Depending on the channel's purpose, it must also inherit IChannelReceiver or IChannelSender interfaces, or both.

One question you may have is how one can, as we asserted at the outset, "create distributed applications with minimal effort and complexity," given the number of namespaces, classes, and interfaces in the preceding description. Why have the .NET designers taken something simple like COM and made it complicated? The answer is, they haven't. .NET ships with two remoting types that support HTTP and TCP/IP protocols. Each provides a client channel, a server channel, and a combined sender-receiver channel. The default formatters support binary and Simple Object Access Protocol (SOAP) serialization.

At this point, it would be beneficial to demonstrate these concepts with an example.

A Server-Activated Example

The projects are in the Sample1 folder and consist of a class library (SimpleObjectLib) and two console applications (ServerActivatedServerExe and ServerActivatedClientExe). The console projects should add a reference to System.Runtime.Remoting.dll and SimpleObjectLib.dll. This section presents the code with few remarks. A detailed discussion will take place in the section Under the Covers: Part 1.

Listing 25.1—The SimpleObject Code

```
namespace SimpleObjectLib
{

        public class SimpleObject : MarshalByRefObject        {
                public SimpleObject()
                     : base()
                {
                      Console.WriteLine(
                         "In SimpleObject constructor.");
                }

                public string ConCatString( string first, string second)
                {
                string concat = null;

                      Console.WriteLine(
                       "In SimpleObject.ConCatString method.");
                      concat = first + " " + second;
                      return( concat);
                }
        }
}
```

Notice in Listing 25.1 that SimpleObject derives from MarshalByRefObject. Any class that is a candidate for remoting *must* derive from MarshalByRefObject. The output for the example is shown below in Figure 25.3.

Figure 25.3: The ServerActivatedServerExe Output

Listing 25.2—The ServerActivatedServerExe Code

```
using System;
using System.Runtime.Remoting;
using System.Runtime.Remoting.Channels;
using System.Runtime.Remoting.Channels.Http;

using SimpleObjectLib;
```

```
namespace ServerActivatedServerExe
{
        class ServerActivatedServer
        {
                static void Main(string[] args)
                {
                HttpServerChannel http = null;

                        http = new HttpServerChannel( 1234);
                        ChannelServices.RegisterChannel( http);
                        RemotingConfiguration.RegisterWellKnownServiceType(
                                        typeof(SimpleObject),
                                        "Simple",
                                        WellKnownObjectMode.SingleCall);
                        Console.WriteLine(
                                        "Press <enter> to exit.");
                        Console.ReadLine();
                }
        }
}
```

The server code in Listing 25.2 is simple and straightforward. An instance of a
System.Runtime.Remoting.Channels.Http.HttpServerChannel is created, specifying the port it will
listen on. Once the channel has been instantiated, it registers itself with the static method
ChannelServices.RegisterChannel(). Finally, the remote object is registered with the static method
RemotingConfiguration.RegisterWellKnownServiceType(). The parameters specify the remote
object, the URI (Uniform Resource Identifier), and the calling mode enumeration. This will be
discussed later in Under the Covers: part 1. The Console.ReadLine() keeps the server up and
running. When the process ends, all channels and registered objects are dropped by remoting
services.

Figure 25.4: The ServerActivatedClientExe Output

Listing 25.3—The ServerActivatedClientExe Code

```
using System;
using System.Runtime.Remoting;
using System.Runtime.Remoting.Channels;
using System.Runtime.Remoting.Channels.Http;
using SimpleObjectLib;

namespace ServerActivatedClientExe
{
        class ServerActivatedClient
        {
                static int Main(string[] args)
                {
                HttpClientChannel http = null;

                        http = new HttpClientChannel();
                        ChannelServices.RegisterChannel( http);

                SimpleObject simple1 = null;

                        simple1 = (SimpleObject)Activator.GetObject(
                                                typeof(SimpleObject),
                                        "http://localhost:1234/Simple");
```

```
        string ret = null;
            ret = simple1.ConCatString( "using",
                            "Activator.GetObject");
            Console.WriteLine( ret);

    SimpleObject simple2 = null;

            RemotingConfiguration.RegisterWellKnownClientType(
                typeof(SimpleObject),
                "http://localhost:1234/Simple");

            simple2 = new SimpleObject();
            ret = simple2.ConCatString( "using the \"new\"",
                                "operator");
            Console.WriteLine( ret);

            return( 0);
        }
    }
}
```

In the client example shown in Listing 25.3 and it's corresponding output in Figure 25.4, two ways of obtaining a remote reference are demonstrated: using the Activator and the *new* operator. Also available to developers is a System.Runtime.Remoting.RemotingServices overloaded method, Connect(). A channel is created and registered. This time, it is an HttpClientChannel. The default constructor attaches to any available port. In fact, if you look at the HttpClientChannel constructors in the .NET class library, a port number specification isn't an option. The static method Activator.GetObject() returns a transparent proxy for SimpleObject. The parameters specify the remote object type and the Uniform Resource Locator (URL). To use the *new* operator to activate remote objects, you must register the object by calling RemotingConfiguration.RegisterWellKnownClientType(). The parameters are the object type and the URL. Calling *new* on SimpleObject returns a transparent proxy. It should be noted, that calling the *new* operator without registering with RemoteConfiguration will work, but a local reference is returned, not a transparent proxy.

As is evident from the preceding example, .NET designers have abstracted much of the remoting complexity and hidden many of the implementation details. The preceding example and a client-activated example, encountered later in the chapter, probably offer a solution for 60 to 70 percent of problem domains. While it isn't essential to understand what is actually going on "under the covers," for those situations where portions of the framework must be adapted or extended, knowledge of the underlying architecture is required.

Under the Covers: Part 1

The server starts up, creates a channel and registers itself, then registers a "well-known type" with remoting configuration. Looking at the server's initial output, Figure 25.3, nothing has been accomplished except the Console.WriteLine() *Press <enter> to exit*. What has happened? The channel starts listening for client connection requests on construction. This is established by looking into the _tcpListener member, an instance of System.Net.Sockets.TcpListener, of the HTTP channel, and determining that the Active property is *true*. It also can be determined that the remote object has been registered with the configuration services by calling the method System.Runtime.Remoting.RemotingConfiguration.GetRegisteredWellKnownServiceTypes(), which returns a WellKnownServiceTypeEntry[] with a list of registered types. SimpleObject is in the list but not yet instantiated.

Start the client. Channels are created and registered, and the Activator.GetObject() is called. No communication has taken place yet between the client and the server. Activator.GetObject() has simply returned a local instance of the transparent proxy. Only when simple1.ConCatString() is called, does the server's output console begin to show signs of life.

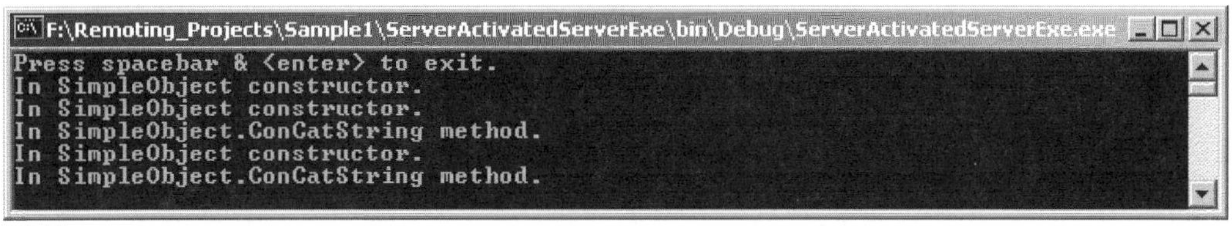

Figure 25.5a: The ServerActivatedServerExe Output

Notice that SimpleObject's constructor (see Figure 25.5a) is called three times, whereas the ConCatString() is called twice. There are a number of things to do in discovering what is actually taking place, but this is a good point to digress for a moment.

If you look at the server code, the call RemotingConfiguration.RegisterWellKnown . . . had as a parameter WellKnownObjectMode.SingleCall. It is an enumeration with two values, SingleCall and Singleton. Using SingleCall creates a new instance of the object for every method call. Singleton mode services all object requests with the same instance. If the mode in the server's code were changed, the server output would look like that shown in Figure 25.5b.

Figure 25.5b: Server Output with Mode Change

Now, back to tracing remote object activation, by doing the following:

- Override MarshalByRefObject's CreateObjRef() in the SimpleObject to aid in tracking the sequence of events.
- MyTrackingHandler in SimpleObjectLib is derived from System.Runtime.Remoting.Services.ITrackingHandler, a utility interface to trace remote object marshaling.
- In the server code, register the tracking handler using System.Runtime.Remoting.Services.TrackingServices.RegisterTrackingHandler().

As the client code calls simple1.ConCatString(), the server creates an instance of SimpleObject(), followed by a call to SimpleObject.CreateObjRef(). By registering a MyTrackingHandler instance, you can see that the remoting subsystem then marshals SimpleObject to obtain a System.Runtime.Remoting.ObjRef.

This ObjRef is a representation of the remote object, including the class's strong name, hierarchy, implemented interfaces, and URI. It also contains details of all the available registered channels. The server's remoting framework stores this reference in a table to track registered objects. With server-activated remote objects, the ObjRef is created only once during the lifetime of the server. This is in contrast to client-activated objects, which we'll encounter next.

Once the server has created and stored the ObjRef, the first instance of SimpleObject is ready for the Garbage Collector (GC). At this point, the server turns to servicing the client's request with a call to SimpleObject(), and then ConCatString(). What has been established? Although this is explained in

Microsoft's .NET Remoting: A Technical Overview, we have used a number of the remoting helper classes and interfaces to confirm a number of points:

- No actual communication takes place between the client and the server until a method or property is called on the remote object.
- Server-activated remote objects registered in SingleCall mode must remain stateless, as there is a new instance with every method call. Singleton mode remote objects could maintain state, but only one instance services all clients, and therefore they should also remain stateless, because of probable corruption.
- An ObjRef is created only once during a server's lifetime, and that is used for all subsequent method calls.

While the preceding holds true for server-activated remote objects, this is not the case for client-activated objects. But before proceeding, it was stated earlier that a real proxy could be customized. This is also true of ObjRef, by inheriting and overriding any of its virtual properties or methods.

A Client-Activated Example

The projects are in the Sample1 folder. The two console applications are ClientActivatedServerExe and ClientActivatedClientExe. Again, add a reference to System.Runtime.Remoting.dll and SimpleObjectLib.dll. SimpleObject has remained unchanged, so we need not bother with the code. Notice that the protocol has been changed to TcpServerChannel and TcpClientChannel. The server's output is shown in Figure 25.6.

```
F:\Remoting_Projects\Sample1\ClientActivatedServerExe\bin\Debug\ClientActivatedServerExe.exe
Press spacebar & <enter> to exit.
In SimpleObject constructor.
In SimpleObject.ConCatString method.
In SimpleObject constructor.
In SimpleObject.ConCatString method.
```

Figure 25.6: The ClientActivatedServerExe Output

Listing 25.4—The ClientActivatedServerExe Code

```csharp
using System.Runtime.Remoting.Channels.Tcp;

namespace ClientActivatedServerExe
{
        class ClientActivatedServer
        {
                static void Main(string[] args)
                {
                TcpServerChannel tcp = null;

                        tcp = new TcpServerChannel( 1234);
                        ChannelServices.RegisterChannel( tcp);

                        RemotingConfiguration.ApplicationName = "Simple";
                        RemotingConfiguration.RegisterActivatedServiceType(
                                                typeof(SimpleObject));

                        Console.WriteLine(
                                        "Press <enter> to exit.");
                        Console.ReadLine();
                }
        }
}
```

This time, a System.Runtime.Remoting.Channels.Tcp.TcpServerChannel is created and registered (see Listing 25.4). The RemotingConfiguration.ApplicationName is Simple, which specifies the URI. In this scenario, server registration of a client-activated object using RemotingConfiguration employs the RegisterActivatedServiceType() method. Then the server waits for a client to connect.

Figure 25.7: The ClientActivatedClientExe

Listing 25.5—The ClientActivatedClientExe Code

```
static int Main(string[] args)
{
        TcpClientChannel tcp = null;

        tcp = new TcpClientChannel();
        ChannelServices.RegisterChannel( tcp);
        UrlAttribute[] urls = new UrlAttribute[1];
        UrlAttribute   url = new UrlAttribute(
              "tcp://localhost:1234/Simple");
        ObjectHandle   handle = null;

        urls[0] = url;
        handle = Activator.CreateInstance( "SimpleObjectLib",
                             "SimpleObjectLib.SimpleObject",
                             urls);
        SimpleObject    simple1 = null;
        string          ret = null;

        simple1 = (SimpleObject)handle.Unwrap();
        ret = simple1.ConCatString( "using", "Activator.CreateInstance");
        Console.WriteLine( ret);

        SimpleObject simple2 = null;

        RemotingConfiguration.RegisterActivatedClientType(
                             typeof(SimpleObject),
                             "tcp://localhost:1234/Simple");

        simple2 = new SimpleObject();
        ret = simple2.ConCatString( "using new", "operator");
        Console.WriteLine( ret);

        return( 0);
}
```

The client code in Listing 25.5 uses Activator.CreateInstance() and the *new* operator to create instances of SimpleObject. Notice that CreateInstance() returns a System.Runtime.Remoting.ObjectHandle rather than a transparent proxy. To obtain the proxy, Unwrap() must be called before accessing SimpleObject's method. The second instance of the SimpleObject proxy is created after calling RemotingConfiguration's RegisterActivatedClientType() method. The client's output can be seen in Figure 25.7.

Under the Covers: Part 2

As in the first example, Listing 25.2, the server creates and registers its channels. When it registers the remote object with remoting configuration, no mode is specified, only the type. This is because the client controls the lifetime of each instance through leasing, discussed later in this chapter. This also means that the client-activated remote objects can have state.

Upon calling RegisterActivatedServiceType(), with the aid of ITrackingHandler, an ObjRef of ActivationListener type is marshaled. This class isn't listed in the .NET class library under the System.Runtime.Remoting.Activation namespace, but it can be found, using the MSIL Disassembler, in the mscorlib.dll in the Activation namespace. It implements the System.Runtime.Remoting.IActivator interface and contains channel and SimpleObject information.

Once the client has started up, compare the server output of Figures 25.3 and 25.6 (duplicated in Figures 25.8 and 25.9).

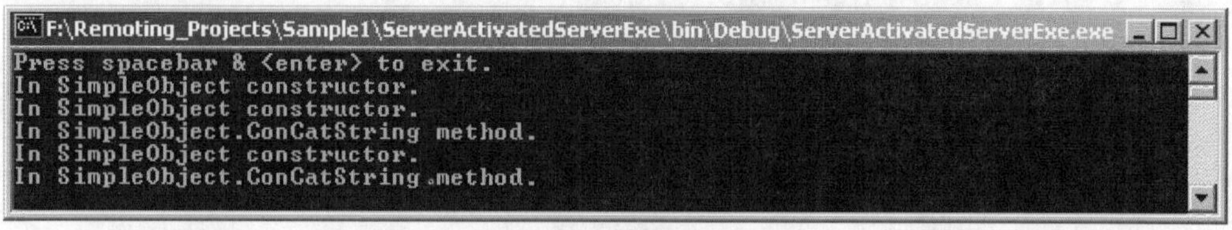

Figure 25.8: Server Output Shown Again

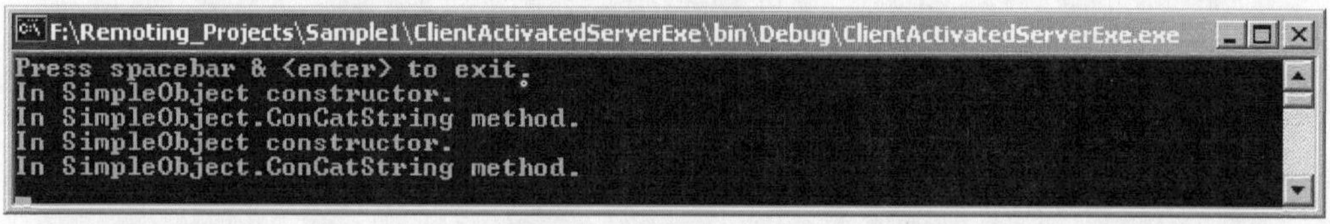

Figure 25.9: Server Output Shown Again

Notice on the server's console screen that the SimpleObject constructor for client-activated objects is called for each creation request. This is also true for the CreateObjRef() method. Remember that server-activated objects require a single ObjRef during the lifetime of the server. Because a client controls the lifetime of the remote object, each instance of the object requires an ObjRef. Using ITrackingHandler, we discover that an ObjRef is marshaled by the server and streamed to the client, where it is unmarshaled to create a transparent proxy. This happens each time the client activates SimpleObject. Also, unlike server-activated objects, which activate the remote objects only when method calls are made, client-activated objects are activated when Activator.CreateInstance() or *new* is called.

Remote Object Lifetime

Unexpected loss of remote connections has been a fact of life since the advent of network communications. Countless lines of code have been written to make endpoints aware of a dropped connection and to recover—either with a reconnection or a graceful shutdown.

DCOM uses a "ping" mechanism. The client pings the server at regular intervals. If the server doesn't receive notification from the client in a specified time, it determines the client has disconnected, for whatever reason, and is free to clean up resources held for the client. How does the .NET Remoting Framework handle a dropped connection?

In the client's application domain, the answer is easy. Once the remote connection disappears, a call on a method or property causes an exception to be thrown. Catch the exception and handle it in some prescibed manner. The exception may be a System.Net.WebException or a System.Runtime.Remoting.RemotingException.

What happens with client-activated remote objects on the server? How does the server detect that the client is no longer alive? The .NET Remoting solution is a form of lease management called Leasing Distributed Garbage Collector (LDGC). Leases implement the System.Runtime.Remoting.Lifetime.ILease interface, which contains three configurable properties:

- InitialLeaseTime is the initial lifetime of the remote object. The default setting is five minutes.
- RenewOnCallTime is the amount of time to renew the lease for, after each method call. The default setting is two minutes.
- SponsorshipTimeout is the amount of time the remoting framework waits for a sponsor to become available. The default setting is two minutes.

The default lease values can be changed while the ILease.CurrentState is set to System.Runtime.Remoting.Lifetime.LeaseState.Initial. Once the object has been marshaled, the lease's current state is set to *active*. Any attempt to alter the properties, once the lease is active, will cause an exception to be thrown. When the lease expires, the CurrentLeaseState property is internally set to *expired* and the remote object will be "garbage collected" at some point.

Leases can be renewed in three ways:

- It is automatic when the client calls a method. The lease time is set to the current lease time remaining plus the RenewOnCallTime.
- The client can renew the lease by using the remote object or transparent proxy as a parameter in calling RemotingServices.GetLifetimeService(). This call returns an ILease, which can be used to call Renew ().
- A sponsor is another alternative to lease renewal. The client can use the supplied System.Runtime.Remoting.Lifetime.ClientSponsor or create a sponsor that implements the System.Runtime.Remoting.Lifetime.ISponsor interface. The client registers the sponsor with ILease.Register(). When the remote object's lease expires, the leasing infrastructure calls the sponsor's Renewal(). The sponsor can then specify a new System.Runtime.Remoting.Lifetime.TimeSpan.

The server can change the default leasing values on *all* remote objects by setting the properties on System.Runtime.Remoting.Lifetime.LifetimeServices. Individual remote objects can also set ILease properties by overriding MarshalByRefObject.InitializeLiftetimeService() as shown in Listing 25.6.

Listing 25.6—SimpleObject.cs

```
public override object InitializeLifetimeService()
{
ILease lease = null;

lease = (ILease)base.InitializeLifetimeService();
        if( lease != null)
        {
                lease.InitialLeaseTime = TimeSpan.FromSeconds( 5);
                lease.RenewOnCallTime = TimeSpan.FromSeconds( 5);
                lease.SponsorshipTimeout = TimeSpan.FromSeconds( 5);
        }

        return( lease);
}
```

Leasing and lease management do not apply to server-activated SingleCall-mode remote objects. Remember that they are created and then offered up to the GC on every method call. Microsoft's

Introduction to .NET Remoting Framework, updated July 2001 in the MSDN library, states that server-activated "Singleton objects are also subject to lifetime management." This seems reasonable, and in fact, InitializeLifetimeService() is called in Singleton mode but not in SingleCall mode.

Leasing configuration, as with much in .NET Remoting, also can be accomplished using a configuration file, which we'll look at later in the chapter.

Using Objects as Parameters and Return Types

The example code for this section of the chapter is in the Sample2 folder. This example is a server-activated sample, and the client will not be using the *new* operator, only Activator.GetObject(). The reason for this is to demonstrate the use of interfaces in remoting, and interfaces can't be created. The server has access to the actual implementation, while the client references the interface. Trying to use *new* or Activator.CreateInstance() on the client results in compiler errors. Because of the use of properties, the server will register the remote objects in Singleton mode. In that manner, the objects are able to maintain state. The example consists of a class library (SimpleInterfaceLib) and two console applications (ClientInterfaceExe and ServerInterfaceExe). Don't forget to add references to System.Runtime.Remoting.dll and SimpleInterfaceLib.dll to the console applications.

So far in this chapter, we have looked at remote objects only from a marshal-by-reference perspective. Marshal-by-reference classes *must* inherit from MarsahlByRefObject. In this section we also look at another type of remotable object, marshal by value. Marshal-by-value classes are declared by using the [Serializable] attribute or implementing the System.Runtime.Serialization.ISerializable interface. These objects are copied (serialized) across the wire and are reconstituted at the other end (deserialized). The objects are independent of each other, and modifying one doesn't change the other.

The SimpleInterfaceLib code is shown in Listing 25.7.

Listing 25.7—SimpleInterface.cs

```
using System;
using System.Collections;

namespace SimpleInterfaceLib
{
        public interface ISimpleInterface
        {
                string this[int index]{ get;}
                ArrayList Names{ set;}

                SimpleMarshal InvokeMethod( ref SimpleParam param);
        }
}
```

The areas of note here are the use of the *this* and the *ref* keywords. The this keyword, in this context, is used as an indexer. The ref keyword means that any changes to *param* in the InvokeMethod will be reflected in the original object. There is also an *out* keyword, not used here, as a parameter modifier. If we were using the out keyword, in this case, param would be passed in as a null, and the object would be created on the server and assigned to param.

Listing 25.8—SimpleMarshal.cs and SimpleParam.cs

```
public class SimpleMarshal : MarshalByRefObject
{
        private string name = null;
        public SimpleMarshal()
        {
```

```
                Console.WriteLine( "In SimpleMarshal constructor");
        }

        public string Name
        {
                get
                {
                        Console.WriteLine( "SimpleMarshal.Name.get");
                        return( name);
                }
                set
                {
                        Console.WriteLine( "SimpleMarshal.Name.set");
                        name = value;
                }
        }
}

[Serializable]
public class SimpleParam
{
        private ArrayList arrayNames = null;
        public SimpleParam()
        {
        }
        public ArrayList ArrayNames
        {
                get
                {
                        Console.WriteLine( "SimpleParam.ArrayNames.get");
                        return( arrayNames);

                }
                set
                {
                        Console.WriteLine( "SimpleParam.ArrayNames.set");
                        arrayNames = value;
                }
        }
}
```

In Listing 25.8 the SimpleMarshal class derives from MarshalByRefObject. The SimpleParam class definition uses the [Serializable] attribute. The ISerializable interface could have been used in place of the attribute. Running this code on the server, results in the output shown in Figure 25.8.

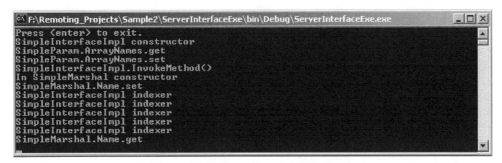

Figure 25.8: ServerInterfaceExe Output

Listing 25.9—ServerInterfaceExe.cs

```
namespace ServerInterfaceExe
{
        class ServerInterface
        {
```

```csharp
        static int Main(string[] args)
        {
        HttpChannel http = null;

                http = new HttpChannel( 1234);
                ChannelServices.RegisterChannel( http);

                RemotingConfiguration.RegisterWellKnownServiceType(
                        typeof(SimpleInterfaceImpl),
                        "InterfaceImpl",
                        WellKnownObjectMode.Singleton);

                Console.WriteLine(
                        "Press <enter> to exit.");
                Console.ReadLine();
                return( 0);
        }
}

public class SimpleInterfaceImpl : MarshalByRefObject,
                                   ISimpleInterface
{
        private ArrayList arrayNames = new ArrayList();

        public SimpleInterfaceImpl()
                : base()
        {
                Console.WriteLine( "SimpleInterfImpl const");
        }

        public string this[int index]
        {
                get
                {
                string ret = null;

                        if( arrayNames.Count == 0)
                        {
                                ret = "No names in list";
                        }
                        else if( index >= arrayNames.Count)
                        {
                                ret = "Index beyond end of list.";
                        }
                        else
                        {
                                ret = (string)arrayNames[index];
                        }
                        Console.WriteLine( "SimpleInterfImpl indexer");
                        return( ret);
                }
        }
        public ArrayList Names
        {
                set
                {
                        arrayNames = value;
                }
        }
        public SimpleMarshal InvokeMethod( ref SimpleParam param)
        {
        ArrayList arrayTmp = new ArrayList();
        ArrayList arrayParam = null;

                arrayParam = param.ArrayNames;
                for( int x = 0; x < arrayParam.Count; x++)
                {
```

```
                    arrayTmp.Add( arrayParam[x] + " InvokeMethod");
            }
            param.ArrayNames = arrayTmp;
            Console.WriteLine( "SimpleInterfImpl.InvokeMethod()");

        SimpleMarshal paramNew = new SimpleMarshal();

            paramNew.Name =  "SimplMarshal from MarshalByRefObj";
            return( paramNew);
        }
    }
}
```

In the main() in Listing 25.9, the code is essentially the same as in our first example. The only changes have been the use of HttpChannel instead of HttpServerChannel and the switch to Singleton mode. HttpChannel combines the functionality of HttpServerChannel and HttpClientChannel. HttpServerChannel receives messages, while HttpClientChannel sends messages. HttpChannel transports messages in either direction.

Just below the main(), the SimpleInterfaceImpl class is defined. It inherits from MarshalByRefObject and ISimpleInterface, by implementing the indexer and Names properties and the InvokeMethod(). When designing remote objects, it is worth considering generic interfaces for their potential reuse.

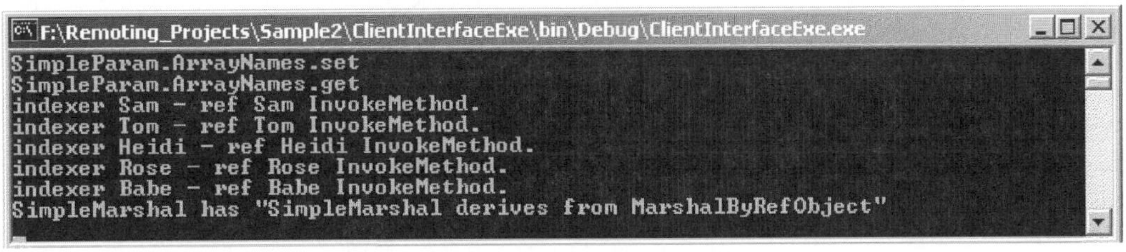

Figure 25.9: ClientInterfaceExe Output

Listing 25.10—ClientInterface.cs

```
static int Main(string[] args)
{
        HttpChannel http = null;

        http = new HttpChannel();
        ChannelServices.RegisterChannel( http);

        ISimpleInterface simple = null;

        simple = (ISimpleInterface)Activator.GetObject(
                            typeof(ISimpleInterface),
                            "http://localhost:1234/InterfaceImpl");

        ArrayList arrayParam = new ArrayList();

        arrayParam.Add( "Sam");
        arrayParam.Add( "Tom");
        arrayParam.Add( "Heidi");
        arrayParam.Add( "Rose");
        arrayParam.Add( "Babe");

        simple.Names - arrayParam;

        SimpleParam param1 = null;

        param1 = new SimpleParam();
```

```
        param1.ArrayNames = (ArrayList)arrayParam.Clone();

        SimpleMarshal param2 = null;

        param2 = simple.InvokeMethod( ref param1);

        ArrayList arrayRet = null;

        arrayRet = param1.ArrayNames;

        for( int x = 0; x < arrayRet.Count; x++)
        {
                Console.WriteLine( "indexer {0} - ref {1}.",
                        simple[x], arrayRet[x]);
        }

        Console.WriteLine( "SimpleMarshal \"{0}\"", param2.Name);
        return( 0);
}
```

In Listing 25.10, the param2 returned by InvokeMethod() is a transparent proxy. The client's output is captured in Figure 25.9.

Events and Delegates in Remoting

Event notification in the remoting framework employs the same paradigm as the rest of the .NET Framework: delegates and events. There are minor differences in construction; and we should point out a constraint before proceeding.

The event originator cannot be registered as a server-activated object in SingleCall mode. Because the object is re-created with each method call, it won't be able to retain a reference to the event's delegate.

The projects are in the Sample3 folder and consist of SimpleEventLib.dll and two console applications, EventServer and EventClient. The delegate, with its method signature, and the event arguments class code are shown in Listing 25.11.

Listing 25.11—RemoteArgs.cs

```
public delegate void RemoteEventHandler(
                    object sender, RemoteArgs args);




[Serializable]
public class RemoteArgs
{
        private string machineName = null;
        private string currentDir  = null;

        internal RemoteArgs()
        {
                machineName = Environment.MachineName;
                currentDir = Environment.CurrentDirectory;
        }

        public string MachineName
        {
                get
                {
                        return( machineName);
                }
```

```
        }

        public string CurrentDir
        {
                get
                {
                        return( currentDir);
                }
        }
}
```

The delegate should come as no surprise; it looks like any other event delegate. The RemoteArgs class doesn't derive from System.EventArgs. To compensate for the lack of an EventArgs parent, the [Serializable] attribute has been attached so it can be marshaled across application domains. The event sink, Listing 25.12, derives from MarshalByRefObject and implements an event handler.

Listing 25.12—SyncRemoteEvent.cs

```
public class SyncRemoteEvent : MarshalByRefObject
{
        public SyncRemoteEvent()
                        : base()
        {
                Console.WriteLine( "In SyncRemoteEvent constructor");
        }


        public virtual void EventHandler(object send,RemoteArgs arg)
        {
                Console.WriteLine();
                Console.WriteLine( "In SyncRemoteEvent.EventHandler");
                Console.WriteLine( "Machine:{0} Dir:{1}",
                                args.MachineName, args.CurrentDir);
                Console.WriteLine();
        }
}
```

SimpleObject has changed very little, except that we have added an event delegate, Listing 25.13.

Listing 25.13—SimpleObject.cs

```
public class SimpleObject : MarshalByRefObject
{
        public event RemoteEventHandler RemoteEvent;
        .
        .
        .
```

In the ConcatString() we insert the event-handling code shown in Listing 25.14 to test whether any remote objects are subscribing to the event. If a subscriber exists, a RemoteArgs instance is created and the event handler is called.

Listing 25.14—SimpleObject.cs

```
public string ConCatString( string first, string second)
{
string concat = null;

Console.WriteLine( "In SimpleObject.ConCatString method.");
        if( RemoteEvent != null)
        {
        RemoteArgs args = null;

                args = new RemoteArgs();
```

```
                        RemoteEvent( this, args);
            }

        concat = first + " " + second;
        return( concat);
    }
}
```

The server creates an HttpChannel to send and receive messages. It registers both server-activated and client-activated SimpleObjects and waits for a client to call a method on the remote object. (See Listing 25.15.)

Listing 25.15—EventServer.cs

```csharp
using System;
using System.Runtime.Remoting;
using System.Runtime.Remoting.Channels;
using System.Runtime.Remoting.Channels.Http;
using SimpleEventLib;

namespace EventServer
{
        class ServerEvent
        {
                static void Main(string[] args)
                {
                HttpChannel http = null;

                        http = new HttpChannel( 1234);
                        ChannelServices.RegisterChannel( http);

                        RemotingConfiguration.RegisterWellKnownServiceType(
                                                    typeof(SimpleObject),
                                                    "Simple",

        WellKnownObjectMode.Singleton);

                        RemotingConfiguration.ApplicationName = "Simple";
                        RemotingConfiguration.RegisterActivatedServiceType(
                                        typeof(SimpleObject));

                        Console.WriteLine( "Press <enter> to exit.");
                        Console.ReadLine();
                }
        }
}
```

Notice that the server-activated registration uses Singleton mode. There is no registration of the SyncRemoteEvent object. Running the server executable produces the output in Figure 25.10, while Figure 25.11 displays the client's output.

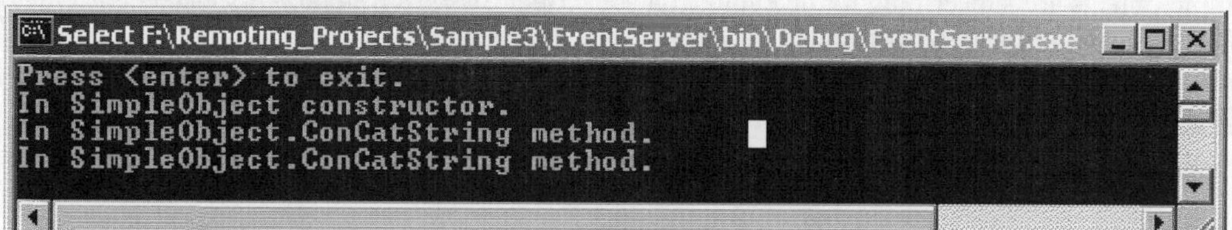

Figure 25.10: EventServer Output

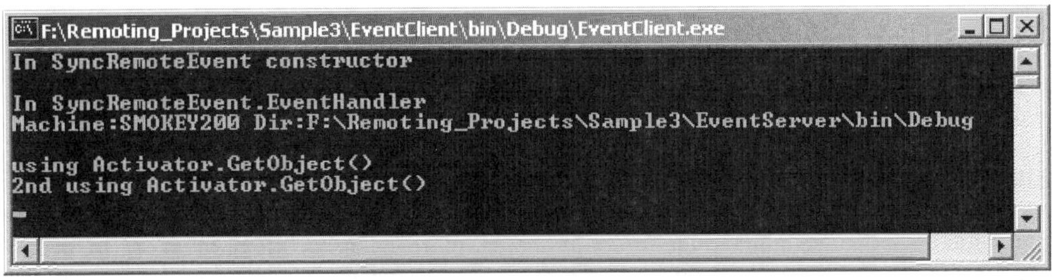

Figure 25.11: EventClient Output

Listing 25.16—EventClient.cs

```
class ClientEvent
{
        public ClientEvent()
        {
                Console.WriteLine( "In ClientEvent constructor");
        }

        static int Main(string[] args)
        {
                SyncRemoteEvent client = null;
                HttpChannel http = null;

                http = new HttpChannel( 2345);
                ChannelServices.RegisterChannel( http);
                //client = (SyncRemoteEvent)ClientEvent.InitClientEvent();
                client = new SyncRemoteEvent();

                SimpleObject simple = null;

                        simple = (SimpleObject)Activator.GetObject(
                        typeof(SimpleObject),
                        "http://localhost:1234/Simple");

                        simple.RemoteEvent +=
                           new RemoteEventHandler( client.EventHandler);

                string ret = null;

                ret = simple.ConCatString( "using", "Activator.GetObject");
                Console.WriteLine( ret);
                simple.RemoteEvent -=
                        new RemoteEventHandler( client.EventHandler);

                ret = simple.ConCatString("2 using","Activator.GetObject");
                Console.WriteLine( ret);
                return( 0);
        }
}
```

The client creates a channel, but in this instance it specifies a port number (see Listing 25.16). The server must have a defined port number to contact the client during the event firing. The event handler is created with a simple *new;* no registration is required. The line commented out above the *new* operator will be discussed later. SimpleObject is a server-activated object because of the Activator.GetObject(). The code for a client-activated remote object could be Activator.CreateInstance() or as follows:

```
RemotingConfiguration.RegisterActivatedClientType(
typeof(SimpleObject),
"http://localhost:1234/Simple");
```

```
simple = new SimpleObject();
```

The client then subscribes to the event and calls SimpleObject.ConcatString(); it then unsubscribes and makes a subsequent call to ConcatString().

While experimenting with remote events, we made an interesting discovery. As the code stands now, the event is fired from within the server's application domain to the client's. The client doesn't actually intercept the event unless the server has some reference to it. If, for example, ClientEvent was derived from SyncRemoteEvent, an exception would be thrown when it is registered with SimpleObject's event delegate—that is, unless the remoting framework is tricked into thinking it is dealing with a SyncRemoteEvent rather than a ClientEvent object. Deceiving the framework results in output such as that shown in Figure 25.12.

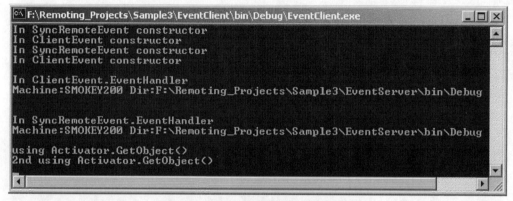

Figure 25.12: Event Client Output

Listing 25.17—EventClient.cs

```csharp
class ClientEvent : SyncRemoteEvent
{
        public ClientEvent()
                : base()
        {
                Console.WriteLine( "In ClientEvent constructor");
        }



        private static object InitClientEvent()
        {
                SyncRemoteEvent client = null;

                RemotingConfiguration.RegisterWellKnownServiceType(
                        typeof(ClientEvent),
                        "Event",
                        WellKnownObjectMode.SingleCall);

                client = (SyncRemoteEvent)Activator.GetObject(
                        typeof(SyncRemoteEvent),
                        "http://localhost:2345/Event");

                return( (object)client);
        }

        public override void EventHandler( object sender,
                                        RemoteArgs args)
        {
                Console.WriteLine();
```

```
        Console.WriteLine( "In ClientEvent.EventHandler");
        Console.WriteLine( "Machine:{0} Dir:{1}",
                                args.MachineName, args.CurrentDir);
        Console.WriteLine();
        base.EventHandler( sender, args);
    }
}
```

The first step in accomplishing direct event interception is to make the EventHandler() in SyncRemoteEvent a virtual method. Then, override the method in ClientEvent. Duping the framework takes place in the static method InitClientEvent(). Register the server-activated object as a type of ClientEvent in either SingleCall or Singleton mode. Then, Activator.GetObject() returns a transparent proxy of the requested type, SyncRemoteEvent. If you look at the output, a ClientEvent instance is created, but the proxy has been downcast to a SyncRemoteEvent instance. The result is that the server doesn't have any reference to ClientEvent. No exception is thrown during registration with the event delegate. Because the EventHandler() is virtual, the proper method is called. Experimenting with this as a client-activated object resulted in failure, no matter what twists and contortions were taken.

Call Contexts

The CallContext class can be thought of as "out-of-band" data or a channel hook. It operates at a thread level within an application domain. To cross application domain boundaries, objects must derive from the System.Runtime.Remoting.Messaging.ILogicalThreadAffinative interface, see Listing 25.18. An object registers with CallContext using the "key/value" paradigm. It is hooked to each method call and is part of IMessage, the __CallContext entry, which is sent over the wire. Using CallContext is simply a matter of calling the static methods SetData() and GetData().

The projects for this example are in the Sample4 folder. There is a standard library (CallContextLib) and two console applications (CallContextServer and CallContextClient). RemoteContextInfo is the class that will contain the out-of-band data. Figures 25.13 and 25.14 are the client and server output, respectively.

Listing 25.18—RemoteContextInfo.cs

```
[Serializable]
public class RemoteContextInfo : ILogicalThreadAffinative
{
        private string machineName = null;
        private string clientDir = null;

        public RemoteContextInfo()
        {
                machineName = Environment.MachineName;
                clientDir = Environment.CurrentDirectory;
        }
        public string MachineName
        {
                get
                {
                        return( machineName);
                }
        }
        public string ClientDir
        {
                get
                {
                        return( clientDir);
                }
        }
}
```

To get and set the call context data, simply use the following code:

```
RemoteContextInfo data = null;

data = new RemoteContextInfo();
CallContext.SetData( "Client", data);

RemoteContextInfo data = (RemoteContextInfo)CallContext.GetData( "Client");
```

Figure 25.13: Client Output

Figure 25.14: Server Output

This is an ideal way for custom proxies or message sinks to pass information from the client to the server or vice versa, without intruding into the functionality of the application.

.NET Remoting Configuration

Remoting configuration files, like other configuration files in .NET, are Extensible Markup Language (XML) files that use the .config extension. Configuration files can be used in remoting in lieu of source code creation and registration. In the examples so far, there hasn't been a desperate need for configuration files, but as we get into customized sinks, the amount and complexity of code required to create and register remote objects increases dramatically. Configuration files also permit configuration changes without code changes.

The naming convention for remoting configuration files is the executable program name and extension, with a .config extension. Thus, for ClientActivatedServerExe.exe, the configuration file would be named ClientActivatedServerExe.exe.config. At this point, it should be evident that less wordy project names are a good idea! The location of the configuration file must be in the same directory as the executable file.

The configuration files are located in the Samples1 with the source files in the directories of the four executable files. They should be moved to the respective "bin\debug" directories.

Listing 25.19 is an example of the configuration file for ClientActivatedServerExe. The XML declaration tag <?xml version="1.0 ?>, although not required by the XML specification, will be used in all examples, because of convention.

Listing 25.19—ClientActivatedServerExe.exe.config

```
<?xml version="1.0" ?>
    <configuration>
```

```
<system.runtime.remoting>
    <application name="Simple">
        <service>
            <activated type="SimpleObjectLib.SimpleObject,
        SimpleObjectLib"/>
        </service>
        <channels>
            <channel ref="TCP Server" name="Client
    Activated Tcp Server" port="1234"/>
            </channel>
        </channels>
    </application>
</system.runtime.remoting>
</configuration>
```

This is the server's configuration file, and like all .NET configuration files, the root element is <configuration>. Remoting configuration is placed in the subelement <system.runtime.remoting>. This is a configuration for a client-activated object. The <application> tag contains the optional *name* attribute that identifies the URI of the remote object. If we dropped the name attribute, the client's configuration tag, below, would have to be changed to <client url="tcp://localhost:1234">.

The two subelements of <application> are <service> and <channels>. An optional subelement is a <lifetime> tag. This defines the leasing lifetime of all remote objects on the server.

The <service> tag contains information about the remote objects and is a server-specific element. The <channels> tag is common to both client and server configuration and contains information about the channels to be used by the remote object. Both of these elements can encapsulate multiple remote objects and channels.

The <activated> element identifies the remote object as being client activated. The *type* attribute gives the remote object's name and assembly. Two optional attributes deal with leasing, *leasetime* and *renewoncall*. These can be used to override the default time associated with those leasing properties.

The <channel> tag on the server contains two attributes. The *type* attribute, as with the other type attributes discussed so far, names the channel type and the assembly to be used. The *port* attribute indicates the port the channel will listen on.

Listing 25.20—ClientActivatedClientExe.exe.config.

```
<?xml version="1.0" ?>
    <configuration>
        <system.runtime.remoting>
            <application name="ClientActivatedClientExe">
                <client url="tcp://localhost:1234/Simple">
                    <activated
            type="SimpleObjectLib.SimpleObject, SimpleObjectLib"/>
                </client>
            </application>
        </system.runtime.remoting>
    </configuration>
```

The client configuration file (see Listing 25.20) is very similar to the server's. The primary difference is the server's <service> tag counterpart, the <client> tag. The <client> element contains the *url* attribute, which, as always, identifies the location of the remote object. Using configuration files in source code is straightforward.

Listing 25.21—ClientActivatedServer.cs

```
static void Main(string[] args)
{
string file = "ClientActivatedServerExe.exe.config";
        RemotingConfiguration.Configure( file);
}
```

Simply call RemotingConfiguration.Configure() with the name of the configuration file as a
parameter (see Listing 25.21). *Remember* that the configuration file must be in the same directory as
the executable file, or the path must be included in the configuration file's name parameter. To see
that the channel has been created and that channel and remote object have been registered, you can
use the RegisteredChannels property from ChannelServices and the RemotingConfiguration's
GetRegisteredActivatedServiceTypes() method.

The server-activated example (see Listing 25.22) demonstrates another facet of remoting
configuration files, the *template*.

Listing 25.22—ServerActivatedServerExe.exe.config

```
<?xml version="1.0" ?>
        <configuration>
                <system.runtime.remoting>
                        <channels>
                                <channel id="Http Server"
                                name="Server Activated"
        type="System.Runtime.Remoting.Channels.Http.HttpServerChannel,
                                        System.Runtime.Remoting"
                                port="1234"/>
                        </channels>
                        <application name="ServerActivatedServerExe">
                                <service>
                                        <wellknown
                                        mode="SingleCall"
        type="SimpleObjectLib.SimpleObject, SimpleObjectLib"
                                        objectUri="Simple">
                                        </wellknown>
                                </service>
                                <channels>
                                        <channel ref="Http Server"/>
                                </channels>
                        </application>
                </system.runtime.remoting>
        </configuration>
```

We have used a template for the <channels> element. How is this benefical? The *id* attribute in the
<channel> element provides a label that can be referred to in the <application> section. Notice, also,
the template is outside the body of the <application>. The <channel> tag attribute *ref* is the link to
channel information. This allows us to create a common file for both the server and the client. In the
example in Listing 25.22, the template is in the same file, but in the real world, the scenario would
likely be in the format shown in Listings 25.23 and 25.24.

Listing 25.23—The Common Template Configuration File

```
<?xml version="1.0" ?>
        <configuration>
                <system.runtime.remoting>
                        <channels>
                                <channel id="Http Server"
                                name="Server Activated"
        type="System.Runtime.Remoting.Channels.Http.HttpServerChannel,
                                        System.Runtime.Remoting"/>
```

```
            </channels>
        </system.runtime.remoting>
    </configuration>
```

Listing 25.24—The Server's Configuration File

```
<?xml version="1.0" ?>
    <configuration>
        <system.runtime.remoting>
            <application name="ServerActivatedServerExe">
                <service>
                    <wellknown
                    mode="SingleCall"
                    type="SimpleObjectLib.SimpleObject,
                            SimpleObjectLib"
                    objectUri="Simple">
                    </wellknown>
                </service>
                <channels>
                    <channel ref="Http Server" port="1234"/>
                </channels>
            </application>
        </system.runtime.remoting>
    </configuration>
```

To access these two files is simply a matter of calling as follows:

```
        RemotingConfiguration.Configure( template configuration file name);
```
and
```
        RemotingConfiguration.Configure( server's configuration file name);
```

RemotingConfiguration reads the directives in the template and applies them to the <application> segment whenever it encounters a *ref* attribute. The usefulness of this approach will become evident when configuring custom channel sink providers, discussed later in the chapter.

Server-activated objects (Listing 25.24) are distinguished from client-activated objects by the <activated> element's corresponding tag <wellknown>. The <wellknown> element's attributes *mode, type,* and *objectUri* mirror the parameters in earlier source code. It should be apparent that this is a server configuration file from the <service> tag.

The examples in this chapter were initially coded using Visual Studio .NET Beta2. RemotingConfiguration.Configure behaves differently in the release candidate. Listing 25.22 executed as expected in Beta2, loading the remoting DLL located in the global assembly cache (GAC). The release candidate, however, threw a "File Not Found" exception. This was unexpected behavior for an assembly in the GAC. To overcome this, highlight the remoting DLL and change Copy Local in properties to *true*.

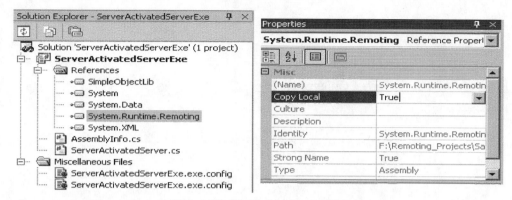

Figure 25.15: Project Properties

The client configuration file for server-activated objects differs only slightly from the client-activated configuration (see Listing 25.25).

Listing 25.25—ServerActivatedClientExe.exe.config

```xml
<?xml version="1.0" ?>
      <configuration>
            <system.runtime.remoting>
                  <application name="ServerActivatedClientExe">
                        <client url="http://localhost:1234/Simple">
                              <wellknown
                              type="SimpleObjectLib.SimpleObject,
                                    SimpleObjectLib"
                              url="http://localhost:1234/Simple">
                              </wellknown>
                        </client>
                        <channels>
                              <channel ref="Http Client"/>
                        </channels>
                  </application>
            </system.runtime.remoting>
      </configuration>
```

The <wellknown> tag contains the ever-present *type* attribute. The additional *url* attribute seems redundant because of the <client> element *url* attribute. Don't be misled. The <wellknown> element's *url* attribute is mandatory, whereas in this case the <client> element's *url* is optional.

Remoting over the Web

It is also possible for Internet Information Server (IIS) to host remote objects. The Web-hosting example is in the Sample1 folder. The console client project is named WebClientExe.

To use IIS as a server, you must take a number of steps:

- The remote object must be server activated.
- Map a virtual directory, on the Web server, to the SimpleObjectLib folder.
- The remote object can't be programmatically configured. It must use a web.config file in the virtual directory's root, see Listing 25.26.

Listing 25.26—Web.config

```xml
<?xml version="1.0" ?>
<configuration>
      <system.runtime.remoting>
```

```
                <application>
                        <service>
                                <wellknown
                                        mode="SingleCall"
                                        type="SimpleObjectLib.SimpleObject,
                                                        SimpleObjectLib"
                                        objectUri="Simple.rem">
                                </wellknown>
                        </service>
                        <channels>
                                <channel
                                        name="Server-Activated Web Client"
                                        type="System.Runtime.Remoting.Channels.
                                                Http.HttpChannel,
                                                System.Runtime.Remoting"/>
                        </channels>
                </application>
        </system.runtime.remoting>
</configuration>
```

You should be aware of a number of items in the configuration file:

- No port number need be specified, as IIS has already been configured to listen on a port, normally port 80.
- The *objectUri* attribute in the *wellknown* element must use the extension .rem or .soap.

The client code remains the same as previous server-activated examples (see Listing 25.27). The client output is shown in Figure 25.16.

Listing 25.27—WebClient.cs

```
        ChannelServices.RegisterChannel( new HttpChannel());

        SimpleObject simple = null;

        simple = (SimpleObject)Activator.GetObject(
                        typeof(SimpleObject),
                        "http://localhost/WebRemoting/Simple.rem");

        string ret = null;

        ret = simple.ConCatString( "using the",
                                        "Web for remoting.");
```

Figure 25.16: WebClientExe Output

Channel Sinks

The examples for this section are in the Sample5 folder. Two projects—CustomSinkLib and SimpleObjectForSinkLib—are libraries. The client and server console projects are SinkClientExe and SinkServerExe respectively. Each of the console projects requires references to System.Runtime.Remoting.dll, SimpleObjectForSinkLib.dll, and CustomSinkLib.dll.

Channel sinks are the means by which messages are passed back and forth between the client and server. Earlier in the chapter, call contexts were explored as a device to transparently pass data across the wire. A channel sink can be an alternative way to achieve the same end. But sinks are not limited to that single function. The HTTP and TCP channels, provided by .NET, have two default sinks in the sink chain—a formatter and a transport sink. The formatter converts an IMessage into a stream, while the transporter streams the data across the wire. Each does a discrete unit of work and hands the result to the next sink in the chain.

The .NET Framework does not restrict the number of links in a sink chain. The sink chain can be viewed as a functional linked list, rather than a linked list of data. Depending on the problem domain, one to many sinks are plugged into a channel's chain, with each sink addressing a single task. This may include logging, security functions, encryption, or any other task that is required on the route from the transparent proxy to the remote object. To become a member of a sink chain, certain criteria must be met.

All channels are divided into senders and receivers. Receivers are generally servers, while senders are clients. Channel sinks can be seen in the same light. They are connected to a channel by a sink provider, either a System.Runtime.Remoting.Channels.IClientChannelSinkProvider or an IServerChannelSinkProvider.

Listing 25.28—ClientSinkProvider.cs

```
public class ClientSinkProvider : IClientChannelSinkProvider
{
private IClientChannelSinkProvider next = null;

    public ClientSinkProvider()
    {
    }

    public ClientSinkProvider( IDictionary props,
                               ICollection provider)
    {
    }

    public IClientChannelSink CreateSink( IChannelSender sender,
                                          string url,
                                          object  channelData)
    {
IClientChannelSink sink = null;

        if( next != null)
        {
                sink = next.CreateSink( sender, url, channelData);
        }

        if( sink != null)
        {
                sink = new ClientSink( sink);
        }
        return( sink);
    }

    public IClientChannelSinkProvider Next
    {
        get
        {
                return( next);
        }
        set
        {
                next = value;
```

```
                        }
                }
        }
}
```

Deriving from the IClientChannelSinkProvider interface, described in Listing 25.28, requires implementing the CreateSink method and the Next property. The server provider code, not shown, in ServerSinkProvider.cs is the same, except for an additional method, GetChannelData(), which has a System.Runtime.Remoting.Channels.IChannelDataStore parameter.

Notice in CreateSink() that if there is a next provider, its CreateSink() is called before the current provider instantiates its sink. In other words, the last provider is the first to create an actual sink and starts the process where the sinks are chained together. It is also evident that as soon as the provider creates its sink, it could be a candidate for disposal, as it has no knowledge of the sink once instantiation is complete.

The order in which providers are attached to a channel determines the order of the sink chain. On the server, the first sink must be the transport sink, and the last must the formatter sink. On the client the order is reversed. If the order is incorrect, results are unpredictable! Sink providers are attached to a channel via a configuration file or programmatically. The order of creation will be clearer with some example code. (See Listing 25.29.)

Listing 25.29—SinkClient.cs

```
Hashtable                         channelData = new Hashtable();
Hashtable                         properties = new Hashtable();
ArrayList                         providerData = new ArrayList();
ClientSinkProvider                clientProvider = null;
ServerSinkProvider                serverProvider = null;
SoapClientFormatterSinkProvider clientFormatter = null;
SoapServerFormatterSinkProvider serverFormatter = null;
MyHttpChannel                     http = null;

clientFormatter = new SoapClientFormatterSinkProvider( properties,
                                                       providerData);
clientProvider = new ClientSinkProvider( properties, providerData);
clientFormatter.Next = clientProvider;

serverProvider = new ServerSinkProvider( properties, providerData);
serverFormatter = new SoapServerFormatterSinkProvider( properties,
                                                       providerData);
serverProvider.Next = serverFormatter;

http = new MyHttpChannel( channelData, clientFormatter, serverProvider);
```

The client creates the SOAP formatter and then the customized provider, which is assigned to the clientFormatter.Next property. The server's order of creation and assignment is reversed. Because MyHttpChannel inherits from HttpChannel, both sender and receiver sinks are required. During construction of the channel, the transport sinks are created and placed in the appropriate position in their respective chains.

Listing 25.30—Shared.config

```
<?xml version="1.0" ?>
    <configuration>
        <system.runtime.remoting>
            <channels>
                <channel id="http"
            type="CustomSinkLib.MyHttpChannel, CustomSinkLib">
                </channel>
            </channels>
            <channelSinkProviders>
```

```
                          <clientProviders>
                                  <formatter id="soap"
                                  type="System.Runtime.Remoting.Channels.

SoapClientFormatterSinkProvider,

                                                  System.Runtime.Remoting"/>
                                  <provider id="custom"
                                  type="CustomSinkLib.ClientSinkProvider,
                                                  CustomSinkLib"/>
                                  </clientProviders>
                                  <serverProviders>
                                          <formatter id="soap"
                          type="System.Runtime.Remoting.Channels.

SoapServerFormatterSinkProvider,

System.Runtime.Remoting"/>
                                          <provider id="custom"
                          type="CustomSinkLib.ServerSinkProvider,
                                          CustomSinkLib"/>
                                  </serverProviders>
                          </channelSinkProviders>
                  </system.runtime.remoting>
          </configuration>
```

The server and client configuration files are shown in Listings 25.31 and 25.32, while a common configuration file is shown in Figure 25.30. The server's provider is listed ahead of the formatter. Not shown, but present nonetheless, is the transporter. The Http and Tcp namespaces supply a client transport sink provider and transport sink as private classes in System.Runtime.Remoting.dll. It is worth noting that the Http and Tcp servers don't have a transport sink provider, simply a transport sink, which has the variable name transportSink.

Listing 25.31—SinkServerExe.exe.config

```
<?xml version="1.0" ?>
      <configuration>
            <system.runtime.remoting>
                  <application>
                        <service>
                              <wellknown
                  type="SimpleObjectForSinkLib.SimpleObject,
                                  SimpleObjectForSinkLib"
                  mode="Singleton"
                  objectUri="Simple"/>
                        </service>
                        <channels>
                              <channel ref="http" port="1234">
                                    <serverProviders>
                                          <provider ref="custom"/>
                                          <formatter ref="soap"/>
                                    </serverProviders>
                              </channel>
                        </channels>
                  </application>
            </system.runtime.remoting>
      </configuration>
```

If it were a requirement that the server send as well as receive, it would be a simple matter to place the following code within the <channel> element, as shown in Listing 25.32:

```
<clientProviders>
        <formatter ref="soap"/>
        <provider ref="custom"/>
</clientProviders>
```

Listing 25.32—SinkClientExe.exe.config

```xml
<?xml version="1.0" ?>
    <configuration>
        <system.runtime.remoting>
            <application>
                <client>
                    <wellknown
        type="SimpleObjectForSinkLib.SimpleObject,
                SimpleObjectForSinkLib"
        url="http://localhost:1234/Simple"/>
                </client>
                <channels>
                    <channel ref="http">
                        <clientProviders>
                            <formatter ref="soap"/>
                            <provider ref="custom"/>
                        </clientProviders>
                    </channel>
                </channels>
            </application>
        </system.runtime.remoting>
    </configuration>
```

In the client's configuration file the formatter is first, followed by the provider. Now that sink ordering is clearer, it is a good point to examine when objects are created. The server is considered first (see Listing 25.33).

Listing 25.33—SinkServer.cs

```
RemotingConfiguration.Configure( "shared.config");
RemotingConfiguration.Configure( "SinkServerExe.exe.config");
```

Earlier in the chapter, we noted that the server's channel listens for requests upon creation, so it should come as no surprise that sink providers and sinks are created at the outset. The call RemotingConfiguration.Configure() with the shared.config file name, which is only a template, triggers nothing. The call using SinkServerExe.exe.config begins the process of instantiation. First, the provider constructors are called, followed by the channel constructor. In the channel's constructor, the provider CreateSink() methods are called, which create their sinks. When the channel constructor returns, the channel is ready to accept requests. The client, on the other hand, is not quite as straightforward. The second call to Configure() in Listing 25.34 creates the providers and the channel. Only with the *new* SimpleObject() instantiation are the providers' CreateSink() methods called.

Listing 25.34—SinkClient.cs

```
static int Main(string[] args)
{
    RemotingConfiguration.Configure( "shared.config");
    RemotingConfiguration.Configure( "SinkClientExe.exe.config");

SimpleObject simple = null;

    simple = new SimpleObject();

string ret = null;

    ret = simple.ConCatString( "Custom", "sink");
    Console.WriteLine( ret);
    return( 0);
}
```

Now that the sink chain has been created, what function do the sinks actually perform? Sinks derive from either System.Runtime.Remoting.Channels.IServerChannelSink or IClientChannelSink interfaces, depending on whether they are senders or receivers. Each implements ProcessMessage() and AsyncProcessResponse() methods and the *get* NextChannelSink property, as well as the System.Runtime.Remoting.Channels.IChannelSinkBase.Properties property. The server also implements GetResponseStream(), while the client implements GetRequestStream() and AsyncProcessRequest(). The first client sink must also implement System.Runtime.Remoting.Messaging.IMessageSink. The interface defines SyncProcessMessage() and AsyncProcessMessage(). One of these methods is called by RealProxy to initiate a remote call to the server.

Listings 25.35 and 25.36 are only a partial source code listing. The ProcessMessage() is the method of primary interest.

Listing 25.35—ServerSink.cs

```
internal class ServerSink : IServerChannelSink
{
        private IServerChannelSink     next = null;

        public ServerSink( IServerChannelSink next)
              : base()
        {
              this.next = next;
        }

        public ServerProcessing ProcessMessage(
                                  IServerChannelSinkStack      stack,
                                  IMessage                            reqMsg,
                                  ITransportHeaders           reqHdrs,
                                  Stream                      reqStrm,
                                  out IMessage                msg,
                                  out ITransportHeaders       respHdrs,
                                  out Stream
        respStrm)
        {
              Console.WriteLine( "In ServerSink.ProcessMessage()");

              SinkHelper helper = null;

              helper = new SinkHelper();
              helper.WriteTransportHeaders( reqHdrs,
                                           "Transport Request Headers");

              ServerProcessing process;

              stack.Push( this, null);
              process = next.ProcessMessage( stack, reqMsg, reqHdrs,
                          reqStrm, out msg, out respHdrs, out respStrm);
              helper.WriteTransportHeaders( respHdrs,
                                           "Transport Response Headers");

              respHdrs["ServerSide"] = "In ServerSink.ProcessMessage()";

              switch( process)
              {

                      case ServerProcessing.Complete:
                      {
                              stack.Pop( this);
                              break;
```

```
                }
                case ServerProcessing.OneWay:
                {
                        stack.Pop( this);
                        break;
                }
                case ServerProcessing.Async:
                {
                        stack.Store( this, null);
                        break;
                }
            }

            return( process);
        }
    }
}
```

Listing 25.36—ClientSink.cs

```
internal class ClientSink : IClientChannelSink
{
        private IClientChannelSink    next = null;

        public ClientSink( IClientChannelSink next)
            : base()
        {
            this.next = next;
        }

        public void ProcessMessage(
                        IMessage                      msg,
                        ITransportHeaders      reqHdrs,
                        Stream                     reqStrm,
                        out ITransportHeaders  respHdrs,
                        out Stream                     respStrm)
        {
            Console.WriteLine( "In ClientSink.ProcessMessage");

            SinkHelper helper = null;

            helper = new SinkHelper();

            helper.WriteTransportHeaders( reqHdrs,
                                    "Transport Request Headers");

            reqHdrs["ClientSide"] = "In ClientSink.ProcessMessage";

            next.ProcessMessage( msg, reqHdrs,
                                    reqStrm, out respHdrs, out respStrm);

            helper.WriteTransportHeaders( respHdrs,
                                    "Transport Response Headers");
        }
}
```

The client's ProcessMessage() has as one of its parameters an IMessage object. At this stage it is informational only, because the formatter has already converted the message to a stream, reqStrm. In this example, the custom sink adds a key/value pair—reqHdrs["ClientSide"] = "In ClientSink.ProcessMessage"—to the transport headers and passes it on to the next sink in the chain. The server responds with two *out* parameters, which are the response headers and streamed return value.

The server code is much the same, forwarding the message to the next sink. The points to highlight are the *stack* parameter and the *return* enumeration from ProcessMessage(). The

System.Runtime.Remoting.Channels.ServerProcessing enumeration describes how the message was processed. As with the client, the IMessage is unused. The stack is a means of keeping track of the sink order during asynchronous remoting. Finally, the server adds a key/value to the response headers.

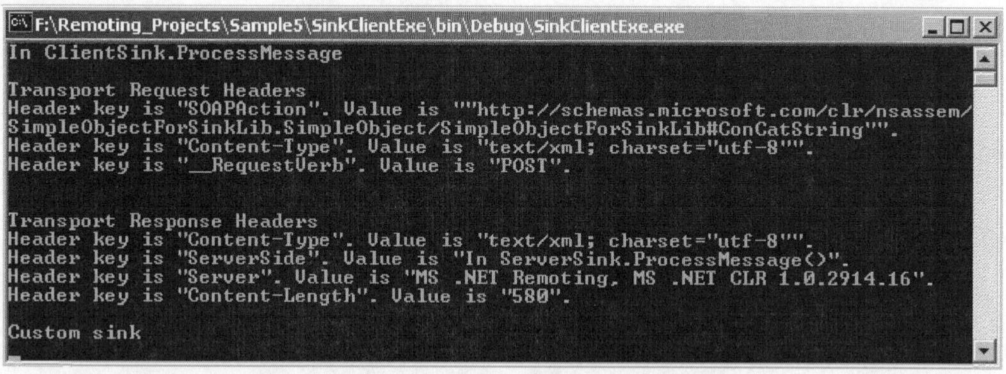

Figure 25.17: SinkClientExe.exe Output

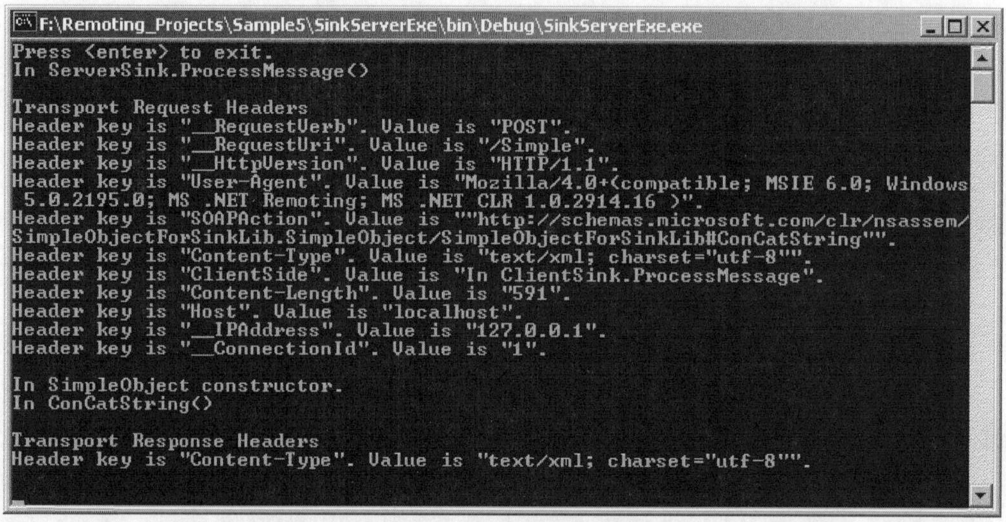

Figure 25.18: SinkServerExe.exe Output

This simple example, whose output is shown in Figures 25.17 and 25.18, explains the basics of constructing a sink. Using essentially the same code, a sink could hang onto the original stream and create its own stream. Ship that stream to the server. Once it receives a response, send the original stream to the server. As should be evident, sinks are a powerful mechanism to extend object remoting.

Summary

The chapter has surveyed the .NET Remoting Framework. We've explored a number of areas and hopefully given developers enough of a grounding to address the majority of their problem domains. However, given the scope of remoting, many areas have been overlooked; among those are asynchronous remoting, customized proxies, and proxy attributes.

The designers of .NET's remoting framework have delivered an easily implementable architecture that is adaptable and can be extended to meet the most demanding of challenges. Not only can sinks and proxies be customized or extended, but channels can be designed and coded using any protocol desired. The remoting framework is truly an extensible architecture. The next chapter will discuss deploying .NET application and the features available to help facilitate this process.

Chapter 26:
Deployment and Packaging

This chapter discusses basic deployment and packaging of .NET applications. It steps you through what is required for a .NET distribution, the different ways to package an application, and how to deploy an application to Windows as well as to the Internet.

Distribution Requirements for .NET

Microsoft provides a .NET Framework redistributable that installs on the application's hosting machine called dotnetfx.exe which allows you to install your .NET application deployment solution. This redistributable component will eventually be available in two versions: a control version and a full version. However, as of this writing, there is only one redistributable package. If you are installing the .NET application on a server, you are also required to have MDAC 2.6 or 2.7 (database components). Applications that use ASP.NET require Internet Information Services (IIS) and .NET Windows Services to be installed as well. Also, .NET will currently run only under Windows 98, Windows Millennium edition (Me), Windows 2000, and Windows NT 4.0 (with Service Pack 6a).

Deploying Simple Applications
with .bat and xcopy

Once the runtime and .NET Framework components are installed on a system, most .NET applications can be deployed by simply copying them onto the host system. In other words, you could write a simple batch file that copies them from a disk to your hard drive. Because the runtime and framework components contain the bulk of the functionality of .NET, the footprints of your applications often remain small, and an application may fit on a floppy disk. Here is a simple example of how you might install the .NET application hello.exe you created in Chapter 3:

- Create a file on a floppy called install.bat.
- Edit the file and type mkdir c:\MyApp<return>.
- Edit the file and type xcopy hello.exe c:\MyApp\hello.exe<return>.
- Save the file.
- Run install.bat from the floppy disk (usually a:\install.bat).

That's all there is to it! The application hello.exe contains all the assembly information it needs to point to the libraries it needs to use, and all this information is added to hello.exe during compile-time. Of course, you may consider using a more elaborate setup program such as InstallShield or Wise Installation to do the copying. That way you can have fancy bitmaps advertising and explaining your hello.exe program and a pretty blue layered screen with the title and version of the software plus security, third-party component installation, and more. However, for many .NET application installations, xcopy will suffice.

What Is an Assembly?

An *assembly* is a group of running programs or libraries that are deployed as a file or set of files in a single unit for implementation. Assemblies are the basic building blocks for all .NET applications and components. Every assembly contains an *assembly manifest* that contains descriptive information about the assembly. This information includes the name of the assembly, the files that make up the assembly, dependencies, version information, and permissions for allowing the assembly to run. .NET consists of both *private assemblies* and *shared assemblies.*

Private Assemblies

A private assembly is one that is known only to the application(s) in a single directory structure. For example, a component is a private assembly if it is placed in the same directory as the application that uses it. If all of your application depends only upon itself, then all of your assemblies can be made private. Private assemblies require you only to copy all the files to a single directory in order to deploy them.

Shared Assemblies

What happens if you need to share a component between different client applications? In this case you need to use a shared assembly. A shared assembly resides in what is known as the global assembly cache (GAC). The GAC also can be used to view all of the shared assemblies (we'll show you how to do this later in this chapter). All shared assemblies need to be assigned a *strong* name. A strong name means that the assembly is digitally signed and needs to be opened with a key. The strong name identity consists of the name, version number, and cultural information of the assembly along with the public key and digital signature. See Table 26.1.

Assembly Attribute	Description	Example in Assembly File
Name	Name of the component	
Version number	Consists of four numbers: Major.Minor.Build.Revision	[assembly: AssemblyVersion("1.0.5.1")]
Cultural information (optional)	A string code representing the cultural attribute—if blank, the default culture is used	For English culture: [assembly: AssemblyCulture("en")]
Digital signature	A unique signature implementing public key cryptography	Usually stored in a file called myfile.snk as a public/private key pair: [assembly:AssemblyKeyFileAttribute(@"sgKey.snk")]
Public key	The key used to decrypt the manifest's hash	Contained in the key file mentioned above

Table 26.1: Information Identifying a Shared Assembly

To install an assembly to the GAC, you can use the command line gacutil.exe:

```
gacutil.exe /i MySharedAssembly.dll
```

Example of Creating a Strong-Named Assembly

The best way to understand how to create a strong-named component is to go through the motions. First, let's create a simple component called SmileyFace.dll. Go to File→New Project and choose Windows Control Library. Type in the project name SmileyFace. See Figure 26.1.

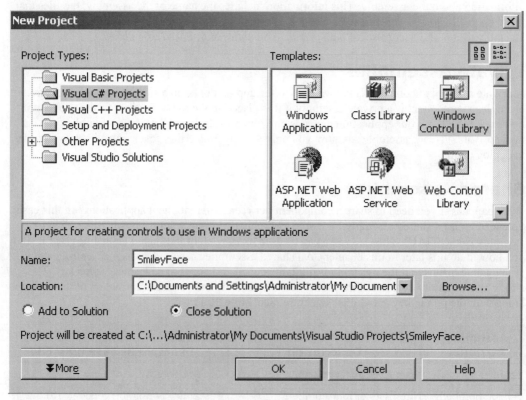

Figure 26.1: Creating the SmileyFace Control

Now double-click the Paint event in the Project window of the control and add the code in Listing 26.1.

Listing 26.1—Added Code

```
        private void UserControl1_Paint(object sender,
System.Windows.Forms.PaintEventArgs e)
        {
            Graphics g = e.Graphics;
            g.FillEllipse(Brushes.Yellow, 0, 0,
                        ClientRectangle.Width,
        ClientRectangle.Height);
            g.DrawEllipse(Pens.Black, 0, 0, ClientRectangle.Width,
                        ClientRectangle.Height);
            g.FillEllipse(Brushes.Black, ClientRectangle.Width/4,
                        ClientRectangle.Height/4, 5, 5);
            g.FillEllipse(Brushes.Black,
                        ClientRectangle.Width*3/4,
                        ClientRectangle.Height/4, 5, 5);
            g.DrawArc(Pens.Black, ClientRectangle.Width/6,
            ClientRectangle.Height/3, ClientRectangle.Width*3/4,
            ClientRectangle.Width/2, 25, 135);
        }
```

This will draw the smiley face in the control. Now open the assembly file AssemblyInfo.cs. Change the assembly information to the following to change the culture and version and assign an encryption key file:

```
[assembly: AssemblyCulture("en")] // culture english

[assembly: AssemblyVersion("1.1.0.0")]  // version 1.1

[assembly: AssemblyKeyFile("..\\..\\keyfile.snk")]
```

To create the key-pair file keyfile.snk we'll use the strong name utility sn.exe:

```
sn -k keyfile.snk
```

Now when we build the assembly, the DLL will have a strong name based on the public and private key in this file. We can actually view the assembly manifest by using the ildasm.exe utility from the command line in the Debug directory where the DLL is contained:

```
ildasm SmileyFace.dll
```

This will bring up the window shown in Figure 26.2.

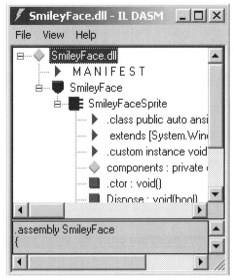

Figure 26.2:ILDASM for Viewing Assemblies

Double-clicking the manifest shows the strong name identity information that we've inserted in our component (public key information, version number, and cultural info). See Figure 26.3.

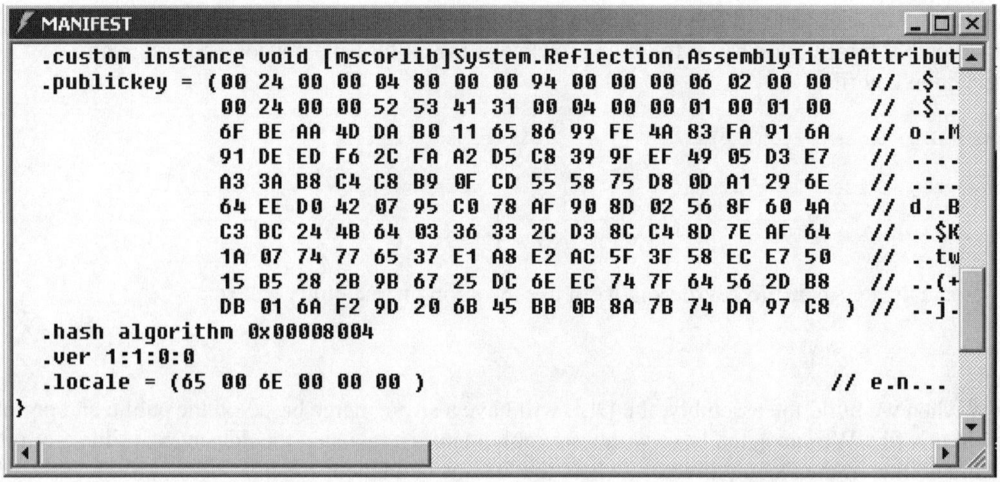

```
MANIFEST                                                              _ □ ×
.custom instance void [mscorlib]System.Reflection.AssemblyTitleAttribut
.publickey = (00 24 00 00 04 80 00 00 94 00 00 00 06 02 00 00   // .$..
             00 24 00 00 52 53 41 31 00 04 00 00 01 00 01 00   // .$..
             6F BE AA 4D DA B0 11 65 86 99 FE 4A 83 FA 91 6A   // o..M
             91 DE ED F6 2C FA A2 D5 C8 39 9F EF 49 05 D3 E7   // ....
             A3 3A B8 C4 C8 B9 0F CD 55 58 75 D8 0D A1 29 6E   // .:..
             64 EE D0 42 07 95 C0 78 AF 90 8D 02 56 8F 60 4A   // d..B
             C3 BC 24 4B 64 03 36 33 2C D3 8C C4 8D 7E AF 64   // ..$K
             1A 07 74 77 65 37 E1 A8 E2 AC 5F 3F 58 EC E7 50   // ..tw
             15 B5 28 2B 9B 67 25 DC 6E EC 74 7F 64 56 2D B8   // ..(+
             DB 01 6A F2 9D 20 6B 45 BB 0B 8A 7B 74 DA 97 C8 ) // ..j.
.hash algorithm 0x00008004
.ver 1:1:0:0
.locale = (65 00 6E 00 00 00 )                                 // e.n...
}
```

Figure 26.3: Manifest Detail Inside the SmileyFace Component

Now we need to add the assembly to the GAC. We can either use the gacutil.exe or simply drag and drop the assembly using Windows Explorer. The GAC is located in the Windows directory under the Assembly subdirectory. If you go to c:\windows\assembly (or c:\winnt\assembly if you use Windows NT or 2000) the Explorer will be transformed into a GAC utility. You can then drag SmileyFace.dll into the GAC from another Explorer window. The results are shown in Figure 26.4.

Figure 26.4: Global Assembly Cache in Windows Explorer

Note that the assembly name, version number, culture, and public key are all displayed reflecting the changes we made to the AssemblyInfo.cs file. We can now run sn.exe -v from the command line to verify that we have a strong-named assembly:

```
sn.exe -v SmileyFace.dll
```

Running sn.exe will produce the following output:

```
Assembly 'smileyface.dll' is valid.
```

Probing for Assemblies

If the assembly is not in the GAC, the runtime uses specific rules to look for it. First, it will look for the assembly in the application base (executing) directory. If it doesn't find it there, it will look for a directory named after the assembly in question and then proceed to look inside that directory. If it can't find it there, and if cultural information is indicated, it will look in a directory with the culture name (e.g., en, de, etc.). If it cannot find the assembly in any of those locations, the runtime asks the Windows Installer to provide the assembly. If none of these actions works, a FileNotFoundException is thrown. As an example, consider our SmileyFace.dll assembly run using c:\MyApp\SmileyFaceTest.exe. In this case, the following locations are probed for the SmileyFace.dll assembly:

C:\MyApp\SmileyFace.dll
C:\MyApp\SmileyFace\SmileyFace.dll
C:\MyApp\en\SmileyFace.dll
C:\MyApp\en\SmileyFace\SmileyFace.dll

Deploying from Visual Studio .NET

Visual Studio .NET provides you the ability to deploy your applications easily. If you click File→Add Project→New Project, that brings up the template dialog in which you can create a deployment project. As you can see in Figure 26.5, you can choose from a few different types of deployment options.

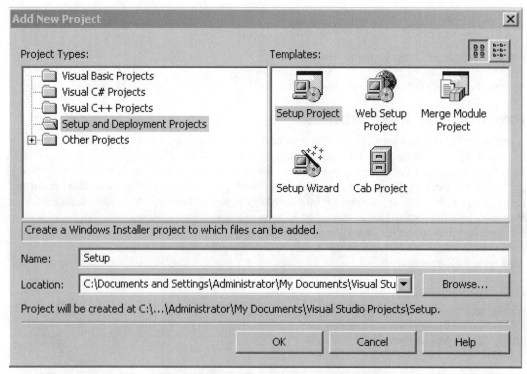

Figure 26.5: Deployment Project Wizard

Packages in Visual Studio .NET

You have two options for packaging your software in Visual Studio .NET: cabinet files and Windows Installer files.

Cabinet Files

Cabinet files (or .cab files) are compressed files of your existing files. A few restrictions apply to using .cab files. First of all, your .cab file can contain only one assembly, so a .cab is good if you are distributing a single DLL component or single executable program. Also a .cab file must have the same name as the assembly it is packaging. For example, our SmileyFace.dll cabinet file would have to be named SmileyFace.cab.

Microsoft Windows Installer Files

Microsoft Windows Installer files (or .msi files) are probably the preferred method of installation. The Windows Installer is the standard installer used for Microsoft Windows 2000, Me, and XP (as well as 98 and even 95). Windows Installer not only installs the application, but it keeps a record of everything it installs including file and registry information. You can also use Windows Installer to repair an application since Installer has a record of what it needs and does a check on what it is missing.

Merge Modules

Merge modules (or .msm files) are used in conjunction with .msi files to install components. The merge module contains all of the file and registry information needed to install your component and can be shared with different .msi files that also need to install the component. Merge modules are useful because they handle the versioning problem each time you create a new .msm file for later versions of your component. In general, you would create a merge module for installing a component that may be used for several different applications.

Setup Project

The setup project allows you to create an .msi file that will install all the necessary files onto a system for running your application. Once you've created your project, you'll need to add files to the project. If you right-click on the setup project and choose Add→File, you can add the files you need to deploy. See Figure 26.6.

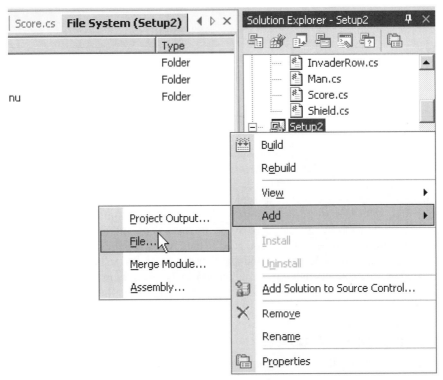

Figure 26.6: Adding Files to the Deployment Project

You also need to bring up the Configuration Manager (under Build→Configuration Manager) to tell it to compile your setup project by checking the Build button. See Figure 26.7.

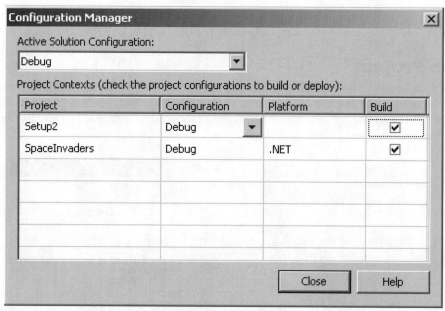

Figure 26.7: Configuration Manager for Setup Project

Once you have added the files you want to deploy (executable files and other assemblies, graphics files, readme files, Help files, even source code if you wish), choose Build Solution from the Build menu. This will create up to five files: Setup.exe, Setup2.msi, setup.ini, InstMsiA.exe, and InstMsiW.exe. These files are everything you need to deploy your application on another system. The files include the distributable runtime and all other dependencies. In other words, we can take the files created by the deployment build, burn them on a CD, bring them to a computer that doesn't have the .NET Framework installed, and run setup.exe to install the application with all the necessary files.

Using the Setup Wizard

The Setup Wizard steps you through creating a deployment package for all the permutations of deployment file options: .cab file, merge module, Windows setup, and Web setup. It makes the setup process even easier than shown in the previous example because it tells you exactly what to do. Figure 26.8 shows the screen from the Setup Wizard with all the deployment options.

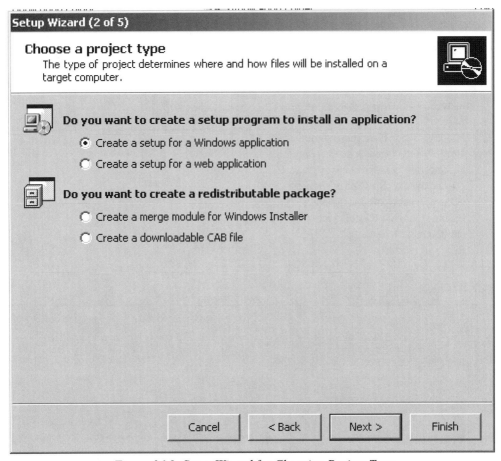

Figure 26.8: Setup Wizard for Choosing Project Type

The next screen (see Figure 26.9) allows us to include outputs from existing projects. This includes primary output such as the executable file or the component, documentation, source code, debug information files, Help files, localized assemblies, and even other setup files referenced in this project.

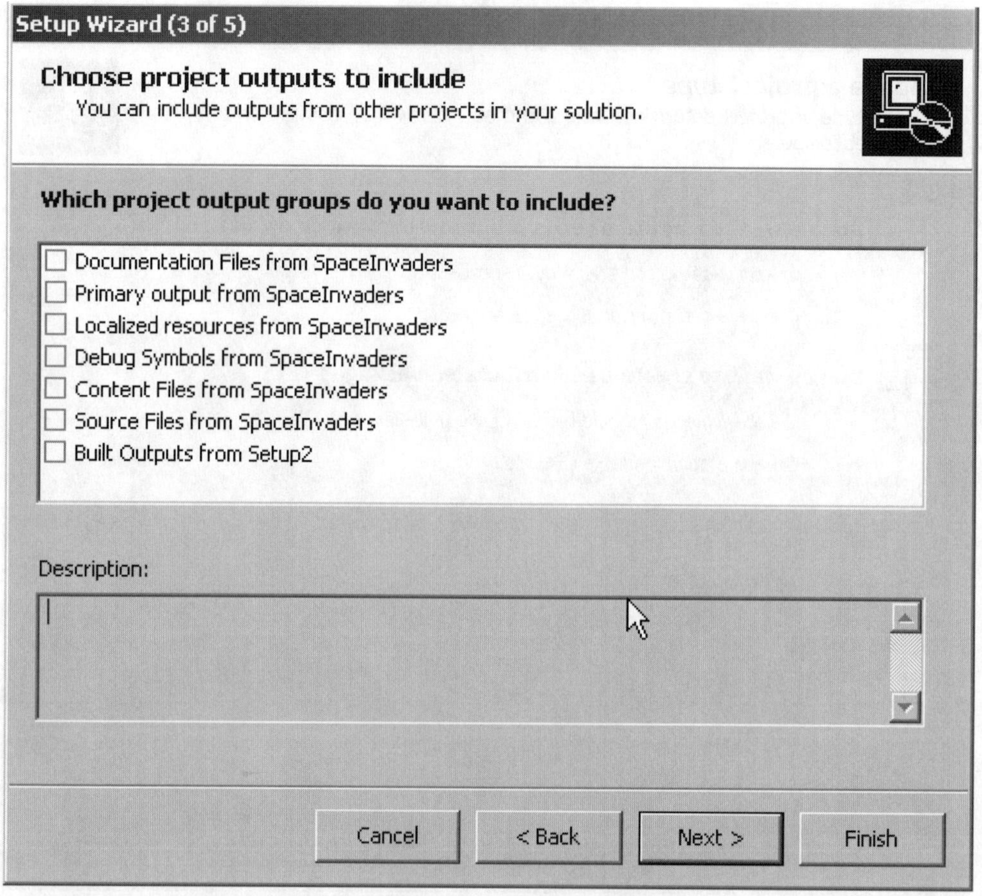

Figure 26.9: Setup Wizard for Choosing Project Output

Finally, we need to choose any additional miscellaneous files we are interested in for this project such as a readme file, graphic and sound files, or HTML files (see Figure 26.10). Don't worry if you forget to add files here, because you can always add them later in the Solution Explorer by right-clicking on the setup project and choosing Add→File.

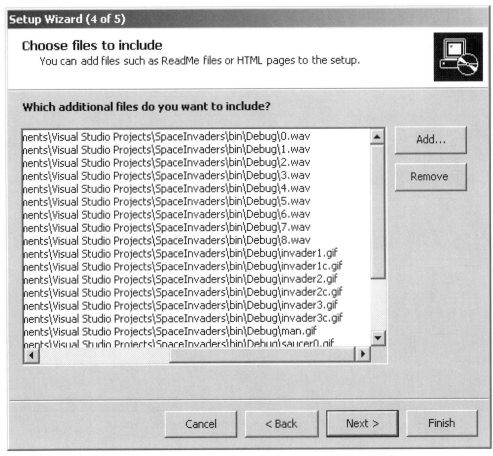

Figure 26.10: Setup Wizard for Choosing Additional Files

When you finish with the wizard, it creates a setup file in a separate setup directory. The setup directory contains the setup.exe and the .msi file to install. When you run setup.exe for the first time, the screen in Figure 26.11 appears with the name of the setup project shown in the title.

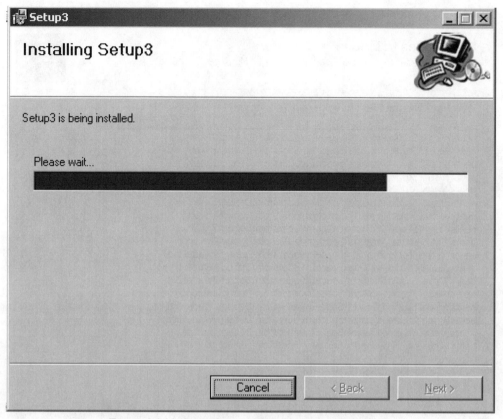

Figure 26.11: Setup Screen When Running Installation

Setup will install the project into the directory c:\program files\<name of your company>\SetupName\.

The File System View

The File System view shows you where your files will be installed. You can use this view to set up additional setup options, such as putting your program in the Start menu or on the desktop.

Putting Your File in the Start Menu

To place the program in the Start menu, first bring up the File System view by double-clicking a project output in the setup project in the Solution Explorer. See Figure 26.12.

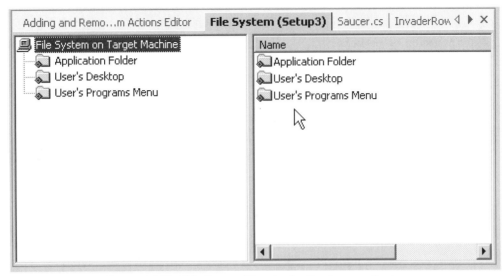

Figure 26.12: File System View in the Deployment Project

Now go into the User's Programs menu and right-click in the left-hand pane on the User's Programs menu to add a folder to the Programs menu. Name the folder after the name of your application. See Figure 26.13.

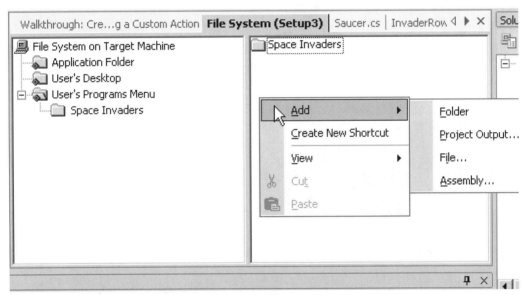

Figure 26.13: Adding a Folder to the Start Menu

Now we need to add a shortcut to the application inside the folder. Right-click in the right-hand pane and choose Create New Shortcut. See Figure 26.14.

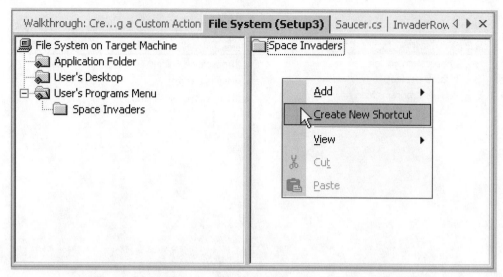

Figure 26.14: Creating the Shortcut in the Application Folder

This brings up the Select Item in Project dialog. Click all the way down into the project folder you just created. See Figure 26.15.

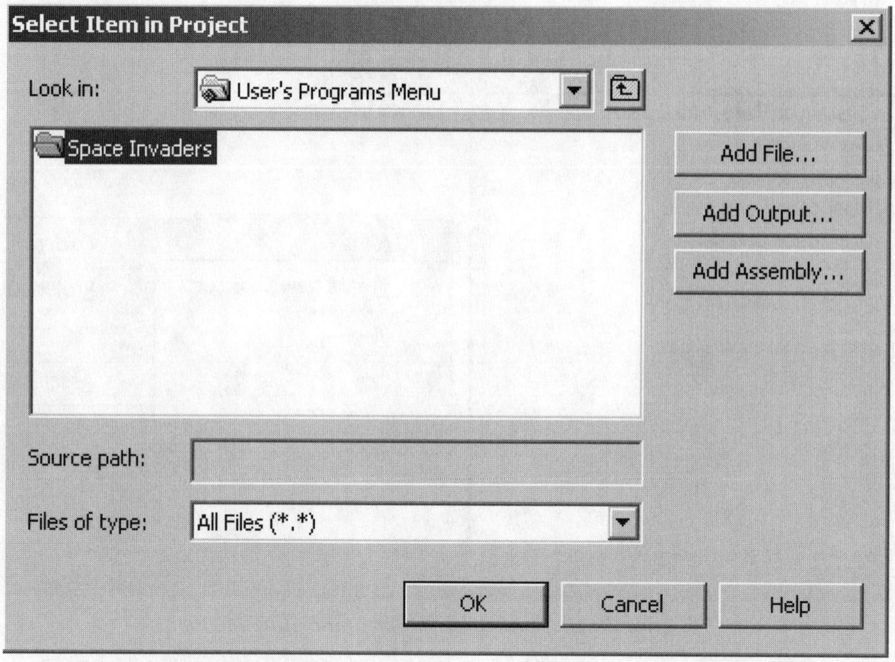

Figure 26.15: Adding a Shortcut in the User's Programs Folder

Double-click the Application folder to find the shortcut for the application. See Figure 26.16.

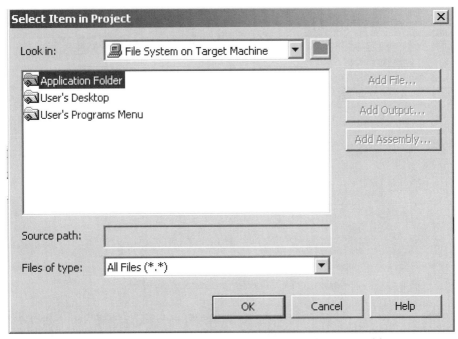

Figure 26.16: Adding a Shortcut from the Application Folder

Look for the application you want to install a shortcut for and click on the Add File button. See Figure 26.17.

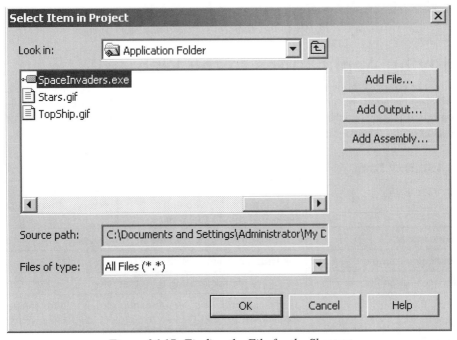

Figure 26.17: Finding the File for the Shortcut

When you are finished, the File System pane should look like the screenshot in Figure 26.18.

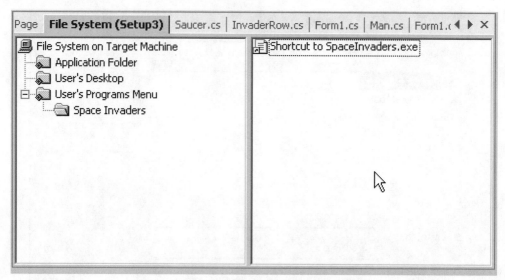

Figure 26.18: Shortcut in File System Window

In most cases you want to add to the Program menu the application's executable file as well as a readme file or any Help files and documentation associated with the application. After the deployment project has been compiled and setup has been run, the application will appear in the Programs menu as shown in Figure 26.19.

Figure 26.19: Application Appearing in the Start Menu

Deploying Applications to the Web

A few files are required for deploying an ASP.NET application: the *.aspx Web pages, the *.asmx Web services, the binary file compiled from the code-behind aspx.cs and asmx.cs files, the local Web configuration file, and the discovery files for the Web services. Table 26.2 shows the different directories and files deployed in a Web application.

ASP.NET Item	Description
Application directory	The root directory of the application. This directory must be made into an IIS Web application directory; otherwise the application might not run.
<AppName>.aspx	The URL for bringing up Web forms.
<webservice>.asmx file	The URL for calling a Web service.
<webservice>.disco file	Discovery file for locating a Web service.
Web.config file	Used to override the default configuration info for the server application.
\bin directory	Contains the binary file for Web services and Web forms.

Table 26.2: ASP.NET Deployed Files and Directories

Web applications can be deployed using FTP tools such as WSFTP or SecureCRT. Listing 26.2 shows the files deployed in a sample GuestBook application and the directory structure.

Listing 26.2—Directory and File Structure of GuestBook Application

```
GuestBookApp (IIS application directory)
   MyGuestBook.aspx
   ViewGuestBook.aspx
   GuestBookServices.asmx
   Thanks.aspx
   Web.config
   GuestBookApp.vsdisco
   GuestBook.mdb
   bin (binary directory for Web services and application)
      GuestBookApp.dll
```

Using the Wizard to Deploy ASP.NET

The Project Wizard really makes your life easy when it comes to deploying an application to the Web. Begin by choosing Add Project→New Project from the File menu. Type the name of the setup project in the Name field and double-click Web Setup Project (see Figure 26.20). This will add a Web setup project to the Solution Explorer.

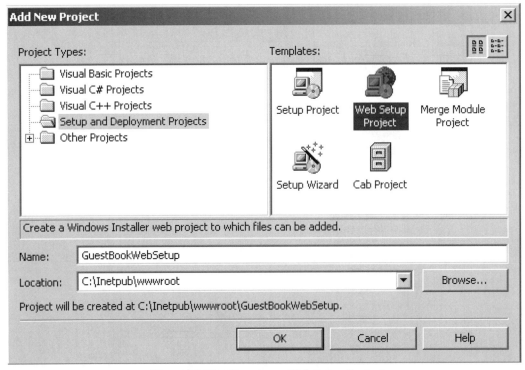

Figure 26.20: Choosing a Web Setup Project

Double-click the setup project in the Solution Explorer to bring up the File System window. Right-click the Web Application folder and choose Add→Project Output, as shown in Figure 26.21.

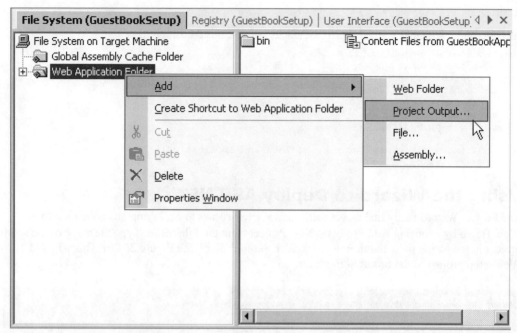

Figure 26.21: Adding Project Files to the Setup Project

This brings up a window in which you can choose the output from the project. Choose Primary Output to package all the local DLLs and DLL dependencies and click OK. See Figure 26.22.

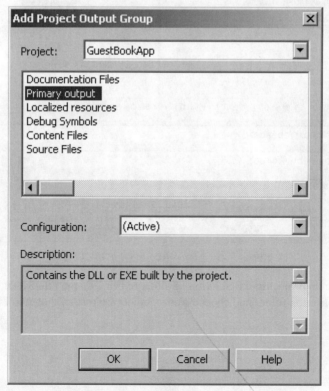

Figure 26.22: Choosing Project Output for the Setup

Next, right-click the Web Application folder, and this time choose Add→File and hold down the CTRL key and click all the files necessary to support your Web application, as shown in Figure 26.23.

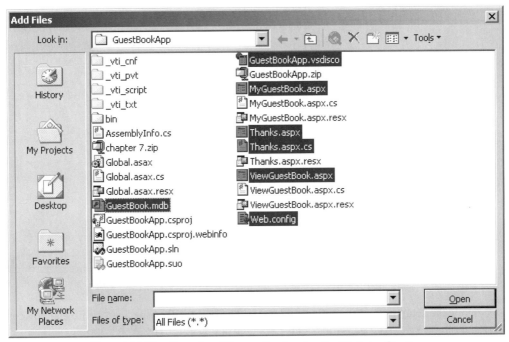

Figure 26.23: Choosing Files to Deploy for the Web Application

When you have finished choosing files, click Open. The File System window should now look like Figure 26.24.

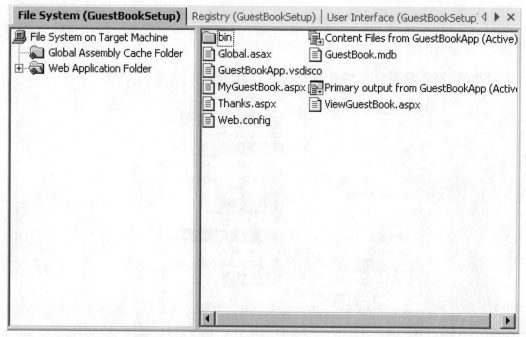

Figure 26.24: File System Window After Adding Necessary Files

Now compile the setup project from the Build menu. The build will create an .msi file that you can deploy and run on your Web server to set up your Web application. The Web setup file will be created in the root of wherever you created your Web project. If you created the project on your localhost, it will place the setup under \InetPub\wwwroot\<projectsetup>.

To run the Web setup, double-click the setup.exe file. You'll be prompted regarding to which virtual directory you would like to install your Web project as well as a port number, as in Figure 26.25.

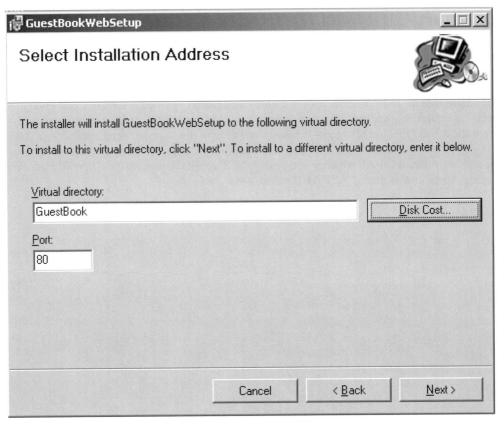

Figure 26.25: Web Setup Wizard from setup.exe

After running the installation on your local drive, you'll find the Web application has installed in the GuestBook directory with the directory structure in Figure 26.26. Note that this matches the directory structure shown earlier in Listing 26.2.

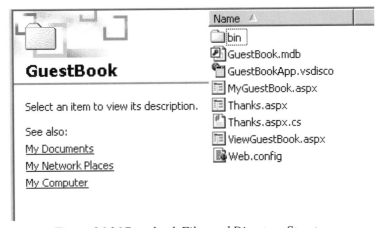

Figure 26.26 Guestbook Files and Directory Structure

If you had copied the setup files to a Web server and run the setup on that Web server, it would have created a <projectsetup> folder in the virtual directory specified in Figure 26.25 and then placed the Web application files and bin directory in that <projectsetup> folder.

Summary

This chapter covers what is necessary to deploy .NET applications. We identified all the necessary files you need to deploy to get .NET applications to run. We illustrated the simplest deployment scenario of copying a file and described the basic unit of a deployed application—the .NET assembly—and how to use that as a private program or a shared program. You learned about the GAC and its role in shared assemblies and how to create strong-named assemblies that give assemblies uniqueness and security. You learned about different deployment packaging options—such as the cabinet file, the Microsoft Windows Installation file, and the merge module—and what is the best time to use each. We delved into how the Visual Studio .NET integrated development environment makes it easy to package and deploy .NET applications with the Setup Wizard. Finally, we talked about how to deploy ASP.NET applications.

Index